VERÖFFENTLICHUNGEN DER

HISTORISCHEN KOMMISSION ZU BERLIN

BAND 66

BEITRÄGE ZU INFLATION UND WIEDERAUFBAU IN DEUTSCHLAND UND EUROPA 1914—1924

Herausgeber

GERALD D. FELDMAN
CARL-LUDWIG HOLTFRERICH
GERHARD A. RITTER
PETER-CHRISTIAN WITT

BAND 7

Walter de Gruyter · Berlin · New York

1986

ANDREAS KUNZ

CIVIL SERVANTS AND THE POLITICS OF INFLATION IN GERMANY, 1914—1924

Walter de Gruyter · Berlin · New York

1986

Gedruckt mit Unterstützung des Stifterverbandes für die Deutsche Wissenschaft, Essen.
Die Schriftenreihe der Historischen Kommission zu Berlin erscheint mit Unterstützung des Senators für Wissenschaft und Forschung, Berlin.

Lektorat der Schriftenreihe

Christian Schädlich

Printed on acid free paper
(ageing-resistant — pH7, neutral)

Library of Congress Cataloging in Publication Data

Kunz, Andreas, 1948-
Civil servants and the politics of inflation in Germany, 1914—1924.

(Veröffentlichungen der Historischen Kommission zu Berlin ; Bd. 66) (Beiträge zu Inflation und Wiederaufbau in Deutschland und Europa 1914—1924 ; Bd. 7)
Bibliography: p.
Includes index.
1. Germany--Officials and employees--Political activity--History--20th century. 2. World War, 1914—1918--Germany. 3. Germany--Economic conditions--1918—1945. 4. Inflation (Finance)-- Social aspects--Germany--History--20th century. I. Title. II Series. III. Series: Beiträge zu Inflation und Wiederaufbau in Deutschland und Europa 1914—1924 ; Bd. 7.
JN3541.K86 1986 354.43004 86-16663
ISBN 0-89925-222-2

CIP-Kurztitelaufnahme der Deutschen Bibliothek

Kunz, Andreas:
Civil servants and the politics of inflation in Germany, 1914—1924 / Andreas Kunz. — Berlin ; New York : de Gruyter, 1986.
(Veröffentlichungen der Historischen Kommission zu Berlin ; Bd. 66 : Beiträge zu Inflation und Wiederaufbau in Deutschland und Europa 1914—1924 ; Bd. 7)
ISBN 3-11-010482-2

NE: Historische Kommission ‹Berlin, West›: Veröffentlichungen der Historischen Kommission zu Berlin / Beiträge zu Inflation und Wiederaufbau in Deutschland und Europa 1914—1924

Satz und Umbruch: Historische Kommission zu Berlin, Berlin 38
Druck: Werner Hildebrand, Berlin 65
Einband: Lüderitz & Bauer, Berlin 61

PREFACE

To anyone familiar with German history or, as the case may be, with daily life in West Germany of today, civil servants, the ubiquitous *Beamte*, are a very visible group in the structure and working mechanisms of German society. This study probes into the social history of German officialdom, the *Beamtenschaft*, during a critical period in German history: the years of the Great War of 1914/18 and the postwar period of reconstruction, which in the German case coincided with political changes of great magnitude: the Revolution of 1918/19 and the founding years of the Weimar Republic. In order to lend greater coherence to a decade of rapid economic, social and political change, the period that extended from 1914 to 1924 is viewed in the present study as a decade of protracted inflation. Thus, an economic process — inflation — is used as an indicator for social (and, perhaps less so) political change. By limiting the time span to a ten-year period, this study does not aspire to present a complete social history of German civil servants in the twentieth century, a task which still awaits its author. However, this study is concerned with two important aspects of a yet-to-be-written social-political history of German officialdom in the twentieth century: first, the interdependence between the civil servants' material conditions and interest-group formation and, secondly, the conduct of interest group politics by the civil servants' representative organizations. One of the main arguments of this book, therefore, is that the economic and social impact of inflation facilitated the entry of civil servants into a more modern type of interest group politics. This development, in turn, produced an impact on what has been termed the "politics of inflation", that is to say, it increased the influence which civil servant associations were able to exert on the conduct of economic and social policies in the early 1920s.

For reasons just explained the study which follows has two foci. On the one hand, it is meant to be a contribution to the still unwritten social history of the German inflation, as well as to the "more traditional" (and, consequently much better known) general political history of Germany during the First World War and the early Weimar Republic. On the other hand, it is a study of interest group politics in an advanced industrial society, using historic events and a specific social group and policy area (civil servants and civil service policy) as points of reference.

The organization of this book reflects the dualism of its approach. Readers interested in the social history of German civil servants in the late nineteenth and early twentieth centuries, as well as readers interested in the social history of the German inflation, will find the lengthy statistical treatise with which this study begins worthwhile their attention despite its "dry" subject matter. Those readers, however, whose interests lie primarily in the sociopolitical aspects of inflation may safely skip (or skim through) this part of the book and turn their attention directly to the chronologically-structured, narrative account of civil servant interest politics in the postwar inflation which begins with CHAPTER THREE. Both groups of readers will, I imagine, profit from a close reading of the story of interest-group formation among German civil servants during war, wartime inflation, and revolution which is told in CHAPTER TWO.

A note on style and usage may be in order at the beginning of the book. It is not always easy — and sometimes impossible — to find adequate translations for the technical terms relating to the German civil service and, for that matter, to other groups and institutions of German society as well. While care has been taken not to overload the text with German words, in some cases it was found to be unavoidable and even called for. For example, the word *Beamtenschaft* is used throughout this study to connote "civil servants as a social group." The German term was given preference to English words such as "officialdom" or "bureaucrats", which may have *similar* meanings, but not the *exact* one intended here. The names of associations, political parties, and the like are given in their German original or, if available, in a standard and accepted English translation. Usually, such names are not italicized. For an explanation of the many acronyms used in this study, the reader is referred to the *List of Abbreviations* which appears on page XVII. Direct quotations from German sources appearing in the text have been translated into English; quotations appearing in the notes have, with some exceptions, been rendered in their German original. American spelling rules have been observed throughout. It may be noted that the American "billion" is equivalent to the British "milliard" (German: *Milliarde*), i. e., to one thousand millions.

The researching and writing of this book, which originated as a doctoral dissertation at the University of California, Berkeley, extended over a number of years, and, as is always the case in enterprises of this kind, the student/researcher/author has incurred many debts of gratitude along the way. I would like to take this opportunity to repay at least some of these, even if limitations of space (and memory) will undoubtedly lead to the unhappy fact of not mentioning *all* individuals to whom such debts are owed. May those who are not mentioned by name accept my apologies and gratitude for the help and assistance they extended to me!

Foremost I would like to thank Gerald Feldman, who supervised this study as a dissertation and continued being "plagued" with the history of German civil servants as one of the editors of the series in which the revised version now appears. He thus shared in all the ups and downs created by this project. As an academic teacher, mentor, and friend I owe him a great deal. I would also like to thank the other three editors of this series, Carl-Ludwig Holtfrerich, Gerhard A. Ritter, and Peter-Christian Witt, for helpful suggestions and critical comments regarding the revising of the manuscript. Reinhard Bendix and Wolfgang Sauer read the manuscript in its disseration form. Special thanks are due to Otto Büsch and the editorial staff at the Historische Kommission, West Berlin, particularly Christian Schädlich, for their editorial advice in the final stages of production of the book.

Research for this study was conducted in a number of archives and libraries in Germany and the United States. To all these institutions and their staffs I owe a special debt of gratitude. In particular, I would like to thank Archivdirektor Dr. Thomas Trumpp of the Federal Archives in Koblenz (FRG), and Dr. Glaser of the Central State Archives in Potsdam (GDR) for their introduction to the relevant source materials. The staff of the University Library at the University of Freiburg was extremely helpful in ordering even the most esoteric journal ever to be published by a German civil servant association, and provided for a pleasant retreat during the earlier writing stages of this book.

Twice while researching and writing earlier drafts of this study I changed my academic environment from Berkeley to Freiburg. I am very grateful to Heinrich August Winkler of the University of Freiburg for his generous advice and support of my work, and for the professional opportunities he extended to me. While in Germany, I also profited from conversations with Hans Rosenberg, Jürgen Kocka, Knut Borchardt, and Hans Mommsen.

Over the years, a fruitful exchange of ideas with colleagues and friends has contributed to the shaping of this study. Only some can be mentioned here specifically: Heidrun Homburg, William C. MacNeil, Robert Moeller, Ulrich Nocken, Irmgard Steinisch — fellow graduate students and friends, now colleagues, from the Berkeley days; Thomas Childers, Larry Jones, Merith Niehuss, Rudolf Tschirbs — coparticipants in the "Inflation Project;" Johannes Bähr, Rudolf Muhs, and James S. Roberts, friends and colleagues from the Freiburg days. For a while I also profited from an exchange of ideas with Jane Caplan, whose own work on the German civil service during the Third Reich is, in some ways, complemental to this study. My new colleagues at the Institute for Economic and Social History of the Free University of Berlin were lucky to only witness the tail end of it all.

Generous financial support for the researching and writing of this study was extended to me by the Regents of the University of California and by the Volkswagen Foundation; publication costs were defrayed by a grant from the Stifterverband für die Deutsche Wissenschaft. I am extremely grateful to these three institutions for this assistence of my work.

The support provided by the Volkswagen Foundation went well beyond financial matters, though. By funding a five-year project of international and interdisciplinary scope on "Inflation and Reconstruction in Germany and Europe, 1914—1924" the Foundation, together with the Historische Kommission at Berlin, provided a most ideal framework for research and scholarly communications in a new area of research. I am grateful to the organizers of this project — who are at the same time the editors of this series — for inviting me to participate in it and for including this study in its series. To a number of other participants in the project I am indebted to for helpful comments and suggestions made on earlier drafts of portions of this study.

The ardeous and time-consuming task of revising a long manuscript was accomplished in 1983—84 during a year-long stay as a Jean Monnet Fellow at the European University Institute in Florence, Italy. I am indebted to Werner Maihofer, president of the Institute, and to Philippe Schmitter and Peter Hertner for their interest in my work and for the excellent working conditions made available to me during a most memorable year at the Badia Fiesolana.

Family life often takes a distant second to scholarly pursuits, especially when deadlines loom large on the horizon. Thus, my final thanks — and apologies — go to my family: to Thomas and Sarah, who even during their well-deserved summer days at Santa Maria a Vezzano often had to survive without their father (and with the galleys), to the people at 117 Main Street, who believed in me through all these years, and, above all, to my wife Wadeane, whose patience, constant encouragement, and unwavering support alone made this study possible. It is but a small repayment of a much larger debt of gratitude that this book is dedicated to her.

Berlin, September 1985 *Andreas Kunz*

CONTENTS

INTRODUCTION

Civil Servants and the Social History of the German Inflation

CHAPTER ONE

The Social and Economic Framework

CHAPTER TWO

Toward Organizational Unity and Interest Representation, 1914 to 1919

CHAPTER THREE

Dividing the Social Costs of War: Postwar Reconstruction and the Emergence of Civil Servant Protest, Spring 1919 to April 1920

CHAPTER FOUR

Illusive Stability, May 1920 to April 1921

CHAPTER FIVE

1921: Accelerated Inflation and the Intensification of Social Conflict

CHAPTER SIX

From Protest to Militancy: The Civil Servant Strike of February 1921 and Its Consequences

CHAPTER SEVEN

From Hyperinflation to Stabilization, July 1922 to June 1924

EPILOGUE

LIST OF TABLES

LIST OF FIGURES

ABBREVIATIONS

ADB	Allgemeiner Deutscher Beamtenbund General Federation of German Civil Servants
ADBZ	*Allgemeine Deutsche Beamtenzeitung*
ADGB	Allgemeiner Deutscher Gewerkschaftsbund General Federation of German Trade Unions (Socialist "Free" Trade Unions)
AEV	Allgemeiner Eisenbahnerverband (National-Liberal) Railroad Workers Union
ANRB	Arbeitsgemeinschaft Nationaler Reichsbahnbeamten
Afa-Bund	Allgemeiner freier Angestelltenbund Federation of Unions of Salaried Employees
AfS	*Archiv für Sozialgeschichte*
ASS	*Archiv für Sozialwissenschaft und Sozialpolitik*
BA	Bundesarchiv Koblenz
BA/MA	Bundesarchiv/Militärarchiv Freiburg
BdF	Bund der Festbesoldeten League of Dependent Employees
BhB	Bund höherer Beamter Federation of Higher Civil Servants
BJ	*Beamten-Jahrbuch*
BT	*Berliner Tageblatt*
Büro RP	Büro des Reichspräsidenten Reich President's Office
CEH	*Central European History*
DAZ	*Deutsche Allgemeine Zeitung*
DB	*Der Beamtenbund*
DBB	Deutscher Beamtenbund Federation of German Civil Servants
DBR	*Deutsche Beamtenrundschau*
DDP	Deutsche Demokratische Partei German Democratic Party
DEV	Deutscher Eisenbahnerverband (Socialist) Railroad Workers Union
DG	*Die Gemeinschaft*
DF	*Die Freiheit*
DGB	Deutscher Gewerkschaftsbund German Federation of Trade Unions (Catholic Trade Unions)

Diss.	Dissertation
DNVP	Deutschnationale Volkspartei German National People's Party
DVP	Deutsche Volkspartei German People's Party
GBZ	*Gewerkschaftliche Beamtenzeitung*
GDB	Gesamtverband Deutscher Beamtengewerkschaften Federation of Unions of German Civil Servants
GDE	Gewerkschaft Deutscher Eisenbahner (Catholic) Railroad Workers Union
GDEB	Gewerkschaftsbund Deutscher Eisenbahnbeamter Federation of Unions of Railroad Civil Servants
GG	*Geschichte und Gesellschaft*
GLAK	Generallandesarchiv Karlsruhe
GStA	Geheimes Staatsarchiv Preußischer Kulturbesitz Berlin-Dahlem
HD	Hirsch-Duncker (National-Liberal) Hirsch-Duncker Unions
HStAD	Hauptstaatsarchiv Düsseldorf
IG	Interessengemeinschaft Deutscher Beamtenverbände Alliance of German Civil Servant Associations
IHG	*Internationales Handwörterbuch des Gewerkschaftswesens*
IWK	*Internationale wissenschaftliche Korrespondenz zur Geschichte der deutschen Arbeiterbewegung*
JCH	*Journal of Contemporary History*
JbNSt.	*Jahrbücher für Nationalökonomie und Statistik*
JMH	*Journal of Modern History*
Korr.Bl.	*Korrespondenzblatt der Generalkommission der Gewerkschaften Deutschlands/des Allgemeinen Deutschen Gewerkschaftsbundes*
KPD	Kommunistische Partei Deutschlands German Communist Party
Monthly Reports	Zusammenstellungen aus den Monatsberichten der Stellvertretenden Generalkommandos
MSPD	Mehrheitssozialdemokratische Partei Deutschlands Majority Social Democratic Party
NSDAP	Nationalsozialistische Deutsche Arbeiterpartei National Socialist Party
PAV	Personal-Abbau-Verordnung
RBBl.	*Reichsbesoldungsblatt*
RDB	Ring Deutscher Beamtenverbände League of German Civil Servant Associations
RDI	Reichsverband der Deutschen Industrie Reich Association of German Industry
Reg.	Regierung
RF	*Rote Fahne*
RfG	*Rundschau für Gemeindebeamte*
RFM	Reichsfinanzministerium Reich Ministry of Finance

RG	Reichsgewerkschaft Deutscher Eisenbahnbeamter und -anwärter National Union of Railroad Civil Servants
RGBl.	*Reichsgesetzblatt*
RhB	Reichsbund der höheren Beamten National Federation of Higher Civil Servants
RköO	Reichskommissar für öffentliche Ordnung Reich Commissar for Public Order
RMdI	Reichsministerium des Inneren Reich Interior Ministry
RPG	Reichspost-Gewerkschaft National Postal Union
RVBl.	*Reichsverkehrsblatt,* Ausgabe A: *Eisenbahnen*
RVM	Reichsverkehrsministerium Reich Transport Ministry
SP	*Soziale Praxis*
SPD	Sozialdemokratische Partei Deutschlands Social Democratic Party
StAH	Staatsarchiv Hamburg
Stenographische Berichte	*Verhandlungen des Reichstags. Stenographische Berichte und Anlagen*
USP(D)	Unabhängige Sozialdemokratische Partei Deutschlands Independent Social Democratic Party
VfZG	*Vierteljahrshefte für Zeitgeschichte*
VDB	Verband Deutscher Beamtenvereine League of German Civil Servant Associations
WSt.	*Wirtschaft und Statistik*
ZAG	Zentralarbeitsgemeinschaft Central Working Community
ZRhB	*Zeitschrift des Reichsbundes der höheren Beamten*
ZStAP	Zentrales Staatsarchiv I, Potsdam

TO WADEANE

INTRODUCTION

Civil Servants and the Social History of the German Inflation

Recent Research on the History of the German Inflation

In recent years the German inflation of the early 1920s has received renewed attention by economic and social historians in the United States and West Germany. Several monographs, collections of essays, and a plethora of scholarly articles on this, in view of our own experience with a decade of protracted inflation, rather timely subject have appeared within the last five years or so. This proliferation of fruitful research suggests that what once has been described as "oases in a historiographical desert" has slowly grown to become "greener pastures in a fertile historiographical grazing around."[1] Given the speciali-

[1] The main responsibility for the improvement of the state of affairs rests with the efforts undertaken by an international research group on "Inflation and Reconstruction in Germany and Europe after the First World War", organized in 1978 under the joint auspices of the Historische Kommission at Berlin and the Volkswagen Foundation. See the report of the preliminary meeting of this group, held in 1976, in Otto Büsch/Gerald D. Feldman (eds.), *Historische Prozesse der deutschen Inflation. Ein Tagungsbericht* (= Einzelveröffentlichungen der Historischen Kommission zu Berlin, vol. 21), Berlin 1978. The then existing state of research and the tasks of future research efforts are discussed by Gerald D. Feldman, *Gegenwärtiger Forschungsstand und künftige Forschungsprobleme zur deutschen Inflation,* in: *Ibid.*, pp. 3—20, where he mentions the "oases in the historiographical desert" (p. 3). The "greener pastures" emerge from the first three of a series of projected volumes published by this research group. See Gerald D. Feldman/Carl-Ludwig Holtfrerich/Gerhard A. Ritter/Peter-Christian Witt (eds.), *Die Deutsche Inflation: Eine Zwischenbilanz* (Engl. title: *The German Inflation Reconsidered: A Preliminary Balance)* (= Veröffentlichungen der Historischen Kommission zu Berlin, vol. 54, Beiträge zur Inflation und Wiederaufbau in Deutschland und Europa 1914—1924, vol. 1), Berlin-New York 1982; idem (eds.), *Die Erfahrung der Inflation im internationalen Zusammenhang und Vergleich* (Engl. title: *The Experience of Inflation. International and Comparative Studies)* (= Veröffentlichungen der Historischen Kommission zu Berlin, vol. 57, Beiträge zu Inflation und Wiederaufbau in Deutschland und

zation of historical research, it is not surprising that the focus of inflation research has shifted according to the primary field of speciality and interest of various scholars engaged in it. Ultimately, however, the goal will have to be, as Gerald Feldman has put it, the drawing of "a total picture of German society between 1914 and 1924, i. e. during a period of sustained socioeconomic and political upheaval,"[2] even if the task of assembling this "total picture" may well have to be deferred to such a point in time when historians have laid the groundwork for the "great synthesis" through a lot more detailed empirical research. Progress has been made in this direction, and a division of research tasks has proven to be fruitful. While economic historians have remained interested primarily in the economic causes and consequences of the inflation process,[3] new approaches have been taken as well. As exemplified best by Carl-Ludwig Holtfrerich's important recent study, West German economic historians have discovered an important international dimension of the German inflation by placing it more concretely into a functioning or dysfunctioning world economy in the period after the

Europa 1914—1924, vol. 2), Berlin-New York 1984; idem (eds.), *Die Anpassung an die Inflation* (Engl. title: *The Adaptation to Inflation*) (= Veröffentlichungen der Historischen Kommission zu Berlin, vol. 67, Beiträge zu Inflation und Wiederaufbau in Deutschland und Europa 1914—1924, vol. 8), Berlin-New York 1986. For the aims of this research project, see the introduction to the first of these volumes, Gerald D. Feldman/Carl-Ludwig Holtfrerich/Gerhard A. Ritter/Peter-Christian Witt, *Inflation und Wiederaufbau in Deutschland und Europa. Ein Forschungsprojekt,* in: Idem (eds.), *The German Inflation*..., pp. 1—21. Recent monographs on the subject include: Gerald D. Feldman, *Iron and Steel in the German Inflation, 1916—1923,* Princeton 1977; Gerald D. Feldman/Heidrun Homburg, *Industrie und Inflation: Studien und Dokumente zur Politik der deutschen Unternehmer 1916—1923,* Hamburg 1978; Carl-Ludwig Holtfrerich, *Die deutsche Inflation: Ursachen und Folgen in internationaler Perspektive,* Berlin-New York 1980, which is likely to become a standard work on the general economic history of the German inflation for years to come. An English version has just appeared.

[2] G. D. Feldman, *Gegenwärtiger Forschungsstand*..., in: O. Büsch/G. D. Feldman (eds.), *Historische Prozesse*..., p. 17.

[3] See: Knut Borchardt, *Strukturwirkungen des Inflationsprozesses* (= Schriftenreihe des IFO-Instituts für Wirtschaftsforschung, vol. 53), Berlin-Munich 1972; idem, *Die Erfahrungen mit Inflationen in Deutschland,* in: Johannes Schlemmer (ed.), *Enteignung durch Inflation?,* Munich 1972, pp. 9—22; Peter Czada, *Ursachen und Folgen der großen Inflation in Deutschland,* in: Harald Winkel (ed.), *Finanz- und wirtschaftspolitische Fragen der Zwischenkriegszeit* (= Schriften des Vereins für Sozialpolitik, vol. 73), Berlin 1973, pp. 9—43; idem, *Große Inflation und Wirtschaftswachstum,* in: Hans Mommsen et al. (eds.), *Industrielles System und politische Entwicklung in der Weimarer Republik,* Düsseldorf 1974, pp. 386—393.

[4] C.-L. Holtfrerich, *Die deutsche Inflation*..., pp. 202—218 and, by the same author,

First World War.[4] In addition, economic historians have probed into the economic and financial policies pursued by the German government and by monetary agencies and institutions as, for example, the Reichsbank.[5] They also have ventured into the social history of the inflation, if under a somewhat narrowly defined paradigm of "distributional conflicts" between socioeconomic groups as the predominant sociohistorical phenomenon of the inflation process.[6]

Perhaps one of the most important aspects of the "new historiography" on the German inflation is the fact that what once had been virtually a domain of economists and economic historians now has developed into a major area of study for *social* historians as well. To be sure, general histories of modern Germany or of the Weimar Republic had always pointed to the impact of the inflation as one of the main sources of the socioeconomic and political problems of the Weimar Republic.[7] Yet political and social historians alike had until recently dealt almost exclusively with the impact of the *hyper*inflation of 1923 and with its connection to the crisis of the Weimar state in that fateful

Die konjunkturanregende Wirkung der deutschen Inflation auf die US-Wirtschaft in der Weltwirtschaftskrise 1920/21, in: G. D. Feldman, et al. (eds.), *German Inflation...,* pp. 207—234, where he puts forward his thesis that the German inflation prevented a major world economic crisis of the magnitude experienced later in 1929, because a "boom situation" prevailed in at least one of the major industrial countries in the 1920/21 depression. The importance of the inflation to the German post-World War I reconstruction effort has been the subject of some of Werner Abelshauser's studies. See, for example, *Inflation und Stabilisierung: Zum Problem ihrer makro-ökonomischen Auswirkungen auf die Rekonstruktion der deutschen Wirtschaft nach dem ersten Weltkrieg,* in: O. Büsch/G. D. Feldman (eds.), *Historische Prozesse...,* pp. 161—174; Werner Abelshauser/Dietmar Petzina, *Krise und Rekonstruktion: Zur Interpretation der gesamtwirtschaftlichen Entwicklung Deutschlands im 20. Jahrhundert,* in: Wilhelm Heinz Schröder/Reinhard Spree (eds.), *Historische Konjunkturforschung,* Stuttgart 1981, pp. 75—114. For a splendid recent analysis of the political economics of inflation in the international and intertemporal context, see Charles S. Maier, *The Politics of Inflation in the Twentieth Century,* in: Fred Hirsch/John H. Goldthorpe (eds.), *The Political Economy of Inflation,* London 1978, pp. 37—72.

5 C.-L. Holtfrerich, *Die deutsche Inflation...,* pp. 93—192. See also Otto Pfleiderer, *Die Reichsbank in der Zeit der großen Inflation,* in: Deutsche Bundesbank (ed.), *Währung und Wirtschaft in Deutschland 1876—1975,* Frankfurt 1976, pp. 115—156, and the recent study by Heinz Habedank, *Die Reichsbank in der Weimarer Republik: Zur Rolle der Zentralbank in der Politik des Imperialismus 1919—1933* (= Forschungen zur Wirtschaftsgeschichte, vol. 12), East Berlin 1981.

6 C.-L. Holtfrerich, *Die deutsche Inflation...,* pp. 218—276.

7 See, for example, Karlheinz Dederke, *Reich und Republik Deutschland 1917—1933,* Stuttgart 1969, pp. 65—81; Hajo Holborn, *A History of Modern Germany 1840—1945,*

year. By doing so, they generally failed to perceive of the inflation as a long-term process and, consequently, as a source of prolonged social and political conflict in the early Weimar years. It is not surprising that East German historians, writing and arguing from the vantage point of Marxists-Leninist economic determinism, were more inclined to view the economic process of inflation as a more crucial social-political variable than their West German colleagues.[8] Historians in both parts of Germany had, moreover, been preoccupied until recently with researching the German Revolution of 1918/19, thereby partially eclipsing other potential areas of concern to the historian of the Weimar Republic such as the post-World War I demobilization, or, in our case, the social and political consequences of protracted inflation and subsequent stabilization.[9]

This is not to say, however, that these last mentioned areas had remained a complete *terra incognita* prior to the unfolding of the "new inflation research" in the late 1970s. There were, after all, these "oases in the historiographical desert" that Gerald Feldman had talked about, which also existed in the social-political history of the German inflation.[10] But generally speaking one could well agree with an assessment

New York 1969, pp. 595—601; Gordon A. Craig, *Germany 1866—1945,* New York 1980, pp. 434—468.

[8] See Wolfgang Ruge, *Deutschland von 1917 bis 1933* (= Lehrbuch der deutschen Geschichte, Beiträge), East Berlin 1974, pp. 175—244.

[9] For a convenient overview of revolution research, see Georg P. Meyer, *Bibliographie zur Deutschen Revolution 1918/19* (= Arbeitsbücher zur modernen Geschichte, vol. 5), Göttingen 1977. Two important recent studies not contained in this bibliography are: Heinrich August Winkler, *Die Sozialdemokratie und die Revolution von 1918/19,* Bonn-Bad Godesberg 1979, and Wolfgang J. Mommsen, *Die deutsche Revolution 1918—1920: Politische Revolution und soziale Protestbewegung,* in: *Geschichte und Gesellschaft* (hereafter cited as *GG*), 4 (1978), pp. 362—391. Problems of demobilization are discussed by Gerald D. Feldman, *Economic and Social Problems of the German Demobilization 1918—1919,* in: *Journal of Modern History* (hereafter cited as *JMH*), 47 (1975), pp. 1—47, as well as the fall issue 1983 of the journal *Geschichte und Gesellschaft,* which is devoted to this subject in comparative international perspective.

[10] See principally: Peter-Christian Witt, *Finanzpolitik und sozialer Wandel in Krieg und Inflation 1918—1924,* in: H. Mommsen et al. (eds.), *Industrielles System...,* pp. 395—425; Claus-Dieter Krohn, *Helfferich contra Hilferding. Konservative Geldpolitik und die sozialen Folgen der deutschen Inflation 1918—1923,* in: *Vierteljahrsschrift für Sozial- und Wirtschaftsgeschichte* (hereafter cited as *VSWG*), 62 (1975), pp. 62—92; idem, *Die große Inflation in Deutschland 1918—1923,* Cologne 1977, the latter a perhaps less satisfactory, brief survey of the inflation and its consequences. See also the useful documentary study by Fritz K. Ringer, *The German Inflation,* New York 1969, and the older, but informative work of Hans Ostwald, *Sittengeschichte der Inflation. Ein Kulturdokument aus der Zeit des Marksturzes,* Berlin 1931.

made in 1976 that in fact very little progress had been made in a systematic examination of the social (not to speak of the political) consequences of the German inflation since the "classic" studies by two contemporary economists, Franz Eulenburg and Costantino Bresciani-Turroni, had been published in 1924 and 1937, respectively.[11] In addition, one of the main objectives of a modern reexamination of the social and political dimensions of the inflation process is to go beyond the narrow confines of contemporary research of the 1920s and 1930s, in which social groups were usually placed into the two categories of "winners" or "losers" of the inflation process, signaling a certain preoccupation with the ultimate *outcome* of the inflation rather than with the study of process itself. What should concern the social historian as well, however, is the manner of survival under extreme economic conditions like inflation, hyperinflation, and economic stabilization, i. e. deflation. This in turn, needs to be done by examining processes of adaptation to inflation, i. e. the "learning process" by which various social groups dealt with the previously unknown phenomenon of extreme inflation in a modern industrial setting. Only in this way can the full historical significance of the inflation be determined and the full impact of subsequent stabilization be assessed.[12]

[11] Jens Flemming/Claus-Dieter Krohn/Peter-Christian Witt, *Sozialverhalten und politische Reaktionen von Gruppen und Institutionen im Inflationsprozeß: Anmerkungen zum Forschungsstand,* in: O. Büsch/G. D. Feldman (eds.), *Historische Prozesse...*, pp. 239—263, p. 239. The contemporary studies referred to are Costantino Bresciani-Turroni, *The Economics of Inflation: A Study of Currency Depreciation in Post-War Germany,* London 1937, and Franz Eulenburg, *Die sozialen Wirkungen der Währungsverhältnisse,* in: *Jahrbücher für Nationalökonomie und Statistik* (hereafter cited as *JbNSt*), 122 (1924), pp. 748—794. A more thorough exposition of the Eulenburg essay will be given below.

[12] G. D. Feldman, *Gegenwärtiger Forschungsstand...*, in: O. Büsch/G. Feldman (eds.), *Historische Prozesse...*, p. 17. Recent studies on the history of social groups in the inflation process include: Werner Abelshauser, *Verelendung der Handarbeiter? Zur sozialen Lage der deutschen Arbeiter in der großen Inflation der frühen zwanziger Jahre,* in: Hans Mommsen/Winfried Schulze (eds.), *Vom Elend der Handarbeit. Probleme historischer Unterschichtenforschung* (= Geschichte und Gesellschaft. Bochumer Historische Studien, vol. 24), Stuttgart 1981, pp. 445—476; Michael L. Hughes, *Private Equity Social Inequity: German Judges React to Inflation, 1914—1924,* in: *Central European History* (hereafter cited as *CEH*), 16 (1983), pp. 76—94; Robert G. Moeller, *Dimensions of Social Conflict in the Great War: The View From the German Countryside,* in: *CEH*, 14 (1981), pp. 142—168; Merith Niehuss, *Arbeitslosigkeit in Augsburg und Linz a. D. 1914 bis 1924,* in: *Archiv für Sozialgeschichte* (hereafter cited as *AfS*), 22 (1982), pp. 133—158; idem., *Arbeiterschaft in Krieg und Inflation. Soziale Schichtung und Lage der Arbeiter in*

The present study, which probes into the social-political history of one social group during inflation and stabilization, needs to be placed into the context of the historiographical developments outlined thus far. Our object of investigation is an occupational group that was very relevant in German society then as it is now: civil servants, the *Beamtenschaft.* Thus our study is meant to be a contribution to the still unwritten social history of the German inflation and, at the same time, a study of some of the political processes that were unleashed by the inflation.

Roughly speaking, this study has two main purposes or foci. The first one may be described as the writing of a social history of German civil servants in a decade of protracted inflation. Socioeconomic conditions and social mobilization are the key words in this portion of our study, in which the social and economic conditions of the *Beamtenschaft* will be examined over the long-term perspective *(Chapter 1)*, while the processes of interest articulation, social mobilization, and interest group formation, which basically unfolded in the period between 1914 and 1919, will be dealt with in a rather long chapter *(Chapter 2)*, covering both the war years and the immediate postwar period of revolution. The conduct of interest politics by civil servant organizations during the postwar periods of inflation and stabilization (1919—1924) is the second major focus of this study. Viewed primarily from the angle of civil servant salary policy and its relationship to levels of social protest and increasing militancy within the *Beamtenschaft,* civil servant interest politics in inflation and stabilization will be explored in the remaining portions of this study *(Chapters 3 to 7)* by and large in form of a chronologically structured narrative. Throughout the entire study, moreover, we will be concerned with the political consequences of social and economic developments by attempting to gauge the political behavior of German civil servants in this period. The various components of these three areas of study, i. e. the social history of an occupational group, the conduct of interest politics in periods of economic inflation and stabilization, and, lastly, the political behavior of social

Augsburg und Linz 1910—1925 (= Veröffentlichungen der Historischen Kommission zu Berlin, vol. 58, Beiträge zu Inflation und Wiederaufbau in Deutschland und Europa 1914—1924, vol. 3), Berlin-New York 1984, and my own *Stand versus Klasse. Beamtenschaft und Gewerkschaften im Konflikt um den Personalabbau 1923/24,* in: *GG,* 8 (1982), pp. 55—86. Several recent dissertations and the contribution to the three anthologies cited in note 1 above have not been cited here.

groups in the inflation-stabilization process will now be examined in some more detail.

The Study of Social Groups in the Inflation Process: Civil Servants as a Case in Point

There can be no doubt that German civil servants, the *Beamtenschaft,* need to be included among the relevant socioeconomic groups to be studied within the framework of the new inflation research outlined above. A sizeable occupational group of nearly one and a half million members, civil servants (and their dependents) occupied an important position in German society in several respects. As an economic interest group, civil servants belonged to the larger stratum of dependent employees and consumers; as a social grouping, they were one of the constituent groups comprising the so-called new Mittelstand.[13] Civil servants were, moreover, an administrative and social elite, even if this role may have applied to the upper ranks of the group primarily.[14] Finally, the *Beamtenschaft* was an important target group for political mobilization, especially as voters and supporters of the liberal center and the moderate right in the spectrum of Weimar politics.

The necessity of including civil servants as a social group in the "group-oriented" study of the social and political consequences of the German inflation has repeatedly been stressed by those favoring the application of such an approach to the social history of the inflation. They have argued that a more or less neo-Marxist inspired class analysis would not do justice to the lingering, often preindustrial traditions of middle class groups in advanced industrial societies, even if, as in the case of German civil servants and white-collar workers, they belonged to the new middle class of dependent employees who also shared some of the modern social values advanced by the blue-collar working class. Owing to the social ambivalence of these groups, however, any attempt

[13] For a lucid introduction to the new Mittelstand, see Emil Lederer/Jakob Marschak, *Der neue Mittelstand,* in: *Grundriß der Sozialökonomik,* vol. 9, part 1, Tübingen 1929, pp. 121—141.

[14] Much of the extensive literature on bureaucracy conceives of (higher) civil servants as a social elite. See also the relevant sections in Wolfgang Zapf, *Wandlungen der deutschen Elite* (= Studien zur Soziologie, vol. 2), Munich 1965. For the European context see John T. Armstrong, *The European Administrative Elite,* Princeton 1972, for the U.S.A. cf. Reinhard Bendix, *Higher Civil Servants in American Society,* Boulder, Colorado 1949.

at forcing them into a traditional Marxist class structure would be counterproductive in the long run, and a group-oriented approach more fruitful in terms of gauging their responses to social, economic, and political developments.[15]

Aside of lingering preindustrial traditions, which need to be defined more clearly and, moreover, should not be overemphasized at the expense of more modern, i. e. industrial forms of behavior existing in middle class groups as well,[16] the study of civil servants defies incorporation into a class scheme because major composite groups of the *Beamtenschaft* would, in a two- or three-class model, have to be assigned to *different* classes. For example, academically trained higher civil servants, a social elite, would have to be included in the upper (or ruling) stratum of society, be it called bourgeoisie, upper middle class, or the like. Middle-grade civil servants would, in a three-class model, become members of the Mittelstand (or: lower middle class), while lower-grade civil servants would be moved near or even into the proletariat.[17] Any class model would, therefore, all but tear apart the *Beamtenschaft* as an

[15] See G. D. Feldman, *Gegenwärtige. Forschungsstand...*, in: O. Büsch/G. D. Feldman (eds.), *Historische Prozesse...*, p. 15. J. Flemming/C.-D. Krohn/P.-Ch. Witt, *Sozialverhalten...*, in: *Ibid.*, p. 242, and G. D. Feldman et al., *Inflation und Wiederaufbau...*, in: Idem (eds.), *The German Inflation...*, p. 19. For the counter proposal of a class-oriented analysis see Gerd Hardach, *Klassen und Schichten in Deutschland. Probleme einer historischen Schichtungsanalyse*, in: *GG*, 3 (1977), pp. 503—524, esp. 503—507.

[16] This is, in my opinion, a perennial problem in the otherwise pathbreaking *oeuvre* of Jürgen Kocka on the *Angestellten.* A good introduction to Kocka's work and his methodology is contained in his recent study of American white collar workers, *White Collar Workers in America 1890—1920. A Social-Political History in International Perspective*, transl. by Maura Kealy, London-Beverly Hills 1980, pp. 1—34.

[17] Such an assignment is made in the three-class model proposed by E. Lederer and J. Marschak in the work just cited in note 13 above. Despite its methodological shortcomings, this study remains the most perspective analysis of the *Beamtenschaft* as a social grouping to appear in the interwar years. See also Theodor Geiger, *Die soziale Schichtung des deutschen Volkes*, Stuttgart 1932, who constructs a five-class model on the basis of the 1925 German occupational census and assigns civil servants to various classes selected according to occupation and income level. Other contemporary sociographic studies of the *Beamtenschaft* include: Wilhelm Kulemann, *Die öffentlichen Beamten*, Berlin 1916; Alfred Weber, *Der Beamte*, in his *Ideen zur Staats- und Kultursoziologie*, Karlsruhe 1927; Erik Nölting, *Zur Soziologie der heutigen Beamtenschaft*, in: *Der Beamte*, 1 (1929), pp. 226—231; Franz Steiner, *Begriff und Wesen des modernen deutschen Beamtentums unter Berücksichtigung des Streikrechts*, Diss., Berlin 1934. The post-1945 study by Hans Maus, *Die soziologischen Formkräfte und Auswirkungen der deutschen Bürokratie als Sozialgebilde*, Diss., Heidelberg 1950, does not live up to its promising title.

existing, clearly identifiable, and historically relevant social group in its own right.

In the context of this study, therefore, it is our contention that despite some important social differentiations within the *Beamtenschaft*, resulting by and large from different levels of education and a corresponding hierarchical separation into higher, middle-grade, and lower-grade civil servants, there were important integrating forces that partially neutralized these differences and thus allow us to view the *Beamtenschaft* as a unique social group even prior to the First World War.[18] For one, there existed a specific civil service code (the *Beamtenrecht*), whose catalog of duties and privileges applied to *all* civil servants alike and governed their relationship with their employer, the government at all levels. The *Beamtenrecht* quasi institutionalized the separation of civil servants from white-collar workers (or salaried employees) in private industry, the *Angestellte,* and, of course, from industrial workers, the *Arbeiterschaft.*[19] To be sure, some lines of social differentiation remained blurred, especially vis-à-vis white-collar workers and, even more importantly, between civil servants and other employees in the public sector who worked under private rather than public law contracts.[20] But as will become clear in the course of the present study, it was precisely a growing tendency of the civil servants' *social* differentiation from non-civil service public employees which characterized social relationships in the German public sector during the inflation and stabilization periods. In other words, war, inflation, and stabilization became decisive factors in a group-formation process that established the *Beamtenschaft* more firmly as a social group than had been the case before 1914. It is not a coincidence, therefore, that in the second

[18] Not suprisingly, the concept of *Stand* ('estate') was then being used. See, for example, Otto Hintze's classic, *Der Beamtenstand* (= Vorträge der Gehe Stiftung), Leipzig 1911, reprinted in his *Gesammelte Abhandlungen,* vol. 2, *Soziologie und Geschichte,* Gerhard Oestreich (ed.), 2nd ed., Göttingen 1964, pp. 66—125. An informed critique of Hintze's approach from a Marxist perspective is Jane Caplan, *The Imaginary Universality of Particular Interests: The Tradition of the Civil Service in German History,* in: *Social History,* 4 (1979), pp. 299—317.

[19] The special social insurance law promulgated for *Angestellte* in 1911 fulfilled a similar function as a group-formation device. See Jürgen Kocka, *Class Formation, Interest Articulation, and Public Policy: The Origins of the German White-collar Class in the Late Nineteenth and Early Twentieth Centuries,* in: Suzanne D. Berger (ed.), *Organizing Interests in Western Europe: Pluralism, Corporatism, and the Transformation of Politics,* Cambridge 1981, pp. 63—81, esp. pp. 73—75.

[20] These were then called *öffentliche Angestellte* and *Staatsarbeiter.*

occupational census taken during the inter-war years, in 1932, civil servants were for the first time counted separately as a "social class", i. e. as a social group.[21]

Interest articulation and organization may be viewed as additional indicators of a specific group identity of the *Beamtenschaft.* Here we note that during the period of inflation civil servants banded together more tightly than before in a separate social movement, the so-called civil servant movement, the *Beamtenbewegung.*[22] There is a striking

[21] Previously, *Beamte* had been counted together with the *Angestellte.* Naturally, the differentiation discussed here may likewise be considered a reflection of the separating tendencies within the *Angestelltenschaft.* The point is that there were obviously two social processes at work at the same time. For a more detailed discussion see CHAPTER ONE of this study.

[22] The *Beamtenbewegung* has not received much attention in recent scholarship, despite the renewed interest in trade-union history and the social history of related occupational groups like the *Angestellte.* The only recent study is by Rainer M. Halmen, *„Das Berufsbeamtentum muß unter allen Umständen erhalten bleiben." Die deutsche Beamtenbewegung zwischen Etatismus und gewerkschaftlicher Orientierung im Übergang vom Kaiserreich zur Weimarer Republik,* in: *Internationale wissenschaftliche Korrespondenz zur Geschichte der deutschen Arbeiterbewegung* (hereafter cited as *IWK*) 18 (1982), pp. 173—205. Some recent organizational histories include Ernst Schrön, *Deutscher Beamtenbund (DBB) 1918—1933,* in: Dieter Fricke (ed.), *Die bürgerlichen Parteien in Deutschland. Handbuch der Geschichte der bürgerlichen Parteien und anderer bürgerlicher Interessenorganisationen,* vol. 1, Leipzig 1968, pp. 422—428; Georg Kalmer, *Vom Staatsdiener zum Staatsbürger. Die Entwicklung der bayerischen Beamtenorganisationen,* in: *Informationsschrift des Bayerischen Beamtenbundes anläßlich seines 50jährigen Bestehens,* Munich 1967. The official history of the Deutscher Beamtenbund, published in 1968, is of limited usefulness because of its organizational bias and rather limited use of reliable source material. See *Deutscher Beamtenbund. Ursprung, Weg und Ziel,* published by the Bundesleitung of the *Deutscher Beamtenbund,* Bonn-Bad Godesberg 1968. The contemporaneous literature on the civil servant movement is more plentiful. See, e. g., Emil Lederer, *Die sozialen Organisationen,* Leipzig-Berlin 1920, pp. 108—114; Wilhelm Kulemann, *Der Gewerkschaftsgedanke in der Beamtenbewegung,* Berlin 1919; Lujo Brentano, *Die Beamtenorganisationen und ihre wirtschaftlichen Ziele,* Munich 1920; Adolf Barteld, *Die deutsche Beamtenbewegung,* in: Anton Erkelenz (ed.), *Zehn Jahre Deutsche Republik,* Berlin 1928. Some of the important works written by persons directly affiliated with the civil servants' movement include: Albert Falkenberg, *Die deutsche Beamtenbewegung nach der Revolution,* Berlin 1920; Fritz Winters, *Die deutsche Beamtenfrage,* Berlin 1918; idem, *Der deutsche Beamtenbund. Seine Entstehung und Entwicklung* (= Templiner Kursushefte, No. 3), Berlin 1931; Ernst Remmers, *Die organisatorische Einheit der deutschen Beamten,* Berlin 1928. A fairly large number of contemporary dissertations were written on the organizational history of the civil servant movement. The most useful ones, partially based on organizational records that have meanwhile been lost, are: Kurt Ritter von Scherf, *Die Entwicklung der Beamtenbewe-*

parallel to salaried employees in this respect, who likewise assembled in a more coherent movement, the *Angestelltenbewegung*, during this time period. The blue-collar working class movement provided the organizational model for both groups.[23]

Viewing civil servants as a "social group in formation" has yet another advantage. It avoids preconceived notions and connotations of preindustrial mentalities and corporate traditions entailed in such terms as *Beamtenstand* and *Beamtentum*, the latter describing an institution rather than a group, moreover, i. e. the professional career civil service or *Berufsbeamtentum*.[24] Our group-approach is more flexible by allowing a greater leeway in dealing with relations between civil servants and other employee groups. The entire area of interest alliances and conflicts between civil servants and the organized working class, for example, is only possible to explore if we allow for a certain openness within the social group *Beamtenschaft* during this period. The same would be true for intra-group conflicts, i. e. for the patterns of relationships at work *within* the *Beamtenschaft*.[25]

The present study, then, examines the *Beamtenschaft* as a unique social group in German society and traces its development — economic, social, and political — over a decade of inflation, i. e. between

gung und ihre Interessenvertretung, Diss., Greifswald 1919; Ernst Krüger, *Die Gewerkschaftsbewegung der deutschen Beamten, ihr Werdegang und ihre Probleme*, Diss., Frankfurt/Main 1924; Wilhelm Schweitzer, *Die Beamtenorganisationen in Deutschland und ihre Stellungnahme zu der Beamtenfrage*, Diss., Würzburg 1929; Martin Oelschig, *Die neuere Entwicklung der Beamtenschaft, die Entstehung der Beamtenvereine und die Beamtenberufsvereine*, Diss., Halle 1933.

[23] The origins of both movements date well before 1914, of course; the point made here is that the final separation of three corporate-type *(ständisch)* branches of the German labor movement, a German peculiarity to this day, happened during the periods of war and postwar inflation. These developments will be discussed in more detail in the course of this study.

[24] Cf. Albert Lotz, *Geschichte des deutschen Beamtentums*, Berlin 1909, and Hans Hattenhauer, *Geschichte des Beamtentums* (= Handbuch des öffentlichen Dienstes, vol. 1), Cologne 1980, two studies that focus on the evolution of a professional civil service in Germany. A study of the same type in English is Fritz Morstein-Marx, *Civil Service in Germany*, in: *Civil Service Abroad: Great Britain, Canada, France, Germany*, New York-London 1935.

[25] The term *Beamtenschaft*, although of pre-industrial origin as well, is definitely the most modern sounding one of the three terms available, pointing, as it does, to the *economic* position of civil servants. The German word *Beamtenschaft* will therefore be used in this study to imply "civil servants as a social group".

1914 and 1924. We shall be concerned with the economic and social conditions of civil servants under the impact of inflation and subsequent stabilization, and with the conflicts and tensions that arose from these conditions. Patterns of social organization, interest articulation, forms of social protest, and group conflicts will initially be explored at the level of the social group. The resulting tensions and conflicts will then be traced to the "higher levels" of interest politics, interest alliances and conflicts, and political decision making.

What, then, are some of the main questions to be raised and issues to be addressed in a study of civil servants and other social groups in successive periods of inflation and stabilization during and after the First World War? To answer this question, we will now examine more closely two works by contemporary observers, both economists, who studied the impact of the wartime and post-World War I currency depreciation on their respective societies: John Maynard Keynes, who astutely observed and described the impact of inflation and deflation on Great Britain, and an essay by the much lesser known German economist Franz Eulenburg, who in 1924 published the perhaps "classic" work on the social consequences of the German inflation.

In his *Tract on Monetary Reform,* first published in 1923, but originally printed as a series of newspaper articles in 1921—22, Keynes made the important observation that any change in the value of money, be it inflation or deflation, was important to society only in so far as it furthered (or altered) existing disparities between social groups. Changes in the level of prices, he wrote, "have produced in the past, and are producing now, the vastest social consequences, because, as we all know, when the value of money changes, it does *not* change equally for all persons for all purposes... Thus a change in prices and rewards, as measured in money, generally affects different classes unequally, transfers wealth from one to another, bestows affluence here and embarrassment there, and redistributes Fortune's favors so as to frustrate design and disappoint expectation."[26] Keynes, who regarded the fluctuations in price levels during and after the First World War as "one of the most significant events in the economic history of the modern world", did so not only because they had affected societies whose economic (and, one may add *social*) organization depended to a greater

[26] John Maynard Keynes, *A Tract on Monetary Reform* (1923), reprinted as Volume IV of *The Collected Writings of John Maynard Keynes,* London 1971, pp. 1—2.

degree than in earlier times and epochs on the rational assumption that the standard of value of money would be moderately stable.[27]

In order to assess the distributional changes produced by inflation and deflation, Keynes divided (British) society in three classes: an investing class, a business class, and an earning class. While he seemed well aware of the unhappy fact that these classes overlapped, because, as he put it, "the same individual may earn, deal and invest", he argued that this division corresponded to social cleavages and actual divergences of interests at work in "present society."[28] The crudity and imprecision of this three-class model remains the Achilles' heel of Keynes' analysis and virtually precludes the acceptance of his findings by the social historian of today. While the "investing class" obviously represents the middle-class element of society and in Keynes' analysis is depicted as the main loser in the inflation process,[29] this characterization seems too global and imprecise to be taken as an acceptable description of the middle class stratum. Indeed, it often seems that Keynes' "investing class" is nothing but the *rentier* class in the Marxian tradition, and hence just one fraction of what we would consider to encompass the middle class stratum.

As the 'investing class' was losing out as a result of inflation, the two other classes, both of which were engaged in production, became winners in the inflation process. The 'business class', Keynes argued, was able to improve its economic position through windfall profits made on the purchase of raw materials and on the repayment of debts to the 'investing class' in devalued currency.[30] The 'earning class' was able to improve its social position in relative and even absolute terms vis-à-vis middle class groups by securing higher wage levels during and after the war. Even the deflationary conditions, which in Great Britain

[27] It may be noted that Keynes was interested in describing the impact of both inflation and deflation upon a society, the latter because several European countries had contracted their money supply as early as 1920 in order to stabilize their financial situation (e. g. Great Britain and the United States), while others allowed a moderate rate of inflation (e. g. France, Italy) and still others (e. g. Germany, Austria) pushed on with an increasing rate of inflation. Both processes, Keynes argued, produced economic and social consequences, albeit different ones. While inflation mainly affected the distribution of wealth between social groups, deflation created an impact on the production of wealth.

[28] J. M. Keynes, *A Tract...*, p. 4.

[29] *Ibid.*, pp. 4—17.

[30] *Ibid.*, pp. 17—25.

prevailed as early as 1920—21, did not change this balance sheet. Wage earners continued to have an advantage over the investing class, since wage rates continued to remain above prewar levels. This alone, Keynes reasoned, made it possible for the working class to later on bear the main penalty of the deflation process, i. e. higher levels of unemployment.[31]

It is in the context of the alleged impoverishment of the middle (i. e. 'investing') class and the gains made by the working class that Keynes drew a parallel to the situation prevailing on the Continent, i. e. in Germany and Austria. In these countries, he wrote, "the burden of hard circumstances" had been placed on the middle class to a much greater degree than in England or France, while at the same time the laboring class had "by no means supported their full proportionate share." A middle-class member himself, Keynes, like many of his contemporaries, was not free of moralizing about the social decline of the latter when he wrote: "The effects of the impoverishment, throughout Europe, of the middle class, out of which most good things have sprung, must slowly accumulate in a decay of science and the arts."[32]

It is not surprising, therefore, that in his overall assessment of the consequences of inflation Keynes stressed the detrimental social and economic impact produced by an alleged redistribution of wealth:

"We conclude that inflation redistributes wealth in a manner very injurious to the investor, very beneficial to the businessman, and probably, in modern industrial societies, beneficial on the whole to the earner. Its most striking consequence is its injustice to those who in good faith have committed their savings to titles in money rather than things. Moreover, inflation has not only diminished the capacity of the investing class to save, but has destroyed the atmosphere of confidence which is a condition of the willingness to save."[33]

Since saving is the sine qua non for capital formation, Keynes' argument runs on, only a healthy middle class of savers and investors could, in the long run, support the standard of living of a growing body of laborers. While the 19th century had provided "a proportionate growth between capital and population, Keynes concluded that "the disturbance of the preexisting balance between classes, which in its

[31] *Ibid.*, pp. 25—30.
[32] *Ibid.*, pp. 27—28.
[33] *Ibid.*, p. 29.

origins is largely traceable to the changes in the value of money, may have destroyed these favorable conditions."[34]

Let us recapitulate the main theses and arguments put forth by Keynes in this somewhat gloomy assessment of the inflation process:

1) Inflation permanently changes the distribution of wealth, or income, between the various social classes of society.
2) The middle class, or 'investor class', as Keynes called it, appears as the main loser of distributional changes prompted by inflation.
3) The working class ('earning class'), by contrast, emerges as a winner in the changes caused by inflation, since its relative position vis-á-vis other groups improved.
4) The erosion of the middle classes' position is viewed by Keynes as an injustice done to this class which would lead to grave social, cultural, and economic consequences.
5) Political consequences, however, were not mentioned by Keynes in this context.

What are, finally, some of the problems with Keynes' analysis? First, as has been mentioned already, the social classification-scheme used by him is too imprecise. Second, in spite of the fact that Keynes himself emphasized the long duration of the inflation/deflation process, he mainly studied their consequences as they had developed by 1920 and 1923, respectively. There is little to be learned about the way in which the distributional changes and the social injuries produced by them came about, other than through deliberate government policy.[35] Let us, then, turn to the second contemporary witness, whose account is somewhat less abstract and more pertintent to the social consequences of the *German* inflation.

In 1924, the year when the trauma of hyperinflation was still very much present in German society, the German economist Franz Eulenburg published his by now classic study on the social consequences of the German inflation.[36] In a number of ways the approaches taken by

[34] *Ibid.*, p. 30.

[35] This aspect is discussed in the subsequent chapter of the *Tract,* in which Keynes explores the relationship between public finances and changes in the monetary value (*ibid.* pp. 37—60).

[36] F. Eulenburg, *Die sozialen Wirkungen...*, in: *JbNSt,* 122 (1924), pp. 748—794. This study was the enlarged version of an address Eulenburg delivered at a meeting of the Verein für Sozialpolitik in September 1924. See *Verhandlungen des Vereins für Sozialpolitik Stuttgart 1924. Theorie des Klassenkampfes, Handelspolitik, Währungsfrage* (= Schriften des Vereins für Sozialpolitik, vol. 170) Munich-Leipzig 1925. The latter work will henceforth be cited as *Währungsfrage.*

Eulenburg and Keynes show parallels and similarities — and similar shortcomings as well. Like Keynes, Eulenburg was mainly interested in an appraisal of the consequences of the German inflation as these presented themselves to him in 1924. "What needs to be done", Eulenburg wrote, "is to determine how the social structure of the various classes of society, how society as a whole has changed as a result of the decline of the currency."[37] For the purpose of such an analysis, Eulenburg divided German society in four (instead of Keynes' three) main "classes": capitalists and property owners, entrepreneurs, the Mittelstand, and the working class. In the course of his study Eulenburg then examines the changed relationship between and, in a broadening of the approach taken by Keynes, *within* these four classes by separating them into various composite social groups as he goes along. The Mittelstand, for example, is divided into six composite groups: artisans (the *Handwerk*), retailers (the *Handelsstand*), houseowners (*Hausbesitzer* — a somewhat unusual category), civil servants, the professions *(freie Berufe)*, and university students.[38] While there are still problems of overlappings and omissions — one is struck by the fact, for example, that the *Angestellte* do not appear as a separate social group in Eulenburg's classification scheme but are subsumed within the *Arbeiterschaft* — the group approach as such led Eulenburg toward more differentiated, often even contradictory conclusions than those advanced by Keynes with regard to the fate of the middle classes and the working class in the inflation.

The Mittelstand, Eulenburg argued, had not been destroyed or expropriated by the inflation. Far from it, *some* middle class groups emerged from the inflation in a socially firmer position than before the war and the Revolution of 1918/19. Among the middle class winners Eulenburg singled out house owners, the *Hausbesitzer,* who could rid themselves of mortgages, and, more important in our context, the middle and lower ranks of the *Beamtenschaft.* The civil servants' position, Eulenburg claimed, had by and large remained protected by his ownership of a post, so to speak, while other middle class groups, whose income had rested solely on monetary proceeds, had lost out:

"Today, when other middle strata have lost a good portion of their income derived from savings and annuities, civil servants appear

[37] F. Eulenburg, *Die sozialen Wirkungen…*, in: *JbNSt,* 122 (1924), p. 753.

[38] *Ibid.*, pp. 771.

stronger than ever [as a social group]. We now understand, why [civil service] positions are in such high demand. The position as such has become property in this case, after a great majority of the Mittelstand has lost its fortunes. For the middle classes, therefore, a civil service position appears as a goal to reach for. It will continue to exist even after interest income *[Rentenkapital]* has disappeared in the chasm of the inflation. The contracts of civil servants have been observed by the government, regardless of the fact that salaries were sometimes paid too late and despite the current personnel reduction measures. By contrast, all other contracts, which had been based on money, could not be kept."[39]

The impact of the inflation on the social conditions of the Mittelstand, Eulenburg concluded, was therefore ambivalent and "as conflicting as this class as such."[40] Major middle class groups, including civil servants, appeared as winners of the inflation together with property owners, especially farmers, entrepreneurs, and all debtors. The main losers were, in Eulenburg's view, the small investors, pensioners, professional people and, in a notable departure from the view held by Keynes, the working class, whose power had been eroded by the inflation and which had all but plunged into a social crisis of major proportions.[41] Similar to Keynes, Eulenburg blamed the inflation for having produced a "general crisis of the educated classes" (the *Bildungsschicht*),

[39] F. Eulenburg, *Währungsfrage*, p. 99. To back up this thesis, Eulenburg mentioned that the number of university students had increased during this period, many of whom came from civil servant families.

[40] F. Eulenburg, *Die sozialen Wirkungen...*, in: *JbNSt*, 122 (1924), p. 779. For an opposing view, in which the Mittelstand appears as the impoverished loser in the distributional conflicts produced by the inflation, see Hans Heiler, *Die Verelendung des Mittelstandes* (= Beiträge zur Statistik Bayerns, No. 106), Munich 1925, pp. 19 ff.

[41] F. Eulenburg, *Die sozialen Wirkungen...*, in: *JbNSt*, 122 (1924), p. 790. It is not surprising that during the discussion of Eulenburg's presentation at the Verein für Sozialpolitik the representative of working-class interests, the trade unionist Paul Umbreit, greatly welcomed the economist's remarks on the situation of labor as a 'scientific proof' of labor's complaints. Eulenburg responded in his closing remarks to what he obviously had taken as an embarrassing praise by pointing out that Umbreit had picked out from his lecture only those points that suited his interests. See F. Eulenburg, *Währungsfrage...*, pp. 123—125 (Umbreit's remarks) and p. 137 (Eulenburg's reply). A useful account of the situation of German labor in the immediate postwar years is Robert Kuczynski, *Postwar Labor Conditions in Germany* (= Bulletin of the United States Bureau of Labor Statistics, No. 380), Washington 1925. For a citation of more recent literature on this topic see note 49 below.

to which he counted professional people and higher civil servants. This crisis, he argued, would in the long run be detrimental to the cultural development of the German people on the whole.[42]

How can one assess Eulenburg's helter-skelter balance sheet of winners and losers in the German inflation? For one, it must be emphasized that his investigation of the fate of smaller social groups makes it, in terms of methodology, a classic in the not so abundant historiography on the subject, even if more recently it has been argued that some of Eulenburg's winners could indeed be losers, and that therefore his overall balance sheet needs to be revised thoroughly.[43] It is as a point of departure, therefore, that Eulenburg's study has retained its importance to today's historian of the German inflation. He was the first to offer a differentiated picture of German society at the end of the inflation process in 1923—24.[44] The three main objectives of his study, i. e. the examination of the inner structure of social groups (intra-group changes and conflicts), the changing relations between social groups (inter-groups conflicts and alliances), and the impact of both of these on society as a whole have remained major tasks for today's historian of the German inflation, as the more modern terms given in parentheses may indicate. However, two other areas of study have to be added, both of which by and large escaped Eulenburg's attention: first, the entire area of interest politics conducted by social groups *during* the inflation, and second, the political consequences of inflation and stabilization in the context of the overall political development of the Weimar Republic.

The Structure and Function of Interest Politics in the Inflation Process: The Case of Salary Policy

Given the importance of interest group politics in the functioning of advanced industrial societies, the activities of a social group and its

[42] F. Eulenburg, *Die sozialen Wirkungen...*, in: *JbNSt*, 122 (1924), p. 790. See also Alfred Weber, *Die Not der geistigen Arbeiter* (= Schriften des Vereins für Sozialpolitik, vol. 163), Munich-Leipzig 1923; Georg Schreiber, *Die Not der deutschen Wissenschaft und der geistigen Arbeiter*, Leipzig 1923.

[43] See, for example, Robert G. Moeller's contribution to G. D. Feldman et al., *The German Inflation...*, pp. 255—288, with the provocative title *Winners as Losers in the German Inflation: Peasant Protest over the Controlled Economy, 1920—1923.*

[44] For a similar, even more comprehensive picture of Austria, which also went through periods of inflation and stabilization between 1914 and 1922, see Julius Bunzel, (ed.), *Geldentwertung und Stabilisierung in ihren Einflüssen auf die soziale Entwicklung in Österreich* (= Schriften des Vereins für Sozialpolitik, vol. 169), Munich-Leipzig, 1925.

relative weight in society can best be measured by the way it conducts interest politics through representative organizations. Since interest organization and articulation is essentially a modern social phenomenon, the degree in which the various social groups responded to the economic pressures of inflation through organized forms of collective action also indicates a social group's willingness to depart from traditional preconceptions and to accept more modern forms of social behavior. By the same token, the willingness of the main addressees of interest politics, government, parliament, and the body politic in general to accept interest politics as a form of legitimate social representation can reflect the modernity of a given society and its political system.[45] Moreover, the renewed and still controversial debate on the concept of corporatism or "neo-corporatism" in advanced industrial societies shows that even the inherent tendency of interest groups to attain political influence through "corporatist arrangements," i. e. by establishing a network of informal interconnections between interest group and body politic, and by exercising quasi-control on public policy through "interest intermediation" are essentially modern phenomena and may therefore be taken as a further indication of the state of development of a given society.[46]

Both tendencies prevailed in the all-pervasive interest group structure of the early Weimar Republic. In view of the importance of interest

[45] For a full discussion of the role of interest groups in modern industrial societies, see G. Wootton, *Interest Groups*, Englewood Cliffs 1970 and Klaus von Beyme, *Interessengruppen in der Demokratie*, Munich 1969. On the formation of interest groups in Western Europe see S. D. Berger (ed.), *Organizing Interests*... For the German case see Heinz Josef Varain (ed.), *Interessenverbände in Deutschland*, Cologne 1973. A splendid bibliography is Hans-Peter Ullmann, *Bibliographie zur Geschichte der deutschen Parteien und Interessenverbände* (= Arbeitsbücher zur modernen Geschichte, no.6), Göttingen 1978.

[46] On corporatism and 'neo-corporatism' in general see Philippe C. Schmitter, *Still the Century of Corporatism?*, in: *Review of Politics*, 36 (1974), pp. 85—131; Philippe C. Schmitter/Gerhard Lehmbruch (eds.), *Trends Toward Corporatist Intermediation*, London-Beverly Hills 1979; and, by the same editors, *Consequences of Corporatist Policy Making*, London-Beverly Hills 1981. See also Ulrich von Alemann (ed.), *Neokorporatismus*, Frankfurt-New York 1982. The German case is discussed by Ulrich Nocken, *Korporatistische Theorien und Strukturen in der deutschen Geschichte des 19. und frühen 20. Jahrhunderts*, in: U. von Alemann (ed.), *Neokorporatismus*..., pp. 17—42, and idem, *Corporatism and Pluralism in Modern German History*, in: Dirk Stegmann et al. (eds.), *Industrielle Gesellschaft und politisches System. Beiträge zur politischen Sozialgeschichte*, Bonn 1978, pp. 37—58.

group politics to the course of modern German history it seems surprising indeed that the role played by economic and social interest groups in the German inflation, or rather in the "politics of inflation," had until recently been almost completely overlooked, especially by economists dealing with the subject. In their 1968 study of the German inflation, the Danish economists Karsten Laursen and Jørgen Pedersen, for example, arrived at the surprising, and in view of recent research totally unfounded conclusion that the German inflation was the result of a "lack of policy" of either government or interest groups.[47] A recent study by Gerald Feldman shows that one of the major socioeconomic interest groups, German industrialists, were indeed very much involved in the conscious planning and conduct of an inflationary monetary policy and were, moreover, supported by organized labor in these efforts, at least up to a certain point.[48]

Alliances between formerly rival interest groups have been identified as a major aspect of interest politics in the inflation process. Historians have raised the question as to when these alliances were forged, what their aims were, what social and economic policies they conducted or supported, and when and under what circumstances they disintegrated again. Regarding the latter, the problem and timing of stabilization has been singled out as a major factor, and it has been argued that on the whole it was easier for rival groups like capital and labor to agree on an "inflation alliance" than to extend such an alliance through the changed economic and social conditions of economic stabilization.[49]

In connection with the theme of alliances and conflicts between interest groups during the inflation, recent research seems to indicate

[47] K. Laursen/J. Pedersen, *German Inflation...*, p. 123.

[48] See G. D. Feldman, *Iron and Steel...*, passim.

[49] On interest alliances between capital and labor during the inflation see Gerald D. Feldman, *Interest Alliances in War and Inflation*, in: S. D. Berger (ed.), *Organizing Interests...*, pp. 169—184. See also Charles S. Maier, *Recasting Bourgeois Europe. Stabilization in France, Germany and Italy in the Decade after World War I*, Princeton 1975, esp. pp. 233—304. The role of industry in these alliances is discussed by Ulrich Nocken, *Industrial Alliances and Conflicts in the Weimar Republic: Experiments in Societal Corporatism*, Diss., University of California, Berkeley 1979, and by Bernd Weisbrod, *Schwerindustrie in der Weimarer Republik*, Wuppertal 1978. The role of labor has, on the whole, received less attention. See Gerald D. Feldman, *Die Freien Gewerkschaften und die Zentralarbeitsgemeinschaft*, in: Heinz Oskar Vetter (ed.), *Vom Sozialistengesetz zur Mitbestimmung*, Cologne 1975, pp. 229—252, and Heinrich Potthoff, *Gewerkschaften und Politik zwischen Revolution und Inflation* (= Beiträge zur Geschichte des Parlamentarismus und der politischen Parteien, vol. 16), Düsseldorf 1979, esp. pp. 177—204.

that major and influential interest groups in German society had very specific interests and motives for supporting an inflationary economic policy in the years between 1919 and 1921. Moreover, it has been pointed out that the German government, whatever its ulterior motives for eschewing stabilization at an earlier date than 1923 might have been (e. g. reparation issue, indirect taxation),[50] also succumbed to the pressures exerted by interest groups in making its political choices.[51] What is important in this context is that the responsibility for the conduct of inflationary policies and the wrecking of the German currency cannot be placed unilaterally upon a government acting on behalf of *one* social group, be it capital or labor, but that a rather complex and complicated pattern of relationships between these two main social groups came into play and exerted interest pressure on the politically weak coalition governments of the early Weimar years.[52]

[50] On reparations and inflation see Hermann J. Rupieper, *The Cuno Government and Reparations. Politics and Economics,* The Hague 1979; Marc Trachtenberg, *Reparation in World Politics,* New York 1981; Stephen A. Schuker, *Finance and Foreign Policy in the Era of the German Inflation,* in: O. Büsch/G. Feldman (eds.), *Historische Prozesse...,* pp. 343—361. That inflation was also a method of indirect taxation used by politically weak government was already noted by Keynes in 1923. See *A Tract...,* pp. 37—60. The interdependence between inflation and taxation policy has recently been reexamined by Peter-Christian Witt, *Tax Policies, Tax Assessment and Inflation. Toward a Sociology of Public Finances in the German Inflation 1914—1923,* in: Nathan Schmukler and Edward Marcus (eds.), *Inflation through the Ages: Economic, Social, Psychological, and Historical* Aspects, New York 1982, pp. 450—474.

[51] It will be argued in the present study that civil servant organizations were one of these groups. Even a cursory look at the relevant government documents, many of which have been published in the series *Akten der Reichskanzlei. Weimarer Republik* will confirm this impression.

[52] Marxist and neo-Marxist West German scholarship singles out the industrialists as the "culprits" of inflation policy, conducted, as it were, at the expense of the working classes, for the sake of economic profit, and for the regaining of political and social power lost in the Revolution of 1918/19. See W. Ruge, *Deutschland von 1917 bis 1933...,* pp. 191—199 for a summary of the East-German position, and C.-D. Krohn, *Die Große Inflation...,* pp. 25—35 for the neo-Marxist position. The counterargument that labor and wage pressures exerted by its organizational and political power was the principal "culprit", a view widely held by contemporary liberal economists of the interwar years, has now been taken up again by economic historians. See Gerhard Kessler, *Die Lage der deutschen Arbeiterschaft seit 1914,* in: Bernhard Harms (ed.), *Strukturwandlungen der deutschen Volkswirtschaft,* Berlin 1928, pp. 433—466 for the contemporary view, and Knut Borchard, *Wirtschaftliche Ursachen des Scheiterns der Weimarer Republik,* in: Karl Dietrich Erdmann/Hagen Schulze (eds.), *Weimar, Selbstpreisgabe einer Demokratie: Eine Bilanz heute,* Düsseldorf 1980, pp. 211—250, for a much more sophisticated restatement of the wage-pressure argument.

In the context of the present study, the role and function of civil servants as an organized interest group will be examined as these related to the politics of inflation and subsequent stabilization. Aside of the general phenomena of interest politics just discussed, which will be used as a framework of reference, some specific observations on the significance and contours of civil servant interest politics need to be made in order to point to the extent as well as to the limitations of our analysis.

One of the principle areas of study targeted by the new research on the German inflation has been the analysis of the process by which social groups were able to adjust to the inflation and thus were able to offset some of its social consequences. In terms of interest politics conducted by organizations of dependent employees — blue-collar workers, salaried employees, and civil servants alike — their respective influence on the formulation and execution of wage (or salary) policy assumes an outstanding historical significance. After all, the material conditions of these three groups depended (and depend to this day) on their pecuniary earnings, regardless whether these were paid in form of a wage *(Lohn)*, salary *(Gehalt)*, or civil service pay *(Besoldung)*. For this reason the main vehicle available to organized civil servants to shape their own destiny, so to speak, was by gaining influence upon the formulation and conduct of civil service salary policy *(Besoldungspolitik)*, a policy area which before 1914 had been a virtual prerogative of government policy makers and parliamentary delegates.[53]

To a large extent, therefore, any study of civil servant interest politics in inflation and stabilization must be a study of salary policy viewed from the organizational perspective. Often accompanied by intense social strife, ranging from mass demonstrations to public service strikes, salary policy emerged as the main source of conflict between civil servants and the state (i. e., the government at all levels) during the inflation years. It will be shown that social conflicts within the German public sector in general, and within the civil service in particular, belonged to the most severe unleashed by the inflation. The struggle over the aims and contours of salary policy was at the core of these conflicts, the great civil servant strike of February 1922, to this

[53] On the conduct of salary policy before 1914, and the exclusion of the associations from it, see Hans Völter, *Die deutsche Beamtenbesoldung*, in: Wilhelm Gerloff (ed.), *Die Beamtenbesoldung im modernen Staat* (= Schriften des Vereins für Sozialpolitik, vol. 184/I), pp. 1—105, pp. 11—14.

day the only major civil servant strike in German history, one of its most remarkable and historically significant manifestations.[54]

It goes without saying that civil servant interest politics was not limited to the area of salary policy. In the course of the stabilization crisis of 1923—24, for example, employment policy became an important concern to civil servant leaders as public employers embarked on a general reduction of personnel in the public sector. It would be beyond the scope and intention of this study, however, to try to offer a complete analysis of civil servant interest politics in its relationship to the formulation and conduct of general civil service policy in the early Weimar Republic. Moreover, this has partially been done elsewhere, particularly with regard to the November Revolution.[55] The main objective of this study will be the examination of social and economic policies conducted by the civil servant associations during inflation, and stabilization. The politics of *Besoldung* und *Abbau* will be set against the changing socioeconomic conditions of the *Beamtenschaft* and the social tensions and conflicts produced by these conditions. In addition, two areas of interest activity will be examined in a more detailed way, since these were supporting policy measures adopted by civil servant organizations at various times during the inflation: (1) the organization and politics of group-controlled economic self-help, and (2) attempts made by civil servant associations to formulate economic policy guidelines, i. e. proposals for the terms of stabilization. The ventures into economic policy-making may offer additional clues about the politics of inflation and stabilization in the early Weimar Republic, as well as serve to enlarge the framework for the discussion of the political responses and the political behavior of civil servants in inflation and stabilization.

Inflation and Political Behavior: Civil Servants as a Test Case

The argument that the German inflation led to clearly indentifiable political responses within major groups of German society is usually made, rather than proven, in the context of middle-class support for right wing political extremism and National Socialism in the Weimar Republic. One does not have to be impressed with the colorful imagery

[54] The February Strike of 1922 will therefore be one of the main foci of this study.

[55] See esp. Georg Kalmer, *Beamtenschaft und Revolution,* in: Karl Bosl (ed.), *Bayern im Umbruch,* Munich 1969, pp. 201—261.

put forth by the British economist Lionel Robbins, who in 1937 called Hitler the "foster child of the inflation,"[56] to be struck by the historical simultaneousness between the hyperinflation and the Munich Beer Hall Putsch of November 9, 1923, which brought Hitler's National Socialists for the first time to the attention of a national audience in Germany. Yet at closer sight this is a historical parallelism at best, and even Robbins probably had long-term developments in the political and economic structure of Weimar Germany in mind when he made his remark in 1937. In the larger debate over the social bases of fascism, it is the role of an allegedly economically expropriated and socially dislocated German middle class as the breeding ground and the recruitment base for right-wing political extremism, be it National Socialism or other forms of militant, anti-republican political conservatism as represented by the German National People's Party (the DNVP), which lies at the core of the middle-class argument connected with the political consequences of the German inflation.[57]

What is to be made of this argument? First of all, the importance of middle-class groups to the rise of right-wing politics and fascism in Germany and Europe in general cannot be denied. At a certain juncture National Socialism did become a political *Sammlung* movement of disgruntled middle-class elements.[58] Whether the economic hardships caused by the inflation played a significant role in the right-wing political mobilization of the German middle class remains unclear, however, and should become more the subject of further empirical research rather than remain a standard assumption made in general studies of the Weimar Republic.[59] Since there was indeed a general turn to the political right in the "inflation elections" of 1924, when the

[56] In the Preface to the English edition of C. Bresciani-Turroni, *The Economics of Inflation...*, p. 5.

[57] Cf. J. Flemming/C.-D. Krohn/P.-Ch. Witt, *Sozialverhalten...*, in: O. Büsch/G. D. Feldman (eds.), *Historische Prozesse...*, pp. 249ff. They point out that in view of a lack in reliable electoral analyses for the early Weimar years the assertion of a right-wing drift of the German middle classes can hardly be substantiated. This gap has by now been partially closed. See the literature cited in notes 61 and 63 below.

[58] For a good summary and an insightful analysis of the role played by the *Angestellte* in this context, see Jürgen Kocka, *Ursachen des Nationalsozialismus*, in: *Aus Politik und Zeitgeschichte. Beilage zu 'Das Parlament'* B 25/80, June 21, 1980, pp. 3—15. See also Wolfgang Schieder (ed.), *Faschismus als soziale Bewegung*, Hamburg 1976, esp. the contributions by H. A. Winkler, M. Kater and H. Mommsen.

[59] A popular version is Gerhard Ziemer, *Inflation und Deflation zerstören die Demokratie*, Stuttgart 1971.

nationalist DNVP briefly became the largest fraction in the German Reichstag, one may wonder whether the stabilization and the way its burdens were — unevenly — distributed among the various groups of German society played a role at least as important as social decline and distributional conflicts caused by inflation even in the subjective perception of the groups involved. By making stabilization the key factor, one could advance the argument that initially, at least, the postwar inflation had a political stabilizing effect by postponing the "day of reckoning", so to speak, which in view of wartime inflation and the inability of the weak Weimar governments to deal with the social costs of the war in as drastic a way as other countries, for instance Great Britain, had to come eventually. The inflation, therefore, may have given the Weimar State a 'lease on life' rather than precipitating its political disintegration. Stabilization and the way it was handled in Germany, then, becomes a crucial factor in the political mobilization and reorientation of social groups in German society, and it is for this reason that the historian of the inflation also has to deal with the consequences of *stabilization* in the political context of the subject.[60]

How can the political behavior of a social group be determined and how can one proceed with regard to the *Beamtenschaft*? One may start out from the assumption that civil servants were, in the context of early Weimar politics, a social group which could be politically mobilized and could become a target group for political parties and movements. The significance of 'occupation' *(Beruf)* as a social category for political mobilization is one of the most striking phenomena of Weimar politics. Even a cursory assessment of party programs and electoral campaign literature reveals the importance of occupational status as a determinant of political campaigning. Sociologists interested in electoral analysis of Weimar politics often substitute these categories with, in our opinion, rather problematic social categories. Terms like upper middle class, lower middle class, and the like, were not relevant in the concrete historical context of Weimar politics.[61] The historian Thomas

[60] On the economic and social dimensions of stabilization, see Ch. S. Maier, *Recasting...*, pp. 355—420; Claus Dieter Krohn, *Stabilisierung und ökonomische Interessen. Die Finanzpolitik des Deutschen Reiches 1923—1927*, Düsseldorf 1974; Uwe Oltmann, *Reichsarbeitsminister Brauns in der Staats- und Währungskrise 1923/24*, Diss., Kiel 1968; Karl-Bernhard Netzband/Hans Peter Widmaier, *Währungs- und Finanzpolitik der Ära Luther 1923—1925*, Basel 1964.

[61] Such a classification scheme is used in the otherwise innovative study by Richard N. Hamilton, *Who Voted for Hitler?*, Princeton 1982.

Childers, whose extensive ecological analyses of Weimar elections make use of the "traditional" social grouping as reference groups, has recently made a similar case for the applicability of the occupational variable in answering the important question concerning the origins of electorial polarization between the extreme right and the extreme left in the Weimar Republic.[62] One of Childers' main theses, moreover, implies that civil servants rather than white-collar *Angestellte* were the main contributors to the Nazi vote as early as 1924 — a thesis which needs to be reexamined in the context of the present study. Taking voting behavior of civil servants as an indicator of political (re)-orientation, we shall undertake, therefore, an in-depth analysis of the "inflation elections" of 1924 from the perspective of the *Beamtenschaft.*[63]

Civil servants had traditionally been a backbone of political liberalism in Germany, be it the so-called national liberalism of the right or the progressive liberalism of the left. Not only as voters, but likewise as active party members and party officials civil servants fulfilled an important function for the liberal parties even before 1914. In the context of Weimar politics, which again produced two liberal parties, the left-liberal German Democratic Party (DDP) and the more right leaning German People's Party (DVP) of Gustav Stresemann, civil service support became again of major importance to both liberal parties. The decline of German political liberalism during the early Weimar years, which has been one of the main subjects in the work of Larry Jones, was to no small degree connected to the loss of civil service support suffered by these two parties and the concomitant fragmentation of the political center.[64] In the context of the present study, we shall approach this

[62] Thomas Childers, *The Social Bases of the National Socialist Vote,* in: *Journal of Contemporary History,* 11 (1976), pp. 17—42; idem, *National Socialism and the New Middle Class,* in: Reinhard Mann (ed.), *Die Nationalsozialisten. Analysen faschistischer Bewegungen* (= Historisch-Sozialwissenschaftliche Forschungen, vol. 9), Stuttgart 1980; idem, *The Nazi Voter. The Social Foundations of Fascism in Germany, 1919—1933,* Chapel Hill 1983, which is the best book on this subject to date.

[63] For an insightful discussion of the "inflation elections" of 1924 and their place in the political development of Weimar Germany, see Thomas Childers, *Inflation, Stabilization, and Political Realignment in Germany 1919—1928,* in: G. D. Feldman et al. (eds.), *The German Inflation...,* pp. 409—431.

[64] See Larry E. Jones, *Inflation, Revaluation, and the Crisis of Middle-Class Politics: A Study in the Dissolution of the German Party System, 1923—1928,* in: *CEH,* 12 (1979), pp. 143—168. Jones has just completed a book-length study on the liberal parties in the Weimar Republic.

problem from the perspective of civil servants and their representative organizations, some of which had close links to the liberal parties. It will be shown that civil service support during the inflation years shifted to the right, i. e. to the DNVP, but likewise — and this is a tendency hardly ever analyzed systematically — initially at least to the left as well, i. e. to the Social Democrats and the other parties of the German labor movement.

Organizational tendencies among civil servants, and the often subtle political connections of the politically non-affiliated civil servant peak associations of the Weimar Republic, the Deutscher Beamtenbund (DBB) and the Reichsbund der höheren Beamten (RhB) can serve as a third determinant of the political leanings of civil servants. Factional strife along political lines *within* the major civil servant peak association, the DBB, must be examined thoroughly for such a purpose, because in contrast to other social movements the civil servant movement remained committed overwhelmingly to the idea of political neutrality even after a Socialist organization, the Allgemeiner Deutscher Beamtenbund (ADB) had been founded in 1922. This is to say that even after 1922 the DBB retained a sizeable left-leaning membership and leadership. Membership figures alone can therefore not be used alone to demonstrate the political preferences of organized civil servants, even if after 1922 politically oriented organizations had e-merged.[65] Shifting political tendencies within the DBB must be analyzed, before any conclusions about the political orientation of civil servants on the basis of organization preferences can be drawn. Organizational affiliation, then, together with the less obvious and more complicated phenomena of internal factionalism and partisan political links can provide us with a framework of reference to analyze the political structure of the civil servant movement during and after the inflation.

Finally, the involvement of civil servants and their organizations in domestic politics of the early Weimar years may be a reflection of the political leanings of the group and its organizations. However, here the danger exists to slip into a general political history of these years if these

[65] Organizational affiliation as an indicator of political preferences has been used by Jürgen Kocka in his studies of the German Angestellte. See his *Zur Problematik der deutschen Angestellten, 1914—1933,* in: H. Mommsen et al., *Industrielles System...,* pp. 792—810, esp. pp. 798—800; idem, *Die Angestellten in der deutschen Geschichte 1850—1980,* Göttingen 1981.

problems are moved into the foreground.[66] Consequently, we shall be less concerned with offering a detailed analysis of the politics of civil servant organizations in the Revolution of 1918/19 or during the Kapp-Lüttwitz Putsch of March 1920, because these events were not causally linked to the economic developments with which we are concerned in this study. It may be argued, though, that in the last year of inflation, i. e. in the hyperinflation of 1923, domestic politics and the social consequences of inflation became intertwined more directly. A brief and necessarily selective discussion of the role played by civil servant organizations in the *Krisenjahr* of 1923, when the occupation of the Ruhr, passive resistance, separatist movements in the Rhineland, and threats of political takeovers from both the extreme left and the extreme right brought the Weimar state near the point of collapse,[67] may therefore add to the understanding of the political behavior of civil servants in inflation and stabilization in the early Weimar Republic.

[66] The political history of the early Weimar Republic has been the subject of numerous studies. A good overview is given in the introductions to the relevant volumes of the *Akten der Reichskanzlei. Weimarer Republik* edition. See also the recent study by the East German historian Kurt Gossweiler, *Kapital, Reichswehr und NSDAP 1919—1924,* Cologne 1982.

[67] The domestic impact of the Ruhr crisis has recently been reexamined by Heinrich August Winkler, *Von der Revolution zur Stabilisierung. Arbeiter und Arbeiterbewegung in der Weimarer Republik 1918 bis 1924,* Berlin-Bonn 1984, chapter 4. On the international implications, see Klaus Schwabe (ed.), *Die Ruhrkrise 1923. Wendepunkt der internationalen Beziehungen nach dem Ersten Weltkrieg,* Paderborn 1984.

CHAPTER ONE

The Economic and Social Framework

The analysis of the economic conditions of social groups in the inflation process is a necessary precondition for more comprehensive studies of the social history of the German inflation and of the politics of inflation and stabilization as defined in the present study. In this introductory chapter, therefore, the economic and social conditions of the *Beamtenschaft* will be examined in the light of hitherto overlooked and thus rarely used statistical materials, relating primarily to the structure and size of the group itself — as well as to those of certain neighboring groups in the public sector — and to the movement of real salaries and wages of civil servants and, again, other public sector employees. Investigating structural changes in the civil service and the German public work force, as done in section one, will serve the dual purpose of introducing the *Beamtenschaft* as a social group and of examining one of the most visible and controversial aspects of the inflation itself, i. e. the allegedly unchecked growth of public employment and public expenditure in these years. The reconstruction of real wage levels, which is the subject of section two, is in itself one of the main desiderata of the new inflation research. Our intentions go well beyond a historical wage analysis, however. By linking the cyclical development of real wage levels to patterns and timing of social protest, and by establishing a connection between wage differentials and propensities for inter and intra-group conflict, we are proposing an interpretative framework for the subsequent chapters of this study.

Structural Changes in the German Civil Service and in the Public Work Force, 1914—1924

"Since the Revolution we have been blessed with an inflation of civil servants of the greatest magnitude," Franz Eulenburg noted in 1924.[1]

[1] F. Eulenburg, *Die sozialen Wirkungen...*, in: *JbNSt*, 122 (1924), p. 775.

Other contemporary observers levelled even more vitriolic charges against an allegedly unchecked growth of governmental employment in Germany during and after the First World War. Very often, this was done in connection with laments about an equally dreaded general encroachment of bureaucracy in all aspects of life.[2] Such criticism was, moreover, not only a domain of scholars interested in social processes caused by the war and by postwar inflation, but also a point of attack for those who regarded the financial burdens created by an army of civil servants an important contributing factor to Germany's financial and economic woes during the postwar inflation. Members of the German business community, for example, were among the most outspoken critics of an allegedly oversized, inefficient, and unaffordable civil service, as were international reparations experts, albeit for very different reasons.[3] The entire problem of the conflict-ridden personnel reductions, undertaken by the German government during the stabilization crisis of 1923—24 partially in response to pressures exerted from the last mentioned two sources, can only be understood in the context of a preceding period of growth in governmental employment. Patterns of growth in public employment and structural changes connected with such growth are therefore a logical place to start with in an examination of the social and economic conditions of the *Beamtenschaft* in the German inflation.[4]

[2] See, for example, E. Schulze, *Not und Verschwendung...*, pp. 454—479 and H. Heiler, *Die Verelendung...*, pp. 23 ff.

[3] An official government memorandum, inspired, however, by business interests and by demands of the reparation authorities noted in 1923: „Es muß Ernst gemacht werden mit einer energischen Vereinfachung der Verwaltung. Die Bürokratie hat überall das Vertrauen verloren. Die Bevölkerung empfindet die starke Belastung des Staates durch die zahllosen behördlichen Stellen als unerträglich." Quoted in *Akten der Reichskanzlei. Weimarer Republik. Das Kabinett Cuno. 22. November 1922 bis 12. August 1923*, Karl-Heinz Harbeck (ed.), Boppard 1968, p. 686.

[4] These problems have not been adequately dealt with either in the contemporary or in the recent literature. Recent studies of the quantitative development of the German civil service, or of the public sector in general, usually exclude the inflation years. See, for example, Thomas Ellwein/Ralf Zoll, *Berufsbeamtentum. Anspruch und Wirklichkeit*, Düsseldorf 1973, Chapter 4 *(Beiträge zur quantitativen Entwicklung des öffentlichen Dienstes)*, and John P. Cullity, *The Growth of Governmental Employment in Germany, 1882—1950*, in: *Zeitschrift für die gesamte Staatswissenschaft*, 123 (1967), pp. 201—217. For a recent presentation of statistical series on public employment in the European context, see Peter Flora, *State, Economy and Society in Western Europe 1815—1975. A Data Handbook*, vol. 1, *The Growth of Mass Democracies and Welfare States*, Frankfurt/M.-London-Chicago 1983, Chapter 5 *(Government Personnel)*, pp. 193—243.

Before we can turn to our analysis, however, some brief remarks must be made on the statistical sources available for such a study. One of the reasons for the great difficulties encountered by scholars interested in the quantitative development of the German public sector is the lack of authoritative and comprehensive statistical data prior to 1927. It was only then that a separate counting of public personnel was undertaken by the German government.[5] In the preceding years, and especially during our period of observation, the number of civil servants (and of other government employees) was almost kept a state secret.[6] Contemporary statisticians were therefore forced to rely almost exclusively on the inaccurate and often cryptic personnel figures listed in the annual budgets of the national and state governments. In addition, some statistical information on employment was published by the two largest single public employers in Germany, the national railways (the *Reichsbahn*) and the postal service (the *Reichspost*) in their yearly operational reports.[7] The perhaps foremost stumbling block for accurate sectoral analyses as well as for the assessment of overall growth of the German public work force is the municipal level of government. In this branch of government overall employment figures continued being based on estimates until 1933, the year when civil servants were counted separately for the first time in connection with that year's occupational census.[8]

The following statistical analysis of quantitative developments in the German public work force during the inflation years is therefore based on some rather scattered statistical sources. German government agencies, for one, did publish some statistical data on public personnel

[5] These were undertaken by the Reich Finance Ministry for the *Hoheitsverwaltungen* only. See Statistisches Reichsamt, *Personalstand der öffentlichen Verwaltung im Deutschen Reich am 31. März 1928 und 31. März 1927. Ergebnisse der Reichsfinanzstatistik* (= Einzelschriften zur Statistik des Deutschen Reiches, no. 18), Berlin 1931.

[6] As noted by E. Schulze, *Not und Verschwendung...*, p. 454.

[7] The findings of these reports were published periodically in the *Statistische Jahrbücher für das Deutsche Reich.*

[8] Altogether 1,480,792 civil servants *(Beamte)* were counted in 1933, which translates into a share of 4.6 % of the total labor force. Some 130,000 of these were women (or 9.2 %), more than one-third (501,000 or 35.9 %) were employed by the two large German government enterprises, the *Reichsbahn* and the *Reichspost.* For further details, see *Statistik des Deutschen Reichs,* vol. 458, Berlin 1937, pp. 36—37. While the results of the 1933 census thus offer an excellent profile of the German *Beamtenschaft* toward the end of the Weimar Republic, these data cannot be marshalled in support for the present analysis of trends that occurred during the *early* years of the republic.

between 1920 and 1924. In using this data, one has to keep in mind, though, that it may have been published for very specific political purposes rather than for providing posterity with an accurate picture of the quantitative development of the German public sector.[9] Secondly, we shall draw on two rather useful contemporary statistical studies; one was undertaken in 1920 by Otto Schwarz, a senior official in the Reich finance administration, the other in 1923 by the noted German statistician Friedrich Burgdörfer.[10] Lastly, some information could be gleaned from statistical information compiled and published by the major German civil servant associations.[11]

Size and Composition of the *Beamtenschaft*

It has been mentioned briefly that the German occupational census did not differentiate between civil servants *(Beamte)* and salaried employees *(Angestellte)* until 1933. Long-range trends on the quantitative development of these two social groups can, however, be determined by mere arithmetic means if the proportional growth of one of the two groups is recalculated. For the *Angestellte*, this method has been applied several times.[12] An impression of the secular trends in the quantitative development of the *Beamtenschaft* over a period of fifty years, i. e.

[9] *Die Entwicklung der Beamtenzahl im Deutschen Reich*, in: *Wirtschaft und Statistik* (hereafter cited as *WSt*), 2 (1922), pp. 131—134. This was an official journal issued by the Reich Statistical Office. See further, *Denkschrift des Reichsfinanzministeriums über den Personalabbau*, May 15, 1924 (hereafter cited as *Denkschrift Personalabbau 1924*), copy in: Zentrales Staatsarchiv Potsdam (hereafter referred to as ZStAP), Büro des Reichspräsidenten, 86, Bl. 78—81. Some rather dubious statistical data was published in an official German report to the reparations authorities entitled *Deutschlands Wirtschaft, Währung und Finanzen*, Berlin 1924, pp. 77, 104, 108.

[10] Otto Schwarz, *Die Entwicklung der Ausgaben und Einnahmen Deutschlands, Englands, Frankreichs und Italiens vor und nach dem Weltkriege (Anhang: Die Beamtenvermehrung seit Kriegsbeginn)*, Magdeburg 1921; Friedrich Burgdörfer, *Tatsachen und Zahlen zum Behördenabbau*, in: *Allgemeines Statistisches Archiv*, 14 (1923—24), pp. 245—255.

[11] The Reichsbund der höheren Beamten, which had good connections to the Statistisches Reichsamt, published statistical materials periodically in its *Zeitschrift*. There is also a file in the archive of this organization relating to the *Zahl der Beamten*, which can be found in ZStAP, Reichsbund der höheren Beamten (RhB), 544.

[12] For a useful summary, see Hans-Jürgen Priamus, *Angestellte und Demokratie. Die National-liberale Angestelltenbewegung in der Weimarer Republik*, Stuttgart 1979, pp. 34—38.

TABLE 1

German Labor Force by Social Groups, 1882—1933 (in Millions)

	1882	1895	1907	1925	1933
1. Wage earners	8.3	9.8	11.9	14.7	15.0
2. Salaried Employees and Civil Servants	1.2	2.1	3.3	5.4	5.5
3. *Salaried Employees*	*.5*	—	*2.1*	*3.9*	*4.0*
4. *Civil Servants*	*.7*	—	*1.2*	*1.5*	*1.5*
5. Self-employed	4.3	4.6	4.8	5.1	5.3
6. Supporting Family Members	1.7	1.8	3.8	5.4	5.3
7. Domestic Servants	1.4	1.5	1.4	1.3	1.2
8. Total[a]	16.9	19.8	25.2	32.0	32.3

[a] Except for figures in italics.

Source: Statistik des Deutschen Reichs, vol. 458, p. 19 for all figures except those in lines 3 and 4 for the years 1882—1925, which are based on estimates.

between 1882 and 1933, is given in TABLE 1, which is based on occupational census material and, in reference to lines 3 and 4, on the aforementioned recalculations. The data presented in this table show that the number of civil servants nearly doubled between 1882 and 1907, the latter the year of the last prewar census. As John Cullity has pointed out, this remarkable increase was connected with Germany's transition from an agrarian to an industrial society.[13] Between 1907 and 1933 the rate of growth levels off; between 1907 and 1925, i. e. during the time-span that encompasses the decade of war, inflation, and stabilization, the total number of civil servants increased by only 300,000 — a figure much too low to account for the complaints about a *Beamteninflation* during these years.

It is clear, however, that the census material is inadequate for our purposes, since the figure for 1925 already compensates for the personnel reductions undertaken in 1923—24. What the census data does suggest, though — and it is here that it has some relevance to our present analysis — is that the growth of civil-service employment between 1914 and 1923 occurred at the end of an extended period of

[13] J. Cullity, *The Growth...*, in: *Zeitschrift für die gesamte Staatswissenschaft*, 123 (1967), p. 205.

civil-service growth. Moreover, TABLE 1 allows some comparisons to growth patterns of other social groups and the relative position of civil servants within the labor force in general. While civil servants remained the numerically smallest group of dependent employees — except for domestic servants, who are of no interest in this context — their relative weight increased because they grew at a faster rate than the blue-collar work force, the *Arbeiter*. Not unlike salaried employees, therefore, civil servants had become more significant as a social group in the decades before the First World War as a result of quantitative growth and by increasing their proportional share of the general labor force.

While these findings provide important background information, they offer few clues about the development of civil-service employment during the decade of war and inflation. For this purpose, other statistical sources had to be tapped. TABLE 2 presents our overall findings.

TABLE 2

Civil Servants in Germany, 1914—1924 (in Thousands)

	1914[a]	1920	1923	1924
Reich Administration	543	688	826	680
of these:				
Higher Civil Servants	*13*	*14*	*17*	*15*
Middle Grades	*189*	*226*	*392*	*333*
Lower Grades	*341*	*448*	*417*	*334*
Länder Administrations	203	312	310	320
Regional and Municipal Administration	250[b]	300	300	300
Total[c]	996	1300	1436	1300

[a] Civil servants employed in *Länder* administrations which after 1918 came under the jurisdiction of the Reich have been computed into the Reich figures for 1914. Figures are based on the annual budgets of Reich and *Länder* unless noted otherwise.

[b] Based on estimates.

[c] Except for figures in italics.

Sources: For 1914 and 1920: *WSt*, 2 (1922), pp. 131—134 and O. Schwarz, *Die Entwicklung der Ausgaben...*, Anlage 12—14. For 1923 and 1924: *Reichsarbeitsblatt*, Sonderheft 30, pp. 25—26.

The figures presented in TABLE 2 show that there was a great fluctuation in the total number of civil servants during this period. This supports the thesis that a pattern of growth and contraction characterized civil-service employment in the inflation period. While in 1914 there had been an estimated number of nearly one million civil servants,[14] their number had increased to 1.3 million in 1920, only to peak at 1.5 million in 1923. Between 1923 and 1924 the number of civil servants decreased sharply to 1.3 million, i. e. to the level of 1920. If the rate of growth is used as an indicator, it appears, therefore, that there were three distinct periods of growth or contraction in civil-service employment during the inflation years. The sharpest increase occurred between 1914 and 1920, an increase of about 30 percent. In the following three years the number of civil servants continued to grow, although at a lesser rate. In the third period, i. e. between 1923 and 1924, the number of civil servants declined.

This pattern of growth and contraction has been established on the basis of the *total* number of civil servants during this period. The series presented in TABLE 2 allow a discussion of this pattern at various levels of governmental employment in Germany. The figures given for the Reich administration follow the pattern most clearly, even if the different civil-service ranks are examined separately.[15] Civil-service employment at the Länder and municipal levels, however, does not follow the pattern as distinctly. Stagnation seems to set in much earlier, and the figures do not reflect the retrenchment measures of 1923—24 as visibly as those at the Reich level. As will become clear later on in this study, the causes of these discrepancies can be found in politics of the 1923—24 personnel reductions.[16] On the whole, however, one can say that civil-service employment in the German inflation was characterized by

[14] It might be noted that this figure is considerably lower than the one appearing in TABLE 2, given there as 1.2 million. It also deviates from estimates given by contemporary writers, which ranged from 1.2 million (Hintze, 1911) to 2 million (Winters, 1918). We believe that the figure given here, which is based on the computations of Schwarz, is the more accurate one, although there is a built-in margin of error since the regional/municipal figure is an estimate only.

[15] The discrepancy in the figures for the middle and lower grades for 1920—23 is a result of pay scale reclassifications undertaken in 1920, not a result of a reversal in the statistical trend.

[16] The *Abbau* was undertaken at the Reich level at first, the Länder only followed reluctantly. It therefore stands to reason that the personnel cuts undertaken at the state level do not appear in the 1924 figure. For a more detailed discussion see pp. 53 ff. below.

a succession of periods of pronounced growth (1914—1920), moderate growth (1920—1923), and contraction (1923—1924). The "inflation of civil servants," which Eulenburg and others wrote about, thus happened indeed. Whether or not the inflation itself was its main contributing factor, however, remains to be investigated.

The war effort,the requirements of an increasingly bureaucratically controlled war economy, and the heightened importance of transportation and communications during the war — all of these factors were undoubtedly responsible for a certain increase of civil service employment during the war years.[17] However, since many civil servants were called into military duty, the increase revealed by the figures for 1914 and 1920 must have taken place in the immediate postwar years. The demobilization of the army and the social processes connected with it were undoubtedly responsible for much of the rise in public employment in 1919. Not only was the German government obliged to rehire civil servants returning from military duty, in addition a large number of war veterans and war invalids were taken into government service as part of dealing with the social costs of the war. It is not surprising, therefore, that similar growth patterns can be observed in some of the other formerly belligerent nations after the Great War.[18]

In Germany, political change added to these general tendencies initiated by war and postwar demobilization. The social gains reached during the November Revolution, particularly the introduction of the eight hour day, increased the real need for manpower in those government enterprises which before 1918 had required longer work hours, particularly the railroads and, to a lesser extent, the postal service. As a consequence, the level of employment increased dramatically in these two areas of public works, which even before 1918 had taken the lion's share of public payrolls. On the railroads, which in 1919 came under the administration of the Reich government, overall employment nearly

[17] This and the following is a synopsis of O. Schwarz, *Die Entwicklung der Ausgaben...*, pp. 46—55.

[18] On the growth of civil service employment in other European countries during and after the First World War, see P. Flora, *State Economy...*, vol. 1, pp. 193 ff. On Britain, see Moses Abramowitz/Vera F. Eliasberg, *The Growth of Public Employment in Great Britain,* Princeton 1957, and, more specifically, *Memorandum on Expenditure, present and pre-war, with particulars of Government Staffs at certain dates* (= Cmd 802), London 1920, a Treasury publication. On France, see Raymond Rivet, *La Statistique des fonctionnaires en France et en divers pays,* in: *Bulletin statistique générale de la France,* (1932), pp. 95—141.

TABLE 3

Personnel in the German Railway Administration, 1912—1928 (Yearly Averages)

Year	*Etatmäßige Beamte*	*Diätarische Beamte* and *Angestellte*	*Arbeiter*	Total
1912	271,013	16,461	452,775	740,249
1913	283,767	16,165	482,799	782,731
1914	—	—	—	670,387
1915	—	—	—	731,944
1916	—	—	—	756,487
1917	—	—	—	816,990
1918	—	—	—	922,355
1919	—	—	—	1,132,185
1920	—	—	—	1,105,557
1921	374,960	63,397	629,080	1,067,437
1922	386,008	60,432	588,222	1,034,662
1923[a]	357,560	44,930	515,028	917,518
1924[a]	288,387	26,708	409,869	724,964
1925	322,123	17,192	410,323	749,638
1926	309,764	10,337	387,469	707,570
1927	306,432	7,749	389,835	704,016
1928	303,577	7,512	389,574	700,663

[a] Excludes Rhineland lines under Allied control *(Regie).*
Source: Statistisches Jahrbuch für das Deutsche Reich, vol. 35—50 (1912—1928).

doubled between 1914 and 1920, as TABLE 3 shows. Employment remained at high levels until 1922, when first attempts of reducing the work force were undertaken. Civil-service employment clearly participated in the general growth of employment in this sector of the public service, rising from 283,767 in 1913 to 374,960 in 1921. Indeed, civil-service employment continued to increase even after 1921, when the number of blue-collar workers had already started to decline.

It was a similar story in the postal administration, where employment likewise increased substantially between 1914 and 1922. Details are given in TABLE 4. Civil-service employment again participated in overall employment increases, rising from 248,195 in 1913 to 311,967 in 1922. Afterwards, there is a significant drop, however, and by 1924 the prewar

TABLE 4

Personnel in the German Postal Administration, 1912—1928[a]

Year	*Beamte*	*Unterbeamte*	*Sonstige*[b]	Total
1912	94,651	144,617	81,296	320,464
1913	97,820	150,375	85,869	334,064
1919	104,666	161,756	156,824	423,246
1920	287,567		156,886	444,453
1921	305,015		·170,153	475,168
1922	311,967		129,355	441,322
1923	253,380		72,376	325,756
1924	247,136		78,077	325,213
1925	250,680		82,052	332,732
1926	252,524[c]		107,815	360,339
1927	248,896		117,899	366,795
1928	244,030		131,363	375,393

[a] Includes personnel at year's end in the postal, telegraph and telephone services of the Reich, Bavaria and Württemberg (1912—1919) and of the *Reichspost* after 1919.
[b] Presumably blue-collar workers *(Arbeiter)* and helpers *(Hilfskräfte);* as of 1926: *Beamte im Nebenamt, Arbeiter,* and *Hilfskräfte.*
[c] As of 1926: *Beamte im Hauptamt.*

Source: As in TABLE 3.

level of employment has been reached again.[19] Viewed together, the two large government-run enterprises, the railway system and the postal service, functioned as a major employment reservoir, if not as a gigantic work-creation program, in the immediate postwar years, a function which was tacitly acknowledged by the government itself.[20]

The increase in personnel was equally dramatic in the other main branch of public administration in Germany, the so-called *Hoheitsverwaltungen,* where employment rose from 56,588 employees in 1914 to 105,976 in 1923. A further breakdown of the aggregate figure into the various administrative departments of the Reich administration, which

[19] For a more detailed account, see Verband Deutscher Post- und Telegraphenbeamten (ed.), *Die Entwicklung der Personalverhältnisse bei der Reichspost- und Telegraphenverwaltung,* Berlin 1923.

[20] This point is made in the semi-official publication *Die Entwicklung der Beamtenzahl...,* in: *WSt,* 2 (1922), p. 133.

TABLE 5

Additions to Staffs in Reich Ministries, 1914—1924 (Annual Budget Figures)

Ministry or Department	Regular Staff			Temporary Staff 1923		Total Staff 1923
	1914[a]	1920	1923	civil service	non- civil service	
A. Administrative Staffs *(Allgemeine Reichsverwaltung)*						
1. President's Office	—	19	18	—	20	28
2. Reichstag	42	50	104	13	230	347
3. Chancellery	21	45	46	6	21	73
4. Foreign Office	1,010	934	1,320	412	1,873	3,605
5. Interior	1,272[b]	843	1,655	606	1,982	4,243
6. Economics	—	811	1,316	241	2,400	3,957
7. Labor	—	10,555	10,792	1,772	13,480	26,044
8. Defense	16,395	2,783	4,588	249	20,926	25,763
9. Military Court	51	47	—	—	—	—
10. Justice	1,059[c]	1,099	1,250	151	204	1,605
11. Treasury	—	8,517	1,645	70	1,475	3,172
12. Transportation/ Waterways	475[c]	612	2,221	158	1,613	3,992
13. Agriculture and Foods	38[c]	149	182	75	313	570
14. General Pension Fund	8	8	—	—	—	—
15. Accounting Office *(Rechnungshof)*	170	169	285	11	22	318
16. Finance	35,792	55,259	83,994	4,870	31,860	120,733
17. Reconstruction	255[d]	654	2,232	596	5,284	8,112
Total A	56,588	82,554	111,648	9,230	81,694	202,572
B. Technical Staffs *(Betriebsverwaltungen)*						
18. Posts and Printing Office	189,181	233,844	246,692	73,496	71,402	391,590
19. Transportation/ Reichsbahn	297,167	371,625	405,660	39,853	526,447	971,960
Total B	486,348	605,469	652,352	113,349	597,849	1,363,550
Grand Total (A + B)	524,936	688,023	764,000	122,579	679,543	1,566,122

[a] Including *Länder* administrations which after 1918 came under the jurisdiction of the Reich.

[b] Excluding: 1) Reich Patent Office with 800 civil servants, listed under Ministry of Justice; 2) Reich Administration of Canals with 423 civil servants, listed under Transportation/Waterways; 3) Biological Institute for Forestry and Agriculture, listed under Ministry of Agriculture and Foods.

[c] Cf. note b) above.

[d] Colonial Office.

Source: F. Burgdörfer, *Tatsachen und Zahlen*. . ., in: *Allgemeines Statistisches Archiv*, 14 (1923—24), p. 250.

has been done in TABLE 5, suggests, moreover, that there were two underlying causes for this development. First, there was a widening of the tasks performed by the central government after the Revolution of 1918/19, and second, there was the appearance of new tasks as a consequence of the war. Two ministries exemplify these two developments rather well, the Reich Ministry of Finance and the Reich Ministry of Labor.

The building up of a central finance and taxation administration under the jurisdiction of the Reich government contributed to the enormous growth of the Reich Finance Ministry's staff in the immediate postwar years. Afterwards, the mounting difficulties in tax assessment and collection in a period of rapid and hyperinflation might have played a part in the hiring of additional personnel. The large number of temporary helpers employed in the finance administration — some 23,000 in 1923 — seems to underscore this impression.[21] The equally astounding growth of the Reich Labor Ministry can be used as a case in point for the second development mentioned above, i. e. the handling of new tasks by the central government as a result of the war. As TABLE 5 shows, this ministry, which had only been founded during the war and then employed a small staff of only several hundred civil servants, grew enormously after the war. In 1923 it employed more than 11,000 civil servants and a temporary staff of nearly 15,000. This most dramatic increase was, no doubt, related to and a consequence of the social problems created by the war, by postwar demobilization, and by general economic reconstruction. It is not surprising, therefore, that this personnel increases in the area of labor relations was not only a German phenomenon, but a development that occurred in other industrialized countries as well during the war and the immediate postwar years. In Great Britain, for example, the Labor Ministry increased its staff from 4,400 in 1914 to 17,324 in 1920.[22] In the German case, therefore, the revolution and the victory of the working class cannot be held responsible alone for the growth of the "worker's ministry."

[21] In contemporary criticisms of bureaucratic growth, the Finance Ministry was often singled out as a main target. See E. Schulze, *Not und Verschwendung...*, p. 440. For an opposing view, see O. Schwarz, *Die Entwicklung der Ausgaben...*, pp. 47—48. A splendid recent analysis of the formation of the Reich finance administration is Peter-Christian Witt, *Reichsfinanzminister und Reichsfinanzverwaltung*, in: *Vierteljahrshefte für Zeitgeschichte* (hereafter cited as *VfZG*), 23 (1975), pp. 1—61.

[22] Figures according to O. Schwarz, *Die Entwicklung der Ausgaben...*, Anlage 15, who quotes from the Treasury memorandum cited in note 18 above.

Rather, the problems and tasks required by postwar reconstruction fostered a development which had already begun during the war.

Thus far we have limited this analysis to developments at the national level of the *Hoheitsverwaltung*, i. e. to the administrative staffs employed within the civil service of the Reich. Some remarks must now be made about similar developments at other levels of government in Germany, i. e. within the public administrations of the various *Länder* and of regional and municipal governments. Statistical data on civil servants employed by the *Länder* (the *Staatsbeamte*) and the municipalities (the *Kommunalbeamte*) is scarce, however, which makes direct comparisons to the Reich level rather difficult.[23]

TABLE 6

Civil Servants in Select Länder Administrations, 1914—1924

	1914	1920	1922	1923	1924
Prussia	86,661	169,470	178,658	173,263	163,555
Bavaria	40,133	43,766	—	52,008	52,043
Saxony	14,738	22,322			
Württemberg	12,666	17,606			
Baden	12,804	18,524			
Hamburg	13,185	14,240			
All Laender	203,078	312,453			

Sources: O. Schwarz, *Die Entwicklung der Ausgaben...*, Anlage 13 (1914 and 1920); ZStAP, RhB, 544, Bl. 6 (Prussian budget figure for 1922); *Reichsarbeitsblatt*, Sonderheft 30, p. 26 (1923 and 1924).

Our finding for the *Länder* administrations are depicted in TABLES 6 and 7. TABLE 6 shows the absolute increase in civil-service employment in selected *Länder* between 1914 and 1920; for two large state administrations, Prussia and Bavaria, the numerical series extend to 1924. The series tend to follow the pattern established at the Reich level. Between 1914 and 1920 there is a significant, in the case of Prussia even dramatic increase in civil-service employment. Afterwards, there is a leveling-off in the Prussian case, but a continued increase in Bavaria. In both cases, however, stagnation in civil-service employment sets in by 1924.

[23] The main source is O. Schwarz, *Die Entwicklung der Ausgaben...*, pp. 54f. and Anlage 13.

TABLE 7

Staffs in Select Branches of Länder Administrations, 1914 and 1920 (Annual Budget Figures)

Administrative Branch	1914[a]	1920	Increase Absolute	%
Parliament and Foreign Affairs	282	252	-30	-11
State Ministry	1,322	1,482	160	12
Interior	62,402	139,429	77,027	123
Social Welfare and Labor	732	3,841	3,109	425
Transportation and Commerce	17,697	20,712	3,015	17
Education	53,111	63,611	10,500	20
Justice	46,049	55,286	9,237	20
Finance	15,469	19,350	3,881	25
Others	5,461	7,845	2,384	44
Total	203,087	312,453	109,366	54
Total except Interior	135,188	173,024	37,836	28

[a] Excluding staffs in administrations which after 1918 came under the jurisdiction of the Reich.

Source: Distilled from O. Schwarz, *Die Entwicklung der Ausgaben...*, Anlage 13.

TABLE 7 presents a sectoral analysis of civil-service growth at the *Länder* level. It shows that in all except one branch of state administration civil-service employment increased between 1914 and 1920. The rate of growth varied greatly, however, in absolute as well as in relative terms. The largest absolute increase by far occurred in the branch "interior administration," which, as one might note, includes the state police forces. As a consequence, much of the increase in this branch can be attributed to a growth in police forces. As a result of the military demobilization and permanent reduction (to 100,000 men) in the size of the German armed forces stipulated by the Treaty of Versailles, large police forces were built up in Weimar Germany, particularly in the State of Prussia. The enormous growth of this branch of government was therefore as result of the political contingencies connected with the loss of the war, the revolution, and the domestic disturbances of the immediate postwar years. If one controls the statistics for the branch "interior," the dramatic total increase of 54 % is reduced to 28 %, which is a figure much more in line with the overall civil-service increase of 30 % established above.

The largest relative increase in civil-service employment at the *Länder* level occured in those branches of government that dealt with labor relations and problems of social welfare.[24] This is a striking similarity to developments observed at the Reich level and another indication that the social costs of war required increased governmental activities in areas that in prewar times had very often been left to private initiative or to clerical and public welfare organizations.

TABLE 8

Municipal Civil Servants in Select German Cities, 1914 and 1920

	1914	1920	Inhabitants in 1920
Berlin	16,646	19,584	1,900,000
Greater Berlin	18,900	23,300	ca. 4,000,000
Munich	7,166	6,734	670,000
Leipzig	4,759	5,492	604,000
Chemnitz	2,157	3,000	313,000
Mannheim	2,095	2,889	229,000
Freiburg i. Br.	554	689	88,000
All cities	103,300	127,295	—

Source: Distilled from O. Schwarz, *Die Entwicklung der Ausgaben...*, Anlage 14c.

At the local level of government, finally, the hiring of employees with civil-service status increased as well. TABLE 8 depicts the overall increase in the number of municipal civil servants in cities with more than 50,000 inhabitants between 1914 and 1920. The overall increase amounts to 27 % and is therefore in line with the general growth of civil service employment (30 %). A sectoral analysis, undertaken on the basis of departmental branches in TABLE 9, reveals once again the by now familiar pattern of a dramatic increase of employment in the area of social welfare, where personnel figures rose by nearly 80 percent be-

[24] The figures given by O. Schwarz in *ibid.*, Anlage 13, translate into a percentage increase of 425 in the branch "Social Welfare", which is considerably higher than the one of 123 % given for the branch "Interior."

TABLE 9

Staffs by Departments in Municipal Administration of Cities with more than 50,000 Inhabitants, 1914 and 1920

Department	1914	1920	Increase Absolute	Increase %
General Administration	17,625	20,357	2,732	16
Debt Administration	240	358	118	49
Police	11,331	14,778	3,447	30
Social Welfare	9,985	17,893	7,908	79
War related	—	3,889		
Fire Department	4,880	5,957	1,077	22
Education	17,198	19,073	1,875	11
Cultural Affairs	1,329	1,870	541	41
Commerce	1,055	1,410	355	37
Construction	4,466	4,596	103	2
Waterways	581	759	178	36
Public Works	20,890	27,228	6,338	30
Others	7,767	9,660	1,893	24
Total	97,347	123,942	26,595	27

Source: As in TABLE 8.

tween 1914 and 1920.[25] This indicates that municipalities, too, had to bear much of the burden connected with the social consequences of the war.

It remains to be discussed whether growth in civil-service employment led to changes in the structure or composition of the *Beamtenschaft.* One development, the disproportional increase of technical staffs *(Betriebsbeamte)* has already been pinpointed as a major trend which led to structural change within the civil service and to potentials for intra-group conflict within the *Beamtenschaft.* If the disproportion in the numerical increase of technical versus administrative staffs was one source of potential intra-group conflict, the uneven growth of the size of the different civil-service ranks, i. e. lower, middle, and higher ranks, was another problem entailed in the overall growth of civil-service employment. As the figures presented for the Reich administration in TABLE 2 above show, the ranks of the lower grades increased at a pace faster than those of the middling or higher ranks of the civil

[25] *Ibid.*, Anlage 14c.

service. Of the 145,000 new civil-service positions created between 1914 and 1920, no less than 107,000 were taken up by lower-grade civil servants, (which translates into an increase of 31.4 %), 37,479 by the middle grades (an increase of 19.9 %), and merely 517 by higher civil servants (an increase of only 3.8 %).[26] One consequence of this development was the expansion of the combined share held by the lower pay groups in the overall civil service pay expenditures to be met by the Reich government: in 1921, these groups made up nearly two-thirds of the total pay expenditures (the *Besoldungsaufwand*) according to a semi-official estimate.[27] In the subsequent years the lower grades' share diminished only marginally, as TABLE 10 indicates. Only with the stabilization of 1923—24 was a more noticeable redistribution of the pay

TABLE 10

Pay Costs for Reich Civil Servants, 1921—1924. By Grades, In Percent of Total Pay Expenditure

Grades	Budget/Year				
	1921[a]	1922	7/1923	12/1923	6/1924
I—V (Lower grades)	64.4	64.1	60.1	60.4	56.9
VI—X a (Middle grades)	33.4[b]	32.4	36.2	35.6	38.7
X b—B 7 (Higher grades)	3.2[c]	3.5	3.7	4.0	4.4

[a] Includes military personnel.
[b] Grades VI—IX.
[c] Grades X—XIII.

Sources: For 1921: *Die Entwicklung der Beamtenzahl...*, in: *WSt*, 2 (1922), p. 134. For 1922—24: H. Heiler, *Die Verelendung...*, p. 22.

[26] For further details, see *ibid.*, pp. 52—54 and *Die Entwicklung der Beamtenzahl...*, in: *WSt*, 2 (1922), pp. 132—133. The somewhat perplexing disruption of the trend after 1920 is a result of a reclassification scheme adopted in the course of the Pay Reform Act of 1920, when certain groups of lower-grade civil servants were upgraded and from then on belonged to a pay group of the middling ranks. The middle grades show an enormous increase in 1923, therefore, while the lower grades have numerically declined.

[27] *Die Entwicklung der Beamtenzahl...*, p. 134. The basis is pay groups II—VI. Generally, however, pay groups I—IV were considered as belonging to the lower grades of the German civil service.

expenditures to the benefit of the middling and higher pay groups achieved. It is not surprising, therefore, that during the inflation years members of the higher pay groups tended to view the overcrowding of the lower ranks of the civil service as a major source of their own predicament of low pay and narrowing pay differentials vis-à-vis the lower grades. In retrospect, higher civil servants regarded the pay policy conducted by the Reich government as having failed primarily because it allegedly succumbed to the pressures of those groups within the civil service whose combined efforts and collective actions were felt most directly, i. e. to those of the numerically strong and socially restive *Unterbeamte.*[28]

Newcomers to the Public Work Force

The war and the peculiar conditions created by the wartime economy led to important changes within the structure of the labor market and of the labor force in Germany, as, in fact, it did in the other belligerent countries. Generally speaking, workers drafted into military service were replaced by temporary helpers, both young and inexperienced male workers and women, who had been drawn into the labor market often on the basis of compulsory labor-service decrees. The return of ex-servicemen after the war to their former places of work then created the conditions of a overcrowded labor market, the regulation of which became one of the foremost objectives of demobilization policies.[28a]

It stands to reason that the public sector and its work force was not to remain untouched by these developments. In the German case, public sector employment during the war became the subject of two important structural changes. First, there was an increase in the use of short-term contractual labor. Contractual public employees *(öffentliche Angestellte)* came to perform what had once been civil service tasks. Second, women were hired in greater numbers, either as contractual

[28] A point stressed by H. Heiler, *Die Verelendung...*, pp. 22—23. The problems relating to narrowing pay differentials will be discussed in full in the following section of this chapter.

[28a] On this, see Gunther Mai, *Die personelle Demobilmachung in Deutschland 1918—1920/24*, in: Gerald D. Feldman/Carl-Ludwig Holtfrerich/Gerhard A. Ritter/Peter-Christian Witt (eds.), *Die Anpassung an die Inflation* (Engl. titel: *The Adaptation to Inflation*) (= Veröffentlichungen der Historischen Kommission zu Berlin, vol. 67, Beiträge zu Inflation und Wiederaufbau in Deutschland und Europa, 1914—1924, vol. 8), Berlin 1986, pp. 202—236.

employees as just defined, as temporary helpers *(Hilfskräfte)*, or even as regular civil service appointees. Both developments, i.e. the inroads made by contractual employees in a formerly civil-service oriented sphere and by women in a formerly male dominated sphere, became to play an important role in the social conflicts entailed by the personnel cutbacks of 1923—24. The fate of these two newcomers to the public work force therefore deserves some more detailed examination.

Let us consider the case of the *Angestellte* in the public sector first, a "peculiar social sub-group" as they have been called.[29] War, demobilization, inflation, and stabilization all left their imprint on the numerical development of this group, which civil servants came to view as a challenge to the continuity of the traditional career civil service.

Prewar statistics on the numerical growth of contractual public employees are extremely sketchy. According to one estimate, some 82,000 of them were employed in the general administrations of Reich, *Länder*, and municipalities in 1913.[30] They numbered much less in the large state-run enterprises (the *Staatsbetriebe*), which seemed to prefer

TABLE 11

Contractual Public Employees in Germany, 1914—1924

	1914	1920	1922	1923	1924
Reich, Administrative Staffs	3,500	46,000	51,000	51,394	27,884
Reich, Technical Staffs	?	?	2,100	9,353	3,932
Prussia, Administrative Staffs	11,300	?	14,900	24,068	18,602
Bavaria Administrative Staffs	30	?	?	2,232	2,471

Sources: 1914: *Einzelschriften zur Statistik des Deutschen Reichs*, No. 18; 1920 to 1924: *Der Behördenangestellte*, No. 15 (October 10, 1923) and *Denkschrift Personalabbau 1924.*

[29] Hans Speier, *Die Angestellten vor dem Nationalsozialismus*, Göttingen 1977, pp. 42—43, provides a insightful profile of this group.

[30] Or 9 % of the public work force, vs. 72 % civil servants and 18 % blue-collar workers. Figures in Thomas Ellwein, *Gewerkschaften und öffentlicher Dienst*, Opladen 1980, p. 37.

employing either civil servants or blue-collar workers. The importance of contractual labor for the performance of civil-service functions increased during the war, as TABLE 11 suggests. If one allows for a sizeable number of contractual employees working in the *Betriebsverwaltungen,*[31] a total overall increase seems likely. In any case, the increase in the area of general administration at all levels of government is supported by the figures cited for Prussia.

Usually, contractual employees were hired during the war to perform administrative duties in the semi-public *Kriegsgesellschaften* established to regulate the German wartime economy. On the local level, personnel hired to administer war-related welfare matters were often contractual employees (or volunteers). The immediate postwar conditions did not change this trend. Demobilization and the laws promulgated to regulate the labor market protected *Angestellte* in the public service from being dismissed arbitrarily to make room for returning civil servants. Many of them were kept on public payrolls to assist in the exceedingly slow dismantling of those agencies which had supervised the controlled war economy. This type of bureaucratic *Abwicklung* became the object of much public criticism.[32]

The hiring of contractual employees instead of career civil servants was also practiced widely in governmental agencies handling new tasks. The Ministry of Labor, for example, employed a large number of contractual employees, as did the newly-created Reich Administration of Finance and Taxation. Quite often contractual public employees were hired (or retained) in areas in which their former training (e. g. as officials in trade unions or professional organizations) was of importance, and where it filled a gap that regular civil-service personnel could not fill, as, for example, in the entire area of labor relations. In areas that required a large number of highly trained clerical employees, as in the administration of finance, the rather inflexible career civil service often could not provide enough personnel at short notice. An important criterion was the temporary nature of the task to be performed and of the employment relating to it. This would hold true for all war-related welfare matters as well, an area which became somewhat of a domain for contractual labor vs. regular civil service appointments. On the whole, therefore, demobilization *tasks* as well as demobilization *policy* favored

[31] There are no exact figures of the number of *Angestellte* in the *Betriebsverwaltungen.*

[32] Cf. E. Schulze, *Not und Verschwendung...*, pp. 459—462.

the increased use of contractual employees in the German public sector after the First World War.[33]

At first, members of the career civil service were not overly alarmed by this development. As long as their own employment remained protected by civil service law, and the *Berufsbeamtentum* as an institution was not called into question, the "newcomers" were tolerated or even viewed as convenient social allies in mutual conflicts with public employers. With the acceleration of inflation in 1920—21 and its positive side effect of generally high levels of employment in the public as well as in the private sectors of the German economy, there were few areas of friction between the two groups. In this sense the inflation became a cushion mitigating potential sources of inter-group conflict. With the end of the "economic boom" and the beginning of personnel cutbacks in the public sector by mid-1922, however, the slogan of a "hidden dismantlement of the career civil service" *(kalter Abbau des Berufsbeamtentums)* as a result of the increased use of contractual labor gained in momentum, leading to a severe social conflict between the two groups in the *Abbau* crisis of 1923/24.[34] Under civil-service pressure those demobilization decrees which then still protected contractual employees from dismissal were lifted, and a concentrated effort to rid the public service of contractual labor was undertaken. The figures presented in TABLE 11 indicate that these efforts were successful indeed: At the Reich level, the number of public contractual employees was cut in half, in Prussia by about one-third.

The story of female employment in the German public sector shows some interesting parallels to that of the *öffentliche Angestellte.* One needs to separate clearly, though, between the position of women within the civil service and the use of female labor for temporary, war-related functions, i. e. as *Hilfskräfte* in public enterprises. Before 1914 women were employed mainly in three branches of the German

[33] See Friedrich Syrup (ed.), *Die Regelung der Arbeitszeit, Einstellung und Entlassung und Entlohnung gewerblicher Arbeiter während der Zeit der wirtschaftlichen Demobilmachung,* Berlin 1919; idem (ed.), *Die Regelung der Einstellung, Entlassung und Entlohnung Angestellter während der Zeit der wirtschaftlichen Demobilmachung,* Berlin 1919, and Bernhardt Lehfeldt (ed.), *Die Freimachung von Arbeitsstellen während der Zeit der wirtschaftlichen Demobilmachung,* Berlin 1919, where details on demobilization decrees, including the handling of public employees and civil servants, are given.

[34] This conflict will be explored more thoroughly in CHAPTER SEVEN of this study. See also A. Kunz, *Stand versus Klasse...,* in: *GG,* 8 (1982), pp. 55—82, where these conflicts are investigated from the perspective of the *Angestellte* as well.

civil service: first, in education, which, however, was not considered an integral part of the civil service and for this and other reasons will be excluded from the present discussion; second, in communications, i. e. the postal, telegraph and telephone services, and third, to a much lesser degree, however, in transportation.[35] The largest employer of women in the public sector were the national and state-run postal services. In 1913, about 30,000 women were employed in this area, mainly as switch-board operators in the postal service's telephone branch. Nearly two-thirds of them had acquired or were slated for civil service positions in the lower ranks of the postal service.[36] About 10,000 women were employed in the transportation sector, although here the civil-service proportion was much lower. For example, of some 9,300 women employed in the Prussian-Hesse Railroad Administration in 1914, only 1,550 had been appointed to regular civil service posts.[37] The employment of women in the area of general administration, where at all three levels of government, national, state, and local some 650,000 civil servants worked in 1914, apparently was so negligible that no exact figures were ever collected or published.

War and postwar demobilization brought noticeable changes and fluctuations in female employment within the public service sector on the whole, as well as within the civil service in particular. In transportation a dramatic increase in the use of female labor during war years was followed by a sharp reversal of this trend during the postwar period. As TABLE 12 indicates, the retrenchment measures taken by the Prussian railroad administration in order to rehire returning employees clearly singled out women as their main target.

If one looks at civil-service employment of women in the Prussian railroads separately, however, a somewhat different picture emerges. As

[35] Except for education there has been no recent study on women in the German civil service. For prewar entry-requirements see Arnold Hirsch, *Weibliche Beamte im Deutschen Reich. Ein Ratgeber für junge Mädchen und deren Eltern*, Baden-Baden 1910. For prewar conditions of women in the postal service, see Verband Deutscher Post- und Telegraphenbeamtinnen (ed.), *Die Frau in der Post- und Telegraphenverwaltung*, Berlin 1917; for transportation, see Else Buß, *Die Frauenarbeit im Dienst der preußisch-hessischen Staatseisenbahnen und ihre Entwicklung während des Krieges*, Diss., Göttingen 1919, pp. 22—47. Developments during the war are discussed in E. Buß, *Die Frauenarbeit...*, pp. 51—66 and in the important study by Hilde Oppenheimer/Hilde Radomski, *Die Probleme der Frauenarbeit in der Übergangswirtschaft*, Mannheim 1918, esp. pp. 127—136.

[36] H. Oppenheimer/H. Radomski, *Die Probleme der Frauenarbeit...*, p. 128.

[37] E. Buß, *Die Frauenarbeit...*, p. 50.

TABLE 12

Female Employment in the German Railway Administration, 1913—1919

Year	A. All Female Employees	B. Women Civil Servants regular track *(planmäßig)*	non-regular track *(außerplanmäßig)*
1913	9,077	—	—
1914	9,167	1,504	47
1915	22,703	1,506	38
1916	55,545	1,484	30
1917	89,051	1,604	—
1918	107,000	1,754	—
1919	17,830	1,928	7,852

Sources:

Column A: Adolph Sarter, *Die deutschen Eisenbahnen im Kriege,* Stuttgart 1930, p. 146 (for 1913 to 1917); E. Buß, *Die Frauenarbeit...,* p. 50 (for 1918); *Die Gemeinschaft,* November 3, 1921 (for 1919).

Column B: E. Buß, *Die Frauenarbeit...,* p. 50 (for 1914 to 1918); *Die Gemeinschaft,* November 3, 1921 (for 1919).

revealed by the figures in TABLE 12, female civil-service employment had remained rather modest during the war, at least as far as regular appointments were concerned. There is a noticeable tendency of assigning more women to non-regular *(außerplanmäßig)* civil-service posts, perhaps a reflection of an adopted policy of appointing the widows of former civil servants killed during military duty to civil-service positions. The figures for 1919 show, moreover, that women in civil-service employment survived the first wave of demobilization related dismissals, whereas, as has been shown, the majority of less-skilled temporary helpers did not.

The available statistics on female employment in the postal service, presented in TABLE 13, show differences as well as similarities to the case of transportation. While the overall increase in female labor war perhaps less dramatic, rising from 30,000 in 1913 to 75,000 in 1917, the increase in civil-service employment of women was more pronounced. Some 10,000 women were appointed to regular service jobs in the same time period (1913—1917); by 1921 this number had risen to 58,000. To be sure, a large number of female *Hilfskräfte* were likewise employed in this branch and, similar to the case of transportation, they were dismissed in the wake of demobilization.

TABLE 13

Female Employment in the German Postal Administration 1913—1933

Year	All female employees[a]	Regular, Civil Service	Temporary, Civil Service	Trainees	Helpers
1913	30,987	6,854	15,388	4,800	3,935
1916	37,304	8,354	16,095	ca. 7,000	5,855
1921	58,000				
1923	51,752				
1924	48,879				
1928	41,027				
1931	37,578				
1933	33,843				

[a] As of 1921: All women civil servants.

Sources: H. Oppenheimer/H. Radomski, *Die Probleme der Frauenarbeit...*, p. 128 (for 1913 and 1916); BA R43I/2552, Bl. 29 (for 1921); *Statistisches Jahrbuch für das Deutsche Reich* (for 1923 to 1933).

Of greater significance, however, seems to be the seemingly uninterrupted trend of an increase civil-service employment of women within the postal service. To some extent this trend might have been linked to specific needs of the postal service, particularly to the growing importance of its telephone service branch. However, there are also indications that women were becoming more important in general administrative and supervisory functions — positions previously almost entirely reserved for male civil servants. More than any other branch of the German civil service (with the exception of education), the postal service became an entry point for women into the middle-level positions in the civil-service hierarchy.[38] In sharp contrast to female helpers *(Hilfskräfte)* employed during the war in the public service, who were quite rapidly dismissed during postwar demobilization (see TABLE 12), the chances of women keeping employment in certain branches of the civil service were not interrupted by the demobilization, regardless of some temporary setbacks, especially in the area of "general administration."[39]

[38] H. Oppenheimer/H. Radomski, *Die Probleme der Frauenarbeit...*, pp. 131—132.

[39] In 'general administration' an increasing number of women had become employed during the war as secretaries and other clerical workers, taking over the function of the

Aside of education and the postal service, the rapidly growing field of social services offered additional job opportunities to women.[40] Moreover, the employment status of woman civil servants' was improved; specific career guidelines were codified in the Salary Reform Act of April, 1920, improving the entrance of women into middle-level civil-service positions. Women civil service associations were instrumental in attaining these and other improvements.[41] On the whole, therefore, women civil servants, too, profited from the policy of full employment in the public sector during the early stages of the inflation.

When in 1923—24 the drastic reduction of civil-service employment was undertaken, however, women civil servants became a main target of personnel cuts. Based on emergency decrees, their legal rights were temporarily suspended, allowing even the dismissal of life-tenured women civil servants under certain conditions, for example if they were married.[42] As a result, women civil servants — similar to public contractual employees — suffered disproportionally under the impact of the notorious *Personalabbau*.[43]

The Personnel Reduction of 1923—24: A Statistical Appraisal

The politics connected with the "infamous" personnel cutbacks of 1923—24, which have been mentioned several times already in the

male *Kanzleidiener*. Very often public employers tried to keep such employment at minimum levels. The government of Baden, for example, in 1917 turned down a request by the Verband Badischer Kanzleibeamtinnen to open up more regular positions for women in the administration. On the other hand, those women hired to permanent positions remained protected by their employer, who in 1919 rejected a petition to dismiss all women hired during the war. Documentation on these matters in Generallandesarchiv Karlsruhe (hereafter referred to as GLAK), 233/3614.

[40] Cf. Charlotte Lorenz, *Die gewerbliche Frauenarbeit während des Krieges*, in: *Der Krieg und die Arbeitsverhältnisse* (= Wirtschafts- und Sozialgeschichte des Weltkrieges, German Series), Stuttgart 1928, pp. 356—357.

[41] Cf. Else Kolshorn, *Die Lage der weiblichen Post- und Telegraphenbeamtinnen*, in: *Jahrbuch für Frauenarbeit*, Berlin 1924, pp. 79—85. Kolshorn was the chairperson of the Verband Deutscher Post- und Telegraphenbeamtinnen.

[42] Article 14 of the so-called *Personalabbauverordnung* of 1923 (*RGBl.* 1923, I. pp. 999 ff.) stipulated that married women were to be dismissed from civil service jobs even if they had obtained life tenure, as long as their economic situation was deemed to be secure.

[43] According to figures given by E. Kolshorn, *Die Lage...*, in: *Jahrbuch für Frauenarbeit*, Berlin 1924, p. 80, 20 percent of all women in the postal administration lost their jobs in 1923—24 as compared to only 12 percent of their male colleagues.

preceding pages, will be fully discussed in a later chapter of this study.[44] It seems appropriate, though, to end the present discussion of quantitative developments and structural changes within the German public sector with some tentative remarks on government policy concerning personnel retrenchment before 1923 and with a *statistical* appraisal of the 1923—24 personnel cuts.

The political controversies connected with the growth of civil service and non-civil service employment in the public sector all relate to the increasing financial burden placed on the public purse by this development.[45] As early as 1919, for example, the Prussian State Ministry had contemplated to undertake sweeping personnel cuts within its administrative jurisdiction, in order to decrease the enormous burdens placed on the Prussian budget by high personnel costs.[46] Due to political considerations and interest pressures, however, such a policy could not be implemented at that juncture, nor could it be pursued in the subsequent years: All efforts undertaken between 1920 and 1922 remained doomed, so to speak.

Another factor must be added here, though. The relative ease with which an inflated public service could be financed at times of inflation may have been one more reason for the failure of implementing retrenchment plans already broached in 1919. The availability of monetary resources for financing an "inflated" bureaucracy was therefore a logical consequence of the economics and politics of inflation. Beginning in mid-1922, however, pressures were mounting that only a sweeping reduction of the size of public payrolls could pave the way for curing the financial problems of the Reich, especially its huge budget deficits, and efforts at reducing the level of government expenditures by trimming public employment were begun in the *Betriebsverwaltungen* of the Reich. But only with the emergency powers granted to the Stresemann government in October 1923 was a decisive reduction of employment levels in the public sector made possible. Its consequences, in statistical terms, are detailed in TABLES 14 and 15. They give an impression of the

[44] See CHAPTER SEVEN below.

[45] It is exceedingly difficult, if not impossible, to express this influence in concrete numbers. For the general picture, see Karl Linck, *Die Beamtenbesoldungspolitik des Deutschen Reiches und ihr Einfluß auf den Reichshaushalt von 1871—1927*, Diss., Frankfurt 1928, esp. pp. 47—70.

[46] President of the Prussian State Ministry, Hirsch, to Prussian Cabinet, May 27, 1919, copy in Bundesarchiv Koblenz (hereafter referred to as BA), R 43I/2551, Bl. 30.

social explosiveness of these mass layoffs in the German public sector during the stabilization crisis of 1923—24.[47]

TABLE 14

Reduction of Personnel in the Reich Administration, 1923—1924

a) Personnel as of October 1, 1923 b) Lay-offs as of March 31, 1924	A) Civil Servants *(Beamte)*	%	B) Contractual Employees *(Angestellte)*	%	C) Workers *(Arbeiter)*	%
1) General Administration	a) 105,976 b) 7,207	7	a) 51,394 b) 24,350	47	a) 50,046 b) 13,411	27
2) Railroads *(Reichsbahn)*	a) 425,852 b) 85,749	20	a) 861 b) 568	66	a) 576,083 b) 186,658	32
3) Postal Service & Printing Office	a) 294,127 b) 41,551	14	a) 8,492 b) 5,279	62	a) 79,384 b) 32,065	40
4) Total I (1+2+3)	a) 825,955 b) 134,507	16	a) 60,747 b) 30,197	50	a) 705,512 b) 232,134	33
5) Total II (A+B)	a) 886,702 b) 164,704 = 19 %					
b) Total III (A+B+C)			a) 1,592,214 b) 396,838 = 25 %			

Source: Distilled from Denkschrift des Reichsfinanzministeriums über den Personalabbau, May 15, 1924, copy in ZStAP, Büro RP, 86, Bl. 78.

An overall target of a twenty-five percent reduction of the public work force at the national level had been set by the governmental decree which initiated the retrenchment measures in the fall of 1923. By March 1924, this target had been met, as the figures in TABLE 14 indicate. The burden of these cutbacks was distributed unevenly between the three social groups which comprised the public work force. This, too, is revealed by the figures presented in TABLE 14. As "newcomers," the contractual employees fared worst with a layoff-rate of fifty percent. Blue-collar workers, the largest group in absolute numbers, were reduced by one-third. Civil servants show a very favorable lay-off rate in comparison, suffering a reduction in numbers of only sixteen percent. If

[47] On the politics of *Abbau*, see the discussion in the CHAPTER SEVEN of this study.

Table 15

Staff Reductions in Reich Ministries, 1923—1924

Ministry/ Department	Civil Servants	%	Contractual Employees	%	Workers	%
Reich President Office	1	6.3	1	16.7	—	—
Reichstag	8	7.0	7	19.5	23	14.1
Chancellory	4	9.5	3	33.3	4	23.5
Foreign Office	77	5.8	599	33.5	35	17.6
Reich Ministry of the Interior	238	16.4	800	54.9	125	23.2
Reich Economics Ministry	224	23.8	1,166	62.3	185	48.7
Reich Economic Council	3	20.0	13	52.0	2	9.1
Reich Labor Ministry	1,439	13.4	8,749	88.6	1,363	53.1
Reich Ministry of Defense	—	—	150	1.8	2,412	11.0
Reich Ministry of Justice	83	7.2	11	15.4	32	20.4
Reich Transport Ministry-Section of Waterways	238	8.8	499	22.5	8,103	53.2
Reich Ministry for Agriculture & Foods	15	7.5	97	56.4	43	16.6
Accounting Office	27	10.0	—	—	3	13.6
Reich Finance Ministry	4708	5.9	10,217	41.7	454	8.1
Reich Ministry for Reconstruction	106	7.6	1,402	36.4	234	37.1
Reich Ministry for the Occupied Territories	36	2.9	336	21.7	393	16.3
Total	7,207	6.8	24,320	47.4	13,411	26.8

Source: As in Table 14.

the area of general administration is examined independently, as done in Table 15, the obvious imbalance between cutbacks in civil service employment (6.8 %) and of contractual forms of labor (*Angestellte*, 47 %; *Arbeiter*, 26,8 %) increases even further. Those ministries with a high proportion of contractual employees, e. g. the Ministry of Labor, took the lead in cutting employment levels for this group by no less than 88.6 %.

Our findings of growth patterns and structural changes within the German *Beamtenschaft* and the public work force during the period of inflation can be summarized in the following five points:

1. War and postwar tasks of demobilization and economic reconstruction led to a significant increase of civil-service employment and thus in the number of civil servants between 1914 and 1920 at all levels of government, national, state, and local.

2. The rate of increase as well as the phenomenon as such was not unlike similar developments in other of the former belligerent European nations. This indicates that the war and the postwar tasks of demobilization and economic reconstruction were the most important causal factors for growth of public employment (including civil-service employment) in the 1914—1920 period.

3. It is peculiar to the German case, however, that bureaucratic growth continued after 1920, albeit at a slower pace. Here the inflation can be cited as a factor, because the accelerated pace of the inflation after 1920 was conducive to full employment in the public sector, allowing for the *continued* financial support of an "army of public servants" by means of the printing presses. In other European countries, public employment receded after 1920, especially in those countries that stabilized their currencies at the expense of economic depression.

4. The growth of civil-service employment led to structural changes within the *Beamtenschaft.* Lower grades and technical staffs *(Betriebsbeamte)* increased at a disproportional rate. The position of women civil servants improved. The relative position of the civil service within the public sector was weakened, however, by the appearance of larger numbers of contractual employees who occupied civil-service positions. Here a source of inter-group conflict developed. Both areas of conflict played a significant part in the personnel reductions of 1923—24.

5. Stabilization necessitated a reduction of the size of public expenditure and hence of public employment. In Germany, first efforts at reducing the size of public employment coincided with the end of the "inflation boom" in mid-1922, but came into full force only during the stabilization crisis of 1923—24. It was only then that the long-overdue task of reducing the size of the state apparatus was finally undertaken.

During the stabilization crisis, personnel reductions were to become a source of intra-group conflicts within the *Beamtenschaft* and of inter-group conflicts within the public work force.

Economic Conditions and Social Behavior, 1914—1924

Considerable controversy still exist about the exact impact which the inflation had on the economic conditions and, as a derivative, on the social position of the relevant social groups in German society. This is true in particular in the case of the *Beamtenschaft.* While most contemporary observers agreed that the economic conditions of civil servants deteriorated during the war and the period of postwar inflation, the *degree* of deterioration and the yardstick by which economic and concomitant social decline was to be measured remained a matter of considerable controversy. To Hans Heiler and others, the economic fate of civil servants was proof of the thesis that a general impoverishment of the new *Mittelstand* and intellectual work *(geistige Arbeit)* had taken place during the inflation.[48] Writers close to the civil servant movement likewise complained about the social decline of the *Beamtenschaft,* although, interestingly enough, the impact of prewar and wartime inflation was stressed more than influences of postwar economic conditions as causal factors for the economic malaise of the *Beamten.*[49] Franz Eulenburg went even further by claiming that the economic conditions of civil servants in the inflation years was no indicator at all for their social position, since in comparison to other groups civil servants had emerged "socially stronger" *(sozial gestärkt)* from the ravages of inflation. The civil servant's security of employment, Eulenburg argued, weighed more heavily than any income losses suffered during the inflation.[50] Costantino Bresciani-Turroni was rather noncommittal on the social consequences of income losses experienced by civil servants during the inflation. He was, however, the first to point toward the uneven distribution of income losses suffered within the

[48] H. Heiler, *Die Verelendung...,* pp. 56—57. See also A. Weber, *Die Not der geistigen Arbeiter...,* and G. Schreiber, *Die Not der deutschen Wissenschaft...,* on the plight of the intellectual worker in the inflation.

[49] Wilhelm Schröder/Paul Lockenvitz, *Der soziale Niedergang der deutschen Beamtenschaft* (= Flugschriften des Deutschen Beamtenbundes, No. 5), Berlin 1921, pp. 3—7.

[50] F. Eulenburg, *Die sozialen Wirkungen...,* in: *JbNSt,* 122 (1924), p. 789. The full impact of the *Abbau* measures, which of course presented a challenge to the civil servant's security of employment, were not known to Eulenburg when he wrote his treatise.

Beamtenschaft by its three main composite groupings, and he showed that the drop in real salaries was proportionately greater for the upper and middle ranks than for the lower ranks of the civil service. In addition, he showed that there was not a steady pace of decline of real salaries, but that there were considerable fluctuations, especially in the phase of accelerated inflation that commenced in the fall of 1921.[51]

The assessment of contemporary observers of the economic situation of the *Beamtenschaft* and other middle class groups varied greatly, therefore — a fact which was long overlooked in post-1945 studies on the social consequences of the inflation. In the latter works, the social decline, or even destruction of *the* Mittelstand became a standard interpretation, and very rarely was this interpretation checked against the real economic situation of middle-class groups, before, during, and after the inflation.[52] Recently, a number of economic historians interested in the distributional effects of the German inflation have taken up the real-wage discussion again and have argued that civil servants were among the main losers of the inflation, primarily because of wage pressures exerted upon a limited national product by the organized working class.[53] Although a much more sophisticated argument, based on a long-overdue reexamination of blue-collar wage levels in the inflation, the notion of civil servants as losers in this distributional struggle is once again more assumed than proven in a detailed and convincing way. The question whether the struggle of adjusting incomes to the rising cost of living led to a distributional conflict between civil servants and other wage earning groups, or if, quite to the contrary, a consensus of interest prevailed among all employee groups, is an important aspect of the linkage between economic and social conditions and social behavior. A discussion of the "levelling of incomes" between *Arbeitnehmer* groups, undertaken in the second part of this section, might lead to a clarification of this unresolved question.[54]

[51] C. Bresciani-Turroni, *The Economics...*, pp. 326—327. Bresciani-Turroni was more interested in the movement of workers' wages. See *ibid.*, pp. 300 ff. Much the same can be said of the more recent study of Gerhard Bry, *Wages in Germany*, Princeton 1960, pp. 214 ff.

[52] Cf. the discussion and the literature cited in the INTRODUCTION to this study, esp. pp. 7 ff. above.

[53] See C.-L. Holtfrerich, *Die deutsche Inflation...*, pp. 224—246, and especially W. Abelshauser, *Verelendung...*, in: H. Mommsen/W. Schulze (eds.), *Vom Elend...*, pp. 445—476.

[54] The following section recapitulates findings published previously by this author as

Real Income and the Phasing of Social Protest

Like other dependent employees, civil servants derive the main portion of their income from a salary received from their (public) employer. From a strictly economic perspective, therefore, a civil servant is not more and not less an employee *(Arbeitnehmer)* than a white-collar *Angestellter* or even a blue-collar worker. Not unlike other wage earning groups, therefore, the level of a civil servant's income relates to the level of the salary or "pay" *(Besoldung)* actually received (nominal salary). Since "money is only important for what it will procure" (Keynes), the real purchasing power of the nominal wage or salary has to be determined as well if one wants to arrive at a better understanding of the decline of income levels and distributional conflicts in the inflation process.[55]

The reconstruction of real wage and salary levels during the decade of inflation is rendered difficult by the lack of reliable statistical data for these years. After all, official time series for the inflation years do not exist, a fact which has prompted most authors who have studied the economic conditions of civil servants to either exclude a discussion of the inflation years entirely, treat it cursorily at best, or begin with the first post-inflation year, i. e. 1924.[56] The argument that a lack of statistical data precludes *any* discussion of real wages and salaries during the inflation has, however, been overstrained. The West German economic historian Werner Abelshauser has made this point in his recent study on the social conditions of the German working class, the

Verteilungskampf oder Interessenkonsensus? Einkommensentwicklung und Sozialverhalten von Arbeitnehmergruppen in der Inflationszeit 1914 bis 1924, in: G. D. Feldman et al. (eds.), *German Inflation...*, pp. 347—384.

[55] This is not to say, however, that *nominal* wages are irrelevant as an explanatory device for certain socio-historical processes during the inflation. For example, it would be unnecessary to "deflate" nominal wages or salaries if one is interested only in comparing wage/salary levels at certain points within or between social groups. Any discussion of distributional changes as a result of declining (or rising) incomes must be based on real wages and salaries, however, because losses or gains can only be measured in reference to a fixed point, usually the "normal" conditions in the last prewar years.

[56] See, for example, Arnold Hülden, *Die Entwicklung der Beamtenbesoldung in den letzten 50 Jahren,* in: *Deutscher Beamtenbund. Ursprung. Weg. Ziel,* Bundesleitung des Deutschen Beamtenbundes (ed.), Bonn 1968, pp. III/59—III/96; Lilian Kleineberg, *Die Entwicklung der wirtschaftlichen Lage der Beamten des Reiches, bzw. Bundes von 1909 bis heute,* Diss., Cologne 1954, pp. 29—33; H. Völter, *Die deutsche Beamtenbesoldung...*, pp. 14—17.

Arbeiterschaft, during the inflation. He and others have argued that difficulties of evaluation rather than lack of sources as such have prevented economists, economic historians and social historians alike from examining the real wage problem in the inflation. In addition, Abelshauser's study shows that important and hitherto untapped regional statistical sources can be helpful in the effort of reconstructing the movement of real wages during the inflation.[57]

The pitfalls of the lack-of-statistics-argument not only applies to workers' wages, but to the movement of real salaries of civil servants in the inflation as well. Here, too, little used statistical material exists which allows us to consider some of the most pressing problems connected with the social conditions of civil servants in the inflation period:

(1) The observation of civil servants' real salaries over an extended portion of the inflation period.
(2) The examination of intra-group differences, i. e. the movement of salary differentials within the *Beamtenschaft.*
(3) The examination of inter-group differences, i. e. the comparison of real income of civil servants and wage earners.
(4) The examination of regional variations in civil service pay levels.

The examination of new or rarely used statistical material on the basis of these four points is one aim of the present analysis. By making completeness, comparability (regional and group-related) and deflation of nominal wages and salaries by means of a verifiable cost-of-living index the main criteria of selection, three numerical series have been selected which comply with these minimum requirements.

The German National Statistical Office *(Statistisches Reichsamt)* collected data on the movement of nominal and real salaries of different Reich civil service pay groups. This was done in a spotty way beginning in 1913, and in a more thorough and continuous fashion since 1920.[58]

[57] See W. Abelshauser, *Verelendung...,* in: H. Mommsen/W. Schulze (eds.), *Vom Elend...,* pp. 451—458. See also C.-L. Holtfrerich, *Die deutsche Inflation...,* pp. 24—43 and A. Kunz, *Verteilungskampf...,* in: G. D. Feldman et al. (eds.), *The German Inflation...,* pp. 349—351.

[58] The results were published periodically in the Reich Statistical Office's journal *Wirtschaft und Statistik* and, in a condensed form, in a special issue of that journal under the title *Zahlen zur Geldentwertung,* which remains one of the most important sources on the statistics of the German inflation. See *Zahlen zur Geldentwertung,* in: *WSt,* 5 (1925), Sonderh. 1, pp. 41—43. Henceforth this publication will be cited by its title only.

TABLE 16, which is based on the data of the Reich Statistical Office, traces the development of the real salaries of Reich civil servants

TABLE 16

Real Monthly Salaries of Reich Civil Servants, 1913—1924[a]
in Marks, Index: 1913 = 100

Year/Month	Higher Grades		Middle Grades		Lower Grades	
1913	608.00	100.00	342.00	100.00	157.00	100.00
1917	260.97[b]	42.90	166.07	48.60	84.22	53.60
1919	244.58	40.20	187.47	54.80	140.24	89.30
1920						
March	123.74[c]	20.40	99.79	29.20	80.02	51.00
April	213.53	35.10	164.40	48.10	119.39	76.00
July	208.92	34.40	160.85	47.00	116.81	74.40
Oct.	217.09	35.70	169.28	49.50	125.49	79.90
Dec.	200.78	33.00	156.56	45.80	116.06	73.90
1921						
April	230.88	38.00	179.33	52.40	132.21	84.20
July	208.16	34.20	161.68	47.30	119.20	75.90
Oct.	325.80	53.60	220.74	64.50	151.93	96.80
Dec.	254.15	41.80	172.20	50.40	118.52	75.50
1922						
April	181.08	29.80	136.00	39.80	102.56	65.30
June	235.23	38.70	176.32	51.60	132.65	84.50
Sept.	266.45	43.80	196.93	57.60	145.40	92.60
Dec.	202.15	33.30	151.73	44.40	103.30	65.80
1923						
Feb.	181.79	29.90	136.44	39.90	92.89	59.20
May	214.27	35.20	160.69	47.00	109.23	69.30
June	249.57	41.00	187.18	54.70	127.18	86.10
Aug.	280.09	46.10	203.79	59.60	130.67	83.00
Oct.	260.65	42.90	189.42	55.40	120.81	76.90
Nov.	193.26	31.80	138.49	40.50	87.34	55.60
Dec.	251.38	41.30	170.41	49.80	92.07	58.60
1924						
April	346.00[d]	56.90	220.00	72.80	129.00	91.70
June	485.00	79.70	304.00	89.00	146.00	93.30
Oct.	449.00	73.80	282.00	82.50	139.00	88.50
Dec.	501.00	82.40	315.00	92.10	158.00	101.00

representing select pay groups for each of the three levels of the civil service. The index numbers, based on the prewar "peace salaries" of 1913, are given as well; they were used as a basis for the wage/salary curves appearing in FIGURE 1. Salaries were changed from "nominal" into "real" by means of an index which from 1913 to January 1920 was based on the cost-of-living index computed by Calwer and, since February 1920, on an index figure computed by the Statistical Office on the basis of an average national cost-of-living index for the actual period of consumption. Beginning with October 1923, the mode of payment was taken into consideration as well.

The widespread misgivings about the cost-of-living index used by the Reich Statistical Office have to be restated at this point as well.[59] The selection of "typical" consumer goods was based on household items purchased in a working class family and therefore cannot be considered as being fully representative for a civil servant's family. On the positive side, however, one may well assume that the nominal salaries deflated by the national cost-of-living index are close enough to their real purchasing value as to allow a reflection of the real income situation of civil servants in the inflation. Regional comparisons are not possible, because the figures are based on a national average. Group-related comparisons, however, are possible, since the earnings of three pay groups belonging to the traditional three-tier hierarchy of the German

Notes to TABLE 16

[a] Average base bay, including all supplement for location class A, for a civil servant in Grade XI, a middle-level civil servant in Grade VIII, and a lower-level civil servant in Grade III, married with two children.

[b] For 1917 and 1919 computed on the basis of Calwer's index of foods.

[c] Since February 1920 computed over a mean national cost-of-living index for the actual period of consumption. As of October 1923, the method of payment is taken into consideration as well.

[d] Calculations for 1924 have been added by this author.

Source: Zahlen zur Geldentwertung..., in: *WSt*, 5 (1925), Sonderheft 1, p. 43 (for 1917 to 1923). For 1924: *WSt*, 4 (1924), pp. 216, 748 (the nominal salaries given there were converted into "real" by using the cost-of-living index for the respective months published in the same journal).

[59] An illuminating discussion of the index question is given by C.-L. Holtfrerich, *Die deutsche Inflation...*, pp. 27—36.

FIGURE 1

Index of Real Salaries/Wages of Reich Civil Servants, Railroad Workers, and of a Metal Worker in Private Industry, 1913—1923

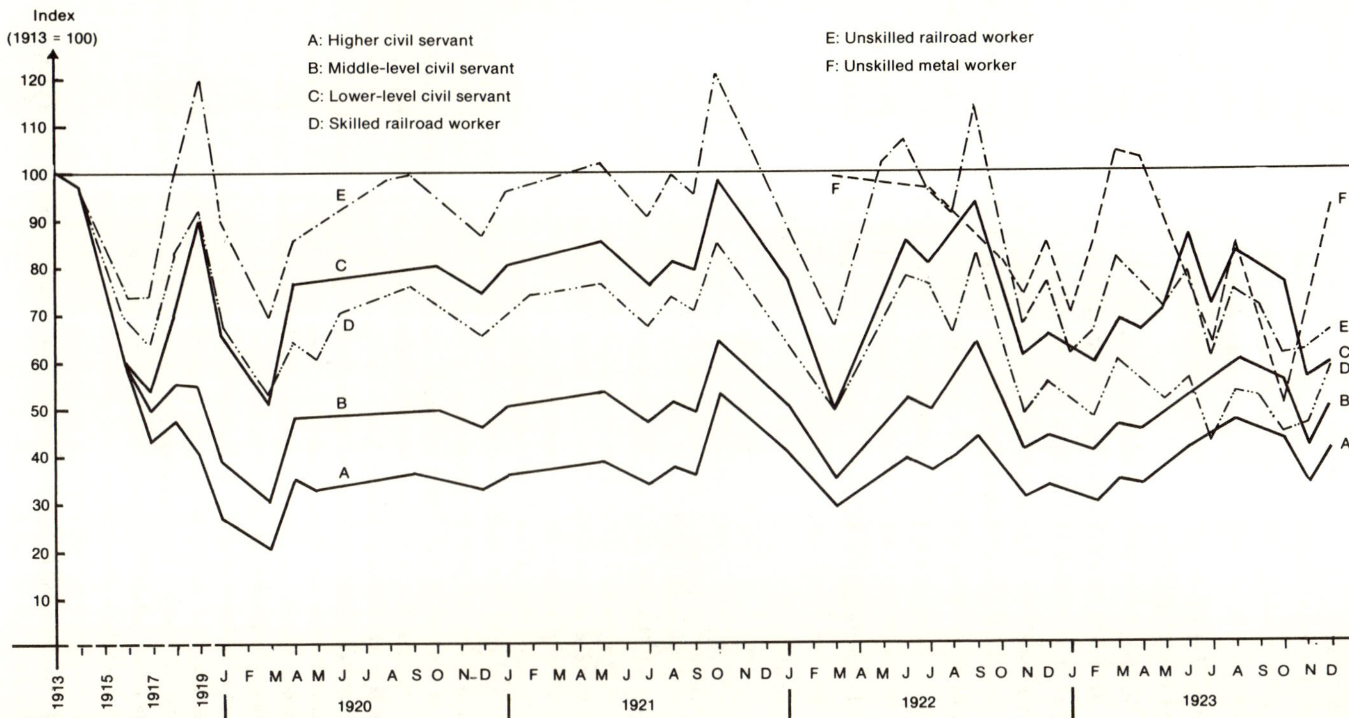

Sources: TABLE 16 (for A to D) and *Zahlen zur Geldentwertung* . . ., p. 40, 44 (for D to F). The weakly earnings given for D to F have been recalculated into monthly earnings

civil service are given: a higher civil servant *(Regierungsrat)* belonging to pay group XI, a middle-level clerk *(Obersekretär)* of pay group VIII, and a lower-level civil servant, a railroad conductor *(Eisenbahnschaffner)* of pay group III.[60] The statistical data compiled for government workers in the service of the Reich government and in private industry allows for some comparisons between the income of civil servants and that of other social groups, moreover.

The second series is based on a statistical survey of wages and salaries in Hamburg undertaken by the Statistical Bureau of the Hanseatic City, which was at the same time a state *(Land)*.[61] A destillation of this data, published in the Bureau's journal, is presented here in TABLE 17 and FIGURE 2. Nominal wages and salaries were deflated on the basis of a special cost-of-living index computed for Hamburg, and therefore allow to draw conclusions about the impact of inflation in a large city which, moreover, was considered as one of the most expensive cities in Germany.[62] Again, "typical" public service groups, including pay rates

[60] The classification scheme used here was only established in 1920 as a result of the Pay Reform Act passed in that year. The Statistical Office compensated for possible changes in classification, however, that is to say the earnings of an *Eisenbahnschaffner* of pay group III (in 1920) was compared with those of an identical reference person in 1914. — It may well be argued that these pay groups selected here were not truly representative of the three levels of the German civil service, but were chosen by the Statistical Office for political purposes. By contrasting the income of a higher civil servant in the first promotional grade (XI) with that of a middle-level civil servant in the next-to-last grade (VIII) and that of a lower-level civil servant in the final promotional grade (III), a partially distorted picture appears since these grades were representative of the three civil-service tiers to a different degree. The implicit aim of these official statistics may well have been to give the appearance of a sharper decline of the salaries of higher civil servants as was actually the case. Consequently, the organizations of civil servants with their predominantly middle, and lower-grade civil service constituency criticized the selection criteria for being "political" rather than "typical." Cf. *Stellungnahme des Deutschen Beamtenbundes zur Denkschrift des Reichsministers der Finanzen über die Besoldung der Reichsbeamten* (= Reichstagsdrucksache, No. 407), Berlin 1925 (hereafter cited as *Stellungnahme DBB 1925*), copy in ZStAP, RMdI, 2598, Bl. 11, pp. 3—5. (I am indebted to Peter-Christian Witt for having brought this point to my attention).

[61] *Die Wirkungen der Geldentwertung auf die Gehälter der Beamten und Staatsangestellten in den Jahren 1919 bis 1923,* in: *Hamburger Statistische Monatsberichte,* 1 (1924), pp. 77—80; *Die Wirkungen der Geldentwertung auf die Löhne einiger typischer Arbeiterberufe in den Jahren 1921 bis 1923,* in: *Ibid.*, pp. 97—100.

[62] For a more exhaustive treatment of the Hamburg survey, see C.-L. Holtfrerich, *Die deutsche Inflation...*, pp. 37f.

TABLE 17

Real Monthly Salaries of State Officials and Public Contractual Employees in Hamburg, 1914—1923[a]. In Marks. Index: 1914 = 100

A) Higher Official. Average Salary 1914: 814

Year	J	F	M	A	M	J	J	A	S	O	N	D
1920	200	162	130	258	250	281	270	279	279	248	224	215
1921	259	283	269	280	302	294	262	267	264	419	321	299
1922	320	249[b]	218	194	218	239	249	261	265	222	146	221
1923	243	244	272	261	263	307	287	382	415	365	195	325
B) Middle-grade Official. Average Salary 1914: 330												
1920	126	102	82	165	161	181	173	179	179	159	144	138
1921	167	182	173	180	194	189	168	171	170	216	165	154
1922	179	139[b]	122	122	137	148	153	157	158	134	88	134
1923	148	148	165	158	159	187	173	230	250	220	118	181
C) Lower-grade Official. Average Salary 1914: 204												
1920	107	87	70	124	120	135	129	134	134	119	108	103
1921	125	137	135	146	142	126	128	128	127	146	112	104
1922	131	102[b]	89	94	106	113	115	116	116	93	61	94
1923	103	103	115	110	110	130	112	150	162	144	77	105
D) Contractual Employee. Average Salary 1914: 167												
1920	101	82	66	124	121	136	130	135	135	120	108	104
1921	125	137	130	135	146	142	126	129	128	153	117	109
1922	135	105[b]	92	97	108	116	118	120	119	96	63	96
1923	106	106	118	113	114	134	115	154	167	148	79	108

TABLE 17 *(Continuation)*

Real Monthly Salaries of State Officials and Public Contractual Employees in Hamburg 1914—1923[a]. In Marks. Index: 1914 = 100

Year	J	F	M	A	M	J	J	A	S	O	N	D
Index: 1914 = 100												
1920	25	20	16	32	31	35	33	34	34	30	28	26
1921	32	35	33	34	37	36	32	33	32	51	39	37
1922	39	31	27	24	27	29	31	32	33	27	18	27
1923	30	30	33	32	32	38	35	47	51	45	24	40
Index: 1914 = 100												
1920	38	31	25	50	49	55	52	54	54	48	44	42
1921	51	55	52	55	59	57	51	52	52	65	50	47
1922	54	42	37	37	42	45	46	48	48	41	27	41
1923	45	45	50	48	48	57	53	70	76	67	36	55
Index: 1914 = 100												
1920	52	43	34	61	59	66	63	66	66	58	53	50
1921	61	67	64	66	72	70	62	63	62	72	55	51
1922	64	50	44	46	52	55	56	57	57	46	30	46
1923	50	50	56	54	54	64	55	74	79	71	38	51
Index: 1914 = 100												
1920	60	49	40	74	72	81	78	81	81	72	65	62
1921	75	82	79	81	87	85	75	77	77	92	70	65
1922	81	63	55	58	65	69	71	72	71	57	38	57
1923	63	63	71	68	68	80	69	92	100	89	47	65

[a] Monthly salaries, excluding children's supplements.

[b] As of February 1922 including expenses for clothing.

Source: Die Wirkungen der Geldentwertung..., in: *Hamburger Statistische Monatsberichte*, 1 (1924), pp. 77—80, distilled from *Übersichten* I and II on p. 78.

Figure 2

Index of Real Salaries/Wages of State Officials, Contractual Public Employees, and Workers in Private Industry in Hamburg, 1920—1923

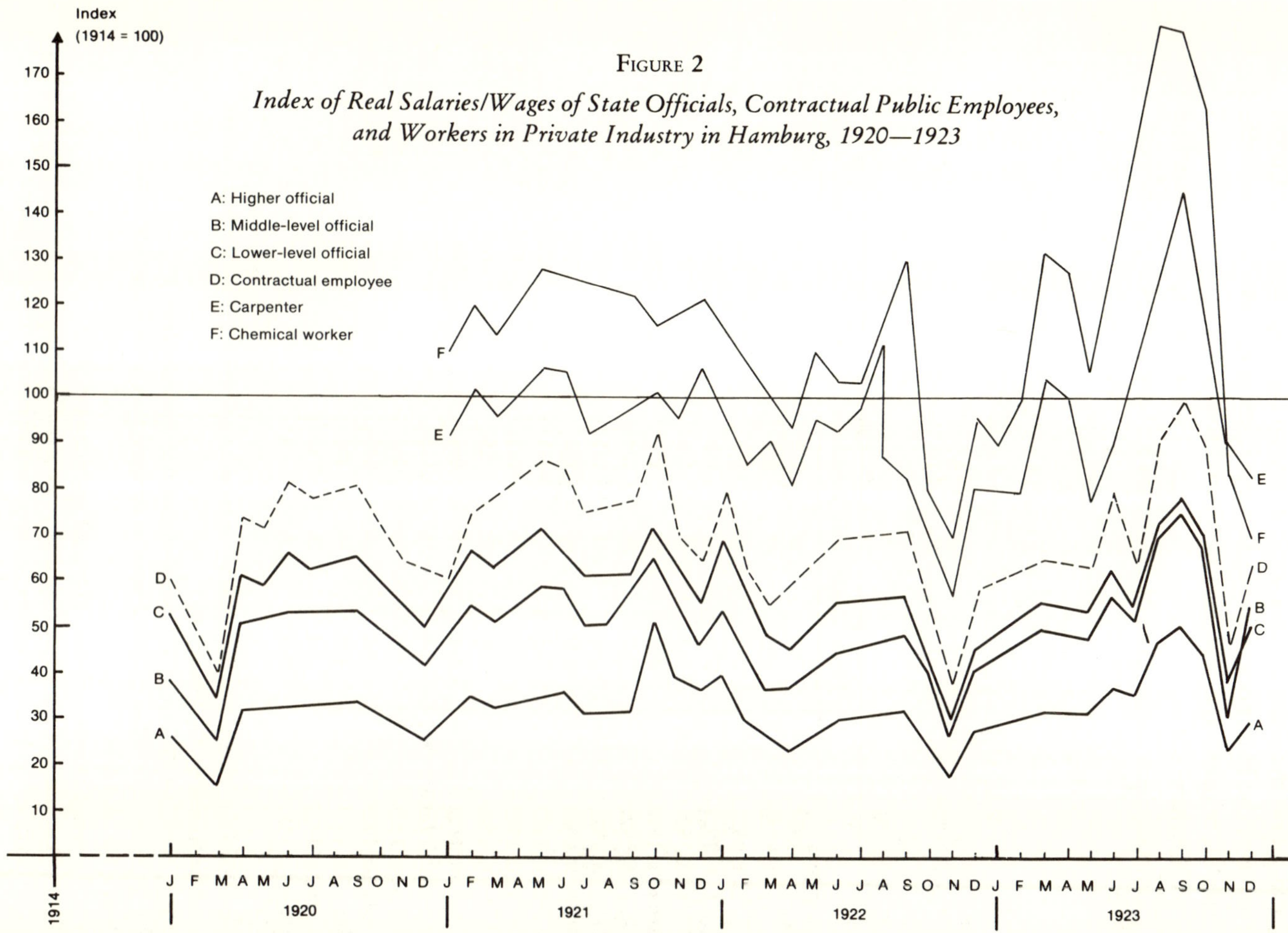

Sources: Table 17 (for A to D) and *Hamburger Statistische Monatsberichte*, 1 (1924),

of a contractual public employee *(Staatsangestellte)*, have been selected and allow the examination of intra-group developments. The great value of the Hamburg material, however, lies in its excellent possibilities for regional and inter-group comparisons.

Our third series, presented in TABLE 18 and FIGURE 3, is based on computations undertaken by Hermann Knecht in 1924 in a contempo-

TABLE 18

Real Monthly Salaries of Bavarian State Officials in Munich, 1914—1923

In Marks. Index: 1914 = 100

	Higher Grades (XIII)		Middle Grades (VII)		Lower Grades (III)	
1914	700[a]	100	203[a]	100	133[a]	100
1. 4. 1920[b]	472	67	238	114	171	133
1. 1. 1921	292	42	147	71	106	80
1. 8. 1921	296	42	145	70	107	81
1.10. 1921	563	80	196	94	133	100
1. 1. 1922	408	58	151	73	106	80
1. 5. 1922[c]	267	38	120	58	92	69
1. 6. 1922	298	43	135	65	101	76
1. 8. 1922	309	44	133	64	109	82
1. 9. 1922	315	45	135	65	102	77
1.10. 1922	273	39	122	59	83	62
5. 1923[d]	199	28	89	43	61	46
6. 1923	341	49	147	71	101	76
7. 1923	254	36	113	54	70	53
8. 1923	368	53	165	79	101	76
17.10. 1923[e]	268	38	120	58	72	54
1.11. 1923	408	58	184	89	112	84
18.11. 1923	184	26	80	39	48	36
12. 1923[f]	245	35	98	47	51	38

[a] Starting salaries *(Anfangsgehälter)* without supplements for spouse and children *(Frauenzuschlag, Kinderzuschlag)*.

[b] From 1.4.1920 to 1.1.1922 simple indexation *(einfacher Index)*.

[c] From 1.5.1922 to 1.10.1922 based on an aggregate cost-of-living index *(Gesamtindex)* for Munich.

[d] Average monthly salaries and average aggregate index.

[e] Ficticious monthly salaries based on actual weekly earnings.

[f] So called "gold-mark" salaries, set after the stabilization of the currency.

Source: H. Knecht, *Die Entwicklung der Löhne und Gehälter...*, pp. 143—160.

Figure 3

Index of Real Salaries of Bavarian State Officials in Munich, 1920—1923

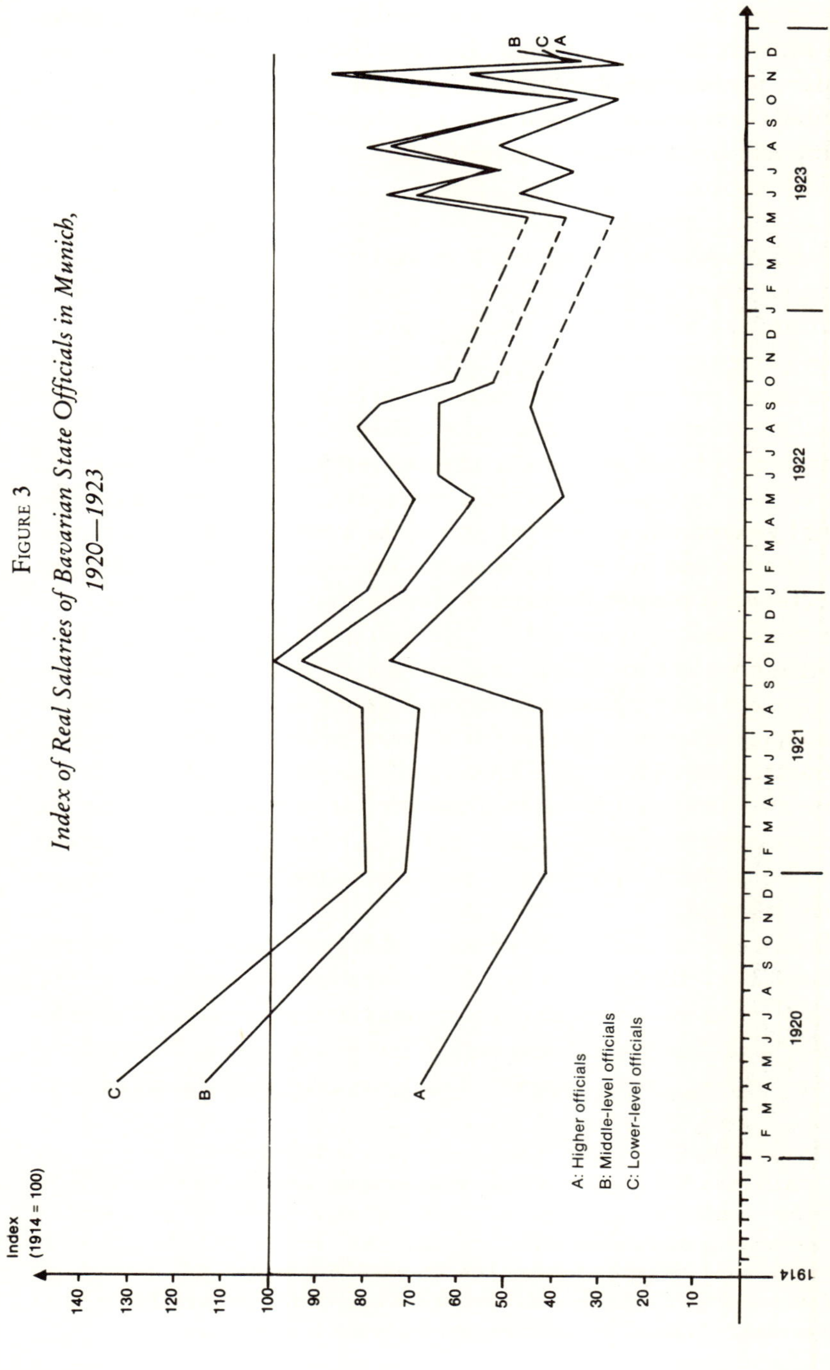

Source: Table 18.

rary dissertation on wage and salary movements of workers and civil servants in Munich.[63] Knecht computed his own cost-of-living index for Munich; its statistical basis changes several times over the period under consideration, and his figures are therefore extremely difficult to double check. As a consequence, the Munich data can only be used selectively and with some reservations.

The statistical data assembled here is useful for the dual purpose of (1) shedding new light on the economic conditions of the *Beamtenschaft* in war, postwar inflation, and stabilization and (2) for reexamining some standard interpretations of the social consequences of the inflation process in general and with regard to civil servants and other employee groups in particular. Both will now be done in the remaining portion of this section, in which we shall deal with the question of whether the inflation prompted the social decline of the *Beamtenschaft*, as argued by Heiler, or aided in the recovery of its social position and status lost during the war years, as argued by Eulenburg. This will be done by examining cyclical patterns in the movement of civil servants' real salaries and by relating those to the more general problems of structure and phasing of social conflict within the *Beamtenschaft* and the public sector in general. In addition, we will be concerned with another phenomenon usually attributed to the inflation: the narrowing of wage and salary differentials between (and within) social groups, the famous (or infamous) "levelling of incomes" noted in the contemporary literature of the 1920s and 1930s. Finally we shall take our findings in these two areas as a point of departure for some comments on the modern concept of a "distributional struggle" between social groups as the all-important aspect of the social consequences of periods of sustained inflation.

Even a cursory look at the behavior of the curves charted in FIGURES 1, 2 and 3 reveal that the notion of *the* inflation as an agent of steadily declining incomes and thus of continuous (and progressively) worsening social decline of the *Beamtenschaft* is misleading. In each FIGURE the curves relating to the salaries of civil servants (A-C) fluctuate pro-

[63] Hermann Knecht, *Die Entwicklung der Löhne und Gehälter der Münchener Arbeiter- und Beamtenschaft in der Kriegs- und Nachkriegszeit bis Ende 1923 mit besonderer Berücksichtigung der Geldentwertung (Inflation)*, Diss., Erlangen 1924. Valuable material is given also by Albert Podschun, *Die Lohn- und Gehaltsbewegung seit der Revolution und ihre bevölkerungspolitische und kulturelle Bedeutung*, Diss., Berlin 1922, but his data only reaches to 1922 and has therefore not been tapped as a source, here.

foundly; periods of decline are followed by periods of recovery. On the whole, the (admittedly low) level reached by real salaries in early 1920 is *not* made worse by the subsequent inflationary developments. On the contrary, there are periods of distinct recovery, e. g. April 1920 to October 1921. This leads one to conclude that the longest sub-period of the *postwar* inflation, the years between 1920 and 1923, was less a source of income losses than a possibility to recoup losses suffered *already* as a result of wartime inflation (1914—1918) and the inflationary upsurge of the immediate postwar and revolutionary period (1918—1920).[64] The fact that salary levels did improve over extended periods of time after 1920 may be an indication that civil servants and those who represented their interests adapted their policies to the inflation by becoming more effective as negotiators in salary negotiations. That this was indeed the case will be shown in a much more systematic and detailed way in the subsequent chapters of this study, where we shall examine civil servant interest politics and its underlying social, political, and economic factors. A further subdivision of the inflation process, i. e. a periodization scheme based more concretely still on the socio-economic conditions of civil servants in the decade between 1914 and 1924, will undoubtedly be a helpful device in structuring our study by identifying phases of relative social calm, phases of intense social unrest, and points of social crisis. A more detailed interpretation of the salary curves presented in FIGURES 1 and 2 makes such a periodization possible.

If one looks at FIGURE 1, for example, it is readily apparent that the decline of salaries[65] commenced during the war years under the impact of wartime inflation. Between 1914 and 1917, the latter obviously a year of crisis, nominal salaries lose between 46 % and 57 % of their real purchasing power. Thus what had already been a prewar trend, namely the gap between civil service salary levels and general economic

[64] Although it may be viewed as part of the conventional wisdom on the German inflation, and as a narrowing of the concept of a decade of inflation spanning the years from 1914—1924, the years from 1920 to 1923 are usually referred to as *the* inflation years in most histories of the Weimar Republic. War and revolution characterized the preceding years (1914—1920), although, as has been pointed out several times in the context of this study, there was also "wartime inflation" and an inflationary upsurge in late 1919 which prepared the grounds for the post-1920 inflation politics.

[65] Henceforth "salaries" is to mean "real salaries of civil servants" unless noted otherwise.

growth,[66] was accelerated to such an extent that in retrospect the conditions existing in 1913 became the positive reference point from which decline was to be measured, if only in the subjective experience of those involved. The war and, quite typically, its political consequences for Germany (political revolution and the Versailles Treaty) were cited as having precipiated the complete economic collapse of the *Beamtenschaft.*[67]

Our own findings *partially* confirm this assessment. While some civil servants, i. e. the lower pay groups, at first seemed to benefit from the general wage movements unleashed by the Revolution of 1918/19 — their salaries stand at 90 % of their prewar value in 1919, while the middle grades reach only 52 %, the higher grades only 48 % — an all time low point is reached by late 1919/early 1920. This was the point in time when, as Heiler reports, the income of a tailor was "princely" compared to that of a higher civil servant, and when the Social Democratic Prussian Minister of the Interior Heine was allegedly unable to find trade union officials willing to become county supervisors *(Landräte)*, because the position was paid too poorly.[68] It is a reflection of the seriousness of the salary decline in the second half of 1919, moreover, that civil servants took their complaints to the streets for the first time: the winter of 1919/20 saw large-scale mass demonstrations conducted by civil servant organizations in Berlin and other large cities.

By March 1920, the salary of a higher civil servant employed by the Reich had been reduced to one-fifth, that of a middle level official to one third, and that of a lower grade *Beamte* to about one half of its prewar value. The figures for Hamburg (16 %, 25 % and 34 %) are even lower and demonstrate the expensive standard of living in a large city (see TABLE 17 and FIGURE 2). All indications point into the direction that in the winter and early spring of 1919-20 an absolute low point had been reached in the movement of civil servant salaries not only in

[66] According to W. Schröder/P. Lockenvitz, *Der soziale Niedergang...*, p. 4, the German national income increased by 52 % between 1898 and 1913, workers' wages by 49 %, the cost of food by 35 %, and civil service pay by only 17.5 %.

[67] W. Schröder and P. Lockenvitz, who were leading members of the main civil servant association, the *Deutscher Beamtenbund,* wrote: „Als dann beim Ausgang des Krieges infolge der Niederlage, des Umsturzes und der harten Friedensbedingungen eine sturzartige Entwertung der Mark eintrat und die Teuerungsziffer ungeheuer in die Höhe ging, wurde die bereits wirtschaftlich geschwächte Beamtenschaft von dieser Entwicklung bis ins Mark getroffen." (*Ibid.*, p. 7).

[68] H. Heiler, *Die Verelendung...*, pp. 20—21.

comparison to the statistically well covered subsequent years (1920—1923), but also in comparison to the less well documented previous years (1914—1919). It stands to reason, therefore, that during winter and spring of 1919-20 coincided with a major offensive toward salary reform undertaken by civil servant organizations.[69]

The Salary Reform Act of April 1920 not only raised civil servant salaries substantially, but, in addition, ushered in a period of relative stable salary levels. If one looks at the curves presented in FIGURE 1, the salaries of the Reich officials, set in April 1920 at 35 %, 48 %, and 78 % of their prewar value, reveal a slight upward tendency and in May 1921 stand at 40 %, 55 % and 88 %, respectively. Despite a noticeable cave-in of salary levels in the fall and winter of 1920-21, stability seems to have been the prevailing trend. This period of relatively stable salary conditions roughly coincides with the period of relative stability of the inflation observed by economists and economic historians.[70] It was the period of inflation when stabilization of the currency became a remote possibility or perhaps, as Gerald Feldman has argued, an "unlikely option" in face of the economic depression and its concomitant aspects of social strife and social instability which currency stabilization had caused elsewhere in Europe at the time.[71] The part played by civil servants and their organizations in the struggle over stabilization can be derived to some extent from the movement of salary levels. While stabilization could have implied a reduction of government expenditures and thus a freezing-in or even reduction of salary levels, we observe that in this period salaries tended to rise slightly. A sudden drop-off in the fall of 1920 (when stabilization was being seriously considered as a political option by the Wirth government) is quickly recovered during December 1920/January 1921 — perhaps an indication that again a potential social conflict between civil servants and the

[69] The conflicts pertaining to the Salary Reform of 1920 are discussed in CHAPTER THREE of this study.

[70] Cf. K. Laursen/J. Pedersen, *The Inflation...*, p. 20, who write: "On the whole these sixteen months [February 1920 to May 1921, A. K.] may be termed a period of relative stability." See also P. Czada, *Ursachen...*, in: H. Winkel (ed.), *Finanz- und wirtschaftspolitische Fragen...*, p. 28, who speaks of a „Phase der relativen Stabilität seit Anfang 1920".

[71] Gerald D. Feldman, *The Political Economy of Germany's Relative Stabilization during the 1920/21 World Depression*, in: Idem et al. (eds.), *The German Inflation...*, pp. 180—206, p. 181.

government as employer has been defused by higher pay at the expense of fiscal and financial contingencies necessary for stabilization.[72]

The twenty months or so between May 1921 and the late summer/fall of 1922 were characterized by an accelerating pace of the inflation rate, approaching rapid and by some accounts, even hyperinflation by mid-1922.[73] During this period civil servant salaries tend to fluctuate rather intensely, revealing a distinct cyclical pattern of upward and downward swings. The most pronounced of these is the long downward swing between October 1921 and March 1922 (again the winter months!) and the subsequent recovery between March and September 1922. The Hamburg and Munich curves display the same pattern. Then follows a renewed down-swing (September to November 1922), which in the Hamburg example is more distinct and leads to a salary level almost as low as the one in March 1920.

It is not difficult to imagine that these cyclical swings, particularly the downward trends and the turning points, coincide with periods of intensification of social conflict between civil servants and public employers during this phase of the inflation process. It is not a coincidence that the only widespread strike ever conducted by German civil servants falls into this period and occurred at the end of the prolonged downward swing in early 1922. The fact that the curves representing salaries and wages of other public employees behave in much the same way, moreover, indicates that the entire public sector was crisis-ridden during this period: protest and strike waves in the public sector became one of the most critical issues in German domestic and social policy in these months.[74]

The hyperinflation brings a change in the pattern. After the low point of November 1922, salaries tend to fluctuate less intensely. There is a general upward tendency until August 1923, followed by a sharp drop between September and November 1923. Salaries are then "stabilized" on a "Goldmark" basis in December 1923 and at a comparatively low level, albeit not as low as during some of the major "crisis points" of the 1920-23 period. In characterizing the phase of the hyperinflation one may state that, on the basis of the present data, a certain calmness

[72] For the full picture, see CHAPTER FOUR of this study.

[73] By then the monthly price increase had reached 50 %, which is often regarded as a sign of "hyper" inflation.

[74] Social conflicts in the German public sector and the strike movements of civil servants in 1921—22 are the subject of the CHAPTERS FIVE and SIX of this study.

seems to set in compared to the violent fluctuations that had characterized much of the previous years. One reason for this may well be that salaries were now adjusted in shorter intervals to the inflation rate, and that by June 1923 automatic indexation prevailed.[75]

The stabilization of the currency prepared in the fall of 1923 and finally achieved on the basis of the famous *Rentenmark* in December 1923 led to the (incorrectly named) "Goldmark salaries" of December 1923. The struggle against the "*Goldgehälter*", which were not all that golden, became a major target of civil servant interest politics in 1924.[76] As indicated by the figures given in TABLE 16, at the end of the stabilization period civil servants' salaries had come close again to their prewar "peace value" for the higher and middle groups (82 % and 92 %, respectively), and had been reached in fact by the lower ranks (101 %).

Let us summarize the findings derived from our interpretation of the movement of real salaries:

1. The decline of the real salaries occurred during the war years (1914—1918) and continued, after a brief recovery, in the postwar revolutionary crisis of 1918—19.

2. This general trend does not continue during the postwar inflation of 1920—23. There is a temporary stabilization of salaries at a level higher than in 1919/20 between April 1920 and May 1921. Afterwards, the figures fluctuate intensely, but there is not an overall downward trend.

3. The stabilization of 1923/24 appears as an important factor in stabilizing civil servants salaries at near prewar levels. However, full recovery was only achieved in several steps by December 1924 and only after salaries have been fixed at a rather low level in December 1923.

4. The periodization of the movement of civil servants' real salaries in the inflation is a meaningful device if one wants to probe into the social history of the *Beamtenschaft* during this period. For the purpose of the present investigation, therefore, sub-periods and phases of the inflation process can be defined on the basis of the periodization scheme just outlined. The sub-periods and phases of the inflation so defined will, in turn, correspond to chapters of this study.

[75] The questions of indexation during hyperinflation will be discussed in more detail in CHAPTER SEVEN.

[76] In fact, these concerns as well as the struggle against the *Abbau* measures during stabilization soon eclipsed the "trauma of hyperinflation." See CHAPTER SEVEN and A. Kunz, *Stand versus Klasse...*, in: *GG*, 8 (1982), *passim.*

Income Differentials and the Structure of Social Conflict

No contemporary observer of the post-World War I inflationary situation in Europe failed to mention the levelling of incomes between different social groups as one of the most striking social consequences of the inflation process. The "levelling" (*Nivellierung*, in German parlance) implied that during war and postwar inflation real incomes did not only decline in absolute terms, i. e. if measured against their prewar levels, but also relative to other, more or less comparable social groups. Narrowing wage (or salary) differentials thus became the true indicator of social decline, a decline which was measured either against the least skilled (educated, trained) member of one's own social group — in the case of the *Beamtenschaft* this would be the lower-level *Unterbeamte* — or against the least skilled (trained, educated) gainfully employed in the labor force, usually an unskilled worker. Thus the phenomenon of narrowing wage differentials can be observed both *within* and *between* social groups. Both tendencies are of equal importance, regardless of the fact that in connection with the fate of middle-class groups in the inflation the last-mentioned one has received more attention.[77] In the context of this study we shall discuss salary differentials within the *Beamtenschaft* and, in a second step, raise the problem of narrowing pay differentials between civil servants and blue-collar workers.

Pay Differentials within the Civil Service: Sources of Intra-Group Conflict

A first glance at FIGURES 1 to 3 on pp. 64—70 above will confirm Bresciani-Turroni's observation that the decline in income was proportionately greater for the upper and middle grades of the civil service than for the lower groups.[78] In fact, it appears as if the members of the lower ranks of the civil service were the winners in an intra-group distributional struggle unleashed by wartime inflation and intensified under postwar conditions. Their reals salaries (Curves C) are closer to prewar levels than either of those of the middle (Curves B) or higher grades (Curves A). As depicted in FIGURE 1, the real salaries of the lower-ranked officials employed by the Reich government approached their prewar level several times, initially under the impact of the Revo-

[77] Even a cursory look at the contemporary literature cited thus far (e. g. Eulenburg, Heiler) will confirm this impression.

[78] C. Bresciani-Turroni, *The Economics...*, p. 326.

lution and the postwar inflationary upsurge in 1919, when the gap between the three pay groups is widened considerably, and again in the course of the postwar inflation, in October 1921 and September 1922. Higher civil servants, on the other hand, appear as the main losers; the index of their salaries (Curve A) falls as low as 20 (in March 1920) and overtakes 50 only once (in October 1921). The middle grades are "sandwiched" in between; their real salaries (Curve B) tend to follow that of the higher groups.

The example of Hamburg (FIGURE 2) reveals some differences, although the general picture is much the same. The distances between the three curves are not as wide; the role of the lower *Reichsbeamte* is played here by the contractual employee (Curve D), whose salary twice approaches the prewar level (October 1921 and September 1923). The general level of real salaries was lower in Hamburg than the national average, moreover. If on extracts yearly averages from the indices given in TABLE 17, it becomes clear that in Hamburg higher-level civil servants only had between 30 % and 40 % of their prewar pay during the postwar period of inflation (1919—1923); the middle grades could claim 40 % to 60 %, while the pay of lower grades oscillated between 50 % and 70 %. 1920 and 1922 again appear as the years with the lowest yearly average of real salaries, i. e. as years of crisis.

At closer sight the "gains" made by the lower grades were, with the possible exception of 1919, merely a reflection of the disproportional losses suffered by the other two groups. We should therefore be less concerned with the successes of the lower groups, whose salaries remained near minimum existence level throughout the inflation, than with the decline of the higher, and to a lesser extent, the middling groups, whose nominal salaries were increased to a lesser degree and thus narrowed the existing differentials in the civil service pay structure. A trend toward a "social wage," i. e. a system of bonuses and supplements based on social considerations (e. g., marriage, number of children) independently of social status or rank in the civil service hierarchy, added on to this tendency. The results are shown in FIGURE 4 below.

FIGURE 4 depicts the differentials in base pay *(Grundgehalt)* in the Reich civil service as they developed between 1913 and July 1923. All salaries appear as multiples of the pay of a lower-grade civil servant of pay group III. FIGURE 4 confirms the impression gained thus far that higher civil servants were the chief losers in the intra-group levelling process. The lead which the higher pay groups (IX—XIII) still have

FIGURE 4

Differentials in Base Pay of Reich Civil Servants, 1913—1923
Pay Group III = 100

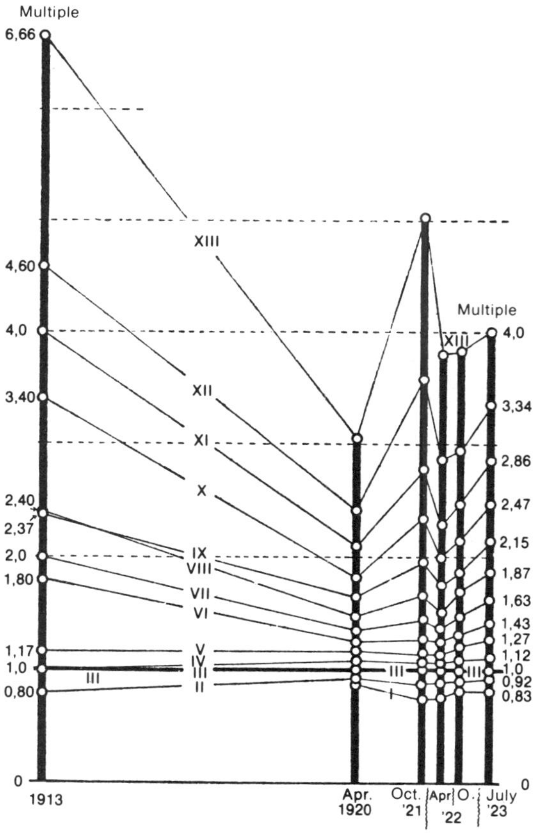

Source: Wirtschaft und Statistik, 3 (1923), p. 416.

over the lower grades (I—V, with III as the reference) in 1913 has been substantially reduced by 1920. If in 1913 a senior ministry official's pay was nearly seven times as high as that of a postman, in 1920 it was only three times as high.[79] There is a widening of the gap again in October 1921, obviously as a result of changes in civil service pay policy, but the differentials were narrowed again only six months later, in April 1922. They remained at about the same "distance" until 1923. If the numerous social supplements *(soziale Zulagen)*, many of which were introduced during the inflation, are computed in, the dislocations and disparities in the civil service pay structure are increased even further to the disadvantage of higher-paid groups. This phenomenon is shown in FIGURE 5, which compares the differentials *(Spannen)* between base pay and total pay (i. e. including all supplements and bonuses) in July 1923 to those existing in 1913.

During the stabilization of 1924 a concerted effort was made to widen pay differentials again, as TABLE 19 shows. Yet even then a significant widening of the pay differentials between April and June 1924 was followed by a renewed narrowing only in December of that year. These fluctuations and changes in the setting of the pay differentials may indicate that they remained controversial and a source of considerable intra-group conflict throughout the inflation years.

TABLE 19

Pay Differentials in the German Civil Service, 1913—1924
Pay Group III = 100

Pay Group	1913/14	Oct. 1921	Oct. 1922	Dec. 1923	Apr. 1924	June 1924	Dec. 1924
III	100	100	100	100	100	100	100
VIII	218	145	147	183	183	203	200
XI	387	214	197	269	270	323	318
XIII	620	347	276	364	362	462	451

Source: WSt, 4 (1924), pp. 413, 748.

[79] Again, war and inflation merely accelerated a pre-war trend. Between 1875 and 1913, i. e. over a period of 38 years, pay differentials had already been narrowed. A *Ministerialdirektor*, for example, who in 1875 made about eighteen times as much as a *Bahnwärter* (the lowest pay group), in 1913 "only" made ten times as much. See *Die Lohn- und Gehaltsentwicklung in den Reichsbetrieben und Behörden*, in: *WSt*, 2 (1922), pp. 378—380.

FIGURE 5

Differentials in Base Pay and Total Pay of Reich Civil Servants, 1913 and 1923
Pay Group III = 1

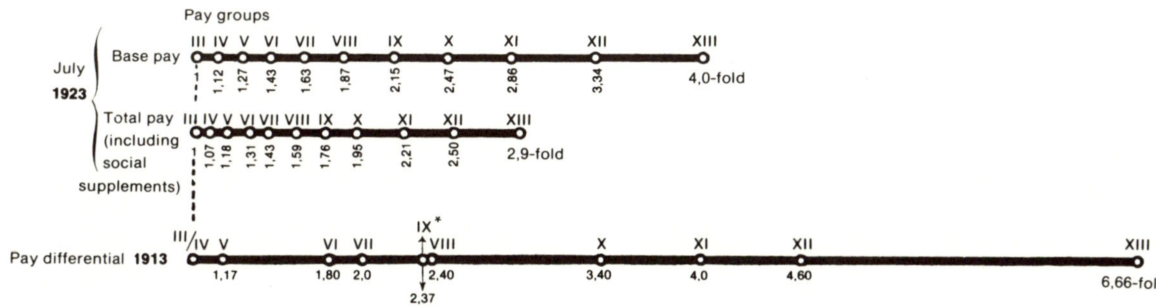

* The lag behind VIII was compensated for a higher rental allowance for these civil servants.

Source: Wirtschaft und Statistik, 3 (1923), p. 416.

Let us summarize our findings:

1. Wartime and postwar inflation accelerated and intensified a prewar trend of narrowing pay differentials within the *Beamtenschaft.*

2. Lower-grade civil servants *(Unterbeamte)* appear as the winners, higher civil servants as the losers in an intra-group distributional struggle fueled by narrowing pay differentials. The increase in the size of the lower ranks, as discussed above, must be taken into consideration as a contributing factor as well. Salary levels and pay differentials *alone* do not explain these conflicts since the salaries of lower officials remained near minimum existence levels.

3. A tendency toward a "social wage" in the civil service pay structure can be observed during the inflation. This too, contributed to narrowing pay differentials.

4. Fluctuations in the size of pay differentials during inflation suggest that they were an important issue in the formulation and conduct of salary policy *(Besoldungspolitik)* during the inflation years.

5. Stabilization at first led to a partial restoration of prewar pay differentials, although a renewed narrowing of differentials in late 1924 suggests that the proponents and supporters of a more 'levelled' pay structure could still exert influence.

6. The struggle over the setting of pay differentials was a major source of intra-group conflict and was likely to diminish the overall bargaining leverage of civil servants' associations by preventing (or rendering difficult) the establishing of a common interest strategy in the area of salary policy.

Civil Servants' Salaries vs. Workers' Wages: Sources of Inter-Group Conflict

Comparing the movement of civil servants' salaries and workers' wages during the inflation years touches upon the central issue of the distributional consequences of the inflation process. In the contemporary literature and in some recent studies undertaken by economic historians, the argument is made that as a result of political and social powers gained in the Revolution of 1918/19, the organized German working class was able to conduct increasingly successful wage movements, leading to higher (real) earnings for blue-collar workers. Since the overall national product was limited, the proportionately greater share received by the workers could only be garnered at the expense of weaker social groups. In this context, civil servants and those forced to rely on small pensions (the *Sozialrentner*) are cited as the main sufferers. Relentless and excessive wage movements on the part of the organized working class, the argument continues, prompted price increases and a wage-price spiral, leading in turn to the inflationary cycle. "Political power" rather than "economic laws" guided wage policy during the inflation, and since employers were forced to make wage concessions, these had to be made at the expense of higher prices and thus ultimately at the expense of less powerful and less tightly organized social groups.[80]

While the question of wage pressure as a cause of inflation cannot be treated thoroughly at this juncture, the question of whether civil servants were the main victims of excessive wage movements conducted by the organized working class has some bearing on our discussion of real wages and salaries during the inflation. Some contemporary observers, for one, seemed to think that civil servants were participants rather than victims in the great wage movements of the revolutionary and immediate post-revolutionary period.[81] In a more recent study of organizational developments and interest politics in the public sector in the Weimar years the argument is made that public employees, including civil servants, even became a driving force in the wage movements of 1921 and 1922.[82] This would lead one to conclude that a "consensus of interest" rather than a "distributional conflict" guided inter-group relations between civil servants and the working class during the infla-

[80] See W. Abelshauser, *Verelendung…*, in: H. Mommsen/W. Schulze (eds.), *Vom Elend…*, pp. 451—476. See also Knut Borchardt, *Wachstum und Wechsellagen 1914—1970*, in: *Handbuch der deutschen Wirtschafts- und Sozialgeschichte*, vol. 2, Stuttgart 1978, pp. 685 ff., esp. pp. 696—703, for a similar argument. For a contemporary discussion of these arguments see Gerhard Kessler, *Die Lage der deutschen Arbeiterschaft seit 1914*, in: Bernhard Harms (ed.), *Strukturwandlungen der deutschen Volkswirtschaft*, vol. 1, pp. 433—466, pp. 445—446.

[81] As noted by Adolf Günther, *Die Folgen des Krieges für Einkommen und Lebenshaltung der mittleren Volksschichten Deutschlands*, in: Rudolf Meerwarth et al., *Die Einwirkungen des Krieges auf Bevölkerungsbewegung, Einkommen und Lebenshaltung in Deutschland*, Stuttgart 1932, pp. 99—279, p. 147: „Indessen sind die unausgesetzten Lohnforderungen, Streiks, und Pressionen der Arbeiter und Angestellten ebenfalls inflationistisch zu werten, und als die Beamten in die Reihen der Fordernden eintraten und schließlich Indexlöhne auf der ganzen Linie herrschten, war eine gemeinsame Front von solchen entstanden, die entweder geradezu Nutznießer der Geldentwertung waren oder diese wenigstens für sich nicht mehr zu fürchten brauchten."

[82] Franz-Josef Furtwängler, *ÖTV. Die Geschichte einer Gewerkschaft*, Stuttgart 1954, p. 344.

tion years. In order to resolve these conflicting interpretations one would need to discuss whether qualitative statements can be substantiated by quantitative data, i. e. whether real wages of workers and real salaries of civil servants developed strikingly different during the inflation period.

There can be no doubt that in the course of the inflation civil servants' salaries declined in real terms against workers' wages. Again it is important to observe, though, that this decline took place during the war and under the impact of wartime inflation, and that it was accentuated during the immediate postwar years (1919-20) under the combined impact of political revolution and the social gains scored by the organized working class. FIGURE 6 depicts this disparity of real income between the two groups rather well. Again, higher civil servants and the middle grades lost proportionately more ground against an unskilled worker than the lower grades. There is a bit of recovery in late 1921, but on the whole FIGURE 6 seems to confirm that civil servants did indeed "lose out" in a distributional struggle with the working class.

This, however, is only half of the story at best. Civil servants did measure their own social decline against the relative (or even absolute) gains of the workers; the fact that the chart reproduced here as FIGURE 6 was published and prominently displayed by the civil servant press is only one indication of this tendency. Higher civil servants were (and remained) the most outspoken critics of social decline and of the consequences of 'relative deprivation' (as one would call it today). However, it appears that this line of argument was *not* the predominant one with the majority of middle-grade and lower-grade civil servants in the years between 1920 and 1922. The reason for this can be found in the movement of real wages and salaries as well.

Our data for Hamburg allows a more differentiated comparison of the tendencies in the behavior of real wages and real salaries during the inflation.[83] FIGURE 2 on page 68 shows that real wage levels of the two categories of workers selected for comparative purposes were on the whole more favorable during the period of observation than salary levels of state officials and public contractual employees. Workers' wages (Curves E and F) tended to be close or above prewar levels; the unskilled chemical worker, for instance, received a real wage which was

[83] That is to say, we can compare the *movement* of wages and salaries, but not the effective *level of earnings* for both groups, since workers were paid on a weekly, civil servants on a monthly or even quarterly basis.

FIGURE 6

Differentials in Income between Civil Servants and Blue-collar Workers, 1913—1922
Pay Group III = 100

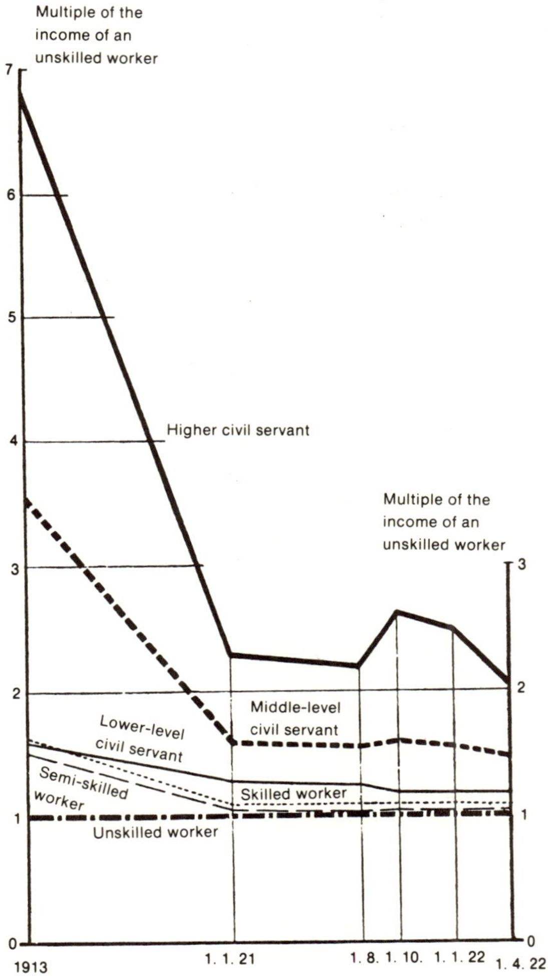

Source: Wirtschaft und Statistik, 2 (1922), p. 232.

below prewar level only eight months out of the three years observed. The real wage of the skilled furniture maker stood altogether twelve months above prewar level, for the rest of the period only slightly below the 'peace wage' at an average of 80 % to 100 %. The workers' distributional advantage increases in the hyperinflation, but declines rapidly beginning in September of 1923. With the stabilization of the currency in December 1923 it has effectively been reversed.[84]

TABLE 20, which lists the yearly averages of the indices of wages and salaries in Hamburg for 1921, 1922 and 1923, provides further clues regarding the relative movement of real wages and salaries. It is appar-

TABLE 20

Indices of Real Wages and Salaries in Hamburg, 1921—1923
Yearly Averages, 1914 = 100

	1921	1922	1923
Higher State Official	36.00	28.75	36.48
Middle State Official	53.64	42.12	53.94
Lower State Official	63.73	50.49	57.84
Contractual State Employee	78.44	62.88	73.06
Printer	81.68	65.36	84.41
Baker	78.92	68.83	83.56
Driver	87.29	73.74	85.43
Longshoreman	101.30	77.96	97.41
Mason	81.11	68.89	86.67
Locksmith	86.67	72.00	78.76
Furniture Maker	100.00	86.15	98.46
Worker in Chemical Industry	116.00	102.00	126.00
Worker in Construction	138.00	120.00	138.00

Source: Die Wirkung der Geldentwertung..., in: *Hamburger Statistische Monatsberichte*, 1 (1924), p. 97.

[84] For a more detailed discussion of workers' wages in the inflation, see W. Abelshauser, *Verelendung...*, in: H. Mommsen/W. Schulze (eds.), *Vom Elend...*, pp. 453—458, G. Bry, *Wages...*, pp. 214—233, and C. Bresciani-Turroni, *The Economics...*, pp. 300—313. On wages in the German mining industry, see Rudolf Tschirbs, *Der Ruhrbergmann zwischen Privilegierung und Statusverlust. Lohnpolitik von der Inflation bis zur Rationalisierung (1919—1927)*, in: G. D. Feldman et al. (eds.), *The German Inflation...*, pp. 308—346.

ent that the indices for state officials are below those of workers' wages in all three years. Contractual public employees, whose wage index stands at about 70 % in the three years, are closer to some of the workers' categories. Income disparities tend to decrease, therefore, the closer one gets to the lower ranks of one group and to the upper ranks of the other group.

Our data for the Reich tend to confirm this last observation (see FIGURE 1 on page 64). The *Unterbeamte*'s real income (Curve C) is closer (or even above) those of real wage levels of workers employed by the Reich government. We conclude that a numerically large group of civil servants (the *Unterbeamte*) held their own against wage levels of workers in the public and private sector (Curve F). The real wage of a skilled railway worker (Curve D), which was leading the real salary of the *Unterbeamte* between 1916 and 1919, drops below it in April 1920, indicating that the civil servants managed to improve their position vis-à-vis public workers.

Another observation can be made from our data: wages and salaries depicted here behave rather synchronous between 1920 and 1923. One reason for this phenomenon is that all wages and salaries in the public sector were based on the earning of a so-called *Stichmann,* i. e. a lower-grade civil servant in Pay Group III whose salary and salary supplements (e. g. cost-of-living increases) were fixed at a level of that of comparable public wage earner *(Betriebsarbeiter)*. The latter's wage, in turn, was determined according to comparable wages paid in private industry.[85] This was done *only* during the inflation period in a systematic and mechanical way, establishing an interdependence of wages/salaries in private industry and wages/salaries in the public sector. In the long run, therefore, civil servants were interested in higher wages for workers: a consensus of interests could (and would) be constructed around the salary issue between workers and civil servants.[86]

The synchronous movement of the curves depicted in FIGURES 1 and 2 suggests that the close link between workers' wages and civil servant salaries — and hence the consensus of interests — lasted through the longer part of the postwar inflation, i. e. from April 1920 to November

[85] For further details on the mechanics of pay determination, see H. Völter, *Beamtenbesoldung...*, p. 29.

[86] This was to become a major aspect of collective bargaining in the public sector during the postwar inflation. From the perspective of civil servants organizations, these developments will be discussed in the subsequent chapters of this study.

1922. In the last phase of the inflation, i. e. the hyperinflation of 1923, however, the synchronism seems to break down, as shown most clearly in FIGURE 1. In 1923 civil servant salaries gain vis-à-vis workers' wages, the latter dropping below the indices recorded for lower grades, and occasionally middle and higher civil servants as well. Since the pay structure within the public sector remained unchanged in this period, the pay mode might have been a decisive factor in creating the "turbulance" in our wage/salary curves, and may have changed a former "consensus" to "conflict." Most civil servants were paid quarterly and in advance. At a time of rapid and hyperinflation this created the advantage of being able to dispose of (or convert in "real assets") large sums at once. Moreover, the prepaid quarterly salary was deducted from the cost-of-living increases paid on a bi-weekly, weekly or later even daily basis in its *nominal* value only, i. e. the value it represented on the day it had originally been paid. The net result was that civil servants received a larger real income than workers or contractual employees with an identical paper mark salary. The higher the base pay, the greater was the advantage. As a consequence, higher civil servants gained also vis-à-vis lower grades during this period.[87] The terms and mechanics of the indexation agreements of June 1923 seemed to have been conducive of this development. (It may be noted that in June 1923 the index of the real wage of the skilled railroad worker falls below that of a higher civil servant!). Figures published in 1924 by the Deutscher Beamtenbund, the leading German civil servant association, confirm this impression.

TABLE 21, which compares the real income of government employees with *the same paper-mark salaries* shows that civil servants had indeed gained an advantage over workers and contractual employees as a result of the complicated mechanics of quarterly pay and continuous (but retroactive) pay adjustment. Not without irony, the Deutscher Beamtenbund called the indexation agreement negotiated between civil servant organizations and the government in June 1923 "the best and only well-functioning one of the inflation period."[88] It stands to reason that

[87] This fact was later pointed out in a government memorandum, drawn up in the Reich Finance Ministry. See *Denkschrift über die Entwicklung der Besoldung der Reichsbeamten von 1896 bis Dezember 1924* (hereafter cited as *Denkschrift Besoldung 1896 bis 1924)* in: *Reichsbesoldungsblatt* (hereafter cited as *RBBl*), 4 (1925), p. 20. Not surprisingly, civil servant associations rejected this argument, at least publicly. See *Stellungnahme DBB 1925.*

[88] *Geschäftsbericht des Deutschen Beamtenbundes für die Zeit vom April 1922 bis September 1924,* Berlin 1924, p. 58.

TABLE 21

Real Monthly Earnings of Government Employees, July to November 1923. In "Indexmarks" computed over the Cost-of-living Index on Day of Payment

1923	Civil Servant	Contractual Employee	Wage Earner
July	101	67	57
August	72	51	60
September	94	47	51
October	106	65	33
November	40	40	39

Source: Geschäftsbericht des Deutschen Beamtenbundes für die Zeit vom April 1922 bis zum September 1924, Berlin 1924, p. 59.

the civil servants' privilege of quarterly pay was a source of complaints for other employee groups, and thus a source of inter-group conflict during hyperinflation and approaching stabilization.

The discussion of inter-group relations between civil servants and blue-collar workers shows that a consensus between civil servants and other public employees emerged as a new element during the inflation period. The interdependence of civil service salaries and wages in the public and private sectors required a common strategy of all *Arbeitnehmer* groups in the increasingly frequent salary and wage negotiations in the public service, especially during the last phases of inflation period. Only with the stabilization crisis of 1923/24, when distribution became above all a question of distributing cutbacks in public expenditure, and when issues such as special salary and employment privileges of civil servants became important again, was "cooperation" and "consensus" preempted by "conflict" and insistence on special status and special interests. While the willingness to engage in interest alliances under the requirement of permanent salary and wage negotiations in an inflation economy characterized the relationship between *Arbeitnehmer* groups during the period of inflation, stabilization was to produce interest collisions that were to govern the relationship between social groups for the remaining years of the Weimar Republic. It is to these conflicts and to the full story of civil servant interest politics in its social, economic and political setting during successive periods of war and revolution (1914—1919), postwar inflation and reconstruction (1919—1923) and stabilization (1923—1924) that we shall now turn our attention to in the main portion of this study.

CHAPTER TWO

Toward Organizational Unity and Interest Representation, 1914 to 1919

Civil servants belonged to those groups in German society which in the summer of 1914 most jubilantly welcomed the outbreak of war. Wholeheartedly, moreover, they embraced the *Burgfrieden,* the "domestic truth" proclaimed by the German Emperor on August 4, 1914. In the words of the *Deutsche Beamtenrundschau,* a conservative associational gazette, the war was certain to lead to a "deliverance from the disturbances of inner strife and partisan politics." Social and political conflict, the same paper argued, would now be replaced by "work for the Fatherland as a whole," by "*vaterländische Arbeit,*" a concept which civil servant associations, too, should elevate to the "guiding principle of their future activities." In doing so, they would contribute to "a great völkisch community" and to "the wholeness of the nation's soul" as the "most solemn and exhilerating phenomena" which the war would bring.[1]

These ideals and the pathos of the first hour, from which other groups were not free either, was to disappear rather quickly under the impact of the military stalemate at the front and the increasing economic hardship and its concomitant social strife at home. Indeed, the war soon became an agent of social polarization rather than integration, and thus fundamentally and irreversibly changed the very fabric of German society. These changes wrought by the Great War amounted to nothing less than a great social upheaval which, as Jürgen Kocka has shown, propelled German society toward a "class society" in its most stringent and visible form.[2] Even if one seeks to avoid the perhaps too

[1] D. Scharringhausen, *Der Krieg und die Beamten,* in: *Deutsche Beamtenrundschau* (hereafter cited as *DBR*), November 16, 1914.

[2] Jürgen Kocka, *Klassengesellschaft im Krieg. Deutsche Sozialgeschichte 1914—1918,* Göttingen 1973. See also the still informative study by Albrecht Mendelssohn-

ideologically-laden terms of "class society" and "class conflict," it may well be argued that the war, often in very subtle ways, changed the patterns of relationships between social groups that had characterized prewar Imperial Germany. For example, the war profoundly altered the complex relationship between organized labor, industry, and the state which, as Gerald Feldman has shown, set the parameters and the limits for a modernization of labor relations in the postwar period.[3] Profound changes occurred likewise within the German middle classes, the *Mittelstand*, as, again, Jürgen Kocka, Heinrich A. Winkler, and Robert Gellately have shown.[4] In this heterogeneous and amorphous social stratum tendencies of organization, engagement in interest politics, politicalization, even radicalization took place in face of increased social and economic pressures. It compelled the various Mittelstand groups to either opt for the forces of the left or those of the political right and thus led to a polarization of the social grouping itself. Polarization tendencies developed along other lines of cleavage as well, for example, along the urban-rural divide. As has been shown by Robert G. Moeller and others, the wear and tear of four years of war greatly added to the latent hostility between the urban and rural segments of German society.[5]

The fate of German civil servants has to be placed within the scholarship on the social impact of the war. It will be argued in this chapter that

Bartholdy, *The War and German Society*, New Haven 1937, which presents the picture from the point of view of a German liberal.

[3] Gerald D. Feldman, *Army, Industry and Labor in Germany, 1914—1918*, Princeton 1966. See also the more recent study by Hans J. Bieber, *Gewerkschaften in Krieg und Revolution. Arbeiterbewegung, Industrie, Staat, Militär in Deutschland 1914—1920*, 2 vols., Hamburg 1981, and H. Potthoff, *Gewerkschaften...*, pp. 25—29.

[4] See Jürgen Kocka, *The First World War and the Mittelstand: German Artisans and White-Collar Workers*, in: *JCH*, 8 (1973), pp. 101—123. See also J. Kocka, *Klassengesellschaft...*, pp. 65—95, which includes a brief discussion of the social and economic situation of civil servants and their organizational attempts. On the so called "old Mittelstand" of shopkeepers and artisans, see Heinrich August Winkler, *Mittelstand, Demokratie und Nationalsozialismus. Die politische Entwicklung von Handwerk und Kleinhandel in der Weimarer Republik*, Cologne 1972, esp. pp. 40—64, and Robert Gellately, *The Politics of Economic Despair. Shopkeepers and German Politics, 1890—1914*, London-Beverly Hills 1974. On the new Mittelstand's propensity for right-wing politics, see Dirk Stegmann, *Zwischen Repression und Manipulation. Konservative Machteliten und Arbeiter- und Angestelltenbewegung 1910—1918*, in: *Archiv für Sozialgeschichte*, 12 (1972), pp. 351—432.

[5] See Robert G. Moeller, *Dimensions of Social Conflict in the Great War: The View from the German Countryside*, in: *CEH*, 14 (1981), pp. 142—168.

the war set in motion a process of fundamental change in the patterns of relationships between civil servants and their associations on the one side, and the government as employer and rival social groups on the other. It will be shown, moreover, that economic and social factors caused or accentuated by the war played a most crucial part in a process of change that eventually would lead to the formation and unification of the *Beamtenschaft* as an economic interest group in the November Revolution of 1918-19.

The central theme of this chapter, then, is the formation of civil servants as an economic interest group, a process which occurred in response to the economic pressures exerted by the First World War. For civil servants, as for comparable social groups like salaried employees in private industry *(Angestellte)*, wartime inflation became the catalyst for social mobilization and organizational concentration. While before 1914 the civil servant movement had been a splintered movement at best, with petty rivalries among the various civil servant classes and "categories" largely precluding organization at the national level, only four years later a powerful peak association, the Deutscher Beamtenbund (DBB), would be formed, an organization which would then represent the entire German *Beamtenschaft.* Civil servants traveled the road to organizational unity during the war years, although the final unification of the movement was achieved only during the German Revolution of 1918-19. War and Revolution form a coherent whole in this respect and will, accordingly, be treated jointly within this chapter.

The chapter itself is divided into five sections. In section one a brief survey of the prewar situation of the *Beamtenschaft* and of the state of the civil servant movement (the *Beamtenbewegung*) is given, so that changes that occurred during the war and in the immediate postwar period can be measured against the prewar situation. The war years have been divided both chronologically and thematically. Section two explores the social and economic origins of interest articulation among civil servants in the first two years of the war, leading to the founding of the Interessengemeinschaft Deutscher Beamtenverbände in early 1917. Section three then examines the relationship between the new interest group and the government as employer within the general sociopolitical system of the Empire. Section four will investigate how, if at all, civil servant organizations were able to deal with wartime inflation and its impact on salary policy, and in the last section the story of the founding of the Deutscher Beamtenbund and its position in the social and political system of the newly founded Weimar Republic will bring to a close our account of the German civil servants' road to organizational unity.

A Splintered Movement: German Civil Servants Before the First World War

Given the peculiar social and legal status of civil servants in German society, it is not surprising that in the second half of the 19th Century civil servants began to assemble in their own organizations. Most of these were fraternal associations *(Standesvereine)*, however, who did not pretend to represent the interests of their members but rather remained concerned mainly with welfare and insurance matters in addition to serving the purpose of general sociability. In the last decade before the turn of the century a gradual change set in, as new types of organizations were founded by some members of the civil service community. Civil servants employed in the large state-run enterprises, particularly those in the postal services, took the lead in founding larger, more centralized associations which then began to make claims at representing the interests of their members vis-à-vis the government in its role as public employer. In 1890 the Verband mittlerer Reichspost- und Telegraphenbeamten was founded, an organization representing middle-grade postal officials. Its statutes proclaimed that "The association has as its purpose ... the representation of the postal assistants' interests."[6] Repressive measures taken by the Reich Postal Administration against this *Verband* soon forced its leaders to preempt the interest clause from the statutes, however, and it receded into the more common role of a fraternal *Verein.*[7]

The fate of this association may be interpreted as an exemplary case of government repression of civil service unionism, but at the same time as a fanal for social and organizational developments within the *Beam-*

[6] Fritz Winters, *Geschichte des Verbandes mittlerer Reichs- Post- und Telegraphenbeamten*, Berlin 1915, p. 44. For summaries of the history of the civil servant movement before 1914, see K. R. von Scherf, *Die Entwicklung der Beamtenbewegung...*, pp. 76—125, M. Oelschig, *Die neuere Entwicklung der Beamtenschaft...*, pp. 129—138, and Ernst Krüger, *Die Gewerkschaftsbewegung der deutschen Beamten, ihr Werdegang und ihre Probleme*, Diss., Frankfurt 1924.

[7] F. Winters, *Geschichte des Verbandes...*, pp. 157—168, W. Kulemann, *Die Berufsvereine...*, vol. 2, p. 220, M. Oelschig, *Die neuere Entwicklung der Beamtenschaft...*, p. 132.

tenschaft that were yet to come. Attempts at interest articulation intensified among German civil servants, primarily as a result of their worsening economic situation in connection with renewed "waves" of price increases *(Teuerungswellen)* which beset the German economy in the last decade before the war.[8] In conjunction with parliamentary struggles over the reform of the civil service pay scale in 1909, a so-called Bund der Festbesoldeten (League of Dependent Employees — BdF) was founded by a number of persons active in the civil servant movement.[9] Viewed with suspicion by government agencies, the BdF tried to cut across occupational and hierarchical divisions within the *Beamtenschaft* by appealing to *all* civil servants rather than to a specific "category," "class," or "group," and thus may be viewed the first attempt at reaching organizational unity within the deeply divided German civil servant movement. Emil Lederer, one of the most astute observers of the social movements of Imperial Germany, even considered the BdF the nucleus of a new, modern civil servant movement, whose importance for the development of German society could, in his opinion, hardly be overestimated.[10]

If, in the long run, this organization did not live up to such high expectations — a fact which was ruefully admitted by Lederer himself in later reports on the development of the civil servant movement[11] — this was primarily due to the fact that the BdF tried to organize public officials *(Beamte)* as well as so-called "private officials" (i. e. salaried employees, or *Angestellte*) at the same time. By subsuming two different social groups, *Beamte* and *Angestellte,* under the artificial rubric of the *Festbesoldete,* the BdF lacked a clear social basis.[12] It thus

[8] This point is made by Emil Lederer, *Die Bewegung der öffentlichen Beamten,* in: *Archiv für Sozialwissenschaft und Sozialpolitik* (hereafter cited as *ASS*), 31 (1910), pp. 660—709, p. 660. Lederer wrote: „Die Bewegung der öffentlichen Beamten ... ist in ihren Wurzeln ökonomischen Ursprungs. Sie hängt zusammen mit der Revolutionierung des Weltmarktes und der Inlandspreise, der allgemeinen Teuerung, die alle überkommenen Vorstellungen von Wert und Preis über den Haufen warf ..." (p. 660). Starting in 1910, Lederer reported regularly on the development of the civil servant movement in the *Soziale Chronik* of the *ASS.* Henceforth these reports will be cited with the authors' name, the year of the journal and the page number given.

[9] There is some documentation on the politics of the BdF in ZStAP, RMdI, 2742. On the history of this organization, see E. Lederer, *ASS,* (1910—1915), as well as K. R. von Scherf, *Die Entwicklung der Beamtenbewegung ...,* pp. 99—100.

[10] E. Lederer, *ASS* (1910), p. 662.

[11] E. Lederer, *ASS* (1913), pp. 659—660.

[12] This fact is stressed in some of the official histories of the civil servant movement.

never could attract a large membership and remained at the fringes rather than moving into the center of the "new" civil servant movement. When in 1913 the BdF joined the small-business oriented Hansabund für Handel, Gewerbe und Industrie as a corporate member, the attachment to an umbrella organization of producer interests became the final act in the demise of this first, but ultimately unsuccessful civil servant peak organization.[13]

There were other organizational developments, however, which indicate that the idea of organization as such had emerged as a form of social protest within the prewar *Beamtenschaft* at this juncture, particularly among its lower ranks. It stands to reason that the slow, but steady rise in the cost of living during the last three decades before the war had an immediate impact on the lower-ranked (and lower paid!) members of the civil service, the so-called *Unterbeamte.* In terms of social mobilization, these groups became especially restive. In 1911, and again in 1913, so-called *Unterbeamtentage* were held in Germany, i. e. large gatherings of associations representing primarily minor officials. At the 1913 meeting a "Social Conference Group of the Associations of Lowergrade Civil Servants" (Soziale Arbeitsgemeinschaft der unteren Beamtenverbände) was founded, a lose federation of associations organizing the lower grades of the civil service.[14] This federation, which had a combined membership of 130,000 in 1914, was to become the organizational prototype of later civil servant peak organizations, because unlike the BdF it was based on associational rather than individual membership. Since the *Unterbeamte* had a working-class background — they usually rose from the manual labor force in the public sector to civil service posts — it is not surprising that the leaders of the Soziale Arbeitsgemeinschaft were interested in establishing a working relationship with the German trade union movement.[15]

The overall assessment of the prewar civil servant movement in Germany is a mixed one. On the one hand, organization had emerged as

See, for example, A. Falkenberg, *Die deutsche Beamtenbewegung*..., pp. 18—19 and F. Winters, *Die deutsche Beamtenfrage*..., pp. 95—96.

[13] E. Lederer, *ASS* (1913), p. 660.

[14] A report of the founding meeting is printed by *DBR*, January 1, 1914. Interestingly enough, this organization has received little attention in contemporary histories of the civil servant movement, although its influence on the movement was considerable, as the present study will show.

[15] For further details, see E. Lederer, *ASS* (1915), pp. 605—607.

a powerful idea among some grades within the civil service — a development which, incidentally, was not merely a German, but a general European phenomenon.[16] Unlike France or Great Britain, however, civil service *unionism*, i. e. the acceptance of trade-union practices by civil servant associations, had not made much progress in Imperial Germany by 1914. The repressive policies conducted by the German government at the national, state *(Länder)* and municipal level vis-à-vis the emerging associations of public employees are as important in explaining this reluctance to duplicate the union model of collective action, as was the civil servants continued reliance on government protection, their often-cited pre-modern traditions, and their inner divisiveness as a social group.

Aside of organization, other forms of social mobilization and social protest began to appear within the German *Beamtenschaft* on the eve of the Great War. While no comparison to the militancy of French *fonctionnaires* during the same period, German civil servants, too, increasingly took their grievances to the streets.[17] The holding of mass meetings may be called the German variant of civil servant protest before the war. It became the means to publicly call attention to the group's worsening economic conditions.

Two examples may suffice to give an impression of the patterns of social protest of the mass-gathering type employed by German civil servants before the war. In 1912, for example, the Bund der Festbesoldeten called a protest meeting to Berlin as a demonstration against the rising cost of food and the worsening economic situation of those groups dependent on fixed incomes. While the government made no direct attempt to prevent the meeting from taking place, the Reich

[16] On organizational tendencies among civil servants in Britain, see Bernhard Leger, *Les syndicats des fonctionnaires en Angleterre,* Paris 1929, and the excellent overview given by Leonhard D. White, *Whitley Councils in the Civil Service: A Study in Conciliation and Arbitration,* Chicago 1932, pp. 246—278. On France, see, among other things, the detailed study by Georges Cahen-Salvador, *Les fonctionnaires, leur action corporative,* Paris 1911, and the recent study by Judith Wishnia, *French Fonctionnaires: The Development of Class Consciousness and Unionization, 1884—1926,* Ph. D. Diss., State University of New York at Stony Brook 1978. Developments among Austrian civil servants are discussed in the aforementioned reports by E. Lederer in: *ASS,* (1910—1915).

[17] On civil servant protest in pre-World War I France, see G. Cahen-Salvador, *Les fonctionnaires...,* pp. 111—183, J. Wishnia, *French Fonctionnaires...,* pp. 138—181, and Michael G. Anderson, *Bureaucrats in Revolt: The Union Movement Among French Civil Servants, 1900—1945,* Ph. D. Diss., University of Chicago 1972, pp. 7—45.

Office of the Interior made certain that no representatives from any Reich or Prussian ministry would attend. At the meeting itself a resolution was adopted, in which an immediate "emergency supplement" *(Notstandszulage)* for civil servants was proposed.[18] One year later, in December 1913, a meeting organized by the Soziale Arbeitsgemeinschaft adopted a similar resolution, calling on the governments of Prussia and the Reich to take immediate steps "to improve the economic situation of the *Unterbeamte.*"[19] As both cases show, collective pressure was applied by civil servants in pursuit of material gains. This called into question the German government's virtual stranglehold over the formulation of civil service salary policy. A closer examination of the government's position toward social protest within the civil service, in both its "organized" form as the formation of civil servant interest associations, and its "spontaneous" form as public gatherings of civil servants, may underscore this last point.

Before the First World War the attitude of the German government toward civil servant associations was characterized, as one contemporary observer phrased it, by "chicanery, disregard, curtailment of activities, disciplinary measures against association leaders, and a deplorable lack of confidence."[20] Even a cursory glance toward the situation in Great Britain, where civil service associations had been recognized as representatives of civil servant interests since 1906 at the latest,[21] shows that despite genuine efforts at keeping social conflict in the civil service at bay by way of a paternalistic, if on the whole quite benevolent social policy, the authoritarian German state failed to grasp the significance of social organization among its employees.[22] A government memoran-

[18] Documentation, including the inter-ministerial correspondence cited here, in ZStAP, RMdI, 2742, Bl. 81—86, and Bl. 93—94. The letter sent by the Reich Interior Office, dated October 1, 1912, is marked „Eilt sehr, Geheim", an indication of the urgency and the importance of the matter.

[19] The resolution is reprinted in: *DBR,* January 1, 1914.

[20] Ludwig Heyde, *Die Beamten und die künftige Sozialpolitik,* in: *Beamten-Jahrbuch* (hereafter cited as *BJ*), 2 (1915), pp. 135—140.

[21] L. White, *Whitley Councils...,* pp. 246—247.

[22] On the social policy conducted by the Reich Postal Administration, see the informative, if overly applauding contemporaneous study by Kurt Kleemann, *Die Sozialpolitik der Reichspost- und Telegraphenverwaltung gegenüber ihren Beamten, Unterbeamten und Arbeitern,* Jena 1914. For a critical appraisal of social policy measures in the Prussian-Hesse Railroad Administration, see Klaus Saul, *Konstitutioneller Staat und betriebliche Herrschaft. Zur Arbeiter- und Beamtenpolitik der preußischen Staatseisenbahnverwaltung 1890—1914,* in: Dirk Stegmann et al. (eds.), *Industrielle Gesellschaft und*

dum, drawn up in 1909 in the Prussian State Ministry, indicates, moreover, that repressive measures taken against civil servant associations were not only acts of whim on the part of senior officials in the different ministries, but instead part of comprehensive government policy designed to stabilize the existing social and political system of Imperial Germany.[23]

The memorandum begins with a reiteration of the "fundamental principle" that a civil servant should submit totally to the interests and the welfare of the state. Any deviation from this iron principle would entail a violation of the Civil Service Code and, if exposed, would therefore be subject to disciplining measures on the basis of Disciplinary Law. The inner commitment to unwavering loyalty to the state, the memorandum stresses, separates civil servants from the rest of the citizenry and curtails their rights as citizens *(Staatsbürger).* These infringements of basic political rights had, above all, an impact on the relationship between civil servants and those political parties whose aims were "the destruction of the very foundation of the state," i. e. the Social Democratic Party and, of lesser importance, the Polish Nationalist Party.

With regard to freedom of speech and freedom of association similar, if more subtle, prohibitions and infringements appear. For one, the Prussian government would not tolerate any longer the practice employed recently by some civil servant associations of placing pressure on government agencies and parliamentary bodies through "agitation" in the associational press. The civil servant press, which had been subject to censorship in the past, should become so again in the future, the memorandum states. Additional pressure could be applied, if necessary, by monitoring subscriptions with the help of the Postal Administration.

politisches System. Beiträge zur politischen Sozialgeschichte. Festschrift für Fritz Fischer (= Schriftenreihe des Forschungsinstituts der Friedrich Ebert Stiftung, vol. 137), Bonn 1978, pp. 315—336.

[23] Denkschrift betreffend der Beschränkung der Beamten in der Ausübung des Rechts auf freie Meinungsäußerung, des Petitionsrechtes, sowie des Vereins- und Versammlungsrechtes, copy in GStA, Rep. 90, 2324, Bl. 71—80. For a more detailed discussion of these developments, including an appraisal of the problem of freedom of association of blue-collar workers in government service (the so-called *Staatsarbeiter*), see Andreas Kunz, *Arbeitsbeziehungen und Arbeitskonflikte im öffentlichen Sektor. Deutschland und Großbritannien im Vergleich,* in: *GG,* 12 (1986), pp. 34—62, esp. pp. 37—42.

The civil servant's right of petitioning, the memorandum states, should be strictly regulated as well. While petitions of individuals could be tolerated if filed in a proper way and through the correct channels, *collective* petitions including those sent by civil servant associations were either not permitted or, at least, "not desired." Furthermore, all petitions, including those sent to parliamentary bodies, required the approval of the civil servant's immeditiate superior. Petitions which in any way advocated changes in existing government policies or in legislative bills pending in the Prussian Diet were strictly forbidden.

With regard to the civil servants' freedom of association, the memorandum points out that a government commission, installed in 1897 at the behest of the Prussian Minister of Finance of that time, Johannes Miquel, had stopped short of recommending to prohibit civil servant associations altogether, but had warned that mass-organization for the sake of coercing government agencies into concessions regarding social demands could not be tolerated by the government. While legally civil servants enjoyed the freedom to combine, their associations were in practice strictly regulated by governmental authorities. These regulations, the memorandum stresses, should again be "sharply accentuated," even if too much open regimentation should be avoided " in order not to stir up the sensitivity of the parliament about alleged infringements on so-called [sic!] basic rights." The Prussian government's insistence on curtailing, if necessary, the organizational activities of its civil servants, and the inherent dilemma faced by it to enforce these curtailments, is captured in the closing phrase of the document. While civil servants, like other citizens, were free to join associations for the benefit of their common interests, the government had the right to prevent its civil servants from participating actively in these associations if the latters' aims were directed against the interests of the state.

The content of this memorandum shows that even before 1914 governmental policies designed to *totally* repress the emergence and activities of civil servant associations had become partially eroded. The renewed "sharp accentuation" of repressive policies advocated in 1909 may also be taken as an admission that previous policies had failed to stem the tide completely. However, this should not becloud the fact that in some administrative branches, especially within the Prussian Railroad Administration, for example, a policy of repression remained the rule right up to the war and indeed beyond.[24] To give yet another

[24] On this, see K. Saul, *Konstitutioneller Staat...*, pp. 326ff.

example. Internal government correspondence indicates that the Reich government's main reason for *not* harassing the Bund der Festbesoldeten, whose activities it was watching with great misgivings, was the fact that the publisher of the BdF's organ *Deutsche Nachrichten* had connections to the former Chancellor von Bülow.[25] On the whole, therefore, the position of civil servant associations remained precarious in prewar Imperial Germany, and it is not surprising that calls for better legal protection and a more explicit guarantee of the civil servant's right to associate freely surfaced with increased urgency in this period.[26] But it would be the war itself, its economic deprivations and concomitant waves of social unrest which would give the strong impulse for organizational concentration within the *Beamtenschaft* and for the government's grudging toleration of civil servant interest politics.

The Impact of War: From Burgfrieden to Social Unrest and Interest Articulation, 1914—1916

The Causes of Social Unrest

The social consequences of the wartime economy and of wartime inflation soon left their marks on the economic situation of the *Beamtenschaft,* as in fact it did for other middle-class groups as well. By 1916 the income of civil servants had lost about forty percent of its prewar value, and little or no government action had been taken to remedy this situation.[27] The economic plight and hardships caused by this tremendous decline in real income prompted a growing feeling of helplessness among civil servants in face of what they subjectively viewed as leading to absolute social decline, even if, in reality, it was only a decline *relative* to other social groups. Increasingly, the government itself was being blamed for betraying the legitimate interests of its "servants," and calls for self-help picked up in the civil servants' organizational press. Already in the spring of 1915 one paper reported that the price of food had reached a level which made it all but impossible for lower-paid

[25] This fact is mentioned in a government memorandum, sent by the State Secretary of the Interior to the Reich Chancellery on July 7, 1917. Copy of this document in ZStAP, RMdI, 2742, Bl. 97.

[26] Understandably, this is stressed in most official histories of the civil servant movement. See, e. g., A. Falkenberg, *Die deutsche Beamtenbewegung...*, pp. 50—53.

[27] See TABLE 22 below and the discussion in CHAPTER ONE of this study.

civil servants to budget their income adequately. Inflation (the *Teuerung*) had a greater impact on lower-paid groups, the same paper argued, because the portion of their salaries spent on foodstuffs was much higher and more inelastic than of those in the higher ranks. Moreover, the paper deplored the fact that increasingly civil servants were being forced to act like wage-earners in private industry, because they were compelled to bargain for higher pay. The writer suggested that only by pegging civil servant pay and cost-of-living increases directly to the cost-of-living index could the latter development be prevented, which he viewed as detrimental to the civil service as an institution of the state.[28]

TABLE 22

Nominal and Real Monthly Earnings of Civil Servants, 1913—1918 (In Marks)

		1913	1914	1915	1916	1917	1918
Higher civil	a	608	608	608	608	660	891
servant	b	608	591	470	358	261	284
Middle-level	a	342	342	342	342	420	598
civil servant	b	342	332	246	202	166	188
Lower-level	a	157	157	157	157	213	342
civil servant	b	157	153	121	93	84	109

a: nominal earnings.
b: real earnings.
Source: Distilled from: *Zahlen zur Geldentwertung,* in: *WSt.,* Sonderh. 1 (1925), p. 43.

Even in the more conservative-oriented civil servant press, attacks were ridden against the excessive price-profiteering *(Preiswucher)* allegedly conducted by industrial and agricultural producers, although price regulation rather than pay increases was still being advocated as the most promising counter-measure against the declining purchasing power of civil servant pay.[29] Price regulation made indeed a lot of sense

[28] D. Scharringhausen, *Teuerungszulagen,* in: *BJ,* 2 (1915), pp. 166—171. It may be noted that this is the same author who wrote the article quoted from at the beginning of this chapter (see note 1 above).

[29] *DBR,* October 16, 1915.

at a time when pay raises granted by the government were clearly inadequate to cover the loss of real income suffered by public employees.[30] Increasingly, the stability of civil service pay rates, a social privilege in normal times if compared to fluctuating wage levels in the private sector, became a millstone around the civil servant's neck at a time of prolonged and intensified inflationary conditions.[31] In view of the steadily worsening economic conditions produced by the war within the *Beamtenschaft*, Emil Lederer remarked in 1915, the German civil servant's almost proverbial virtues of "willingness to sacrifice" and "doing without" was being put to a hard test. Lederer predicted that in the long run the civil servants' patience would wear thin, and their wishes and demands for an improvement of their situation in relative proportion to other social groups would not be able to be set aside much longer by public employers.[32]

Not only would Lederer's prediction turn out to be correct, similar observations were being made at the same time by perhaps less partial observers, i. e. by military agencies in charge with surveillance of the general mood of the German population.[33] In the course of 1916 these highly secret reports began sounding warnings that the economic situation of civil servants and other dependent employees had deteriorated to a degree as to cause deep dissatisfaction and embitterment within these Mittelstand groups, whose continued support was essential to the smooth running of the state apparatus and thus to the war effort as well. A report filed in mid-July 1916 noted that the situation of lower-grade civil servants was particularly pressing. They were unable to make ends meet with the pay they were receiving and had resorted to applying for extra financial support in increasing numbers.[34]

[30] As of October 15, 1916 the supplements to the children's bonus had been increased somewhat for the lower pay groups. For further details, see *Denkschrift Besoldung 1924*, in: *RBBl.*, 4 (1925), pp. 13—15.

[31] H. J. Bieber, *Gewerkschaften . . .*, p. 436 makes this comparison. — The *intensity* of the wartime inflation is the main difference to the *Teuerung* of the decade before the war. While many of the developments discussed here had already begun before the war, the war itself greatly intensified and accelerated them. For a similar interpretation, see E. Lederer, *ASS*, (1915), p. 912.

[32] E. Lederer, *ASS*, (1915), p. 914.

[33] These reports were collected by the Deputy Commanding Generals of the twenty army corps districts in Germany. A compilation, covering the years 1916 and 1917 can be found in GLAK, Abt. 456, E. V. 8, Bd. 70. They will henceforth be cited as *Monthly Reports* with date and page numbers added.

[34] *Monthly Reports*, June 14, 1916, pp. 9—10, 58.

In the fall of the same year, the Deputy Commanding General of the army corps district of the Mark reported that the mood among Mittelstand groups living on fixed incomes had greatly deteriorated. This was the case especially for state and municipal civil servants, the report noted. While wage earners and salaried employees had seen their income doubled and tripled, civil servant pay had essentially remained at the same level since the outbreak of the war. The report claimed that in some cases skilled workers in key war-related industries were making more money than a higher civil servant, if the latters' weekly take-home pay was compounded to an annual salary. Social frictions and bitterness had been the result of this wage policy, whose overall impact the report viewed as potentially dangerous to the war effort. "The cheerful support of the *Beamtenschaft* at a time when fewer officials had to solve greater tasks," the report concluded, "is essential to the survival of the state and the Empire."[35] In a follow-up report the same army corps district warned two months later that the difficulties encountered by many civil servants to adequately feed and clothe themselves and their families had pushed dissatisfaction to a level high enough as to lead to "grave political consequences." The military agency urged the civilian authorities to enact immediate measures in an effort to counteract these tendencies and suggested to award long-overdue cost-of-living increases to civil servants.[36]

It comes as no surprise that similar views were held by civil servants themselves. Throughout 1916 the number of petitions sent to government agencies increased rapidly, and the economic distress of the civil servants was painted in the darkest colors. Even the otherwise staunchly patriotic and conservative Verband Deutscher Beamtenvereine (VDB), which in prewar times had viewed itself as an organic connection *(Bindeglied)* between civil servants and the government rather than as a representative of civil servant interests,[37] now felt compelled by the prevailing circumstances to act more like an interest-group organization and began to petition the government in the economic interests of its members. Still, the VDB, with some 500,000 members the largest civil servant association of Imperial Germany, clearly felt uncomfortable in its new role, never failing to excuse its

[35] *Ibid.*, September 8, 1916, p. 3.

[36] *Ibid.*, November 3, 1916.

[37] This role had been stressed at the VDB's last prewar meeting. See the report in *DBR*, June 16, 1914.

"suggestions" for higher pay with the economic plight of its members, the alleviation of which should not be regarded as an act of interest politics but rather as one of "social justice."[38] The exact impact of these and similar petitions is difficult to ascertain. By and large, it seems, government authorities had retained their prerogative of handling civil service matters on their own terms, although toward the end of 1916 the Reichstag did take some initiative, which might be an indication of increased organizational as well as public pressures.[39]

In spite of economic hardships that were much more severe compared to the prewar situation, protest meetings, for example, had virtually disappeared from the scene in 1914 and 1915. The *Burgfrieden* mentality and preventive government measures undoubtedly played some part in this temporary disruption of the prewar trend. In 1916, however, this situation began to change as the economic and social pressures induced by the war revitalized expressions of social protest. In October of 1916 several civil servant associations organized the first major wartime *Teuerungsversammlung* in Berlin.[40]

Still, this was muted protest at best. The immediate strategy of defense employed by civil servants to counteract the economic vicissitudes of the war remained, above all, organization and interest politics.[41] While social unrest and direct forms of social protest were a doubtful enterprise for most civil servants in times of national crisis, interest-group politics seemed a more legitimate and promising road to travel. Organization thus became the most striking result of wartime inflation and its economic and social consequences within the *Beamten-*

[38] See the petition of the VDB, in: *DBR*, May 16, 1916.

[39] *DBR*, November 16, 1916. In a formal parliamentary motion the National Liberal Reichstag delegate Riesser had requested information on what the government was doing about the „schwere Bedrängnis der Beamten." The government spokesman announced that 1.5 million marks had been earmarked for cost-of-living supplements in the new budget (a trifling sum!). The Reichstag had then voted additional monies for that purpose.

[40] Reported by Albert Falkenberg, *Deutsches Wirtschaftsleben und Beamtenschaft,* in: *BJ*, 3 (1916), pp. 53—61.

[41] This is pointed out by Falkenberg in the article just cited. He suggested the creation of a central organization of consumer interests, in which civil servant organizations were to play a major role, to counterbalance similar concentration tendencies on the producer side. The Interessengemeinschaft participated in the Kriegsausschuss für Konsumenteninteressen, in fact IG Chairman Remmers held a seat in the board of directors *(Vorstand)* of this umbrella organization. For further details see E. Remmers, *Die organisatorische Einheit...*, pp. 32—34.

schaft. It is not surprising, therefore, that the year 1916 saw the birth of the modern German civil servant movement.

Toward Organizational Concentration: The Interessengemeinschaft Deutscher Beamtenverbände

While the euphoric approval of the war and the unconditional support of the war effort did not diminish within the *Beamtenschaft* until at a later stage of the war, in mid-1917 at the earliest, the renunciation of interest representation and interest politics advocated in 1914 as part of the *Burgfrieden* syndrome soon gave way to increased activity in the organizational realm and in the area of interest politics. The main targets in these efforts, which commenced in late 1915, were first, the organizational concentration of the existing civil servant associations at the national level, i. e. the construction of a civil servant peak organization *(Spitzenverband),* and second, a more assertive and effective representation of civil servant interests vis-à-vis public employers and vis-à-vis rival, usually better organized social groups as, for example, the working class.

Organizational *Sammlung* had been, as has been shown above, a long-range goal within the German civil servant movement even before 1914. In spite of prewar failures, the idea of establishing a peak association as the all-important prerequisite for a more effective form of interest representation had been kept alive in the civil servant movement. One forum for *Sammlung* ideology became the *Beamten-Jahrbuch,* the "theoretical journal for the entire civil servant movement" (so its sub-title), which had been founded in early 1914 and was edited jointly by the left-liberal Reichstag Deputy Heinrich Potthoff and by Albert Falkenberg, a leading figure in the civil servant movement.[42] In his contributions to this journal, Falkenberg relentlessly propounded the idea that only organizational concentration could turn the splintered civil servant movement into a powerful social force in its own right. This in turn, he regarded a necessary precondition for a

[42] Albert Falkenberg (1871—1945) had originally been a middle-level postal official in Hamburg, but soon embarked on an organizational career. From 1908 to 1910 he served as an editor to the *Deutsche Postzeitung,* the mouthpiece of the Verband der mittleren Post- und Telegraphenbeamten. In 1910 he became the editor-in-chief of the *Deutsche Nachrichten,* the official gazette of the Bund der Festbesoldeten, and, starting in 1914, the co-publisher of the *Beamten-Jahrbuch.* His subsequent career will emerge from this study.

more direct participation of civil servants in the conduct of civil service policy, as well as a prerequisite for improving their material conditions. If civil servants wanted to have an impact on their own destiny, Falkenberg argued, they had to organize and conduct interest politics at the national level rather than weaken their strength by internal divisions.[43]

Yet a social movement cannot be created by the force of the pen alone. It was the war and its economic and social pressures which turned civil servants into a pressure group: The war became the catalyst for an organizational *Sammlung*. Initiatives toward such a goal were taken up in 1915 by Ernst Remmers, often regarded the *spiritus rector* of the modern German civil servant movement. Remmers was a former middle-grade postal official, who later rose to become chairman of the large association of lower-grade postal civil servants, the Verband der unteren Post- und Telegraphen-Beamten, co-founded by him in 1908. In 1913, he also became the first general secretary of the Soziale Arbeitsgemeinschaft.[44] Remmers was thus a man of practical organization work rather than theoretical discourse like Falkenberg. As a leading member of the left-liberal Fortschrittliche Volkspartei, Remmers was also politically well connected. He was a shrewd tactician who possessed the organizational and political skills necessary to overcome the almost insurmountable task of unifying the more than seven-hundred different civil servant associations which then existed in Imperial Germany. His experience with the Soziale Arbeitsgemeinschaft — an umbrella organization for several already-existing associations — became the basis, or the model, for a new civil servant peak association to be founded during the war: the Interessengemeinschaft Deutscher Beamtenverbände (IG).

Throughout 1915 and 1916 Remmers used his influence and connections to bring together a number of civil servant associations into a

[43] See the following articles contributed by Falkenberg to the *Beamten-Jahrbuch: Die Aufgaben der Beamtenbewegung im modernen Rechtsstaat*, in: *BJ*, 1 (1914), pp. 23—31; *Die Zukunftsarbeit der deutschen Beamtenverbände*, in: *BJ*, 1 (1914), pp. 65—75; *Zur Vereinheitlichung der deutschen Beamtenbewegung*, in: *BJ*, 2 (1915), pp. 107—111.

[44] Remmers had also been a co-founder of the ill-fated Bund der Festbesoldeten in 1909. Like Falkenberg, Remmers had originally been a middle-level postal official, but left the Postal Service in 1894 to devote himself entirely to organizational efforts. In 1908 Remmers founded the first general association of lower-grade postal officials, the Verband der unteren Post- und Telegraphenbeamten. His subsequent career will emerge from this study. There is a brief biographical sketch of Remmers in: *Internationales Handwörterbuch des Gewerkschaftswesens* (hereafter cited as *IHG*), ed. Ludwig Heyde et al., 2 vols., Berlin 1931—1932, vol. 2, p. 1313.

single umbrella organization. His efforts were crowned with success, when in late 1916 some twenty-five organizations, with a combined membership of some 300,000, agreed to form an *Interessengemeinschaft,* i. e., a loose federation of associations held together by a "community of common interests." After a series of preliminary negotiations within a specially appointed committee, the Interessengemeinschaft Deutscher Reichs- und Staatsbeamtenverbände (at its first general meeting in October 1917 the name was shortened to Interessengemeinschaft Deutscher Beamtenverbände — IG) was formally established in February 1917.[45] Remmers became its first chairman (or: general secretary), while Falkenberg became the editior of the new peak association's mouthpiece, poignantly called *Die Gemeinschaft* (The Community).

In one of the first proclamations issued by the IG, Falkenberg attempted to put together an associational credo for the new organization. He emphasized the need for organization as a general precondition for a group's acceptance as a factor in a nation's economic and cultural life. Accordingly, the Interessengemeinschaft's purpose could not be "minor politics" *(Kleinpolitik)*, but rather was called upon to find the "general line" *(große Linie)* in the major issues concerning the civil service. While the independence of the IG's affiliates should and would not be infringed upon by the peak association, the "great tasks" of the future could only be accomplished if "thinking in small categories," the "*Kleinstaaterei*" still prevailing in the civil servant movement, was abandoned once and for all. The political analogy used by Falkenberg here was not an accident. He compared the unification of the civil servant movement with the alleged political unification of the German nation in times of war. "The German nation's will to unify, which has been awakened by the war, must find expression in the German *Beamtenschaft's* willingness to unify *(Einheitswille),*" Falkenberg wrote.[46]

The rapid organizational growth of the Interessengemeinschaft seemed to indicate that a great proportion of the German *Beamten-*

[45] Cf. A. Falkenberg, *Einigungsbestrebungen,* in: *BJ*, 3 (1916), pp. 195—196, and idem, *Die Interessengemeinschaft Deutscher Reichs- und Staatsbeamtenverbände,* in: *BJ*, 4 (1917), pp. 93—96. There is a discrepancy in the literature concerning the founding-year of the IG. Falkenberg later cited February 1916 (*Beamtenbewegung*..., p. 19), while Remmers refers to February 1917 (*Die organisatorische Einheit*..., p. 20). In view of contemporaneous press reports (e. g. *Der Tag,* June 12, 1917) 1917 seems to be the correct year.

[46] Quoted in A. Falkenberg, *Die deutsche Beamtenbewegung*..., pp. 21—22.

schaft was prepared indeed to support integration under the general guidelines of social unity *and* interest representation. In October 1917, only six months after its official founding, the IG's membership figures had nearly doubled with some forty affiliates and 400,000 members; by January 1918 some 500,000 civil servants were affiliated with the IG through some fifty member-associations, and in mid-1918 nearly 600,000 civil servants, or roughly one half of the entire German *Beamtenschaft,* belonged to associations affiliated with the Interessengemeinschaft.[47]

The relative ease with which the IG accomplished what had failed several times before 1914 can be explained by a number of factors. The war itself was certainly the most important variable, because it had demonstrated the economic vulnerability of civil servants much more clearly than the prewar *Teuerung,* which had moved at a much slower pace. The organizational structure adopted by the IG was a second factor. While all prewar attempts had been based on the founding of a completely new organization — the BdF was but one attempt in this direction — the IG guaranteed the independence of its affiliated organizations in exchange for the latters' willingness to delegate certain powers to the new peak association and its leadership. Under this scheme, the IG would become responsible for all matters relating to *general* civil service policy, as, for example, civil service law *(Beamtenrecht),* civil service pay *(Beamtenbesoldung),* and economic self-help organizations *(Beamtengenossenschaften).* Finally, the IG made no attempts at organizing salaried employees and chose instead to establish itself as a third social movement alongside (and not in competition with) the white-collar movement (the *Angestelltenbewegung*), where similar tendencies of concentration had been sparked by the war,[48] and the blue-collar labor movement (the *Arbeiterbewegung*).

There were limits to the IG's appeal, though, both regional and social. It had almost no following in southern Germany, where separate, regionally-based concentration movements were underway.[49] The failure to integrate the south German associations would remain one of

[47] *Die Gemeinschaft* (hereafter cited as *DG*), July 16, 1918 (Bericht der Hauptversammlung der Interessengemeinschaft).

[48] On the white-collar movement during the war, see Siegfried Aufhäuser, *Weltkrieg und Angestelltenbewegung,* Berlin 1919, and the relevant literature cited in note 4 above.

[49] On the opposition of the South German associations, see E. Remmers, *Die organisatorische Einheit...,* pp. 25—32.

the most difficult problems and strongest liabilities that the IG passed on to its successor, the Deutscher Beamtenbund (DDB) in the postwar period. Moreover, the IG had a limited social basis. It appealed primarily to lower-grade civil servants and middle-grade *Betriebsbeamte* in the postal and railway administrations. Middle-grade administrative officials *(Hoheitsbeamte)* remained allied with their traditional *Vereine* and its loosely-structured umbrella organization, the conservative Verband Deutscher Beamtenvereine (VDB). Several attempts were made to merge the Interessengemeinschaft and the VDB, and in the fall of 1917 a joint "National Steering Committee" *(Reichsarbeitsausschuss)* was finally established to prepare and co-ordinate a possible merger. As a result of these preliminary measures, the final merger between the two umbrella organizations would rather quickly be achieved once the political situation had dictated such a move during the days of the November Revolution of 1918/19. Finally, higher (i. e. academically trained) civil servants remained outside the new peak organization. Toward the end of the war, higher civil servants made efforts to put together a *Spitzenverband* of their own by founding a Federation of Higher Civil Servants (Bund höherer Beamter or BhB).[50]

In summarizing these organizational developments one can say that the war provided the catalyst for concentration efforts among civil servant associations. Even if total integration was not achieved and some organizational rivalries persisted, a more modern type of interest representation had found an expression within the Interessengemeinschaft Deutscher Beamtenverbände. In this respect the war had indeed given a clearer profile to the civil servant movement if compared to prewar situations.[51] It remains to be shown whether organization and interest articulation could be followed up by interest politics, i. e. whether the war could also provide an entry point for civil servant organizations to participate in the formulation and execution of civil service policy.

[50] For further information on the founding of the BhB in the early spring of 1918, see *Zwei Jahre Bund höherer Beamter,* in: *Zeitschrift des Bundes höherer Beamter,* January 15, 1921.

[51] I would therefore disagree with J. Kocka, *Klassengesellschaft...,* p. 84, who suggests that the German civil servant movement did not acquire a clearer profile during the war.

Toward Interest Representation: The Struggle for Recognition, 1916—1918

For many social groups in Germany, most notably for organized labor, the war and the mechanisms of the war economy with its emphasis on the complete mobilization of human resources became a catalyst for the breakthrough into full fledged interest-group politics. Gaining recognition as a negotiating partner of both government and employer organizations was, in the case of organized labor, the fundamental precondition for setting in motion a process of integration into decision-making at the highest levels in the areas of social and economic policy, as well as for opening up the entire area of collective bargaining at regional, branch, and factory levels. Participation became the key to labor's successes, and the passage of the Auxiliary Service Bill in late 1916, the "triumph of labor," as Gerald Feldman has called it, was the first major step in a process of realignment and reorientation between capital and labor that would lead to acceptance of fundamental trade-union demands like the eight-hour day and the abolition of company unions in the so-called Stinnes-Legien Agreement concluded between industrialist and labor leaders in late 1918.[52] By that time corporatist relationships had developed, and were given an institutional framework in the so-called *Zentralarbeitsgemeinschaft* (ZAG) of employers and blue-collar trade unions, under participation of some white-collar unions as well. The ZAG was to have a lasting impact on social policy legislation in the early Weimar Republic.[53]

Civil servant associations, it may be noted, did not participate in these corporatist arrangements. Indeed, they did not fully participate in the entire process of recognition and social realignment unleashed by the war. As a latecomer to the social arena, civil servant organizations were prevented from pressing for concessions that had been made to

[52] G. Feldman, *Army...*, Chapter 4. See also J. Kocka, *Klassengesellschaft...*, Chapter 2, who takes a somewhat more critical view of these developments than the one presented here. On the Stinnes-Legien Agreement, see Gerald D. Feldman, *German Business between War and Revolution: The Origins of the Stinnes-Legien Agreement*, in: Gerhard A. Ritter (ed.), *Entstehung und Wandel der modernen Gesellschaft. Festschrift für Hans Rosenberg*, Berlin 1970, pp. 312—340.

[53] For an excellent overview of these developments, see Gerald D. Feldman, *German Interest Alliances in War and Inflation*, in: Suzanne Berger (ed.), *Organizing Interests in Western Europe*, Cambridge 1981, pp. 159—184. Cf. also the contributions by Charles Maier and Jürgen Kocka to the same volume.

other employee groups by their inexperience in trade union matters, their inner divisiveness, and, perhaps most importantly, by a still unclear attitude about their own position within a broadly conceived *Arbeitnehmer* movement. This was true for the two most basic demands to be made by an interest-group organization: (1) recognition as the legitimate representative of the interests of its members, and (2) recognition as a partner in negotiations. Both matters involved government policy as well, since the government also functioned as the employer of civil servants and other public employees. The issue at stake was, therefore, whether public employers, especially the governments of the Reich and in Prussia, would formally recognize the civil servants' right to associate and, in a second step, recognize civil servant associations as a bargaining agent for civil servant interests.

Civil Servants and the Reform of the Associations Law in 1916

The outbreak of the war and the *Burgfrieden* produced an impact on the two principle rights withheld from civil servants, i. e. the full right of association and the right to engage actively in partisan politics.[54] While these two issues are certainly intertwinded, we shall concentrate in the subsequent analysis on the problem of association as the more pertinent (and less studied) issue. It will be placed into the context of organizational behavior and the emergence of civil servant interest politics during the First World War.

Just as the Prussian government was forced to make concessions with regard to the appointment of SPD members to elected civil service positions at the municipal level,[55] it felt obliged rather early in the war to suspend the practice of enforcing a declaration of non-membership in the SPD or SPD-oriented trade unions from prospective employees, civil service and non-civil service.[56] By the same token, membership in civil servant associations ceased being a major source of conflict between civil servant associations and the governments in Prussia and in

[54] On German civil servants' political rights, see Hermannjosef Schmahl, *Disziplinarrecht und politische Betätigung der Beamten in der Weimarer Republik*, Berlin 1977.

[55] Despite serious objections raised by some district governors in Prussia, the practice of not recognizing these elections was discontinued by the state authorities during the war. There is some documentation on this matter in ZStAP, RMdI, 2172.

[56] Meeting of the Prussian cabinet, December 31, 1914, Geheimes Staatsarchiv Preußischer Kulturbesitz, Berlin-Dahlem (hereafter cited as GStA), Rep. 90, 2324, Bl. 132—141.

the other German states. In the fall of 1914 the Bavarian minister of finance, for example, grudgingly accepted the activities of civil servant interest organizations as a "phenomenon of modern life," even if not a very pleasant one, during a speech in the Bavarian Diet. He expected, however, that in return the organizations would use their influence to insure the continued discipline within the civil service.[57] Widely reported in the civil servant press, the incident was interpreted there as a first step toward a less repressive attitude not only of the Bavarian state government, but of "government" as such. Membership in "striking unions" continued being illegal for Bavarian civil servants, however, as well as for blue-collar workers in government service, which prompted one observer to comment that in reality the position of the Bavarian state government had not changed at all.[58]

Indeed, if one probes into the internal operations of the government bureaucracy on this issue, it appears that senior officials in the relevant ministries remained sceptical, if not hostile, toward the emerging associations of public employees. This hostility increased even further, once the associations began putting pressures on parliamentary bodies to obtain material support in face of mounting *Teuerung*. These procedures high-ranking government officials still found "highly objectionable."[59] Their worries increased even more, when in mid-1916 civil servant associations began pressing for *formal* recognition as bargaining agents for civil servant interests. The reform of the Associations Law, undertaken by the Imperial government in 1916 as one of the concessions made to the Social Democrats and to the Socialist Trade Unions whose stigmatization as "political associations" was to be changed by the reform,[60] was seized upon by civil servant organizations to enhance their standing vis-à-vis the government. Although ultimately unsuccessful, the struggle for inclusion in the reform of the Associations Law must be regarded as the first major offensive conducted jointly by those

[57] *DBR*, October 1, 1914, reports on the speech.

[58] E. Lederer, *ASS* (1915), p. 915. In early 1916 the Prussian minister of public works still insisted on a clause in the personnel regulations newly adopted for the railroads in 1915, in which membership in "striking unions" was explicitly prohibited. See *Soziale Praxis* (hereafter cited as *SP*), March 9, 1916, col. 534. For a more detailed discussion, see A. Kunz, *Arbeitsbeziehungen...*, in: *GG*, 12 (1986), pp. 42—51.

[59] Reich Office of the Interior to Reich Chancellery, January 10, 1916, ZStAP, RMdI, 2738, Bl. 53.

[60] Cf. G. D. Feldman, *Army...*, pp. 121—123.

civil servant associations that had just assembled in the Interessengemeinschaft.

In April 1916 the leaders of fifteen civil servant associations met to devise a strategy to insure that civil servants, too, would benefit from the proposed revision of the Associations Law then pending in the Reichstag.[61] There had been rumors that civil servants and their associations would, in fact, be specifically *excluded* from the improvements in the legal position of associations entailed in the reform bill. The assembled civil servant leaders decided to send a joint petition to the Reichstag and to the Bundesrat, in which the civil servants' demands concerning the new law would be formulated. Obviously, this was a clear departure from the prewar practice of not interfering with governmental legislative bills, and as such a clear sign of a new sense of power. As Anton Hoefle, the director of the Technikerverband and a leading member of the Center Party, who was also the driving force behind the organizations' initiative, told his colleagues, "The opportunity for such a move is splendid, because the war has demonstrated that organizations are indispensable to our modern national economy."[62]

Whether or not the petition created an impact during the parliamentary deliberations of the bill is difficult to ascertain. Several left-wing parties did, however, introduce a resolution calling for the recognition of civil servant associations in such a way that provisions of disciplinary law could not be used any longer by the government to overrule the stipulations of the new Association Law. Government representatives refused to make any concessions, though, and argued that civil servants and contractual employees in the public service could not be regarded as

[61] Reports of this meeting in *DBR*, May 16, 1916.

[62] *DBR*, May 16, 1916. — Anton Hoefle was one of the most interesting personalities to emerge from the civil servant movement, and he was to play a leading, albeit controversial, role during the Weimar years. In 1918 Hoefle became one of the directors of the newly founded Deutscher Beamtenbund. Only one year later, however, he led the secession of the DBB's Catholic (Center Party) wing and subsequently became chairman of the Gesamtverband Deutscher Beamtengewerkschaften, the civil servant section of the Catholic Trade Unions. Hoefle was the only civil servant leader to made a political career as well, although it ended abruptly and tragically. After his election to the Reichstag in 1920, Hoefle, a personal friend and confidant of Wilhelm Marx, in 1923 rose to become minister of posts, a position he held in both cabinets formed by Marx between 1923 and 1925. In 1925 Hoefle, by then minister of reconstruction as well, was implicated in a corruption scandal and was forced to resign. He committed suicide that same year while in police custody. There is short biographical sketch of Hoefle in *IHG*, vol. 1, p. 777.

regular employees *(Arbeitnehmer)* and that therefore the anticipated legal changes in the status of employee organizations could not be applied to civil servant associations. While in the case of public wage earners *(Staatsarbeiter)* the government was forced to make concessions as a result of trade-union and SPD pressures,[63] it won out in the civil service question. Despite the fact that during the plenary debate in the Reichstag the civil servants' cause was taken up forcefully by the Progressive Party — and here a connection between parliamentary strategy and interest-group politics, transmitted primarily through Remmers in his dual position as IG-chairman and member of the Progressive Party, may be assumed — no amendment regulating the legal status of civil servant associations was written into the new law.[64] In a way, therefore, the initiative of the organizations had failed, and there was some resignation in the words of Remmers, spoken at the first congress of the IG in October 1917, when he demanded that the government should place more confidence into the political and organizational skills of civil servants by recognizing their organizations and by cooperating with them in all questions relating to civil service policy.[65]

The offensive undertaken by the associations regarding the reform of the Associations Law may be interpreted as the first example of a modern-type interest politics conducted by civil servant organizations in Germany. Characteristically, the very position of the civil servant organizations within society and vis-à-vis the government in its role as employer was at stake. Civil servants tried, if unsuccessfully as of yet, to benefit from changes in the relationship between state authorities and interest organizations that had appeared in the first two years of the war. In doing so they increasingly ran into the difficulty of having to explain why, as a socially privileged group long protected by the state they served, civil servants were actually in need of measures which the less privileged groups like blue-collar workers had wrested from their employers, often with the help of the state, to achieve an amount of social protection equal to those of civil servants. It is the partial erosion of the state's protection — best revealed in the governments unwillingness and financial incapacity of living up to its duty of protecting the

[63] G. D. Feldman, *Army...*, p. 122.

[64] *Stenographische Berichte der Verhandlungen des Deutschen Reichstags* (hereafter cited as *Stenographische Berichte*), vol. 307, pp. 1011—1021.

[65] IG meeting 1917, reported in *DG*, July 1, 1917.

material needs of the *Beamtenschaft,* thereby creating social-status anxieties within the group — which explains the civil servants' turn toward the seeking of additional, outside mechanisms of protection like interest associations and social policy legislation. The relative success of the labor movement in protecting workers' interests became a reference point for the activities of civil servants, as the struggle for inclusion within the reform of the Associations Law has demonstrated. This acceptance of labor and the labor movement as a kind of "model social movement" and "model interest group" was a decisive switch from prewar conditions, when civil servants and the majority of their associations had emphasized their *distance* from the blue-collar trade unions.[66]

These tendencies toward social reorientation on the part of the organized civil servants in the course of the first two years of the war were not, as of yet, paralled by government (i. e. employer) recognition, even if in the struggle for the reform of the Associations Law parliamentary support had been mobilized for the first time in connection with a civil service issue promoted, if not created, by civil servants' interest organizations. The parliamentary struggles revealed for the first time, moreover, a close alliance between civil servant interests and the bourgeois parties of the center, an alliance that was to continue even under changed political conditions in the Weimar Republic. It is to the relationship between civil servant organizations and the political sphere as it developed during the war years that we shall now turn.

Government, Parliament and Civil Servant Interests (I): The Struggle for Recognition

Political parties were among the first to recognize the potential importance of the "new civil servant movement" as a social movement, a movement which, moreover, could be harnessed for political goals. As has been mentioned above, the leaders of the Interessengemeinschaft

[66] What I am arguing here is a change in reference groups on the part of the *Beamtenschaft.* While prior to 1914 the (even then only relative) secure position of the civil servant, especially his greater job security, provided a point of reference for the working class and for trade-union policy, the deterioration of their economic position after 1914 propelled civil servants to regard the power of the organized working class (i. e. the value of organization and of collective action) as a model. This leaves the question open whether or not a socially privileged group should be allowed to use (or: misuse) the weapon forged by a socially less privileged group. The behavior of salaried employees *(Angestellte)* is a similar case in point, as Jürgen Kocka has shown in his work.

were closely connected with the forces of German political liberalism. Indeed, conservatives charged that the new peak association was nothing but a creature of the left-liberal Progressive Party.[67] Initially, this allegation was not totally unfounded. At the IG's first general meeting in October 1917, the only two parliamentary delegates who attended were both members of the Progressive Party: the Reichstag deputy Hubrich, who was also a high-ranking official in a civil servant association,[68] and Carl Delius, a delegate to the Prussian Diet and one of the most outspoken supporters of the "new orientation within the *Beamtenschaft.*"[69] To Delius and other liberals, the organizational developments within the *Beamtenschaft* sparked by the war were not only to lead to a social reorientation of civil servants, but to their *political* reorientation as well. This political reorientation was to imply, above all, the civil servants' full acceptance of their role as *Staatsbürger* (citizens) instead of the submissive and politically docile *Staatsdiener* (state's servant) attitude, which had made them all too willful an instrument in support of conservative political forces during the prewar days. Consequently, civil servants were viewed by liberal leaders as a new target group for the liberal cause, and as supporters of the political and constitutional reforms advocated by left-liberal and other left-wing parties, especially the suffrage reform in Prussia.[70] It comes as no surprise, therefore, that similar demands for political reform were echoed in the Interessengemeinschaft's press.

The close links between the civil servant movement and the champions of political reform in the Empire could lead one to conclude that the IG was primarily interested in political change. Quite to the contrary, however, IG leaders were very much convinced of the feasibility of working *within* the *existing* political system if only their organizations were allowed to participate in some of the reforms undertaken to

[67] The conservative *Kreuzzeitung*, quoted in *DBR*, June 16, 1917. This charge was not totally unfounded. Remmers, for example, was treasurer of the left-leaning Volksbund für Freiheit und Vaterland, the staunch opponent of the ultra-nationalist Fatherland Party.

[68] Hubrich was a leading member of the Verband der unteren Post- und Telgraphenbeamten.

[69] So the title of an article written by Delius for the left-liberal *Berliner Tageblatt*, excerpted in *DBR*, June 16, 1917.

[70] *Ibid.* As a left-liberal delegate of the Progressive Party to the Prussian Diet, which was then still elected on the anachronistic three-class voting system, Delius greatly emphasized this point.

gradually liberalize this system. At its 1917 meeting, and at later occasions as well, the IG demanded recognition as the legitimate professional representative *(Standesvertretung)* of the *Beamtenschaft* as a first step of integration into the socio-political system. As a second step, the IG proposed the quasi-institutionalization of governmental recognition by being allotted a seat in the upper house of the Prussian legislature, the *Herrenhaus*, whose reform was being discussed in late 1917. At the middle and lower administrative levels the process of institutionalization of influence was to be accomplished by establishing civil servant committees *(Beamtenausschüsse)* and civil servant chambers *(Beamtenkammern)*.[71]

The government responded to these demands, some of which were again modeled after similar gains scored by blue-collar workers in the Auxiliary Service Law of 1916, with great hesitation, however.[72] The establishing of civil servant chambers and committees was among the many "unfulfilled wishes" of the *Beamtenschaft* mentioned by Remmers in an address to the Society for Social Reform in the spring of 1918.[73] With regard to the IG's demand of representation in semi-parliamentary bodies like the *Herrenhaus* in Prussia, the state secretary of the interior advised the Reich chancellor in mid-1917 that these were "far-reaching demands indeed." He questioned the usefulness of consulting with civil servant representatives in matters not directly related to civil service policy, and he advised the chancellor not to respond to the IG's demands.[74] The incident shows again the limited political leverage which the IG still possessed in 1917.

Less than a year later, however, the integration of the Interessengemeinschaft into the socio-political system of the Empire had made further progress, and the peak association's political significance and leverage had increased accordingly. At the IG's second congress, which convened in June of 1918 in Berlin, a much larger group of parliamen-

[71] *Wünsche der Beamten zur Reform des preußischen Herrenhauses*, in: *DG*, December 16, 1917.

[72] This was the case especially regarding the question of participation and representation through committees and "workers's chambers", which had been conceded to workers in the Auxiliary Service Law of 1917. On this, see G. D. Feldman, *Army...*, pp. 225—237 and *passim.*

[73] *Für Sozialpolitik nach dem Kriege* (= Schriften der Gesellschaft für soziale Reform, vol. 8), Jena 1918, pp. 38—39.

[74] Draft letter, State Secretary of the Interior to Reich Chancellor, July 4, 1917, ZStAP, RMdI, 2742, Bl. 97.

tary representatives, now spanning the political spectrum from the left-liberal Progressive Party to the moderate-conservative Deutsche Reichspartei, attended, which may be taken as an indication of the increased importance with which the IG was now being viewed in the bourgeois political camp. Delegates from the Social Democratic Party and the Socialist Trade Unions — not to speak of the radical-left Independent Socialists — were conspicuously absent, though, which shows that the IG had either remained a bourgeois-oriented association, or that links to the labor movement, which might have existed already at this juncture, were at least not publicly disclosed.[75]

If the attendance of political spokesmen can be interpreted as a sign of the increasing importance of the IG and of its closer links with the parliamentary sphere, it is of equal, if not greater significance that government representatives attended the IG's second meeting as well. They had come not as 'official watchdogs,' as had been the case before 1914, but as invited guests of the association and its leaders. According to the inter-ministerial correspondence, the Reich as well as the Prussian government had found it "useful" at his point to send a delegation to the meeting, although still none of the ministers or state secretaries themselves "were inclined to attend."[76] The fact that the government had sent an official delegation to an IG congress at last was noted by Chairman Remmers "with great pleasure and satisfaction," in his opening remarks.[77] Speaking for the government delegation, Privy Councillor von Jacobi of the Reich Office of the Interior promised to take the civil servants' wishes to their respective ministers and see to it that, if possible, they would be granted.[78]

The spokesman for the Reichstag delegation, the Center Party Deputy and leading Christian Trade Unionist Johannes Giesberts, praised the founding and the promising organizational development of the Interessengemeinschaft as a step toward a more socially and politically active officialdom. Against almost insurmountable obstacles, the leaders of the IG had managed to integrate the rival factions within the

[75] IG meeting 1918, reported in *DG*, July 1, 1918.

[76] State Secretary of the Interior to IG, June 20, 1918, informing the organization that Privy Councilor von Jacobi would attend the meeting as the official representative. A *Vermerk* appended to the copy of letter explains the position of the other ministries. Only the Reich Office of Justice refused to send a delegate at all. The correspondence can be found in ZStAP, RMdI, 2738, Bl. 179ff.

[77] IG meeting 1918, reported in *DG*, July 1, 1918.

[78] *Ibid.*

Beamtenschaft, thus ending factional strife within this social group and rendering the conduct of civil service policy easier for both parliament and government. Giesberts applauded the fact that the government had made concessions regarding the acceptance of the IG as a negotiating partner and pointed out that this entailed an immense progress compared to prewar days, when it was potentially dangerous for a civil servant to even belong to an association. "We are on the right track," Giesberts concluded, "by establishing a relationship between government, parliament, and the *Beamtentum* based on trust through the energetic policies conducted by your Interessengemeinschaft."[79]

Similar hopes were raised by Remmers himself in his report to the IG delegates. Reviewing the two main targets of IG politics in the previous eight months, i. e. the reform of civil service pay scales and the preparations for a modern civil service code, Remmers asserted that these tasks could only be accomplished by way of a trusting cooperation between government and civil servants on the one hand, and parliament, civil servants and government on the other. Consultation of civil servant leaders at both levels (or stages) in the formulation of civil service policy he regarded as the most important demand to be raised in the future. Not mere petitioning, Remmers claimed, but the opportunity to explain the content of petitions in direct talks with senior government officials and parliamentary leaders was the prerequisite to successful civil servant interest politics. In this context he praised the Prussian minister of finance for having taken a first step into this direction by inviting IG leaders for talks about the civil servants' economic plight during the war and the granting of cost-of-living increases. While the results of these talks had not been all too favorable, since the IG's proposals had not been followed by the ministry, the invitation alone, Remmers suggested, had been a most decisive turning point in the IG's struggle for recognition as the representative of civil servant interests.[80]

In Remmer's view the IG (and thus the "new" civil servant movement as such) was not only to function as a representative of special interests, however. Quite emphatically he tried to place civil servant

[79] *Ibid.* — Giesberts' remarks are noteworthy not only as a reflection of the Center Party's interest in civil service matters at this juncture, but also because Giesberts later rose to the position of minister of posts in several Weimar cabinets and thus became a target of the type of civil servant interest politics he was now advocating.

[80] *Ibid.* The meeting had widely been regarded as a breakthrough for the organizations. The IG's *Gemeinschaft,* for example, spoke of the beginning of a "new area in the history of the civil servant movement." See *DG,* March 1, 1918.

interest politics within the larger framework provided by general social policy *(Sozialpolitik).* Civil service policy, he told his audience, had to become an integral part of *Sozialpolitik* if it was to be successful. The goal of civil servant interest politics should therefore not only be the attaining of narrow group interests *(nackte Standesinteressen),* but likewise the support of the general welfare of the nation (the *Allgemeinwohl*) and of the interests of other social goups. "Our own plight," Remmers said, "should remind us of the plight of others and of that of the nation in times of war."[81]

Two aspects in Remmers' speech are interesting. First, the mentioning of cooperation strategies between civil servants and other social groups under the common denominator of *Sozialpolitik.* Presumably, such cooperation would extend to working class organizations, and here above all the Socialist trade unions. A cautious reorientation toward the labor movement had indeed taken place in the previous months, even if still under the tutelage of the bourgeois social reform movement. In April 1918, Remmers had attended a meeting of the Society for Social Reform, where some of the most prominent German trade union leaders were present as well. To this audience, Remmers had articulated forcefully the civil servants' commitment to social policy and their willingness to cooperate with other employee groups in pressing for the continuation of social policy legislation after the war.[82] The reiteration of this theme in his general policy address at the 1918 IG congress shows that Remmers and other leading figures of the Interessengemeinschaft were convinced that only cooperation with other employee groups could ensure the success of a more effective type of civil servant interest politics.

The second aspect of Remmer's speech worth examing in some more detail is the notion that civil servant interest politics had to remain within the framework of the national welfare, the *Allgemeinwohl,* particularly at times of war. Undoubtedly, this was a more traditional

[81] IG meeting 1918, reported in *DG,* July 1, 1918.

[82] *Für Sozialpolitik...,* p. 37. With regard to possibilities of cooperation between civil servants and other *Arbeitnehmer* groups Remmers said in full: „Im übrigen ist sich die Beamtenschaft wohl bewußt, daß sie zusammenstehen muß mit den übrigen Schichten, die an der Fortführung der Sozialpolitik interessiert sind. Nur *der* Staat, der die Sozialpolitik für die Arbeiter und Angestellten fortführt, wird sie auch fortführen für die Beamtenschaft. Wir sind uns des Zusammenhangs aller Fragen bewußt, darum stellen wir uns auch hier Schulter an Schulter mit den anderen Schichten des Volkes.“ (p. 39).

element than the reorientation toward employee politics discussed above. It reflects, to a degree, the civil servants' traditional point of view of equating their welfare with that of the nation as a whole, i. e. the notion of the *Beamtenschaft* as the *allgemeiner Stand* par excellence. The dualism between these two poles, civil service policy as "employee politics" within the framework provided by a common stake in social policy, and civil service policy as a separate set of problems in the context of the general welfare of the state, was to remain a major problem for civil servant interest politics in the years to come.

Despite the persistence of traditional elements, the foregoing analysis of the changing pattern of relationships between civil servants, the government, and the parliamentary/political spheres may have shown that liberal and progressive forces were on the march within the civil servant movement. Represented by the Interessengemeinschaft, some groups of civil servants had begun to demand recognition as an interest group in exchange for the continued support of the existing political system, a system which in addition they wanted to see partially reformed. In connection with the latter, the IG became one of the supporters of the broadly-based constitutional reform movement of late Imperial Germany. The IG's position and influence as an interest group can only be judged in terms of practical interest politics, however, and we shall therefore return at this point to the question of how successful civil servants as an organized interest group were in combatting the social consequences of wartime inflation.

The Limits of Wartime Interest Politics

The Crisis of the Civil Service in 1917

In the spring and summer of 1917, a social crisis of major proportions developed at the German "home front." Food shortages and ever rising prices precipitated the crisis, which took on a political dimension as well by fueling the desire for peace; its most visible and acrimonious symptoms were the great strike movements of April 1917. While these strikes, conducted by blue-collar workers, have received much attention in the contemporary and recent literature,[83] it is less known that

[83] See, for example, G. D. Feldman, *Army...*, pp. 333—348, H. J. Bieber, *Gewerkschaften...*, pp. 441 ff., and J. Kocka, *Klassengesellschaft...*, pp. 51—57.

for civil servants and other middle class groups 1917 became a "year of crisis" as well.

1917 marks the statistical low point in the development of civil servant salaries during the war.[84] This alone is an indication that a crisis point had been reached. Subjectively, civil servants began viewing their economic situation as dangerous to the very existence of their group.[85] The notion gained grounds that the war had led to a general crisis of the civil service, which, if remained unchecked, could turn into a "crisis of the state" and of the entire social order. This point of view was most forcefully stated in a widely noted article, entitled *Die Krisis in der Beamtenschaft,* which appeared in the Berlin weekly *Der Tag* in May 1917. Its author, the Center Party Reichstag deputy Joseph Kuckhoff, was a high-school teacher by profession and thus a civil servant himself, whose position as a member of the Reichstag undoubtedly increased the weight and the political implications of his argument.[86]

From what could best be described as a position of social conservatism, Kuckhoff argued that the three main groups or strata which comprised the *Beamtenschaft* had fallen below the level of the social rank to which they had belonged before the war. Higher civil servants, who had once held a "determining influence on the nation's social, cultural and educational life" had lost this position to social upstarts who lacked the cultural refinement to adequately replace them. Quite emphatically, Kuckhoff warned that the higher civil servants' replacement from their allotted rank within the upper bourgeoisie would, in the long run, drain the nation's main source for replenishment of the educated classes, the *Gebildete.*[87] Middle-grade civil servants, Kuckhoff maintained, had suffered decline as well. Their position within the petit-bourgeois middle class, he held, should be improved because only there could they fulfill their "natural function" as a source of inter-

[84] By 1917 real salaries of Reich civil servants had declined to 43 percent (higher grades), 49 percent (middle grades) and 54 percent (lower grades) of their peacetime value. See the discussion in the CHAPTER ONE of this study and TABLE 22 on page 102 above.

[85] See, for example, a petition of several civil servant associations in Baden, dated April 4, 1917, in GLAK, 233, 24255.

[86] (Joseph) Kuckhoff, *Die Krisis in der Beamtenschaft,* in: *Der Tag,* edn. B., No. 106, May 8, 1917.

[87] A similar argument is made by Otto Most, *Zur Wirtschafts- und Sozialstatistik der höheren Beamten in Preußen,* in: *Schmollers Jahrbuch,* N. F., 39 : 1 (1915), pp. 181—218.

generational upward social mobility. The lower ranks of the *Beamtenschaft*, finally, should at least be kept at a social level comparable to that of the skilled manual worker. Within the unruly lower strata of society, Kuckhoff warned, the *Unterbeamte* were an island of social and political stability, and the government would do well, not to let this conservative element slip through its hands.

Kuckhoff did not limit himself to a mere recounting of the deplorable state of affairs concerning the *Beamtenschaft* and its composite groups. In addition, he made some interesting, almost prophetic observations on the way and the means with which this situation should — or should not — be improved. In this context the strength of the organized working class became important to Kuckhoff as a negative point of reference. While blue-collar workers and salaried employees had been able to adjust wages to the declining value of the currency through the powers of organization and collective actions vis-à-vis the (equally highly organized) forces of capital, civil servants had been unable to assert themselves in an equally forceful manner vis-à-vis the government as employer; salaries in the civil service had thus been unable to keep up with rising prices. To be sure, from his position of clerical social conservatism Kuckhoff did not really complain about the lack of organizational power on the part of the civil servants, and he did not seem to mind the absence of collective bargaining procedures in the public sector. Instead, he called on the benevolence of the government to improve the civil servants' plight precisely for reasons of *preventing* the appearance of wage disputes and their concomitant symptoms of social conflict in society as a whole and of social strife within the *Beamtenschaft* as a group. As he wrote:

"The war clearly shows the critical situation in which the *Beamtentum* finds itself today. [The war] has accelerated the appearance of a crisis which would have come sooner or later ... A *Beamtenstand* torn out of its normal conditions of life represents a great danger to the state. Historically, the *Beamtentum* has always been the most conservative element in a Prussio-Germany afflicted by the forces of 'social progress.' Civil servants are accustomed to simplicity of lifestyle and a quiet appreciation of life *(ruhige Daseinsfreude)*. Hence they represent a part of society that is opposed to social transformation, and they do not want to share the fate of other occupational groups which are thrown back and forth by modern developments. Our social community *[Gemeinschaft]* has a great interest in keeping the *Beamtenschaft* in this position. It must be prevented that civil servants, even those employed in the large government enterprises, are drawn into the wage struggles *(Lohnkämpfe)* of modern economic life."[88]

Kuckhoff's admonitions and dire predictions must not only be interpreted as an expression of a specific type of social conservatism with its emphasis on tradition, stability, and social harmony which was rampant in the more conservative wing of the Center Party and in the Catholic labor movement. His views correspond as well to those shared by other conservative forces within German society, including the upper ranks of the *Beamtenschaft* themselves (of which Kuckhoff was, after all, a member) and the conservative wing of the civil servant movement.[89] Moreover, throughout 1917 military and civilian government agencies made similar observations about the plight of the *Beamtenschaft*, and they drew similar conclusions as well.

The "official worries" about the deteriorating situation of the *Beamtenschaft* appeared once again in the reports of the Deputy Commanding Generals on the mood of the civilian population in wartime Germany. In early 1917 one report noted that the economic situation of the Mittelstand in general, and that of civil servants in particular, was producing an adverse effect on the very fabric of German society and on the political allegiances of these middle-class groups. While civil servants and teachers were essential to all efforts of improving and maintaining a "mood of patriotism and perseverance" in the population at large, parliamentary bickering about cost-of-living increases for these groups had been hurting these efforts.[90] The insufficiency of cost-of-living increases granted by the government thus far, another report noted, was leading to the social decline of a stratum of society "which through generations had been the mainstay of culture and education," and whose willingness to make personal sacrifice a precondition for educating its children had supplied the state with its most well-trained and loyal public servants. It was unfortunate, therefore, the report continued, that as a result of the conditions and necessities of war the qualitative element in "population policy" *(Bevölkerungspolitik)* was being replaced by quantitative considerations alone, as the care for the lower strata of society was increased at the expense of the middling and

[88] J. Kuckhoff, *Die Krisis...*, in: *Der Tag*, edn. B, No. 106, May 8, 1917.

[89] See *Eingabe des Verbandes Deutscher Beamtenvereine zur Notlage der Beamten*, in: *DBR*, August 1, 1917, where similar points are stressed.

[90] *Monthly Reports*, February 3, 1917, p. 10.

upper groups. This, the report surmised, could not be in the best interest of the state.[91]

By mid-1917 the reports began to warn about political consequences of the civil servants' economic malaise. Embitterment would eventually prompt civil servants "to join the ranks of the Social Democratic Party," one report observed.[92] Citing an account by the Württemberg War Ministry on a protest meeting of lower and middle grade civil servants in Stuttgart, another report emphasized that these groups had expressed their grievances in a way not to be misunderstood and were "about to drift to the left toward the Majority Social Democrats."[93] By the summer of 1917, the "crisis of the civil service" had entered the official reports as topic. "The situation of the middling and lower ranks of the *Beamtenstand* has become more and more dangerous," a report filed in August 1917 noted. Even the families of those higher civil servants who did not possess private fortunes were becoming financially strapped, the report claimed, and were increasingly unable to meet the "general dearness of the cost of living," because their personal savings had become more and more depleted.[94]

While the "Crisis of the Civil Service" as outlined by Kuckhoff and corroborated in the reports of the Deputy Commanding Generals certainly depicts the economic plight of the *Beamtenschaft* in 1917 rather well and in vivid terms, it needs to be reexamined and partially redefined in more modern terms as well. Actually, there appeared to have been *two* crises within the *Beamtenschaft,* or rather two separate socioeconomic trends produced by the war and by wartime inflation. For one, civil servants experienced a *relative* loss of economic position and social status, relative because social decline was measured against the social resistance or even social advancement of other groups. The working class, the *Arbeiterschaft,* emerged as the reference group from

[91] *Monthly Reports,* May 5, 1917, pp. 20—21. Similar arguments were made in a widely circulated, anonymous pamphlet, written allegedly by a middle-level civil servant and entitled *Teuerungszulagen und Besoldungspolitik,* Berlin n. D. (1917). For a critical appraisal of this pamphlet, see D. Scharringhausen, *Teuerungszulagen und Bevölkerungspolitik,* in: *BJ,* 4 (1917), pp. 122—127. See also Karl Bälz, *Beamtenrecht und Familie. Ein Beitrag zur sozialen Frage* (= Der deutsche Krieg. Politische Flugschriften, no. 89), Berlin 1917, and Georg Strutz, *Das Beamtenproblem nach dem Kriege, insbesondere in Preußen,* Stuttgart 1918. Both authors address the population argument.

[92] *Monthly Reports,* June 3, 1917, p. 17.

[93] *Monthly Reports,* July 3, 1917, p. 21.

[94] *Monthly Reports,* August 3, 1917, p. 16.

which civil servants measured their own social decline. Secondly, there was an *absolute* decline of *all* social groups compared to their prewar situation. This, however, was of lesser importance in a line of argumentation which implied that civil servants had dropped in the social hierarchy further and at a faster pace than other social groups.[95] Thirdly — and perhaps most importantly in the context of the present study — the crisis of 1917 prompted civil servant associations to make their bid for a more active role in the formulation and execution of civil service salary policy.

Salary Policy and Wartime Inflation

Pressing for changes in government salary policy became one of the main targets of practical interest politics conducted by the IG in the last two years of the war. In view of the fact that the price increases of the war years was interpreted by associational leaders as the very motor of the civil servants' organizational formation,[96] it is not surprising that efforts to diminish the impact of wartime inflation assumed highest priority in the organization's initial attempts at conducting interest politics. Salary policy *(Besoldungspolitik)* became the main catalyst for successful and cohesive civil servant interest politics; it alone could appeal to members and to those who had remained outside the new organization. Salary policy was to become the yardstick by which the success of civil servant interest politics would be measured during the war as well as during the much more conflict-ridden salary struggles under postwar inflationary conditions.[97]

As early as 1916, leaders of several civil servant associations had decided to formulate general guidelines concerning salary policy. The underlying assumption of proposing such guidelines was that only a thorough revision of the existing civil service pay structure and a more flexible adjustment of pay rates to the general economic conditions could, in the long run, guarantee the material well-being, if not the economic and social survival of the *Beamtenschaft*.[98] On the whole, how-

[95] Cf. D. Scharringhausen, *Arbeiterlöhne und Einkommenssteigerung während des Krieges,* in: *DG,* September 16, 1917.

[96] Emphasized by Albert Falkenberg, *Die Organisationsfrage der Beamten,* in: *DG,* April 1, 1917.

[97] On the function and significance of civil service salary policy in the inflation period, see the discussion in the INTRODUCTION esp. pp. 18—23 above.

[98] Report of the meeting in: *Die Beamten und ihr Vereinsrecht,* in: *BJ,* 3 (1916).

ever, the organizations had made little headway in establishing their influence on the formulation and implementation of civil servant salary policy in the early years of the war. Accordingly, at the first general meeting of the Interessengemeinschaft in June 1917 not much progress in terms of actual achievements in the salary question could be reported to the delegates by the IG leadership. Comprehensive "principles for a revision of civil service pay" had been drawn up, obviously in response to the economic crisis situation within the *Beamtenschaft* discussed above. One of the central demands voiced in these guidelines was that "henceforth civil service pay should not depend on the financial situation of the state, but rather on the civil servants' material needs of life."[99] Resolutions were passed by the delegates demanding higher cost-of-living supplements, a better supply with basic foodstuffs, and the government's acceptance of the IG as a representative of civil servant interests in the preparation and execution of these measures.

In a comprehensive revision of the system of wartime cost-of-living supplements, which the Reich government and the Prussian state government undertook in the summer of 1917 — no doubt in partial response to the critical situation within their respective services — proposals submitted by civil servant organizations still mattered comparatively little. In the new scheme, permanent cost-of-living supplements replaced the irregular bonuses paid thus far. The new system, which later was adopted by the other German federal states as well, favored married civil servants with children, lower paid groups as opposed to the higher ranks, and, for the first time, city dwellers as opposed to civil servants residing in small towns and in rural areas by fixing levels of cost-of-living increases to location classes *(Ortsklassen)*.[100] While the first two measures were a reflection of the tendency

[99] IG Meeting 1917, in: *DG*, November 1, 1917. On some theoretical conceptions of adjusting civil service pay to mounting inflation, cf. Thomas Kleinheinz, *Neue Gedanken zum Gehaltsproblem der Beamten*, in: *BJ*, 3 (1916), pp. 30—36, and Alois Zeiler, *Grundsätzliches zur Ordnung des Beamtengehalts*, in: *BJ*, 4 (1917), pp. 97—108. See also Zeiler's *Der Beamtenschaft Not und Rettung*, Munich 1918, in which he develops his famous theory for adjusting civil service pay directly to rises in the cost of living. Zeiler's proposals were to play an important role in the postwar period of inflation. See CHAPTER SEVEN, pp. 352—355 below for a more detailed discussion.

[100] For a detailed description of these measures, see *Rundschau für Gemeindebeamte* (hereafter cited as *RfG*), August 11, 1917, and *Denkschrift Besoldung 1924*, pp. 13—14. See also Karl Rothmeier/Karl Heinrich, *Die Kriegsbeihilfen für Beamte in Bayern und den anderen Bundesstaaten*, Munich n. D. (1917), and R. Schmidt, *Die Kriegsteuerungs-*

toward a social wage already discussed above, the rationale for the latter was the presumably lower cost of living in rural areas and small towns. By affirming the existence and the necessity of a social factor in civil servant pay, and by formulating a method of regional differentiation of cost-of-living increases, the government had, by decree, introduced two new principles into the civil service pay structure that would become major sources of conflict and prime targets for civil servant interest politics. Civil servant representatives, who had not been consulted before these measures were adopted, were still unhappy with the level of the increases, although they did welcome the fact that a more regular and permanent granting of the cost-of-living increases would now allow for a more timely adjustment of salaries to the prevailing economic conditions.[101]

Fiscal considerations continued to outweigh civil servant demands in the shaping of wartime salary policy, however, even after a breakthrough into direct negotiations with government agencies on the salary issue had finally occurred in early 1918. While the Prussian finance minister was then prepared to listen to what civil servant leaders had to say, he was not willing to yield to organizational pressures with regard to fundamental policy considerations, such as the *Ortsklassen* principle or the differentiation of increases according to pay levels. Even the size of the "war bonus" was not really up for negotiation yet, with organizational proposals hopelessly outpacing subsequent government pay awards.[102] As a consequence, the economic plight of civil servants continued virtually unabated.

In the spring und summer of 1918, urgent requests for immediate economic support increased within the *Beamtenschaft* and were reported by the civil servant press. In February 1918, for example, the Civil Servant Association of Cologne complained that the "enormous depreciation of the currency" had rendered hopeless all efforts made by civil servants to keep an "adequate household." In order to protect civil servants from complete economic collapse, immediate and substantial pay increases were needed.[103] Corruption in the formerly proverbially

zulagen usw. bei der Reichs- Post- und Telegraphenverwaltung, in: *Archiv für Post und Telegraphie,* 40 (1920), pp. 128—147.

[101] *Denkschrift Besoldung 1924,* p. 25 and *Anlage* 1.

[102] *DG,* March 1 and April 1, 1918.

[103] *Entschließung des Verbandes Cölner Beamten- und Lehrervereine,* February 9, 1918, reprinted in: *DG,* March 1, 1918.

incorrupt German civil service was becoming a problem as well. Civil servants were being forced to resort to "dishonest means in order to stay above water," the IG's *Gemeinschaft* reported,[104] and in a widely noticed statement the Bavarian Minister of Cultural Affairs von Knilling warned that as civil servants were rapidly being proletarianized, the German *Beamtenstand*, "the most honest and reliable one in the world" was getting close to "being corrupted in all its parts."[105] Easy access to loans had been part of the problem, because many financially pressed civil servants had become overburdened with debts in the previous years and were now unable to meet their payments. Embezzlement of public funds and other forms of corruption were all too often regarded as the only way to prevent a total financial collapse.[106]

The worsening economic conditions of the *Beamtenschaft* and the problem of corruption and indebtedness were issues discussed at the second meeting of the Interessengemeinschaft in mid-1918. With regard to the latter, the IG proposed the granting of a special pay award to cover debts incurred by civil servants and a special government loan program that would prevent the accumulation of debt at exorbitant interest rates paid to "private usurers." In order to improve the general economic situation of the *Beamtenschaft* the IG called for immediate legislative preparations for a comprehensive salary reform. As short-term measures, higher cost-of-living supplements and the granting of a special "purchasing allowance" *(Beschaffungszulage)* were advocated, the latter to deal with the very real problem of poor clothing which was gnawing at the civil servant's social self-esteem as well as on his public image.[107] It is of some importance that these decisions and the resolu-

[104] *DG*, March 1, 1918.

[105] *Der wirtschaftliche Niedergang der Beamten und Lehrer*, in: *DG*, September 9, 1918. Postwar statistics reveal that the level of corruption within the German civil service did indeed increase during the war and in the immediate postwar years. Accepting bribes (*passive Bestechung*), a most serious offense for a civil servant, picked up during the war years (from 37 cases in 1914 to 62 in 1918), only to rise dramatically in the postwar period (343 cases in 1922). Cf. *Statistik des Deutschen Reichs*, vol. 370, p. 55, where these and other figures are reported. See also *Die Kriminalität der deutschen Beamtenschaft 1882—1928*, in: *DG*, December 5, 1931, which is an appraisal based on the survey of the Reich Statistical Office.

[106] See *Friedensurlaub und Wirtschaftsnot der Beamten*, in: *DG*, July 18, 1918, where one case of corruption involving the financing of a civil servants's vacation is discussed in detail.

[107] IG meeting 1918, in *DG*, 1, 1918, where this issue is discussed at length. On the

tions drafted on their basis were not simply viewed as supporting material for yet another petition to be sent to the government, but rather as the blueprint for negotiations to be conducted with public employers. Accordingly, the IG leadership was ordered by the delegates to enter into negotiations on the basis of the resolution with the Prussian Ministry of Finance and the Reich Treasury Office.[108] The outcome of these negotiations was disappointing, however. In September 1918 the Prussian government, after consulting with the organizations, granted another "war bonus" to civil servants, the last one to be granted by the old regime. Since the organizations again regarded the pay award as "totally insufficient," it might safely be assumed that still their voice did not carry too much weight within the realm of policy making.[109] Their direct influence on salary policy remained limited, even if the government had moved from repression to toleration with respect to the existence and functioning of civil servant interest organizations.

The reform of the political structure of the Empire in the wake of the so-called October Reforms of 1918, the last German "revolution from above," did not drastically change the civil servant organizations' leverage on the conduct of civil service policy, although the October Reforms did confirm the civil servants' full political rights as *Staatsbürger*.[110] In any case, such reforms that were undertaken were soon eclipsed by the "revolution from below" of November 1918, which was to lead to fundamental changes in the relationship between civil servant organizations and the government as employer. The organizations' — by and large unsuccessful — struggle to improve the civil servants' economic and social position through influence on wartime salary policy meant that the basic confrontation between organized civil servants and the government as employer was yet to come. It was to be a part of the heavy burden which the rapidly disintegrating Imperial regime left to the revolutionary governments and to the parliamentary democracy of the Weimar Republic.

problem of civil servants' poor clothing and loss of social status resulting from it, see the perceptive remarks made by G. D. Feldman, *Army...*, p. 465.

[108] *DG*, July 1, 1918.

[109] *DG*, September 16, 1918.

[110] Documentation in GStA, Rep. 90, 2324, Bl. 279—282.

The Impact of Revolution: Civil Servants and the Birth of the Weimar Republic

The Revolution of November 1918 did not interrupt, but rather accelerate and complete many of the developments within the German *Beamtenschaft* and its social movement set in motion by the war. Seemingly overnight — but in reality as the endpoint in a much longer process of organizational formation — the revolutionary events in the fall and winter of 1918/19 and the challenges they entailed for civil servants as exponents of the old regime brought about the unification of the civil servant movement, governmental recognition of civil servant associations, the latters' integration into the sociopolitical structure of the newly formed republic, and, as a result of all of this, the civil servants' forceful entry into interest group politics. While the last mentioned development will move into focus in much of the following chapters of this study, the first mentioned ones shall now be discussed briefly as the concluding episode in our story of the civil servants' march toward organizational unity.

Organizational Unity Achieved: The Founding of the Deutscher Beamtenbund (DBB)

In the organizational realm, the November Revolution led to the integration of the German *Beamtenschaft* within a single organizational framework. The founding of the Federation of German Civil Servants (Deutscher Beamtenbund or DBB) in early December 1918 at the instigation of Ernst Remmers of the Interessengemeinschaft was a somewhat hastily achieved victory in the quest for organizational unity which, as we have seen, had characterized organizational politics in the civil servant movement during the war years.[111] With a total member-

[111] The most detailed account of the founding of the DBB is provided by E. Remmers, *Die organisatorische Einheit...*, pp. 49—58. See also F. Winters, *Der Deutsche Beamtenbund...*, pp. 21—25, A. Falkenberg, *Die deutsche Beamtenbewegung...*, pp. 83—93, and W(ilhelm) Flügel, *Werden und Wesen des Deutschen Beamtenbundes,* in: Ernst Remmers/ Albert Falkenberg (eds.), *Beamten-Handbuch,* Berlin-Friedenau n. d. (1921), pp. 45—52. Recent accounts include Erhard Schrön, *Deutscher Beamtenbund (DBB) 1918—1933,* in: Dieter Fricke et al. (eds.), *Die bürgerlichen Parteien in Deutschland. Handbuch der Geschichte der bürgerlichen Parteien und anderer bürgerlicher Interessenorganisationen vom Vormärz bis zum Jahre 1945,* vol. 1, Leipzig 1968, pp. 422—428, and a documentation compiled by the DBB's post-1945 successor organization entitled *Deutscher Beamtenbund. Ursprung. Weg. Ziel. Zur 50. Wiederkehr der Gründung des Deutschen Beam-*

ship of over one million civil servants,[112] the new federation was a formidable interest organization by any standard. To rival organizations within the German labor movement, to public employers, and to a national audience in general it must have come as somewhat of a surprise to see that the German *Beamtenschaft* had finally overcome its inner divisiveness, and that associations representing divers categories of civil servants (with often equally diverse social backgrounds and values) such as higher ministerial officials, school teachers, locomotive engineers, tax collectors and postal clerks had at last unified in a single federation and were ready to combat the economic, social and political pressures created by wartime inflation, military defeat, and political revolution.

Like its predecessor, the Interessengemeinschaft, the DBB was an umbrella organization, i. e. a federation of independent member associations of which there were a good many. In 1919, for example, the DBB consisted of some twenty-eight affiliates, varying greatly in size and importance.[113] A large organization like the Federation of German Railroad Civil Servants (Gewerkschaftsbund Deutscher Eisenbahnbeamter or GDEB), which could muster over 200,000 members and was

tenbundes am 4. Dezember 1918, Bundesleitung des DBB (ed.), esp. pp. II/17—II/31. On the more general contours of civil servant interest politics in the revolutionary period, see Georg Kalmer, *Beamtenschaft und Revolution. Eine sozialgeschichtliche Studie über Voraussetzung und Wirklichkeit des Problems,* in: Karl Bosl (ed.), *Bayern im Umbruch,* Munich-Vienna 1969, pp. 201—261, and the more recent, somewhat problematical interpretation by Rainer M. Halmen, *„Das Berufsbeamtentum muß unter allen Umständen erhalten bleiben". Die deutsche Beamtenbewegung zwischen Etatismus und gewerkschaftlicher Orientierung im Übergang vom Kaiserreich zur Weimarer Republik,* in: *IWK,* 18 (1982), pp. 173—203. Entirely based on published source materials, Halmen's study dwells on the thesis of an underlying etatism within the German civil servant movement, which, as he argues, led to pseudo-unionization at best. As the present study will show, this approach does not do justice to the complexity of the topic.

[112] The official figure of "ca. 1.5 million", given in *Die Verbände der Unternehmer, Angestellten, Arbeiter und Beamten im Jahre 1918* (= Sonderheft zum Reichsarbeitsblatt, no.22), Berlin 1920, is a gross overestimate and may reflect membership in late 1919. For DBB membership figures in later years and those of important DBB affiliates, see TABLE 23 on pp. 134 f.

[113] The number of associations *indirectly* affiliated with the DBB was much larger, of course. In all, there existed some 472 civil servant associations in 1919 with a combined membership of 1,289,343. Cf. *Die Verbände ... im Jahre 1919...,* pp. 20*—23* and the tables provided there in *Übersicht* 16. Contrary to the year given in the title of this publication (i. e. 1918), the figures relating to civil servant associations usually refer to 1919.

TABLE 23

Civil Servant Associations in Germany, 1918—1932

Association	Year Founded[a]	1918/19[b]	1920	1922[c]	1924	1926	1928	1930	1932
DEUTSCHER BEAMTENBUND (DBB)	1918	(1 000 000)[d]	1 058 804	774 309	845 045	902 889	1 058 510	1 069 306	993 257
Reichsgewerkschaft Deutscher Eisenbahnbeamten (RG)	1919 [e]	250 000	300 000[f]	—	—	—	—	—	—
Gewerkschaft Deutscher Reichsbahnbeamten	1922	—	—	—	19 850	80 000	110 000	83 000	91 000
Reichsverband Deutscher Post- und Telegraphenbeamten	1908	100 498	—	129 000	120 000	123 183	137 000	138 000	136 000
Verband Deutscher Post- und Telegraphenbeamten	1890	40 518	—	51 065	23 000	25 320	26 000	23 000	21 000
Verband Deutscher Reichspost- und Telegraphenbeamtinnen	1912	22 870	—	33 526	37 720	38 636	33 377	36 550	36 965
Reichsverband der Kommunalbeamten und Angestellten (Komba)	1921	—	—	164 542	153 302	153 336	184 374	154 000	155 285
Verband Preußischer Polizeibeamten	1915	53 000	—	?	50 000	58 130	64 512	53 100	61 400
Deutscher Lehrerverein	1871 [g]	113 214	—	117 632	125 000	145 000	154 112	125 000	119 000
Gewerkschaft Deutscher Verwaltungsbeamten	1918 [h]	11 606	—	12 006	12 505	8 000	10 000	—	—
ALLGEMEINER DEUTSCHER BEAMTENBUND (ADB)	1922	—	—	(350 000)	354 274	178 296	166 610	177 070	171 800
Reichsgewerkschaft Deutscher Eisenbahnbeamten (RG)	1919	—	—	250 000	(200 000)[i]	—	—	—	—

Deutscher Eisenbahnerverband (Beamtensektion)	1916[k]	(80 000)	—	40 000	40 000	45 852	52 376	52 400	?
Deutscher Justizbeamtenbund	1918[l]	17 100	—	(20 000)	11 000	?	22 400	21 000	?
Allgemeine Deutsche Postgewerkschaft	1922[m]	—	—	?	20 000	23 500	23 500	44 200	?
Allgemeiner Preußischer Polizeibeamtenverband	1925	—	—	—	—	6 071	6 000	5 800	?
Reichsgewerkschaft Deutscher Kommunalbeamten	1922	—	—	?	2 700	30 000	13 200	15 100	?
Reichsgewerkschaft Deutscher Verwaltungsbeamten	1919	4 000	5 400	5 000	2 000	1 800	1 800	2 500	?
GESAMTVERBAND DEUTSCHER BEAMTENGEWERKSCHAFTEN (GDB)	1920	—	(420 000)	342 642	399 478	302 977[n]	—	—	—
RING DEUTSCHER BEAMTENVERBÄNDE (RDB)	1920	—	(30 000)	90 000	65 000	54 000	32 000[o]	—	—
REICHSBUND DER HÖHEREN BEAMTEN (RhB)	1918[p]	40 000	55 085	75 000	100 700	100 000	100 000	100 000	?

[a] In some cases founding year of precursor organization.
[b] Figures refer to late 1919 in most cases.
[c] Figures given are for late 1922, i. e. *after* the founding of the ADB.
[f] All figures in ( ) are estimates.
[e] From 1919 to 1920: Gewerkschaftsbund Deutscher Reichsbahnbeamten (GDEB).
[f] As of June 1922 to ADB.
[g] Affiliates with DBB in 1920 only.
[h] Nominally independent, but most member associations in DBB.
[i] Dissolves in 1925.
[k] Figures refer to civil servant section only. Affiliate of ADGB.
[l] Until 1922 a DBB affiliate.
[m] Civil servant membership only.
[n] As of October 1926 to DBB.
[o] As of 1928 to DBB.
[p] Originally founded as Bund höherer Beamter (BhB). Affiliated with DBB until 1920.

Sources: Reichsarbeitsblatt, Sonderh. 22, 25, 30, 52 (= *Jahrbuch der Berufsverbände im Deutschen Reich*) and organizational statistics.

itself an umbrella for some forty-six affiliated associations, had little in common with a small group of 125 civil servants united in an Association of Civil Servants of the National Printing Office (Verband der Reichsdruckerei-Beamten).[114]

According to its statutes, the DBB professed to be "a federation of civil service and teachers' associations on a trade-union basis." Its main objective was "to promote the legal, economic and professional affairs of German public officials."[115] For this purpose, the DBB reserved itself the right to act as the principle negotiator in general economic and political questions — while, at the same time, observing strict "political neutrality." Like its predecessor, the Interessengemeinschaft, the DBB considered itself to be the peak association of the entire German *Beamtenschaft* and thus lay claim to the right of negotiating exclusively in all matters that were of general concern to civil servants as a group. The affiliated organizations, in turn, sent delegates to the peak association's important governing bodies, the annual (later biannual) meetings (*Verbandstage* or, later on, *Bundestage*) and the General Council *(Bundesausschuss)*, the latter being the most important policy-making body between the general meetings.[116] Although delegation to these two bodies was done on a proportional basis (one delegate per 10,000 members), preventive measures were taken to protect small associations by giving to them the right to send at least one delegate regardless of their size in membership.

Nonetheless, the financially powerful *Großverbände* of postal and railroad civil servants soon attained a certain predominance within the federation. At the DBB's first regular annual meeting in May 1919, the founding team of men like Remmers, Hoefle, and Falkenberg was partially replaced by representatives of the large branch associations, who were elected to the DBB's most important day-to-day governing body, the Executive Board *(Bundesvorstand)*. Most importantly, the chairman of the largest DBB affiliate, Max Lange of the Railroad Civil Servant Union, took over as DBB chairman, while Remmers, the

[114] Figures given in *ibid.*, *Übersicht* 16.

[115] *Ibid.*, pp. 21*—22*, where the statutes are reprinted in full lenght. An abridged version is contained in *Deutscher Beamtenbund. Ursprung. Weg. Ziel...*, pp. II/21—II/22. In 1920, and again in 1928, the DBB's statutes were changed and amended.

[116] A good discussion of the DBB's structure at the time of its founding is contained in K. R. v. Scherf, *Die Entwicklung der Beamtenbewegung...*, pp. 105—119. See also E. Schrön, *Deutscher Beamtenbund...*, in: D. Fricke, et al. (eds.), *Die bürgerlichen Parteien...*, vol. 1, p. 423 f.

"founding chairman", became one of the peak association's two business managers *(Direktoren)*.[117] The domination of the large, tightly organized, and, later on, increasingly militant organizations of railroad and postal civil servants (i. e. the *Betriebsbeamte*) over the much smaller and splintered associations of the *Hoheitsbeamte* was to become a most difficult internal problem for the DBB in the subsequent years.

This was the case even more so in view of the fact that clear-cut civil service unionism, i. e. the restructuring of civil service associations along trade-union lines and such concomitant phenomena as organizational concentration, trade-union behavior and tactics (including militant forms of collective action like strikes), made inroads above all among the *Betriebsbeamte.* Organizational concentration was particularly successful among railroad and postal civil servants, as TABLE 24 suggests. On the railways, the nearly one hundred different associations

TABLE 24

Civil Servant Associations by Administrative Branches 1918—1930

Administrative Branch	1918	1922	1925	1927	1930
1. General and "Peak" Associations	33	28	39	55	56
2. General Administration	36	29	37	48	54
3. Public Corporations, Mining, and Commerce	46	46	48	70	69
4. Finance, Taxation, and Customs	35	30	32	35	36
5. Agriculture and Forestry	24	15	21	24	20
6. Transportation and Communications					
A) Railroads	93	25	40	57	59
B) Postal Service	14	15	18	19	17
7. Police	15	13	33	47	51
8. Judicial Administration	33	24	25	68	98
9. Education and Church Administration	63	80	89	96	112
10. Armed Forces (Civilian Employees)	33	11	21	23	29
11. Public Insurance	9	8	10	10	9
12. Public Health	16	24	25	20	20
13. Other Agencies	12	11	6	7	7
14. Municipal Administration	10	18	20	22	23
15. Total	472	377	472	611	668

Source: Reichsarbeitsblatt, Sonderh. 22, 25, 30, 36, 52 (= *Jahrbuch der Berufsverbände im Deutschen Reich*).

117 See *Bericht über die Hauptversammlung und die Verhandlungen des 1. Vertreter-*

that had existed prior to 1918 had, in 1919, formed the above mentioned GDEB, a still loosely organized federation of some forty-six associations. One year later, the GDEB was restructured along trade union lines as the National Union of German Railway Civil Servants (Reichsgewerkschaft Deutscher Eisenbahnbeamten or RG). The former forty-six affiliates were grouped into only nine "branch unions" *(Fachgewerkschaften)*, who delegated much of their powers to a national leadership that increasingly took on a militant, left-wing posture.[118] With a membership of nearly 300,000 in 1920,[119] the RG was an impressive union by any standard and definitely the most powerful, militant, and politically radical civil servant union in the early Weimar Republic.[120] Its choice of affiliation could make or break a *Spitzenverband*. The RG's history, perhaps the most striking example of radical unionism among German civil servants, coincided with the period of the postwar inflation and stabilization. It was this organization which would unleash the most severe confrontation between civil servants and the state in the inflation period: the civil servant strike of February 1922.[121] Yet less than three years later, in early 1925, only remnants of this once powerful organization were to join forces with the Socialist trade unions.[122]

There were similar developments among organizations representing the different grades of postal officials. Under the leadership of the

tages des Deutschen Beamtenbundes, n. p. n. d. (Berlin 1919) (hereafter cited as *DBB Protocol 1919*), pp. 159—161.

[118] On the history of the GDEB and the founding of the Reichsgewerkschaft, see the GDEB's first annual report *Geschäftsbericht des Gewerkschaftsbundes Deutscher Eisenbahnbeamten für die Zeit vom 1. Juli 1919 bis zum 1, Juli 1920*, n. p. n. d. (Berlin 1920) (hereafter cited as *GDEB Report 1920*). See also K. R. v. Scherf, *Die Entwicklung der Beamtenbewegung...*, pp. 123 f. There is some documentation on the RG's internal structure in Hauptstaatsarchiv Düsseldorf (hereafter referred to as HStAD), Regierung Düsseldorf (hereafter cited as Reg. Düss.), 15762.

[119] RG to Reich President's Office, June 12, 1920, ZStAP, Büro RP, 149, Bl. 30, announcing its founding and reporting a membership figure of 300,000.

[120] Militant in this context is to imply, above all, the espousal of the strike as a means to achieve union objectives, which for a German civil service union can be described as a posture of militancy. In its letter to the Reich President's Office just cited, the RG had stressed its commitment to the "unlimited right of coalition."

[121] This strike, and the RG's role in it, will be the subject of CHAPTER SIX of this study.

[122] Less than 40,000 members were brought into the DEV at the time of the merger, which indicates that the once powerful national union had been reduced to its radical core. On the merger itself, see Deutscher Eisenbahnerverband (ed.), *Protokoll der gemeinsamen Tagung des Deutschen Eisenbahnerverbandes und der Reichsgewerkschaft Deutscher Eisenbahnbeamten am 27. Juni 1925 in Köln*, Berlin 1925.

largest postal civil servant union, the Reichsverband Deutscher Post- und Telegraphenbeamten (which organized primarily the lower grades of the postal administration) six major postal associations in 1921 merged into a single umbrella organization, the Reichsgewerkschaft der Post- und Telegraphenbeamten (or: Reichspostgewerkschaft — RPG).[123] This organization proved to be more shortlived than its counterpart in the railroad administration, however. Internal conflicts and similar tendencies of militancy and radicalism led in the case of the postal officials to an even earlier collapse of the merger across social lines.[124]

The position of the *Fachverband* as the dominant pillar of the DBB's internal structure was, initially at least, heatedly contested.[125] Critics of this organizational principle came chiefly from three camps. First, from within the associations of the *Hoheitsbeamte* who were fearful of being consistently outvoted by the large railroad and postal associations. Second, from within assosiations organized on a territorial basis, who were pressing to adopt a structure based on territorial considerations thus making state, regional and local organizations (Landesverbände, Provinzialverbände, Ortskartelle) the core of the peak association's internal structure. Such organizations were, in fact, later established i. e. the DBB came to rest on a dual organizational structure based on civil service branches *and* on territorial considerations.[126] The third group of critics came from within the so-called "horizontally-structured" organizations; they objected to the DBB's principle of "vertical" organ-ization along branch lines. Very much a specificity of the German civil

[123] There is some documentation on the RPG in HStAD, Reg. Düss., 15761.

[124] The RPG broke apart in 1922 in the wake of the February Strike just mentioned above. See CHAPTER SIX below for further details.

[125] The following account is based on an examination of the minutes of the DBB's meeting in 1919. See *DBB Protocol 1919*, esp. pp. 33—66.

[126] Pressures for a territorial basis of organization came above all from the South German associations and those in the East Elbian states and Prussian provinces. The *Landesverbände* were to represent the interests of the state officials *(Landesbeamte)* vis-à-vis the state governments. The most influential *Landesverband* was the Bayerische Beamtenbund (BBB), since, curiously enough, there did not exist a state association for Prussia at that time. Instead, several regional associations *(Provinzialverbände)* had been founded in Prussia, particularly in its East Elbian provinces. At the bottom of the "territorial structure" was the *Ortskartell*, a local organization whose purpose it was to unite all DBB members in a given locality. As a result of the DBB's dual structure, many civil servants had, in fact, dual membership, belonging to a *Fachverband* and a territorial association at the same time.

servant movement, the issue of "vertical" vs. "horizontal" organization needs to be discussed in some more detail.

In principle, the DBB adopted a "vertical" structure, i. e. a structure that was based on the various branches of the German civil service (e. g. posts, general administration, education, etc.) rather than on the socially divisive "horizontal" ranks of the civil service hierarchy, i. e. higher grades, lower grades, etc. The DBB's organizational guidelines, adopted at the first general meeting in 1919,[127] called for member organizations to affiliate in one of six (later seven) so-called "pillars" *(Säulen)* that stood for the different civil service branches,[128] regardless of whether the particular association organized higher, middle-level, or lower-grade civil servants. Opposition to this principle of "vertical" organization along branches and across social boundaries came above all from those associations which already had organized its members on the basis of social rank, e. g. the Federation of Higher Civil Servants (BhB) and the Soziale Arbeitsgemeinschaft of Lower-Grade Civil Servants.[129] As a compromise, both these horizontally-structured organizations were given a seat on the DBB's executive board. However, this was done on a temporary basis only, i. e. until a final solution to the question of "vertical" vs. "horizontal" organization could be found. The secession of the BhB from the umbrella organization in mid-1920 would serve as a reminder, though, that the issue was never really resolved.[130]

Antagonisms between the different ranks were, after all, rooted in and a reflection of the traditional structure and career divisions of the German civil service which the Revolution and the republican regime had been unable to change. It comes as no surprise, therefore, that these social division would continue to be reflected in the German civil

[127] For this and the following, see *DBB Protocol 1919*, pp. 34 ff.

[128] The "pillars" were: railways *(Reichsbahn)*, postal service *(Reichspost)*, Reich administration *(Reichsverwaltung)*, state administration *(Länderverwaltungen)*, municipal administration *(Gemeindeverwaltung)*, education *(Lehrer)*, and police *(Polizeibeamte)*. The last one was only added in 1928; previously, police officials had been subsumed under state administration.

[129] On these two organizations, see pp. 96 and 110 above.

[130] The organizational conflict between DBB and BhB was fueled by the latter's refusal to participate in the general strike against the right-wing Kapp Regime in March 1920. See *Bericht über die Verhandlungen auf dem außerordentlichen Vertretertag des Deutschen Beamtenbundes*, Berlin n. d. (1920) (hereafter cited as *DBB Protocol 1920*), pp. 5—28. There is some documentation on this in ZStAP, RhB, 194.

servant movement as well. Those associational leaders who favored the vertical structure attempted to overcome these divisions in the organizational realm by supporting an integration model for civil servants based on civil service branches rather than on career levels, which, after all, were *social* tiers at the same time. But the persistence and, toward the end of the Weimar Republic, renewed proliferation of horizontally-structured organizations along civil-service ranks shows that the more pluralist model advocated by the DBB could not entirely replace the more class-oriented one promoted by its critics.[131] As we shall see later on, the entire spectrum of organizational problems just discussed would, at certain junctures, impair the DBB's freedom of maneuver and decrease its effectiveness as a peak association.

A few words must be said about another potential source of organizational strife: the DBB's relations with the German trade union movement. As is well known, the German labor movement, including its trade union wing, was at that time deeply divided along political-ideological and religious lines. The trade unions in particular were split into so-called *Richtungsgewerkschaften,* whose origins date well back in the middle of the Nineteenth Century.[132] In 1919 there existed three major federations of labor: (1) the Socialist or "Free" Unions, united in the General German Federation of Labor (Allgemeiner Deutscher Gewerkschaftsbund or ADGB). With more than seven million members in 1919, the ADGB was by far the largest of the three federations. Politically, the Free Trade Unions stood close to the parties of the left, i. e. the Majority Social Democrats (MSPD) and the Independent Socialist (USPD). A smaller minority later on adhered to the German Communist Party (KPD) as well. (2) The Catholic (or Christian) Trade Unions, who were close to the Center Party and in late 1919 had merged in the German Federation of Labor (Deutscher Gewerkschaftsbund or

[131] In early 1923, for example, a horizontally-structured Reichsbund der oberen Beamten was formed, which claimed to represent the interests of some 80,000 *obere Beamte,* i. e. civil servants in the upper reaches of the middling grades or entry levels of the higher grades (pay groups VII to XII). Its request to be recongnized as a separate negotiator was denied by the Reich Interior Ministry, however, after consultation with the other peak associations. There is some documentation on this in ZStAP, RMdI, 2739, Bl. 302, 313, 353, 359—360. In the late 1920s a second, then more successful attempt was made to found a peak association of this type.

[132] If one disregards its obvious ideological bent, the most complete survey of the history of the German trade union movement is Frank Deppe et al. (eds.), *Geschichte der deutschen Gewerkschaftsbewegung,* Cologne 1977.

DGB). In early 1919 the Catholic unions could claim to represent a little more than one million blue-collar workers. (3) The so-called Hirsch-Duncker Unions (Verband Deutscher Gewerkvereine or H.-D.), who had close ties to the German liberal parties. As the smallest of the three federations, the Hirsch-Duncker unions could merely claim 200,000 blue-collar workers as members in early 1919.[133]

While before 1914 the three federations of labor had primarily tried to organize blue-collar workers *(Arbeiter)*, during and after the First World War they had stepped up their efforts to recruit salaried employees *(Angestellte)* and, to a lesser degree, civil servants *(Beamte)* as well. With regard to the *Angestellte*, these efforts proved to be successful indeed. By 1921 the German white-collar movement, the *Angestelltenbewegung*, had been separated into the same three political camps that characterized the *Arbeiterbewegung*, i. e. major white-collar unions had allied with either of the three federations of labor. Thus by 1921 the ADGB could claim to represent some 600,000 salaried employees, who were organized in a separate peak association, the General Federation of White Collar Unions (Allgemeiner freier Angestelltenbund or Afa-Bund). The Catholic unions had the allegiance of some 400,000 white-collar workers, who were members in a peak association called General Association of German White Collar Unions (Gesamtverband Deutscher Angestelltengewerkschaften or Gedag). The Hirsch-Duncker unions, finally, had affiliated with the Federation of Salaried Employees (Gewerkschaftsbund der Angestellten or GDA), which had slightly over 300,000 members in 1921.[134]

Labor's appeal to civil servants proved to be more complicated and, on the whole, less successful. The main reasons for this was the founding of the DBB in 1918. Unlike salaried employees, civil servants had managed to unify their movement within a single organizational framework. The existence of the DBB did not, however, preclude attempts by the federations of labor to add a "third pillar" to their

[133] A brief, but useful sketch of the profile of the three federations of labor at the beginning of the Weimar Republic is contained in Ludwig Preller, *Sozialpolitik in der Weimarer Republik*, Düsseldorf 1949 (reprint Kronberg/Taunus 1978), pp. 182—191. Membership references are based on the exact figures given in Dietmar Petzina et al. (eds.), *Sozialgeschichtliches Arbeitsbuch III*, Munich 1978, p. 111.

[134] For a brief profile of the white-collar unions, see, again, L. Preller, *Sozialpolitik* . . ., p. 191 f. Membership figures given here are based on D. Petzina et al. (eds.), *Sozialgeschichtliches Arbeitsbuch* . . ., p. 112. For references to recent *Angestellten* literature, see note 4 on p. 92 above.

respective organization, and to recruit civil servants into a separate civil service branch. These efforts on the part of labor will be a part of our story in the subsequent chapters of this study, thus only some introductory remarks shall be given at this point.

Once the Revolution had given civil servants the right to become members in trade unions, the three labor federations — or their affiliated unions — swiftly proclaimed to organize civil servants as well as blue-collar workers and salaried employees. Their initial efforts in this direction remained limited, though, as was revealed by a governmental survey conducted in 1921 for the purpose of gathering information on civil servant membership in trade unions. Of the three federations of labor, only the Catholic unions had been successful in recruiting civil servants. In its response to the government's query, the DGB claimed a membership of 420,000 civil servants *and* salaried employees; some 200,000 of these were likely to have been civil servants.[135] The DGB was the only labor federation, moreover, which at that point had formed a separate civil service branch, the General Association of German Civil Service Unions (Gesamtverband Deutsche Beamtengewerkschaften or GDB), which was headed by the renegade DBB Director Anton Hoefle.[136] The chief membership reservoir of the GDB was the Christian Railroad Workers' Union (Gewerkschaft Deutscher Eisenbahner or GdE), which had simply been forced to transfer its sizeable civil-servant constituency to the DGB's new civil service branch.[137]

[135] Reich Ministry of the Interior to DBB and other peak organizations, ZStAP, RMdI, 2324, Bl. 298. For the GDB's reply, dated May 7, 1921, see *ibid.*, Bl. 339. The reason for the ministry's initiative was to solve the pressing question of which peak associations should be recognized for negotiating purposes.

[136] The GDB had been founded in December 1919 shortly after the Catholic unions had formed the DGB. Hoefle had apparently been involved in the founding although he was still a director of the DBB at that time. He resigned from this post shortly afterwards to assume the leadership of the GDB. (Cf. *DBB Protocol 1920*, pp. 163, 217.)There is some documentation on the GDB, including its statutes and a civil service program for the Center Party in ZStAP, RhB, 201.

[137] The GDB became the umbrella for associations of all public employees organized by the Catholic unions, i. e. civil servants as well as blue-collar workers and salaried employees in government service. In 1926, however, the civil servant branch of the GDB returned under the wings of the DBB, which dealt a severe blow to the Catholic unions' organizational efforts. The remaining public employees formed the Gesamtverband Deutscher Verkehrs- und Staatsbediensteter, which concluded an organizational pact with the DGB. Cf. Hubert Jipp, *Gesamtverband deutscher Verkehrs- und Staatsbediensteter*, in: *IHG*, vol. 1, p. 608 f. See also the recent major study of the Catholic unions by Michael Schneider, *Die Christlichen Gewerkschaften 1894—1934*, Bonn 1982, esp. pp. 465—478.

This pattern of transferring members to a newly established civil servant branch was likewise used by the Hirsch-Duncker unions, where in 1921 some 30,000 civil servants were registered as members[138] — again predominantly in the federation's railroad organization, the General Association of Railwaymen (Allgemeiner Eisenbahnerverband or AEV). Later on, the Hirsch-Duncker unions, too, established a separate civil service branch, the Ring Deutscher Beamtenverbände (RDB).[139] Finally, there were the Socialist "Free" Trade Unions. The ADGB did not respond to the government's query regarding civil servant membership, but it can be ascertained from other sources that in contrast to its eight million members (i. e. blue-collar workers and salaried employees) the Free Trade Unions' appeal to civil servants had remained negligible, to say the least. According to one source, 80,000 civil servants were paying members in the ADGB's railroad union, the German Association of Railwaymen (Deutscher Eisenbahnerverband or DEV) in 1919.[140] Other ADGB affiliates, especially those unions organizing blue-collar workers in the public sector, might have had a small civil service constituency as well,[141] but on the whole the ADGB did not actively recruit civil servants at that point. Partially, this was the result of an understanding with the DBB not to interfere with the latter's organizational efforts. From the perspective of the ADGB, the rationale behind this policy of non-interference was the aim to draw the DBB into the camp of the Free Trade Unions "wholesale," so to speak, i. e. as its "third pillar" representing civil servants. This policy and the resulting tensions in the relationship between ADGB and DBB will become a major focus of this study and thus will be discussed later on in

[138] This figure was given in the H.-D. unions' reply to the government survey mentioned in note 135 above (ZStAP, RMdI, 2324, Bl. 341). Insisting that its civil service membership was increasing rapidly, the RDB asked the ministry to keep this figure in "strictest confidentiality."

[139] Cf. *Freiheitlich-nationaler Kongreß des Gewerkschaftsrings deutscher Arbeiter-, Angestellten- und Beamtenverbände, 27—29. November 1920 in Berlin,* n. p. n. d. (Berlin 1920), pp. 99—102, which is a speech on civil service matters delivered by AEV Chairman Hugo Scaruppe. See also Wolfgang Schröder/Gerd Haferstroh, *Verband der deutschen Gewerkvereine (Hirsch-Duncker) (VDG) 1869—1933,* in: D. Fricke et al. (eds.), *Die bürgerlichen Parteien...,* vol. 2, pp. 684—710.

[140] K. R. v. Scherf, *Die Entwicklung der Beamtenbewegung...,* p. 123.

[141] These were the Verband der Gemeinde- und Staatsarbeiter and the Deutscher Transportarbeiterverband, which then organized postal employees. See F. J. Furtwängler, *ÖTV...,* pp. 307—327, 337—343, who does not provide membership figures, however. See also H. Potthoff, *Gewerkschaften...,* pp. 58—66.

more detail.[142] Suffice it to say at this juncture that even the rather limited civil-servant membership garnered by the ADGB and the two other labor federations qualified them in the eyes of the governmental bureaucracy to be consulted in civil service matters along with the "pure" civil servant peak associations, the DBB and, later on, the Federation of Higher Civil Servants (RhB).[143]

With this observation we have reached the second "conclusion of an ongoing struggle" brought about by the revolutionary events of 1918/19, i. e. the recognition of civil servant associations as representatives of civil servant interests and their acceptance as negotiating partners in matters concerning civil service policy. Both of these were, of course, preconditions for the associations' entry into full-fledged interest group politics, and it is to the relationship between civil servant interests, the government, and the political parties in the early Weimar Republic to which we shall now turn in the concluding section of this chapter.

Government, Parliament, and Civil Servant Interests (II): From Recognition to Representation

Given the impressive stature of the newly-founded DBB as the peak association of the German *Beamtenschaft*, it is not surprising that the revolutionary governments in Germany soon recognized the DBB as the main, although, as has been shown, not the only representative of civil servant interests. Previously, the revolutionary regimes established in Prussia and the Reich had quite explicitly confirmed the civil servants' full right of coalition,[144] although the question whether this implied the right to strike as well remained unclear and became one of the most controversial issues in the early Weimar period.[145] In any case,

[142] Cf. CHAPTER FIVE below.

[143] See the document cited in note 135 above.

[144] In the famous "Proclamation to the German People" issued by the Council of People's Commissars on November 12, 1918. It declares: „Das Vereins- und Versammlungsrecht unterliegt keiner Beschränkung, auch nicht für Beamte und Staatsarbeiter." *RGBl.* 1918, p. 1303.

[145] This will become more evident in the further context of this study. The most exhaustive treatment of the subject matter from a legal perspective is Ludwig Bendix, *Das Streikrecht der Beamten*, Berlin 1922, where many of the relevant official pronouncements are reprinted. Bendix was one of the few German jurists in support of a *limited* right to strike for civil servants.

however, the Revolution precipitated the formal recognition of civil servant interest organizations as negotiators in civil service affairs. Thus a major source of conflict between civil servants and the state as employer — a conflict which, as we had seen, had preoccupied the organizations during the war years — had become history, so to speak, with one stroke of the pen.[146]

Given the openness of a revolutionary situation, it is not surprising that civil servant leaders were not just interested in gaining recognition for their associations, but also used the hour of political transition to see to it that lines of influence to the governmental and political-parliamentary spheres would be established and, if possible, institutionalized within the socio-political structure of the new "people's state" of Weimar. In the critical days of the November Revolution the DBB pursued a double strategy in establishing links to the new political system as it was being formed. One strategy was to penetrate the high ministerial bureaucracy in an effort to move closer to the decision-making process relevant to the interests of its members, i. e. in the area of civil service policy. This strategy was connected with several attempts undertaken by the DBB to press for the creation of a National Civil Service Ministry. The second strategy was to intensify earlier efforts at gaining representation within the parliamentary sphere by establishing closer links with political parties. Here the obvious target was to influence legislation once it had reached the parliamentary level. Both strategies will now be considered briefly in their historical setting.

The Quest for a Civil Service Ministry

As envisioned by civil servant leaders, the vehicle for a more permanent representation of civil servant interests in the realms of high-policy making was to be some kind of central authority for civil service affairs, preferably a National *(Reich)* Civil Service Ministry.

From the perspective of the organizations, the centralization of the highly *de*centralized government agencies active in civil service policy

[146] This is not to say, however, that recognition led to immediate acceptance as partners in consultation and negotiation. This process would only be achieved in the wake of the interest struggles conducted by the DBB in the subsequent weeks and months. Even the terms and mechanics of negotiation — which organization would represent whom, when, and where — was ultimately the endpoint of a longwinded, bureaucratic process that extended over a number of years. Documentation on this in ZStAP, RMdI, 2324 and 2325.

made good sense indeed.[147] Not only would the central civil servant organization, i. e. the DBB, be able to negotiate with only *one* central government agency in important civil service matters instead of having to deal with a multitude of different ministries and government agencies, but there were additional expectations that a civil service ministry would be staffed with "experts" from within the organizations themselves and thus become a useful tool of civil servant interests.

Requests for a central agency, board, or ministry for civil service affairs surfaced immediately after the collapse of the old regime. On November 11, 1918, Remmers telegraphed "Reich Chancellor" Ebert, asking his permission to form a central civil service council *(Beamtenrat)* in support of the new government.[148] No council of this type was ever formed, but the notion that only a *central* civil service agency could deal effectively with the pressing social and economic problems faced by the *Beamtenschaft* persisted. In their first post-Revolution declaration, issued on November 14, the major civil servant associations led by Remmers' Interessengemeinschaft demanded the creation of a special "*Reichsamt*" for civil service affairs.[149] About a week later, on November 25, Remmers formally petitioned the Council of People's Commissars to establish a "Central Authority for Civil Service Questions" *(Zentralstelle für Beamtenfragen).*[150] The next steps taken in the matter are not as well documented. Remmers himself recalls in his memoirs that during a crucial meeting with Ebert — which took place either on November 13 or November 14 — the influential Majority

[147] In contrast to other highly industrialized and bureaucratized countries, Imperial Germany did not possess a central ministry, department, or supervisory body for civil service matters. In Prussia, for instance, several ministries had been active in civil service affairs, often conducting a rather independent social and civil service policy for their administrative jurisdiction. The Ministry of Public Works is a good case in point. At the Reich level, the Ministry of Posts is a similar case. Nominally, the Reich Office of the Interior was the "classic" *Beamtenministerium* before and after 1918. However, matters of pay were negotiated in the Reich Finance Ministry (after 1918) or in the relevant *Ressorts* (i. e., Reich Transport Ministry, Reich Ministry of Posts) for the mass of the *Betriebsbeamte.*

[148] Remmers to Ebert, November 11, 1918, ZStAP, RMdI, 2738, Bl. 193. Ebert had by then already resigned as the last "Imperial" Chancellor, of course.

[149] *Erklärung der Deutschen Beamtenschaft,* in: ZStAP, RMdI, 2164, Bl. 22, reprinted also in *DBR,* November 16, 1918. A "Reichsamt" was the equivalent to a ministry in Imperial Germany.

[150] Interessengemeinschaft (Remmers) to Council of People's Commissars, November 22, 1918, ZStAP, 2165, Bl. 21.

Social Democrat agreed to give the matter "favorable consideration," while the ranking Independent Social Democrat of the Council of People's Commissars, Hugo Haase, allegedly even went one step further and reportedly said, "This we can do."[151] Nothing was done, however, prior to the convening of the Constituent National Assembly. In early February of 1919, Remmers, now a vice-chairman of the National Assembly's Civil Service Committee, tried to use his newly-acquired political power to bring the matter to a decision. The best he could do, however, in a series of talks with the new Reich Minister of the Interior, Hugo Preuss — who like Remmers was a member of the Democratic Party — was to attain a promise that a special "Section for Civil Service Affairs" (a *Referat*) would be created within the Reich Ministry of the Interior.[152] The final decision that such a *Referat* would indeed be organized must have been made by mid-February, 1919. In the list of "Principal Demands," presented by the DBB to the Reich government on February 28, 1919, the proposal for a Civil Service Ministry has been dropped — an indication perhaps that a compromise had been reached on this issue.[153]

The initiative undertaken by the organizations had paid off. To be sure, their request for a National Civil Service Ministry had been denied by the Reich government. As Remmers recalls, financial considerations and the objections of the South German States, which were always fearful of centralization tendencies that would encroach upon their rights and prerogatives, played a role in the Reich government's decision against a separate ministry.[154] To some degree, however, Remmers' account offers more excuses than explanations. The failure of the quest for a civil service *ministry* also shows that the political influence of the DBB was still limited in early 1919 and no match to the political leverage of the labor unions, whose successful drive for a Reich Labor Ministry had originally provided the model for the DBB's initiative.[155]

[151] See E. Remmers, *Die organisatorische Einheit...*, pp. 11—42. Remmers' rationale for a civil service ministry is revealing. Why should not a civil service ministry be placed alongside the planned ministry of labor of the *Arbeiterschaft,* he told Ebert.

[152] This decision is mentioned on a handwritten marginal note on the back of the document cited in note 149 above.

[153] DBB to Reich government, February 28, 1919, ZStAP, RMdI, 2183, Bl. 47.

[154] E. Remmers, *Die organisatorische Einheit...*, p. 42.

[155] On the Labor Ministry, see the discussion in CHAPTER ONE, p. 40 above.

The considerable gap between what had been demanded by the DBB and what had been conceded by the government was closed somewhat by the latter's willingness (upon the DBB's insistence) that a DBB representative should head the new civil service section in the Reich Interior Ministry. No one less than Albert Falkenberg, then one of the DBB's two executive directors, was singled out for the job. The decision to send Falkenberg into the ministry, where he was to act as the DBB's agent in the high ministerial bureaucracy, was taken by the DBB executive board on March 8, 1919.[156] At first, Falkenberg had some reservations about accepting the new post. According to his own testimony, he was not entirely happy about leaving the civil servant movement, a movement which he himself had helped to build. Furthermore, he predicted quite correctly that the main problem with his new job would be to assert himself vis-à-vis the conservative, established ministerial buraucracy. With some reluctance, therefore, Falkenberg assumed his new post in the ministry in April of 1919.[157]

Falkenberg's appointment is a classic example of interest-group attempts to increase the leverage on policy making by means of personal representation.[158] Viewed from the government's perspective, it reflected a trend prevailing in post-revolutionary Germany of appointing "experts" to important political and administrative positions.[159] In a sense, there was a certain amount of experimentation involved in these appointments, because they were based on the assumption that "experts from the field" would function better in such post than traditionally-trained career civil servants. On the other hand, an entire bundle of conflicts were built into such experiments. Not only were career civil servants unhappy about what they regarded political ap-

[156] E. Remmers, *Die organisatorische Einheit...*, p. 42.

[157] *DBB Protocol 1919*, p. 32, and A. Falkenberg, *Die deutsche Beamtenbewegung...*, pp. 103—104. In some respects, Falkenberg's elevation to a high civil service post at the ministerial level was quite an advance for a man who had started out as a lower-ranked postal official. Details on Falkenberg's civil service career between 1919 and 1921 can be gleaned from his personal file in the Reich Ministry of the Interior, now kept in ZStAP, RMdI, PA/267.

[158] Remmers' election to the National Assembly was an obvious complement; see below, pp. 152—153.

[159] A list of similar appointments of "experts" in other ministries would, no doubt, be quite long. A celebrated case is the appointment of Colonel Koeth to head the Demobilization Office in 1918—19. On this see G. D. Feldman, *Economic and Social Problems...*, pp. 7—8 and *passim.*

pointments, the appointees themselves often had difficulty in bringing their governmental work into line with their former, and all too often, continuing role as interest-group representatives. Falkenberg is a good case in point. His influence on civil service policy remained rather limited. He hardly asserted himself against the other senior officials in the Interior Ministry, especially vis-á-vis his immediate superior the ultra-conservative State Secretary Lewald.[160] Furthermore, he seemed uncomfortable during negotiating sessions with his former associational colleagues, even more so, perhaps, since he still held the position of a DBB vice-chairman.[161] But it was above all his limited influence on the formulation of civil service policy which bothered him and the DBB.[162]

In the wake of the political turmoil unleashed by the abortive Kapp putsch of March 1920, the DBB later on made a second bid for a new government agency to handle civil service matters. The DBB, whose position had been strengthened by its participation in the general strike which had brought down the Kapp regime, demanded that a separate Department of Civil Service Affairs *(Reichsamt für Beamtenfragen)* be created within the Reich Ministry of the Interior. The new department would be under the direct supervision of the minister; its head, presumably Falkenberg, would have the rank of a deputy state secretary *(Unterstaatssekretär)*. The DBB claimed that only such an organizational restructuring and upgrading of the existing *Beamtenreferat* would guarantee its "decisive influence on civil service policy as well as on general economic and social policy."[163]

[160] The considerable frictions which existed between Falkenberg and "Excellenz Lewald" are documented in Falkenberg's personal file. In February 1920, for example, Lewald demanded an explanation from Falkenberg why he had left the Democratic Party to join the SPD (ZStAP, RMdI, PA/267, Bl. 12). At several occasions, Lewald demanded written statements on Falkenberg's activities as a DBB leader (*ibid.*, Bl. 13).

[161] One gains this impression when reading the protocols and minutes of meetings in which Falkenberg presided or participated. There are a number of these, relating to the institutionalization of the *Beamtenräte* as *Beamtenausschüsse* in: BA, R 43I/2630, and on the problem of economic self-help organizations of the *Beamte* in BA, R 43I/2634. Obviously, Falkenberg had been put in charge of these two policy matters.

[162] A notable exception is the question of the *Beamtenausschüsse.* Here Falkenberg's influence might have played a role in pushing through the DBB's concept of assigning a *limited* function to these committees, which the DBB regarded as organizational rivals. Documentation on this matter in GStA, Rep. 90, 470. See also A. Falkenberg, *Die deutsche Beamtenbewegung...*, pp. 111—115.

[163] DBB to Bauer, March 24, 1920, demanding talks on the subject and forwarding an

Once again, however, the DBB failed to reach its objective. Although the Reich government entered into negotiations with the interest organization, and Falkenberg's promotion to the rank of an acting *Ministerialdirektor* as the head of a somewhat enlarged civil service section was finally agreed upon,[164] the idea of establishing a semi-separate agency failed, again, in part, because of massive opposition of the *Länder.* On July 9, 1920 the Reichsrat rejected the creation of an independent civil service department within the Reich Ministry of the Interior. "While the political demands of workers and salaried employees have always found the support of the government" the DBB's *Gemeinschaft* wrote, "civil servants have once again been rebuked."[165] Not least because of this renewed defeat, Falkenberg's position in the ministry had become shaken. Several months later, in April 1921, the DBB and the government agreed to withdraw Falkenberg from the ministry.[166] Falkenberg's departure was a tacit admission on the part of the DBB that its strategy of exerting influence on civil service policy by means of *direct* representation in the policy making process had not worked out as well as had originally been anticipated in the days immediately after the Revolution.

The DBB and the Political Parties of the Weimar Republic

In any given parliamentary system of government, a second important addressee of interest pressures is the political party system and the parliamentary sphere in general. Civil servant interest organizations in Weimar Germany were no exception to this rule, in fact the relationship between the DBB and the political-parliamentary sphere offers a splendid illustration of just how intrinsic and effective a network of cross-connections between interest group and the body politic can be. In the following pages, a (necessarily brief) analysis of the emergence of these cross-connections and their early application in the civil servants' quest to protect their social privileges will be given.

organizational plan for the proposed Department of Civil Service Affairs, BA, R 43I/990, Bl. 2—12.

[164] Minutes of the meeting in *ibid.*, Bl. 21.

[165] *DG*, July 16, 1920. The (unsigned) article was probably written by Falkenberg himself, who still functioned as the editor in chief of the *Gemeinschaft.*

[166] ZStAP, RMdI, PA/267, Bl. 26, which is Falkenberg's notice of intent to quit his government job. It clearly emerges from this document that the DBB wanted to withdraw Falkenberg from the Ministry.

As has been mentioned already, the establishing of links between interest organizations and political parties may be viewed as one essential element for the conduct of an effective type of interest politics for any social group. Attaining influence in the parliamentary sphere is particularly important in the case of civil-servant interest politics, however, since much of civil service policy, including the all-important area of salary policy, is subject to legislative action and parliamentary approval.[167] Already the leaders of the Interessengemeinschaft had been well aware of this interdependence and had tried to establish closer ties to some of the political parties of the Empire.[168] It stands to reason that in the parliamentary state of Weimar interconnections between the newly-founded DBB and the partially restructured party system would be a matter of great urgency and concern to civil servant leaders once the threat of a council democracy had been averted and a National Constituent Assembly was about to be elected.[169] DBB leaders did not have to start from scratch, however. At closer scrutiny, lines of continuity in the relationship between the wartime peak association, the Interessengemeinschaft, and the postwar one, the DBB — and thus between the wartime and postwar political arenas — appear. These continuities help to explain the amazing speed with which the DBB was able to occupy key positions in the political-parliamentary structure of the new republican state of Weimar.

The most illuminating example by far is provided by Ernst Remmers, the DBB's founder and first chairman. In the Empire a leading member of the Progressive Party, Remmers became a member of the circle of left-liberals who in 1919 founded its Weimar successor, the German Democratic Party (Deutsche Demokratische Party or DDP).[170]

[167] Political scientists interested in contemporary public sector politics maintain that what they call "the legislation model" of wage policy is especially susceptible to interest pressures, since normal collective bargaining procedures do not exist. Cf. Berndt Keller, *Determinants of Wage Rates in the Public Sector: The Case of Civil Servants in the Federal Republic of Germany*, in: *British Journal of Industrial Relations*, 19 (1981), pp. 345—360.

[168] See pp. 118—119 above.

[169] On the pivotal importance of the National Assembly in the DBB's political tactics during the revolutionary period, see Albert Falkenberg, *Die Nationalversammlung*, in: *DG*, January 1, 1919. The DBB had sent a list of candidates of its own choice to represent civil service interests in the assembly. Reported in *DG*, January 16, 1919.

[170] See Lothar Albertin, *Liberalismus und Demokratie am Anfang der Weimarer Republik*, Düsseldorf 1972. See also Werner Stephan, *Aufstieg und Verfall des Linksliberalismus 1918—1933. Geschichte der Deutschen Demokratischen Partei 1918—1933*, Göttingen 1973, and Reinhard Opitz, *Der deutsche Sozialliberalismus*, Cologne 1973.

Remmers was subsequently elected to the National Assembly as a DDP deputy, where he served as the vice-chairman of the assembly's civil service committee. His election had been financially supported by the DBB, and he made no secret of his associational connection.[171] Links between DBB and DDP were not confined to the person of Remmers alone, however. One of the first proclamations issued by the DDP's civil service section in early 1919 bears his signature as well as those of Albert Falkenberg, who would later switch to the (M)SPD, Fritz Winters, a member of the DBB's leadership circle, and Wilhelm Flügel, later the long-time chairman of the DBB, as members of the DDP's Civil Service Committee.[172]

While the relations between the DBB and the Democratic Party were particularly close — and continued to be so throughout the history of the Weimar Republic — it must be remembered that the DBB espoused a policy of non-affiliation with any single party and was thus interested in establishing links to the entire political spectrum of Weimar politics, with the sole exception of the extreme left and, later on, the extreme right. One way to achieve this goal was to pressure political parties into coopting prominent DBB members into advisory boards and internal party committees, usually those that dealt with civil service matters.[173] Parties with an expressed interest-group character like the DDP and, above all, its right-liberal rival, the German People's Party (Deutsche Volkspartei or DVP) were particularly susceptible to such pressures. In the period immediatly after its founding, the DBB's connections to the DVP were established and maintained with the help of the BhB, an

[171] The DBB had given the sum of 10,000 marks to promote his candidacy (*DBB Protocol 1919*, p. 144). In the Assembly's directory, Remmers' profession was given as „Vorsitzender des Deutschen Beamtenbundes." (Reported by *DBR*, March 16, 1919).

[172] There is a membership list entitled *Mitglieder des Demokratischen Beamtenausschusses*, in ZStAP, RhB, 196, Bl. 27, which contains the names of Falkenberg, Winters and Flügel. In fact, of the eleven names listed, ten could be identified as leading members of civil servant associations. The way the coopting was done also emerges from documents in this file. On March 29, 1919, for example, the Federation of Higher Civil Servants (BhB) proposed a candidate for the committee (*ibid.*, Bl. 28), who then promptly appears on the list as a committee member. In the cover letter for the list (DDP to BhB, May 23, 1919, *ibid.*, Bl. 26) the DDP informed the BhB of its selection and requested that, for the time being, the list should be kept strictly confidential. The incident shows how promptly a party (here the DDP) responded to a civil servant organization's request for representation on internal party committees.

[173] It may well be assumed that the methods employed by the DBB were similar to those just described in note 172 above.

organization which had very close contacts to this party. The BhB's founding chairman, Thiele, was a member of the DVP's central committee, and he was apparently the co-author of the DVP's first civil service program.[174] Other leading BhB members were members of the DVP's committee on civil service affairs and, at the same time, held important positions in the DBB. For example, one Dr. Tapfer, a high postal official *(Postrat)*, was at the same time a member of the BhB executive, a DBB vice chairman, and a member of the DVP's civil service committee. Privy Councillor Hüfner, the chairman of the DBB's important committee on legal affairs, likewise held important functions in the BhB and the DVP.[174a]

But even those parties that were based on an ideology or religious appeals, like the Social Democrats (SPD) and the Catholic Center Party, later on appointed civil service experts to committees dealing with civil service matters; these experts were often, although not always, members of the DBB's inner leadership circle.[175] Both parties also had to accomodate the leaders of the civil servant branch of their own respective trade union movements, which precluded the type of exclusive influence exercised by the DBB on the two Liberal parties. In the right-wing German National People's Party (Deutschnationale Volkspartei or DNVP) the DBB's influence was initially rather limited and held in check by agrarian interests, who were certainly no friends of the *Beamte* or their organizations. Only later on were some lines of influence established with the help of some of the DBB's more conservative regional associations in the East Elbian provinces.[176]

[174] The fact that there is an edited version of this program in ZStAP, RhB, 193, Bl. 59, would support this conclusion.

[174a] All this emerges from the minutes of the DVP's civil service committee for 1919, which are likewise kept in the RhB file (!) just cited in note 174 above. On the DVP's relations to civil service interests, see also Lothar Döhn, *Politik und Interesse. Die Interessenstruktur der Deutschen Volkspartei*, Meisenheim 1970, pp. 245—273.

[175] After his switch to the (M)SPD in 1920, Falkenberg was the DBB's chief representative on the (M)SPD's civil service advisory board *(Reichsbeamtenbeirat)*. Max Lange, the DBB's chairman in 1919/20 and afterwards one of the peak association's managing directors, likewise had a seat on this board. The DBB's main contact to the Center Party was, initially, Anton Hoefle. After Hoefle's departure to the Catholic trade unions, Hubert Lenz, a leading official in a postal organization and as of 1924 one of the DBB's vice chairmen, took over this function.

[176] Both DNVP experts on civil service matters, the Reichstag deputies Schmidt-Stettin and Deglerk, were members of the DBB, although neither one held a very prominent position in the interest organization. Schmidt-Stettin played a role in the

Another method used by the DBB in its dealings with political parties was to insure that the political profile of its inner leadership circle was varied enough, i. e. that it extended from the moderate right to the moderate left of Weimar Germany's political spectrum. Admittedly, this was also a reaction to *internal* pressures and the search for an often precarious political balance within a "neutral" organization.[177] There was, however, a kind of windfall profit to be gained from establishing such a political equilibrium, since leading members of the DBB (i. e. members of its executive board or council) could function as a liaison to the leadership of their respective political parties. In the latter capacity, DBB members often became delegates to parliamentary bodies, although interestingly enough these delegates tended to be drawn from the second rank of the DBB leadership once Remmers had lost his seat in the Reichstag.[178]

Finally, the DBB was represented in Weimar Germany's innovative (if by and large powerless) "economic parliament," the Preliminary Reich Economic Council (Vorläufiger Reichswirtschaftsrat or RWR), established in 1920. Of sixteen seats apportioned there to civil servants and to the free professions, the DBB together with its economic organization, the Beamtenwirtschaftsbund (BWB), were allowed to fill five. Repeatedly, the DBB tried to increase its representation in the RWR, although these moves were blocked by the government bureaucracy and thus remained unsuccessful.[179]

DBB's provincial association of Pomerania, Deglerk was the chairman of a local railroad association in Breslau. Other lines of influence were, again, established with the aid of the more conservative BhB. On this, there is some documentation in ZStAP, RhB, 195.

[177] This emerges, among other things, from the elections of the DBB's executive board, which in the early years of the peak association's history were accompanied by severe internal strife along political (as well as social) lines. See, for example, the elections in May 1920 (*DBB Protocol 1920,* p. 144), where Anton Hoefle is reelected to one of the directorships amidst oubursts of "political plot" *(politische Mache)* from the floor.

[178] Otto Schuldt, the chairman of the GDEB/RG between 1919 and 1922 is a good case in point. A Reichstag deputy for the DDP and one of his party's main spokesmen on civil service matters, Schuldt never held a high-level post in the DBB. After 1920 there seems to have been a certain division of labor, therefore, between the DBB's inner leadership circle on the one hand, and its parliamentary contacts on the other hand. Schuldt himself was instrumental in furthering such a *Arbeitsteilung,* which, of course, implied that a certain amount of independence would be given to interest-group representatives in parliamentary bodies. See his article *Beamtenpolitik in den Parlamenten,* in: E. Remmers/A. Falkenberg (eds.), *Beamten-Handbuch...,* pp. 31—38.

[179] In 1921, for example, the Reich Economics Ministry quite emphatically rejected a demand for increased representation made by the DBB with the argument that other

The overall picture that emerges of the DBB's corporatist connections in the early Weimar years is that of an interest organization well connected to the centers of governmental, bureaucratic, partisan, and parliamentary power. Improved relations to the other federations of blue-collar workers and salaried employees increased the DBB's leverage even further.[180] If speed is any indication of success, therefore, the DBB's quickness in establishing the all-important lines of influence between 1919 and 1920 was a successful operation indeed. A brief glance at one of the DBB's first victories as an interest organization, the protection of the the civil servant's so-called "well-earned rights", may serve as an example that these lines of influence could indeed become operative as soon as they were established.

The Defence of "Well-earned Rights": Interest Politics and Revolution

The November Revolution presented an entire set of problems to civil servant leaders regarding the social position of their constituents. This was the case especially in the earlier stages of the Revolution, when for a brief moment at least the very existence of the civil service, and hence the survival of the *Beamtenschaft* as legally and socially privileged group seemed at stake. From the perspective of civil servants and their organizations, the commitment of the revolutionary forces to a former prop of the old regime was doubtful at best and could not be taken for granted.[181] The protection of pension claims and security of employ-

social and economic groups could follow suit, which in turn would lead to a general reorganization of the RWR. Reich Ministry of Economics to Reich Chancellor, November 8, 1921, copy in ZStAP, RMdI, 2739, Bl. 142.

[180] It was again Ernst Remmers who was instrumental in establishing better contacts to the Socialist Free Trade Unions, although Falkenberg likewise had good contacts to leading members of the Socialist trade union movement, e. g. to Rudolf Wissell, the later Minister of Economics and Minister of Labor. This emerges from a letter sent by Falkenberg to Wissell on February 8, 1919 (GStA, Rep. 470, Bl. 182—184), in which he refers to their pre-1918 cooperation. In the letter itself, Falkenberg urged Wissell to accept the DBB as the representative of the democratic, progressive currents whithin the *Beamtenschaft*, opposed to the conservative *Geheimratsbürokratie*, which had misused the civil-servant-council concept to undercut the DBB's influence. On Remmers' contacts to Legien, the head of the Free Trade Unions, see E. Remmers, *Die organisatorische Einheit...*, pp. 58—64, where the correspondence between the two men in late 1918/early 1919 is reproduced.

[181] Ebert's often-quoted proclamation to the civil servants of November 9, 1919 *(An die deutsche Beamtenschaft)*, in which he asked civil servants to remain at their posts

ment, the civil servants' often-cited "well-earned rights" *(wohlerworbene Rechte)* became a matter of highest priority, therefore, in the days and weeks immediately following the collapse of the old regime. It entailed, of course, a struggle for the continued existence of the traditional concept of the German career civil service, the *Berufsbeamtentum.*[182] In this struggle Ernst Remmers was to play a major role, who skillfully used his associational position as DBB chairman and his influential parliamentary position as vice-chairman of the National Assembly's Committe on Civil Service Affairs to achieve the goals set by the DBB.

In mid-February of 1919 Remmers approached the President of the Reich Ministry (i. e. Reich Chancellor), the Majority Social Democrat Scheidemann, and requested that either a firm guarantee be given by the government regarding the civil servants' special rights, or, better still, a constitutional provision for the protection of the coveted "well-earned rights" would be prepared. Scheidemann's explicit reply that the Reich government had stated repeatedly, civil servants were not about to lose any of the acquired rights and pension claims apparently did not satisfy Remmers.[183] A few days later, the DBB formally asked the government to write civil servant rights into the new constitution.[184] To back up this request, Remmers arranged for a DBB delegation to meet with government leaders and with members of the National Assembly's committee in charge of the drafting of the constitution in Weimar.[185] In the course of this meeting, which took place on March 18, 1919, an agreement was

"until the hour of departure *[Ablösung]* has come," understandably failed to convince civil servants in view of the last mentioned clause. It stands to reason that the conservatively-oriented civil servant press in particular used Ebert's remarks as proof that the Socialists were planning the abolition of the civil service. See *DBR*, November 16, 1918, where the matter is discussed on the front page.

[182] For this reason the struggle for the preservation of the "well-earned rights" hardly ever fails to be mentioned as one of the great successes of civil servant interests politics in the Revolution. See, for example, Hans Hattenhauer, *Geschichte des Beamtentums* (= Handbuch des öffentlichen Dienstes, vol. 1), Cologne 1980, pp. 308—309.

[183] Remmers to Scheidemann, February 20, 1919, BA, R 43I/2551, Bl. 4—5, and Scheidemann to Remmers, February 20, 1919 (draft letter), *ibid.*, Bl. 5. See also A. Falkenberg, *Die deutsche Beamtenbewegung...*, p. 55, where Scheidemann's letter is reprinted.

[184] DBB to Reichsregierung, *Wahrung von Beamtenrechten*, February 28, 1919, ZStAP, RMdI, 2183, Bl. 47.

[185] A detailed account of this meeting is given in *DG*, April 1, 1919. See also E. Remmers, *Die organisatorische Einheit...*, pp. 64—66.

reached between parliamentary leaders, government representatives, and DBB negotiators that a special passage concerning the protection of the civil servants' special rights and privileges would indeed be written into the new constitution. Over the objections of the Weimar Constitution's chief author, Hugo Preuss, who feared that other groups would begin to make similar claims thus turning the constitution into a blueprint for the protection of special interests, the civil servant's "well-earned rights" and with it the continued existence of a career civil service were guaranteed by a constitutional provision.[186] It is not surprising, therefore, that Remmers himself later regarded the role played by the DBB in this matter as the first success of the new peak organization and as a "great victory for the *Berufsbeamtentum.*"[187]

The DBB's performance in the defence of the civil servant's "well-earned rights" was undoubtedly a major success. It showed that the new civil servant peak association was ready and capable to defend the interests of its members. In other words, civil servants had in fact become an interest group — and a most effective one at that. They were ready to face the economic and social struggles which the postwar period of reconstruction and inflation were to bring.

[186] Civil servants' rights were later confirmed in Articles 128 to 131 of the Weimar Constitution. For a reprint of the text and a contemporaneous evaluation, see A. Falkenberg, *Die deutsche Beamtenbewegung*..., pp. 56—58. For a recent appraisal, see H. Hattenhauer, *Berufsbeamtentum*..., pp. 320—328.

[187] E. Remmers, *Die organisatorische Einheit*..., p. 66. See also *DBB Protocol 1919*, pp. 20—21.

CHAPTER THREE

Dividing the Social Costs of War: Postwar Reconstruction and the Emergence of Civil Servant Protest, Spring 1919 to April 1920

"The organization shall be our weapon to hold our own and to triumph in the fierce competition and interest struggles with other groups," Hofrat Blum, a leading member of the DBB, told his colleagues at this organization's first general meeting in May, 1919.[1] Blum's words were both prophetic and a reflection of recent experiences. In the previous weeks, immediately after the November Revolution, the DBB and its member associations had received a first taste of the value of organization in a series of fierce wage struggles in the public sector. In the months to follow, the DBB was to become engulfed in struggles of even greater proportions, struggles which aimed at improving the economic and social position of a *Beamtenschaft* shaken by the combined impact of wartime inflation and the renewed price increases suffered in the immediate postwar period.[2] It was to be a struggle over who was to bear the greater share of the social costs of war, and at whose expense powerful organized groups were able to offset social decline

[1] *DBB Protocol 1919*, p. 36. Hofrat Blum, a leading member of the conservative VDB, was the head of the DBB's section on organizational matters. He used the term *Stände* for groups, by the way.

[2] According to the index compiled by Richard Calwer, the cost of food had risen from 2.48 to 2.87 (1913 = 1) between November 1918 and May 1919. From May to December 1919, the same index rose to 5.08. The rate of increase clearly picks up after July 1919, and intensifies even further in the winter months of 1919—20, reflecting an "inflationary upsurge" in these months. Figures according to C.-L. Holtfrerich, *Die deutsche Inflation...*, p. 42, Table 9, who also provides an informed discussion of the limitations of the Calwer index. For the general economic picture in 1919, see also C. Bresciani-Turroni, *The Economics...*, pp. 29—30, 303—305.

and economic privations suffered during the war years. Wage policy *(Lohnpolitik)* became one of the centers of this conflict, because it was the main vehicle used by the organized working-class to improve the situation of the *Arbeiterschaft.* As the working-class revolution of November 1918 slowly turned into a gigantic wage movement, conducted by the organized working-class and their unions often against the convictions of Socialist-led governments, and as political power and influence were rapidly turned — if not perverted — into group-related economic gains, civil servants, too, were beginning to use their newly-acquired political and social leverage to improve their economic situation. The civil servants' main objective was to arrest, if not reverse, social decline suffered as a consequence of wartime inflation.[3] Their organizations' vehicle to reach this objective was salary policy. It is for this reason that in the spring of 1919 salary policy moved into the foreground of civil servant interest politics once again, after the initial problems of organization, political transition, and social rearrangements brought by the November Revolution had been solved.

This is not to say, of course, that the salary question had played no role at all during the Revolution itself. From the very onset, civil servant organizations had coupled their support of the moderate forces of the Revolution with demands for economic help in an attempt to offset the privations suffered during the war. In their proclamation of November 14, for example, the IG and other leading civil servant organizations had expressed "their confidence that the governments and administrations in Reich, Länder, and municipalities will do their utmost to secure the economic situation of a *Beamtenschaft* that has been hardest hit by the war."[4] About a week later, Remmers had informed the Council of People's Commissars that civil servants expected a comprehensive revision of civil service salary policy.[5] Branch associations and local civil servant organizations had become active in this matter as well. In a letter to the Council of People's Commissars, the Federation of German Municipal Civil Servants pointed out that the revolutionary government was not only obligated to protect acquired civil servant rights and pension claims, but that it should work toward improving the deplorable and demeaning economic situation of the *Gemeindebeamte,* who were "especially hard pressed by the prevailing inflationary conditions" since their pay

[3] Cf. the discussion in CHAPTER TWO of this study, esp. pp. 127—130.

[4] The proclamation of November 14, 1918 is reprinted in *DBR,* November 16, 1918.

[5] Interessengemeinschaft to Council of People's Commissars, November 22, 1918, ZStAP, RMdI, 2165, Bl. 21.

scales had been too low even before the war.[6] A few weeks later the same organization had made very specific proposals for an "appropriate improvement of civil service pay," suggesting that civil service pay scales be tied to the rising cost of living in such a way as to allow for the adjustment of pay to the rate of inflation in shorter intervals. More generous cost-of-living allowances should be paid to civil servants until such time when the principle of automatic adjustment could be implemented as part of a general revision of civil service pay schedules.[7] Similar proposals had been put forward by the Civil Servant Association of Baden, which demanded that civil service pay be realigned to the income levels of "comparable social strata" as well as to the general standard of living,[8] and by the Civil Service Council *(Beamtenrat)* in Hamburg, where the demand for an "adjustment of civil service pay and pensions to the changed economic conditions" ranked second only to the call for the convening of a National Constituent Assembly.[9] Finally, the DBB had demanded a reform of civil service pay and pension scales in its proposals regarding the "Protection of Civil Servant Rights" sent to the Reich government on February 28, 1919.[10]

As indicated by these efforts on the part of the organizations, a sweeping reform of the pay scale soon emerged as a important, if long-range goal of civil servant interest politics during the revolutionary period. This was even more so, because *immediate* success in the question of salary reform was, unlike in the case of the securing of "well-earned rights," not easily to be attained. While it was expensive enough to guarantee social privileges like pensions and life-employment through constitutional provisions, it would be even more costly to raise existing civil service salaries and to tie pay scales permanently to a cost-of-living index. Fiscal considerations by and large precluded the introduction of more flexible pay scales in early 1919. Instead, the new constitutional governments in the Reich and in Prussia, which had been installed after the elections to the constituent assemblies, opted to

[6] Bund Deutscher Gemeindebeamter to Council of People's Commissars, November 19, 1918, ZStAP, RMdI, 2165, Bl. 11.

[7] Forderungen der preußischen Gemeindebeamten und Gemeindeangestellten, in: *RfG,* January 25, 1919.

[8] Forderungen der Beamtenschaft. Aufgestellt vom Verband der Beamten- und Lehrervereine Badens, n. d. (1918), GLAK, 233, 3429.

[9] A copy of these *Forderungen,* which are not dated but obviously were put together before November 15, 1918 is to be found in StAH, 122-4-4, Bd. 2.

[10] DBB to Reich Government, February 28, 1919, ZStAP, RMdI, 2183, Bl. 47.

continue with the method of compensating for changes in the cost of living by increasing the so-called "wartime cost-of-living supplements" *(Kriegsteuerungszulagen)*, a method which had been introduced during the war by the governments of the old regime and which had been continued by the revolutionary regime between November 1918 and January 1919.[11] For this reason, the struggles between civil servant organizations and public employers, especially the Reich and Prussian governments, continued to be a struggle over the "war bonus" even after the war had ended, and over the rationale of what the organizations critically called *Zulagenpolitik* (literally: bonus or supplement policy).[12]

In the long run, these conflicts would not only entail a struggle between civil servants and public employers to compensate for the detrimental impact of wartime and postwar inflation, but also turn into a fierce competition between civil servants and rival social groups over the distribution of the social costs of the war.[13] Lastly, it was to be a

[11] Similar developments occurred in the other former belligerent European countries, where increases in the cost of living led to changes in the formerly rather inflexible structure of civil service pay. See Herman Finer, *The Principles and Practice of Remuneration in the British Civil Service*, in: Wilhelm Gerloff (ed.), *Die Beamtenbesoldung im modernen Staat*, T. 1 (= Schriften des Vereins für Sozialpolitik, vol. 184/1), Munich-Leipzig 1932, pp. 114—117. In the second part of the same publication, see François Perroux, *Beamtenbesoldung in Frankreich...*, pp. 11—24, and Erich Gruber/Richard Pfaundler, *Die Besoldungsverhältnisse der Beamtenschaft und die neuere Entwicklung der Besoldungspolitik in Österreich...*, pp. 126—131.

[12] *Zulagenpolitik* was not only a German phenomenon. In Great Britain, a *Teuerungszulage* was known as the cost-of-living bonus or as the "war bonus" (H. Finer, *The Principles...*, p. 114), in France as "indemnité exceptionnelle du temps de guerre" (F. Perroux, *Beamtenbesoldung...*, p. 20). In both countries, this variable element had been introduced during the war, and payment of these special wartime supplements was continued after the war for a while until structural reforms of the pay scales were undertaken in March 1920 and October 1919, respectively. In Austria, a pay reform was undertaken in March 1920 as well, in which a permanent cost-of-living supplement to base pay was established (E. Gruber/R. Pfaundler, *Die Besoldungsverhältnisse...*, p. 127). This brief comparison shows that the German case, with which we are concerned, was by no means a singular event, but that we are dealing with a structural problem created by wartime inflation in *all* belligerent nations. Naturally, the solutions found in the various countries differed, depending on the special political and economic circumstances which prevailed in each country.

[13] On this, see the perspective remarks made by Anton Golecki in the introduction to *Akten der Reichskanzlei. Weimarer Republik. Das Kabinett Bauer, 21. Juni 1919 bis 27. März 1920*, Anton Golecki (ed.), Boppard 1980, p. LX. (Hereafter the various volumes of this document edition will be cited as *ARK. Kab.* and the name of the cabinet added,

contest between the priorities of fiscal and budgetary policies on the one hand, and the introduction and extension of social-policy measures to the public service sector on the other hand. This explains the enormous social explosiveness which the often rather technical and complicated issue of civil service salary policy produced in 1919 and during the entire inflation period. The conflicts of 1919 brought to the fore the question of the legality of civil servant (and public service) strikes, a question which was to remain one of the most controversial and volatile issues throughout the early years of the Weimar Republic.[14] As will be shown in the following pages, the struggle over the formulation and content of salary policy prompted widespread protest movements within the *Beamtenschaft,* including strike threats and fears of increased political radicalism. These social and political implications of civil service salary policy during the postwar inflationary upsurge of 1919 are the subject of this chapter of our study. We shall begin with a discussion of the first real crisis in salary policy in April 1919 and carry the story up to the spring of 1920, when the German government, with the help of the organizations of civil servants, attempted to stabilize the situation with the enactment of the Salary Reform Act of April 1920.

Toward the First Conflict: The "April Crisis" of 1919 and the Strike Issue

Only ten days after the November Revolution, the new regimes in Prussia and the Reich had granted a cost-of-living increase to civil servants — a small reward for the latter's willingness to support the moderate forces in the internal political and social struggles unleashed by the Revolution.[15] Financially, this pay increase added to the growing bill of postwar social costs which the revolutionary regimes were forced to pay. For Prussia alone the additional expenditure created by the salary supplement totalled some 250 million marks — a considerable sum even for the largest German state, which had just been forced to grant a substantial wage increase to railroad workers. In December 1918

e. g. *ARK. Kab. Bauer.* Full citation of each volume will be provided when first cited.)

[14] Hagen Schulze, introduction to *Akten der Reichskanzlei. Weimarer Republik. Das Kabinett Scheidemann, 13. Februar bis 20. Juni 1919,* Hagen Schulze (ed.), Boppard 1971, p. XL.

[15] This and the following is based on A. Falkenberg, *Die deutsche Beamtenbewegung...,* pp. 76 ff.

railroad workers had been given an additional "demobilization supplement", which soon was extended to lower-ranked civil servants as well. Railroad workers and civil servants were thus paid-off to avoid labor struggles in the key transportation sector during the demobilization of the military forces.[16] A newly-founded railroad civil servant union, the Bund der Beamten der Preussischen Staats- und Reichseisenbahnen (later renamed into Gewerkschaftsbund Deutscher Eisenbahnbeamter, or GDEB) had been instrumental in negotiating the transfer of the special "demobilization bonus" to lesser railroad officials.[17]

It takes little imagination to foresee the net result of granting a special supplement to *one* civil service group. Other groups, especially postal officials, began demanding a similar supplement, causing considerable strife and animosity within the civil servant movement as a whole. Finally, the DBB stepped in. Under its leadership a compromise between the railroad officials and other civil servant groups was hammered out. In March 1919, after a series of "long and difficult negotiations" a new and more uniform pay system was agreed upon. It provided for higher cost-of-living supplements that were differentiated according to the level of base salaries (with higher-paid civil servants receiving less) and according to place of residence or "location". The division of supplements according to location was pushed through by the government against the wishes of the organizations. Government negotiators argued that inflation was having less of an impact in small towns and rural areas; therefore, a classification of "most expensive, expensive, and less expensive" should rule cost-of-living supplements. The organizations opposed such a differentiation out of principle and with the assertion that "less expensive localities" simply did not exist in Germany at that time. The government insisted, however, not least for financial reasons. For Prussia alone, the "March Agreement" of 1919 added 1.3 billion marks to a budget already grown way out of proportions. Any changes in the classification scheme would only add to an already enormous expenditure.[18]

[16] See G. D. Feldman, *Economic and Social Problems of the German Demobilization...*, in: *JMH*, 47 (1975), pp. 16—18 for further details.

[17] See the annual report of this organization for 1919—20, where these developments are discussed in greater detail. Gewerkschaftsbund Deutscher Eisenbahnbeamter, *Geschäftsbericht für die Zeit vom 1. Juli 1919 bis zum 1. Juli 1920*, n. p. n. d. (Berlin 1920), pp. 124—128.

[18] Again, A. Falkenberg, *Die deutsche Beamtenbewegung...*, pp. 77—78 is the source here.

In view of the considerable conflicts that had surfaced in the January/March negotiations and in view of the fragility of the compromise to which the railroad civil servant union (GDEB) had acquiesced only reluctantly, it must be considered a severe tactical mistake on the part of the Prussian government that it decided to revoke the railroad civil servants' demobilization supplement before it was to expire officially on March 31, 1919, and — in an even more controversial and potentially dangerous decision — decreed that the new cost-of-living increase just negotiated would, in the case of railroad civil servants, be reduced by the amount paid previously as demobilization supplements. Almost immediately the GDEB responded with strike threats, setting in motion a sharp confrontation between civil servants and the state, the first one the newly-founded Republic was to face. It brought to the fore the issue of the civil servant's right to strike for the first time, an issue that had been debated in theory,[19] but now would have to be solved in a much more direct and practical way by the Prussian state government, a coalition government led by Majority Social Democrats who were certainly not opposed to the right of strike as such. The problem of public service strikes, however, had not been thought out sufficiently by Social Democrats and Socialist trade unionists, especially as far as strikes involving civil servants were concerned, whose position as *Arbeitnehmer* had long been eclipsed by their status as privileged, but at the same time severely regimented state servants.[20] The struggle between civil servants and the government as employer during the "April Crisis" of 1919 was to become the first of a series of conflicts that would ultimately solve the strike question in a very practical, if painful way.

When the Prussian government revoked the demobilization supplement, the railroad civil servant union reacted swiftly. On March 25, 1919 the GDEB passed a resolution at a meeting in Halle, which demanded the continuation of the bonus until March 31 and, more importantly, the assurance that it would not be deducted from the new cost-of-living increase for the simple reason that it had been granted to railroad civil servants for "special achievements" during the demobili-

[19] See Fritz Winters, *Zur Frage des Streikrechts der Beamten,* Berlin 1919, which presents the official DBB policy toward the civil servant strike and gives a summary of the pros and cons. See also Paul Kamke, *Der Streik der Staatsbeamten. Ein Kampf- und Weckruf,* Frankfurt n. d. (1919).

[20] On the attitude of the labor unions toward public service strikes in 1919, see H. Potthoff, *Gewerkschaften...,* pp. 112—116, 158—168.

zation. The resolution also called for an adjustment of civil servant pay to the allegedly higher wages of railroad workers on the basis of a number of proposals sent by the Civil Service Advisory Council to the Prussian Ministry of Public Works. This council was an elected body and staffed by union officials, among them the chairman of the GDEB, Max Lange, who also was chosen by the Halle delegates to chair the committee that was to negotiate with the Ministry of Public Works. In unmistakable language, the GDEB called on the government to respond to its demands within the next two weeks. If no response was forthcoming, an eight-hour work stoppage would commence. Should the goverment decide to reject the demands outright, a full strike would commence.[21]

This was the first time a German government had been confronted with a strike-threat by its civil servants. The political and economic ramifications of a railroad strike were incalculable and potentially disastrous. Of this the Prussian government had been prewarned by sporadic participation of civil servants in rail strikes called by workers' organizations.[22]

On April 3, the GDEB sent a revised version of its March 25 resolution to the Ministry of Public Works, now headed by Democrat Rudolf Oeser. Apparently this version was more moderate in tone and did not contain an explicit ultimatum.[23] In the meantime, however, senior

[21] *Beschlüsse in Halle*, BA, R 43I/2640, Bl. 4. Hagen Schulze (*ARK. Kab. Scheidemann*, p. 134, note 9) falsely ascribes this document to an „Allgemeiner Eisenbahnerverband". On the whole, Schulze tends to misinterpret the April events as a strike movement among railroad *workers.* On strike movements in the revolutionary period, see Gerald D. Feldman/Eberhard Kolb/Reinhard Rürup, *Die Massenbewegung der Arbeiterschaft am Ende des Ersten Weltkriegs (1917—1920)*, in: *Politische Vierteljahresschrift*, 13 (1972), pp. 84—105.

[22] Shortly before the GDEB had issued its strike resolution, the Prussian Ministry of Public Works had warned the Prussian State Ministry that a strike by railroad officials was imminent. Such a strike was likely to develop into a general transportation strike, the State Secretary in the Ministry of Public Works, Hoff, wrote, because a great number of civil servants were in daily contact with blue-collar workers, whose right to strike was uncontested, and who had in the recent past achieved considerable gains by issuing strike threats. Ministry of Public Works to State Ministry, March 22, 1919, GStA, Rep. 90, 631, Bl. 2.

[23] The April 3 resolution is mentioned in a summary of the GDEB's actions during the April Crisis, prepared by that organization in form of a petition to the Prussian government. Copy in GStA, Rep. 90, 631, Bl. 23—26. See also *Die drohende Kohlenkrise und die Eisenbahnbeamtenschaft*, Berlin 1919, a GDEB publication.

officials in the Ministry of Public Works had drafted a proclamation aimed at outlawing civil servant strikes in Prussia. On April 3, the very day the revised GDEB resolution had been sent to the Public Works Ministry, senior officials of several Prussian and Reich ministries met to discuss the proposed proclamation. The course of this meeting and its impact on the higher political level are instructive to the understanding of the political dimension of public service strikes at this juncture, and thus need to be retold in greater detail.[24]

At the beginning of the meeting the delegates representing the Prussian ministries of the Interior and Culture voiced serious objections to the draft proposal. According to the delegate from the Ministry of Culture, his boss, the Social Democrat Haenisch, felt that Social Democratic ministers should not infringe upon the right to strike of civil servants or any other public employee, since the attainment of this right had been a programmatic demand of Social Democracy before 1918. He then proposed to issue a proclamation to civil servants that would appeal to their sense of duty rather than pushing legalisms. If civil servants went on strike, he argued, the government would eventually be forced to negotiate or even eventually capitulate, which would make things worse than they were now. — Therefore a "softer" proclamation was called for. The representative of the Reich government agreed and warned that the generally tense political situation should not be aggravated even further by a decree of this type. Civil servants should be calmed down by being reminded of the potentially catastrophic consequences of a political turmoil, which would in the end endanger the continued existence of the civil service as an institution. Since other Prussian ministries, especially Public Works and Justice, insisted on the original proposal, however, the matter was deferred to the cabinet for decision.

When the Prussian cabinet met on the following day, the ministers of interior and culture had apparently given up their objections. The cabinet decided that a somewhat softened version of the proclamation should be drawn up jointly by the ministries of Justice and War. The Prussian minister of finance, Südekum, a Social Democrat, made several suggestions concerning the proposed proclamation.[25] It should

[24] Minutes of this meeting in ZStAP, RMdI, Bl. 13 and Bl. 39, the latter the personal notes taken by the Reich government's representative, von Bornstedt. This account is based on both documents.

[25] Minutes of the cabinet meeting in GStAP, Rep. 90, 631, Bl. 10 and Rep. 84 a, 3145,

emphasize, he argued, that the railroad administration had become a deficit enterprise, and that in spite of this development the Prussian government had tried to improve the economic situation of civil servants to the utmost capacity of its financial strength. To a large extent, Südekum told his colleagues, civil servant salaries had to be paid by tax payers "whose income is to no small measure less than that of the *Beamten.*" He pointed out that the civil servants' own representative organization, the DBB, had renounced the civil servant strike officially and that the action taken by the Prussian government therefore only reflected what the vast majority of civil servants themselves felt about this issue — a claim definitely not quite correct as far as the DBB's position was concerened.[26] Südekum's arguments did not fail to impress his colleagues, however. The cabinet unanimously agreed to publish the anti-strike proclamation as fast as possible.

The decree, which was issued three days later on April 7, 1919, followed in its main contours the suggestions made by Südekum. It declared that a striking civil servant was subject to disciplinary punishment since civil service strikes had no legal basis. By proclaiming that "major civil servant organizations were in agreement with the government," the Prussian government obviously tried to divide the civil servant movement over this issue. The extremely tense relationship between the DBB and the GDEB — nominally a DBB affiliate — was well known, and the Prussian government was playing on this inner division of the movement when it emphasized that "those who continued to work in a possible case of a strike would be protected by the state with all its power." To unleash a railroad strike "at a time when the Fatherland is imperiled by dangers from outside and by shortages of food and raw materials" was irresponsible, a "crime against the nation," and a "pernicious struggle against the *Volksgesamtheit.*"[27]

In the following days it looked as if this "pernicious struggle" was indeed to take place. As had been predicted by some more imaginative

Bl. 75. A memo by von Bornstedt in BA, R 43I/2640, Bl. 16, discusses the political implications.

[26] Officially, the DBB acknowledged the strike as the "ultimate trade union weapon" *(letzte gewerkschaftliche Mittel).* However, this weapon was to be used only when the existence or economic survival of the *Beamtenschaft* was at stake. Cf. F. Winters, *Zur Frage des Streikrechts...,* p. 23.

[27] Text of the proclamation in BA R 43I/2640, Bl. 15, and in A. Falkenberg, *Die deutsche Beamtenschaft...,* pp. 59—60. Falkenberg later commented: „Diese Art, Beamtenpolitik zu treiben, kann als glücklich nicht bezeichnet werden." (*Ibid.,* p. 60).

members of the Prussian cabinet, the anti-strike decree merely added fuel to an already explosive situation. Unrest among railroad civil servants grew to most serious proportions. On April 10, the Prussian government met in an emergency session.[28] Oeser, the Minister of Public Works, reported to the cabinet that the situation on the railroads had deteriorated rapidly. He warned that if a railroad strike was conducted simultaneously with a strike by miners in the Ruhr it would lead to a complete standstill of railroad traffic and thus eventually to shortages in raw materials and food supplies. In view of these circumstances, he added, the civil servants' right to strike had to be regarded not as a theoretical, but as a very practical problem, a problem which, moreover, contained an important foreign policy dimension as well: In connection with the return of Polish troops from France to Poland, which the German government had pledged to undertake upon insistence of the Entente powers, the spectre of a transport strike had become a "highly sensitive foreign policy issue." Oeser then offered a solution. He alluded to the fact that even the Social Democrats had once agreed that the right to strike within the railroad service should be curtailed not only for civil servants, but even for wage earners. Opponents of the strike within the civil servant movement, he added, had urgently requested the issuing of guidelines regarding the civil service strike, guidelines that would be stiffer than the Proclamation of April 7.

While Oeser was backed up by the Minister of War, Reinhardt, several cabinet members strongly objected to any further measures on the part of the government. Otto Braun, the Social Democratic Minister of Agriculture (and later longtime Minister President of Prussia) warned that any further public discussion of the strike issue should be avoided lest the strike question itself would become the major issue of confrontation. In spite of these objections, which were shared by other cabinet members as well, Oeser made another attempt to force his point. He argued that in a "socialized enterprise" like the railroads the right to strike might have to be scrapped entirely. He claimed to have the "better cards" in any confrontations with the unions — civil servant and workers — that might result from such a decision. The majority of the cabinet remained unimpressed, however, by this policy of confrontation and decided not to take any further steps.

[28] The following account is based on the official (but brief) minutes in GStA, Rep. 90, 631, Bl. 20, and on a lengthier version in BA, Nachlaß Südekum, 105.

The political alignment in the Prussian cabinet on the strike issue is revealing: The Democrat Oeser, originator and defender of a course of confrontation with railroad civil servant unions, was supported by a military man, the Minister of War Reinhardt, and, tacitly at least, by those ministers most directly involved with civil service matters, i. e. Heine (Interior) and Südekum (Finance), who both belonged to the right wing of the MSPD. The Center Party representatives, am Zehnhoff (Justice) and Stegerwald (Welfare) initially supported Oeser's course, but then backed down by questioning the "psychological impact" of the proclamation. The main opposition came from those MSPD cabinet members who either belonged to the center (Braun, Haenisch) or left wing (Hirsch) of this party.

When on the following day the Reich cabinet met to discuss the issue of civil servant strikes, a similar political alignment surfaced.[29] While the DDP ministers Schiffer (Finance) and Gothein (Treasury) supported Oeser's course in Prussia and argued that a similar declaration should be issued by the Reich government, the Centrist Giesberts criticized the fact that the Prussian government had failed to consult with the Reich on this important matter and had acted in haste by issuing the decree of April 7. Now he, as minister of posts, had come under increased pressure to issue a similar proclamation for his administration. It was Scheidemann, the Social Democratic president of the Reich ministry, who argued most forcefully *against* an anti-strike order for civil servants. He pointed out that in the working class movement the "right of association," which the revolutionary government had just granted to civil servants, was generally held to include the "right to strike." If this right should be denied to civil servants, other means of settling labor disputes in the public sector would have to be found. Scheidemann mentioned arbitration courts in this context, but he hastened to point out that only the scheduled revision of the Civil Service Code could bring clarification on this issue. The Reich cabinet then decided that the minister of posts would try to avoid commenting on the Prussian decree if questioned about it in the Reichstag. Should the issue be forced by the opposition parties, Giesberts was empowered to reply that the strike question would be settled within the framework of the yet-to-be-drafted new Civil Service Code. With this response the Reich cabinet had effectively dodged the issue, a fact that would be-

[29] Cabinet meeting, April 11, 1919, *ARK. Kab. Scheidemann,* p. 153.

come a serious handicap in later disputes between civil servants and the Reich government.

While these discussions had been conducted at the high government levels in Prussia and the Reich, the Prussian minister of public works, Oeser, had continued negotiating with the railroad civil servant union, the GDEB. On April 4, the very day the Prussian cabinet had decided to go forward with the controversial decree, he had met with union leaders and offered a compromise with regard to their demands. The controversial demobilization supplement would not be deducted from the cost-of-living increase for the months of January and February, but only for March. Moreover, this compromise settlement would apply to the technical staffs *(Betriebsbeamte)* only. Oeser refused to make any further concessions and did not inform the GDEB delegation about the Prussian cabinet's decision to issue a strike ban, although this decision had been taken only a few hours before.[30]

Union leaders were therefore taken by complete surprise when the decree was issued three days later. The GDEB called a meeting of its executive council to Berlin, where the delegates met from April 12 to April 14 to map out a counter-offensive. While they welcomed the fact that the government had agreed to compromise on some of the GDEB's demands, they insisted on a *total* fulfillment. No ultimatum was issued, however, which was as a clear signal of the union's willingness to conduct further negotiations. The criticism of the union delegates centered around the notorious decree. They were enraged that the government had issued the decree while still negotiating with the union, and thus had violated established negotiating practices. For a number of other reasons the decree was viewed as unjustified. First, the union claimed that it had not issued a strike threat, a claim that was not entirely correct if the March 25 resolution is taken into consideration. Second, the decree was seen as an attempt to drive a wedge into the *Beamtenschaft* by dividing between officials "willing to work" and those "unwilling to work" in the case of a strike, and thus was a blatant attempt at undercutting union solidarity. Third, the public had been misinformed about the actual content of the GDEB's demands. The government had tried to create the impression that the financial burden of the cost-of-living supplement was a result of railroad civil servant

[30] For this and the following, *Erklärung des Eisenbahnbeamtenbundes,* GStA, Rep. 90, 631, Bl. 24—26.

demands, while actually the economic situation of *all* civil servants was at stake.

With regard to the strike question as such the GDEB did not succumb, although it slightly softened its stance. While insisting that ultimately the union alone would have to decide whether or not to call a strike of railroad civil servants, a partial disclaimer was added:

"The railroad civil servant union realizes that as a representative of the *Beamtenschaft* on the nation's railroads it carries a high amount of responsibility. A strike vote will only be taken in full regard of this responsibility and only if grave circumstances will call for such a step. Furthermore, all other means to reach an agreement, including arbitration, would have to be exhausted first."[31]

Despite moderation in language, however, actions taken by the GDEB conference of delegates seemed to indicate that the test of strength between the union and the government was not yet over. An executive committee was appointed by the delegates, whose task it was to coordinate to GDEB's next steps in its struggle with the government. The committee was comprised of two delegates from the central leadership (among them the union's chairman, Max Lange), and two delegates from its branch affiliates *(Fachverbände)* and its regional districts, respectively. The seventh member, a railroad engineer from Magdeburg, was a member of the Prussian legislative assembly and the GDEB's contact to the parliamentary sphere. The committee's first order of business had been the drafting of the resolution mentioned above, which was hand delivered to the Ministry of Public Works on April 16. It set off a new round of talks between the union and government officials.[32]

In the end the organization prevailed. The Prussian government backed down and reinstated the contested demobilization supplement for all railroad civil servants. On April 26, the Prussian Minister of Finance Südekum informed the legislative assembly's budget committee about the governmental decision, which quite misleading he described as a conciliatory act on the part of the government toward its civil servants. He failed to mention that in fact the government had, for the first time, been *forced* by a civil servant organization to reverse itself on a decision regarding civil service policy. Moreover, the conflict had demonstrated quite clearly that the government as employer had

[31] *Ibid.*
[32] *Ibid.*

gravely underestimated the power of organized civil servants. Südekum did not fail, however, to point out the fiscal implications of public sector wage policy:

"I cannot spend more than what I have. The new cost-of-living increases not only push us to the limits of the state's financial resources, they go well *beyond* the state's financial capabilities. I shall do the utmost to meet civil servant requests, but I shall not be pushed beyond a certain line which I believe to mark the border to financial solvency and of justified demands to the government."[33]

Südekum warned that as a result of the renewed wage increases the Prussian budget deficits would reach unprecedented levels, deficits that could not be met by further loans or new taxes. In the end, he said, all dependent employees would suffer. They would find out soon enough that "money wages" were not "real wages." New price increases, Südekum predicted, would wipe out most of the gains scored by organizational interests in the previous wage and salary movement.[34]

Südekum's course of fiscal austerity might very well have been the sounder way to travel than the "wage revolution" that took place in post-revolutionary Germany in 1919. But wage policy had become a very political, or politicized, matter by that time not only in the private, but also in the public sector of the economy. Economic and fiscal considerations and policies were for this reason only one part of the problem at best. The other part was to carry through these economic arguments politically against an increasingly powerful set of organized interests, who were opposed to the singular wisdom of economic considerations and chose to blackmail the government in order to reach their goals. But to a degree the Prussian government was to be blamed as well. It had not yet fully understood the fact that in the public sector, too, even among the formerly docile *Beamten,* collective bargaining procedures had emerged, which precluded the handling of civil service matters by decree and governmental fiat. By ignoring these changes, the government precipitated social conflicts that were bound to be severe. The strike issue, which had come of age during the April Crisis of 1919, was only a first taste of even greater conflicts that were yet to come.

[33] *DG,* June 16, 1919, a reprint of the official stenographic report.
[34] *Ibid.*

Price Reduction vs. Pay Increases: Salary Policy as a "Motor of Inflation" in mid-1919

The conflict between government and civil servants in the April Crisis of 1919 had been a "partial conflict," so to speak, because only one, albeit a rather militant group of the *Beamtenschaft* had been involved. Railroad civil servants and their organizations continued to be the militant force within the civil servant movement and remained ready to consider the strike as an option for conflict solution even after the DBB had emerged as the chief negotiator in the area of salary policy. Furthermore, the events of April 1919 had demonstrated to all civil servant the power of collective action. Such concessions as were made by the government had proven that the position of public employers was more vulnerable than expected and that, faced with increased militancy on the part of its "servants," the government had apparently become susceptible to interest pressures.

To be sure, some civil servant organizations and their leaders were worried that the reputation of the civil service as an institution and of the *Beamtenschaft* as a group was being impaired by the bargaining over cost-of-living increases and the social tensions connected with it. They also questioned the overall economic usefulness of these increases and claimed that the "excessive wage increases" given to workers in private industry were pushing up production costs and thus price levels, which in turn meant that pay awards were soon overtaken by general price increases. Only a reduction of price and wage levels, they argued, would prevent the further social decline *(Deklassierung)* of the *Beamtenschaft.*[35] But these were minority opinions at best. To the majority of civil servants, especially to the unruly rank-and-file members, the balance sheet of the postwar inflation was a much simpler one: "Since the cost of living had tripled [sic!], cost-of-living increases should do so as well," a resolution of the local "cartel" of Hanover to the DBB's general meeting in May, 1919 declared. Civil servant pay, the same resolution continued, "needs to be brought into line again with the general cost of living and with workers' wage levels, not only for economic, but also for political reasons, i. e. to prevent an impending strike of the lower ranks

[35] Verband der Beamten- und Lehrervereine Badens to the Baden state government, May 5, 1919, GLAK, 233, 24222. The author of the petition was most probably Hans Völter, a trained economist and the business manager of this Verband. Völter would soon be appointed to a directorship of the DBB in Berlin, becoming something of an economic expert to the DBB.

of the *Beamtenschaft* which undoubtedly would lead "to the total collapse of our economy and of the state."[36]

Similar arguments were made in a petition, sent to several government ministries and agencies by an association of lower-grade civil servants on May 5, 1919. The *Unterbeamte,* the petition claimed, had been hardest hit by "the steady depreciation of the currency and the increase of the prices for all necessities of life." Lower civil servants, underpaid even before the war, were now unable to lead a halfway decent life. "Worries, distress, shame, and embitterment" had been the result. Again, the increasing discrepancy between civil service pay levels and workers' wages in private industry were marshalled as evidence for an intolerable economic situation. It was an outrage, the petitioners claimed, that a young skilled worker was earning more after an employment of only three years than a much older low-level clerk *(Kanzleidiener)* in government service, who had served his country first for thirteen years in the armed forces and then for twenty years in his civilian civil service post.[37]

Not the government, but interest groups responded first to these and similar grievances and to calls for immediate economic aid. At the DBB's general meeting on May 12, 1919, the delegates followed a proposal introduced by a number of local cartels and affiliated associations. They resolved that the cost-of-living allowances, which had been in effect since January 1, 1919, should not only be raised, but also be revised and distributed more evenly and uniformly among the different ranks and pay groups of the civil service hierarchy. Existing differentials in cost-of-living supplements according to base pay and location should be eliminated, or at least be reduced — the first a concession made to the lower pay groups, the second to civil servants living in rural areas who objected to the policy of differentiating the children's bonus on the basis of 'cost-of-living districts' *(Teuerungsbezirke).* Finally, and most importantly, the DBB demanded an immediate payment of a

[36] *DG,* May 16, 1919, where this resolution is reprinted together with other *Anträge zum Vertretertag.*

[37] Verband der unteren Beamten der obersten Reichs- und Staatsbehörden to several government ministries and agencies, May 5, 1919, BA, R 43I/2578, Bl. 6—8. This Verband organized mainly veterans who had acquired the right to a civil service post, the so-called *Militäranwärter.* The exact figures, as stated in the petition, are: For the *Kanzleidiener* a yearly income of 4660 marks (1840 base pay, 480 rental allowance, and 2340 cost-of-living allowance), for the skilled worker yearly earnings of 6387 marks (= 17,50 marks per day).

lump-sum, across the board, to all civil servants to cover the costs for replenishing clothes, shoes, houseware, etc. worn out by the war years.[38] This "purchase allowance" *(Beschaffungszulage)*, as it was called, became the main point of controversy between civil servant interests and the government in mid-1919. The DBB had not asked for a specific sum, leaving this up for negotiation, but in a later document 1200 marks was mentioned as the price to be paid to "quiet down the great disturbances existing within the *Beamtenschaft* at the present time."[39] In any case, the potential costs placed on the public purse by such a pay supplement for civil servants were staggering.

It is not surprising, therefore, that the "cost argument" was emphasized by government leaders in a meeting with a DBB delegation, which took place on July 4, 1919 in Weimar. The meeting had been arranged by Remmers, who had used his influence as a delegate to the National Assembly to bring together parliamentary experts on civil service questions, leading members of the Reich cabinet, and representatives of the DBB. In a sense, it was the first "bargaining session" between civil servant leaders and the Reich government, and it was duly heralded in the organizational press as "the dawn of a new era."[40]

The negotiations themselves were exceedingly difficult. The Bauer government had just embarked on a policy of price reductions in order to stem the inflationary tide; new wage increases in the public sector were certainly detrimental to such efforts. Thus, after the DBB spokesman had restated the organizations' position, and after Chancellor Bauer had raised hopes that an agreement would be reached, the advocates of the price-reduction scheme poured water into the wine. Finance Minister Erzberger pointed out that the Reich government had

[38] See DBB Protocol 1919, pp. 24—25 and *Eingabe des Deutschen Beamtenbundes betr[effs] Gewährung einer Beschaffungszulage...*, reprinted in *DBR*, August 1, 1919, pp. 231—232. Apparently, the petition was sent to the government in late May or early June of 1919.

[39] Beamtenausschuß beim Amtsgericht Charlottenburg to Minister President Hirsch, June 25, 1919, GStA, Rep. 90, 473, Bl. 19. The Ausschuß invited Hirsch to discuss the issue at a public meeting two days later. Hirsch's answer, sent by special courier to the committee on June 27 (*ibid.*, Bl. 20) stated that he was interested in discussing the matter but that he would be unable to attend.

[40] A report of this meeting is printed by the *Allgemeine Deutsche Lehrerzeitung*, July 17, 1919, reprinted by the *Gewerkschaftliche Beamtenzeitung* (hereafter cited as *GBZ*) on July 25, 1919. Another report is given in *Die Gemeinschaft*, July 16, 1919 *(Verhandlungen des Deutschen Beamtenbundes mit der Regierung in Weimar)*. The official protocol of the meeting could not be found in government files.

just begun to work toward a reduction of price levels and had earmarked nearly two billion marks for this purpose. The Prussian Minister of Cultural Affairs, Haenisch, seconded and emphasized that demands for higher pay and supplements would not lead to a lasting improvement of the economic situation of the *Beamtenschaft.* Only a reduction in the general price level, and thus in the cost of living, would be of any help in the long run. The financial possibilities of the state of Prussia, Haenisch added, were nearly exhausted. Therefore, he was in no position to make any promises regarding pay increases. Reich Interior Minister David, like Haenisch and Bauer a Majority Social Democrat, made the most forceful argument against wage increases. A reduction of the price of food rather than pay increases was the policy to be pursued, he said. Wage increases would ultimately fuel the "feverishly-working printing presses," with the net result that the value of the currency would decline even further. Their continued pay demands made civil servants an "accessory to the crime of bankrupting the state," David told civil servant leaders, and it was the government's duty to prevent such a financial collapse. Already, government enterprises were running up billions in deficits. Pay increases would therefore have to be financed through new tax increases, increases which in turn would be passed on to the civil servants. Thus only a "drastic reduction in price levels," or at least a policy leading toward such a goal, was the road to travel.

DBB leaders were unimpressed and remained adamant in their demands for "more cash." Price reductions, Remmers argued, might have worked a month ago, but now civil servants needed cash to purchase desperately needed items like food and clothes. Even politically moderate civil servants, he warned, had become involved in sporadic work stoppages, organized by more militant forces. The organizations were about to lose their hold over their members, which would not be in the best interest of civil servants or the government. The position of the organizations could not be supported through radical economic cures, threats of disciplining, or even dismissals. The government should show more interest and activity in civil service questions, Remmers said, and negotiations about a general reform of civil service pay should be taken up between the organizations and the government. In a final point, Remmers touched upon the issue of excessive workers' wages. As soon as possible, he argued, wage levels in the private sector should be reduced so that civil servants realized that there was evenhandedness and justice in the government's policy. As long as such a wage reduction would or could not be undertaken, the government should provide material support to its civil servants.

After Remmers' interjection, Bauer, somewhat surprisingly, declared that the Reich government was prepared and willing to make concessions as long as the Prussian government would go along with it (Haenisch had apparently already left the meetings). Both the special purchase allowance as well as a reduction in the number of *Teuerungsbezirke* would be considered by the cabinet.

On the next day DBB leaders met with parliamentary delegates who signalled support for their efforts.[41] On the same day the Reich cabinet met and decided that a special pay supplement would be granted to civil servants; the exact amount and time of payment would have to be negotiated between the Reich ministries, the Prussian government, and the other Länder. It was also decided to reduce the number of *Teuerungsbezirke* from three to two, and to begin consultations on the reform of civil service pay in the Finance Ministry, and of the recodification of civil service law *(Beamtenrecht)* in the Interior Ministry. Ostensibly, the organizations would be consulted in both cases.[42] It looked as if the organizations had scored a resounding victory.

But a snag soon developed. The very same day that the Reich cabinet met, the Prussian Finance Minister Südekum, a right-wing Social Democrat, wrote to Bauer and violently objected to the decisions that were about to be taken by the Reich government. Südekum informed Bauer that the Prussian government was strictly opposed to a special civil-service pay supplement because of the condition of the Prussian finances. He warned that promises, or half-promises containing the clause 'if Prussia agrees', were bringing the Prussian government into an "impossible situation" since it weakened its position vis-à-vis left-wing radicals among the railroad personnel, with whom Prussia was presently engaged in a "struggle for life or death."[43]

Responding on behalf of Bauer, Finance Minister Erzberger emphasized that the Reich and Prussia would ultimately decide jointly on this issue, and that no final decision had been taken by the Reich government. Erzberger, too, voiced "grave doubts" about a renewed spending of huge sums of public money and emphasized that any pay increases

[41] Reported by *DG*, July 16, 1919.

[42] Cabinet meeting, July 5, 1919, *ARK. Kab. Bauer*, p. 55.

[43] Südekum to Bauer, July 5, 1919, BA, R 43I/2583, Bl. 9, and in BA, Nachlaß Südekum, 105, Bl. 113.

would depend on the finding of additional funds through new, more resourceful means of taxation. Nothing, he told Südekum, would therefore happen before September.[44]

This delayed schedule the government was unable to keep, however. Mounting unrest within the *Beamtenschaft,* especially among the unruly, radically inclined railroad civil servants, called for more immediate action. Throughout June and July civil servants had participated in the great wage movements that took place in central Germany, movements which soon took on a political character as well. In a particularly spectacular incident, radical railroad employees, civil servants as well as workers, had taken over the railroad district of Erfurt in Thuringia, had removed high officials from their posts, and had elected one of their own as *Präsident* (district administrator). The Reich government later sent troops to quell the "Spartacist uprising," which in turn prompted a wave of protest strikes. Only after the Prussian Minister of Public Works, Oeser, had made some concessions to the strikers could order in Erfurt be restored.[45]

In the meantime the strike movement had spread, and wildcat strikes of railroad employees occurred in Silesia and the greater Berlin area. Again, civil servants must have participated in these movements, because a representative of the GDEB took part in negotiations with the Prussian government to end the strikes.[46] While the strike movement in Berlin was under control by July 3, new wildcat strikes broke out in Frankfurt-on-the-Main, Hanover, Magdeburg and Elberfeld, the latter being one of the central railroad districts of the Ruhr. Only in Hanover did civil servants *not* participate in these strikes; a police report made a special note of this.[47] It was this situation which Südekum on July 5 described as a "battle for life or death" between the state authorities in Prussia and the railroad men.[48]

[44] Erzberger to Südekum, July 9, 1919, copy in BA, R 43I/2583, Bl. 9. Apparently, Südekum had also contacted Erzberger on July 5, so the latter's response is a reply to both queries.

[45] Reports of the "Erfurt uprising," which was widely noted in the press, in *SP,* June 6, 1919, *ibid.,* July 17, 1919, and in *DG,* July 1, 1919. The last two reports are accounts given by Wilhelm Funk, the General Secretary of the GDEB, whose organization had been involved in the "uprising." See also the GDEB's *Geschäftsbericht 1919—20...,* pp. 19—20.

[46] *SP,* July 3, 1919.

[47] *Ibid.,* July 10, 1919.

[48] See the documents cited in note 43 above.

The railroad organizations, among them the GDEB, tried to disassociate themselves from the strike movement and its political overtones.[49] The DBB issued a warning to civil servants not to participate in the strikes and called on its members to adhere to union solidarity and discipline. While the DBB was prepared to pursue the interests of its members "with all legal means," a DBB proclamation said, wildcat strikes and a "misuse of civil servants for *political* ends" would endanger the *economic* improvement of the *Beamtenschaft.*[50] Characteristically of the trade-union approach to political radicalism, economic gains were played out against political goals.[51] In this sense, the DBB's proclamation was perhaps a pay-off for the concessions made by the government in the negotiations of July 4.

The delay in implementing these concessions, however, which had emerged as a result of the conflicts between Prussia and Reich over the pay issue, threatened to undercut the DBB's efforts to quiet things down. Although Chancellor Bauer had publicly confirmed that the Reich government would "look favorably upon the demands raised by civil servants," including the special supplement, in his programmatic speech to the National Assembly on July 23, civil servant leaders remained sceptical. "Unrest within the *Beamtenschaft* has risen to a feverish level," the DBB's *Gemeinschaft* noted in response to Bauer's speech, "and it appears questionable whether the organizations will be able to protect the dikes against the pressures of the rank and file much longer, unless the promised economic aid is forthcoming soon, very soon."[52] DBB leaders were especially upset over the fact that public contractual employees *(öffentliche Angestellte)* had won a wage contract *(Tarifvertrag)* from the Reich government, which set salaries of contractual employees well above civil service pay levels. Even the civil servants' right to future pension claims, Falkenberg argued in the *Gemeinschaft,* did not warrant such a discrepancy, and he wondered why, if such high salary levels could be granted to contractual em-

[49] The organizations issued a statement condemning the strike. Printed by *SP,* July 7, 1919.

[50] Proclamation published in *ibid.,* July 10, 1919 (my italics).

[51] It may be noted that the striking civil servants in Erfurt had demanded the "democratization of the civil service" and the dismissal of all higher Reichsbahn officials in their district, whom they regarded as supporters of the old regime. See *Die Erfurter Vorgänge,* in: *DG,* July 1, 1919.

[52] Albert Falkenberg, *Die Not der wirtschaftlich Schwachen,* in: *DG,* August 1, 1919.

ployees, the civil servants' "much more reasonable demands" were still being rejected.[53]

On July 29, a few days after Bauer's programmatic speech in the National Assembly, the issue of the controversial supplement and the question of realigning civil service pay to salary levels of contractual employees were the subject of a lengthy discussion in the Reich cabinet.[54] A decision in both matters was urgently needed, not only because of the mounting unrest within the *Beamtenschaft* over the delay, but likewise for political reasons. The National Assembly had scheduled a civil service debate for August 1, and the Reich government's decisions concerning the pay issue was certain to play a major part in what could become a major parliamentary battle between coalition and opposition parties.[55] It was perhaps for political reasons, therefore, that Interior Minister David, in his opening statement to the cabinet, now pleaded for an immediate granting of a special pay supplement for civil servants. It looked as if at this juncture the Reich government was set to go ahead with the pay increases in order to avoid a political confrontation with the opposition of the right in the National Assembly. Obviously, the issue of civil servant pay had become a highly political issue. Still, the plans of the Reich government met fierce resistance by the members of the Prussian government who attended the cabinet meeting. Finance Minister Südekum insisted that Prussia was in no position to come up with the money for the proposed supplement which, as he claimed, would cost half a billion marks, while Prussia's floating debt had already reached eight billion marks. Südekum held that civil servant organizations, which he had consulted, had indicated understanding for Prussia's strapped financial position. "It is not a question if we can give out a new pay supplement," Südekum said, "but if we are able to continue paying salaries at all in the usual way."

[53] *Ibid.* To clarify his point, Falkenberg cites the following figures: A higher-level contractual employee would earn 9,600 marks in his third year of service; a civil servant in a comparable position (a *Regierungsrat*) would earn only 5,800 marks, including the portion of his salary withheld as future pension claims. On *öffentliche Angestellte*, see the discussion in CHAPTER ONE of this study.

[54] Cabinet meeting, July 29, 1919, BA, R 43I/2583, Bl. 27—29 (excerpt). Also in *ARK, Kab. Bauer*, pp. 147—151.

[55] The debate had been scheduled in response to a parliamentary motion of the two conservative parties in the Assembly, the German People's Party (DVP) and the German National People's Party (DNVP); the motion had been introduced initially on March 28, 1919. The „Errettung der Beamten aus der wirtschaftlichen Not“ was a main feature of the interpellation. For the *Antrag*, see *Stenographische Berichte...*, vol. 336, no. 202.

Südekum's views were strongly supported by his cabinet colleague, the Prussian Minister of Public Works, Oeser. The price reductions, Oeser claimed, had worked, and things were reasonably quiet now on the railroads. To grant a special pay award now would only improve the position of the "radical elements." From a financial point of view the pay increase was irresponsible. For his administration the costs would amount to half a billion marks, adding on to a deficit of some 3.4 billion marks.

The members of the Reich cabinet remained adamant in their conviction, however, that something had to be done right away. Bauer claimed that he and the Reich government were bound by his programmatic speech to the National Assembly with regard to the salary reform law, since he had promised the immediate preparations for such a step. Concerning the controversial pay supplement, Bauer suggested that it was easier to give something voluntarily now than be forced to do it later on. Erzberger, the Reich minister of finance, agreed with Bauer and suggested that the price-reduction policy should not be pursued at all costs. Finally Falkenberg, the "DBB representative" in his official function as *Referent* in the Reich Ministry of the Interior, spoke up and questioned Oeser's allegation that the *Beamtenschaft* had calmed down. Quite the opposite was the case, he argued, and he claimed the discrepancies between the earnings of civil servants and contractual public employees were the main reason for the high level of unrest.

The renewed impasse between the Reich and Prussia obviously could not be resolved. Hirsch, the Prussian minister president, acknowledged that there were compelling reasons for a pay award, but kept insisting at the same time that Prussia would not be able to meet the costs of a special pay supplement for its employees. He suggested that further negotiations at the inter-ministerial level as well as between the government and the organizations were necessary to solve the remaining problems. To this "compromise" the cabinet agreed — the problem had been tabled rather than solved.

As had been predicted, the economic plight of the *Beamtenschaft* was a major, if not *the* major theme in the comprehensive civil service debate which took place in the National Assembly on August 1, 1919, i. e. only three days after the cabinet's decision.[56] In his explanation of the parliamentary motion, the DVP Deputy Most, an expert in civil service affairs, stressed that the "rescue of the *Beamtenschaft* from economic

[56] *Ibid.*, vol. 329, pp. 2206—2233.

distress" had been a major reason for his party and the DNVP to introduce the motion.[57] Most was well-informed to concede openly that the civil servants' social decline had its origins in prewar and wartime developments, but he still accused the *current* government of having neglected civil servant affairs and thus having made the situation even worse. To him, the refusal to give aid to economically hard-pressed civil servants reflected a "degradation of intellectual work *[geistige Arbeit]* in a Socialist age." Most buttressed his point with the increasing disparity in the earnings of manual workers and civil servants: it was an intolerable situation, he argued, that a fully-educated jurist in his late thirties war earning less an income now than a young miner in the Ruhr. Most called on the government to remedy these inadequacies in current wage and pay levels, which, as he claimed, was responsible for the fact that the "best and the brightest" were leaving the Civil Service, that morale was low, that a "general decline of civil service tradition" had taken place, and that the *Beamtenschaft* was slowly but steadily being "proletarianized."[58]

Minister of the Interior David himself responded to the parliamentary motion. A comprehensive pay reform, he said, had already been necessary *before* the war and was then supported by his party, but rejected by "the gentlemen of the old order." Since during the war this lingering problem had been shelved as well, "we merely had to accept one more difficult legacy." Nonetheless, David promised to begin work on a salary reform bill as soon as the budgetary situation had been consolidated. Until then, the government was committed to meet the needs of its civil servants by paying out cost-of-living increases "as long as the current financial situation allows us to do so." Whether the desired special supplement could be granted, however, was still uncer-

[57] *Ibid.*, pp. 2209 ff. Before and during the war, Most had published several scholarly articles on the social situation of higher civil servants in Prussia. See, e. g., his *Zur Sozialstatistik der höheren Beamten in Preußen*, in: *Schmollers Jahrbuch*, vol. 39 (1915), no. 1, pp. 181—218.

[58] A similar point was made by the co-sponsor of the motion, although with much more aplomb and Nationalist pathos in the subsequent debate. The DNVP Deputy Deglerk accused the Social Democrats, the "source of all evil in post-revolutionary Germany," of the crime of having destroyed the *Berufsbeamtentum:* "Sie [i. e. the Social Democrats] haben unser Heer und unsere Wirtschaft zertrümmert ... Erhalten Sie uns wenigstens die letzte Säule, die uns geblieben ist, unser gutes deutsches Beamtentum, das kostbarste Erbe einer großen Vergangenheit." (*Stenographische Berichte ...*, vol. 329, p. 2227).

tain, David told the assembly, but he mentioned that a new round of talks had been scheduled with the organizations in effort to reach a compromise solution.[59]

During the extended debate which followed, nearly all the speakers in one way or another supported the civil servants' cause, although the Social Democrats were eager to broaden the issue by insisting that "all economically-weakened groups" should be helped equally.[60] Remmers on the other hand, who represented not only the views of his party, the DDP, but likewise those of the major civil servant interest organization, the DBB, warned his fellow deputies and the government delegates that the long delay in the settling of the special allowance issue had caused "embitterment and unrest" within the *Beamtenschaft,* and that social tension had reached a most dangerous level as a consequence. While the strike was a weapon which, as Remmers put it, did not "appeal too much to civil servants," the DBB would not renounce this right under the present circumstances. The special pay supplement, he insisted, had to be awarded at all costs, and the salary reform had to be taken up fast and thoroughly. In addition, Remmers demanded that the organizations of civil servants should be recognized as a major force in the setting of salary levels in the civil service, as an equal partner to the financial authorities of the state. The most recent practical experiences with government officials during the negotiations of June and July probably played a role in Remmers' overall sceptical assessment of the extent of civil servants' influence on government policy:

"If in the course of the revision of the civil service pay scales the Reich Finance Ministry and the Prussian Finance Ministry will keep the upper hand, things will be quite the same for the *Beamten* in the new democratic people's state *(Volksstaat)* as they had been in the old authoritarian state *(Obrigkeitsstaat).* It will be checked how much money is available in the public coffers, and only then will a reform of the civil service pay system be undertaken."[61]

The level of militancy, radicalism and unrest within the *Beamtenschaft,* of which Remmers and others had spoken, and the difficulties which organizational leaders faced in their efforts to control their unruly rank and file, emerges from a protest meeting, organized by the Soziale Arbeitsgemeinschaft a few days after the assembly debate. Some

[59] *Ibid.,* p. 2212.

[60] *Ibid.,* p. 2214 (speaker is the Deputy Kronen).

[61] *Ibid.,* pp. 2220—2221.

6,000 civil servants, mostly members of the lower ranks, gathered in Berlin on August 6, 1919. Sharp accusations, directed mainly against the Prussian Finance Ministry, were made by a radical spokesman of the Soziale Arbeitsgemeinschaft, Hugo Kamossa. He told a cheering crowd that "he would understand if disappointed civil servants allowed themselves to be carried away and called a strike." Remmers, Falkenberg and other DBB leaders present at this meeting encountered difficulties in calming down the emotions of the crowd.[62] When several days later DBB leaders met again with government negotiators, it was not without justification, therefore, that they warned again about the dire consequences which a rejection of their demands would produce within the rank and file of their organization.[63]

Three days later, on August 15, the Reich and Prussian cabinets met in a joint session to discuss the issue. Südekum still kept up his opposition by arguing, not very convincingly, that a strike of civil servants was more than unlikely since civil servants did not have the right to strike. Such legalisms were easily rejected by members of the Reich government, who warned that radicalized civil servants were "being drawn into the Communist camp," and that any further neglect of the salary issue would open the door to corruption. The majority of the Prussian cabinet members were swayed by these arguments, and the decision of the granting of the special "purchase supplement" was finally made.[64]

After a long and difficult battle, civil servants interests had finally won out over fiscal considerations. In his final assessment of the protracted conflict over the special pay award, Falkenberg called the weeks between July 4 and August 15 "one of the most important period of struggle in the history of the civil servant movement." While Falkenberg seemed well aware of the soundness of fiscal arguments put forth by the DBB's main opponent, the Prussian government, he nevertheless

[62] *Aktenvermerk betr. Versammlung der Sozialen Arbeitsgemeinschaft der Unterbeamten,* dated August 6, 1919, GStA, Rep. 84a, 2718, Bl. 95—96. There is another report on the same meeting in *GBZ,* August 25 (1919).

[63] Reports on this meeting, which took place on August 12, 1919, in BA, R 43I/2583, Bl. 47—48, and, a less reliable version, in *DG,* August 16, 1919.

[64] Cabinet meeting, August 15, 1919, BA, R 43I/2583, Bl. 31 (excerpt). The cabinet agreed on a supplement of 1,000 marks for married civil servants and an additional 200 marks for each child. Unmarried civil servants only received an increase of 600 marks. This was in accordance with the compromise hammered out between government and organizations on August 12. The National Assembly then swiftly passed the bill, and on August 26, 1919 the *Zulage* was paid out (*ARK. Kab. Bauer,* p. 189, note 3).

stressed that social and political consideration had to take priority under the existing conditions. The social danger of a civil servant strike had become a living reality, he claimed. Political radicalism, which usually went hand in hand with such a form of extreme social conflict, was a threat to the very existence of the state. Under these circumstances economic, i. e. fiscal arguments, he held, were of lesser importance.[65]

Falkenberg's analysis was quite correct and to the point. The struggle between government and civil servant interests in the spring and summer of 1919 had posed the fundamental question, whether economic arguments and fiscal policy would remain the strait jacket of civil service pay policy. Just as workers were insistent upon the fact that their wages had to meet certain social requirements, civil servants now usurped this "social wage argument" for themselves as well. A social component had entered salary politics, and social pressures like mass protest, strike threats, and ultimately the strike itself — always readily transformed into political pressure as well — were and would from now on be applied to salary policy, an area which had once been the sole domain of government decision making. In this respect, the events of July and August only set the stage for the continued and increasingly acrimonious confrontations between government and interest groups in the area of civil service salary policy.

Finally, a note must be added on the role played by civil servant pay increases in public-sector wage policy in general. A few weeks after civil servants had reached their aims, talks between workers' organizations and government representatives were conducted in the Reich Finance Ministry, whose aim it was to apply the *Beschaffungszulage* that had been granted to civil servants to *all* public employees.[66] The arguments were predictable: what one group had reached could not be denied to the other. In short, civil service pay increases put pressures on wages in the public sector, and indirectly on those in the private sector as well.[67] The spiral-effect at work here was to become a characteristical feature, if not a "motor" of the postwar German inflation.

[65] Albert Falkenberg, *Die ‚letzte' einmalige Teuerungszulage,* in: *DG,* August 16, 1919.

[66] Minutes of this meeting in ZStAP, Büro RP, 92, Bl. 92.

[67] In a cabinet meeting on October 17, 1919, Reich Minister of the Treasury Mayer mentioned that if the *Beschaffungsbeihilfe* were paid workers in the Reichsbetriebe, it would likewise have to be paid to workers in private industry eventually. For the mining industry alone this would amount to one billion marks. *ARK. Kab. Bauer,* p. 312.

The Postwar Inflationary Upsurge and the Crisis of Winter 1919—20

In the fall and winter of 1919 the German economy went through and inflationary upsurge of major proportions.[68] Its impact on the economic situation of civil servants and other dependent employees was both predictable and immediate. As the cost-of-living began to soar upward, markedly outpacing the much more steady rate of increase of the previous months, the economic gains scored in the first half of 1919 were all but wiped out.[69] The civil servants' worsening economic situation is perhaps best captured in reports drawn up by local civil service committees. In one of these reports, filed by the *Beamtenausschuß* of the Prussian district administration in the city of Magdeburg, a direct link was established between the civil servants' increased economic plight and the very reliability and integrity of the civil service. The "enormous increase of all prices and the decline of the value of the currency" had led to mounting indebtedness of the *Beamte,* the report noted, and it would sooner or later lead to their complete economic collapse. If the high level of indebtedness was not checked immediately, a very foundation of the Prussian state would be in danger: the incorruptibility and dependability of its civil service. While prices of all necessities of life had not only doubled, but risen many times over, the report continued, workers had seen their wages increased by a multiple of their prewar "peace wages." To the writers of this report, it was an intolerable situation when "civil servants of long standing are earning a lesser income than unskilled industrial workers, which has now become quite the rule." The committee called on the Prussian State government to take immediate action to alleviate the "terrible plight of its civil servants" and to make certain that in the forthcoming general increase of civil service pay "the increases in the cost of the essentials of life and the depreciation of the currency will be fully taken into consideration."[70]

[68] Details on the economic situation in C. Bresciani-Turroni, *The Economics...*, pp. 29—30.

[69] The Calwer index of food prices rose nearly one percentage point in September 1919, the steepest monthly increase recorded to that point. Whether the pay raise awarded to civil servants in August had a direct bearing on the sharpness of this increase, can only be speculated upon. It does not seem to be totally implausible, however. The index continued its fast rise through November and December. Cf. note 2 above and the literature cited there.

[70] Beamtenausschuß der Regierung Magdeburg to Beamtenausschüsse at the Regierungen in Prussia and to the DBB, December 3, 1919, GStA, Rep. 180, 16884.

A similar report, drafted by a civil service committee in Danzig, singled out the high salaries allegedly made by contractual public employees on the basis of a national wage contract *(Reichstarifvertrag)*, which the white-collar unions had just negotiated with the Reich government. While the committee did not deny that the salary scale awarded to the *öffentliche Angestellte* was "justified and in line with the inflationary conditions prevailing today," it made clear that the Reich government was obliged to concede a pay scale of equal level to its civil servants. The committee called on the DBB to remedy this situation, if necessary by attacking the government in full force. From now on the DBB should demand *(fordern)* rather than request *(bitten)*. "Now the Deutscher Beamtenbund has an opportunity to demonstrate that it is the rightful representative of civil servant interests."[71]

Clearly, dissatisfaction with the performance of the peak association in Berlin was mounting within the rank and file. It was out of the question, therefore, that the outcome of the negotiations over the Salary Reform Bill, scheduled for April of the following year, could be awaited to alleviate the civil servants' economic distress. The DBB was called upon to act immediately. A new confrontation between government and interest organization was sure to take place.

On November 27, 1919, DBB representatives met with Chancellor Bauer and other members of the Reich cabinet, among them the new minister of the interior, the Democrat Erich Koch. DBB leaders pointed out the economic situation of the *Beamte* had deteriorated to such a degree that a substantial increase in the cost-of-living supplements was necessary prior to the anticipated general pay increase connected with the Salary Reform in April of the following year.[72] An increase of 150 percent might have been mentioned as the target already during this meeting, but was definitely raised as a demand by the DBB executive committee *(Gesamtvorstand)* in a special meeting on December 10.[73] The Reich government then made a grave tactical mistake. Without reconsulting the organizations, the cabinet on December 12

[71] Beamtenausschuß Danzig to Gewerkschaftlicher Bund der Regierungsbeamten Preußens [a DBB affiliate], October 2, 1919, *ibid.*

[72] Lengthy reports of the meeting in *DG*, December 1, 1919, *DBR*, December 1, 1919, and *GBZ*, December 10, 1919, which attests to the importance of these talks.

[73] *DG*, December 16, 1919. Other demands were: cancelling of all pay differentials on regional bases (the notorious *Teuerungsbezirke*), and equal pay for unmarried civil servants. Guidelines for the Salary Reform were adopted as well, in which the "timely adjustment of pay to the economic conditions" figured prominently.

decided to raise cost-of-living allowances by 50 (rather than 150) percent. The Budget Committee of the National Assembly had agreed to such an increase, which was to take effect as of January 1, 1920.[74]

A wave of protest swept through the *Beamtenschaft.* The pay award was regarded as too small and, moreover, as a breach of good faith on the part of the government, which had taken the decision unilaterally, i. e. without renegotiating with the organizations. Protest meetings were held, strike threats surfaced. The ever unruly railroad civil servants and — for the first time — postal officials were the main source of unrest. Sporadic strikes of railroad officials occurred in Elberfeld, Dortmund and Frankfurt-on-the-Main in response to the "50 percent *Diktat*".[75] Protest meetings of postal officials were held in Essen, Düsseldorf, Dortmund and other cities of the Ruhr; partial strikes were reported, and strike committees were formed to coordinate protest actions between railroad and postal officials. "The organizations are unable to control the situation any longer," a report from Düsseldorf exclaimed.[76]

That emotions were running high indeed emerges from the course of a protest meeting, held by the local DBB cartel in Düsseldorf on December 19. The fifty-percent increase was a "slap in the face and a challenge [to the organizations]," one speaker said. Another one chided the government for "having made efforts only to placate the workers or those who were shouting 'strike,' while the *Beamtenschaft* had been forced to beg for every penny." Now civil servants, too, were prepared and willing to use "the ultimate weapon." The leaders of the DBB, the crowd demanded, should take immediate, forceful action *("energisch zupacken").*[77]

In Frankfurt, the postal organizations and the local DBB cartel called for a cost-of-living increase of 300 percent and for the establishing of an arbitration committee to settle pay disputes in the public sector. The cartel set an ultimatum to the government to fulfill these demands; in

[74] Cabinet meeting, December 12, 1919, BA, R 43I/2583, Bl. 63 (excerpt).

[75] This was mentioned in a meeting of the Prussian cabinet in mid-December, BA, Nachlaß Südekum, 106, Bl. 4—6.

[76] Arbeitsgemeinschaft der Post- und Telegraphenbeamten des OPD Bezirks Düsseldorf to Oberpost-Direktion Düsseldorf, December 19, 1919, copy in BA, R 43I/2583, Bl. 80.

[77] Bericht über die Versammlung des Deutschen Beamtenbundes, Ortskartell Düsseldorf, December 19, 1919, copy in *ibid.*, Bl. 81. There are a number of similar reports from other cities in the same file, Bl. 82ff.

case of non-compliance "passive resistance" would ensue.[78] In response to these threats, Minister of Posts Giesberts informed his cabinet colleagues on December 30 that "passive resistance and unconcealed strike-threats" had been voiced by civil servants within his administration. The situation had become serious, he claimed, and he proposed that the Reich government should take a decision on the question of the legality of civil servant strikes.[79]

Just how serious and potentially explosive the situation had become by late December 1919 was revealed by a number of mass meetings and mass demonstrations, organized by the DBB cartel of Greater Berlin on December 28, a Sunday. Thousands of civil servants gathered in several large meeting halls in Berlin and, in spite of adverse weather conditions, in an open-air protest rally in the Berlin Lustgarten.[80] They listened to rousing speeches of some of their more militant local leaders, who "talked strike" unless the government reversed its decision and agreed to grant an increase of 150 percent. The more moderate exponents of the DBB's top-level leadership, among them Falkenberg, Hoefle, and Remmers, encountered obvious difficulties in their efforts to calm things down and prevent the worst from happening. After the meetings had ended, a protest march of some 40,000 civil servants, most of them lower-grade *Unterbeamte* and among them many postal civil servants in their uniforms, moved from the Lustgarten to the Wilhelmstraße, Berlin's government district. They carried banners proclaiming that

[78] Mentioned in a letter sent by the Reich Minister of Posts, the Centrist Johannes Giesberts, to the postal administration of Frankfurt-on-the-Main, December 18, 1919, copy in BA, R 43I/2640, Bl. 26. Giesberts gave these instructions to the Frankfurt office, „Wer zur passiven Resistenz aufruft ... macht sich mitschuldig am Verbrechen gegenüber unserer Volksgemeinschaft; er vergeht sich gegen seine Pflicht als Beamter und wird die Folgen tragen müssen."

[79] Giesberts to Reich Ministry of the Interior and to the Chancellery, December 30, 1919, *ibid.*, Bl. 28. In October the Reich government had once again deferred a decision on issuing a formal interpretation of the strike question. Its rationale had been that the level of discontent within the *Beamtenschaft* was high enough as it was, and that an anti-strike proclamation would only increase social unrest needlessly. The Prussian government had once again regarded this a grave mistake. There is a lengthy protocol of this meeting in GStA, Rep. 90, 631, Bl. 38—47.

[80] Reports on these meeting and on the protest marches in *DG*, January 1, 1920 (*Demonstration*) and in *GBZ*, January 10, 1920 *(Riesendemonstration der Beamtenschaft)*. The events were also reported widely by the local dailies of Berlin. See, for example, *Berliner Lokalanzeiger*, no. 626, December 29, 1919 *(Riesenkundgebung der Beamtenschaft)*, clipping in BA, R 43I/2583, Bl. 77.

civil servants, too, had the right to receive a sufficient level of pay for their work.[81] The demonstrators were stopped just short of the Chancellery by armed guards, but a deputation consisting of local DBB leaders and the Social Democratic Deputy Willy Steinkopf, was admitted to the Chancellery to deliver a protest resolution.[82] The resolution voiced "sharpest protest" against the planned increase of only fifty percent and charged that the government, against all established trade-union practice, had refused to negotiate with the organization about the level of the cost-of-living increase. The originally-desired increase of 150 percent, the resolution declared, must be viewed as a minimum demand of the *Beamtenschaft,* which has therefore ordered the DBB to reenter into negotiations with the government about the granting of this demand.[83] The deputation's attempt to hand-deliver this resolution to the chancellor himself, failed; they were received by a high Chancellery official instead, who on the same day forwarded the resolution to Bauer.[84] Similar incidents happened at the Reich Ministry of Finance, a second target of the protest marchers. Here, too, the person in charge, Finance Minister Erzberger, refused to meet with a delegation of the protesters, who were forced to hand a copy of their resolution to a minor ministry official. While this behavior caused great animosity among the demonstrators, who had meanwhile marched to the square in front of the Reichstag, the crowd dissolved later in the afternoon without having caused greater incidents or even acts of violence.[85]

[81] The emphasis was on "too" *(AUCH),* a hint that other groups were receiving sufficient wages and salaries, while civil servants were not. There is a photography of the marchers in *DBB. Ursprung, Weg, Ziel...* opposite p. I/96.

[82] On December 25, 1919 Steinkopf had informed the government of the planned march in a personal note to "comrade" Bauer. He had requested that the DBB deputation would be met by the Chancellor himself, a request which according to a marginal comment on the letter was quite emphatically denied. Steinkopf to Bauer, December 25, 1919, BA, R 43I/2583, Bl. 67.

[83] The original specimen of this resolution is to be found in BA, R 43I/2583, Bl. 73.

[84] This emerges from the signatures on the above cited document. Bauer initialled the resolution on December 28. The receiver of the resolution was the Geheime Regierungsrat Arnold Brecht, whose observations, likewise jotted down on the original resolution, reveal some of the dramatics of the moment. Brecht wrote: „Diese Entschließung wurde mir heute 11 1/2 Uhr vormittags von dem Postsekretär Beyer in Gegenwart des ihn einführenden Abgeordneten Steinkopf überreicht. Währenddessen zogen draußen in vollster Ruhe die demonstrierenden Beamten — dem Anschein nach waren darunter besonders viele Postbeamte —, schätzungsweise 25,000 Personen und mehr vorüber."

[85] The report in the *GBZ,* January 10, 1920 is the source here.

Still, the protest meetings and mass demonstrations of December 28 were a signal that could not be missed by the government. Falkenberg's judgement, that after the events of December 28 there were even fewer doubts than before that civil servants were willing and prepared to fight for their demands, was more than correct.[86] Obviously, social tensions within the *Beamtenschaft* had reached a dangerous level, a level which the more militant organizations were only all too prepared to use as a leverage in future bargaining with public employers. This fact emerges very vividly from a letter, sent by the railroad civil servant union (GDEB) to the Prussian Ministry of Finance on January 2, 1920. The GDEB wrote:

"There is still some time left, but soon it will be too late. If in its misery the *Beamtenschaft* is handed over to the radicals, civil servants, too, will come to the conclusion that they can reach their goals by force. They will become more aware of a fact which [the radicals] keep reminding them of: that they are in a position to strangle the state economically *[die Hand an der Gurgel des Staates haben].*"[87]

The scenario envisaged here was not as far removed from reality as moderate civil servant leaders and government leaders would have wished. In the following days a strike movement developed in the industrial regions of the Rhineland and Westphalia, a strike movement that was principally carried by railroad workers, but in which railroad *civil servants* were to play a prominent part. It soon took on the political overtones alluded to in the GDEB's letter, but its importance in the context of the struggle for economic gains of the *Beamtenschaft* lies in the fact that it moved the government to make concessions regarding the embattled cost-of-living increase. On the basis of police reports filed during these days and weeks, it is possible to reconstruct the extent of this strike movement and to pinpoint the part played in it by civil servants more clearly. A report, drawn up in the Westphalian city of Hamm on January 2, 1920, mentioned that railroad civil servants there were demanding a 300 percent increase of their cost-of-living allowance.[88] In Mülheim/Ruhr civil service personnel employed by the

[86] *DG*, January 1, 1920.

[87] GDEB to Prussian Minister of Finance Südekum and other Prussian and Reich ministries, BA, R 43I/2583, Bl. 89—95.

[88] The report, dated January 2, 1920, is kept in a file containing „politische Agentennachrichten" in HStAD, Reg. Düss., 15972.

Rhenish Westphalian Water Works were threatening to strike, a report filed two days later warned, and a "catastrophe was sure to happen if the water was cut off."[89]

Social tensions in the German public sector increased to a dangerous pitch, when on January 5 railroad workers went on strike in the Rhenish-Westphalian industrial region.[90] Railroad civil servants, already radicalized by the events of the previous two weeks, suddenly saw their chance to increase their bargaining power by the use of force. Elberfeld in the Wupper valley, an important railroad intersection for the Ruhr, became one of the centers of civil servant militancy. On January 6, the local DBB organization in Elberfeld reported that a general strike, including a strike of civil servants, was imminent. A strike vote *(Urabstimmung)* had been called, and a strike was sure to happen unless the government accepted the DBB's demands within the next forty-eight hours. The citizen's council of Elberfeld spoke of a "menacing threat of a general strike in the Wupper valley," unless the demands of the railroad men and of other civil servants were met immediately.[91] Two days later, the Wuppertal civil servants called on the DBB leadership in Berlin to begin "immediate preparations for a general strike of civil servants in the entire country." Once the forty-eight hour deadline elapsed, such a strike could be called right away.[92] In the meantime the railroad workers' strike had spread. According to local strike reports, the situation was most serious in those cities where civil servants had declared themselves in solidarity with the striking railroad workers and had refused to conduct emergency operations. Apparently, this had happened in Hagen, Hamm, and in Münster.[93] There were limits to the solidarity between workers and civil servants, however. A report filed after the end of strike stressed that on several stations in the Elberfeld railroad district civil servants had returned to work once it became clear that political rather than economic aims were being pursued by the striking workers.[94]

[89] Report, dated January 4, 1920, in: *ibid.*

[90] The immediate causes of this strike were conflicts that had developed in a bargaining session between the railroad workers' unions and the Prussian Railroad Administration. Mentioned in *ARK. Kab. Bauer,* pp. 511—512, note 2.

[91] Telegrams of the DBB Ortskartell and the Landesbürgerrat Elberfeld to the Reich Chancellery, January 6, 1920, BA, R 43I/2583, Bl. 96—97.

[92] Beamtenschaft of the Wupper valley to DBB, January 8, 1920, copy in *ibid.*, Bl. 98.

[93] Reports, dated January 8 and 12, 1920, HStAD, Reg. Düss., 15972.

[94] Report, dated January 17, 1920, *ibid.*

During the strike, however, the temporary solidarity between *Beamte* and *Arbeiter* at the local level greatly worried the government, and definitely increased the bargaining power of civil servant leaders in Berlin. In a meeting of the Reich cabinet on January 9, Minister of the Interior Koch pleaded for a "generous raise of civil service salaries, so as not to be forced to do so by a strike." His predecessor, the Social Democrat David, still insisted that all that was needed was "to demonstrate to the public the interdependency between pay raises and the depreciation of the currency," but apparently Koch's view prevailed. Government leaders had to come to a tentative decision in the matter at this point, because talks with the organization had been scheduled for the following day.[95]

On January 10, DBB leaders met with members of the Reich and Prussian cabinets and representatives of the other Länder in the Reich Finance Ministry.[96] The atmosphere was tense: both sides knew what the stakes were in the current round of negotiations. Accordingly, Reich Finance Minister Erzberger opened the meeting with a warning shot: civil servants had participated in strikes in several places; this, he added, was not in accordance with the legal position and the duties of a civil servant. A DBB spokesman countered by saying that the government could not *ad infinitum* claim to have no money for its civil servants. The DBB's minimum demand of a 150 percent increase should be granted. Any other solution "would lead to a situation, which he personally would regret very much: the most immediate danger was that civil servants refused to work and declared solidarity with the *Arbeiterschaft.*" A spokesman for the railroad civil servant union put it

[95] Cabinet meeting, January 9, 1920, based on minutes taken by Koch himself, BA, Nachlaß Koch-Weser, 22, Bl. 35. There is no official protocol of this meeting in the Chancellery files; the cabinet probably decided on the 150 % raise as a strategy for the talks with the organizations scheduled for the following day.

[96] *Bericht des badischen Bevollmächtigten beim Bundesrat [sic], Kempf, über eine Besprechung im Reichsfinanzministerium mit den Beamtenvertretern,* January 10, 1920, GLAK, 233, 24256. There is a second, but briefer report on the same meeting in ZStAP, Büro RP, 92, Bl. 122. Reich Minister of the Interior Koch, in his unmistakably sarcastic way, gave this account of the meeting in his diary: „Herrgott! Schon äußerlich gräßlich. Diese formelle, stereotype Redegewandheit ... Jeder der Beamtenvertreter fängt seine Rede damit an, daß er den Ausführungen seines Kollegen nichts hinzuzufügen hat, aber ... Keiner verkennt die schwierige Lage der Regierung, aber jeder muß fordern, daß die Beamten als Rückgrat des Staates ... [...]. Die Führer bekämpfen den Streik, aber sie sind verpflichtet, sich an die Spitze zu stellen, um Unheil zu verhüten." BA, Nachlaß Koch-Weser, 22, Bl. 35 f.

more bluntly: if the government did not grant the 150 percent increase, railroad operations in Prussia would cease within twenty-four hours. This challenging remark was picked up by Südekum, the ever belligerent Prussian minister of finance, who claimed that if civil servants were willing to take such a step, they would also have to bear the consequences. Any action of this type would mean a "suicide of the *Beamtenschaft,*" because a collapse of the state would affect civil servants. If, as one of the DBB representatives had claimed, civil servants regarded themselves as *Arbeitnehmer,* then civil servants would from now on be treated like other employees, i. e. lose their special privileges and protection.

Yet clearly, government negotiators were fighting with their backs against the wall. Erzberger called on the DBB to publicly condemn the increasing level of corruption and sluggishness within the civil service. After DBB leaders had promised to issue a proclamation concerning these issues,[97] Erzberger announced that cost-of-living increases would be raised by 150 percent as of January 1, 1920. The government had reversed itself on the decision of December 15, 1919.

At first glance, the government's concessions appeared like a stunning victory for civil servant interests, a victory which had revealed the usefulness of the *combined* power of pressure from below and interest politics at higher levels. But that, to some degree at least, it might have been a Pyrrhic victory, was noted by no one less than Albert Falkenberg in the pages of the *Gemeinschaft,* where he wrote:

"This new paper money will not lead to a fundamental improvement of the situation. [Issuing] paper money will not suffice, because its circulation leads to renewed pressures on the value of the currency and ultimately to an increase in the cost of living. *Circulus vitiosus!*"[98]

Falkenberg, much in line with the government's insistence on better performance, then advocated higher productivity of work as the panacea for the economic woes of Germany and its *Beamtenschaft.* Public employees, and civil servants in particular, Falkenberg argued, had to increase their productivity, if the common goal of bringing the German national economy back to work was to be achieved.[99] As it turned out,

[97] Published on the front page of the *Gemeinschaft* on January 16, 1920 *(An die deutsche Beamtenschaft).*

[98] Albert Falkenberg, *Die Erhöhung der laufenden Teuerungszulagen,* in: *DG,* January 16, 1920.

[99] The low productivity of administrative work performed by civil servants had been subject to much public criticism, especially within the *Arbeiterschaft.* Miners in the

this, too, would not break the "vicious cycle" Falkenberg had talked about, at least not over the short run. The struggle for higher pay was to continue nearly unabated. Its next stage was the struggle for a complete overhaul of civil service pay, for *Besoldungsreform.*

In Search of Stability: The Salary Reform of April 1920

The intensification of social unrest within the *Beamtenschaft* in late 1919, the low level of performance, and the increasing tendencies toward corruption within the civil service all had sent signals to government policy makers that a comprehensive reform of civil service pay scales and the entire pay structure was urgently needed. During the negotiations of December 1919 and January 1920, the organizations had promised to "keep quiet" with regard to pay demands until April, the month targeted by the government for the completion of the task of a comprehensive pay reform which government leaders had promised to civil servants during the parliamentary debate in the National Assembly in August 1919.[100]

Preparations for the Pay Reform Bill were begun in August in the Reich Ministry of Finance, initially at the lower ministerial level. They extended through the fall and winter of 1919-20, but only in early February of 1920 was the final draft bill (the *Referentenentwurf*) completed and its content made public.[101] The delay was not only a result of the usual bureaucratic foot-dragging, but also — and not least — a consequence of the immense complications involved in the task. To give but one example: the more than 180 pay groups *(Besoldungsgruppen)* that existed until then were to be reduced to only thirteen, a task which required extensive re-classification of existing civil service grades.[102] The intrinsic details of the pay reform need not concern us in

Ruhr, for example, whose "excessive wages" were often cited by civil servant leaders as a rationale for their pay demands for civil servants, were particularly enraged about the low level of bureaucratic productivity, or rather the complete lack of it. On this, see Gerald D. Feldman, *Arbeitskonflikte im Ruhrbergbau 1919—1922,* in: *VfZG,* 28 (1980), pp. 168—223.

[100] See pp. 181—184 above.

[101] Documentation, including the inter-ministerial correspondence and several draft versions of the bill, in ZStAP, RMdI, 2593.

[102] On this, see Hans Völter, *Die deutsche Beamtenbesoldung...,* in: W. Gerloff (ed.), *Die Beamtenbesoldung...,* T. 1, pp. 15—16, L. Kleineberg, *Die Entwicklung...,* pp. 27—49, A. Hülden, *Die Entwicklung...,* in: *DBB. Ursprung, Weg, Ziel...,* pp. III/61-III/62.

greater detail at this point. Suffice it to say that some of the important general demands raised by civil servant organizations in the preparatory stage the reform were observed in the draft bill. The organizations had, however, been largely excluded from any *direct* participation in the preparation of the bill. In August 1919, the DBB had appointed a ten-member committee to prepare general guidelines for the pay reform in an effort to minimize the type of intra-group strife that had characterized the last prewar *Besoldungsreform* of 1909. While the government had made repeated promises to cooperate with the DBB committee, an input by the organization on the formulation of the draft bill does not emerge from the documents.[103]

In its guidelines, published in November 1919, the DBB expounded as a main target of the new pay structure the introduction of more uniformity within the civil service pay schedules under the principle of "equal pay for equal duty and performance" *(gleiche Leistung, gleiche Bezahlung).*[104] The aim was to do away with the hierarchically-separated career levels between higher, middle and lower grade civil service appointments, which were by and large based on the education of the entering appointee rather than by performance on the job.[105] To achieve this aim within the realm of the pay structure, the DBB demanded that any mentioning of the three different career levels was to be avoided.[106] Furthermore, the maximum pay rates applicable in the

[103] At least not from the files of the Interior Ministry cited in note 101 above. It should be mentioned here, however, that the files of the Reich Finance Ministry, which are likewise kept at the Zentrales Staatsarchiv Potsdam, were closed at the time when research for this study was undertaken there.

[104] *Richtlinien für die Besoldungsreform,* printed by *SP,* November 11, 1919. An earlier version was published by the *GBZ,* August 8, 1919 *(Richtlinien für die Beamtenbesoldung).*

[105] There was, of course, a remote possibility to advance to a different career level *(Laufbahn)* by way of additional education and entry examinations. But before 1920 this was a difficult chore at best, and in the case of the higher ranks (the *höhere Laufbahn*) a near impossibility. The organizations of lower and middle-grade civil servants insisted that this situation needed to be changed in accordance with the "democratic spirit of the times" by opening up the hierarchy, and by eliminating the *Laufbahnen* or rather their separation into three distinct levels, entirely. See the petition of an organization of middle grade civil servants, sent in September 1919 to the Prussian government, copy in BA, R 43I/2578, Bl. 32—39.

[106] The position of the DBB emerges from a letter sent by the Reich Finance Ministry to the Prussian State Ministry on March 29, 1920, copy in BA, R 43I/2559, Bl. 24—26. In a round of talks on March 5, the DBB had demanded, the letter states, „daß zur Förderung des sozialen Ausgleichs innerhalb der Beamtenschaft jede Trennung in obere, mittlere und untere Beamte streng zu vermeiden sei."

lower ranks were to overlap with the starting salaries paid in the next higher levels, that is to say, the highest pay rate achieved by a lower-grade civil servant would overlap with the lowest pay rate of a middle grade civil servant, who in turn could rise to a pay group that stood parallel to the pay level of a higher civil servant.

The DBB considered this principle of linkage *(Verzahnung)* between the different career levels as a step toward the democratization of the Civil Service in the new parliamentary state of Weimar. Understandably, this principle was vehemently supported by lower and middle-level civil servants,[107] while higher-civil servants rejected *Verzahnung* as one step further toward a leveling of incomes within the civil service and between skilled and less-skilled work in general, a leveling process which had already been set in motion by the narrowing of differentials between the pay scales of the various classes during the war and the immediate postwar years.[108] The controversial principle of *Verzahnung,* then, and the narrowing of pay scales to a much smaller ratio than the one which had existed before the war, both of which had been demanded by the DBB and were on the whole conceded by the government, made the Pay Reform Act of 1920 a "revolution" of some sorts, but it also revealed that severe intra-group conflicts still existed within the *Beamtenschaft.*[109]

Some other sources of intra-group conflict may be mentioned in this context. There was the lingering problem of pay differentials between rural and small town dwellers, and those civil servants living in large cities. Cost-of-living increases granted between 1917 and 1919 had been fixed according to base pay *and* location, with rural dwellers and small towners receiving less of an increase under the assumption that the cost of living was lower in rural areas and small towns than in large cities. While all civil servants agreed that a variable element of pay had to be written into the new law — the DBB guidelines demanded "an adjust-

[107] Some radical associations of the *Unterbeamte* even demanded a strictly uniform career *(Einheitslaufbahn)*, which was to be based entirely on performance. According to this scheme, a judge would start his career as a lowly court-usher *(Gerichtsdiener)* rather than as a high-level *Gerichtsassessor.* Moreover, all civil service appointees would start out at the same pay level, and promotions and pay raises would again be based on "performance" only. See *GBZ,* August 8, 1919, which advocates this scheme.

[108] On the position of higher civil servants, see Bergs, *Das Besoldungsgesetz in seinen sozialen Auswirkungen auf die Beamtenschaft,* in: *Zeitschrift des Reichsbundes der höheren Beamten* (hereafter cited as *ZRhB*), August 31, 1919.

[109] Albert Falkenberg, *Zwischenakt,* in: *DG,* March 1, 1920.

ment of pay scales to the prevailing economic conditions —",[110] there was less agreement over the modalities of how and on what basis such an adjustment was to be determined. Rural civil servants, for one, objected to any form of gradation of cost-of-living increases on the basis of location.[111]

The most volatile source of intra-group strife connected with the preparation, deliberations, and final passage of the Pay Reform Act was the re-classification issue. When in early February 1920 the details of the draft bill prepared in the Reich Finance Ministry became known, a wave of protest of the various civil service classes and groups was unleashed, putting group-solidarity to a hard test. While the peak association had finally been called into the negotiating rooms of the ministries of Finance and Interior,[112] affiliated associations tried to exert pressures upon the government to improve the classification (and thus the pay rate) for their respective groups.[113] Members of the middle-grade administrative staffs were especially aggrevated by the fact that similar groups within the technical staffs had been allotted a higher place in the new classification-scheme.[114] Women civil servants in the postal administration protested against having been placed summarily into a low — in fact the lowest — grade and demanded partial re-classification into a higher grade as a reward for years of hardest work in middle-level civil service posts during the war, when they had sustained the operation of the postal and telephone services. Their low classification, they argued, was a "dequalification of female labor" and

[110] See the documents cited in note 104 above.

[111] On this, see Ernst Remmers and Paul Lockenvitz, *Die Verhandlungen über die Ortsklasseneinteilung* (= Flugschriften des Deutschen Beamtenbundes, no. 6), Berlin 1921, pp. 7—9. On the regional dimension of social conflict within the Beamtenschaft during the inflation, see Andreas Kunz, *Variants of Social Protest in the German Inflation: The Mobilization of Civil Servants in City and Countryside 1920 to 1924*, in: G. D. Feldman/C.-L. Holtfrerich/G. A. Ritter/P.-C. Witt (eds.), *Die Anpassung an die Inflation*..., pp. 323—353.

[112] According to a note published by the *GBZ* on February 10, 1920, these talks took place on February 3 and 5. Very little was divulged in the civil servant press about the content of the talks, though, and the existence of official protocols could not be ascertained. For this reason, the exact substance of the negotiations can unfortunately not be reconstructed here.

[113] Numerous petitions are contained in BA, R 43I/2578.

[114] Reported by *Die Arbeitsgemeinschaft*, the mouthpiece of an alliance of several associations of middle-grade civil servants. Copy in *ibid.*, Bl. 107—116, 190—195.

not in accordance with equal rights of women as guaranteed by the Weimar Constitution.[115]

The greatest amount of pressure by far was exerted by the powerful railroad civil servant unions, however. Already during the preparatory stages of the bill they had apparently been able to put enough pressure on the Reich Finance Ministry that they were moved up one step in the new classification scheme.[116] Protests of other civil servant groups and of the Prussian government *against* this decision had compelled the Reich government to reconsider its decision, however. In response, the railroad civil servants unions sounded alarm against a revision of their classification as it appeared in the draft bill issued by the Finance Ministry. The government was warned that "700,000 organized railroad civil servants are prepared to fight with all means available" if it came to a test of strength.[117] Apparently unmoved by these threats, the Reich cabinet during its initial deliberations of the Pay Reform Bill on March 1 and 2 decided to move railroad civil servants down one grade, although a special bonus *(Betriebszulage)* was granted to those civil servants engaged in difficult and hazardous work.[118] One day later, the

[115] Verband der Reichspost- und Telegraphenbeamtinnen, Bezirksverein Frankfurt, to Reich Chancellor, telegram, February 27, 1920, *ibid.*, Bl. 166. In its guidelines, the DBB had emphasized the "equality aspects," but had also demanded that the appointment of women to civil service positions should remain within a "healthy equilibrium to the number of male civil servants" (*GBZ,* August 8, 1919). For a further discussion of this subject, which cannot be treated exhaustively here, see Claudia Hahn, *Der öffentliche Dienst und die Frauen-Beamtinnen in der Weimarer Republik,* in: *Mutterkreuz und Arbeitsbuch. Zur Geschichte der Frauen in der Weimarer Republik und im Nationalsozialismus,* Frauengruppe Faschismusforschung (ed.), Frankfurt 1981, pp. 49—77. See also the discussion in CHAPTER TWO of this study, esp. pp. 49—53 above, and the literature cited there.

[116] The numerous *Unterbeamte* in the Reichsbahn administration were to be moved from Grade II to Grade III in the new pay schedule. This implied, of course, that all other railroad officials would be advanced one pay group or grade as well. The rationale behind all this was that railroad civil servants should be paid more than other civil servants, because their work was more difficult and dangerous.

[117] *Erklärung der Personalvertretung im Reichsverkehrsministerium,* February 22, 1920, BA, R 43I/2578, Bl. 174—176. The chairman of this personnel board was a leading member of the GDEB.

[118] Cabinet meetings, March 1 and 2, BA, R 43I/1354, Bl. 2 ff. and Bl. 25 ff. During the same meetings, Reich Minister of Posts Giesberts made an unsuccessful attempt to have female civil servants in his administration moved up one grade, from Grade III to Grade IV. This came in obvious response to the pressures of the association of female postal civil servants cited in note 115 above.

Reich government sent the bill to the Reichsrat in an attempt to insure a speedy parliamentary passage. At the government level, the pressures of the railroad civil servant unions had been all but ignored. This defeat would become a major contributing factor to the continued high level unrest and militancy among railroad civil servants during the further debate of the Pay Reform Bill.

One of the chief reasons for the rejection of the railroad civil servants' demands by the Reich cabinet was the high costs which they entailed, especially since there were well-founded fears that other groups would follow suit if a higher classification were granted to railroad personnel. Except in this context, the issue of the costs of the Pay Reform did not overly concern the Reich cabinet at this juncture.[119] The situation was quite different in the financially hard-pressed state of Prussia. The fact that Prussia had just been forced to turn over the right of levying taxes to the Reich government in the wake of the sweeping tax reforms undertaken by Erzberger undoubtedly increased its sensitivity toward additional expenditures entailed in a revision of civil-service pay scales for the numerous officials employed by the state of Prussia.[120] This emerges from a discussion between the Prussian minister of finance, and two of his ranking ministerial officials in the Prussian Finance Ministry, which took place on March 3, 1920, i. e. one day after the Reich cabinet had given its final approval to the Pay Reform Bill. These deliberations are instructive as to (1) the enormous costs created by the entire undertaking, (2) as to the impact of wage pressures in the public sector on financial policy, especially budget policy, and (3) with regard to the relationship between public expenditures and the inflation process. For these reasons, they deserve to be reproduced verbatim:[121]

[119] The issue of costs was never brought up in any of the cabinet meetings where the bill was discussed. Details on the public expenditures incurred by the reform of the pay schedule, totalling more than 9 billion marks annually, are given in the bill that was finally sent to the Reichstag *(Stenographische Berichte...*, vol. 342, p. 2662). There is no statement on how these costs would be covered. Obviously, it was expected that the Erzberger tax reform would provide the necessary funds. On the origins, content, and the ultimate failure of the tax reform to raise these additional revenues, see Peter-Christian Witt, *Tax Policies, Tax Assessment, and Inflation: Toward a Sociology of Public Finance in the German Inflation 1914—1923*, in: Nathan Schmukler/Edward Marcus (eds.), *Inflation through the Ages*, New York 1983, pp. 450—474.

[120] It may be noted that Prussia, for reasons of uniformity, had to legislate a reform of its pay structure at the same time.

[121] Source are the notes taken by Südekum himself, in: BA, Nachlaß Südekum, 106, Bl. 77—78.

Südekum: The most important issue is the problem of meeting the expenditures of the civil service pay reform. The total cost of the new pay schedule is 3,959 million marks. Of these, 1,271 million marks are already covered by the current budget, 2,688 million marks need to be covered additionally. [Südekum then discusses additional sources of revenue and continues]: An uncovered deficit of 1 billion [remains]: How can we cover this? We are in the position of a small pensioner, whose expenditures cannot be reduced any further. Without secure funding I cannot face the Landtag. Can our sources of revenue be increased? The entire pay reform has been caused by the depreciation of the currency. Therefore, we should simply consider this billion as a tax revenue from the Reich in our budget. This is not entirely out of the question. The entries made thus far are rather small; they are based on 1917.

Busch: This is a fictitious item. Our entire national economy is not operating.

Löhlein: If this is the decisive factor, we have reached the end of the line.

Busch: But the Reich has the coal tax! And the printing presses!

Just how the Prussian government in the end solved its fiscal dilemma created by the costs of the pay reform does not emerge from the discussion. But the tendency toward passing the responsibility toward those who were able to print the money to pay for costs created by rising civil service expenditures, i. e. to the Reich government, seems clear, even more so, because the Reich had usurped most of the taxation privileges formerly held by the *Länder.* That printing money, in turn, meant greater budget deficits at the national level, but likewise led to higher prices, more inflation, and renewed wage demands in the public sector must have been clear to a man of Südekum's caliber; he himself had preached it to organizational leaders time and again. The fact that he now had to opt for such a policy shows that in early 1920 the inflation had developed its own rules and dynamics, of which the wage-price spiral was but one, albeit an important aspect. In the public sector it would from now on continue to put pressures on budgetary deficits, all the more because periodic cost-of-living increases to civil servants had then become a legal requirement, stipulated by the new pay law, rather than a voluntary social measure undertaken by the government or by parliamentary bodies.

The political turmoil of the abortive Kapp Putsch in mid-March 1920, the resignation of the Bauer Cabinet on March 27, 1920 and the subsequent installation of an interim cabinet under the chancellorship of the Social Democrat Hermann Müller,[122] interrupted the social struggle and political controversies connected with the Civil Service Pay Reform Bill. As a result of these political developments, the cards had been reshuffled somewhat. The position of the organizations, including that of the railroad civil servant unions, had been improved as a result of their active participation in the general strike which brought down the Kapp regime. Civil servant leaders had participated in the famous negotiations between trade union leaders and government representatives on March 18, which had led to the forced resignation of the Bauer Cabinet.[123] On the government side, the appointment of the Centrist Joseph Wirth to head the Reich Finance Ministry had elevated a man into office, who as finance minister and later as chancellor would become a most formidable adversary to civil servant interest pressures.[124]

A renewed contest between the Reich government and the radical civil servant unions erupted in mid-April, when the unions restated their claim that railroad civil servants should be moved up one grade in the new pay schedule. In addition to their usual strike threats, the organizations threatened to sabotage the transfer of the railroad civil servants from Prussian into Reich service, unless their demands were met. The cabinet, which discussed the matter on April 19 and 20, remained firm, however, leaving it up to the National Assembly to

[122] For a good summary of the political developments in March 1920, see A. Golecki, introduction to *ARK. Kab. Bauer,* pp. LXXXIII—XC, and Martin Vogt, introduction to *Akten der Reichskanzlei. Weimarer Republik. Das Kabinett Müller I, 27. März 1920 bis 21. Juni 1920,* Boppard 1971, pp. IX—XXIV. The most thorough treatment remains the study by Johannes Erger, *Der Kapp-Lüttwitz Putsch. Ein Beitrag zur deutschen Innenpolitik 1919/20,* Düsseldorf 1967.

[123] Minutes of this meeting in *ARK. Kab. Bauer,* pp. 710—725. For the role played by the DBB, see A. Falkenberg, *Die deutsche Beamtenbewegung...,* pp. 105—111, and J. Erger, *Der Kapp-Lüttwitz Putsch...,* pp. 206—219. Interesting material on the activities of the DBB are contained in GStA, Rep. 84 a, 217. On the strategy pursued by the trade unions, see Hans H. Biegert, *Gewerkschaftspolitik in der Phase des Kapp-Lüttwitz Putsches,* in: *Industrielles System...,* H. Mommsen et al. (eds.), pp. 190—205, and H. Potthoff, *Gewerkschaften...,* pp. 261—286.

[124] Wirth was to play a key role in the protracted battle between civil servant organizations and the Reich government over the issue of pay. For the rationale of his financial policies, see the short biographical sketch given by Ingrid Schulze-Bidlingmaier in the introduction to *Akten der Reichskanzlei. Weimarer Republik. Die Kabinette Wirth I und II, 10. Mai bis 16. Oktober 1921. 26. Oktober 1921 bis 22. November 1922,* 2 vols., Boppard 1973, pp. XVI—XVII.

make any changes if so desired by the parliament.[125] Several cabinet members were outraged over the threats made by the unions, and even more so by the apparent willingness of the Assembly's Budget Committee to succumb to them.[126] Only through the direct intervention of Finance Minister Wirth was a favorable vote in the National Assembly blocked. This led to sharp protests by the railroad civil servants unions and to a scathing personal attack on Wirth's policies and his suitability for a ministerial post.[127]

The organizations' last minute push was to no avail, however. On April 28, 1920 the Pay Reform Bill passed the National Assembly without the desired upgrading of the railroad civil servants having been written into the law.[128] However, the conflict was only postponed, because the Assembly decided that a revision of the classification-scheme entailed in the new pay law was to take place within the following months. Other, equally important supplementary tasks such as the compilation of a schedule for the new 'location classes' *(Ortsklassen)* were similarly left to the new Reichstag. In a sense, therefore, the new law was a torso, a fact that was immediately pointed out by the organizations.[129] On the other hand, the legal provisions for a variable

[125] Cabinet meetings, April 19 and 20, 1920, *ARK. Kab. Müller I*, pp. 138—139.

[126] Koch-Weser noted in his diary on April 4, 1920: „Trostlose Lage. Eisenbahner drohen mit Streiks, wenn sie nicht 2 Milliarden mehr bekommen. Das Kabinett ist dagegen, sagt aber die Sache liegt beim Ausschuß, der ohnehin berät. Der Ausschuß bewilligt schlank, und Wirth bringt die Sache noch heute ins Plenum. Das Kabinett erfährt nichts mehr. Glatte Kapitulation. Das ist Futter für die Rechte. Unerhörte Nachgiebigkeit." BA, Nachlaß Koch-Weser, 27, quoted also in *ARK. Kab. Müller I*, p. 139, note 2.

[127] Resolution of the railroad civil servants in the Reichsbahn District of Berlin-Ost, April 27, 1920, BA, R 43I/2583, Bl. 134. In the text of the resolution there are these comments on Wirth's performance in the Assembly's Budget Committee: „Ein Mann, der in so kritischen Zeiten die Herrschaft über sich verliert, ein Mann, der in einer solchen Weise den Vertretern des gesamten Eisenbahnpersonals gegenübertritt, eignet sich nicht für den zur Zeit wichtigsten Ministerposten."

[128] *Stenographische Berichte...*, vol. 333, p. 5578. In the course of the third and final reading of the bill (*ibid.*, pp. 5564 f.) the only opposition came from the ranks of the USPD. Its speaker on civil service matters, Luise Zietz, criticized among other things that the *minimum* number of work hours for civil servants had been set at 48 hours per week. Quite correctly, she regarded this as an indirect attack on the eight-hour day, because longer work hours were not legally possible. In spite of these complaints, the clause was kept in the final wording of the law. The issue of work hours in the public service was to become even more controversial later on not least because of this clause.

[129] Cf. Albert Falkenberg, *Das Alte und das Neue Jahr*, in: *DG*, January 1, 1921. The

element in civil service pay was invoked almost right away: on May 8, 1920 a cost-of-living increase of fifty percent was granted as a further adjustment to the "general economic conditions."[130]

Despite some obvious beneficial aspects of the new pay structure there was little immediate "gratitude" displayed by the beneficiaries. Quite the opposite was the case: a renewed flood of protest petitions descended upon the government.[131] Protest meetings were called, and the allegedly still higher wages and cost-of-living increases awarded to blue-collar workers were cited as proof that civil servant pay was still not in tune with rapidly rising prices.[132]

Civil servant pressures for higher pay were still placing a heavy burden on government policy makers at a time when the government was getting more serious about stabilizing the currency. Attaining more stability in civil service pay — and thus indirectly in government spending and budgetary policy — was one precondition for a fiscal and monetary policy conducive to stabilizing the currency. It was then that the question arose whether *Besoldungspolitik* would be more manageable in a period of "relative stability," the beginning of which coincided with the passage of the Pay Reform Bill, or whether civil servant pressure would continue to function as a "motor of inflationary tendencies" and thus remain a most crucial variable in the German government's push toward stabilization.

final version of the Pay Reform Act was published in the *Reichsgesetzblatt* on April 30, 1920 (*RGBl.*, 1920, pp. 805—832). See also Willy Steinkopf, *Was muß der Beamte vom Besoldungsgesetz wissen?*, Berlin 1920, and O. Ruthenburg, *Das Besoldungsgesetz für die Reichsbeamten vom 30. 4. 1920*, Berlin 1920.

130 *RGBl.* 1920, p. 938.

131 This emerges from the content of documents filed in BA, R 43I/2579.

132 Resolution of the GDEB, Magdeburg district, May 18, 1920, *ibid.*, Bl. 22.

CHAPTER FOUR

Illusive Stability, May 1920 to April 1921

The year 1920, or, more precisely, the fifteen months between February 1920 and April 1921, have been singled out by economic historians as a phase of "relative stability" in the course of the German inflation.[1] In addition, it has been argued recently that during this phase stabilization emerged as an option available to German policy makers at the time.[2] The purpose of this chapter of our study is to show that such stability that might have existed in 1920 was "illusive" at best if the level of social conflict rather than the rate of inflation is used as an indicator. As will be shown, conflicts between civil servants and the government as employer actually increased through much of this period. The phenomenon of economic stability itself — or rather the policy of stabilization pursued by the German government to maintain it — were at the core of social struggles waged with increased intensity in the German public sector during this period. Interest alliances between civil servants and other public employee groups came to be formed, whose sole objective it was to prevent stabilization and its high social costs for *all* public employees, civil servants, blue-collar workers and public contractual employees alike. These alliances were but one aspect, albeit an important one, of what has been called the "inflation alliance" between the major German socioeconomic groups, i. e. an alliance whose purpose it was to perpetuate rather than to terminate the inflation.[3] In the fall and winter of 1920-21, when the struggle over civil service salary policy turned into a social *and* political crisis of major proportions for

[1] Cf. the discussion in the CHAPTER ONE of this study, esp. pp. 74 f. above.

[2] G. D. Feldman, *Political Economy...*, in: Idem et al. (eds.), *The German Inflation...*, passim.

[3] Cf. Ch. Maier, *Politics of Inflation...*, in: F. Hirsch/J. Goldthorpe (eds.), *The Political Economy...*, p. 41 ff., who speaks of an "inflation coalition" in existence between social groups.

the first time, the working mechanisms of this social alliance can be observed for the first time. It would, however, accompany social struggles in the public sector during the subsequent phase of accelerated inflation, when a series of wage movements would lead into the great outburst of militancy in the German public sector: the February Strike of 1922. All in all, therefore, the civil servants' first struggle against stabilization occurred at the beginning of the most conflict-ridden period in the German public sector during the inflation years. It came, moreover, at a time when the political, social, and economic framework of civil servant interest politics had been subject to some important changes.

The Political and Economic Situation in mid-1920

In the late spring and early summer of 1920 the organizational, political, and economic framework of civil servant interest politics underwent a number of important changes. In the area of domestic politics, June 1920 became a turning point in the history of the fledgling Weimar Republic.[4] In the first regular elections to the Reichstag, held on June 6, 1920, the parties of the so-called Weimar Coalition of Social Democrats, Center Party, and the left-liberal Democratic Party lost their parliamentary majority, while the more or less radical, anti-republican parties on the left and right of the political spectrum managed to increase their electoral vote considerably.[5] In response to their defeat at the polls, the Majority Social Democrats all too willingly departed from "the burden of power," as the West German historian Susanne Miller has aptly called it,[6] and turned the responsibilities of governance over to a bourgeois coalition cabinet led by the Centrist Konstantin Fehrenbach. As a minority government still dependent on the tacit parliamentary support of the SPD, the Fehrenbach Cabinet was the first in a series of internally weak coalition governments spanning from the DDP on the left to the moderate conservative German People's Party (DVP) on the right. At various times, the SPD re-

[4] Martin Vogt, introduction to *ARK. Kab. Müller I*, p. LXIII.

[5] For a good discussion of the election results and of the political options which arose from them, see Peter Wulf, introdution to *Akten der Reichskanzlei. Weimarer Republik. Das Kabinett Fehrenbach 25. Juni 1920 bis 4. Mai 1921*, Boppard 1972, pp. VIII—XX.

[6] So the title of her important study *Die Bürde der Macht. Die deutsche Sozialdemokratie 1918—1920*, Düsseldorf 1978.

entered the government as a coalition partner, and the DVP dropped out as a consequence. These shifting coalitions and unstable cabinets were one characteristic of the "era of Catholic democracy" (A. Rosenberg)[7] between 1920 and 1922. As will become clearer in the following chapters of this study, this volatile political situation would have some consequence for the conduct of civil service policy as well.

If one seeks to probe into the deeper reasons for the loss of electoral support suffered by the Weimar Coalition in the 1920 Reichstag elections, the role played by civil servants as voters might provide some answers.[8] The successes scored by the Independent Socialists, which had increased their vote from 7.6 to 18.8 percent, were most likely and primarily a result of a switch of electoral support of blue-collar workers, but it cannot be discounted that white-collar workers and lower-grade civil servants voted more heavily for the radical parties of the left as well.[9] On the whole, however, the voting behavior of civil servants is a more decisive factor in explaining the heavy losses suffered by the left-liberal DDP, and of the gains made by the two conservative bourgeois parties, the DVP and the Nationalists, the DNVP. While in 1919, in the elections to the Constituent Assembly, a good portion of the *Beamtenschaft* had undoubtedly supported the DDP as the best guarantor for needed political change without too much Socialism, and as a counterweight to the influence of the working class through the political labor movement,[10] the poor performance of the DDP in vital civil service questions may have prompted them to cast their vote in 1920 for the two bourgeois parties who did not have to claim responsibility for the conduct of civil service policy and salary politics in the previous months. It is not surprising, therefore, that the "defense of the civil service" was a most important theme in the electoral campaigns of both DVP and DNVP in 1920, and one may well assume that their appeals

[7] Arthur Rosenberg, *Geschichte der Weimarer Republik*, ed. by Kurt Kersten, 15th ed., Frankfurt 1973.

[8] The following discussion is based on the figures given by Wulf, introduction to *ARK. Kab. Fehrenbach*, pp. IX—X.

[9] Judging from the campaign materials contained in GStA, XII. HA, IV, no. 81, the USPD made at least a concerted effort to target these groups in its election campaign.

[10] A DDP campaign flyer for the 1919 elections, entitled „Was ist der Beamte in der sozialistischen Republik?" stressed this aspect and extolled the notion that the organized working class and its political branch, the labor parties, were about to dismantle the *Berufsbeamtentum*. Specimen in GStA, XII. HA, IV, no. 126.

found the necessary resonance among civil servants.[11] The catastrophic decline of the DDP's popular vote from 18.8 percent to 8.4 percent, and the increase of the DVP's vote from 4.4 percent to 13.9 percent, reflects a shift of civil service support in large cities, where both parties had their predominant political base.[12] The DNVP, which increased its vote primarily in rural areas, may well have profited from the dissatisfaction and embitterment of rural civil servants, whose specific demands had not been met in the interest struggles connected with the Salary Reform of April 1920.[13]

Contemporary observers, especially those within the civil servant movement, were keenly aware of the fact that the Reichstag elections of June 1920 had been a warning signal given by civil servants in protest against the civil service policies conducted by the government and the parties in control of the National Assembly in the previous seventeen months. In one of the rare political analyses ever to appear in the pages of the *Gemeinschaft,* Albert Falkenberg wrote: "Civil servants have judged that the policy conducted by the government before June 6, 1920 had been a policy contrary to their own interests. They have expressed their mood through the ballot." To Falkenberg, the outcome of the elections was proof that no parliamentary government could conduct civil service policy against the wishes of the *Beamtenschaft.* This should be a warning sign to the newly elected Reichstag, he maintained. Only by cooperating closely with the civil servants' own representative organizations could the political parties regain or retain the confidence of civil servants. More than before, the direction of civil service policy would in the future be mapped out by the organizations.[14]

[11] This impression emerges from the campaign materials of these two parties, contained in GStA, XII. HA, IV, no. 126 (DVP) and nos. 180—181 (DNVP). A DNVP flyer, (*ibid.*, no. 181) deals very concretely with struggles for the cost-of-living increases and the salary reform of the previous months, attacking especially the Social Democrat Südekum and his policy of fiscal conservatism in Prussia.

[12] A DVP flyer issued after the elections jubilated: „Bei der Reichstagswahl am 6. Juni haben die Beamten ‚rechts' gewählt ... Kollegen und Kolleginnen! Ihr habt richtig gehandelt..." (*ibid.*, no. 162).

[13] The DNVP was especially active in the predominantly rural state of Pomerania, where it controlled the regional DBB association. See the report of the third Pommersche Beamtentag, held in Stettin on July 18, 1920, in the *Pommersche Tagespost* (a DNVP paper) of July 20, 1920, clipping in ZStAP, RMdI, 2185, Bl. 97.

[14] Albert Falkenberg, *Der neue Reichstag und die Beamten,* in: *DG,* July 16, 1920. The avowed principle of political neutrality usually precluded the interpretation of partisan politics in the *Gemeinschaft.*

Falkenberg's admonitions to the new Reichstag were, to some degree, a response to a loss of direct influence in the parliament which civil servant associations had suffered as a result of the elections. Key representatives of civil servant interests like Remmers had lost their electoral mandate, and fewer civil servants had been elected to the new Reichstag.[15] On the whole one gains the impression from Falkenberg's article that civil servant leaders were worried that their direct influence in the parliamentary and governmental spheres had decreased as a consequence of the elections, and of the political changes they had produced.

It is interesting to note that in this context Falkenberg brings up the idea of an organizational alliance between civil servants and the labor movement as one way to increase the leverage in parliamentary struggles and in the governmental decision making process. He speculated that in the months ahead civil service policy would have to be broadened and brought into line with general "employee policy" *(Arbeitnehmerpolitik)* to be conducted jointly by civil servant associations and white and blue-collar trade unions. The lessons of the political *Arbeitnehmer* alliance forged during the abortive Kapp Putsch, Falkenberg claimed, were only the beginning of a complete reorientation toward trade-union policy *(Gewerkschaftspolitik)* within the civil servant movement. For the first time the notion of an organizational alliance between civil servants, salaried employees, and blue-collar workers had been articulated in the civil servant press, and it is important to note that this alliance was to be built around common strategies to be pursued in trade union wage policy *(Lohnpolitik)* and civil service pay policy *(Besoldungspolitik).* Cooperation between the three social groups was thus to be centered around social and economic issues, and not, as in previous attempts, around political concerns.[16]

As the forthcoming events would show, an alliance would be difficult to forge in the realm of organizational politics as such. What would develop eventually, however, was the notion that there existed a general

[15] *Ibid.* It was a sign of the time and of the political shift to the right that the Reichstag committee on civil service affairs would be chaired by a DNVP delegate, the Deputy Deglerk (reported by *DG*, June 9, 1921). On parliamentary representation of civil servant interest in the Reichstag, see also Otto Schuldt, *Beamtenpolitik in den Parlamenten,* in: *Beamten-Handbuch,* pp. 31—38. Schuldt, the chairman of the GDEB, was the ranking DBB leader elected to the new Reichstag as a delegate for the DDP.

[16] *Ibid.* On the DBB's tactics during the Kapp Putsch, see the brief discussion given in CHAPTER THREE of this study and the literature cited there.

consensus between different employee groups in the areas of social and economic policy. The economic conditions in 1920—21, which were characterized by a relative stabilization of the inflationary trend and by governmental attempts to achieve greater economic stability even at the price of social discontent, were instrumental in the construction of an "inflation consensus" among rival social groups. It was on the basis of an "inflation consensus" that organizational alliances would be formed between civil servants and other *Arbeitnehmer* groups.

One of the priorities of the Fehrenbach Government, pursued with vehemence by the new and old Finance Minister Wirth, was to reach a more stabilized budget as the all-important prerequisit to move toward economic and monetary stability.[17] The latter, in turn, was a precondition for making headway in the pressing reparations question.[18] The target of a more balanced budget prompted Wirth to pursue a financial policy based on two logical principles: public expenditures had to be cut and government income had to be increased. Both of these principles would place a heavy burden on those groups in German society which had become used to see their demands being met by the public purse and the printing presses. As the discussion in the previous chapter has shown, civil servants, in spite of their complaints, had certainly become one of these groups.

Any program involving financial austerity measures on the part of the Reich government would make itself felt in the public sector right away, since wage demands would have to be kept at bay, even at the cost of increased social unrest. It is here where the explanation of the pivotal importance of the public sector in the social conflicts and struggles of 1920 and beyond lies. As has been pointed out by Gerald Feldman, the basic dilemma for the German government in the period of relative stabilization was "how the battle against internal unrest and unemployment was to be reconciled with the struggle against budgetary deficits and the recurrent wage-price spiral."[19] To Feldman, the battle over civil service pay scales provided an obvious illustration of the losing struggle against inflation in this period. As will become clear, the

[17] The now following discussion owes much to the insightful analysis given in G. D. Feldman, *Political Economy...*, in: Idem et al. (eds.), *The German Inflation...*, passim.

[18] A useful discussion of the reparations question is contained in P. Wulf, introduction to *ARK. Kab. Fehrenbach*, pp. XXXIV—XLIV.

[19] G. D. Feldman, *Political Economy...*, in: Idem et al. (eds.), *The German Inflation...*, p. 196.

inflation alliance forged between civil servants and workers in a joint offensive for higher wages and pay in the fall of 1920 was indeed a *decisive* factor in rendering futile any effort by the German government to attain sounder budgetary conditions and thus monetary and economic stability.

Salary Policy vs. Financial Stability

Although the Pay Reform Act of April 1920 and the cost-of-living increases granted in May had, on paper at least, raised civil servant salaries substantially, these measures failed to produce social tranquillity within the *Beamtenschaft.* Partially, this was a result of the law's incompleteness, especially with regard to the re-classification problem and the revision of the schedules for the new "location classes" *(Ortsklassen).* In addition, however, members of the lower ranks of the civil service still regarded their pay rates as insufficient in contrast to wages paid to workers in private industry. In a letter to the editor of the *Gemeinschaft* one lower-level civil servant complained, for example, that compared to workers' wages the earnings of *Unterbeamte* were so meager as to "endanger their economic survival." The writer accused the DBB leadership of having perverted the idea of organizational unity by misusing the bargaining power of the mass organizations of the *Unterbeamte* to neutralize their specific interests. He warned that a revolt of the lower ranks would ensue unless their material needs were met immediately.[20]

When in July the new quarterly salaries were paid out, a third grievance developed, adding fuel to an already high level of social unrest among civil servants. Despite warnings from some of its regional agencies, the government in Berlin had decided to deduct a portion of an advance that had been granted to civil servants in the previous March from July paychecks. The net result of this measure was that salaries for the next three months were cut substantially and thus viewed as totally insufficient by their recipients. An outburst of hostility and resentment took place in response to this measure, especially among railroad civil servants whose militancy had surfaced before under similar circumstances. Local police reports captured the mood within the *Beamtenschaft* particularly well. In Hagen, for example, railroad civil servants called a protest meeting and threatened to strike unless the government re-

[20] *Was soll nun werden? Ein Wort zur Beamtenbesoldung,* in: *DG,* July 1, 1920.

versed itself on the issue.[21] The same report warned of the dire economic, political, and military consequences of a transportation strike in the Ruhr, the latter because the railroads would be crucially important in cases of internal unrest. A similar report, filed in August, pointed toward the political implications of civil servant unrest. Commenting on the danger of a strike by lower grade postal officials in several cities of the Ruhr, the report emphasized that the local presses of the radical left-wing parties had stepped up their coverage of the alleged economic plight of the *Unterbeamte.* As the report warned: "These circles are eagerly awaiting a strike call by the lower ranks of the postal and railroad services as a first step toward a general strike in the transportation sector, which in turn could be used to trigger off a major domestic crisis."[22] Even in far-away Bremen, bourgeois oriented civil servant associations sent out warnings that they would be unable to prevent a strike vote of the *Beamtenschaft* in their city, if the Bremen state government and the Reich government in Berlin again rejected their demands for higher pay.[23]

These pressures, originating from the rank and file, forced the DBB to take action in the matter. An initial attempt to have the controversial advance changed retroactively into a "special bonus" and thus eliminated met with fierce resistance by the Reich Finance Ministry and ultimately failed.[24] In late August, therefore, DBB leaders met to discuss the possibilities of a new wage offensive. They decided to seek an increase of the cost-of-living allowance from the current 50 to a hefty 100 percent.[25] In early September, the DBB sent its demands to the Reich government. At the insistence of Finance Minister Wirth, the cabinet flatly rejected them in a meeting on September 22. Wirth had threatened to resign unless the DBB's pay demands and a set of other demands made by his cabinet colleague, Minister of Posts Giesberts, were scrapped.[26] Wirth argued that the financial situation of the Reich

[21] This report, dated July 24, 1920, is to be found in HStAD, Reg. Düss., 15973.

[22] Reported by the Reichszentrale für Heimatdienst, Ruhrgebiet, August 26, 1920, ZStAP, RMdI, 2594, Bl. 278.

[23] Meeting of the Hauptausschuß der Bremer Beamtenvereine, August 16, 1920, mentioned in a police report, dated September 10, 1920, HStAD, Reg. Düss., 15973.

[24] DBB circular, dated July 12, 1920, copy in Staatsarchiv Hamburg (hereafter referred to as StAH), 122-4-4 Bd. 4. The only concession apparently made by the Reich Finance Minister was that the advance could be repaid (i. e., would be withdrawn) in several installments.

[25] Reported in: *GBZ,* September 25, 1920.

[26] Giesberts had announced that he intended to upgrade several classes of civil

simply did not warrant any further increases of the budget. On this he was adamant. "The finance minister cannot continue granting civil servant requests without taking into consideration the menace of the financial collapse of the Reich," he told his colleagues.[27]

Not surprisingly, the DBB rejected the argument that its demands had been excessive and were partially responsible for the financial woes of the state. Indeed, its demands had been formulated by taking into full consideration "the critical financial situation of the Reich" and on the basis of the "scarcest needs" of the *Beamtenschaft,* the DBB argued. Civil servants were unwilling to be singled out for "special sacrifices." In the long run, the government's decision would only lead to the further social and political radicalization of segments of the *Beamtenschaft.*[28]

In the fall of 1920 these predictions appeared to move one step closer to reality. Social unrest within the *Beamtenschaft* began to increase again, and at an alarming pace. The causes of this development were twofold. For one, food prices began to rise after having been rather stable in the previous weeks.[29] Secondly, salaries paid out in October had again been diminished by withholding a portion of the by now notorious pay advance of March. Protests were forthcoming right away. The radical railroad civil servant union urged the government to pay out the portions of the salaries that had been withheld immediately. No economic argument, the Reichsgewerkschaft claimed, could outweigh the material needs of the civil servants. Even if an increase in paper-mark salaries was meaningless unless prices were controlled at the same time, the necessity to meet the bare essentials of life was a matter of greater importance than any economic argument.[30]

servants within his administration. This meant that other civil service groups would come with similar demands, and additional costs would have to be met by the Finance Minister.

[27] *ARK. Kab. Fehrenbach,* pp. 189—192 (cabinet meeting) and pp. 186—187 (Wirth's letter of resignation).

[28] Albert Falkenberg, *Beamtenopfer,* in: *DG,* October 1, 1920.

[29] The official cost-of-living index compiled by the Statistisches Reichsamt rose from 10.15 to 10.71 in the month of October. Between May and September this index had actually declined slightly from 11.02 to 10.15. By December 1920, the index stood at 11.58 again. Cf. *Zahlen zur Geldentwertung...,* p. 33. For the full picture, see CHAPTER TWO of this study.

[30] Reichsgewerkschaft Deutscher Eisenbahnbeamten- und Anwärter to Reich Cabinet, October 20, 1920, BA, R 43I/2583, Bl. 143.

Similar lines of reasoning surfaced at the DBB's general meeting in late October, where the *Besoldungsfrage* was one of the central points of discussion. DBB Chairman Flügel, responding to criticisms that the leaders of the organizations had not been assertive enough in its dealings with the government, promised to defend to the utmost the "well-balanced, but indispensable demands" raised by civil servants. Otto Schuldt, the chairman of the Reichsgewerkschaft and a DDP Reichstag deputy, claimed that civil servants already were carrying more than a fair share of the burdens placed on German society as a whole. "For this reason alone we must demand that civil servants, too, shall receive what is rightly theirs," he told his audience.[31] The DBB congress then adopted a resolution, in which the government was warned "not to destroy the economic strength of the *Beamtenschaft* and with it the backbone of the state."[32] DBB leaders had received a clear mandate to begin a new pay offensive.

The new *Besoldungsbewegung* began on November 5, when DBB representatives met with Reich Finance Minister Wirth to explore the conditions for a successful new wage drive. Wirth was unwilling to make any assurance, however, so DBB leaders met with a group of Reichstag deputies on the following day to check on the political constellation in the Reichstag. They received the general message that a pay offensive based on the September demands would be a hopeless endeavor. Consequently, the DBB scaled down its demands somewhat, presenting them formally to the Reich government on November 10, 1920.[33] A new struggle between civil servant organizations and the government had begun, but this time, the government reacted swiftly. Wirth informed the leaders of the coalition parties about the renewed demands,[34] and he arranged a meeting with the finance ministers of the *Länder*.[35] Obviously, he was gathering support for a major confrontation with the interest group.

The meeting with the finance ministers took place only one day after the DBB's demands had been received, on November 11, 1920. When

[31] Protocol of the meeting reprinted in *DG*, November 1, 1920.

[32] *Ibid.*

[33] Reported in *DG*, December 1, 1920.

[34] Wirth to Reichstag Deputies Schiffer, Spahn, and Hugo, undated draft letter, BA, R 43I/2583, Bl. 190—192.

[35] Meeting of the Baden State Government, November 8, 1920, GLAK, 233, 24256, where the Baden Finance Minister Köhler mentions that Wirth had just informed him by telephone about the matter.

Wirth informed his colleagues that the DBB's pay demands tallied up to a total of 2.3 billion marks, he could be certain of their response. The Bavarian representative pointed out that previous civil service pay increases had caused bitterness and resentment among other social groups, especially among farmers and members of the old Mittelstand. Should the Reich government and the Reichstag decide on a new pay raise, the central government alone would have to pay for it, including the share for state civil servants. Similar objections were raised by the Prussian Minister of Finance Lüdemann, a Social Demorat. While the economic plight of the civil servants might well justify their demands, he said, the state could not increase its budget any further. The Finance Minister of Baden, Köhler, put it more bluntly. He objected on the rationale of pay increases that would ultimately have to be financed by the printing presses.[36]

Backed up by the Länder governments, the Reich cabinet decided in a later meeting that an increase of the cost-of-living supplements as proposed by the DBB was out of the question. Wirth was asked to prepare a draft proposal for a bill that would call for a much more modest (and less costly) increase of the cost-of-living supplement to the children's bonus.[37] Several days later, on November 20, the cabinet agreed to this slight raise of the children's bonus, and even this increase would pertain only to civil servants in urban areas; those civil servants residing in small towns and rural areas would receive no increase at all.[38]

The organizations were stunned. Of the three demands put forth by the DBB only one, a minor one, had been partially granted. In a sharply-worded letter to Chancellor Fehrenbach, the DBB spoke of a "fateful decision" of the government that would not be "to the best of the nation and the state." Its final hopes, the DBB wrote, were now placed on the Reichstag, which in the end would have to decide on the "future of the German *Beamtenstand.*"[39] Unless the parliament overturned the government's decision, the DBB's *Gemeinschaft* argued, the vision of the *Beamtenschaft* as a "new proletariat" was certain to become reality.[40]

[36] Meeting with Finance Ministers of the Länder, November 11, 1920, *ARK. Kab. Fehrenbach*, pp. 274—276.

[37] Cabinet meeting, November 11, 1920, *ARK. Kab. Fehrenbach*, p. 277.

[38] Cabinet meeting, November 20, 1920, *ibid.*, pp. 293—294.

[39] Letter printed in *DG*, December 1, 1920.

[40] Albert Falkenberg, *Das neue Proletariat*, in: *Ibid.*

The government's decision against a higher cost-of-living allowance, coupled with the delay in a vote on the revision of the pay schedules by the Reichstag's Budget Committee, intensified social unrest among the organizations' rank-and-file members. In a series of reports to the Reich Ministry of Posts, the regional postal administrations *(Oberpostdirektionen)* warned in late November and early December about incidents of passive resistance; work slow-downs, work stoppages, and even strike sentiments had increased among postal civil servants. "In their desperation," one report noted, "civil servants will not hesitate any longer to make use of the ultimate trade-union weapon *(zum letzten Mittel greifen),*" i. e. go on strike.[41]

Unrest reached especially dangerous levels in the Rhenish-Westphalian industrial regions, where prices had climbed at a faster pace than in other areas of Germany. In the Ruhr cities of Essen and Duisburg, for example, DBB local organizations had conducted protest meetings and threatened to strike unless substantial economic relief was forthcoming immediately. The Prussian Commissar for Public Order, Weismann, who reported on these incidents, warned the government of the grave economic and political consequences which a public service strike in the Ruhr might produce. If railroad civil servants went on strike, workers and other transportation employees might follow suit, triggering off a transportation strike that would all but paralyze the Ruhr. Weismann warned about foreign policy implications: coal deliveries to France would have to be curtailed or suspended entirely, giving the French the long-desired opportunity to seize the Ruhr. Weismann argued that only a speedy and extensive relief for the restive *Beamtenschaft* could prevent such a chain of events.[42] That civil servants in the industrial regions of the Ruhr were economically hard pressed indeed, emerges from reports filed by other government agencies. The Prussian minister of justice, for instance, was alarmed that officials in his administration were forced to rely on semi-legal side jobs to make ends meet financially — an only insufficiently disguised euphemism for an increasing level of corruption.[43]

Representatives of the major political parties, especially those with a sizeable civil service constituency, were becoming equally worried and

[41] Reports contained in BA, R 43I/2583, Bl. 80—82.

[42] Staatskommissar für öffentliche Ordnung to Reich Ministers, Prussian Ministers, and Reich President's Office, November 15, 1920, GStA, Rep. 90, 631, Bl. 101.

[43] Prussian Minister of Justice to President of Prussian State Ministry, November 11, 1920, GStA, Rep. 84 a, 3145, Bl. 216—217.

bestormed the government to take immediate action on behalf of the *Beamtenschaft.* Endorsing the DBB's last pay proposal, the Democratic Party urged Chancellor Fehrenbach to increase the cost-of-living allowance to the sought-after level of seventy-five percent "in order to maintain a healthy officialdom free of corruption."[44] Not only one of the coalition partners, but the chancellor's own party as well sounded warnings that unless the DBB's demands were met, civil servants would go on strike and probably gain the support of the workers in a walk-out.[45]

Of the three coalition parties, the DVP clearly felt most uncomfortable in being forced to support a policy conducted against the wishes of the *Beamten,* a group which had supported it so heavily in the June elections. The DVP introduced a motion in the Reichstag committee where the matter was under study, which called for a general increase of the cost-of-living allowance as proposed by the DBB, even if at a somewhat lesser rate of sixty percent.[46] This was a clear departure from coalition politics, and the ranking DVP representative in the cabinet, Vice Chancellor Heinze, later tried to intervene at the cabinet level in favor of this general increase.[47]

The position of the two main opposition parties in the Reichstag, the MSPD and the DNVP was predictable: the Social Democrats favored a more generous increase for the lower pay groups,[48] while the Nationalist Party demanded a percentage increase that would benefit higher civil servants.[49] At the same time, the DNVP warned civil servants not to engage in any strike actions. This, the DNVP's civil service section claimed, would in the long run be "disastrous to the position of the civil servant in society and the state."[50]

[44] Reichsgeschäftsstelle DDP to Reich Chancellor, November 26, 1920, BA, R 43I/2584, Bl. 13.

[45] Center Party Frankfurt/Main to Reich Chancellor, December 3, 1920 (telegram), BA, R 43I/2560, Bl. 104.

[46] Reported by *Kölnische Zeitung,* no. 1035, December 10, 1920, clipping in BA, R 43I/2560, Bl. 106.

[47] In a *Chefbesprechung* with Fehrenbach and Koch, either on December 6 or 7. Mentioned by Koch in his diary, BA, Nachlaß Koch-Weser, 27, Bl. 329.

[48] SPD Zentralstelle für Beamtenagitation to Reich Chancellor, November 23, 1920, BA, R 43I/2584, Bl. 11—12. The SPD later introduced a motion in the Reichstag in this matter.

[49] *Kölnische Zeitung* (as in note 46).

[50] Deutschnationale Beamtenschaft to Reich Chancellor, November 23, 1920, BA, R 43I/2584, Bl. 9—10, forwarding a resolution adopted by the DNVP's civil service section on November 22, 1920.

With opposition to the government's policy mounting in the political arena, talks of an impending political crisis began to circulate. As a minority government, the Fehrenbach Government needed the support of the SPD to usher its bill through the Reichstag. In view of the DVP's unorthodox action in the Reichstag, moreover, the matter threatened to cause a coalition crisis as well. By early December, therefore, the problem of the cost-of-living increases for civil servants had created a major political crisis.

Against all political and social pressures, however, the government remained firm. In a cabinet meeting on December 2, 1920, the decision was taken to issue an anti-strike decree in order to prevent the transformation of social unrest with the *Beamtenschaft* into a goal-directed strike movement.[51] The government's move could not have come any later, because tensions had been mounting within the *Beamtenschaft,* especially among the ever unruly railroad civil servants. On December 3, Transport Minister Groener informed his cabinet colleagues that the railroad civil servant union was rapidly losing its grip over the rank and file. As reported to him by a reliable source from within one of the unions, local strike committees had been set up by civil servants in the industrial centers of the Ruhr. These committees defied orders and decisions taken by the central union leadership in Berlin. The committees had begun negotiating pay increases for railroad employees in the occupied territories through direct contacts with French authorities. This, Groener worried, was playing into the hands of the French and their desires to take over the complete control of the Reichsbahn in the occupied zones.[52]

Groener's source was likely to have been a leading official in the conservative, anti-strike, and Center Party oriented Catholic Civil Servant Federation (GDB), because only a few days later this organization informed the government that they were about to lose control over their rank and file. The GDB chided the government for "having allowed for things to get out of hand" by ignoring the organizations petitions and proposals. In the end, the GDB argued, this would reconfirm and justify the position of those radicals in the civil servant

[51] Cabinet meeting, December 2, 1920, *ARK. Kab. Fehrenbach,* pp. 319—322, p. 322. It may be remembered that unlike the Prussian state government the Reich government had not yet issued a formal decree outlawing civil servant strikes.

[52] Groener to Minister of Justice and Minister of Finance, December 3, 1920, BA, R 43I/2560, Bl. 94.

movement "who want to hit with the clenched fist on the table." Ultimately, the government alone would have to accept the responsibility for such a showdown.[53]

For the time being, however, the government remained unmoved by threats of an impending strike of its civil servants and began to step up its preparations for a possible violent confrontation with the radical wing of the civil servant movement. Minister of Posts Giesberts, ordinarily one of the exponents of a moderate and conciliatory policy toward civil servant interests, issued a decree banning strikes by civil servants in his administration, and the Prussian government publicly reconfirmed its anti-strike decree of April 1919.[54] Adopting a more moderate course, Reich Finance Minister Wirth suggested in a letter to his cabinet colleagues that the government should appeal to the goodwill of the civil servants, to their sense of duty, and, most likely, to their understanding of the unhappy fact that the Reich's precarious financial position simply did not allow a general cost-of-living increase at this time. An increase of only ten percent would cost 564 million marks, Wirth warned, and with a budget deficit totalling some seventy billion marks already, any further increase of the deficit would be detrimental to the well-being of the state and thus of its employees as well. Of this, Wirth suggested, civil servants should be informed, and they should be asked if they were willing and prepared to pay closer attention to the country's financial plight, or if they were bent on working toward the financial collapse of the state by insisting on their demands.[55]

On December 8, 1920, the embattled cost-of-living increase bill reached the floor of the Reichstag. Rumors of a government crisis intensified, when in the last minute the coalition parties tried to reach a compromise with the DNVP in order to forestall a possible parliamentary defeat that would have forced the cabinet to resign.[56] In a cabinet

[53] Gesamtverband der Beamten- und Staatsangestelltengewerkschaften to Reichstag, Reichsrat, and Reich government, December 6, 1920, BA, R 43I/2584, Bl. 32.

[54] A draft version of this decree and the relevant interministerial correspondence is to be found in BA, R 43I/2640, Bl. 45—73. See also the report in: *SP*, December 15, 1920.

[55] Wirth to State Secretary in the Reich Chancellery, December 5, 1920, BA, R 43I/2640, Bl. 60—61. (The letter is falsely dated November 5.) Wirth proposed that civil servants were to be enlightened about these hard facts in a formal speech *(Ansprache)*. He also proposed rigorous disciplinary measures to be taken against civil servants should a strike occur.

[56] BA, Nachlaß Koch-Weser, 27, Bl. 343. In his sarcastic way, Koch called the parliamentary debate a „widerliches Gezänk".

meeting on the following day, the government decided to stand firm on its bill, but, as a sign of good will and in view of the impending Reichstag vote, agreed that January salaries would be paid out to civil servants by mid-December already, i. e. before Christmas.[57] With this amendment, the bill passed the Reichstag one day later.[58] Against all pressures and intense lobbying of interest groups and political circles, the government had prevailed in the first round of the battle.

It was to be a Pyrrhic victory, however. Politically, the cabinet crisis lingered on even after the Reichstag vote. DVP-oriented papers unleashed a campaign against Finance Minister Wirth, who was singled out as the main culprit of the civil servants' dissatisfaction and their loss of confidence in the government.[59] In a sharp response to these attacks, Wirth threatened to resign unless the DVP muzzled its press and apologized formally to him.[60] The incident shows how politically explosive the issue of civil service policy had become.

From the civil servants' perspective the "loss of confidence" diagnosed by the *Kölnische Zeitung* was perhaps even an understatement. The political bickering in the Reichstag and the token resistance put up by the opposition parties, who then failed to vote jointly against the government bill, most likely did not endear parliamentary democracy to the civil servants. As far as the *Beamte* were concerned, the political parties had misused their interests and concerns for agitational purposes during the debate, and had sold them out, so to speak, in the final vote. Civil servants and their organizational leaders were particularly enraged that their justified demands had been rejected on the grounds that they would lead to similar demands of other social groups. Not without some good reasons they regarded this as a degrading of their own specific interests and needs through the government and the parliament. To them, therefore, the final decision in the matter was merely postponed, but not cancelled.[61] The social consequences of the political decisions taken in early December 1920 were to become signif-

[57] Cabinet meeting, December 9, 1920, BA, R 431/2584, Bl. 78 (excerpt).

[58] *GBZ*, December 16, 1920 reports on the Reichstag vote. The bill as passed by the Reichstag provided for an increase of the cost-of-living supplement to the children's bonus only.

[59] *Kölnische Zeitung*, December 10, 1920. Other attacks appeared in the *Tägliche Rundschau*, another DVP oriented paper.

[60] Cabinet meeting, December 20, 1920, *ARK. Kab. Fehrenbach*, pp. 361—362.

[61] Albert Falkenberg, *Aufgeschoben — nicht aufgehoben*, in: *DG*, December 16, 1920.

icant historically: in the winter of 1920-21 Germany was to be only a breath away from a major civil servant strike.

Salary Policy as a Political Conflict: The Crisis of Winter 1920-21

The belligerent mood within the *Beamtenschaft* after the Reichstag vote and the options available to civil servant leaders at that time emerge from an anonymous letter, which the state secretary in the Reich Chancellery received on December 11, 1920.[62] According to a marginal note on the document, the author of the letter was "a leading figure in the civil servant movement, and it is for this reason that considerable weight was attached to it then by the ministerial bureaucracy, and hence must be attached to it now in the reconstruction of these events.

In his report on the existing state of the civil servant movement the author of the letter made it clear that the way chosen by the government to quell the latest wave of unrest within the *Beamtenschaft* was the wrong one and would, in the long run, be disastrous. The net effect of granting an advance on January salaries would be that by February the salaries would be spent, and new pay demands would then have to be presented by the organizations in response to new pressures from the rank and file. If the government had cooperated with the organizations earlier, the writer claimed, a better solution could have been found. Against their will, the organizations had been pushed into conducting something like a permanent "blackmail policy."

It is perhaps even more important that in this report an attempt is made to speculate on the deeper causes of the continued unrest in the public sector. In pointing out that all public sector wage movements had in the past originated in the industrial regions of the Ruhr and the Rhineland, the author put forth the argument that their origins had to be searched for in the social animosities created by a glaring discrepancy between the earnings of miners and the income of civil servants employed in government-run mines. In addition, the practice of supplying

[62] Copy of the letter in BA, R 43I/2560, Bl. 112—113. The letter is unsigned, but a note sent by the State Secretary in the Chancellery Albert to all cabinet members and the Reich President's Office on December 14, together with a slightly edited version of the letter, claimed that it had originated „in Fachkreisen." According to several clues in the letter, its author might well have been a leading member in a railroad civil servant union, most likely a one affiliated with the Catholic trade union movement.

miners with foods at lower rates had stirred unrest among the people in the Ruhr: "If Herr Stinnes is allowed to buy potatoes in Mecklenburg for 48 marks and then sells them to his employees for 25 marks, it is not surprising that the rest of the population in the Ruhr is losing its breath," the writer complained.[63] Even industrial leaders had, in private conversations at least, supported higher wage rates in the public sector, if only to dispel the notion that "the state, the scroundrel, keeps its employees hungry, while the privately operated mines can feed their people."[64] If the government and the political parties in the Reichstag continued with this preferential treatment for the miners, the industrial centers of the Ruhr would continue being a seedbed of social unrest among public employees, and especially of recurring strike threats by railroad civil servants. In confrontation with such threats the government would continue being forced to back down eventually, which would lead to an erosion of its authority not only over its employees, but in a more general sense as well. It would be more prudent, therefore, the author of the letter concluded, to *negotiate* wage concessions now than be *forced* to make them later.[65]

The document has been recited in some length because it illustrates rather well, even if from a very subjective perspective, some of the underlying causes of civil servant unrest in a short-range and long-range perspective. While it was to have no immediate impact on the chain of events in the December days of 1920, its content and timing is a product

[63] The writer speculates in this context whether Stinnes had embarked on an "aggressive anti-socialization policy." The coal mines in the Ruhr had been slated for nationalization; a good number of mines were (and had been since the mid-nineteenth century) government-owned enterprises. Cf. Peter Wulf, *Regierung, Parteien, Wirtschaftsverbände und die Sozialisierung des Kohlebergbaus 1920—1921*, in: *Industrielles System...*, H. Mommsen et. al (eds.), pp. 647—657.

[64] The writer cites a conversation with Privy Councillor Quaatz, a spokesman for Rhenish industrialists, who apparantly had indicated support for such pay increases.

[65] Responding to these complaints, the Labor Ministry later on defended the special wage levels of the miners with the „besondere Schwierigkeit und der Bedeutung ihrer Arbeit für sämtliche Zweige des Wirtschaftslebens und alle mit ihm verbundenen Berufe." The Labor Ministry conceded, however, that the payment in kind which miners were receiving as an additional wage-supplement, was often exceeding their actual needs and consumption, especially with regard to the coal allowance *(Kohlendeputat)*. Reich Labor Ministry to Reich Chancellery, January 12, 1921, BA, R 43I/2560, Bl. 184. On miners' wages see G. D. Feldman, *Arbeitskonflikte...*, in: *VfZG*, 28 (1918), pp. 168—223, and R. Tschirbs, *Der Ruhrbergbau...*, in: G. D. Feldman et al. (eds.), *The German Inflation...*, pp. 308—346.

and a result of these events. Moreover, the line of argumentation shows that in the all-important wage issue a certain solidarity between various groups of public employees — in this case railroad workers and civil servants — against those of another social group, e. g. miners, existed, i. e. interests that went beyond established "class lines." These new alliances would become of some importance in the further course of events.

After the Reich government and the Reichstag had rejected their demands, DBB leaders were put under enormous pressure by militant affiliates to begin preparations for a strike vote.[66] On December 10, 1920 the DBB executive met "in a mood of extraordinary excitement and commotion," as one participant later recalled. Only the "cold-blooded maneuvers" of some members of the executive's moderate faction prevented the adoption of a strike vote.[67] In a public statement issued later on, the DBB stressed that the political situation of the Reich did not warrant a strike at this time, but insisted on its economic demands as well as on the civil servants' right to use the "ultimate trade-union weapon" to protect vital interests.[68] In a letter to the Ministry of Posts, the DBB emphasized the last point by protesting against Giesberts' anti-strike decree on the grounds that "the constitutionally guaranteed right of coalition implied the right for a joint work-stoppage" to attain improved economic conditions.[69] This toughness in language could not precloud the fact, however, that the DBB had all but abdicted from the envoking of this right at a very critical moment. Radical member organizations justifiably spoke of a

[66] On December 8, i. e. one day before the crucial vote in the Reichstag, three militant affiliates of the Reichsgewerkschaft had agreed to call a strike-vote immediately. They had demanded the resignation of the current RG leadership, accusing it and the DBB of unnecessary prolongation of the vote *(Verschleppungstaktik)*. ZStAP, RMdI, 2185, Bl. 125—126, copy of the resolution adopted by the three branch associations. The same file contains explicit guidelines for a civil servant strike on the railroads.

[67] ZStAP, RMdI, PA/267, Bl. 13, an exposé drafted by Albert Falkenberg for his superior, State Secretary Lewald. The final vote was 31 against and only 12 members in favor of the strike, an indication that Falkenberg's account might have been somewhat dramatized. Figures on the vote given in *Der Beamte,* Karlsruhe, January 1, 1920.

[68] The statement was distributed by the semi-official Wolff Telegraphic Bureau. Copy in GStA, Rep. 631, Bl. 115. The Catholic civil servant organizations published a similar declaration, which likewise criticized the Reichstag vote, but refrained from *any* mentioning of the strike issue *(ibid.)*.

[69] DBB to Minister of Posts Giesberts, December 14, 1920, copy of the letter in ZStAP, RMdI, 2185, Bl. 155—156.

turnaround of the DBB on the strike issue and predicted a sharp internal confrontation as a result of it.[70]

In a letter to its own regional organizations, the DBB tried to justify its position. The economic situation of the *Beamte* had been improved somewhat by the pay awards granted. The successful outcome of a strike was dubious, because other large trade unions would most likely refuse to participate, and "firm solidarity in the ranks of our own member organizations" was doubtful according to reports received by the DBB executive. Furthermore, the Reichstag had endorsed the anti-strike decree issue by Giesberts, with only the small radical left supporting the DBB's position in this matter. This meant that severe countermeasures could be taken by the government against striking civil servants; a success of the strike was doubtful on that account, too. On the other hand, a general strike by civil servants could not afford being lost under any circumstances. In view of these developments the DBB had concluded that negotiation rather than strike action was a more promising road to travel.[71] There can be no doubt that the DBB leadership was, in fact, afraid of the consequences which a strike might produce on its own organization. A similar situation was to appear a year later, when once again the DBB had to decide on whether or not to use the "ultimate trade union weapon," which, it should be stressed again, the DBB rhetorically at least still claimed to possess.[72]

Militant DBB affiliates were less cautious, however. The Reichsgewerkschaft went ahead with its strike vote among railroad civil servants. Its result was an overwhelming call for strike action by the RG's rank and file.[73] Railroad civil servants had been further antagonized by the fact that on December 16 the Reichstag, in a vote on the revision of the Salary Law of April 1920, had revoked the special allowances granted to railroad personnel in the original bill. Merging now with parallel wage movements among railroad workers,[74] a strike bloc between railroad workers and railroad civil servants was forged.[75] The

[70] *GBZ*, December 15, 1920.

[71] DBB to Landesverbände and Provinzialkartelle, reprinted in DG, January 1, 1921.

[72] On this see CHAPTER SIX below.

[73] Nearly 82 %, i. e., more than the required two-thirds, had voted for the strike. *RG Geschäftsbericht 1920—21*, p. 122.

[74] In early November the Socialist railroad workers' union, the DEV, had begun a wage movement, which had run parallel to the one conducted for civil servants by the DBB. Details in *Korrespondenzblatt des Allgemeinen Deutschen Gewerkschaftsbundes* (hereafter cited as *Korr. Bl.*), January 5, 1921.

[75] *Der Freie Beamte*, January 8, 1921.

struggle between government and civil servants had thus entered a third and decisive phase. In this stage of the conflict, an alliance of railroad unions representing a total of 1.2 million members — 700,000 workers and nearly 400,000 civil servants — was ready to take on the Reichsbahn Administration under the leadership of Reich Transport Minister Groener, the former general of the Imperial army, whose military background and traditional perceptions of state authority and public order were to make him more than inflexible in the handling of labor disputes in his administration. A potentially violent confrontation between these two sides seemed imminent by mid-December 1920.

The railroad unions began their wage offensive with a joint petition, sent to the government on December 22. They demanded an increase of the cost-of-living allowance for workers by one mark per hour, and for civil servants a percentage increase scaled according to salary groups, with lower groups receiving a steeper increase than the higher ones.[76] In the letter of explanation appended to their demands, the organizations spoke of tendencies toward proletarianization and of a "mood of desperation" among their members. If government and parliament were unwilling to grant economic aid, "the organizational leadership would be forced to adhere to the will of the rank and file and use the last trade-union weapon, the strike." In the latter case, the organizations were in agreement "to conduct the battle, which had been forced upon us, jointly," and they would not tolerate attempts at breaking this organizational alliance *(Einheitsfront).*[77]

On the very same day the DBB approached the Reich government. Referring to the initiative of the railroad unions, the DBB suggested that negotiations should commence immediately in order to defuse the conflict. It warned the government about the "seriousness of the situation" and of its escalation to a "chain of uncontrollable events." Very much in accordance with the DBB's previous decision, there was no mentioning of the possibility of a strike.[78] The government had come under pressure to act, and the question was whether the hard-line approach advocated by Groener in a cabinet meeting only a few days

[76] The range was from an increase to 90 % (i. e. a 40 percent increase) for the lower groups to 60 % (an ten percent increase) for the higher groups.

[77] Copy of this petition in BA, R 43I/2584, Bl. 85—88. Next to the RG, the petition was signed by the three leading railroad workers' unions, the Socialist DEV, the Catholic GDE, and the National-Liberal AEV.

[78] DBB to Reich Government, December 22, 1920, BA, R 43I/2579, Bl. 96.

earlier could indeed be pursued. Groener had based his "policy of toughness" on the prospects of dividing the interests of workers and civil servants, and by regaining the control over the civil servant union and its actions. This apparently had misfired, as the joint petition of the railroad organizations indicated. While Groener's position had found the support of Reich Finance Minister Wirth, the majority in the cabinet was swayed toward making concessions before things got out of hand even further.[79]

Domestic political disturbances, as well as potential international complications caused by a railroad strike, finally prompted the cabinet in a meeting on December 29, 1920 to change its policy.[80] The final decision for a more conciliatory policy was taken on January 2, 1921 in the absence of Finance Minister Wirth, who was still opposed to making any concessions.[81] An alarming report from the Rhenish-Westphalian industrial region, which claimed that in case of a rail strike the railroad in the occupied zone would be placed under the military administration of the allied powers and a seizure of the unoccupied portions of the Ruhr might follow, may have tipped the balance in favor of wage concessions and against fiscal considerations.[82]

At the same time, the Reich government made use of this report to demonstrate to foreign powers that their commitment to a more balanced budget as a precondition for reparation payments and economic stabilization was being sabotaged by the interventions of the Allied Rhineland Commission. "While on the one hand the payment of billions was being demanded, the saving of billions was made impossible by the policies of the Rhineland Commission," a government memo-

[79] Cabinet meeting, December 18, 1920, *ARK. Kab. Fehrenbach*, pp. 359—360.

[80] There is no official protocol of this meeting. Koch noted in his diary on December 29, 1920: „Beamtenfragen. Wirth hat seine Vertreter nicht instruiert. Es wird über sein Nein hinweggegangen. Reichsregierung ist grundsätzlich zum Nachgeben bereit. Dadurch wird doch wenigstens ein kleiner Anschein von Initiative bewahrt und nicht wieder nur der Drohung des Streiks nachgegeben. Haltung des Reichsfinanzministers jammervoll. Will sich selbst salvieren anstatt zu führen. Die Beamtenfrage ist aber hochpolitisch geworden. Die Kommunisten rechnen mit Beamtenstreik, die Franzosen wollen die rheinischen Eisenbahnen übernehmen, um selbst die Kohlen rauszuholen." BA, Nachlaß Koch-Weser, 27, Bl. 353.

[81] Cabinet meeting, January 2, 1921, *ARK. Kab. Fehrenbach*, pp. 368—389.

[82] The report was sent to the Chancellery. Its authorship is unclear, but it was probably written by a unionist or by a civil servant association leader in the Ruhrgebiet. Copy in BA, R 43I/180, Bl. 3 and BA, R 43I/2560, Bl. 141—143, the latter a slightly edited version (see note 83 below).

randum declared.[83] That these international entanglements, especially a harsh reaction by the French, were not totally unrealistic is borne out by the fact that apparently British and Belgian members of the Rhineland Commission met separately with representatives of the railroad unions in order to persuade them to cancel the idea of a railstrike.[84] Earlier, the railroad unions had tried to assure the Entente Powers that a possible strike would *not* affect the occupied zone,[85] a promise which the Rhineland Commission had obviously ignored.

Partially as a consequence of these potential international complications, then, the Reich government decided to resume negotiations with the organizations. A preparatory meeting took place in the Finance Ministry on January 3, 1921, where it was decided that separate talks would be conducted first on the railroad issue between the railroads unions and the Reich Transport Ministry, and then for all other civil servants and public employees between DBB and the Finance Ministry.[86] Tactically, this was a clever move on the part of the government: it divided the interest of the civil servants, since the Reichsgewerkschaft took part in the talks to be conducted in the Transport Ministry.

With relative ease a compromise was reached in the negotiations conducted in the Transport Ministry on January 5. The organizations agreed to a scaled-down version of their original demands. Groener urged the cabinet to accept this compromise as a blueprint for the negotiations with the DBB and a model for the final wage agreement.[87]

[83] *Ibid.* — The Chancellery sent an edited version of the report to the Foreign Office, requesting to forward the report to German embassies in "enemy countries" *(feindliches Ausland)* as well as to those in the main neutral countries. „Von besonderer Bedeutung dürfte die Sache für die Amerikaner sein," the cover letter said. State Secretary in the Reich Chancellery to State Secretary in the Foreign Office, BA, R 43I/2560, Bl. 140.

[84] Oberbergrat Jordan to [unknown addressee], January 4, 1921, BA, R 43I/180, Bl. 70. Jordan believed that the Transport Ministry had been too timid in the matter and stressed that the Rhineland Commission would not tolerate a railstrike in the occupied territories under any circumstances.

[85] Reichsgewerkschaft, Section Cologne, Trier, and Mainz to Interalliierte Rheinland Kommission, Koblenz, December 20, 1920, copy in ZStAP, RMdI, 2185, Bl. 126—127. The RG later denied the authenticity of this letter, which was publicized in the press, obviously to undercut accusations of "collaborating with the enemy."

[86] Minute on a meeting in the Reich Finance Ministry, January 3, 1921, BA, R 43I/2560, Bl. 148.

[87] Groener to Reich Minister of Finances and Cabinet, January 6, 1921, copy: PA AA, RM 17, Bd. I. A handwritten marginal note on this document indicated that the expenditures entailed by the agreement would total 2,852 million marks.

The matter was indeed taken up by government negotiators in talks with the DBB, which took place two days later in the Finance Ministry. The DBB's bargaining position had been all but eroded by the separate agreement negotiated by its strongest member association. Not without justification, the DBB press spoke of a collapse of the organizational unity among civil servants at the expense of an alliance between workers and civil servants in the transportation sector.[88] The railroad unions, on the other hand, had behaved admirably, as one of the participants reported: they had been the more moderate force and had put pressure on DBB negotiators to accept the railroad compromise. The unity of the civil servant organizations, so often proclaimed to the outside, was more than shaky at closer scrutiny, the same source reported.[89]

Indeed, the DBB had been forced to drop all of its demands, most importantly the idea of a minimum increase for the lower groups, and it had to give up its opposition to a differentiation of the cost-of-living increase according to regional principles under the *Ortsklassen* scheme. Intense internal pressures by organizations of rural civil servants *(Landbeamte)* had forced the DBB to bargain for a general increase independent of location. In the end, however, the government's position prevailed, which implied that since the cost-of-living was less high in rural areas and in small towns, pay scales for *Landbeamte* should be increased at a lesser rate than for civil servants residing in large cities.[90] With the indirect help of one of its own affiliates, the DBB had suffered a severe set-back.

Only a development beyond its own control enabled the DBB to recapture some of its lost ground during the following days. As it turned out, the executive councils of the participating railroad unions rejected the compromise negotiated by their leaders. The union quickly put the blame on Finance Minister Wirth, who had openly disapproved of the wage concessions made to the railroad men during a meeting of the Finance Committee of the Reich Economic Council.[91] These misgiv-

[88] *DG*, January 16, 1921.

[89] State Secretary Stieler of the Transport Ministry to State Secretary in the Chancellery, January 8, 1921, BA, R 43I/2560, Bl. 158.

[90] *DG*, January 16, 1921. („Vor der Entscheidung“).

[91] RG to Reich Chancellor, Reich President, and Reich Minister of Transport, January 10, 1921, BA, R 43I/2560, Bl. 164. The RG was especially enraged that Wirth had put the costs of the measure at 6 billion marks, while they held that it amounted to only 1.3 billion. On the source of yet a different figure, see note 87 above. The 3 billion

ings were echoed by one of Wirth's own cabinet colleagues, Interior Minister Koch, who blamed the Finance Ministry for having caused higher expenditures through false delaying tactics in the previous days.[92]

In any case, the rejection of the compromise by the DEV's rank and file required either renegotiation or the acceptance of an all-out confrontation with the strike-inclined railroad men. These options were discussed in a meeting between members of the cabinet and party leaders on January 13.[93] Chancellor Fehrenbach told the Reichstag delegation that the government would remain firmly committed to the provisional settlement. Speaking for the SPD, Otto Wels cautioned that according to information made available to him, the French would occupy the Ruhr in case of a strike. If this was the case, one could not let a final agreement fail for sole reasons of additional public expenditures. Moreover, a strike had to be avoided at this juncture at all costs in order to keep Communist agitation at bay. Speakers for the coalition parties replied that public finances and the authority of the government precluded any further giving-in to the civil servants' demands. The additional costs, Wirth said, would run up to one-and-a-half billion marks, a sum which the already overgrown budget could not afford. Minister of Posts Giesberts held that the government had succumbed to ultimatums of railroad employees already four times in the recent past; now it was to happen a fifth time. No responsible German trade union, he added, could endorse such a behavior. Labor Minister Brauns emphasized that formal negotiations with the railroad unions had taken place and that the latter should adhere to their results. SPD Deputy Hermann Müller replied that trade union leaders had done their utmost to push for an acceptance of the compromise, but had failed. The SPD

mentioned there are the projected costs for *all* Reich civil servants. The six billion would include Länder and municipalities as well, and the 1.3 billion would refer to the costs for the railroad administration only. The matter shows, how figures were misused for political purposes.

[92] BA, Nachlaß Koch-Weser, 27, Bl. 359. Commenting on the cabinet meeting on January 12, Koch wrote: „Wirth verkorkst alles um sich herum. Durch sein Zögern hat er die Sache entweder gefährdet oder teuerer gemacht als Groener."

[93] *Protokoll über die Besprechung mit den Parteiführern über die Teuerungszuschläge*, January 13, 1921, BA, R 43I/2560, Bl. 196—197. Representatives of the USPD and the KPD had not been invited. The question of financial cover for the new expenditures was not discussed in the meeting. The cabinet in a follow-up meeting decided on a complicated scheme to raise 2.3 billion marks in additional taxes.

could not give a binding promise that it would be able to support the government's position in a possible showdown, because too many trade unionists were in its ranks. Thus far the government had not yet exhausted negotiations with the peak associations of labor. Other party delegates, including the DNVP representative, agreed that a political front against the railroad organizations was out of reach for the moment, and that the results of the negotiations between government and unions had to be awaited first. In a follow-up meeting the cabinet decided to stand firmly on the compromise of January 5 as a negotiating position for the upcoming talks with the unions.[94]

These talks took place on the following day, January 14, which was to become the day of the decisive battle over the wage increases in the public sector. Time was running out, because the railroad unions had called for mass demonstrations to begin on the following Sunday (January 16) as the opening signal for a general rail strike. To avert such a development, which was not in the interest of the moderate majority of the union leadership, the railroad workers' unions had called on their respective peak organizations to mediate in the conflict in order to find a way to break out of the deadlock. Accordingly, the peak associations of the trade union movement, especially the Socialist General Federation of Trade Unions (ADGB) had entered the picture as a mediator.[95] The sole exception was the railroad civil servant union, the Reichsgewerkschaft, which had not asked its peak organization, the DBB, but continued to act in its own behalf.

The decisive meeting between peak associations and government leaders took place in the morning of January 14. The railroad unions presented a new wage proposal that was considerable higher than the one negotiated earlier.[96] The proposal relating to the cost-of-living increase of civil servants met with the fiercest resistance on the part of the government. As a representative of the Finance Ministry pointed

[94] Cabinet meeting, January 13, 1921, *ibid.*

[95] *Korr.-Bl.*, January 29, 1921.

[96] *Besprechung am 14. Januar 1921 mit den Spitzenorganisationen*, BA, R 43I/2560, Bl. 198—202. According to the list of participants, leading members of the three trade union federations (ADGB, DGB, and Gewerkschaftsring) were present, as well as representatives of the major railroad unions and most cabinet members. Groener apparently did not participate in the meeting. The proposal called for an increase of workers' wages between 70 and 40 pfennigs per hour, and for an increase of the cost-of-living supplement for civil servants, varying according to pay group and *Ortsklasse*. Civil servants in the lowest rural *Ortsklasse* were not awarded an increase at all.

out, it was too much in favor of the lower pay groups and would therefore add onto the leveling of income within the civil service. Furthermore, the government claimed that the increases sought in the rural "location classes" were too high, and in total disregard of the fact that the inflation was less virulent in rural areas, where many civil servants were "economically self-sufficient" *(Selbstversorger).* Chancellor Fehrenbach defended the position of the government by pointing out that the plight among civil servants and workers was, on the whole, less intense than for millions of small pensioners. He then chided the union leaders for their lack of understanding for the financial malaise of the state. The wage increase for Reich employees alone would cost 2.8 billion marks, and since the Reich government would most likely be forced to pay the share of Länder and the municipalities as well, a total of six billion marks would be required. Moreover, the organizations were unable to guarantee that a strike would be called off if the government gave in. The strike threat, Fehrenbach claimed, was politically motivated, and forces were at work who were about to seize this opportunity regardless of any wage concessions that the government might make. In view of these facts and in order not to undermine the authority of the state even further, Fehrenbach concluded, the government had to insist upon its position.

Clearly exasperated by this uncompromising attitude, Adolf Cohen, the ADGB mediator, pleaded with the government representatives to make some concessions. Wage demands, he insisted, were only a response to rising prices for basic food stuffs. Only recently farmers had raised the price of potatoes, abandoning all previous promises not to do so. As a consequence of recent price increases, Cohen argued, the standard of living of workers had declined by 25 percent. Fehrenbach, however, was unmoved. The standard of living of other groups had dropped even more sharply, he argued. Wage increases alone were not the solution to this problem. Only a sharp reduction of prices would help — and there were some indications that the current international crisis on commodity markets might lead to a price decline *(Preissturz)* in Germany as well.

Union leaders remained unimpressed. While these arguments might well be true, DEV Chairman Scheffel replied, they would not be understood by the workers; who wanted "money in the pocket". Scheffel, too, pleaded for some concessions on the part of the government to avoid the complete collapse of the talks. Fehrenbach, however, did not give in. He announced that he would first have to consult with Reichstag leaders and with the full cabinet. Without concrete results, therefore, the talks were broken off.[97]

Immediately afterwards, Fehrenbach received a delegation of the DBB. DBB Chairman Flügel bitterly complained that his organization had been excluded from the top-level talks with the other unions. The interests of three-fourth of the *Beamtenschaft,* he added, had therefore not been taken into consideration. Flügel emphasized that the DBB's demand for a minimum increase for the lower pay groups entailed an important social dimension, and he told the Chancellor that civil servants living in rural areas were extremely antagonized by the disregard of their concerns in the cost-of-living allowance proposed by the government. Without too much ado the meeting was then closed, perhaps and indication of the comparatively limited leverage which the DBB could muster at this juncture.[98]

While Fehrenbach and other ministers had conferred with the DBB delegation, two cabinet members, Minister of Labor Brauns and Economics Minister von Raumer, had inofficially conferred with ADGB leaders Grassmann and Cohen in an attempt to break the deadlock and to reach a compromise. They had agreed to form a special negotiating committee, to be composed of one representative of each peak association, including the DBB, leaders of the political parties, and representatives of the ministries of Finance and Transportation. The committee's task would be to work out a compromise. In exchange for the offer, union leaders had signalled their support for a ceiling of 70 percent for the embattled cost-of-living increase. Brauns and von Raumer then proposed to the cabinet that renewed talks to be conducted this very afternoon, and that the cabinet would then make its final decision later in the evening.[99] Fehrenbach and the other cabinet members accepted

[97] Koch, who was obviously unimpressed with Fehrenbach's performance in the meeting and his abrupt style of negotiation, noted in his diary: „Fehrenbach will nicht auf Details eingehen und redet mit seinem eindringlichen oder aufdringlichem Pathos über Finanznot, Autorität der Regierung und die Notlage, in der sich auch seine mit einem Arzt verheiratete Tochter befindet und erklärt — es hatten nur zwei Gewerkschafter gesprochen — man sei am Ende der Verhandlungen. Statt sachlich Klarheit zu schaffen, Geschwätz! Es ist zum Jammern, und wenn es zum Streit kommt, ist die Ungeschicklichkeit der Regierung daran mit Schuld." BA, Nachlaß Koch-Weser, 27, Bl. 360—361.

[98] *Besprechung... mit Vertretern des Deutschen Beamtenbundes.* January 14, 1921, 12:30 p. m., BA, R 43I/2560, Bl. 203.

[99] *Ibid.* (notation on a follow-up meeting of the cabinet immediately after the talks with the DBB).

this proposal, but only after Reichstag leaders had indicated their support for a continuation of the negotiations. Labor Minister Brauns was appointed to chair the committee.[100]

At the meeting of the committee, in the early evening of January 14, Brauns introduced a compromise which basically set the rates of the cost-of-living increase for workers and civil servants to the half-way point between the proposals made by the railroad unions and those made by the Reich Finance Ministry. Attempts made by the DBB delegate, Remmers, to introduce a minimum pay standard for the lower groups and to raise the percentage rate to be paid in rural areas of location-class "E" were blocked, because they did not receive the support of any of the other organizations, much less of the government delegates. The DBB, it seemed, was effectively isolated. After long and intensive bickering about the final level of the increase, during which the conservative fiscal policies of the Reich Finance Ministry collided once again head-on with the wage policies pursued by the labor unions and the Labor Ministry, a compromise was hammered out.[101]

On the same evening, the cabinet gave its agreement to the compromise-solution reached in the committee.[102] On January 15, the railroad organizations issued a joint statement urging their members not to take part in the protest meetings announced by radical left-wing groups for the following day.[103] The immediate danger of a strike had, in the last minute, been averted. A wage movement in the public sector had been brought to a close which, as one contemporary commentator wrote, had been "one of the largest and most important ones ever to be conducted in the history of the modern German labor movement." The same writer did not fail to mention that the significance of this wage movement was, above all, that for the first time civil servants had fought side by side with workers for economic and social gains. For this reason alone, he argued, a new era in public-sector labor relations had begun.[104]

[100] *Besprechung... mit den Führern der politischen Parteien,* January 14, 1921, 5:40 p. m., *ibid.,* Bl. 207.

[101] *Verhandlungen der Kommission für die Erörterung der Teuerungszuschläge...,* January 14, 1921, 6:45 p. m., *ibid.,* Bl. 208—211.

[102] Cabinet meeting, January 14, 1921, 10 p. m., *ARK. Kab. Fehrenbach,* pp. 409—410.

[103] Text of the proclamation in BA, R 431/2560, Bl. 188.

[104] Theodor Kotzur, *Zum Abschluß der Eisenbahnerbewegung,* in: *Korr. Bl.,* January 29, 1921. Kotzur was the civil service expert of the DEV.

From the perspective of railroad civil servants, the alliance with the organized working class had indeed turned out to be beneficial. Not only had their organization been accepted as an "equal among equals," the events had proven, moreover, that civil servant demands could be attained more forcefully with the backing of the workers vis-à-vis an increasingly stubborn government as the bargaining adversary. From the point of view of the DBB, however, the "railroad alliance" must have appeared as a real threat to its own power as an interest group and as the foremost representative of civil servant interests. For the DBB, therefore, the outcome of the January crisis was more a defeat than a victory, in spite of the fact that in the last phase it had been able to at least participate in the bargaining sessions.

To the government, finally, the events of winter 1920-21 showed that the primacy of fiscal and economic policies could not be maintained against trade-union power in the public sector, or even vis-à-vis its civil servants. The compromise of January 14, 1921 was therefore a defeat and a severe set-back of its economic and financial policy, which had been based on wage reductions (in real terms) as a precondition for attaining greater economic stability.

The January Crisis of 1921 was the first major confrontation between civil servants organizations, trade unions, and the government as employer over wage policy in the public service. This confrontation had occurred at the end of a period of relatively stable economic conditions. It stands to reason that in the following months, in which the rate of inflation was to accelerate after all attempts at stabilization had failed, social conflicts in the public sector and the confrontations of the type just described would accelerate and intensify as well.

CHAPTER FIVE

1921: Accelerated Inflation and the Intensification of Social Conflict

In the summer and fall of 1921 the public sector became the center of social conflict in Germany. Civil servants and their organizations played an important, if not crucial role in a series of social struggles which were to last for nearly a year until the spring of 1922. Conflicts that were fought out in the public sector during these months were to foreshadow those that later on would characterize the stabilization period of 1923—24.

The causes of the intensifying social conflicts in 1921 are to be found in the renewed upturn of the inflationary conditions of the German economy. After the temporary lull of 1920-21, the cost of living began to rise once again in the spring of 1921.[1] In the subsequent months, which in the context of this study have been subsumed under the rubric of "accelerated inflation," civil servant organizations conducted three major wage movements *(Besoldungsbewegungen)* in an effort to offset the loss of real income which their members were experiencing during this period.[2] These wage movements, which one author later described as having surpassed all other labor struggles of the inflation years in

[1] Between May and October 1921 the cost-of-living index rose by 34 percent from 11.20 to 15.04. From October to December 1921 it rose by another 28 percent (from 15.04 to 19.28). In February 1922 the index stood at 24.49, which translates into another increase of 27 percent. Over the entire period of "accelerated inflation," i. e. from May 1921 to February 1922, the cost of living slightly more than doubled in nine months' time. Between February and June 1922, i. e. in four months, the index rose from 24.49 to 41.47 (or 70 percent), which indicates that accelerated inflation had given way to rapid inflation. Index figures according to *Zahlen zur Geldentwertung...*, p. 33. For a characterization of the period, see C. Bresciani-Turroni, *The Economics...*, pp. 32—33.

[2] The period of civil servant interest politics to be discussed now coincides with the

both extent and importance,[3] are the subject of the next two chapters of this study. The very fact that one has to deal with these movements in two rather long chapters is an indication of their complexity and historical significance. Clearly, by 1921-22 a climax has been reached with regard to social conflicts within the *Beamtenschaft* and, more importantly perhaps, with regard to conflicts between civil servants and other social groups and with the government as employer.

The salary struggles unleashed by the first two wage movements in the summer and fall of 1921 produced a profound impact on the ever precarious relations between civil servants and the German labor movement. This theme will be explored in the following pages. The conflicts that arose during 1921 set the stage for the most serious crisis in the triangular relations between civil servants, the labor movement and the state in the winter of 1921-22, when a third wage movement conducted in the public sector turned into a strike movement and produced the first (and, to this day, the last) major civil servant strike in German history: the so-called February Strike of 1922. This strike and its social and political implications and consequences — by all accounts one of the most explosive social conflicts in the history of the German inflation — will be the subject of the next chapter of this study.

Confrontation With Labor: The Wage Movement of August 1921,

In May 1921, the period of relative stability of the inflation came to an end. As prices began to rise once again, the social impact of the inflation became a much discussed topic again in the organizational press. In early May the DBB's *Gemeinschaft* reprinted an article which had originally appeared in the SPD's theoretical journal *Sozialistische Monatshefte*. The article speculated on the organizational consequences of the renewed price increases. Its author, Max Schippel, pointed out that in the earlier stages of the inflation serious conflicts had erupted between civil servants and the workers — an obvious reference to the struggles between the DBB and the railroad workers' unions in the winter of 1920-21 — and he raised hopes that in the forthcoming salary and wage movements in the public sector these "artificial rivalries" would be overcome. In face of pressing economic and social problems,

phase of the long downswing in civil servants' real salaries discussed in CHAPTER ONE of this study. See above, pp. 75 f.

[3] F. J. Furtwängler, *ÖTV*..., p. 344.

Schippel argued, a new interest alliance between wage and salary earners, i. e. between blue-collar workers *(Arbeiter)*, salaried employees *(Angestellte)* and civil servants *(Beamte)* needed to be reconstructed.[4]

The notion that a renewed wage offensive in the public sector would not only become the testing ground in the prolonged struggle between civil servant interests and the government as employer, but also bring up again the crucial and unresolved question of organizational alliances between civil servants and the organizations of labor, was taken up by Wilhelm Schröder, a member of the DBB's inner leadership circle, in the pages of the *Gemeinschaft.* Schröder conceded that there was indeed a strong interdependence between wage contracts *(Tariflöhne)* in the public sector and the setting of civil servant pay levels, in spite of the fact that the latter had to be done through legislative procedures rather than in form of collective agreements between public employees and public employers. The interdependence of wages and civil servant pay, Schröder argued, necessitated close cooperation between civil servants and the other wage and salary earners in the public enterprises of *Reichsbahn* and *Reichspost,* just as much as cooperation was called for in other areas of social policy like working hours and working conditions. Yet Schröder likewise emphasized that there were certain differences between civil servants and the other employee groups, differences based largely on the special legal status of the civil servant, who, after all, was subject to public rather than contractual law. These social and legal differences, Schröder argued, placed certain limits on cooperation strategies between civil servants and organized labor, because they could very well become a source of differences of interest. Moreover, the political division of the trade union movement into three rival factions, he claimed, presented a threat to the DBB's avowed principle of political neutrality, on which alone its internal unity was based. The DBB simply could not afford to establish too close a relationship with only *one* of the *Richtungsgewerkschaften* of the German labor movement. "The *Beamtenschaft,*" he insisted, "must at all costs conduct an independent policy and refrain from establishing partisan political affiliations."[5]

[4] Max Schippel, *Soziale Wirkungen des Valutaelends,* in: *DG,* May 15, 1921. See also P. Class, *Beamtengehalt und Teuerung,* in: *Ibid.,* August 11, 1921.

[5] Wilhelm Schröder, *Der Deutsche Beamtenbund und die anderen Gewerkschaften,* in: *DG,* July 7, 1921.

Thus according to Schröder, a spokesman of the DBB's centrist faction, cooperation rather than affiliation with labor was the road to travel in the forthcoming wage movements. Even cooperation would in the long run depend on labor's willingness to acknowledge, without reservations, the special legal status of the *Berufsbeamtentum.* Any measure or demand proposed by labor that was likely to endanger this special status or the continued existence of independent civil servant organizations would jeopardize cooperation strategies between civil servants and the working class.

By rejecting the idea of affiliation, Schröder was indirectly commenting on high-level talks between DBB and ADGB which were being conducted at the same time. The aim of these negotiations was a "cooperation agreement" between the two confederations as a first step toward a possible merger. A revival of similar talks that had taken place in 1919, the ADGB had stepped up its pressure on the DBB in the spring of 1921 to come to a final decision on whether or not it would join the Free Trade Union movement as its third "pillar" representing civil servants in a socially broadly based "employee movement" *(Arbeitnehmerbewegung)*. The urgency with which the ADGB pursued the matter at this juncture had two causes. First, the ADGB had concluded a similar cartel agreement with the leading leftwing white-collar organization, the Federation of Salaried Employees (Afa-Bund), in April of 1921. This was the first step toward the goal of constructing the "three pillars" of the new, more broadly based Socialist trade-union movement, and a step toward the "corporatist" *(ständisch)* model of three semi-independent confederations under the Free Trade Union banner. This model was favored by the ADGB leadership and, even more so, by the leaders of the Afa-Bund. Now the "civil-servant question" *(Beamtenfrage)* was taken up by these circles in the Free Trade Unions in an effort to secure an organizational base for the "third pillar" of the movement.[6] The second reason was that opposition to the "corpora-

[6] For the background from the Free Trade Unions' perspective, see Allgemeiner freier Angestelltenbund (ed.), *Angestelltenbewegung 1921—1925,* Berlin 1925, pp. 474—484; the section is entitled „Die dritte Säule". See also, Salomon Schwarz, *Handbuch der Gewerkschaftskongresse,* Berlin 1930, pp. 158—165. For a semi-official account from the DBB perspective, see E. Remmers, *Die organisatorische Einheit...,* pp. 58—64, and F. Winters, *Der Deutsche Beamtenbund...,* pp. 26—30. It stands to reason that from hindsight of the early 1930s DBB officials tried to present the entire affair as a simple tactical maneuver on their part to undercut recruitment efforts made by the Free Trade Unions. As will become clear, this is an apologetic view at best.

tist" three-pillar principle had gained momentum, most notably within the unions of public employees in the ADGB, i. e. the Transportarbeiter-Verband and the Deutscher Eisenbahnerverband (DEV). The two last-mentioned organizations joined up forces by amalgamating as a "Transport Alliance" *(Verkehrsbund)*, partially with the aim of organizing civil servants in a more coordinated and systematic way.[7] This step was clearly in opposition to the policy pursued by the central leadership of the ADGB, whose executive *(Vorstand)* was geared toward attracting the DBB to its banner. This, too, explains the pressure that the ADGB put on DBB leaders with regard to an organizational agreement between the two federations.

These developments in the Free Trade Union movement were being watched closely by the DBB, as the aforementioned article by Wilhelm Schröder indicates. The DBB's centrist faction showed clear apprehension about a contractual 'cartel' with the ADGB, not to mention the direct opposition displayed by the DBB's right wing. Even the avowed trade unionists within the DBB's left wing, whose main spokesman was Albert Falkenberg, the editor of the *Gemeinschaft* and a member of the (M)SPD, argued that the time was not ripe for an organizational agreement between DBB and ADGB, at least not, of the type concluded with the Afa-Bund.[8] But the ADGB insisted on a speedy clarification of the DBB's position. On July 6, 1921, therefore, the DBB's executive board *(Bundesvorstand)* endorsed a draft proposal for an agreement between the two organizations.[9] There were a number of dissenting

[7] On the *Verkehrsbund* and other organizational developments in the German public sector during these years, see F. J. Furtwängler, *ÖTV...*, pp. 337—343. Furtwängler gives a brief discussion of the civil servant problem as seen from the perspective of the Free Trade Unions. See *ibid.*, pp. 317—336.

[8] See Albert Falkenberg, *Die Organisationsfrage der Beamten — Wege und Ziele,* in: *BJ*, 8 (June/July 1921), pp. 131—135, esp. pp. 133—134. See also his earlier contribution to the *Gemeinschaft, Der Neutralitätsgedanke in der Beamtenbewegung,* in: *DG*, April 7, 1921. A response to this article was printed in the same paper under the title *Beamte und Arbeiter* (*DG*, April 28, 1921), the author of which expressed his unconditional support for an alliance with Socialist labor.

[9] The text of the proposed agreement is reprinted in *DG*, July 14, 1921, and in the ADGB's *Korr. Bl.*, 1921, p. 448. Its key passages reads as follows: „Zur wirksamen Vertretung der gemeinsamen Interessen der Arbeiter, Angestellten und Beamten vereinbaren die unterzeichneten Spitzenorganisationen unter Wahrung ihrer vollen Selbständigkeit und unter Ausschluß aller parteipolitischen und religiösen Bestrebungen folgende Abmachungen:

1. Die drei Spitzenverbände verpflichten sich und die ihnen angeschlossenen

votes, however, signalling opposition within the DBB against the proposed agreement. Final approval was therefore deferred to the DBB council *(Bundesausschuß)*, the organization's ranking body in important policy matters between two general meetings *(Bundestage)*, which was scheduled to meet in mid-August.

In the meantime the DBB leadership was kept busy responding to critics in its own as well as in rival organizations, particularly within the Christian Trade Union movement (DGB). The latter stood in sharp opposition to a possible "merger" between ADGB and DBB. Emphasizing that the DBB was not about to be forced to decide on "either Christ or Marx," Falkenberg tried to stultify such criticism. He likewise warned opponents in his own organization not to become the tools of those who worked toward the destruction of a united organizational front *(Einheitsfront)* with the leading labor organization to further their own egotistical interests.[10] But as the bourgeois-liberal *Soziale Praxis*, certainly not a friend of closer ties between DBB and ADGB, pointed out, the organizational and political options circumscribed (and downplayed) by Falkenberg were indeed the main issue confronting the DBB in the coming weeks. While it could be regarded as a positive effort, this paper wrote, to work toward the general improvement in the relationship between civil servants and the working class, the content of the proposed agreement between DBB and ADGB well exceeded such efforts. The proposed *Vereinbarung* seemed to indicate "that the third

Verbände, in der Wahrung der gemeinsamen Arbeiterinteressen zusammenzuwirken. Jede Organisation hat ihr eigenes Programm selbst durchzuführen. [...]

2. Alle beteiligten Verbände erkennen ihren organisatorischen Besitzstand gegenseitig an...

3. Die beteiligten Verbände stehen auf dem Boden der demokratisch-republikanischen Verfassung des Deutschen Reiches. Sie verpflichten sich, jeder Verletzung und jeder ungesetzlichen Änderung dieser Verfassung im Reich und in den Ländern geschlossen entgegenzutreten, aber jede politische und religiöse Überzeugung in ihren Mitgliederkreisen unbestritten zu dulden.

4. Für die Stellungnahme zu wirtschaftspolitischen Fragen und eine gemeinsame Einwirkung auf die Wirtschaftspolitik ... ist richtungsgebend die Lage der Mitglieder als Arbeitnehmer und Verbraucher. Erster Grundsatz in der Wirtschaftspolitik soll sein, daß stets das Allgemeinwohl den Privatinteressen voranzustellen ist."

The third point shows that the proposed agreement entailed an important political dimension, i. e. a commitment to the parliamentary state of Weimar. This obviously was a consequence of the cooperation between the three federations during the abortive Kapp Putsch of March 1920.

[10] Albert Falkenberg, *Wochenschau*, in: *DG*, July 14, 1921.

large employee movement, too, was about to split into the same political factions which had been formed within the workers' movement and later on in the white-collar union movement as well."[11] It was the altogether not unfounded fear, then, that a closer alliance between DBB and the Free Trade Unions might lead to a political schism, if not to the complete disintegration of the outwardly powerful, one-million-member confederation of civil servants' associations, which loomed large in the public debate on the future relationship between the two organizations.

These worries were premature, however. On August 15, 1921, the DBB council rejected the proposed agreement with the ADGB. The timing of this vote is important if one seeks to answer the question of why, at this juncture, the DBB decided against an organizational pact with the Free Trade Unions. By mid-August of 1921 a wage movement conducted by the organizations in the public sector had reached a critical point. Serious conflicts had arisen between the civil servants' representatives and those of the participating labor organizations with regard to the aims and strategies to be pursued in the salary and wage drive. As a consequence, the attempt of putting together a negotiating cartel had all but been frustrated by specific interests and seemingly irreconcilable differences between the various social groups that comprised the public work force. Civil servant interests were pitted against those of wage earners and salaried employees; the admonitions given by Schippel and Schröder had not been followed by either side. Practical interest politics might therefore have played an equally, if not more important role in the failure to reach a closer organizational base between labor and civil servant organizations in mid-1921 than ideological differences and organizational rivalries usually cited in this context.[12] It is to the analysis of practical interest politics and its underlying economic and social factors that we shall now turn in our attempt at providing a more thorough explanation for the confrontation between civil servants and organized labor in mid-1921.

During June and July of 1921 the targets and main objectives of a new wage offensive had been mapped out by the DBB in response to urgent requests from its affiliate organizations. The *Beamtenrat* in Hamburg,

[11] *SP*, August 8, 1921.

[12] As done by most of the authors cited in note 6 above. See also F. J. Furtwängler, *ÖTV...*, pp. 345—347, and Thomas Ellwein, *Gewerkschaften und öffentlicher Dienst*, Opladen 1980.

for example, had informed the DBB leadership that salaries in Hamburg were just barely high enough to cover the rising costs for the essentials of life, i. e. food and rent, while no money was left for other necessities for instance, clothing, an item of great importance to the social self-esteem of civil servants.[13] In a series of internal meetings the DBB formulated a catalog of pay demands, ranging from a "sufficient" increase in base pay to the abolition of local differentiations in the cost-of-living allowances, to a proposal for the complete indexation of civil service pay: "We must demand", the DBB wrote, "that a reliable standard to adjust civil servant pay to the declining purchasing power of the currency is devised and applied in a more expeditious way."[14] Indexation of salaries had always been a popular demand with civil servant organizations, while labor unions were more reluctant to put wages on a "sliding scale." The government had consistently opposed such a measure.

Before presenting its demands to the government, however, the DBB contacted the peak associations of labor in an attempt to forge an organizational alliance of civil servants and other public employees around the salary issue. On August 5, DBB representatives and labor leaders met to discuss the DBB's proposals. While the idea of an *Einheitsfront* across organizational lines appealed to labor delegates, they were clearly unhappy with several of the DBB's specific demands. The meeting adjourned with labor leaders insisting that they needed the approval of their affiliated organizations on several points. It was decided to keep the content of the talks in strictest confidence and to meet again in a week's time.[15]

[13] Beamtenrat Hamburg to DBB, May 31, 1921, StAH, 122-4-100.

[14] Deutscher Beamtenbund (ed.), *Die Besoldungsbewegung des Deutschen Beamtenbundes* (= Flugschriften des Deutschen Beamtenbundes, No. 4), Berlin 1921, pp. 3—5, quotation p. 5. The position of the organizations had not become any easier in the wake of the cabinet reshuffle of May 1921. Wirth, the bulwark against civil service pressure, had become chancellor, and an exponent of agrarian interests, the Centrist Andreas Hermes, who was actually the Minister of Food and Agriculture, had been appointed as a caretaker of the Ministry of Finance. Groener and Giesberts had retained their posts, while a Social Democrat, Georg Gradnauer, had moved into the Ministry of the Interior. For further details, see Ingrid-Schulze-Bidlingmaier (ed.), *Akten der Reichskanzlei. Weimarer Republik. Die Kabinette Wirth I und II*, Boppard 1973, pp. XIX—XXIX and Ernst Laubach, *Die Politik der Kabinette Wirth 1921/22*, Lübeck-Hamburg 1968.

[15] Only a non-revealing statement that preliminary talks had been conducted was released to the press. No details on the content of the talks and the scope of the demands were given, however. See *Die Besoldungsbewegung...*, p. 7.

Before this second meeting could take place, however, the situation was made more complicated by the decision of several railroad unions to form a separate negotiating cartel, and by excluding the main representative of railroad officials, the Reichsgewerkschaft Deutscher Eisenbahnbeamter (RG) from it. On August 9, the railroad organizations formed a "Committee of Sixteen" *(Sechzehnerausschuß)* under the leadership of the Deutscher Eisenbahnerverband (DEV), an ADGB affiliate. Moreover, in a definite breach of the decisions and agreements reached on August 5 among the peak associations, the railroad cartel went public with its demands, threatening to strike if they were not met by the government.[16]

The DBB's attempt at taking the leadership in the forthcoming wage and salary drive had clearly been frustrated by this separate initiative taken up by railroad workers' organizations. Moreover, the railroad organizations had agreed on the level of the increases to be sought in the wage offensive, setting 3600 marks as a ceiling for wage and salary demands, a figure definitely lower than the one envisioned by the DBB. Lastly, the element of surprise had been lost, since the public and the government had become alerted to the general prospects of a new wage offensive in the public sector as a result of the publicity that had accompanied these talks.

The Reich government immediately began preparations for a counter offensive. The content of a memorandum drawn up in the Reich Chancellery on August 9, i. e. on the same day on which railroad unions had put together their negotiating cartel, shows that the government was well informed and clearly worried about the prospects of an organizational alliance in the public sector encompassing both workers and civil servants. Not only would the government's bargaining position be weakened if confronted with an alliance of all public employees, the government also feared that labor unrest would produce a spillover on civil servants. The latter, to be sure, had become unruly and restless themselves, but their social radicalism and strike tendencies could be contained more easily if confronted alone. One of the foremost aims of government strategy, the memorandum suggested, should therefore be to divide civil servant and workers' interests and prohibit the formation of a "united front" among public employees.[17]

[16] *Ibid.*, p. 8 and *Vossische Zeitung*, no. 366, August 6, 1921, which published these demands.

[17] Unsigned draft memorandum, dated August 9, 1921, BA, R 43I/2562, Bl. 150—153.

As the subsequent events will show, this task was fulfilled much better by the organizations themselves than could have been masterminded by any high-level bureaucrat. On August 11, the labor organizations quite abruptly called off the meeting with the DBB scheduled for this day, ostensibly because of the commemoration of the Weimar Constitution. Taken by surprise, the DBB issued a press release, stressing that "good reasons" and not organizational conflicts had caused the cancelling of the talks. In a separate meeting in the afternoon of the same day, the DBB Salary Committee decided to step up its proposed increase in civil servant base pay from 4000 to 5000 marks per year; together with the cost of living increase this amounted to a total increase of 8000 marks, a figure well above the "ceiling" of 3600 marks set by the railroad unions' Committee of Sixteen.[18] Even if this was not designed as an act of defiance on the part of the DBB leaders, a confrontation course with labor in the upcoming negotiations was now more certain than before.

One day later, on August 12, the crucial meeting between the DBB and the peak associations of labor took place.[19] While there was still a general willingness to reach a common platform, problems soon developed as the meeting went on. After the DBB representatives had outlined their proposal of a uniform increase in civil servant base pay, coupled with an equalization of staggered cost-of-living allowances, labor representatives first objected to the form of the proposed increase. Any changes in civil servant base pay, they argued, would necessitate the cancellation of wage contracts on the labor side, and would thereby lead to "intolerable delays" in the current wage drive. Although the raise of base salaries was clearly in the interest of civil servants, for only base pay accrued to future pension claims, DBB negotiators compromised on the issue. They agreed that in a first round of bargaining only an increase in the cost-of-living supplements would be pursued, and the conversion into base pay be left to a second round.

Once this issue had been settled, controversy arose about the level of the proposed increase. As reported by a participant of the meeting, labor leaders were vehemently opposed to the DBB's demands, claiming that they were "excessive" and "purely agitational." They would endanger the success of the entire wage offensive, and, moreover, could

[18] *Die Besoldungsbewegung...*, pp. 7—8.

[19] The following discussion is based on the account of the meeting given in *ibid.*, pp. 8—10 and on the documents cited in noted 20 and 23 below.

not be explained to the members of their own organizations. Moreover, the exact impact of inflation was yet unknown, and one should only demand remedies for the present economic distress, not for anticipated rises in the cost of living. To one DBB observer it looked as if labor leaders had acted as "voluntary government spokesmen."[20]

Faced with stiff opposition of this kind, the DBB scaled down its demands somewhat, proposing 4200 marks as a compromise solution. Labor leaders still rejected this compromise, insisting on their own figure of 3600 marks, i. e. the level established by the railroad cartel. The meeting ended with the DBB "reclaiming its freedom to negotiate independently", an only vaguely concealed euphemism for the collapsed *Einheitsfront.*[21]

It comes as no surprise that once these talks had failed each side accused the other of having caused the disruption. The DBB's final assessment of the matter reveals, though, that not only organizational rivalries, but also deep-rooted social antagonisms and conflicting economic interests had been at play. To DBB leaders, it was "intolerable" to witness that the aims of civil service pay policy were "dictated" to them by the organizations of railroad workers. "The solidarity of all *Arbeitnehmer,*" the DBB concluded, "can only be reached if the existence of a very real social diversity between *Arbeiter, Angestellte* and *Beamte* is recognized."[22]

Labor was quick in responding that excessive demands and the lack of trade-union practice shown by the DBB was to blame for the disruption of the talks. *Der Deutsche,* the mouthpiece of the Christian Trade Unions, wrote, for example:

"The incident reveals the complete lack of judgement and the incompetence of the DBB leadership. [DBB negotiators] were unable to justify either the proposed procedure or the level of their pay demands.

[20] *Soziale Arbeitsgemeinschaft Deutscher Beamtenverbände, Bericht über die Sitzung des geschäftsführenden Ausschusses am 12. August 1921,* BA, R 43I/2579, Bl. 150—152. The meeting took place immediately after the talks between DBB and the labor organizations. The "observer" was Hugo Kamossa, the General Secretary of the Soziale Arbeitsgemeinschaft, who had participated in the talks. He reported that above all the General Secretary of the Christian Gewerkschaft Deutscher Eisenbahner (GDE), Roth, and the Chairman of the Socialist Deutscher Eisenbahnerverband (DEV), Scheffel, opposed the DBB's demands. — In a resolution adopted at this meeting the Soziale Arbeitsgemeinschaft strongly supported the DBB position (*ibid.,* Bl. 152).

[21] *Die Besoldungsbewegung...,* p. 10.

[22] *Ibid.,* pp. 11 and 14.

They presented a pitiful picture of an organization making demands at random. It is an outrage, how, in a time of deep economic depression, billions [in pay demands] are thrown around in a ruthless way."[23]

The "governmental line" adopted by the Christian Unions undoubtedly reflects their support for the Center Party coalition cabinet and its financial policies. Excessive wage and salary demands were bound to put further strains on the already overburdened budget of the Reich, particularly at a time when financial austerity measures were being considered by the Wirth government in order to make headway in the thorny reparations question. The Christian Union's harsh criticism might also be interpreted, however, as an attempt to influence the outcome of the high-level organizational talks between ADGB and DBB by emphasizing the unreliability of the civil servant organization in trade union matters. Indeed, the DBB suspected that the entire strategy adopted by the railroad organizations in the preceding talks had been "masterminded" by the Gesamtverband Deutscher Beamtengewerkschaften (GDB), the Christian Trade Unions' civil servant branch. An integral part of this alleged strategy had been to join forces with DBB-opponents within the Free Trade Unions, i. e. the *Verkehrsbund* organizations, and apparently this strategy had worked out.[24] The disruption of the negotiating cartel between labor unions and civil servant associations for the pending wage movement in the public sector had cast a shadow over the important decisions to be taken by DBB and ADGB in the affiliation question.

On August 16, the DBB council convened in Berlin. Two issues, linked together by the recent developments, had been placed on the agenda: first, the "securing of the material existence of the *Beamtentum,*" and second, the "proposed agreement with the ADGB."[25] With regard to the first issue, the council endorsed the steps taken thus far by the DBB leadership in the salary movement. With regard to the latter, the council, at the behest of the Reichsgewerkschaft, adopted a resolution which all but killed the prospects for an organizational alliance with the ADGB. The reason for this posture, as stated in the resolu-

[23] Quoted in *DG*, August 18, 1921 *(Wochenschau).*

[24] Reported by *DG*, August 18, 1921, which claimed to have acquired a copy of the protocol of a meeting in question. *Der Freie Beamte,* September 10, 1921 reports on the same incident under the heading „Minierarbeit der ‚Christen'". The *Freie Beamte* was the mouthpiece of the SPD's civil servant section.

[25] Announced in *DG,* July 28, 1921.

tion, was "that the DBB council had not been assured of adequate protection of civil-servant interests in a written agreement with the ADGB."[26] The oppositional stance adopted by the DEV, an ADGB affiliate, in the preceding salary talks was cited as a proof for this kind of non-representation of civil servant interests through the ADGB. The DBB's trade-union wing obviously had suffered defeat, although it is interesting to note that even members of the DBB's left wing who previously had supported the alliance with the ADGB now took a somewhat different view. In his commentary on the negative vote taken by the council, Albert Falkenberg, one of the leading proponents of the agreement only a few weeks earlier, now chose to defend the DBB's decision and argued that the *Beamtenschaft* was unwilling to succumb to a *Diktat* of labor in economic as well as organizational questions.[27]

For the time being, therefore, civil servants had opted against closer ties with organized labor. The reasons for this are to be found in their inability to overcome certain social traditions, but also, and perhaps more importantly, in very concrete conflicts of interest in matters of policy, accentuated by the necessities of wage and salary policy under conditions of accelerating inflation. In shifting our focus now briefly to the internal discussions within the Free Trade Unions, it will become clear that the failure to reach an organizational pact with the DBB was as much the result of the ADGB's inability to overcome internal dissent on what was viewed as a very controversial issue, as it had been the civil servant federation's inabilty to break with its traditional perceptions of the role and position of the *Beamtenschaft* in German society.

Quite by coincidence the ADGB council *(Ausschuß)*, the forum of the ADGB member associations and nominally the body controlling the policies of the ADGB executive, met the very same day on which the DBB council was scheduled to vote on the agreement with the ADGB. On August 17 — the DBB's decision was not yet known — the ADGB leaders discussed the recent price increases and their impact on workers' wage levels. In the context of these discussions, the recent

[26] *DG*, August 18, 1921. Ernst Remmers, in his position as a leading member of the DBB's organization commitee, had supported the content of the agreement, for which he was primarily responsible. He viewed it as the best way to reach closer cooperation between the DBB and the Free Trade Unions, while at the same time maintaining the DBB's principle of political neutrality. Remmers had justified his position in the *Gemeinschaft* immediately prior to the Bundesausschuß meeting. See his *Die Neutralität des Deutschen Beamtenbundes*, in: *DG*, August 4, 1921.

[27] *DG*, August 18, 1921.

wage and salary negotiations in the public sector, the role of the Transport Alliance, and the policies pursued by the DBB became a point of controversy. The delegate of the Transport Workers Union, Schumann, sharply attacked the negotiations undertaken by the DBB and the ADGB executive in order to reach a organizational agreement. The DBB's excessive pay demands in the recent wage drive, Schumann claimed, must be judged as a clear expression of the civil servants' lack of ability in trade union tactics and policy. In response to this situation, the railroad organizations had been compelled to draw up their own wage demands. He chided the ADGB executive for having claimed publicly that the central organization had not officially participated in the salary and wage negotiations on August 12. This posture, he said, had weakened the Transport Alliance's position in its conflict with the DBB. He himself, Schumann claimed, had been the official spokesman for the ADGB in the August 12 talks.[28] Leipart, the ADGB chairman, replied that the important thing at this point was to save "in the last hour" the pact with the DBB and not to complicate matters even further by internal quarrels. He rejected Schumann's accusation that the ADGB executive had undercut the position of the Transport Alliance and pointed out that the DBB's inital invitation to the wage talks had indeed been sent to the Transport Workers Union, and not to the ADGB's central office. The delegate of the Afa-Bund, Fries, supported Leipart's point of view, and deplored the damage caused by the internal fighting over the civil servant issue. This had made the agreement with the DBB rather impossible, he said, and the Christian Trade Unions were delighted about it, because their tactic apparently had worked. The Transport Alliance, Fries claimed, should never have engaged in a tactical alliance with the Christian and the Hirsch-Duncker Unions against the DBB. To this massive criticism Schumann could only reply that even the *Verkehrsbund* had continued to pursue a policy of reconciliation with the DBB.

When on the following day the ADGB council met again, the predictions of the Afa-Bund delegate had become reality. The DBB had frustrated all hopes for an organizational agreement with the negative

[28] Protokoll der 13. Sitzung des Ausschusses des Allgemeinen Deutschen Gewerkschaftsbundes. 1. Geschäftsperiode (Berlin 1921), p. 18. (Hereafter cited as *ADGB Ausschuss Protocol 1921.*) In a move to minimize the damage done by the disruption of the salary talks, the ADGB *Vorstand* had issued a statement proclaiming that it had not taken part in these talks officially.

decision taken by its council. In response to this development, the past and future relationship between ADGB and DBB was added on to the agenda of the meeting as a main point of discussion.[29]

Leipart began with a review of the negotiations between DBB and ADGB since 1919. He complained that the ADGB policy of bringing together three independent federations representing wage earners, salaried employees, and civil servants, respectively, as the foundations of a more broadly based trade-union movement had been frustrated from the very beginning by the Transport Alliance and its policy of organizing blue-collar workers, salaried employees, and civil servants of one economic branch into a single organization. Only the cooperation of three independent peak associations, Leipart claimed, could insure that the social identity and the specific interests of the three employee groups be maintained. Ultimately only the "three-pillar principle," he argued, could attract middle-class groups like *Angestellte* and *Beamte* to the Socialist trade-union movement.[30]

Using these general remarks as a point of departure, Leipart strongly defended the ADGB executive's policy toward the DBB. The DBB was, after all, an impressive organization with a membership of more than a million civil servants. The DBB leadership, moreover, contained persons who, as Leipart claimed, were "compatible to us," i. e. friends of the socialist unions. There had been good prospects that these forces would win out in the DBB's internal struggle regarding an agreement with the ADGB. The "unpleasant developments" in connection with the recent wage and salary negotiations in the public sector, Leipart held, were at least partially responsible for the defeat suffered by the ADGB's friends within the DBB leadership. Leipart still rejected the idea of founding an organizational rival to the DBB within the Free Trade Union movement. Instead, he proposed to adopt a wait-and-see attitude, not least because the DBB had left open the possibility of taking up the organizational question again at a later date. This policy,

[29] *Ibid.*, pp. 26—31 (*Die organisatorischen Beziehungen zum Beamtenbund*).

[30] The origins of the so-called *Drei-Säulen-Theorie* as a trade union principle of organization along "corporatist" *(ständisch)* lines are to be found in the *Angestellten* branch of the Free Trade Unions. Leading Socialist white-collar unionists like S. Aufhäuser and O. Urbahn argued that only a white collar union independent from the predominantly working-class based *Arbeitergewerkschaften* would be attractive to white-collar workers. Cf. the deliberations of the ADGB *Verbandsvorstände* on December 15—18, 1920, in: *Beschlüsse der 1.—12. Sitzung des Ausschusses des ADGB,* Berlin 1928, pp. 50—59, where the term „*Heeressäulen*" is used.

Leipart insisted, would be pursued by the ADGB executive even at the expense of stiff opposition from the Transport Alliance or other member organizations.[31]

Such opposition was indeed forthcoming right away. The chairman of the Railroad Workers' Union, Scheffel, bitterly complained that the policy pursued by the ADGB leadership would ultimately lead to what he called an "artificial organizational division" of workers, salaried employees, and civil servants in the transportation sector. In addition, the DBB's militant railway officials' union, the Reichsgewerkschaft, would be invited to step up recruitment among those railroad workers occupying civil servant posts, and thus endanger the organizational base of his own organization, the DEV. Scheffel suggested that neither the political direction, nor the trade-union character of the DBB could be trusted: "The anti-union character of the civil service federation," he said, "has not changed to this day."[32]

Scheffel's position was strongly supported by Schumann, his colleague from the Transport Alliance's other affiliate, the Transport Workers Union. The DBB, Schumann claimed, had become increasingly "reactionary" in the past two years. Taking this organization into the Free Trade Unions "whole-sale" was therefore out of the question. One hundred thousand strictly trade-union oriented civil servants in the Transport Alliance, he argued, were worth more to the Free Trade Unions than the one million reactionary civil servants of the *Beamtenbund.* He himself was delighted that the organizational agreement had been rejected by the DBB. This should encourage the ADGB to reconsider its policy pursued thus far. "The 'three-pillar concept' leads to inner divisiveness," he warned; "it is a burden to the free unions, and of no use to us."[33]

Even within the ADGB executive itself opposition to the official ADGB policy toward the DBB emerged. Brunner, a member of the executive and a former chairman of the DEV, pointed out that the DBB's decision to reapproach the ADGB "at a suitable time" was an embarrassment for labor, since until then the ADGB had always taken up the initiatives in this respect. Brunner supported the policies suggested by the Transport Alliance, arguing that an agreement with the DBB would be "a millstone around the neck of the trade unions."[34]

[31] *ADGB Ausschuss Protocol 1921,* pp. 27—28.
[32] *Ibid.,* p. 29.
[33] *Ibid.,* p. 30.
[34] *Ibid.,* p. 31.

The most outspoken defenders of the executive's policy were the delegates from the Afa-Bund, who, after all, spoke for an organization that had vital interests in the pursuit of the corporatist three-pillar principle. To them, the attacks of the *Verkehrsbund* delegates revealed nothing except high-pitch organizational egotism. The Afa-Bund delegate Hoffmann, in a surprising shifting of arguments, claimed that in the final analysis the DBB's differences with labor did not matter at all. Instead, the DBB's firm opposition to labor in the salary talks was a good sign of increasing trade-unionism among civil servants, because the DBB had finally recognized the priorities of economic factors in the conduct of interest politics. In this sense the DBB had proven itself as a genuine trade union, and the coming weeks, in which the salary issue would be negotiated at governmental level, might actually bring the organizations closer together once again.[35]

After the debate had been closed, the ADGB leaders adopted a resolution which "took notice" of the DBB's decision but expressed hopes for coming to a final agreement with the DBB "in an appropriate period of time." If by then an agreement could not be reached, the ADGB executive would allow its affiliate organizations to begin preparations for the founding of a separate civil servant organization within the Free Trade Union movement.[36] This was not a compromise solution, because the Transport Alliance was opposed to *any* separate organization of civil servants. Accordingly, their representatives voted against this resolution, which had been introduced by an Afa-Bund affiliate and the Union of Municipal Workers. The outcome shows that the internal conflicts within the ADGB over the organization of civil servants and, more fundamentally, over the entire organizational structure of the erstwhile labor confederation with regard to its middle-class constituents, had not been resolved. The civil servant movement would continue to play an important part in this conflict, which, as may well be argued, point to fundamental problems of social organization and social regrouping in the early years of the Weimar Republic.

After the DBB had reclaimed its independence in the salary negotiations, a petition was sent to the Reich Ministry of Finance on August

[35] *Ibid.*, p. 29.

[36] Resolution is reprinted in *ibid.*, p. 28, *Korr. Bl.*, 1921, p. 439 and S. Schwarz, *Handbuch der Gewerkschaftskongresse...*, p. 159. The liberal *Vossische Zeitung* (no. 398, August 25, 1921) quite correctly claimed that this resolution was nothing but a „mehr oder minder deutliche Konkurrenzdrohung" on the part of the ADGB.

18, in which the DBB's original pay demands of August 2 were restated. Most notably, the high figure of 8500 marks in civil servant pay increase was reintroduced, as well as the indexation clause.[37] On August 22, negotiations began in the Finance Ministry between the government and the five peak associations representing civil servants: the two non-affiliated civil servant associations (DBB and RhB) and the three confederations of labor (ADGB, DGB, and the Hirsch-Duncker unions). The five organizations had been unable to formulate joint wage demands, which improved the bargaining position of the Reich government in its role as public employer.

To emphasize the importance of the salary question in the current political situation of the Reich, Chancellor Wirth himself opened the bargaining session. He lectured the organizational leaders on the dire financial situation of the Reich and the critical situation in both domestic and foreign affairs, all of which, he claimed, called for moderation in wage negotiations. Such moderation, however, was not forthcoming, particularly not from the DBB, which kept insisting on its high-level demands and especially on a minimum cost of living increase for the lower grades. Government negotiators rejected this demand out of principle. For reasons of state, they argued, any levelling of incomes between the different civil-service grades had to be prevented, and a minimum increase for the lower groups would lead to such a levelling of civil-servant pay rates. Thus, they defended the established government policy that cost of living increases had to be awarded according to percentage-rates, so that the "levelling of incomes" would not be increased any further. This was the position also of the association of higher civil servants, the RhB. The exact opinion of the participating labor organizations does not emerge from the documents, but it seems clear that they pretty much left the DBB without open support, regardless of the fact that the minimum increase would also be in the interest of the lower-grade civil servants represented by their organizations. Twice the talks broke down over this issue. The government finally felt compelled to garner the support of the Reichstag leadership in an attempt to overcome the impasse. While the Reichstag parties made any final settlement contingent upon the organizations' consent, they

[37] *Die Besoldungsbewegung...*, pp. 14—15. Unless indicated otherwise, the following account is based on *Die Verhandlungen über die Erhöhung der Teuerungszulagen*, Appendix to *Die Besoldungsbewegung...*

signalled support for the government line of negotiation.[38] Increasingly isolated, the DBB at first scaled down, and later even dropped its demand of a minimum increase for the lower pay groups.

The controversy over the minimum increase, and the apparent disagreement between the organizations on this issue and on the level of the increases to be sought, had weakened their bargaining position to such a degree that the final settlement was not only based on percentage rates of increase, but also considerably lower in the amount to be granted. Not even labor's more moderate target of covering the rise in the cost of living since May had been met, not to speak of the DBB's objective of seeking remedies for past and future price hikes.[39] Viewed from this perspective, the salary initiative had turned into a debacle for the organizations.

It comes as no surprise, therefore, that the two sides blamed each other for the failure of the wage movement. The ADGB claimed that the DBB's excessive initial pay demands had swayed public opinion against the salary offensive and had thus strengthened the government's bargaining position. The *Korrespondenzblatt*, the ADGB's official gazette, further suggested that the previous events had shown that a wide gap still existed between civil servants and the working class.[40] The DBB responded by rejecting the argument that civil servant demands had been the major factor in the unfortunate outcome of the negotiations. Civil servant spokesmen emphasized that the DBB's demands had been justified since real income of civil servants had been declining at a faster rate than workers' wages even before 1914, and definitely during and after the war.[41] The DBB issued a statement in which the government and the political parties of the Reichstag were warned "not to continue with a disastrous salary policy that was leading

[38] *Besprechung mit den Parteiführern und den Spitzenorganisationen der Beamten, Angestellten und Arbeiter der Reichsbehörden*, August 24, 1921, BA, R 43I/2562, Bl. 188.

[39] Only the cost-of-living allowances to base pay and location bonuses were increased, with the rate of increase depending on *Ortsklassen*. The increase thus varied between 13 and 20 percent, depending on *Ortsklasse*, and thus fell short in matching the rise in the cost-of-living index of nearly 30 percent. Further details in: *WSt.*, 1 (1921), pp. 426—429.

[40] *Korr. Bl.*, 1921, pp. 555—557.

[41] *DG*, September 1, 1921. This theme was expounded in Wilhelm Schröder/Paul Lockenvitz, *Der soziale Niedergang der deutschen Beamtenschaft* (= Flugschrift des Deutschen Beamtenbundes, no. 5), Berlin 1921, a statistical treatise written to justify the DBB's pay demands.

more and more to the economic immiseration of the larger proportion of the *Beamtenschaft.*"[42]

Despite all the clamor on the organizational front in the wake of the wage offensive, the organizations of both civil servants and labor settled their differences surprisingly fast and united in common front of defense. A new wage movement was viewed as the only remedy for making good for the debacle in August. A joint rebuttal was drafted and sent to the Reich Ministry of Finance, in which the organizations demanded the expeditious renegotiation of the salary and wage levels in the public sector.[43]

There are some indications that the swiftness with which a joint counterattack was begun by the leadership came as a result of rank-and-file unrest in both organizational camps. Apparently *die Basis* was unhappy about the fact that organizational discord had lessened the potentialities in the salary movement just completed. The DBB local organization *(Ortskartell)* in Cuxhaven, for example, called the outcome "insufficient to improve the economic situation of civil servants and other public employees." It called on the organizations in Berlin to take "the most rigorous action" to insure the immediate payment of a substantial across-the-board bonus for all public employees. Otherwise civil servants in Cuxhaven would unite with salaried employees and wage earners in an attempt at "taking by means of force what has not been given voluntarily" by the government.[44] In a letter to the DBB's *Gemeinschaft* one middle-grade civil servant tried to correct the impression advanced by the right-wing press that a contractual agreement between DBB, ADGB and Afa-Bund would imply a "[d]eparture of the *Beamten* into the socialist camp." The continual struggle between public employees and public employers for economic and social gains, the writer maintained, necessitated the close cooperation between all peak associations representing *Arbeitnehmer* in the public sector. Cooperation between the DBB and the Free Trade Union movement should therefore not be confused with partisan politics, but rather be viewed as a sign of progress in the development of German trade unionism.[45] Aside of the incongruity in this argumentation, the exam-

[42] *Entschließung des DBB Bundesvorstandes,* August 30, 1921, reprinted in: *Die Besoldungsbewegung...,* Appendix, p. 2.

[43] *DG,* September 8, 1921.

[44] DBB Ortsgruppe Cuxhaven to Beamtenrat Hamburg, August 27, 1921, StAH 122-4-4, Bd. 4.

[45] *DG,* September 8, 1921.

ple may show that the idea of an agreement with the ADGB had not been laid to rest within the DBB's rank and file.

There were similar currents within the ADGB membership. In Rostock a working alliance *(Arbeitsgemeinschaft)* of municipal workers, contractual employees, and civil servants criticized the peak organizations in Berlin for having failed to put together what, on a local level, in Rostock had worked for years: a united front of all public employees vis-à-vis public employers in wage negotiations. The *Arbeitsgemeinschaft* called on the central organizations "to conclude an agreement soon in the interest of all working people, an agreement which would provide for unlimited cooperation between the peak associations."[46] The message "from below" seemed to be in this case, too, that the two sides should overcome their differences for the benefit of their members. Only if organizational rivalries and ideological differences could be overcome by the demands of practical interest politics, as practiced already at local levels, could public employers be prevented from playing on the disunity of wage and salary earners and civil servants in the public service.

The wage movement of August 1921 marks the beginning of interest politics and social conflict in the German public sector during the period of accelerated inflation. The course and consequences of the August events can therefore be used to extrapolate certain problems and patterns of relationships that were to reappear and characterize interest politics and salary policy in the subsequent weeks and months, culminating in the breakdown of interest politics during the great civil servant strike of February 1922.

First: The events of August 1921, subsumed here under the heading "confrontation with labor," reveal a very complex and complicated pattern of relations between civil servants and the organized working class. The conflict between DBB and ADGB as it unfolded during the salary and wage offensive indicates that economic interests and traditional social preconceptions mattered as much as organizational rivalries, based on political differences, in the unsuccessful attempt to bind the two organizations together. Clearly, these three levels — economic, social, and political/organizational — reinforced each other, and it is not always possible to isolate them properly. But since preference has been given in this analysis to economic factors and their resulting

[46] *Entschließung der Arbeitsgemeinschaft der städtischen Arbeiter, Angestellten und Beamten,* September 16, 1921, repr. in: *Korr. Bl.*, 1921, pp. 581—582.

consequences in what has been called "practical interest politics," it now seems plausible to argue that any consensus between the organizations of civil servants and the working class had to be based on an initial consensus in key areas of practical interest politics. The latter consensus had not been achieved in the August salary and wage offensive, and it remains to be seen if the worsening economic conditions in the second half of 1921 would lead to a working relationship between civil servant organizations and the labor movement in salary politics.

Second: The August events show that at this point in time labor organizations and civil servant associations had become interested in curing the social impact of inflation by means of economic rather than traditional social policy measures. An economic problem, i. e. inflation, was to be dealt with in economic terms, i. e. by gaining influence on economic policy making. There were, however, marked differences in the approach taken by the two organizations in this respect. To the DBB, inflation remained above all a question of adjusting civil servant pay to the rising cost of living by means of some form of direct indexation. Only in this way, the DBB's economic experts argued, could a timely adjustment of the otherwise rather inflexible civil servant pay be achieved, and delays caused by the governmental and parliamentary stranglehold on salary policy be avoided. Concretely, this would mean that the variable element in civil service pay, the cost-of-living supplement (the *Teuerungszuschlag*) which had been instituted by the Salary Reform Act of 1920, would be changed according to a cost-of-living index established by the Reich Statistical Office and the DBB in joint consultation. While the idea of indexation had been popular with civil servant associations even before 1914, the proposals for a "sliding scale" developed primarily by Alois Zeiler, a higher civil servant himself, became an integral part of the DBB's response to the inflationary spiral in mid-1921.[47] From then on the problem of indexation was to play a major role in the conflicts between organized civil servants, the labor movement, and the government over the shaping of salary policy during the inflation.

While the DBB was using economic arguments in its attempt to attain the indexation of civil servant salaries, the ADGB in mid-1921 embarked on a full-scale effort to influence the redirection of the Reich's economic and financial policies. In a catalog of demands, sent to

[47] See Alois Zeiler, *Eine selbsttätige Anpassung von Gehalt und Lohn an die Wirtschaftsentwicklung* (= Flugschrift des Deutschen Beamtenbundes, no. 7), Berlin 1922.

the Reich government on August 27, 1921, the ADGB suggested that the renewed acceleration of the wage-price spiral could only be put under control through a decisive turnaround in the direction of current economic, financial, and wage policies. New wage increases, the ADGB argued, would only lead to a new "flood of paper marks" and to new price increases. Raising income taxes, as planned by the Wirth Government, would, on the other hand, lower the purchasing power of wages and salaries of dependent employees to "intolerable levels." The ADGB demanded instead a tax reform program that would balance the Reich budget without resorting to the printing presses: by seizing capital assets of those groups in society which had not been affected by the depreciation of the currency, i. e. the industrial plants of big business and the landholdings of big agriculture. In addition, the ADGB proposed a complete redirection of the German economy from profit orientation to a "supply economy" *(Bedarfswirtschaft)* that would increase production while at the same time lower production costs and thus the prices of consumer goods.[48] Perhaps also as a result of the controversies surrounding the wage and salary negotiations in the public sector in the summer of 1921, organized labor had finally realized that in the race between paper-mark wages and consumer prices its clientel could not be on the winning side any longer under the prevailing economic conditions of accelerating inflation.

In this respect the ADGB's response to the problem of inflation differed markedly from the one of the DBB. While the civil servant assocation still relied on salary policy as a panacea for dealing with inflation, the more experienced labor organization had recognized the limitations of sole reliance upon wage policy to handle the worsening economic and social conditions of the working classes. It remains to be seen whether this distinctly different assessment of the value and function of wage policy in accelerated inflation would continue to provide areas of conflict between civil servant interests and those of organized labor, or whether the ADGB's much more comprehensive evaluation would serve as a model for the DBB to depart from the exclusive concentration on indexation possibilities in favor of a more encompassing economic policy as a basis for its economic demands.

[48] ADGB to Reich Chancellor, August 28, 1921, BA, R 43I/2023, Bl. 136—138 (*Forderungen der Gewerkschaften in der Steuerfrage und Wirtschaftspolitik*). The dating of this document is interesting, because it is generally held that only in *late* 1921, with the so-called "November Demands" did the ADGB formulate an economic program of its own On this, see H. Potthoff, *Gewerkschaften ...*, pp. 296—299.

The following weeks and months would offer ample opportunity to civil servants and their organizations to resolve these and other matters of controversy between them and the organizations of labor. As the cost of living continued to surge upward virtually unabatedly, the contours of a renewed wage drive soon emerged within the public sector. Once again it would raise the unresolved issue of a social alliance between civil servants and the other public employees and their organizations. In addition, the new wage movement was to lead to a sharp confrontation between civil servants and the state as employer over the very aims of civil service salary policy.

Confrontation with the State: The Wage Movement of October 1921

The failure of the August wage movement and the continued increase in price levels prompted the DBB to start preparations for a new salary offensive almost immediately after the August settlement had been rejected by the five peak associations. At stake in the new offensive were not only those objectives that had not been realized in the preceding struggles, but also, and perhaps more importantly, the DBB's prestige as the main representative of civil servant interests. Mounting discontent within the organization's rank and file signalled to its leadership that some form of spectacular success was urgently needed in order to recapture some of the prestige lost in the August debacle.

To set things on the right track at the very beginning, the DBB in early September requested a meeting with Reich President Ebert to "discuss an important and fundamental matter concerning civil service policy."[49] Taking civil servant demands to the Reich president, the supreme arbitrator above partisan politics and, in addition, the constitutional head of the civil service and thus the civil servants' supreme employer *(Dienstherr)*,[50] was a shrewd and calculated move on the part of the DBB leaders. Not only would such a step generate a positive response within the DBB's own ranks, an audience with the Reich president would furthermore demonstrate the political significance of civil service salary policy to the public at large. Ebert's considerable weight in the governmental and parliamentary spheres, moreover,

[49] *DG*, September 22, 1921.

[50] On Ebert's role in this context, see G. Hoffmann, *Sozialdemokratie...*, pp. 75—80.

would hopefully increase the organization's leverage in the upcoming salary offensive.[51]

The meeting took place on September 13, 1921.[52] In his opening remarks DBB Chairman Flügel told Ebert that the economic plight of civil servants had become unbearable. The measures adopted thus far by Reich government and Reichstag had been insufficient and inadequate, especially with regard to the lower ranks of the civil service. The August settlement, Flügel argued, had benefited higher civil servants disproportionally, which had sparked social and political discontent among the lower grades. Flügel warned that the DBB would be unable to contain discontent in the lower ranks of the civil service, unless a minimum salary standard was introduced for the lower pay groups. Social discontent, moreover, could very easily turn into political radicalism, Ebert was told, and it was not unlikely that the *Unterbeamte* would sever their ties to the Beamtenbund for the sake of following leaders "who were preaching radicalism."[53] In order to prevent such a development, the DBB's principle demand of a minimum subsistence level of pay *(Existenzminimum)* for the lower ranks should be granted by the government and the Reichstag. In addition, the DBB, like the other trade unions, should be consulted in the formulation and implementation of economic policy.

In his reply Ebert pointed out that the latest price increases had resulted from the current transition from a "controlled" to a "free" economy *(Zwangswirtschaft* to *freie Wirtschaft).* They should therefore be regarded as a temporary, transitional phenomenon only. While he had always been an ardent supporter of the minimum wage standard, such a standard could only be fixed in normal times, not in times of economic transition. Civil servants would therefore have to live with the inadequacies of the current pay structure. Participation in economic policy decision making, Ebert added, was guaranteed to the DBB through its seat in the Reich Economic Council; a separate institutional arrangement was therefore not required. Ebert emphasized that above all civil servants should retain their confidence in the good-will of the

[51] This line of reasoning was used in internal circular, which the DBB sent to its affiliate organizations. Copy in GLAK, 233, 24211.

[52] Protocol of this meeting in BA, R 43I/2562, Bl. 224—225; another report in *DG*, September 22, 1921. Next to DBB Chairman Flügel, Falkenberg, and the head of the powerful Union of Lower Postal Civil Servants Kugler — a member of the SPD — participated in the meeting.

[53] *Ibid.*

government. Perhaps as a conciliatory gesture in view of his generally evasive, if not negative, response to the DBB's wishes, he agreed to contact the chancellor concerning some of the specific demands raised by the DBB leaders.

Of the two "fundamental questions" raised by the DBB leaders in this meeting, i. e. a minimum wage standard for lower-level civil servants and consultation with the unions in the economic affairs of the nation, the quest for a participatory voice in the higher realms of economic policy making was perhaps the more innovative demand. Undoubtedly, the offensive launched by the ADGB a few weeks earlier must have played a major role in the DBB's sudden interest in *Wirtschaftspolitik*. It had strengthened the position of those members of the DBB's inner leadership circle who had always pleaded for a greater involvement of the DBB in general economic policy, not least because the economic well-being of the civil servant depended on the economic well-being of the state and that of the nation's economy.[54] The mere fact that economic questions had now become an integral part of DBB interest policy indicates that a learning process had been set in motion within the DBB's leadership. Faced with fundamental economic decisions regarding the very structure of the German economy, and with increasingly detrimental economic conditions during accelerating inflation, DBB leaders seemed to have concluded that civil servants ought to have an independent voice in general economic affairs and cease relying on the efforts of other organized interests in these matters. It would take another year, however, and the experience of hyperinflation before the DBB was to come forward with a comprehensive economic program of its own.[55]

The question of a minimum subsistence level raised by DBB leaders in their talk with Ebert likewise put a new element, or point of controversy, into salary policy in the period of accelerated inflation. Setting minimum wage standards in the public sector had been opposed persistently by the government, which could count on a broad majority in

[54] The foremost representative of this group was Hans Völter, an economist by training and a former *Syndikus* of the Badischer Beamtenbund in Karlsruhe. Völter advanced rapidly in the DBB hierarchy, becoming a *Direktor* in 1920. See his *Beamtentum und Wirtschaft* (= Flugschrift des Deutschen Beamtenbundes, no. 2), Berlin 1920.

[55] In November 1922 the DBB presented an economic program which aimed at improving the increasingly difficult economic situation of the Reich. See *DBB Geschäftsbericht 1924*, pp. 40—41. The program will be dealt with in a more comprehensive manner in CHAPTER SEVEN below.

the Reichstag in this matter, including the SPD. Any attempt by civil servant organizations to reach a minimum cost of living increase for the lower pay groups had little or no chance to succeed, as was pointed out by the Reich minister of the interior in response to an inquiry by the Reich Chancellery.[56]

One final conclusion can be drawn from the talks between DBB leaders and the Reich president. Organizational leaders had clearly become worried about the high level of unrest within the *Beamtenschaft*, and they foresaw the potentially damaging organizational and political consequences of civil servant unrest more clearly than most high government officials responsible for the formulation of civil service salary policy. A detailed analysis of the new salary offensive, conducted by the organizations in October of 1921, shall be used to substantiate this point. Our focus will now shift somewhat to the higher levels of government decision making in order to ascertain the impact of civil servant demands on the formulation not only of civil service policy, but on finance and budgetary policy as well. In a second step, the impact of the October wage movement on organizational politics and on the relationship between civil servant interests and those of big business shall be analyzed. With regard to the latter issue the question will be raised whether a common front against the interests of capital was an instrumental factor in a renewed rapprochement between the civil servants and organized labor, i. e. between DBB and the Free Trade Union movement.

By mid-October 1921 a new wage movement had gathered momentum in the public sector. Its first round were a series of preliminary talks, conducted between the organizations of civil servants, labor unions, and the Reich Finance Ministry, where plans for a salary reform had been drawn up by government officials at the lower ministerial level. The organizations, on the other hand, had agreed to formulate and present a joint catalog of demands for public employees. These included the controversial minimum pay increase for the lower ranks of the civil service, and, significantly, an appeal to the government not to tinker with the eight-hour workday in the public sector. Moreover, the organizations called on the government to adopt measures to insure an easier and more expeditious adjusting of wages and salaries to the

[56] Reich Ministry of the Interior to State Secretary in the Chancellery, October 7, 1921, BA, R 43I/2563, Bl. 28.

prevailing rate of inflation.[57] While falling a bit short of the DBB's proposal for automatic indexation, this last mentioned demand does indicate the labor had come around somewhat on this issue. The wide scope of these demands, particularly the defense of the eight-hour workday, indicate that the public sector had emerged as a battle ground in the fight against attempts at rolling back social gains made by the working classes after the Revolution. The question of the eight hour day would play a major role again in the events leading to the civil servant strike of February 1922.

In this round of bargaining, however, the question of a minimum increase for the lower grades was to play the leading role. At the higher governmental level there was a great sense of urgency to resolve the civil servant pay issue, which toward the end of October 1921 had taken on considerable political significance.[58] Quite in contrast to the DBB's conviction that the salaries of the lower grades needed to be raised to a minimum level, the government seemed determined to disproportionally raise the pay of higher civil servants. This option was discussed in a cabinet meeting on October 27. Interestingly enough, the most forceful plea for raising the pay of the higher groups was made by Vice Chancellor Bauer, a Social Democrat. He argued that the government should not "proletarianize" its higher civil servants. Each social group, he said, was entitled to be kept at its "appropriate social rank." This principle needed to be applied to higher civil servants as well, who had suffered disproportionate social decline as compared to other groups. Bauer's point of view was strongly supported by high career civil servants present at the meeting. State Secretary Stieler of the Reich Transport Ministry noted that the unions' pay demands amounted to a total of 3.67 billion marks: they should therefore not oppose an additional six million for the higher pay groups. Ministerial Director von Schlieben of the Reich Finance Ministry argued that since "the interest of the organizations ended with Pay Group V," the government itself had to step in to improve the economic position of the higher pay groups. The

[57] I am following here the detailed account of this salary drive given in *DG*, November 3, 1921 *(Die neue Besoldungsaktion)*.

[58] To illustrate this level of significance, the following example may suffice: On October 24, 1921, DVP Chairman Stresemann sent a letter to Chancellor Wirth urging him not to delay the civil-service pay question because of the impending reshuffling of the Cabinet (Stresemann to Wirth, BA, R 43I/2563, Bl. 80). The first Wirth Cabinet had resigned only one day earlier; the new Cabinet discussed the salary issue in one of its first meetings on October 27, after it had been installed officially on October 26, 1921.

only opposition came from the Minister of Economics Schmidt, a Social Democrat, who argued that the salaries paid by the government to its higher civil servants could never approach the level or even compete with salaries paid in private industry to higher management personnel. For this reason salaries for higher civil servants should not be raised excessively.

The point of view advanced by the Finance Ministry and supported by Bauer and Stieler prevailed, however. The forthcoming negotiations between the Reich Finance Ministry, the organizations, and the state governments, the cabinet stipulated, would be conducted on the basis of the Finance Ministry's proposals.[59] In the bill that was later sent to the Reichstag the government again made the point clear that in its opinion the proposals advanced by the organizations would have resulted in an intolerable worsening of the economic position of the higher and middling pay groups in the *Beamtenschaft:*

"A further erosion of the higher pay groups' economic position is not only unjust, it will also lead to a point when persons without private fortunes are less and less attracted to the higher and middle ranks of the civil service. Many well qualified and capable public officials, moreover, will be encouraged to leave the service of the Reich, lured away by better-paid positions in commerce and industry. It stands to reason that such a development is detrimental to the best interests of the Reich."[60]

While DBB leaders were likely to be unimpressed with such an argument in view of their own contention that the main issue was not the recruitment problem in the higher echelons of the civil service, but rather the social and political radicalization of the lower ranks, they failed in their efforts to alter the government's policy in favor of their own proposed minimum increase for the lower pay groups. Even intensive lobbying at the Reichstag Committee on Civil Service Affairs, where the government bill was being deliberated in early November of 1921, failed to produce the desired minimum increase for lower-grade civil servants. On November 11, the pay-award bill passed the Reichstag as an amendment to the Salary Law of April 1920.[61] In its confron-

[59] Cabinet meeting, October 27, 1921 (excerpt), BA, R 431/2563, Bl. 88—89. Also in *ARK. Kab. Wirth*, p. 347.

[60] *Begründung zum Entwurf einer dritten Ergänzung des Besoldungsgesetzes*, in: *Stenographische Berichte...*, vol. 384, no. 2935, p. 5.

[61] *RGBl.*, II, 1921, pp. 13 ff.

tation with the government the DBB, which had led the other organizations in the struggle for the minimum cost-of-living increase for the lower grades, had suffered a severe setback.

To be sure, the pay raises and cost-of-living increases granted to civil servants as a result of these measures were substantial, if not enormous in view of the dire economic and financial conditions of Reich, *Länder*, and municipalities. Between 12 and 13 billion marks alone were placed on an already overstrained and deficit-ridden Reich budget. The coverage of such an enormous expenditure was discussed by the Reich cabinet in the vaguest terms only, leading one to conclude that essentially they intended to resort to the printing presses.[62] A heavy burden was placed on *Länder* and city governments as well. According to the *Besoldungssperrgesetz* of 1920 they had to duplicate all wage and pay measures adopted for civil servants and other employees of the Reich. While the state governments had been consulted during the negotiations by the central government, city administrators had not, and it is therefore understandable that the *Deutscher Städtetag* swiftly proclaimed that the wage and salary increases could not be met by the cities, and called on the Reich government to cover all or at least part of the costs.[63]

In sheer size, then, the pay awards granted to civil servants in the wake of the October wage movement were impressive and could be called a major success of civil servant interests. The net effect in terms of civil-servant salary levels was that in October 1921 — all wage and salary awards were retroactive as of October 1, 1921 — civil service salaries reached their highest level during the inflation period. If measured in real terms against prewar levels, the pay of higher civil servants had reached 54 % in October (37 % in August), that of middle-level officials 65 % (51 % in August), and lower civil servants had nearly reached the prewar level with 97 % (82 % in August).[64] This leads one to conclude that the social explosiveness of the October settlement cannot be found in salary *levels*, but rather in salary *differentials*, which had

[62] During the cabinet meeting on October 27 the problem of financial coverage was not mentioned at all. In the meeting on November 2, a total expenditure of more than 20 billion marks for Reich, *Länder*, and municipalities was mentioned (including 8 billion for workers' wages), but the question of how these expenditures were to be met was, again, not discussed in full. Cf. the documents cited in note 58 above.

[63] Reported by and quoted in *DG*, November 17, 1921.

[64] Cf. *Zahlen zur Geldentwertung*..., p. 43 and the charts and tables presented in CHAPTER ONE of this study.

been changed as a result of the October settlement. For one, the "distance" *(Spannen)* in the pay rate between higher and lower grade civil servants had been increased for the first time since these differentials had been fixed in the Salary Law of 1920. Moreover, in its attempt to alleviate the "great dislocations in income levels" caused by the war and by postwar inflation, the government had increased the pay of lower civil servants to a lesser degree than the wages of a skilled worker in government service.[65] While these changes were quite insignificant in the overall gains and losses that they entailed, an "iron principle" had been violated as far as lower-grade civil servants were concerned, namely, that there should be no rollback in the gains that had been made by this group during the struggles for the Salary Reform of 1920.[66] Seen from the perspective of the lower ranks, the wage movement of October 1921 had therefore been a disaster. Not only had their principle demand of a disproportionally large pay increase in form of a minimum allowance for the lower pay groups been rejected, the government had added insult to injury by awarding such a disproportionally large increase to higher civil servants instead. Massive protest was certain to follow.

The relatively high pay levels, and the considerable financial burden which the government had placed on the public purse as a result of these income levels were certainly not honored with social peace and tranquillity within the *Beamtenschaft.* Higher civil servants still claimed that their income level was too low and that the inflation, rampant since 1914, had far outpaced civil servant salaries.[67] The most forceful protest

[65] For further details, see *WSt.,* 1 (1921), p. 536.

[66] One may argue that the relative improvement of the position of higher civil servants was minimal at best, since they gained only two percentage points if measured against the pay of a lower-level civil servant (i. e. from 45 in August to 43 in November). However, the significance of these gains do not lie in their size, but rather in the closing of the differential as such. It was a matter of the politics of pay rather than of economic improvement. *Any* alteration in the pay structure to the favor of the higher groups, even if relatively small, was opposed by the lower ranks as a return to the "injustice" of the prewar pay structure. Moreover, if other pay groups are selected as "typical" for the three-tier structure of the German civil service, the gains scored by the higher groups in the November pay settlement increase to a certain extent.

[67] On a preprinted postcard to Chancellor Wirth, the Westfälische Philologenverein, a RhB affiliate, made this point clear by depicting graphically that the cost of living had risen sixteen-fold since 1913, while civil servant pay, even after the latest increase, had been raised only seven, four, and three and a half-fold, respectively. „Ist das gerecht?" the card asked. One specimen of what apparently was a mailing blitz is contained in BA, R 43I/2563, Bl. 163.

emerged, however, from the lower ranks of the civil service. While the inflation in Germany was nearing "Austrian proportions," one paper noted, the *Unterbeamte* were being forced down into the proletariat. Only unconcealed class interests, the same paper claimed, had guided government negotiators — higher civil servants themselves — in their effort to alter the pay structure in favor of the higher pay groups. Lower civil servants would continue to be deceived until they band together more tightly in their own representative organization, the Soziale Arbeitsgemeinschaft, and begin imposing *their* will on the DBB.[68] Protest surfaced in mass rallies organized by local DBB cartels in Berlin, Hamburg, and other major German cities.[69] As had been the case before, such protest was an easy prey to radical political agitation. Expounding the "maltreatment of the *Beamte,*" the KPD's *Rote Fahne* called on lower-grade civil servants to remain steadfast in their just struggle against a "counterrevolutionary bureaucracy of the privy councillors *(Geheimratsbürokratie).*" This struggle, the paper enlightened the *Unterbeamte*, could not be won with parliamentary means, but only by "joining forces with the fighting proletariat."[70] Such tirades were not meant to be hollow propaganda rhetoric, but signalled a rising interest on the part of the KPD in the plight and welfare of the "proletarians of the civil service;" the long-range aim was the widening of the KPD's sociological base as a political party. These attempts were by no means unsuccessful either. In Hamburg the local Beamtenrat was forced to call off a planned protest meeting, because there were indications that KPD agitators would take over the meeting. When Hamburg's KPD called its own protest meeting for lower civil servants in response to the Beamtenrat's decision, it apparently was well attended.[71]

DBB leaders were keenly aware of the increasingly radical mood of their rank and file members. The renewed defeat suffered in the October salary offensive, Albert Falkenberg warned in the *Gemeinschaft,* would undoubtedly lead to "justified discontent" among the lower ranks of the civil service. Since the cost of living was bound to continue on its upward surge, a third salary offensive might be inevitable, adding

[68] *GBZ,* November 15, 1921.

[69] Reported by *DG,* November 17, 1921.

[70] *Die Rote Fahne* (hereafter cited as *RF*), November 11, 1921.

[71] Materials in StAH, 122-4-3 and 122-4-17, Bd. 3, For a more thorough treatment of civil servant protest in Hamburg, see A. Kunz, *Variants…,* in: G. D. Feldman et al. (eds.), *Die Anpassung…,* pp. 328—342.

on to the twenty billion marks that had just been paid out in the second phase of the prolonged salary struggle between civil servants and the government.[72] It is interesting to note that Falkenberg for the first time admitted to the shortcomings of repeated salary increases. "An increasing inflation of the currency and a higher cost of living," he asserted, would be the ultimate outcome of a new wage drive. In the long run, only a more equitable distribution of the tax burden would increase the purchasing power of civil-servant incomes, as well as lead to an improvement of the general financial situation of the Reich. Using surprisingly radical wording, Falkenberg called on civil servants to join the fight for tax reform and a juster tax policy:

"If those, who have seen their income be reduced by direct withdrawal of taxes only knew that the financially solvent groups of our nation, i. e. the profiteers of war, revolution, and reparations, are still protected by the same state, whose existence their tax payments guaranteed, they would become an invincible fighting force to change such a method of taxation."[73]

This frontal attack against the "profiteers of war, revolution, and reparations" (one may note that "inflation" is not mentioned!) was an only barely disguised attack against big business and big landowners. The same theme was expounded again, and even more intensely, when in early November 1921 the leading organization of German industry, the Reichsverband der Deutschen Industrie (RDI), made a controversial credit offer to assist the Wirth government in the attempt at overcoming the financial crisis of the Reich.[74] A key element in the industrialists' design was the denationalization of the railroads and other public enterprises, in order to deal with their inflated personnel structure more effectively and to turn them into profitable enterprises again.[75] In how far the much-publicized salary struggles of the previous

[72] *DG*, November 3, 1921.

[73] *Ibid.*

[74] On the "credit action" of industry, see E. Laubach, *Die Politik der Kabinette Wirth...*, pp. 84ff.

[75] The section on railroads and state-run enterprises reads: „Insbesondere müssen die in Reichs- und sonst in öffentlicher Hand befindlichen Betriebe derart behandelt werden, daß sie nicht weiter die öffentlichen Finanzen belasten, sondern sie entlasten." (*Die Kabinette Wirth I und II...*, p. 368, note 1). Cf. also Silverberg's elaboration on this point in a discussion between RDI, labor organizations, and the government on November 10, 1921 (*ibid.*, p. 369), where he proposes an enabling law *(Ermächtigungsgesetz)*

weeks and months, and the enormous costs which they had produced, had played a role in the RDI's demands can be anyone's guess. The industrialists had, however, consistently opposed the "overbureaucratization" in all levels of government, and had always argued that only drastic measures could lead to a reduction of the inflated bureaucracy.[76]

To civil servant interests, the industry's proposals seemed to imply the final goal of a "radical reduction *(Abbau)* of the *Berufsbeamtentum.*"[77] The DBB issued a statement condemning the attempt by the industrialists "to misuse the emergency situation of the Reich for an effort to turn the railroads and the other government enterprises . . . into private ownership." This self-serving plot, directed against the common good, had to be prevented "with all available means."[78] It is interesting to note that the idea of an organizational alliance between DBB and the Free Trade Unions was broached again, or at least talked about, in this context. Seizing upon a common enemy, big business, was thus not only a way to deflect attention from the defeat just suffered in the previous wage movement, but also to demonstrate once again the necessity of constructing "a common front of *Arbeitnehmer* of all social ranks and all political persuasion."[79] The mere fact that the idea of an organizational alliance was still a matter to be pursued indicates, moreover, that in spite of the working relationship established between the DBB and the labor organizations during the previous wage and salary offensive, not too much progress had been made on solving the question of the DBB's future relationship to the Free Trade Union movement. In the concluding section of this chapter we shall return to the realm of organizational politics, therefore, and examine more closely the relationship between the DBB and the labor movement in the fall of 1921.

in order to change the Reichsbahn into a private corporation. On the politics of industry at this juncture, see G. D. Feldman, *Iron and Steel...*, pp. 284—287.

[76] For the statistical dimension of personnel size, see CHAPTER ONE of this study. The politics of *Abbau* will be a major theme in CHAPTER SEVEN below.

[77] *DG*, November 17, 1921.

[78] Resolution reprinted in *ibid.*

[79] *Ibid.* See also *DG*, November 24, 1921 *(Wochenschau)*, where the inner solidarity of the *Beamtenschaft* against the RDI offensive is stressed: „Mit der Eisenbahnbeamtenschaft sind auch alle anderen im DBB organisierten Beamten darüber einig, daß dieser selbstsüchtige, mit dem Allgemeinwohl unvereinbare Versuch der Industrie mit allen Mitteln abgewehrt werden muß."

In Pursuit of the Organizational Alliance: Civil Servants and the Labor Movement in the Fall of 1921

It has been shown above that organizational tensions in the transportation sector, i. e. between the DBB-affiliated Reichsgewerkschaft Deutscher Eisenbahnbeamter and the three railroad unions attached to the three federations of labor, played a leading role in the confrontation between the DBB and the labor movement in the summer of 1921. Both movements regarded the Reichsbahn with its nearly 400,000 civil servants and more than 600,000 blue collar workers as a key organizational testing ground. All developments in this sector would invariably produce repercussions on the relationship between the peak organizations themselves. This interrelation became apparent once again in early September 1921, when the first elections to the newly established representative staff advisory boards *(Beamtenbeiräte)* were held within the Reichsbahn administration.[80] Since the elections were based on union slates, they pitted "pure" civil servant organizations (in this case the Reichsgewerkschaft) against the "mixed" organizations of labor. The latter sought to represent the interests of wage earners, salaried employees, and civil servants alike, either within one single organization *(Einheitsverband)* — as was the case in the ADGB Transport Alliance's railroad branch, the Deutscher Eisenbahnerverband (DEV) —, or within single unions and a *separate* civil servant branch, which was the organizational principle employed by the Christian Trade Union-affiliate Gewerkschaft Deutscher Eisenbahner (GDE), and by the Hirsch-Duncker Unions' Allgemeiner Eisenbahnerverband (AEV). Both of these organizations had transferred their civil servant members to a separate civil servant umbrella organization within their respective movements.[81] At stake for the DBB was its claim of being the logical and only "true" representative of civil servant interests. For ADGB leaders the outcome of the elections would provide a clearer indication whether the Transport Alliance's concept of an all-embracing union of public employees, civil servants, salaried employees, and blue-collar

[80] Since legislation on the problem of civil service councils had not been passed by the Reichstag, these special advisory boards had been set up in the Reichsbahn administration by decree in 1921. Cf. *Reichs-Verkehrs-Blatt,* Ausgabe A, 1921 for details. Similar bodies had been established in the Reich postal administration.

[81] These were the Gesamtverband Deutscher Beamtengewerkschaften (GDB) and the Ring Deutscher Beamtenverbände (RDB). On the organizational strength of these federations, see TABLE 23 on pages 134—135.

workers, was the best vehicle to attract civil servants to the Free Trade Union banner, or whether the concept of a "corporatist" structure of the Free Trade Union movement, based on an organizational agreement with the DBB, was the more promising road to travel. In addition, these elections would also be an indicator of the *political* preferences of railroad civil servants in late 1921, since the three labor organizations represented political directions as well. The Reichsgewerkschaft as a politically "non-affiliated" organization did not officially, but it should be noted that its top-leadership stood left-of-center politically in 1921. In this sense a vote for the Reichsgewerkschaft was also a vote of political preference.[82]

TABLE 25

Elections to Representative Staff Boards in the Reichsbahn Administration (September 1921)

Union Slate/ Total Number of Votes and Seats	*Hauptbeamten-beirat* at the RVM		*Ausschuß* for Prussia		*Ausschuß* for Bavaria	
Total votes & seats	369,394	17	254,276	13	37,122	5
Reichsgewerkschaft	230,803	11	183,803	10	12,230	2
DEV	61,268	3	29,085	1	7,767	1
GDE/Deutsche Verkehrsbeamtengew.	74,317	3	38,421	2	17,091	2
AEV	2,957	0	2,955	0	—	—

Source: Reichsverkehrsblatt, Ausg. A (Eisenbahnen), 1921.

The results of the elections are depicted in TABLE 25. They reveal that the Reichsgewerkschaft, which had garnered some 230,000 of the 370,000 votes cast, came out as a clear, albeit not unchallenged victor in the elections to the Central Civil Servant Advisory Board *(Hauptbeamtenbeirat)* at the Transport Ministry and in those for the Committee *(Ausschuß)* for Prussia, where it received 183,000 of 253,000 votes. Only

[82] Officially, the Reichsgewerkschaft claimed to be "politically non-affiliated," which implied that various political factions existed in this organization. Its leadership, however, had tended to be left-of-center since 1919, and would move even further to the left as our subsequent discussion will show. There is no written history of this organization. For these political tendencies, its *Geschäftsberichte* are instructive, however.

in Bavaria was the RG slate overtaken by a labor organization. The success of the Christian (i. e. Catholic and conservative oriented) GDE tells something about the political inclinations of railroad officials in the *Ordnungszelle Bayern.* In the other elections, especially in the crucial elections to the Central Advisory Board, labor organizations did less well. Here the Christian unions came in a distant second, with nearly 75,000 votes, and the Free Trade Union's DEV only reached third place, with some 61,000 votes polled for its slate. The 3,000 votes cast for the Hirsch-Duncker union slate were marginal. Counted together, however, the votes cast for labor organizations (nearly 140,000) compare more favorably to the 230,000 cast for the RG.

The election results can be used to analyze the organizational and political preferences of railroad civil servants in 1921, as well as the potential chances and political implications of a pact between the DBB and the Free Trade Unions. Clearly, a majority of railroad *Beamte* regarded the civil servant movement as its logical representative, although a sizeable minority did not. Still, it had been a good showing for the Reichsgewerkschaft, which in turn would strengthen the position of this powerful union within the DBB leadership. Since the RG was opposed to an agreement with the ADGB on account of its sharp differences with the DEV, the position of the "trade-union wing" within the DBB's inner circle had been weakened as a result of the elections and of the bitter strife between RG and DEV which had characterized the elections campaign. In his commentary on the elections, Albert Falkenberg admitted that the "fratricidal strife" between RG and DEV had increased to such an extent "as to make the establishing of an organization alliance [with labor] unreachable for a long time to come."[83] He especially deplored that the RG had been accused of election fraud by DEV spokesmen, and that the ADGB had allowed this to be done in the pages of the *Korrespondenzblatt,* the official ADGB gazette.

This accusation had indeed been made by Theodor Kotzur, the DEV's expert on civil service matters, in his assessment of the election results published by the *Korrespondenzblatt.* Kotzur spoke of "election terror" by the Reichsgewerkschaft, which had been put in charge by the Transport Ministry to organize the elections. Kotzur insinuated that election fraud had been committed, because some 43,000 votes from Breslau and Cologne had purposely not been forwarded to Berlin in

[83] Albert Falkenberg, *Wochenschau,* in: *DG,* September 29, 1921.

time to be counted, and finally he accused the RG (and with it the DBB as well) of having orchestrated their "victory" through their excessive and "agitational" pay demands during the wage movement in August. Displaying a stiff dose of wishful thinking, Kotzur still claimed the elections had proven "the onward-march of Free-Trade unionism among railroad civil servants."[84]

The "fratricidal strife" between RG and DEV, which again put their peak associations at loggerheads as well, likewise prevented leaders of both organizations to come to grips with another significant aspect of the September elections in the *Reichsbahn* administration: the results revealed an overwhelmingly left-leaning, and hence more democratic potential, within the Reichsbahn's *Beamtenschaft*. After all, if counted together an overwhelming majority of some 300,000 railroad civil servants had cast ballots for one of the two left-oriented unions, RG and DEV, while (with the exception of Bavaria) the center-right leaning GDE, which had strong ties not only to the right-wing of the Center Party, but also to the DNVP,[85] had been outvoted by a great margin, as had the nationalist-democratic AEV, which had ties to both DDP and DVP. Yet instead of combining their efforts at strengthening the "democratic potential" within the *Beamtenschaft*, organizational strife between the two sides would diminish, if not squander away, this potential in the subsequent weeks and months.

Shortly after the September elections in the Reichsbahn had propelled the animosities that existed between the Transport Alliance organizations of the ADGB and the DBB to a new and dangerous level, the main political arm of the German labor movement, the SPD, was deeply drawn into the conflict. The timing of this development was not a coincidence, nor had the SPD been excluded from the previous struggles between DBB and ADGB. After all, some of the DBB's leading officials were SPD members and active in that party's civil servant section, the *Reichsbeamtenbeirat*. The most prominent of these was undoubtedly Albert Falkenberg, who aside of his position as the

[84] Theodor Kotzur, *Beamtenrätewahlen im Eisenbahnbetrieb*, in: *Korr. Bl.*, 1921, pp. 649—650.

[85] A „Berufsständischer Ausschuß für die Beamten beim Landesverband Magdeburg der DNVP" had suggested in a circular to its members to cast their ballots for the GDE slate in the upcoming elections. The same circular was sent to the Deutschnationale Beamtenschaft, the civil service section of the DNVP. Reported in *DG*, September 29, 1921. — The GDE's *Generalsekretär* Roth apparently was a member of the DNVP.

head of the DBB's press organization and as editor of *Die Gemeinschaft* also wrote leading articles for the *Vorwärts* and for the newsletter of the *Reichsbeamtenbeirat*, the *Freie Beamte.*[86] Thus the SPD's civil servant section had always functioned as a kind of "neutral meeting ground" for DBB and ADGB leaders. On the other hand, the party had often walked on a tight-rope when conflicts had erupted between the two organizations. Now, in the fall of 1921, the SPD was drawn more deeply into the conflict between DBB and ADGB, because the party itself was embarking on a new course, a course in which civil servants and their organizational direction became an item of considerable importance. The new course was aimed at broadening the social base of the traditional working-class party by changing the erstwhile "class party" *(Klassenpartei)* of the proletariat into a more sociologically heterogeneous "people's party" *(Volkspartei)*, primarily by becoming more attractive as a party to members of the middle classes.[87] This step was to be taken by adopting a new party platform at the SPD's 1921 party congress, which met in Görlitz in late September of that year. There the delegates adopted a new platform, the so-called Görlitz Program, which proclaimed that henceforth the SPD was to be "the party of all working people in city and countryside" *("die Partei des arbeitenden Volkes in Stadt und Land")* — a clear departure from the class-struggle concept that had guided the party since the adoption of the Erfurt Program in 1892.[88]

[86] At its 1919 party congress the SPD had founded a Zentralstelle für Beamtenagitation, which later was expanded into a civil servant section (Reichsbeamtenbeirat) at the party's central office in Berlin. Leading members of civil servant associations and several Reichstag deputies, e. g. Willy Steinkopf and Max Seppel, were members of this advisory board in civil service matters. The leading figure of the Reichsbeamtenbeirat was Franz Krüger, a member of the SPD Parteivorstand, and Hermann Wäger, who was the editor of the *Freie Beamte.* For the programmatic and practical aims of the Reichsbeamtenausschuß, see two proclamations entitled *An die deutsche Beamtenschaft,* in: *Der freie Beamte,* May 1 and 22, 1922. For an in-depth discussion on the SPD's approaches to civil servants and the organizational measures taken within the party to achieve this goal, see G. Hoffmann, *Sozialdemokratie...*, pp. 118—137 and *passim.*

[87] On the "class party/people's party" issue in German Social Democracy, see Hans Mommsen (ed.), *Sozialdemokratie zwischen Klassenbewegung und Volkspartei,* Frankfurt 1974. See also S. Miller, *Die Bürde...*, and Heinrich August Winkler, *Die deutsche Sozialdemokratie und die Revolution von 1918/19,* Bonn-Bad Godesberg 1979. The older study by Richard N. Hunt, *German Social Democracy 1918—1933,* New Haven 1964, is still useful on this subject.

[88] The *Programmdebatte* is best discussed by Heinrich August Winkler, *Klassenbewegung oder Volkspartei? Zur Programmdiskussion in der Weimarer Sozialdemokratie*

It was clear to the originators of the Görlitz Program that reaching out to the middle classes meant, among other things, the stepped-up appeal to the middling and lower ranks of the *Beamtenschaft.* In this context the concept of the civil servant as a dependent employee, as an *Arbeitnehmer,* was emphasized, an employee whose economic plight the party should take more notice of. The numerous resolutions presented to the party congress dealing with civil service questions, particularly with salary questions, indicate that civil service matters were indeed becoming more and more a point of debate within the party.[89] This fact was also registered in the civil servant press.[90] Yet SPD civil service experts were keenly aware of the fact, too, that the party still lacked a special civil service program, a *Beamtenprogramm,* which, in turn, might become a serious obstacle in the party's efforts to attract civil servants to the SPD. It was in this context that, again, the trade-union concept of the *Arbeitnehmer* was used. In its commentary to the Görlitz Program the *Freie Beamte* wrote:

"The program does not have a special section on the *Beamtentum.* Civil servants' demands have been integrated with those raised by other *Arbeitnehmer* groups. In the context of this program, civil servants belong to the 'working people in city and countryside.' All 'manual and intellectual workers' are to assemble in a 'community of struggle for democracy and socialism.' In this way, a lasting solidarity between civil servants, white-collar workers, and manual workers can be established."[91]

Theoretical and programmatic pronouncements are usually more easily made than actually carried through. While it was one thing to coopt civil servants into the "working people in city and countryside," it was quite another thing to actually achieve such unity in reality. The area of organizational politics, also discussed at Görlitz, is a case in point. In spite of the plea for a common *Arbeitnehmer* front under the Socialist banner as envisaged by the new party platform, a motion brought before the congress that would have required mandatory

1920—1925, in: *GG,* 8 (1982), pp. 9—54. The implications of Görlitz for civil servants are treated by G. Hoffmann, *Sozialdemokratie...,* pp. 121—124, who fails to bring in the trade-union issue, however, with which we are concerned primarily.

[89] *Die Beamtenforderungen auf dem Görlitzer Parteitag,* in: *Der Freie Beamte,* October 1, 1921.

[90] *Der Görlitzer Parteitag und die Beamten,* in: *DG,* October 6, 1921.

[91] *Der Freie Beamte,* October 1, 1921.

membership of SPD *Arbeitnehmer* in either ADGB, Afa-Bund, or DBB (!) was not carried by the delegates. The organizational unity expressed in this motion, the *Freie Beamte* commented, did not yet exist in reality. In addition, the DBB's political and organizational direction was still unclear, the same paper argued, and "widely differing factions" were struggling for supremacy in the DBB's inner leadership circle.[92]

It is understandable that this incident was down-played by Falkenberg in his commentary on the Görlitz Congress.[93] Indeed, the SPD-leaning wing of the DBB leadership was confused and irritated, because the defeat of the motion could be interpreted as a call on SPD members in the DBB to leave the organization in favor of either ADGB or Afa-Bund. Undoubtedly through pressures applied by the DBB's left wing, the ADGB executive issued a statement to clarify the issue. It emphasized that the three-pillar concept was still the guiding principle of the ADGB in organizational politics since the negotiations with the DBB had not been broken off entirely. SPD civil servants could and should therefore remain in the DBB "as long as ADGB and Afa-Bund have not issued a new slogan *(neue Parole).*"[94] Again, the ADGB executive had backed up the DBB's left wing in a attempt to save the negotiations between the two organizations. Again, this had been done with the risk of alienating groups within its own organization.[95] The tone had become a bit more impatient, however, and the mentioning of a possible "*neue Parole*" could be taken as an indication that the ADGB's tolerance level had limits in view of the fact that negotiations had all but ceased since the DBB's rejection of the agreement in late August.

A show of goodwill on the part of the DBB was urgently needed! It came in early October 1921, when the Afa-Bund held its first congress in Düsseldorf. For the first time a DBB representative, the DBB Director and former Chairman Max Lange,[96] attended a meeting of a Socialist trade union. Afa-Bund Chairman Aufhäuser emphasized this fact in his opening remarks and expressed hopes that soon the DBB might appear as an ally *(Bundesgenosse)* rather than as a guest of the Free Trade

[92] *Ibid.*

[93] Cf. *DG,* October 6, 1921.

[94] Reported in *Der Freie Beamte,* October 10, 1921.

[95] The statement led to rank-and-file protest within the DEV-controlled *Beamtenräte* movement in Saxony. Mentioned in: *Ibid.*

[96] In 1921, Lange was one of the DBB's three salaried top officials, the *Direktoren,* so his presence at the Afa-Bund meeting must be viewed as highly significant.

Union movement.[97] Leipart, the ADGB Chairman, stressed that the Free Trade Unions rather than the Christian Unions were the DBB's logical ally in the representation of civil servant and general employee interests.[98] Lange himself in his address to the Afa-Bund delegates spoke of the hopes and aspirations, but also of the enormous difficulties still faced by the DBB's trade-union wing in its struggle to reach an agreement with the Free Trade Unions.

Lange's speech is a central document, recapturing in brief many of the social and economic forces contributing to civil servant *Arbeitnehmer* politics. It also shows, though, that there was still a considerable ballast of traditional emphasis on social rights and privileges active in the *Beamtenschaft,* which provided a buffer, so to speak, against the acceptance of a modern *Arbeitnehmer* perspective. Lange said:

"The executive of the Deutschen Beamtenbund has asked me to convey greetings to your first trade-union congress. We are observing your struggles and aspirations with great interest... for we are convinced that your ways will, in many respects, have to be ours as well. With a clear aim in mind, your leaders have prepared the ground for an all-encompassing *Arbeitnehmer* perspective. In my organization, too, the economic situation of civil servants as *Arbeitnehmer* and consumers is now being recognized. More and more we have taken the path of broadly-based employee- and consumer politics. In this respect, we believe, the aims of workers, salaried employees and civil servants are identical. For this reason, cooperation between the large peak associations is a virtual necessity. This firm conviction had been expressed in an agreement, which the leaders of ADGB, Afa-Bund, and DBB have been negotiating. This agreement is meant to be a symbol of strength and a reservoir of concentrated energy to counteract the formation of the enemy forces of the intellectual and manual workers. You know, ladies and gentlemen, that you yourself responded to the call of your leaders much faster than the *Beamtenschaft* did to theirs. Civil service law and certain traditions have encouraged a special development of the concept of the civil servant. This in turn was responsible for the fact that the awareness of the civil servant about his position as an *Arbeitnehmer* and consumer did not mature as rapidly as it did among salaried employees. The current economic pressures, which the *Beamtenschaft*

[97] *Protokoll vom 1. Gewerkschaftskongreß des Allgemeinen freien Angestelltenbundes,* Berlin n. d. (1921), p. 5.

[98] *Ibid.,* p. 15.

is facing, have been a good teacher, though. The tempo, with which civil servants have approached the *Arbeitnehmer* movement, had been too slow in the past. It has now picked up and continues to increase in proportion to a loss in the belief of the reliability and traditional benevolence of the government as employer. Yet in some circles of the *Beamtenschaft* worries do exist that certain social protections . . . will be lost if civil servants embrace the new tendencies too fast and without reservation. A greater proportion of the *Beamtenschaft* has realized, though, that cost of living increases alone cannot lead to a victory over the forces of capital, which are determined to keep the trade union movement at bay. We are actively supporting these ideas . . . The hour will come, when the wish mentioned only just now by your chairman, Mr. Aufhäuser, will become reality and the Deutscher Beamtenbund will approach you and say: 'Let me be the third one in your alliance.'"[99]

While Lange's speech indicates that the DBB's trade union wing had remained interested in the alliance with the Free Trade Unions, the negative response which his words found in his own organization indicates that his opinion was that of a distinct minority only. Since Lange's speech had been widely quoted in the bourgeois press as proof of the DBB's alleged gravitation toward the Socialist labor movement, the DBB, in a surprising reproach of one of its own leading officials, issued statement in which the "continued validity" of the DBB council decision of August 16 was emphasized, which had prohibited a "unilateral merger with one of the existing trade unions."[100]

The lingering factional strife over this issue within the DBB leadership now began to produce exasperation in ADGB and SPD circles. While no one was interested in a destruction *(Zertrümmerung)* of the DBB, a high-ranking member or the SPD civil service section warned, the DBB in turn should hurry up and clarify its relationship to the different political branches of the trade-union movement.[101] Top-level negotiations resumed between DBB and ADGB leaders in early November, but when in mid-November the SPD's *Reichsbeamtenbeirat* met, Falkenberg had to admit once again that the DBB needed more time to overcome its internal differences in order to avoid the complete

[99] *Ibid.*, pp. 18—19.

[100] *DG*, October 20, 1921 *(Afabundtagung und Deutscher Beamtenbund).*

[101] Hermann Wäger, *Beamte und Gewerkschaften*, in: *Der Freie Beamte*, October 22, 1921. — Perhaps as warning to his own adversaries in the DBB, Falkenberg published Wäger's article *verbatim* in the *Gemeinschaft* (*DG*, October 27, 1921).

disintegration of the federation. "It does not make much sense to be placed into a state of dreams," he ruefully said, "hard facts are ruling the trade-union world."[102]

The fact was that negotiations between DBB and ADGB again had reached an insurmountable impasse. In mid-December the ADGB council met. Leipart had to admit that the talks between ADGB and DBB had all but failed. The DBB leadership as well as the large postal and railroad civil servant unions had declined an organizational agreement in order not to upset the precarious political balance within their respective organizations. Leipart now proposed a double strategy to be employed by the Free Trade Unions. On the one hand, the ADGB would go ahead in organizing civil servants already in its ranks in a more systematic way by establishing a central civil servant committee, a *Beamtenzentrale.* The latter was to function as a cadre-organization for a future *Beamtensäule* of the Free Trade Unions; it was to be run jointly by civil-service experts of Afa-Bund and the Transport Alliance. On the other hand, the connections between ADGB and DBB should not be broken off completely, so that the "comrades" in that organization could continue in their efforts of establishing trade-union principles there and, perhaps at a more distant point in the future, negotiations concerning an organizational pact could be resumed once again. To this compromise solution, which, however, was a decisive move toward the founding of a "free" civil servant organization independent of the DBB, the leaders of the ADGB's affiliated organizations gave their agreement.[103]

The second phase in the prolonged conflict between the DBB and the Free Trade Union movement in the period of accelerated inflation had come to an end. The possibilities for a broad *Arbeitnehmerbewegung* under the Socialist banner, with the DBB as one of its mainstays, had not vanished altogether, but they had been greatly diminished by the conflicting economic and social interests and the resulting organiza-

[102] *Tagung des Reichsbeamtenbeirates in Berlin am 12. und 13. November 1921,* protocol in: *Der Freie Beamte,* November 19, 1921. — Taking the *Besoldungsfrage* as a point of departure, one resolution presented to the meeting once again demanded „... daß die drei Hauptorganisationen DBB, Afa und ADGB *gemeinsam* mit der Regierung verhandeln und *gemeinsam* die neuen Gehälter der Beamten, Angestellten und Arbeiter festsetzen." Reprinted in *ibid.* (italics in the original).

[103] *Protokoll der 14. Sitzung des Ausschusses des Allgemeinen Deutschen Gewerkschaftsbundes. 1. Geschäftsperiode,* Berlin 1922, pp. 35—36.

tional rivalries that had emerged during the wage movements of mid- and late-1921. In the third and most severe social crisis in the German public sector, which was to commence in the winter of 1921-22, these organizational conflicts were to play an important role again and would be brought to a conclusion. As German civil servants moved from protest to militancy in the wake of the third public sector wage movement of 1921, solutions to the social and organizational issues would take on a more radical tinge as well. The February Strike of 1922, the culmination of three years of endemic social unrest in the public service of the fledgling Weimar Republic, would propel civil servants into the forefront of social strife for a brief moment, although the reverberations of this moment of militancy would be long and painful. It is to the history of these conflicts in the winter of 1921-22 that our attention will turn to in the next chapter of this study.

CHAPTER SIX

From Protest to Militancy: The Civil Servant Strike of February 1922 and Its Consequences

"Railroad strike! Battle against democracy!" Eduard David jotted into his diary on February 2, 1922.[1] David's comment came in response to a strike of railroad civil servants; on the previous day, February 1, the Reichsgewerkschaft Deutscher Eisenbahnbeamter had issued a strike call, and within a matter of hours railroad traffic, the nation's lifelines, had ground to a halt in most parts of Germany. Militant civil servants had finally lived up to their promise of "taking the state by its throat."[2]

The February Strike of 1922, the first (and last) major civil servant strike in German history, has attracted the attention of contemporary observers and historians alike. Contemporary observers tended to follow David's description of the strike and concentrated therefore on its *political* dimension.[3] Perhaps as a consequence of this rather myoptic interpretation, recent accounts of this strike, too, have concentrated on its political aspects and implications, while its social and economic

[1] BA, Nachlaß David, 19, Bl. 4. The Social Democrat Eduard David had been Minister of the Interior in 1919.

[2] „An der Gurgel des Staates." This quip was attributed to the radical chairman of the Reichsgewerkschaft, Ernst Menne. On Menne and his career, see note 43 below.

[3] This was done by two other Social Democrats, who in their recollections gave detailed accounts of the strike. See Carl Severing, *Mein Lebensweg*, vol. 1, Cologne 1950, pp. 339—346, and Friedrich Stampfer, *Die ersten vierzehn Jahre der deutschen Republik*, Karlsbad 1935, 2nd ed., 1947, pp. 258—263. See also Hans Friedl, *Der deutsche Eisenbahnerstreik*, in: *Archiv für Eisenbahnwesen*, 47 (1924), which is a semi-official account from the perspective of the German railroad administration. A contemporaneous dissertation by Heinrich Windeler, *Der Eisenbahnerstreik vom Februar 1922 als Beamtenproblem. Ein Beitrag zur Beamtenfrage und zur Geschichte der Inflationsperiode*, Diss., Leipzig 1924, might take a broader approach, but a copy of this dissertation could not be secured despite an intensive search.

origins have escaped the attention of students of the political history of the early Weimar Republic.[4] Accounts given in the contemporaneous organizational publications of civil servant associations and other trade unions are more open to the social dimension of the strike, but they usually provide a distorted picture because of the severe organizational conflicts which the strike itself unleashed or accentuated.[5] Finally, the February Strike attracted the attention of jurists, who either attacked or defended the civil servants' right to strike from a legal perspective.[6]

On the whole, the history of the civil servant strike of February 1922 has not been written, just as the entire history of strikes and strike movements in the Weimar period has been sadly neglected.[7] There are two reasons, therefore, for retelling the history of the February Strike at this point. First, and most importantly, this strike marks the culmination in our story of social conflict in the German civil service and of civil servant protest in the inflation period. What had begun as a protest movement in 1919, now, in the winter of 1921-22, was to become a movement of militancy accompanied by severe social, political and organizational strife. Secondly, the history of the February Strike deserves to be retold because it was a transportation strike conducted by railroad civil servants, and became one of the most serious labor struggles in Germany during the interwar period. Lastly, the February Strike of 1922 still stands as the only major civil servant strike in

[4] See esp. E. Laubach, *Die Politik der Kabinette Wirth...*, pp. 153—157, who follows Stampfer's account closely. See also G. Hoffmann, *Sozialdemokratie...*, pp. 92—102, who confines herself to a discussion of the SPD's policies during the strike, and Ch. S. Maier, *Recasting...*, pp. 270—272, who concentrates on the policies pursued by the Wirth government.

[5] The official DBB version is Albert Falkenberg, *Der Eisenbahnerstreik 1922*, in: *BJ*, 9 (1922), pp. 47—60. The most detailed account from the perspective of the Socialist trade unions is contained in *Angestelltenbewegung 1921—1925...*, pp. 73 ff., 82 ff., 97 ff., and Richard Seidel, *Die Gewerkschaftsbewegung und das Streikrecht der Beamten*, Berlin 1922. A summary of the Free Trade Union's opinion on public service and civil service strikes is given by H. Potthoff, *Gewerkschaften...*, pp. 158—177.

[6] One of the many attacks is Wilhelm Kulemann, *Der Eisenbahnerstreik im rechtlichen Licht*, in: *Deutsche Juristenzeitung*, (1922), col. 137 ff.; one of the few defenses is Ludwig Bendix, *Das Streikrecht der Beamten. Ein Wort zur Verständigung*, in: *Der Freie Beamte*, (1922).

[7] For an assessment of the deplorable state of research on the history of strikes in the Weimar Republic, see Gerald D. Feldman, *Streiks in Deutschland 1914—1933: Probleme und Forschungsaufgaben*, in: Klaus Tenfelde/Heinrich Volkmann (eds.), *Streik. Zur Geschichte des Arbeitskampfes in Deutschland während der Industrialisierung*, Munich 1981, pp. 271—286.

German history and for this reason, too, needs to be restudied from a socioeconomic perspective.[8]

Toward the Strike

The Stillborn Wage Movement of December 1921

It has been argued in the preceding chapter that the salary agreement reached between civil servant organizations and the government in the fall of 1921 had caused deep dissatisfaction within the lower ranks of the *Beamtenschaft*, in spite of the fact that salary levels had attained — on paper at least — an all time high as a consequence of the pay increases that had been awarded. The main cause of the continued unhappiness on the part of the lower ranks was the disproportional increases of the salaries of higher civil servants, which had upset the existing pay differentials in the civil service at the expense of the lower ranks. While socially such a policy was certainly defensible, politically it was a disaster, because the powerful organizations of lower civil servants were almost certain to put increased pressure on their central leadership to remedy the "injustice" done to the lower pay groups. Accordingly, the DBB began preparations for a renewed salary drive almost immediately after the agreements of October 1921 had been negotiated. In a series of preliminary talks with labor unions the DBB managed to garner their support for a new wage offensive in the public sector. Labor's quick support was not only due to the fact that it always had an open ear for the specific interests of the lower grades, the "proletariat" of the civil service, but also a direct response to the economic situation in the late fall of 1921. The cost of living had risen sharply in October and November,[9] and the inflation had eaten up most of the pay increases

[8] This has hardly been done in the more recent associational literature published by the present-day Deutscher Beamtenbund, an organization which rejects the civil servant strike. See esp. *Die Beamten und das Streikrecht* (DBB Dokumente, no. 4), Bonn-Bad Godesberg 1969, pp. 11—23. Not surprisingly, this publication reprints excerpts from Severing's account of the strike (pp. 16—17). The summary of the history of German civil servant strikes contained in William McPherson, *Public Employee Relations in West Germany*, Ann Arbor 1971, pp. 171—191, is little more than a summary and a translation of key passages from the last mentioned DBB publication.

[9] The index rose from 15.04 to 19.28 between October and December, 1921, which means that civil servant salaries lost about 20 % of their real purchasing power in only two months' time.

before they had even paid out — a result of the complicated and longwinded mechanisms of wage bargaining in the public sector. With the rate of inflation approaching "double-digit" levels, the long duration of a wage movement rendered futile all efforts at adjusting wages and salaries in a timely way, and a more frequent use of the bargaining weapon was viewed by labor as a logical remedy.[10] Civil servant leaders, on the other hand, while likewise committed to new wage movements in shorter intervals, increasingly felt that some form of automatic adjustment of wages and salaries in the public sector should be introduced in order to avoid the social strife accompanying successive wage movements. It is for this reason that the "sliding scale" would become a major point of controversy in the third wage movement to be conducted in the German public sector in 1921.

On December 3, 1921, only shortly after the "October agreements" had finally passed the Reichstag, the peak associations under the leadership of the DBB sent a joint petition to the Reich government, in which they demanded once again a substantial raise of base pay and an increase in the cost-of-living allowance for civil servants.[11] The demands were drawn up as to benefit the lower pay groups more than the higher ones; similar measures were proposed for public workers and contractual employees. Thus in splendid unity from the onset, organizations representing civil servants, blue-collar workers, and contractual salaried employees in the public service used the concentrated power of a united front of all *Arbeitnehmer* in a renewed squeeze on the financial situation of the Reich, the patience of the government, and the understanding of the public.

To the Wirth government, which had just embarked on a series of financial austerity measures in an effort to insure a more balanced budget for 1922 as a prerequisite for a better bargaining position in the difficult reparations question, renewed wage demands by its public servants to the tune of some fifty to sixty billion marks could not have come at a worse time.[12] The government's reaction was therefore predictable, but the harshness with which Reich Finance Minister

[10] For a background discussion of labor's position, see *Die Gewerkschaften für die Beamten,* in: *Vorwärts,* December 6, 1921, morn. edn.

[11] The petition is reprinted in *GBZ,* December 15, 1921 and in the *Vorwärts* article just cited.

[12] On the political options of the Wirth government at this juncture, see E. Laubach, *Die Politik der Kabinette Wirth...,* pp. 145 ff. and Ch. S. Maier, *Recasting...,* pp. 265—269.

Hermes responded to the organizations' demands set a new tone in the relationship between government and civil servants. Hermes flatly refused to even enter into negotiations with the organizations. Neither the recent movement of the cost-of-living index, nor a comparison with wage levels in private industry and in the professions justified wage demands of such magnitude, he complained. The organizations' demands, Hermes insisted, "failed to take into consideration the condition of the national economy, the concerns of other groups of the population, the state of the nation's finances, and the requirements of foreign policy."[13]

The abrasiveness of Hermes' letter, the belatedness of the reply, and above all the categoric refusal to enter into negotiations greatly incensed the organizations. In an equally abrupt manner they approached Hermes demanding "immediate talks."[14] In an effort to increase the pressure on the Reich finance minister, they took their complaints to the chancellor as well. They assured Wirth that they were well prepared to substantiate the level of their wage demands, but insisted that this was usually done *during* rather than *before* salary and wage negotiations. They argued that Hermes had violated standard negotiating practices by cutting off the talks before they had even begun, and they raised hopes that neither Reich government nor Reichstag would endorse such a violation.[15]

Support for the organizations' point of view quickly emerged in the left-wing press. In several front-page articles, the *Vorwärts* took up the civil servants' side, despite the fact that the SPD was a coalition partner in the Wirth Cabinet. In a front-page editorial, Reichstag Deputy Steinkopf, the SPD's leading expert on civil service matters, admonished readers that the civil servants' economic demands were justified and a necessary consequence of the general economic situation, just as necessary as the wage demands of other employees. *All* social groups, Steinkopf argued, were being forced to keep demanding higher pay

[13] Reich Finance Minister to Organizations, December 13, 1921, BA, R 43I/2563, Bl. 215. The *Vorwärts* reproduced the letter on its front page (December 15, 1921, ev. edn.), which is an indication of the considerable political importance of the matter. The paper commented: „Die Öffentlichkeit sollte aus dem wiederholten Nachgeben der Beamtenschaft nicht voreilig den Schluß ziehen, daß die Gefahr eines Beamtenstreiks in Deutschland gering einzuschätzen ist."

[14] Organizations to Reich Finance Minister, December 14, 1921 (copy), BA, R 43I/2563, Bl. 214.

[15] Organizations to Reich Chancellor, December 14, 1921, *ibid.*, Bl. 213.

from employers in order to purchase the bare essentials of life; civil servant demands should therefore not be singled out in this context and used as a negative example.[16]

While the *Vorwärts'* editorial stance clearly showed that the SPD attached great political importance to the civil servant question at this juncture, drumming up parliamentary support was a different matter, even as far as the SPD Reichstag delegation was concerned. When on December 17 the Reich ministers of finance, transportation, and posts met with delegates from the Reichstag parties to discuss the problem of "economic aid" for civil servants and other public employees, the organizations and their parliamentary supporters scored a partial victory at best. Hermes remained firm in his rejection of the demands of December 3 as a basis of negotiation. Since the economic *malaise* of civil servants was, however, acknowledged and deplored by many of those present at the meeting, a compromise was reached. It stipulated that an advance on January salaries would be paid out before Christmas in an effort to provide some form of temporary relief and to take some of the pressure out of the current confrontation. While this compromise was very much in line with the government's policy, it was not in the best interest of civil servant organizations. The latter were opposed to the payment of advances since, in their opinion, this would only lead to problems in the subsequent months. It was more of a concession to civil servant leaders, therefore, that Hermes agreed to enter into negotiations with the organizations, albeit not on the basis of the December 3 demands. The assurances given by the finance minister to this effect were an indication that his confrontation course had met considerable resistance within both cabinet and Reichstag.[17]

While the cabinet quickly endorsed the compromise hammered out between parliamentary leaders and the three cabinet members,[18] the subsequent negotiations with the organizations, conducted under strictest secrecy in several Reich ministries, soon led to an impasse. Government negotiators remained locked in the position that the advance to be paid out in December would be an advance on January

[16] Willy Steinkopf, *Soziale Beamtenfragen*, in: *Vorwärts*, December 17, 1921, ev. edn. Steinkopf had close ties to the DBB.

[17] This meeting is reported by *Vorwärts*, December 18, 1921, Sun. edn. *(Die Notlage der Beamten)*.

[18] Meeting in the Chancellery *(Chefbesprechung)*, December 17, 1921, mentioned in BA, R 43I/2563, Bl. 246 and in *ARK. Kabinett Wirth*, p. 494, n. 9.

salaries, and not an advance on future pay increases yet to be negotiated. The latter mode had been proposed by the organizations in response to increased pressures from rank-and-file members.[19] Several protest meetings had been held, in which strike threats had surfaced and calls for a "radical solution" had gained in momentum. In the most widely noticed meeting of this kind, a protest meeting of postal officials in Berlin, a resolution had been passed which called for a strike to be conducted even against the declared will of the DBB leadership if no acceptable solution in the salary issue was found soon.[20] The incident prompted the bourgeois press to speculate that the rank and file had presented an ultimatum to their organizational leaders, who were defending it in the high-level talks against their own conviction. Such an accusation was viewed as grave enough by the organizations to be rebuked by Albert Falkenberg in an editorial on the front page of the *Vorwärts.* Civil servants, Falkenberg wrote, were no longer willing to accept the limits of the state's financial capacity as a strait jacket for their justified economic demands. If no other occupational group refrained from adjusting its wages and salaries to the increased devaluation of the currency, Falkenberg argued, why should the *Beamte* be the *one* group to do so.[21]

The negotiations between civil servant organizations and the Reich Finance Ministry failed to produce an agreement; they were broken off and postponed until early January. Faced with mounting pressures from below and mounting criticisms from the press that once again excessive civil servant demands had frustrated a combined wage and salary offensive in the public sector by turning it into a "stillborn movement" from the start, the DBB leadership decided to pursue a more offensive policy. In a letter, sent to Chancellor Wirth on December 28, the DBB rejected as "preposterous" *(ungeheuerlich)* a claim which some government negotiators had leaked to the press implying that the DBB's false tactics and its insistence on excessive wage demands had undercut the government's good intentions in the salary issue, and had therefore produced the unhappy result of no wage and

[19] Reich Minister of Transportation Groener to State Secretary in the Chancellery, December 23, 1921, BA, R 43I/2563, Bl. 246—247, where Groener reports on the negotiations conducted with the RG and the railroad workers' unions and indicates that he had pursued a hard line.

[20] *Vorwärts,* December 21, 1921, morn. edn. *(Gehaltsbewegung der Beamten).*

[21] Albert Falkenberg, *Beamtenpolitische Polemik,* in: *Ibid.* Falkenberg's editorial came in response to an article which had appeared in the *Berliner Tageblatt* a few days earlier.

salary increases in the public sector before Christmas. The obvious intentions of these press reports, the DBB surmised, were to once again divide the interests of civil servants and other employees in the public sector.[22] The DBB did not resort to protest at the government level alone, however. In a press campaign of its own, launched as a part of the counter offensive, the DBB extolled the importance of the solidarity between the various strata of German society as a prerequisite for the ultimate success of economic reconstruction and the improvement of all conditions of life. "The enemy within," the DBB's *Beamten-Korrespondenz* wrote, "is he who plants hatred and discord between our fellow Germans *(Volksgenossen)* for reasons of profit..." The *Beamtenschaft* had been the target of such attempts in recent weeks, the DBB paper surmised, and the net result had been a general misunderstanding of the real economic plight of civil servants, especially in the public press. A culprit was easily to be found: "Heavy industry needs to turn public opinion against the *Berufsbeamtentum* in order to prepare the grounds for the day, when it will assume ownership of the railroads, the postal service, and other public enterprises for reasons of profit."[23]

Such polemics notwithstanding, the fate of the December wage movement would not be decided with the pen, but rather in a very real confrontation between public employers and public employees. Railroad workers and their organizations were the first to challenge the results of the December negotiations through direct action, setting a dangerous precedent of new and more militant forms of conflict solution in the public sector: the issuing of ultimatum-style demands, coupled with strike threats, and subsequent strike actions in form of wildcat strikes in order to coerce public employers into accepting their demands. A strike of railroad workers in late December of 1921 was the first major conflict to be fought and settled in this way. It marks the beginning of an acrimonious strike movement that was to engulf the public sector in the winter of 1921-22.

[22] DBB to Reich Chancellor, December 28, 1921, BA, R 43I/2563, Bl. 249.

[23] *Der innenpolitische Verständigungsprozeß*, in: *BK-Beamtenkorrespondenz: Mitteilungen des Deutschen Beamtenbundes*, no. 1, January 5, 1922 (quoted from a copy found in GStA, Rep. 84 a, 2719). One of the papers most critical of DBB politics was the *Deutsche Allgemeine Zeitung (DAZ)*, which had ties with the industrial wing of the DVP. The DBB's campaign against industrial interests has to be connected with the RDI's notorious credit action of November 1921, which has been discussed in the previous chapter. For similar attacks against the industrialists' alleged designs to "privatice" public enterprises, see *DG*, September 29, 1921 *(Wochenschau)*.

The Railroad Workers' Strike of December 1921

Some of the economic relief measures adopted by the Reich cabinet on December 17, 1921 had specifically excluded blue-collar workers as potential beneficiaries. This, as might be expected, had caused great consternation with labor leaders of those unions representing mainly workers, and had once again pitted civil servant interests against those of blue-collar workers. The weakening of the bargaining alliance, which had been employed by the organizations thus far, was an almost necessary consequence, as was a marked increase of rank-and-file pressure on negotiators acting in behalf of workers' interests. The latter was especially the case on the ever volatile railroads. When Transport Minister Groener, the champion of a government policy of dividing civil servant and workers' demands, met with union leaders on December 23, he defended the government's wage policies toward workers by arguing that the measures prepared for civil servants were merely a compensation for what workers had already received in form of advances on their weekly wages *(Lohnabschläge).* Any attempt at raising workers' wages in the public sector, Groener argued, would only complicate matters in the industrial centers by leading to a rise of wages in private industry and ultimately, therefore, to new price increases. Such a wage policy, Groener held, was fundamentally wrong and fiscally irresponsible. Hence it would not be pursued by the Reich government or the railroad administration under the present economic and political circumstances.[24]

Groener's tough style of negotiation was criticized by the unions and the left-wing press alike as "authoritarian" and likely to instigate conflicts rather than provide solutions.[25] And conflicts were forthcoming, indeed. In the Rhenish-Westphalian industrial region, especially in Elberfeld, Essen, and Cologne, railroad workers issued an ultimatum and threatened to strike on December 28, unless wage measures were extended to railroad workers by that day at the latest. Their cause was taken up and defended by a number of DEV locals, while the national leadership of the Socialist railroad union at first refused to endorse the ultimatum. The strike mood gained momentum quite rapidly. On December 28, the day the ultimatum was to expire, the situation had

[24] Groener to State Secretary in the Chancellery, December 23, 1921 (see note 19, above).

[25] *Vorwärts,* December 24, 1921, morn. edn.; *DG,* January 5, 1922.

become "serious" in the eyes of the *Vorwärts,* and the paper speculated that Finance Minister Hermes' sharp rejection of the initial demands put forth by the organizations were the deeper cause of the current conflict.[26]

Hermes himself refuted this accusation in a cabinet meeting on the same day, when the danger of an imminent strike on the railroads was discussed. The cabinet not only supported Hermes' point of view, but likewise endorsed proposals made by Groener and Minister of Posts Giesberts that this time the government should remain firm lest the demands of workers in the public service "grow into boundless proportions." Vice Chancellor Bauer, the ranking SPD man in the Wirth Cabinet, defended the government's tough line by pointing out that a strike would have to be regarded as a breach of a collective agreement *(Tarifbruch),* the consequences of which should be pointed out to the strikers in no uncertain terms.[27] It is not without irony, when the *Vorwärts* in a final appeal to reason spoke of mistakes made by both sides in precipitating the current conflict. While the government could not and should not succumb to an ultimatum, the SPD organ wrote, it should accept some of the responsibilities of having led things develop to this point. In a last-minute attempt at preventing a major conflict in the key transportation sector, the SPD called on railroad workers to be patient and to exercise more restraint. A railroad-strike, the *Vorwärts* argued, would be most dangerous to the nation's economy and the "general welfare." Moreover, should it fail, it would be an dangerous defeat for the entire labor movement.[28]

Despite these pleas for moderation, the strike broke out on December 29. Starting in the industrial centers of the West, the strike movement spread, shutting down rail traffic as far as Berlin.[29] With great reluctance, the DEV assumed the leadership of the struggle in an attempt to take from it the "odor" of a wildcat strike.[30] The ADGB leadership, in turn, assumed the role of a mediator in the conflict. In a

[26] *Vorwärts,* December 28, 1921, ev. edn. *(Die Eisenbahnerbewegung).*

[27] Cabinet meeting, December 28, 1921, *ARK. Kab. Wirth,* pp. 493—494. Groener had requested that the item be placed on the agenda of this meeting.

[28] *Vorwärts,* December 30, 1921, morn. ed. *(Der drohende Eisenbahnerstreik).*

[29] *Ibid.,* December 30, 1921, morn. edn. *(Der Eisenbahnerstreik greift um sich).*

[30] The DEV later claimed that this decision was forced upon the union to prevent worse things from happening and act as controlling force. *Vorwärts,* December 31, 1921, Sun. edn.

meeting with Chancellor Wirth, ADGB leaders obtained the concession that Groener would be compelled to renegotiate with the railroad unions regarding the wage issue. The unions, however, insisted on a major concession, a *große Geste,* as a condition to get the strikers back to work and the railroads back into operation.[31] With surprising speed, the government agreed to make such a gesture. On December 31, the cabinet decided to increase regional cost-of-living supplements (so-called *Überteuerungszuschüsse*) by one mark per hour for railroad workers. Since these supplements were primarily paid to workers in the expensive industrial regions of the West, in Berlin, and in other large cities, it was hoped that the mood in the centers of the current strike movement would become more favorable for a settling of the dispute. In addition, the government promised not to take disciplinary action against strikers and agreed that further negotiations, covering all wage demands, would be resumed in January of 1922.[32] The government had made major concessions to the strikers, and on their basis an agreement between the organizations and the Transport Ministry was reached. On New Year's Day of 1922, "new year's peace also reigned on the German railroads," the *Vorwärts* was happy to report.[33]

For the Free Trade Unions and the SPD as a labor party and a member of the Coalition Cabinet, the rather swift settling of a potentially disastrous and crippling labor dispute in the all-important transportation sector was a major success. To be sure, an additional financial burden had been placed on public coffers in order to pacify railroad workers, a fact realized and criticized by some far-thinking Social Democrats.[34] But the dreaded alternative of "class struggle" instead of "coalition politics," advocated by the SPD's challengers on the far left, the Communist Party, had been checked.[35] As far as the trade union

[31] Groener to Reich Chancellor, December 30, 1921, BA, R 43I/2124, Bl. 2—4. The DEV had been compelled to publicly disavow the strike as prerequisite for entering into negotiations.

[32] Cabinet meeting, December 31, 1921, *ARK. Kab. Wirth,* pp. 496—497.

[33] *Vorwärts,* January 1, 1922, Sun. edn. *(Neujahrsfrieden im Eisenbahnbetrieb)* and January 3, 1922, ev. edn. *(Das Streikergebnis).*

[34] See, for example, an article by Eduard Bernstein entitled *Reichsfinanzen 1922,* in: *Vorwärts,* December 31, 1921, sun. edn., where he points to the important linkage between the strike of the railroad workers and the future of public finances. Bernstein advocated a better tax system as the only remedy to avoid conflicts of this kind in the future.

[35] *Koalition oder Klassenkampf? Die Lehren der Bewegung,* in: *RF,* no. 3, January 3, 1922.

movement was concerned, mediation had replaced militancy as the main lever in settling labor disputes in the public sector. The ADGB had proven to be able to deal with labor struggles in the public sector and with militants in its own ranks, particularly within the radicalism-prone DEV. The settling of the strike showed that some measure of trade-union discipline had taken hold in the often uncontrollable railroad workers' union.

There is another, a negative side of the balance sheet as well, however. Viewed from the government's side, the strike and its settlement had also set a dangerous example of conflict-solution in the public sector. After all, the workers had been paid off by the government to some degree, and the latter seemed to have buckled under when confronted with a strike in the transportation sector. To other groups in the public sector this seemed to indicate that in spite of tough rhetoric, the government was essentially weak if only challenged forcefully enough. In other words, economic demands could be reached with brutal force. To the militant union of railroad civil servants, the Reichsgewerkschaft Deutscher Eisenbahnbeamter (RG), the December strike became a blueprint for its own strategies and designs in the forthcoming conflict with public employers.

The policies pursued by the RG during the workers' strike did not necessarily endear civil servant demands to labor unions. In the initial stage of the strike the RG had sent several of its leading officials to the center of the strike movement in the western industrial region, ostensibly "to gather information." The real reason had been, however, that several of the RG's local organizations had made attempts to join the strike in an effort to support the workers' cause, as well as to press for civil servant demands. The RG's central leadership in Berlin had remained undecided, however, whether or not to call a strike of railroad officials. "The civil servants are biding their time," the *Vorwärts* commented on the RG's wait-and-see attitude.[36] In the later stages of the strike, especially after the movement had reached Berlin, the RG's position had shifted somewhat. The radicals within the RG leadership now seemed to have gotten the upper hand, and a strike call on the part of the RG seemed imminent. "The civil servants are joining," the USPD's *Freiheit* rejoiced somewhat prematurely on December 30.[37]

[36] *Vorwärts*, December 30, 1921, morn. edn.

[37] *Die Beamten schließen sich an!*, in: *Die Freiheit* (hereafter cited as *DF*), December 30, 1922, ev. edn.

The swift settling of the strike only one day later prevented the RG from joining the walkout — provided that indeed it had planned to do so — and spared Germany a civil servant strike and a complete shutdown of rail traffic at this point. To the workers, on the other hand, the RG's indecisive actions and vascillating policies seemed to indicate that this civil servant union, and indeed the entire civil servant movement, was an uncertain ally at best.

The militancy among the RG's rank-and-file members, local organizations in the western industrial region, and in parts of its central leadership in Berlin did not abate, however, with the settling of the railroad workers' strike. Quite to the contrary, the relatively successful outcome of the workers' strike increased pressures within the civil servant movement to score equally impressive gains by using force instead of relying on longwinded and ultimately fruitless negotiations. The use of the "ultimate trade-union weapon" became the *ultima ratio* even for militant civil servant organizations, and the government was beginning to feel the pressures of having to deal with a major civil servant strike in the foreseeable future. On January 5, 1922, Transport Minister Groener warned Chancellor Wirth in a letter that plans for such a strike had been drawn up by local RG organizations in Essen, Elberfeld, and Cologne, i. e. in the same cities from which the railroad workers' strike had started, and that these plans had not been discarded after the settling of the last strike. Groener surmised that the RG leadership in Berlin had taken up these plans in order to assume the control over a renewed confrontation in the transportation sector, and that the civil servant union was trying to forge an alliance between militant civil servants and those portions of the *Arbeiterschaft* in the railroads still dissatisfied with the compromise reached to settle the December strike. Groener had few doubts that railroad workers would join a possible walkout called by the civil servant union, and he warned that the result would be a most crippling strike conducted by the entire railroad personnel. As a remedy, he urged Wirth to speed up the pay negotiations scheduled to take place initially in the Finance Ministry, whose results would then set the parameters for similar negotiations in the transportation sector scheduled to be conducted in the Transport Ministry.[38]

These negotiations began on January 5. They lasted for a week, until January 12, but they failed to produce an agreement acceptable to the

[38] Groener to Reich Chancellor, January 5, 1922, BA, R 43I/2124, Bl. 16.

organizations. The level of the pay increases conceded by the government — an hour raise of 75 pfennigs for workers and a salary increase of 2000 marks for civil servants — was regarded as "totally insufficient" by the organizations in view of a cost of living still increasing by leaps and bounds.[39] The government's inflexibility, but also internal conflicts between civil servant representatives and labor leaders, contributed to the collapse of the wage movement. In the course of the talks, DBB negotiators had become increasingly alarmed over the fact that priorities were assigned to the issue of workers' wages, while in the question of civil servant pay government negotiators chose to hide behind the sovereignty of the Reichstag in matters of civil service pay. DBB leaders regarded this as a way to weaken their bargaining position, if not as an attempt to do away with bargaining procedures in civil service salary policy altogether. The latter had always been the declared aim of conservative bureaucrats in the Reich Finance Ministry, who were now supported by the equally conservative attitude of Reich Finance Minister Hermes. Since labor organizations had not protested against the splitting of the issues of workers' wages and civil servant pay, the DBB decided to protect the "vital interests of civil servants" by lobbying at the relevant Reichstag committees. This, in turn, prompted labor to declare that the DBB had willfully sabotaged the bargaining alliance in the ongoing wage movement.[40]

These development reveal again how vulnerable cooperation strategies between civil servant associations and labor organizations were. Once again the responsibility for the meagre results of the wage movement could be placed on the organizational rival rather than on the third party, the government. Neither it, nor the left-wing press, which once again alleged that the DBB had misused the wage movement for purely agitational purposes and had thereby contributed to its failure, were prepared to grasp the impact which a successful workers' strike and an unsuccessful round of negotiations for civil servant demands would produce within the civil servant movement at this juncture.[41] Pushed relentlessly by its radical wing, the DBB had come under extreme pressures to settle its dispute with the government by making use of less peaceful means.

[39] Reports of these talks in *GBZ,* January 15, 1922 and in ZStAP, RhB, 55 (notes of the participating RhB delegate).

[40] Reported by *DF,* January 17, 1922, morn. edn.

[41] See, for example, *DF,* no. 29, January 28, 1922 *(Beamtenbewegung und freie Gewerkschaften).*

The Ultimatum of the Reichsgewerkschaft

By mid-January 1922 social unrest within the *Beamtenschaft* had reached a most critical and potentially explosive level. Railroad civil servants took the lead, and a renewed strike on the troubled railroads seemed imminent, a strike which would this time be carried by civil servants like train engineers and middle-level supervisory personnel rather than by railroad workers. The prevailing mood among civil servants as a result of discontent over the settling of the pay issue was captured well in a secret police report which the Reich Commissar for Public Order sent to the Reich Ministry of the Interior on January 19, 1922. The report stressed that the recent pay awards had incensed not only civil servants in the more militant railroads, but the *Beamtenschaft* as a whole. Even the "orderly and quiet elements," had articulated their sharp opposition to the government's policy, claiming that the pay increases granted by the government did not even match the latest increase in the price of bread. Large families, the report stated, were particularly hard pressed, because the children's bonus had not been raised at all. Citing confidential reports from within the civil servant movement as a source, the report stressed that the peak associations of civil servants and workers had been forced to defend their initial, admittedly high demands in view of the paltry concessions made by the government over a prolonged period of time. Sentiments for a "forced solution" were on the rise within the civil servant movement, and a strike of enormous proportions was inevitable unless the government showed more willingness to adjust civil service pay to the rising rate of inflation. The Reich Commissar warned of the grave economic and political dangers of a major transport strike, which, as he claimed, always carried the seed of a general strike and could thus lead into an attempt of a violent overthrow of the government by the extreme left. As to the extent of the strike itself, the report stressed the fact that in case of a renewed walkout in the public sector the government would probably be faced with a united front of workers and civil servants. Because of the extreme unrest at the rank-and-file level, the organizations would be unable to prevent or even control a possible strike, lest their credibility, which already had been damaged by the outcome of the wage movement, be totally destroyed.[42]

[42] Reich Commissar for Public Order to Reich Minister of the Interior, January 19, 1922, ZStAP, RMdI, 2185, Bl. 178—179. This report was obviously based on information originating from within the civil servant movement.

The scenario envisaged here by an informed government report was to become a reality in many ways during the subsequent days. On January 24, the leaders of the Reichsgewerkschaft assembled in Berlin. At the behest of the RG's radical wing, which only a few days earlier had assumed control over the organization's executive committee,[43] an ultimatum was drawn up and sent to the Chancellery, where it was received two days later, on January 26. Two major demands were raised. First, the government was asked to reconsider the DBB's salary proposals of December 3 as a basis for immediate pay increases for civil servants, as well as for a guiding principle of future increases by restudying the feasibility of automatic indexation. Secondly, the RG demanded that all plans be dropped by the government to tamper with the eight-hour work day in the public sector. The latter was a preventive demand, which aimed at forestalling governmental plans to rescind the schematic application of the eight-hour day on the railroads. The government was given five days to either accept or reject these demands; in case of a rejection, the RG would call a strike.[44]

It was unlikely indeed that the government would succumb to an ultimatum of this kind. In a sense, therefore, the issuing of the ultimatum was equivalent to calling the strike itself, i. e. a pretense for a "settling the score" rather than a way to reenter into negotiations. While it was not acceptable trade-union practice, as pointed out by

[43] In November 1921 the radical wing of the RG had pushed through the election of Ernst Menne as chairman of the organization. Menne, a militant middle-level railroad official from Erfurt, had been implicated in a revolt of railroad men there in 1919 whose aim it had been to support the establishing of a Central German council republic (cf. CHAPTER THREE, p. 179 above). Since then, he had risen in the GDEB/RG hierarchy, and, according to police reports, had consistently tried to use his union position to further political ends. His party affiliation remains unclear, however; he is variously described as a member of the (M)SPD, the USPD, and the KPD in the police files (ZStAP, RKöO, 453, Bl. 8—9). Throughout 1921 Menne and his deputy Scharfschwerdt, the chairman of the union of engineers and already a member of the RG executive in charge of press and agitation, had pushed toward a strike. Now, in November 1921, they had effectively taken over the leadership of the RG, which until then had been held by the DDP Reichstag deputy Otto Schuldt, a representative of the RG's moderate faction. Together with Menne and Scharfschwerdt, other radicals had been voted into key positions within the RG's inner leadership circle, while the position of the moderates had declined. (This account is based on a report, sent by the State Commissar of Public Order to the Reich Chancellery on March 18, 1921, BA, R 43I/2125, Bl. 31.)

[44] Text of the ultimatum in *DG*, February 2, 1922, and in the official strike report of the RG, copy in BA, R 43I/2124, Bl. 258—261 (hereafter cited as *RG Strike Report*).

observers in the labor movement both then and in retrospect, it should be remembered that the same method had been used by railroad workers prior to the December strike — a fact which generally escaped the attention of the critics of the RG from within the trade union camp. This is not to say that the RG's strategy was a sound one — a question to be discussed later on in some more detail. But it may serve as a reminder that the RG's action was not completely new as a strategy in trade union struggles, and therefore not merely a lack of trade union experience of a "union on the war path," as Friedrich Stampfer has claimed, nor a "demonstration of political inexperience competing successfully with other foolish acts of [a] peculiar union," as Carl Severing later wrote.[45] The RG's decision to challenge the state directly reflects a much more general phenomenon of deteriorating possibilities of mitigating social conflict under the impact of accelerated inflation, i. e. at a time when "traditional" methods of collective agreements and trade union practices began to break down. In this sense, the ultimatum of the RG, and the struggles which where unleashed by it, are of greater significance than the two contemporary observers and some recent studies have chosen to believe.[46]

The government's response to the ultimatum was both immediate and sharp. Prewarned by press reports even before the RG's letter was officially received, Transport Minister Groener issued a decree prohibiting the conduct of a civil servant strike in his administration. Any striking public official, the decree stipulated, would be formally charged with misconduct and removed from his post.[47] Once the RG's ultimatum had been received in the Chancellery and the Transport Ministry on January 27, Groener's tough stance toward a possible strike became the government's chosen policy in the matter. In its official response to the ultimatum, formulated apparently in a cabinet meeting on January 27,[48] the government restated its position that the DBB's pay demands of December 3 could not be met under any circum-

[45] C. Severing, *Mein Lebensweg...*, vol. 1, p. 340; F. Stampfer, *Die ersten vierzehn Jahre...*, p. 260.

[46] See the literature cited in note 7 above.

[47] *Erlaß vom 25. Januar betreffend den Beamtenstreik*, in: *Reichsverkehrsblatt*, Ausg. A (Eisenbahnen) (hereafter cited as *RVBl. A*), no. 3, January 26, 1922, p. 45.

[48] An official protocol of this meeting could not be found. The minutes of a *Chefbesprechung* held on this day (BA, R 43I/2124, quoted in *ARK. Kab. Wirth*, p. 530, note 6) does not contain a discussion of the ultimatum. The subsequent chain of events shows, however, that a decision was reached within the cabinet on this day.

stances. An additional burden on the Reich budget of fifty to sixty billion marks, which these demands entailed, was intolerable under the existing economic and political conditions in the Reich. The government insisted that in the course of the salary negotiations of mid-January the DBB had all but dropped these demands; renewed negotiations on their basis were therefore out of the question. Only with regard to the problem of automatic adjustment of pay to the inflation did the government indicate a willingness to negotiate with the organizations, but only after preliminary talks with political parties and the Länder governments had been completed. The government stressed the fact that with regard to the latter issue things had been set in motion already, and that a sub-committee of the Reichstag had already begun its deliberations and hearings on the "sliding scale" proposal. Taken these facts into consideration, the RG's ultimatum was, according to the government, not only incomprehensible *(unverständlich)* but also irresponsible *(unverantwortlich).* Any strike action, the government warned, would be regarded as a flagrant violation of civil servant duties *(Beamtenpflichten),* and any civil servant found guilty of such misconduct would be dealt with "in the appropriate manner."[49]

Deeds followed words. One day later, on January 28, Groener revoked the extended leave of absence granted to high-ranking RG functionaries. They were ordered to report back to their former places of work immediately.[49a] Meant as a challenge to the RG's resolve to go ahead with its strike plans, Groener's action only strengthened the solidarity within the civil servant movement in view of what was considered an infringement upon civil servants' trade-union rights. While the government's reply to the ultimatum had at least sounded a conciliatory note by promising discussions of the "sliding scale" issue, Groener's repressive measures seemed to indicate that forces within the government were more interested in a test of strength than in conciliation and compromise solutions. Groener had been "poorly advised," the DBB press concluded; his measures would only fuel discontent and militancy within the civil servant movement on the whole. The DBB

[49] Official response of the government reprinted in *Schultheß Europäischer Geschichtskalender,* vol. 38 (1922), pp. 11—12.

[49a] Reich Minister of Transportation to Regional Reichsbahn Offices, Mailgram, January 28, 1922, copy in BA, R 43I/2640, Bl. 92. The fact that Groener sent a copy of this directive to the State Secretary in the Reich Chancellery indicates that he wanted to keep Wirth informed on the steps and countermeasures taken by his ministry.

was not prepared to renounce the civil servant's right to strike, the paper wrote, because it was an "emergency measure" required if the existence of the civil service was endangered; no anti-strike decree could change this fact.[50]

If indeed certain forces within the government were interested in a test of strength in order to settle the strike issue once and for all, the same could be said about the militant wing of the civil servant movement. Here, too, the opinion was widely held that a showdown was better at this juncture than renewed and fruitless negotiations. In both cases, in the cabinet as well as in the civil servant movement, the position of the moderates had been weakened by the course of events; their objective of reaching compromise solutions had become less and less feasible. Internal conflicts within the civil servant movement, which surfaced in the final days and hours before the ultimatum was to expire and the strike to be called, can serve to further illustrate this point.

Even within the Reichsgewerkschaft itself there was considerable controversy over the strike issue. On January 28, the RG's branch union representing upper-ranked officials *(gehobene Beamte)* resolved at a general meeting in Berlin to oppose a possible strike-call by its central organization. The resolution claimed that a strike was unnecessary, since the government had agreed to reconsider the entire salary question. More importantly, the branch union accused the RG leadership of having violated organizational statutes by not having called a strike vote. On the whole, the resolution concluded, a strike at the present time would be "against the interests of the entire German *Beamtenschaft.*"[51]

Internal tensions within the railroad civil servant union were compounded by tensions between the RG and railroad workers' organizations over the conduct and execution of a renewed labor struggle in the transportation sector. Only in the rank and file of the DEV was some support for a strike, a police report noted; the DEV leadership itself was reluctant, if not hostile toward supporting a walkout by civil

[50] *DG*, February 2, 1922.

[51] Reported by the business-oriented *Deutsche Allgemeine Zeitung* (hereafter cited as *DAZ*), January 30, 1922, ev. edn. The RG statutes did, however, allow for the conducting of a strike without a strike vote under certain circumstances, e. g. in cases of "immediate danger" („in Fällen unvorhergesehener, dringender Gefahr"). In such cases a two-third majority of the RG's enlarged executive committee *(erweiterter Vorstand)* was necessary.

servants, not least because of its long-standing organizational rivalry with the RG. The other two railroad workers' organizations, the national-liberal AEV and the Christian GDE, opposed a general strike on the railroads almost out of principle and would definitely not support the RG in its struggle. Still, the RG could count on the majority of its own members to observe a strike call, which as the report noted, would lead to a widespread shutdown of rail traffic, since key groups like train engineers and conductors were in support, if not the driving forces behind the strike.[52]

The DBB and the Strike Issue

The potential severity of a possible struggle with the authorities of the state, of which the inital steps taken by Groener were only a mild foretaste, probably convinced even the most militant members of the RG leadership that the support of allies would certainly not hurt in their efforts, even if the strike itself could be conducted mainly by the RG and its affiliated unions. Since the support of labor was doubtful at best, the RG's most logical and most important potential ally was the DBB, its very own peak association and its nearly one-million members. It therefore stands to reason that the RG put intense pressure on the DBB to issue a declaration of solidarity, to provide financial backing and, if possible, make provisions for turning the railroad strike into a general civil servant strike. The DBB, in turn, was caught in a difficult position. On the one hand, the RG had used the DBB's demands of December 3 as a basis for its ultimatum, and by doing so had clearly elevated the conflict above specific railroad concerns. By making *general* civil servant grievances the basis of its actions, the RG had struck a positive chord within other DBB affiliates and their rank-and-file members, as well as within the left wing of the DBB leadership itself. On the other hand, DBB leaders had not been informed in advance about the RG's plans and had been presented with a *fait accompli* when the ultimatum was issued. This was not only a violation of DBB statutes (the peak organization was, after all, responsible for the major questions concerning civil servant policy), but also increased the apprehen-

[52] Report Reich Commissar for Public Order, January 30, 1922, entitled *Zur Lage im Eisenbahnerstreik*, BA, R 431/2124, Bl. 39—40. Henceforth these and other situation reports on the strike will be summarily cited as "strike report" with date and source added.

sion of DBB leaders of being outmaneuvered and controlled by its largest, most powerful, and most militant affiliate organization. The strike issue had therefore unleashed an internal power struggle within the DBB, a struggle which was superimposed, so to speak, on the conflict between civil servant organizations and the government as employer.

DBB leaders seemed keenly aware that the civil servant movement had arrived at a most critical juncture, when on the afternoon of January 30, 1922, the DBB executive committee *(Bundesvorstand)* convened for a special meeting.[53] The only order of business for the meeting, which was conducted under somewhat unusual and clandestine circumstances in the backroom of a Berlin hotel, was to debate and decide on a request for solidarity and support issued by the RG. The implications and consequences of this decision to be taken by the DBB's organizational leadership were far-reaching indeed. If it accepted the RG's request, the DBB itself would be drawn into a potentially disastrous confrontation with the government. A rejection of the RG's demands, however, could lead to the further disintegration, if not the total collapse of the DBB's ever fragile internal consensus along factional lines. The strike question had once again become the crucial testing point for the organizational survival of the DBB.

The meeting began with the report of a special committee, which had been appointed by the DBB executive after the request of the RG had reached the DBB's central headquarters in Berlin. The committee had formulated five principle questions as a basis of its deliberations: First, whether the inner cohesion of the DBB was strong enough to endure a potentially divisive call for a general civil servant strike; second, whether there were sufficient funds available to cover the costs of a large-scale strike; third, whether a possible strike could be conducted

[53] The following account is based on the verbatim protocol of this meeting, a copy of which is to be found in BA, R 43I/2125, Bl. 12—20. The history of this document — to my knowledge the only protocol of a DBB *Vorstand* meeting in existence — is revealing. It was sent to the Prussian State Commissar for Public Order by a "reliable source from within the DBB" — no doubt by a member of its conservative wing — and forwarded to the Reich Chancellery by the Commissar. (Cf. the cover letter to the protocol, *ibid.*, Bl. 11.) It is because of this historical coincidence that this protocol became a part of governmental record and thus survived the destruction of the DBB Archive in 1944. The decision-making process within the DBB can therefore be reconstructed at this critical juncture with the necessary closeness to documentary evidence. All subsequent quotations have been taken from this source unless indicated otherwise.

by the DBB alone or if allies were needed; fourth, whether the general political situation of Germany warranted a strike by its civil servants at the present time; fifth and last, what impact the RG's actions would produce on the DBB. According to its spokesman, the committee had agreed unanimously that the DBB's inner stability was too precarious to last through a conflict of this magnitude. There was not enough money to support a strike, since only two organizations (the RG and the postal unions) possessed strike funds. The support of the peak associations of labor was doubtful at best, and public sentiments were set against public service strikes. As a consequence, the strike would have to be fought alone, which in turn would lessen its chances of success. While some members of the committee had argued that chances of outside support could be improved by pushing the issue of work hours and the eight-hour day into the foreground of the conflict, a greater faction of the committee had claimed that the internal and international situation of the Reich simply did not allow for a major conflict in the public sector. Any public service strike, and a civil servant strike in particular, would be an act of grave irresponsibility toward the nation as a whole. There was general agreement within the committee, finally, that the RG had diminished the chances of a successful strike by acting alone and by issuing the ultimatum without having notified the DBB in advance.

Given this generally negative evaluation of the strike issue by the majority of the committee, it is not surprising that the draft resolution put before the full executive committee all but refused to throw the DBB's support toward the RG and the forthcoming strike. Although the circumstances which had led to the RG's ultimatum were fully endorsed in the first passage of the resolution, the consequences arising from the "anti-social salary policy" of the Reich government should, according to the committee, differ from the confrontation course chosen by the RG leaders. The committee suggested continued negotiations instead, and rejected the strike in a second, and, as it turned out, most controversial passage of the draft resolution.[54]

[54] The passage reads in full, "If in spite of these circumstances the DBB executive still cannot recommend the use of the ultimate trade-union weapon, this is done in view of the government's official pronouncement in the Reichstag on January 21, in which a thorough revision of civil service pay rates has been promised. Despite repeated disappointments, the DBB expects that the Reich government will keep its promise and enter into negotiations on a civil service pay reform immediately."

With this resolution, the moderate faction of the DBB leadership had issued a challenge to the organization's left wing. It would obviously not remain uncontested in the subsequent debate, which only commenced after the DBB's legal expert, Privy Councillor Gress, made some introductory remarks on the legality of civil servant strikes. At the behest of DBB Chairman Flügel, Gress restated the DBB's position that civil servant strikes were legal, because civil servants had acquired the full right of coalition during the November Revolution. In a curious disclaimer, however, Gress also stressed that "a striking civil servant ceases to be a civil servant the very moment he begins to strike" — an obvious warning shot fired against the pro-strike faction.

The latter remained unimpressed, however. Once the floor had been opened for debate, the RG's cause was taken up and defended forcefully by the chairman of the Association of Justice Officials, Bente, a representative of the DBB's left wing. With this resolution, Bente told his colleagues, the DBB would all but capitulate in face of government pressure. His organization could and would not participate in such a capitulation. He refuted the argument that the domestic and international situation was any worse now than it had been during the wage movements of August and October of the previous year, when the possibility of a civil servant strike was first discussed. No other occupational group, he added, cared about the general political situation of the country when pursuing its economic demands. The DBB should therefore not make its decision contingent upon the affairs of state or on the support of social allies, but rather depend on its own strength. "We have agreed that the ultimate trade-union weapon is to be used if our demands are rejected," Bente said, "and we have made a solemn promise to support the cause of other civil servant groups. Our cause is a just one, and our use of power would not be quite so modest if we already had more inner cohesion." Citing his own organization as an example, Bente appealed to the delegates to support the RG both morally and financially and to reject the proposed resolution.

In the further course of the debate, disunity among the DBB's rival factions intensified to such a degree, that finally the meeting had to be interrupted. The left wing, under the leadership of the RG delegation, worked out a counter-resolution. Its key passage read that the DBB would urge its affiliated organizations to support the RG's struggle, should negotiations between the RG and the government produce no immediate results.[55] Members of the right wing and the centrist faction

[55] The text of the counter-resolution reads in full: "The Deutscher Beamtenbund

voiced sharp opposition to what even Albert Falkenberg called "an open declaration of solidarity" with the Reichsgewerkschaft, which he could not support. Spokesmen for the right wing argued that the RG was only using the strike issue in an attempt to take over the DBB. The railroad union remained adamant, though, and a disruption of the meeting (and of the DBB) seemed imminent. In this situation Ernst Remmers, the great tactician, proposed a compromise solution: If adopted by the DBB executive committee, the RG's resolution would be disclosed to the public and to the affiliated associations *without* the controversial last clause. The latter would merely serve as a "general policy guideline" for the DBB executive in the case of a strike. With this restriction added, the centrists of the DBB executive committee could agree to a pro-strike resolution. Against the opposition of the right wing, the resolution was passed, and its content (except for the disputed clause) was later published in the DBB press.[56]

The conflicts which had overshadowed the meeting of the DBB executive committee, and the compromise that was reached in order to prevent the breaking-apart of the organization, provide a key to the understanding of the policies pursued later on by the DBB during the strike. Faced with the pressure of its radical wing, the DBB had embarked on what was to become a fatal zig-zag policy in the strike issue. Moreover, it had left the ultimate responsibility for support or non-support of the strike to its affiliated associations. In a sense, the DBB had relinguished its responsibilities as a peak association. During the strike, this would seriously hamper the DBB's role as a negotiator; after the strike, it would produce a major internal crisis, which, in turn, would ultimately lead to the DBB's split into two rival peak organizations.

With a defeat suffered in the meeting, the moderate faction of the DBB leadership concentrated its efforts on semi-official attempts at mediation between the Reichsgewerkschaft and the government. These efforts were hampered by the fact, however, that DBB leaders had not

expects that the Reich government will avoid the impending conflict with the Reichsgewerkschaft by reentering into negotiations about the proposed demands immediately. Should this expectation turn out to be wrong, the Deutscher Beamtenbund hereby recommends to its affiliated organizations to support the Reichsgewerkschaft, depending on their power and ability to do so."

[56] The text of the resolution, without the last sentence, was published in the *Gemeinschaft*, on February 2, 1922.

received a clear mandate by the radical wing to undertake such steps and, secondly, by the fact that the government had received support fore its "course of confrontation" from parliamentary leaders, including their consent that any strike attempts by civil servants would be answered with emergency decrees based on Article 48 of the Weimar Constitution.[57] On the evening of January 30, therefore, the lines of confrontation had hardened considerably; mediation had become an almost insurmountable task.

Immediately after the meeting of January 30, Remmers and Flügel of the DBB went to the Reich Chancellery to inform the chancellor of the DBB resolution and to offer to mediate in the conflict. They were not received by Wirth, however, but referred to the Reich Finance Ministry.[58] A similar attempt at mediation with Groener in the Reich Transport Ministry failed as well.[59] The DBB's bargaining position seemed too fragile to government leaders to attach greater importance to it. While the bourgeois press speculated that the DBB's maneuvers might well lead to a last minute compromise,[60] such hopes were premature and unfounded, since the momentum had already passed to the radical wing of the civil servant movement. The final strike decision would be made by the leaders of the Reichsgewerkschaft alone, who in turn were faced with mounting rank-and-file pressure to go through with the terms of their ultimatum.

By the afternoon of Tuesday, January 31, preparations for a strike were running at high gear in the industrial region of the Ruhr, particularly in Essen, where postal officials, policemen, and municipal streetcar drivers had apparently agreed to participate in a strike.[61] Similar inci-

[57] Joint meeting of the cabinet and leaders of the political parties, January 30, 1922, mentioned in a document filed in Nachlaß Groener, which is reprinted in *ARK. Kab. Wirth*, p. 537. The Reich government announced its position and intentions publicly in a meeting of the Hauptausschuß of the Reichstag. Reported by the *Berliner Tageblatt* (hereafter cited as *BT*), no. 53, February 1, 1922.

[58] DBB circular no. 7, reprinted in *DG*, February 9, 1922. The meeting with Hermes took place on the next day.

[59] Mentioned in a police report, dated January 31, 1922, copy in BA, R 43I/2124, Bl. 41. The same report noted that despite the internal disunity within the DBB on the strike issue, the important consequence of the meeting of January 30 was that "a sizeable proportion of the *Beamtenschaft* could be won over to a possible strike."

[60] *DAZ*, no. 5, January 31, 1922. The paper reported that DBB leaders had again contacted Groener, as well as leading members of the Reichstag.

[61] Strike report, January 31, 1922, BA, R 43I/2124, Bl. 45.

dents of "civil servant solidarity" were reported from Berlin. The same report stressed that workers were beginning to show solidarity as well. In Hagen, for example, a general meeting of railroad employees had ignited such radicalism that even the conservative GDE local felt obligated to support the strike call. Strike committees, the report noted, had been appointed in a number of cities in the Ruhr, and they had tried to establish contacts with workers' committees in large firms. In Breslau, public utility workers had agreed to support the civil servants' cause. There was a general tendency, the report observed, that not the ultimate success of the strike itself was viewed as the important long-range goal, but rather "to give a demonstration of power to the government in order to be taken seriously in the future."[62] Another police report, filed on January 31 as well, stressed that the position of the Reichsgewerkschaft had been improved at the rank-and-file level by the resolution adopted by the DBB the day before. The report speculated, however, that a large proportion of the *Beamtenschaft* would probably not support a strike, and therefore not all railroad districts would be afflicted uniformly by a walkout. Still, serious interruptions, or even a total breakdown of rail service could very well develop, particularly in the railroad districts of Elberfeld and Essen, even if the attitude of railroad workers toward a walkout was still uncertain.[63]

On January 31, the RG's executive committee met to take the final vote on the strike. The long duration of the meeting, which lasted all night until six o'clock in the morning of the following day, is an indication that the RG's radical wing still faced considerable opposition within its own organization.[64] After a ten hour battle against the strike opponents, the radical wing, led by RG Chairman Menne and his deputy Scharffschwerdt, managed to get a narrow 20 to 15 majority vote in favor of a strike, a vote that fell short of the two-thirds majority, however, required by the statutes. Shortly after this vote had been taken, Flügel and Remmers of the DBB telephoned to notify the RG leaders that a breakthrough had been made in the negotiations at the Reich Finance Ministry.[65] Although the anti-strike forces within the

[62] *Ibid.*

[63] Regional strike report for Prussia, copy in ZStAP, RMdI, 2185, Bl. 167.

[64] Reports of this meeting in BA, R 43I/2124, Bl. 50 (a police report dated February 1, 1922), in *BT*, no. 53 February 1, 1922, and in BA, R 43I/2124, Bl. 27, which is a flyer entitled "Menne und Genossen" distributed by the Catholic railroad union (hereafter cited as *Menne und Genossen*).

[65] DBB circular no. 7, *DG*, February 9, 1922, reports on the incident somewhat

RG had received desperately needed support through the DBB's last-minute effort, the radicals remained in control and committed to "their strike," as a critic noted bitterly.[66] Train engineers and their powerful union, the Gewerkschaft Deutscher Lokomotivführer, were determined to go ahead with the strike even if the RG executive committee should rescind its vote. They put pressures on the RG's moderate faction to remain firmly committed to the strike, despite the fact that the situation had changed considerably as a result of the DBB initiative.[67] The fierce internal struggle lasted until the early morning hours of the next day, but the moderates lost out in the end. It was decided that the strike would be called, since the government had not fulfilled all terms set by the ultimatum of January 24. The strike was scheduled to begin at midnight of the same day, i. e. in the night from February 1 to February 2.[68]

The RG used the remaining hours to complete its final preparations of the walkout. Its radical leaders, organized now in a central strike committee, went into hiding.[69] Couriers were sent to local organizations, carrying the strike-call and guidelines for the conduct of the strike.[70] Local strike committees were formed or activated, the latter was the case especially in the radical, strike-prone districts in the Western Industrial Region.[71] The rather organized manner in which the RG braced itself for the impending struggle shows that the strike was not nearly as "chaotic" an affair as depicted by rival unions.[72]

The government, in turn, used the time to enact preventive measures against the now imminent walkout of its civil service railroad personnel and the menace of a slowdown or even standstill of railroad traffic. A Presidential emergency decree was issued by Ebert on February 1 at the

differently. Here it is claimed that RG representatives did not show up for a meeting with DBB leaders despite repeated tries on the part of the DBB delegation. Thus, the RG never learned about the "breakthrough."

[66] *Menne und Genossen* (see note 64).

[67] Police report of the meeting in BA, R 43I/2124, Bl. 50.

[68] *RG Strike Report* (see note 44).

[69] *DAZ*, no. 55, February 2, 1922.

[70] There is a copy of these directives for a strike in ZStAP, RköO, 453, Bl. 152—155. The authenticity of this document, which was exposed by the bourgeois press after the strike (see *BT*, March 8, 1922), is unclear, though. The *Rote Fahne* (March 17, 1922) called it a fabrication. — The directives encouraged acts of sabotage by the strikers.

[71] The relevant documents are in HStAD, Reg. Düss., 15618.

[72] As charged in a resolution of the Catholic GDE, copy in BA, R 43I/2124, Bl. 52.

behest of Groener and Wirth, in which Article 48 of the Weimar Constitution was invoked to "restore public security and order in the country." The decree prohibited a walkout of civil servants in the Reichsbahn, and made it a criminal offense to agitate for such a walkout, engage in acts of sabotage, or prohibit nonstrikers from the performance of their duties. In addition, the Reich Transport Minister was empowered to take all emergency measures that seemed necessary in order to guarantee the continuation of the flow of emergency supplies.[73] The content of the decree was immediately made known to the regional district administrations of the Reichsbahn and posted in railroad yards, stations, and other public buildings.[74] In addition, Groener instructed the heads of the Reichsbahn's administrative and operational districts by telegraph to enforce the provisions of the emergency decree with utmost severity.[75] They were advised to contact local police departments in order to attain warrants for the arrest of strike leaders, for the impounding of strike funds, or to counteract strike propaganda. A police ordinance, issued already by the police commissioner of Berlin, was cited as a model.[76] While the mere participation in the walkout was not an offense against any of the provisions of the Emergency Decree, it was still a violation of civil service law and was to be dealt with through disciplinary action. Similar instructions were given by the Prussian State Commissar of Public Order to the provincial heads of government in Prussia.[77] With clockwork precision, it appeared, the German state authorities were getting ready for a major showdown with their disobedient public servants.

The Strike Days

The strike finally began on Thursday, February 2. All expectations harbored in the Reich Transport Ministry and proclaimed loudly in the

[73] *Verordnung des Reichspräsidenten betr. Verbot der Arbeitsniederlegung durch Beamten der Reichsbahn,* in: *RGBl.* 1922, p. 187 and in *RVBl.* A. 1922, p. 67.

[74] Specimen in HStAD, Reg. Düss., 16892.

[75] Groener to Reichsbahn District of Cologne, February 1, 1922, copy in HStAD, Reg. Düss., 16892. The RG had decided not to call a strike in the occupied zones, to which Cologne belonged. Reported by *DAZ,* no. 55, February 2, 1922.

[76] See C. Severing, *Mein Lebensweg...,* vol. 1, p. 341, for details. Severing himself, as Prussian Minister of the Interior, was instrumental in the issuing of this ordinance and in other measures taken against the RG.

[77] Oberpräsident of the Province of Westphalia to Regierung in Düsseldorf, February 2, 1922, HStAD, Reg. Düss., 16892.

rightwing press that the isolation of the Reichsgewerkschaft within the civil servant movement, its tensions with the labor movement, and the internal strife over the strike issue between moderates and radical factions within the striking civil servant union itself would seriously cripple a walkout from the very start, proved to be wrong.[78] The strike set in with a large-scale walkout of railroad officials, leading to an almost instant stoppage of rail traffic in Northern and Western Germany.[79] The first general strike report, issued on the afternoon of the first day of the strike, noted that nearly all train engineers had walked off their jobs, and a majority of the train conductors as well, especially in the western districts. Other strike centers were Hamburg and Berlin, where hardly any passenger and freight trains were running except for some local lines. There had been no cases of sabotage, the report noted, and blue-collar railroad workers had thus far remained "neutral." Many of them had appeared for work but had refused to take over functions performed by the striking civil service personnel. In several Reichsbahn districts, however, workers had demanded the lifting of the Presidential Emergency Decree and had threatened to join the strike unless the anti-strike order was scrapped.[80] In the Elberfeld District, for example, 7,500 employees, far more than the 1,300 registered RG members, walked off their jobs; therefore a good number of them must have been railroad workers. Toward the end of the strike, nearly 10,000 persons were listed as "absentees."[81] A similar situation developed in two cities of the Ruhr, Mülheim and Essen, where more than two-thirds of *all* railroad employees were on strike and operations had ceased altogether. Train stations and yards had been occupied by the police, although there had been no clashes with the strikers. In Remscheid, a major industrial center in the Bergisches Land, rail operations had ceased as well and local industries were already fearful of coal shortages, since they had only a supply for three to four days.[82] At the local level, the adverse affects of a rail strike were thus felt almost immediately.

[78] See, for example, the report in *DAZ*, no. 55, February 2, 1922 *(Der Streik der Eisenbahnbeamten. Keine Streikneigung in Süddeutschland. Verschärfte Gegensätze).*

[79] As later claimed by the RG. See *RG Strike Report.*

[80] Strike report, February 2, 1922, BA, R 43I/2124, Bl. 50ff.

[81] Polizeiverwaltung Elberfeld to Regierungspräsident Düsseldorf, February 28, 1922, report on the strike in the Elberfeld Reichsbahn District, HStAD, Reg. Düss., 16892 (hereafter cited as *Elberfeld Strike Report*).

[82] Strike report for the administrative district of Düsseldorf, dated February 2, 1922, *ibid.*

Anti-strike sentiments were running high in southern Germany. In Württemberg, for example, the regional RG leadership was predominantly moderate and had refused to issue a strike call, claiming that the policy pursued by its central organization was "a policy of fools" *(Narrenpolitik).*[83] Together with a delegation of the Württemberg DBB they had tried to establish contacts with the Reich government (via the Württemberg State government) in an early mediation effort, proposing that the Reich government should enter into negotiations with a representative of the RG's moderate wing.[84] Rail traffic was running about normal as well in the areas under Allied occupation, where the Interallied Rhineland Commission (IARC) had forbidden railroad personnel to go on strike, announcing stiff measures based on the existing military regulations *(Kriegsrecht)* if the order was violated.[85] As has been mentioned above, RG leaders had negotiated separately with the IARC in the days before the strike and had given assurances that no strike would be called. This promise was kept, although with the continuation of the strike rail traffic was to be more and more hampered even in the occupied territories, especially since traffic into the occupied zone all but ceased.[86]

Public response to the strike remained overwhelmingly negative, at the national as well as on the local level. Exceptions were, again, the KPD and, occasionally, the USPD oriented press.[87] The strikers tried to increase their level of support both within the labor movement and within the public by issuing flyers and posters, in which the economic plight of the civil servants was described and, more importantly, the extension of work hours on the railroad was cited as a first attack against the eight-hour day in general. Not totally unfounded, the press was accused of having begun a "campaign of lies" *(Lügenfeldzug)* against the striking civil servants and their aims.[88] Rival organizations in opposition to the strike carried on their own campaign, exposing the al-

[83] *Menne und Genossen* (see note 61).

[84] Württemberg State President Hieber to Reich Chancellor, telegram, February 2, 1922, BA, R 43I/2124, Bl. 64.

[85] Copy of the order, issued by General Degoutte and posted in railroad stations and yards in the occupied zone, in HStAD, Reg. Düss., 16892.

[86] *Elberfeld Strike Report* (see note 81).

[87] *Ibid.*, „Die Öffentlichkeit bekundete sowohl bei Ausbruch des Streiks als auch während seines ganzen Verlaufs keine Sympathie für die Bewegung." At the national level, the KPD's *Rote Fahne* supported the strike most forcefully.

[88] Flyer issued by the RG local in Essen, specimen in HStAD, Reg. Düss., 15618.

legedly non-trade-union like measures taken by the RG in an obvious attempt at preventing their rank-and-file members to join the walk-out.[89]

The overall situation on the first day of the strike presented itself in the following way: the RG's strike call had been observed by railroad personnel, mostly civil servants, and occasionally by blue-collar workers as well, in the northern and western parts of Germany. Vital areas like the industrial centers of the Ruhr and the cities of Berlin and Hamburg, were seriously affected by the strike. While the strike had not spread nation-wide, railroad traffic had become seriously disturbed, since major rail centers had been affected by the walkout. The enactment of emergency operations had been slow. The strike had thus far remained a rail strike only; no other civil servants had joined the struggle of their railroad colleagues.

The government's response to the strike had been both swift and tough. Several leading RG officials were arrested in Berlin. The RG's strike fund was impounded by the chief of police in Berlin at the order of the Prussian minister of the interior, the Social Democrat Severing.[90] Understandably, both these measures had caused anger in trade-union circles and in the papers of the extreme left, while the SPD's *Vorwärts* tried to downplay the incidents. In contrast, both the left-liberal and right-wing bourgeois press strongly supported the government's actions.[91] The government's strategy clearly was designed to force the strikers back to work and to break the power of the radical civil servant union once and for all. An early attempt by the DBB leadership to mediate in the conflict was therefore doomed to fail.

In the afternoon of February 2, Flügel and Remmers went to the Chancellery and offered their "good services" in the settling of the strike. They emphasized that there was a great inclination among lower-grade postal officials to join the walkout and proposed that the Reich finance minister begin immediate talks with the DBB on basic changes in civil servant pay. With such a promise they would be able to

[89] See, for example, a flyer issued by the Christian trade union affiliate GDE entitled *An die Eisenbahner zur Aufklärung*, specimen in: *Ibid.* The aforementioned flyer *Menne und Genossen* (see note 61), issued by the same organization, is another example.

[90] C. Severing, *Mein Lebensweg*..., vol. 1, p. 342. The RG leaders were later released at the insistence of the ADGB and other trade unions.

[91] *Vorwärts*, February 3, 1922, morn. edn.; *Germania*, no. 83, February 3, 1922 *(Das Streikverbrechen).*

exert their influence on the greater part of the railroad officials.[92] Alerted by the state secretary of the Chancellery, Reich Transport Minister Groener categorically rejected the DBB's proposals since it would give the appearance as if the government was backing down.[93] Groener's view prevailed, and no talks were scheduled. For the time being, a course of confrontation remained the prevailing government policy.

A second attempt by the DBB to mediate in the conflict, undertaken on the following day, February 3, failed as well. This time DBB Chairman Flügel was accompanied by the DBB's ranking Social Democrat, Falkenberg, in a visit to the chancellor's office, where they requested a meeting with Chancellor Wirth "to explain to the chancellor the DBB's attitude toward the strike."[94] When asked by a high official in the Chancellery, who had received them, what this position was, they declared that DBB "disapproved of *[missbilligen]* the strike." Reminded of DBB's January resolution in support of strike, Flügel and Falkenberg tried to argue that this resolution did not contain an explicit approval *(Billigung)* of the present strike, which in their view had been unleashed against all trade union principles, but should only be interpreted as a general defense of the civil servant's right to strike. When they were reminded that the DBB was being held responsible for the current conflict since the RG was, after all, a DBB affiliate, the DBB leaders responded by saying that they should not be made liable for the fact that one group of their federation was "dancing out of line." Informed by the Chancellery official about the visitors and their request, Chancellor Wirth let them know that he was too busy to see them at this point, but that he would contact them again in the course of the day. Wirth's refusal to receive the DBB delegation dealt a severe blow to the conciliatory policy which obviously had been adopted by the leadership of the civil servant peak association. Apparently, they were not being taken seriously as negotiating partners, and their zig-zag policy toward the strike and its supporters had not paid off.

An attempt by the ADGB to bring the DBB and the government together at the negotiating table failed as well. Fearful that radical elements in their own organization might decide to join the strike, the ADGB had decided to mediate in the conflict, and to work toward a

92 Minute of a meeting in the Chancellery, February 2, 1922, BA, R 43I/2124, Bl. 56.

93 Groener to State Secretary in the Chancellery, February 2, 1922, *ibid.*, Bl. 69.

94 Minute of a meeting in the Chancellery, February 3, 1922, *ibid.*, Bl. 88.

rapid settlement of the strike. On the evening of the first day of the strike, ADGB Chairman Leipart had met with Reich President Ebert and offered the ADGB's services as a mediator.[95] Informed by Ebert about the offer, Wirth invited union leaders for talks to be held in the Chancellery at three in the afternoon. The invitation was sent out at 12:15 p.m., i. e. minutes after the DBB delegation had been in the Chancellery. Moreover, Leipart was telephoned by the Chancellery in order to stress the point that DBB representatives had *not* been invited to participate in the talks.[96] Obviously, the government was determined not to deal directly with the striking civil servants in any form whatsoever.

The government's tough position was undoubtedly influenced by reports that emergency operations on the railroad were improving and that the regional railroad administrations were staying in control of the situation. As a consequence, the strike movement had not spread further. Southern Germany had still not been afflicted at all. While strike sentiments had increased among civil service personnel in some districts, in other areas strikers had voiced interests in an unconditional return to work. On the other hand, strike sentiments had spread among railroad workers in several districts. In Berlin the local DEV organization had voted to join the strike, acting under intensive pressure from rank-and-file members and against the declared will of the union's central leadership. Indeed, the DEV local had offered to assume the leadership of the entire movement. By way of contrast, the resolve of the Reichsgewerkschaft and its strike committee had been weakened by the police measures taken against the organization and the freezing of union accounts.[97] As long as there would be no full-scale support of the strike movement by railroad workers and their unions, the government seemed convinced that it would persevere in the conflict through a policy of sheer force. There were supporters of such a policy even in those segments of German society most directly afflicted by the strike. Industrial circles, for example, were supportive of the government's policy of holding out at all costs, despite the fact that shortages in the

[95] *Vorwärts*, February 2, 1922, morn. edn.

[96] Wirth to Leipart, February 3, 1922, BA, R 43I/2124, Bl. 70, and a handwritten notation on a telephone conversation, *ibid.* In the first draft of the letter an insertion which reads „und der Deutsche Beamtenbund“ has been crossed out.

[97] Strike report, February 3, 1922, 5:30 a. m., *ibid.*, Bl. 72.

supply of coal had forced several major industrial firms to cease operations.[98]

Wirth's willingness to receive union leaders indicates, however, that the chancellor, unlike Groener, did not feel committed to a policy of total confrontation, but rather remained interested in a solution of the conflict through negotiations. In the course of the meeting, which took place in the afternoon of February 3, Leipart presented the position of the unions. He emphasized that pressure was being exerted on the union leadership by rank-and-file members in favor of joining the walkout. Labor was opposed to the strike, because it had been called in violation of the most basic trade-union regulations. On the other hand, the workers were upset about the government's anti-strike decree. Leipart then proposed that the unions would issue a joint appeal to end the strike, as long as the government was willing to continue negotiations on the civil servants' demands and, more importantly, would suspend the Presidential anti-strike decree. Afa-Bund Chairman Aufhäuser warned that a union appeal would only be successful if the controversial decree was withdrawn immediately. He added that the DBB had not approved of the strike and should therefore be consulted as a negotiating partner at a later point. In his reply, Wirth stressed the fact that according to the government's point of view civil servants did not have the right to strike at all. He agreed with the idea of a union proclamation to end the strike, and offered a repeal of the Presidential Decree at a later date. Wirth insisted, however, that the latter issue should remain excluded from the proclamation. He then asked the union leaders to return later in the evening with a draft proposal of the proclamation.[99]

Immediately afterwards the cabinet convened.[100] Wirth informed his colleagues on the situation in the strike and about his talks with the union leaders. Hermes and Groener were enraged that negotiations had taken place. Hermes emphasized that this had weakened the government's position by giving indications that the government was already prepared to negotiate. Groener, after reporting that the strike had thus far been confined to northern Germany, warned that one could not deal with labor unions on civil servant questions. Wirth's policy found the

[98] Strike report, February 3, 1922, 6 p. m., *ibid.*, Bl. 99—100.

[99] Meeting with union leaders, February 3, 1922, 3 p. m., *ARK. Kab. Wirth*, pp. 534—536.

[100] Cabinet meeting, February 3, 1922, 5 p. m., *ibid.*, pp. 537—539.

support of other cabinet members, however. Vice-Chancellor Bauer, the ranking Social Democrat in the cabinet, argued that the belligerent mood of the workers necessitated the intervention of the trade unions, and that the ADGB's mediation efforts was likely to "break the backbone of the strike movement." Minister of Posts Giesberts insisted that negotiations with the peak organizations of labor were necessary at all costs, and even proposed to make concessions regarding the Emergency Decree to insure that progress would be made. Workers, he argued, were unwilling to differentiate between a right to strike for workers and civil servants. Wirth promised to emphasize in his discussion with union leaders that the workers' right to strike had not been impaired by the Decree. He then adjourned the cabinet meeting, because the labor leaders had arrived.

The unionists had brought along a draft version of the proclamation. In it, the unions accused the Reichsgewerkschaft of having placed the interests of a small group above those of all *Arbeitnehmer,* and indeed above those of the general public, by having called the strike. In addition, Germany's international negotiating position had been severly damaged on the eve of the Genua conference. The labor unions appealed to the striking railroad men to return to work, and urged the Reichsgewerkschaft to call off the strike at once. The controversial anti-strike decree, the proclamation promised, would be lifted as soon as the strike had ended. The chancellor agreed to the content of the proclamation, and on the following day it was published by the major German newspapers and posted in railroad shops.[101]

Radical forces within the trade union movement were unimpressed with the handling of the all-important issue of the Presidential Emergency Decree. The ADGB's influential Berlin local warned that unrest among workers would only abate if the decree, an attack against the right of coalition of *all* employees, was withdrawn right away.[102] Judging from this and similar responses "from below," the attempts of union leaders to end the strike failed, because they met stiff resistance at the lower organizational level and among rank-and-file members, not to speak of the fact that most strikers were not represented by the blue-collar unions in the first place.

[101] Text of the proclamation in BA, R 43I/2124, Bl. 179—181, and in *Angestelltenbewegung 1921—1925 . . .*, pp. 396—398. The proclamation was signed by ADGB, Afa-Bund, the Catholic unions, and by the Hirsch-Duncker unions.

[102] ADGB local of Berlin to Reich Chancellor, February 4, 1922, BA, R 43I/2124, Bl. 91—92, forwarding a resolution co-sponsored by the local Afa-Bund organization.

The DBB's negotiating position had remained a subject of controversy. On February 3, immediately following his talks with union leaders, Chancellor Wirth, flanked by the hardliners Groener and Hermes, had received a DBB delegation. Only after the DBB leaders had openly disavowed the current strike movement and the actions of the Reichsgewerkschaft, were they reaccepted as negotiating partners by the cabinet members. DBB leaders promised to work toward a settling of the strike, while Hermes agreed to continue negotiations on the pay issue. Wirth indicated that these talks would be conducted in the Chancellery under his personal supervision.[103] In a press release issued on the following day, the DBB tried to correct the impression that it had acted against the interests of the striking railroad officials when it had publicly condemned the strike.[104] This rather desperate attempt shows that the DBB had maneuvered itself into an nearly impossible position by first supporting the strike and then, for the sake of negotiation, disavowing it. It is not surprising, therefore, that at the local level these maneuvers of the leadership in Berlin were interpreted as a "total failure" of the DBB, and only added fuel to the determination of the rank-and-file to remain tough and unbending in the conflict with the authorities of the state.[105]

In an equally abrupt manner, the Reichsgewerkschaft repudiated the call of the four peak associations of labor to end the strike. In a counter-proclamation the RG pointed out that it was conducting the strike not for special privileges of civil servants, but for two goals important to the entire working class: (1) the prevention of a partial revoking of the eight-hour day and (2) the automatic adjustment of wages and salaries to the depreciation of the currency. In an appeal for more solidarity, the RG described its actions as "a struggle for the interests of all *Arbeitnehmer*" and proclaimed that the "united front" of railroad civil servants and workers would remain unshaken.[106]

103 Minute of the meeting in *ibid.*, Bl. 163.

104 Reprinted in *DG*, February 9, 1922.

105 Report on a meeting of the DBB local of Hamborn, HStAD, Reg. Düss., 15594. One of the speakers exlaimed, „Wir rufen der Regierung zu! Regierung bleibst du hart, so bleibt die Beamtenschaft stahlhart. Wenn die Beamtenschaft geschlossen bleibt, ist der Sieg unser."

106 The declaration of the Reichsgewerkschaft was published by the *RF*, no. 61, February 5, 1922. The KPD organ used the occasion to call for "solidarity with the strikers."

At the local level, however, solidarity between workers and striking civil servants was put to a hard test. RG leaders openly accused labor representatives of acting as strike breakers.[107] Workers, in turn, often showed little enthusiasm for backing up a civil servant strike. Why should the worker fight alongside with the civil servants now, who in earlier instances had refused to lend their support to the concerns of the workers? was a recurring argument raised by workers in local meetings.[108] To be sure, the counter argument that "solidarity would lead to victory," and that the civil servants were struggling for workers' demands, too, was articulated as well, and in the subsequent days the strike itself would become a catalyst for greater solidarity between workers and civil servants.

Contrary to all expectations, the strike movement spread rather than abated. Some regions of southern Germany now were affected by the strike, and, perhaps more importantly, municipal workers in Berlin went on strike on February 5. Now that a joint strike movement of workers and civil servants was underway, the situation had become alarming indeed.[109] In a series of lengthy discussions with parliamentary leaders, the Reich cabinet tried to develop a strategy of defense, while at the same time leave room for negotiations to settle the dispute. The hardliners in the cabinet, above all Groener, still categorically refused "to sit on the bargaining table with striking civil servants," while a more flexible attitude was advocated by other cabinet members, among them Chancellor Wirth, and, above all, by ranking SPD parliamentary leaders. They argued that it made little sense to "ride on principles" in face of the very real political and economic dangers that could arise from a strike movement in the public sector. As a compromise between the two factions, the cabinet decided to negotiate from now on with all peak associations of labor, i. e. including the DBB. Furthermore, the cabinet agreed that those leaders of the Reichsgewerkschaft who were

[107] RG leader Willms in a meeting organized by the DBB local in Essen, February 5, 1922, HStAD, Reg. Düss., 16892. Willms addressed his remark to a DEV representative, who had tried to speak at the meeting.

[108] Report on a meeting in Wesel, organized by the local KPD and USPD organizations on February 5, 1922. Report is dated February 7, 1922, and is to be found in: *Ibid.*, 15618.

[109] Baden State Minister Remmele to Reich Chancellor, February 5, 1922, BA, R 43I/2124, Bl. 114 (notation on a telephone call), and Reich Minister of the Interior to the Lord Mayor of Berlin, Boess, February 4, 1922, copy in: *Ibid.*, Bl. 116—119.

known to be opposed to the strike could participate in these talks as members of a DBB delegation.[110]

When union leaders met with the members of the Reich cabinet in the morning of the following day, the RG was not represented at the meeting, however. RG leaders had declined to work under the tutelage of the DBB. Instead, they had given a direct mandate to negotiate on their behalf to the Reichspostgewerkschaft (RPG), ostensibly in exchange for the latter's willingness to join the strike if the negotiations should fail to produce an agreement on the foremost aim of the settlement talks: the preventing of disciplinary measures against strikers.[111] The DBB's bargaining position had certainly not been improved by this act of defiance on the part of the RG, and DBB leaders were increasingly walking a tightrope in trying to settle a strike which they had publicly disavowed, but whose aims they had espoused. In the course of the bargaining session the DBB's position improved markedly, however.[112] DBB Chairman Flügel spoke first, apparently at the insistence of Chancellor Wirth, and he skillfully passed the burden of explanation for the current conflict onto the government. The government's delay in reviewing pay scales for the middle and lower ranks, and, above all, the controversial hours-of-work bill, Flügel said, had led to the high level of unrest within the *Beamtenschaft.* The hours-of-work question, he added, had been made more serious by the fact that in several Reichsbahn districts new work schedules had been released on the basis of a draft bill, and working hours had been extended beyond the customary eight hours. These work schedules would have to be withdrawn, Flügel emphasized, if the conflict was to be settled. Furthermore, a settlement would have to be found in which there were "no winners or losers" — a clear hint concerning the problem of disciplinary measures against strikers.

Placing the work-hour question into the center was a clever move on the part of the DBB. It produced the double-effect of rallying support

[110] Cabinet meeting and talks with party leaders, February 5, 1922, *ARK. Kab. Wirth*, pp. 539—548. The last mentioned clause was introduced by Hoefle, who participated in the meeting as a delegate for the Center Party. He cited Thieme and Rusch as moderate leaders of the RG.

[111] Cf. *RG Strike Report* (see note 44).

[112] The following account is based on two separate protocols of the meeting. The first and official one is contained in BA, R 43I/2124, Bl. 210—212. The second one are the minutes taken by the RhB delegate present at the meeting and is to be found in ZStAP, RhB, 55, Bl. 320—322.

of the representatives of some of the other labor unions and putting the government on the defensive in an issue, which, of course, was of vital interest to the entire trade-union movement. The excuse offered by Wirth and Groener that "everything was tentative", and that talks about the work-hours bill would be held later on, did not impress union leaders, especially those representing the Socialist Free Trade Unions. The sharpest opposition came from Afa-Bund Chairman Aufhäuser, a left-wing representative, but other leading trade unionists, like ADGB Chairman Leipart and DEV Chairman Scheffel, voiced objections as well — not primarily against more flexible work-hours on the railroads as such, but above all that decisions had been taken by the Reichsbahn Administration in this vital issue without prior consultation with the unions. There was a sense of irritation that apparently a *fait accompli* had been tried out by the Transport Ministry in the vital issue of work hours. Only the delegate of the Catholic Trade Unions, Roth, supported the government's position. He felt that a "schematic application" of the eight-hour day on the railroads was impossible. It is not surprising that the Catholic unionists likewise wanted to leave the decision of disciplinary actions to the government alone, so that "the authority of the state would be maintained." Roth hinted that the entire strike had been conducted for political rather than social and economic purposes.

If, with the exception of the Center Party-oriented Catholic Unions, unity prevailed among labor and civil servant leaders on the work-hours issue, there was an even greater agreement on the validity of the salary proposals put forth by the DBB. The revision of the pay scales to benefit the lower and middling ranks was a "social question" to which union leaders were fully committed. Under the combined pressure of civil servant and labor leaders, the government finally agreed to discuss the pay-scale issue, together with the question of automatic indexation, as the first order of business in a follow-up meeting in the Reich Finance Ministry planned for later in the afternoon, in which originally only the question of special cost-of-living allowances was to be debated. The prospect of yet another pay increase to civil servants, which was certain to be followed up by wage demands on the part of the workers, seemed to materialize as a "pay-off" for a strike settlement. In view of the combined union pressures, economic and fiscal arguments had dropped in the rating. Chancellor Wirth's objections that a renewed pay increase would only lead to a further depreciation of the currency, and that a stable dollar-exchange rate was in the long run better than any pay or wage increase, went unheard. In order to find a way out of the current crisis, Wirth and the Reich cabinet once again had to compromise on their economic principles and conceptions.

During the negotiations in the Reich Finance Ministry, Flügel reiterated his view that the widening of pay differentials within the civil service pay structure, undertaken in the course of the November pay increase, was the prime cause of the current state of crisis.[113] The lower ranks of the *Beamtenschaft,* he said, had gained the impression that an act of social injustice" had been committed by the government. Only a speedy revision of the pay scale, he argued, could serve as a remedy, and he challenged Finance Minister Hermes to give a binding promise that such a revision would be undertaken. To save face, Hermes accused the Reichstag of having prolonged the matter after he had already agreed in principle to such a review. He promised to put pressure on the Reichstag committee where the matter was being discussed, and he stressed that the Reichstag had already appointed a sub-committee to study the problem of automatic indexation. After a discussion, which according to Hermes himself had been "peaceful and to the point,"[114] the organizations and the finance minister formulated a joint statement, which expressed their mutual agreement that a revision of the current pay scales was urgently needed.

On the all-important pay issue, therefore, the government had given in to the demands of the organizations. Whether this would be enough to break the deadlock on the strike settlement, however, was another question. The strike had developed its own dynamics and problems, problems that were independent of the salary issue and even of the work-hour question. Above all, the government still refused to negotiate with the striking union, the RG, which alone was in a position to call off the strike. For RG leaders, moreover, the question of disciplinary measures and forced lay-offs of striking rank-and-file members had replaced the original strike aims as the foremost objective.[115] To more moderate and more flexible members of the cabinet, to which Chancellor Wirth himself must be counted, it may well have been clear at an

[113] Minutes of this meeting in ZStAP, RhB, 55, Bl. 322—323.

[114] In his follow-up report to the cabinet (see note 119 below for exact citation).

[115] *RG Strike Report* (see note 44). The RG claimed that its bargaining agent had insisted on a full discussion of the subject of disciplinary punishment of strikers, but that the issue had been excluded from the talks. For this reason the RG regarded the results as unacceptable and decided to continue the strike.

earlier stage that only direct negotiations with the strikers on subject of disciplinary measures would lead to a settlement in the long run. They were, however, besieged by hardliners in the cabinet and by outside forces to remain in an uncompromising attitude on both issues. Such pressure was applied, for example, when a delegation of industrial leaders met with Wirth in the afternoon of February 6, and called on the chancellor not to give in to any of the demands of the striking railroad men. They claimed that workers in the private sector had thus far remained unaffected by the strike because the government had adopted a tough approach to the conflict. Giving in now, even partially, would endanger all efforts of building up animosity toward the strike at the factory level. As fas as the industrialists were concerned, the government's resolve could not be pronounced enough. They suggested that the government make greater use of emergency operations with the aid of the controversial *Technische Nothilfe* (Teno), established for such purposes in 1919.[116]

Similar views were held within the ranks of the opposition parties of the political right. There, too, pressures for a "policy of toughness" toward the strikers were applied. In a meeting with Chancellor Wirth the Chairman of the DVP, Stresemann, echoed the complaints voiced by business leaders about the delays of employing the Teno to break the strike. He also wondered why strike leaders were released again after initially having been arrested. For domestic and foreign policy reasons, Stresemann insisted, the government had to deal firmly with what he viewed as a political strike fueled by the far left.[117] In an ever more severe attack, the DNVP declared that the railroad civil servant strike was "a crime to the German people that would lead to the most serious economic and political consequences." It comes as no surprise that the DNVP questioned the resolve of "a government under the controlling influence of the Social Democrats" to deal with the strike in an uncompromising way. The release of the strike leaders, rumors that the

[116] Meeting with representatives of industry, February 6, 1922, 4 p. m., BA, R 43I/2124, Bl. 204. The Berlin industrialists von Siemens and von Borsig were the chief spokesmen of the four-member delegation. The industrialists were obviously interested in testing the Teno's usefulness as a strike-breaking instrument in large-scale walkouts in the public sector, which would have implications in future labor struggles in the private sector as well. See H. Potthoff, *Gewerkschaften...*, pp. 158—177 for a thorough discussion.

[117] Meeting with representatives of the Deutsche Volkspartei, February 6, 1922, *ARK. Kab Wirth*, pp. 551—553.

government was about to negotiate directly with the strikers, and the possibility that disciplinary measures would not be enacted against striking civil servants were cited as proof that the government had embarked on a "policy of weakness". Only an unwavering attitude of the government would lead to an end of the strike, the DNVP warned, and would prevent similar strikes in the future.[118] Caught between pressures for "more resolve" from the right and for more flexibility from the political parties from the left, the trade unions, and the DBB, the cabinet decided in the evening of February 6 to table the final decision on the extent and mechanisms of disciplinary measures to be enacted against the strikers to the next day, when, as Wirth put it, the impact of the previous negotiations would be more clearly discernable.[119]

The strike situation, as it presented itself on the following day, February 7, could hardly lead to the conclusion that the previous negotiations had paved the way for a settlement of the conflict. If anything, the situation had become more serious. Strike reports, filed on February 7, stressed that civil servants had closed ranks in support of their colleagues on the railroads. Postal civil servants had become especially restive and were eager to join the walkout.[120] A further regional spreading of the strike to encompass Württemberg was only narrowly avoided.[121] Also, the economic consequences of a prolonged transportation strike were finally making themselves felt more acutely, especially in the industrial centers of the Ruhr. Several larger mines had been forced to slow down operations temporarily by calling shift layoffs. As a consequence, several steel mills had been forced to extinguish furnaces for lack of coal. Lastly, food supply had become critically low in some cities of the Ruhr, which, as a report from Essen noted, "might enable the Communists to stir up the workers to engage in reckless actions."[122] The underlying warning was, of course, that the strike

[118] DNVP Reichstag delegation to Reich Chancellor, February 7, 1922, BA, R 43I/2124, Bl. 201—202.

[119] Cabinet meeting, February 8, 1922, 6 p. m., *ARK. Kab. Wirth*, pp. 548—551.

[120] Strike report, February 7, 1922, BA, R 43I/2124, Bl. 145—149. According to a later testimony of its chairman, the RPG would have joint the strike if it had lasted only one day longer. Notation in a police report, ZStAP, RKöO, 453, Bl. 50. The same report noted that the RPG had given 50,000 marks in support for the strikers.

[121] Strike report, February 7, 1922, BA, R 43I/2124, Bl. 221.

[122] *Ibid.*

might lead into a general labor uprising engineered by the radical political left, i. e., the Communist Party.

That political consequences of this nature were not just dreamed-up by overzealous police agents emerges from internal KPD directives issued during the strike days. On February 2, already, i. e. only one day after the beginning of the rail strike, regional party organizations had begun with active preparations for a general strike at the direct order of the KPD central headquarters in Berlin. According to internal correspondence, the KPD regarded the conditions as being favorable for a general strike in view of the labor struggle on the railroads.[123] At the local level, the KPD organized mass meetings in support of the strike, to which representatives of labor unions and civil servant associations opposed to the strike were invited as well in an obvious attempt to compromise them.[124] On February 7, a whole series of such meetings were held in Berlin and other large cities.[125] Throughout the conflict, moreover, the KPD cooperated closely with the left-wing of the RG and with the RG's central strike committee in Berlin by throwing its entire propaganda apparatus behind the railroad civil servants' cause. In some respect, the *Rote Fahne* became the mouthpiece of the strikers and their union.[126]

These developments had, of course, not remained unnoticed in government circles, as the numerous police reports indicate. The documents also show that on February 7, in the wake of KPD-organized mass-meetings and other occurences, the government had begun to judge the domestic political impact of the strike as potentially dangerous. It was for political reasons, therefore, that a settling of the conflict in the public sector was urgently needed.

Further attempts to move toward a solution had been made at the 'higher' levels of decision making. During the night of February 6/7 the

[123] KPD Bezirksleitung Süd-West to local organizations („alle aktiven Kampfleitungen"), February 2, 1922, HStAD, Reg. Düss., 16892.

[124] KPD Hamburg to Beamtenrat Hamburg, February 6, 1922, StAH, 122-4-3. The Beamtenrat declined the offer.

[125] Reports in *RF*, no. 65, February 8, 1922.

[126] KPD circular no. 62, February 8, 1922, copy in HStAD, Reg. Düss., 15618. This is the full account of the February Strike from the perspective of the KPD. — A somewhat overly laudatory account of the KPD's policies and tactics during the February Strike, is the East German study by Hans Maur, *Zur Rolle der KPD im Februarstreik der Eisenbahnarbeiter und -beamten im Jahre 1922*, in: *Wissenschaftliche Zeitschrift der Universität Greifswald. Gesellschafts- und sprachwissenschaftliche Reihe*, 2—3 (1965), pp. 289 ff.

DBB had approached Transport Minister Groener in order to reach an agreement on the last obstacle toward a settlement of the strike, the problem of disciplinary measures. Groener had flatly refused to make any concessions, claiming that the emergency operations on the railroads had improved well enough that the government would prevail in the confrontation with the strikers.[127] In the cabinet, where the subject of disciplinary measures was discussed in the afternoon of February 7, Groener pursued the same course. He insisted that the "authority of the state" had to be maintained at all costs in a conflict which the chancellor himself had labeled a "revolt of the civil servants" *(Beamtenrevolte).* Groener then proposed a comprehensive catalog of disciplinary measures, which in one way or another would affect *all* civil servants that had participated in the strike.[128] Wirth, who at this point had been informed by the DBB and the Socialist unions that the strike would only be called off if Groener's *Herr im Hause* approach to the problem of reprimands was softened a bit,[129] disagreed with Groener, who in his opinion was out to subjugate the union rather than end the strike. He informed the cabinet that the DBB had indicated its (and, implicitly, the RG's) willingness to bring the strike to an end, provided that a formulation of the reprimand-clause could be found to which both sides could agree without losing face. This, Wirth insisted, was the policy which he as chancellor would pursue.

The chancellor had, in fact, thrown the weight of his office and his prerogative of determining the guidelines of policies behind the approach of continued negotiation, which he obviously favored. The majority of the cabinet was prepared to follow him on this course. Opposition remained stiff, however, from Groener's side, who warned that "he would be no part of a governmental defeat in this matter," as well as from Finance Minister Hermes, who argued that "the authority of the Reich Transport Ministry should not be impaired under any

127 Mentioned in *ARK, Kab. Wirth,* p. 554, note 1. The account given there is based on the Groener Nachlaß.

128 Cabinet meeting, February 7, 1922, 4 p. m., *ARK. Kab. Wirth,* pp. 554—557. Groener wanted to begin disciplinary actions against "originators and promoters" of the strike. More passive participants would be reprimanded and forfeit their pay for the days of the walkout.

129 ADGB and Afa-Bund to Reich Chancellor, February 7, 1922, BA, R 43I/2124, Bl. 200. The unions warned that blue and white-collar workers were joining the strike in increased numbers. They urged Wirth to drop all plans regarding disciplining of strikers except those guilty of acts of sabotage and of assault of nonstrikers.

circumstances." Wirth responded to these implicit threats by emphasizing that after his talks with the DBB the final decision would be taken by the full cabinet. He then adjourned the cabinet session to meet with a DBB delegation, which had already been waiting.

This meeting, which had been arranged by Hoefle of the Catholic Unions, was to become the crucial step toward breaking the deadlock between government and the striking railroad civil servants. For the first time, representatives of the striking union took part in the talks, which goes a long way in explaining the success of this final round of bargaining.[130] Speaking for the Reichsgewerkschaft, its General Secretary Döbling assured the chancellor that the RG was in a position to call off the strike immediately. His union, he claimed, had control over its members. What he wanted to know first, however, was whether the government was prepared to stand by its promise to review the pay scale and to withdraw the controversial hours of work bill. According to the official minutes of the meeting, Remmers of the DBB rather than the chancellor responded to Döbling's query. He claimed that there were no reasons to doubt the sincerity of the promises made by the finance minister in the previous day's meeting. Wirth confirmed this by stressing that the entire cabinet stood behind the finance minister's promise. After DBB Chairman Flügel had expressed his gratitude for the chancellor's assurance, Döbling, too, seemed convinced.

The discussion then turned to the subject of disciplinary punishment of strikers. Referring to the DBB's last effort in this matter in the Transport Ministry, Remmers complained that Groener still was insistent upon reprimanding *all* strikers. The second RG representative, Thieme, then suggested that disciplinary punishment should be confined to the leaders of the strike movement. Although Wirth stressed that the transport minister's right to begin investigations into the matters involving disciplinary action could not be infringed, he prom-

[130] The following account is based on the offical protocol of the meeting, to be found in BA, R 43I/2124, Bl. 208—209. A summary of this document is contained in *ARK. Kab. Wirth*, p. 557, note 2, where Döbling is falsely described as a delegate of the DBB. The RG later published its own version of these talks in a memorandum on the issue of disciplinary measures. See *Denkschrift der Reichsgewerkschaft Deutscher Eisenbahnbeamten und Anwärter betreffend Maßregelungen von Eisenbahnbeamten aus Anlaß des Streiks* (hereafter cited as *RG Denkschrift Maßregelungen*), copy in ZStAP, RMdI, 2185, Bl. 347—356. This document's content cannot always be trusted, however, as far as its accuracy is concerned. See note 161 below for further details.

ised to see to it that a formulation could be found in the cabinet to which both sides could agree.

The chancellor then returned to the cabinet room, while the wording of the agreement was still drafted by Chancellery officials. After his report to the cabinet, in which he announced his intention to take the question of disciplinary punishment out of the jurisdiction of the ministries and into that of the full cabinet, Groener bluntly stated that he was in no position to agree to such a step as long as he had not seen the actual text of the agreement. Perhaps in an attempt to put Groener on the defensive, Wirth brought up the matter of the work-hours decrees which had allegedly been issued in two Reichsbahn districts. Although Groener denied that current laws had been violated in any way in these decrees, he had to concede to an official investigation about the origins of these special directives within his ministry.

Then the text of the agreement, which had been handed to the chancellor in the meantime, was read to the cabinet. Groener agreed to it after consulting with high officials of his ministry. The agreement stipulated that if the Reichsgewerkschaft broke off the strike immediately, disciplinary punishment of strikers would be undertaken on the basis of guidelines agreed to by the full cabinet. Furthermore, the Reich government agreed to refrain from *mass* disciplining of civil servants and *mass* dismissals of contractual employees.[131] It looked like a complete victory of the moderates in the cabinet. In a surprise move, Groener then presented a set of guidelines to the cabinet for approval, which apparently had been drafted in his ministry and which were harsher than the general agreement to which he had just given his consent.[132] The transport minister threatened to resign if the cabinet did not approve of these guidelines. Unanimously, the cabinet approved. Wirth then went to meet again with the organizational leaders and to get their consent to the general agreement.[133] A few minutes

[131] Copy of the agreement in BA, R 43I/2124, Bl. 143. Cabinet meeting February 7, 1922, 8 p. m., *ARK. Kab. Wirth,* pp. 557—559.

[132] Text in *ARK. Kab. Wirth,* p. 559, note 5. A full discussion of these guidelines and their implications will be given below.

[133] According to the RG version of the meeting, Wirth assured organizational leaders that he would fully cooperate with them in the *Maßregelungen* question. He told them that they would be satisfied with the guidelines "to be prepared" (!) by the cabinet. See *RG Denkschrift Maßregelungen* (see note 130), p. 12. If indeed Wirth had said this at this moment, he would have lied to the organizational leaders, since the content of the guidelines had already been agreed upon by the cabinet.

later he returned to cabinet room with the agreement of the organizations and their promise that the strike would be ended immediately. In the night of February 7, the RG central office in Berlin called off the strike and ordered its members back to work. As had been promised by RG leaders, the union's rank-and-file obeyed their orders, even if only after a twenty-four hour delay caused by communication problems, and by double-checking through regional RG strike committees on the authenticity of the telegraphic order from Berlin.[134] By February 9, rail traffic was almost back to normal, and at the suggestion of Groener, the Reich government agreed to revoke the controversial Presidential anti-strike order that had been issued under emergency decree on February 1.[135] One of the most severe labor struggles in the Weimar Republic, and the first civil servant strike in German history, had finally been brought to a close.

It was only natural that both sides claimed to have emerged victoriously from the conflict. The Reichsgewerkschaft, which had carried the main burden in what it called the "most powerful struggle in German trade-union history," claimed it had reached most of its strike-goals: A review of the pay scale had been promised by Chancellor Wirth "in a most solemn form;" the work-hour draft-bill would be revoked and replaced by a new version to be prepared jointly by the organizations and the government; RG leaders had been recognized as negotiators for the strikers by the government; and lastly, disciplinary punishment of strikers would be limited to a few strike-leaders. All notices given out already to non-tenured civil servants would be rescinded. "All in all," the RG declared, "these concessions have justified the gigantic strike action" undertaken by the civil servants. With regard to the long-range consequences of the strike, the RG hinted that its position within the civil servant movement and the labor movement in general would have to be redefined. Since the RG had carried the strike alone, it had become a factor of power with which the German government, the DBB, and the other trade unions would henceforth have to deal.[136]

If viewed from a more detached vantage point, the RG's claims of success appear rather hollow. Such concessions that had been made in

[134] *RG Strike Report* (see note 44) and strike report, dated February 8, 1922, in HStAD, Reg. Düss., 15618.

[135] Meeting in the Chancellery, February 9, 1922, BA, R 43I/2124, Bl. 239.

[136] *Erfolge und Auswirkungen des Streiks,* a flyer issued by the RG, specimen in: *Ibid.*, Bl. 255. See also *RG Strike Report,* and *RG Geschäftsbericht 1922,* where similar conclusions are drawn.

the pay issue and the work-hour question were made to labor leaders and DBB representatives against the will of the striking civil servant union. The RG had regarded them as non-binding promises — quite correctly as it turned out. Wirth's willingness to negotiate with RG leaders toward the end of the strike may be viewed as a success indeed, although it, too, had its price. The fact that RG negotiators agreed to disciplining of striking civil servants, even to a limited extent, and, more importantly, to disciplinary measures against members of their own union leadership, indicates defeat rather than success on this key issue. The evaluation given by the ADGB's *Korrespondenzblatt* immediately after the strike was pretty much to the point. "Has it ever happened before," this paper wrote, "that disciplining measures became a negotiated portion of a strike settlement?"[137] As it would turn out in the subsequent weeks and months, some circles in the government were indeed committed not to let the revolt of the *Beamte* go unpunished. The unsuccessful struggle over the disciplinary measures, which was to continue on through 1922 and 1923, would expose the decline of the RG's power and influence suffered as a consequence of a partially lost strike.

The government's position as the main contestant of the striking civil servant union had not remained unscathed either. At a crucial juncture in the development of the strike, the government had been forced to change its uncompromising attitude toward the strikers and abandon the "policy of toughness" advocated by Groener and Hermes. The chancellor's willingness to negotiate with the strikers was viewed as a conciliatory gesture by the strikers and their union, although it was perhaps more a clever tactical move on the part of Wirth and other "moderate" cabinet members to end the strike. The chancellor's tough-talk in the Reichstag on February 9, where he called the strike a "revolt of the civil servants" and unequivocally rejected the civil servants' right to strike, seems to point in this direction.[138] The chancellor's public disavowal of the strike and its leaders could not prevent the beginning of a severe political and parliamentary crisis, however, during which Wirth was attacked from the right for having been "too soft" on the strikers by his willingness to negotiate with them, and from the left for having allowed Groener to handle the strike on his own terms.

[137] *Korr. Bl.*, February 25, 1922.

[138] During the government's formal report to the Reichstag. These political developments and implications will be discussed in greater detail below.

Finally, the internal cohesion of the DBB, and its credibility as the peak association of all civil servants, had suffered as a consequence of the strike. The internal factional strife, which had already appeared in the crucial pre-strike meeting of January 30, was intensified by the unfortunate, often dubious mediating role played by the DBB during the strike. The DBB's own evaluation that its leaders had functioned as mediators in the strike movement "most conscientiously" and "in the interest of the entire *Beamtenschaft*,"[139] would neither placate its left-wing, which felt that the central civil servant organization had indeed *betrayed* the interests of the striking civil servants,[140] nor the members of its right-wing who argued that the DBB should have disavowed the strike from the very beginning.[141] These internal organizational conflicts, which centered around the strike issue in general and around the DBB's vascillating policy during the February strike, would only a few weeks later plunge the DBB into its most severe organizational crisis.

The Political and Organizational Consequences of the Strike

The Public Reaction

The response of the various political groupings of Weimar Germany to the February Strike can best be ascertained by means of a survey of the political press. The fragmentation of the Weimar press into an ideologically and politically divided *Richtungspresse* renders any discussion of a seemingly neutral "public opinion" toward the strike difficult, if not impossible, but it does enable the historian to gauge the political response to the strike in a rather succinct way. The following survey of the political press will therefore serve the dual purpose of presenting an overview of the political implications of the strike, as well as giving an

[139] In an official statement, issued by the DBB *Bundesleitung* immediately after the strike. See DBB circular no. 9, reprinted in *DG*, February 16, 1922. See also Albert Falkenberg, *Der Eisenbahnerstreik von 1922*, in: *BH*, 9 (1922), pp. 47—56.

[140] *GBZ*, March 15, 1922 *(Beamtenbund und Eisenbahnerstreik)*.

[141] The National Association of Police Officers claimed, for example, that the DBB, had failed entirely during the strike (letter to DBB reprinted by *DG*, March 16, 1922). The same organization, a federation of various police officers' associations, contacted the Reich Ministry of the Interior immediately after the strike and emphasized that policemen had not participated in the strike or supported the strikers in any way — an accusation that had been made by the right-wing press. Copy of the letter in ZStAP, RMdI, 2185, Bl. 192.

introduction to its broader political, social, and organizational consequences.

Within the German labor movement, its political as well as its trade-union branches, opinions on strike were as deeply divided as the movement itself. During the strike, support for the strikers and their goals had been coming from the extreme left-wing of the labor movement, i. e. the Communist Party (KPD) and the left-wing of the Independent Socialists (USPD). Accordingly, the KPD's *Rote Fahne* praised the civil servant strike as the beginning of a new solidarity between workers and civil servants against the common class enemy.[142] The other left-wing labor party, the USPD, was internally split over the strike issue. Members of its right wing viewed the strike as an irresponsible act and an example of glaring trade-union dilettantism undertaken by the Reichsgewerkschaft for "agitational purposes" and to outmaneuver those labor unions which also organized civil servants. Siegfried Aufhäuser, the chairman of the Socialist Afa-Bund and a representative of the USPD's right-wing, deplored the fact that major forces in his party had supported the radicals in the RG and had listened to their appeals for solidarity between railroad civil servants and railroad workers.[143] Aside of the very real misgivings of an experienced trade-union leader like Aufhäuser about an irresponsible and poorly conducted strike, organizational politics might have played a role as well, because the Afa-Bund was opposed to a close cooperation between civil servants and workers on a sectoral (railroad or transportation) basis.[144] These hidden motives in Aufhäuser's argumentation were duly exposed by the Communist press, and might have played a role in the determination of the USPD's left-wing to continue supporting the RG cause in the forthcoming parliamentary confrontations with the government.[145]

The (M)SPD did not have the same internal conflicts over the strike in its ranks. It had opposed the strike during its course, and it continued doing so once the conflict had been settled.[146] To be sure, Majority Social Democrats did not deny the economic causes of the strike, nor

[142] *RF*, no. 67, February 9, 1922 *(Der Kampf der Beamten)*.

[143] Siegfried Aufhäuser, *Agitation oder Verantwortlichkeit?*, in: *DF*, no. 67, February 9, 1922. The *Freiheit* supported this line of reasoning in several other editorials. Cf., for example, *Randbemerkungen zum Eisenbahnerstreik*, in: *Ibid.*, no. 68, February 9, 1922.

[144] See the discussion in CHAPTER FIVE of this study.

[145] *RF*, no. 72, February 11, 1922 *(Wer treibt Katastrophenpolitik?)*.

[146] *Vorwärts*, February 8, 1922, morn. edn., *(Der Eisenbahnerstreik beendet)*.

did they question the civil servants' right to strike for economic gains. Similar views were shared by SPD-oriented trade unionists. They chastised the "non-trade-union character" of the strike and the irresponsible actions of the RG leadership.[147] Small wonder, therefore, that the SPD's civil service experts (and other leading SPD members) later on gloated over the "defeat" suffered by the RG, and that the SPD was determined to support the government's position in the Reichstag.[148]

At the local level, however the membership of the three labor parties showed greater solidarity than their respective leaders. Against common adversaries, be they ultra-left wing syndicalists or right-leaning Catholic trade unionists, the lessons drawn from the February Strike were that an attack by the government against the right of coalition and the eight-hour day had been withstood by the striking civil servants on behalf of the entire working class. At a public meeting in the Ruhr city of Hamborn, called by the KPD on February 10, a resolution was adopted which stressed this fact. In the course of this meeting, the speakers for the KDP and the USPD confirmed their unconditional support for the cause of the Reichsgewerkschaft and its members. The KPD delegate, who gave the main speech, warned that the erosion of the eight-hour day was sure to spread from the public to the private sector eventually, especially to the mining industry. Both speakers criticized the harsh measures that had been taken by the government against the striking civil servant union, and demanded that all disciplinary measures be revoked at once. The SPD spokesman tried to downplay the importance of the strike and questioned its usefulness to the working class, without, however, condemning it entirely. The civil servants should first adopt the views of the proletariat, he said, before one could even speak of a solidarity between civil servants and the working class. A *common* oppositional stance of the three labor parties toward the Syndicalists, who used the occasion for vicious attacks against political parties and trade unions in general, and against an attempt by a speaker of the Catholic railroad union who argued that the strike had been unjustified from a trade-union perspective, was

[147] A. Wuschik, *Streikbetrachtungen*, in: *Ibid.*, February 22, 1922, ev. edn. The author was a trade unionist from an ADGB public service union.

[148] Cf. Hermann Wäger, *An der Gurgel des Staates*, in: *Der Freie Beamte*, February 11, 1922; Franz Krüger, *Beamtenrecht und Streikrecht*, in: *Ibid.*, February 18, 1922; and Hermann Wäger, *Beamtenstreik*, in: *Ibid.*, April 8, 1922. See also C. Severing, *Mein Lebensweg...*, vol. 1, p. 344.

easily forged, and the joint resolution cited above was readily adopted.[149]

Within the bourgeois press, opposition to the February Strike was coupled with attacks against the civil servants' right to strike and public service strikes as such. The left-liberal, DDP-oriented *Berliner Tageblatt* wrote that legal measures were urgently needed to prevent similar strikes, not only among civil servants, but among other employees in "socialized," i. e. government-run enterprises.[150] The editor of the *Soziale Praxis,* Ludwig Heyde, spoke of the strike as a "revolt against the entire public" which the railroad civil servants had committed. Heyde reminded his readers that in the previous months his paper alone had warned about excessive wage demands in the public sector and had criticized the "continously-operating printing presses of the Reich" in the wake of wage concessions made by the government. The "revolting civil servants," he wrote, had not acted in self-defense, but had committed an act of assault, i. e. the direct opposite of self-defense.[151]

A similar line of reasoning was used in an editorial of the *Germania,* the official mouthpiece of the Center Party. Here the strike was portrayed as an "act of terrorism" by a minority group, whose results in the long run would not be to the benefit of the laboring classes on the whole. Even if in the end the strike might not lead to wage gains in the public sector, a further depreciation of the currency would set in because of scarcity of coal and other detrimental effects caused by a transportation strike. The paper emphasized that only a rapprochement between the rival social groups and classes, and the establishing of

[149] Police report on a public meeting of the three Socialist Parties in Hamborn, February 10, 1922, HStAD, Reg. Düss., 16892. Several documents pertaining to the relationship between the labor parties at the local level during the strike are reprinted in Hans Maur, *Zur Einheitsfrontpolitik der KPD im Eisenbahnerstreik 1922,* in: *Beiträge zur Geschichte der Arbeiterbewegung,* (1972), pp. 237—259.

[150] Erich Dombrowski, *Gesetzgeberische Notwendigkeiten,* in: *BT,* no. 66, February 8, 1922. See also, Karl Delius, *Die Stellung der Beamtenschaft im neuen Staat,* Berlin n. d. (1922), in which this DDP Reichstag deputy presents the official party position on the strike. A more exhaustive treatment of the DDP's (and the DVP's) attitude toward the strike will be contained in Larry E. Jones's forthcoming study of the Liberal parties in the Weimar Republic.

[151] Ludwig Heyde, *Betrachtungen zur Revolte der Eisenbahnbeamten,* in: *SP,* February 22, 1922. It may be remembered that Heyde had been a staunch supporter of a more aggressive civil servant interest politics during the war years (cf. CHAPTER TWO above).

a "united front against the threat to our national survival" would prevent similar "fractricidal strife" in the future.[152]

The further to the right one moves in the political spectrum of Weimar politics, the more uncompromising, even vicious the criticisms of the strike become. The DVP-oriented *Deutsche Allgemeine Zeitung* was jubilant that the Reichsgewerkschaft had suffered a "decisive defeat," and it applauded the "policy of strength" conducted during the strike by some [!] members of the cabinet. Any government which conceded the right to strike to its public officials, the *DAZ* wrote, would destroy its own foundations. Civil servants, on the other hand, would have to learn a lesson from the strike as well: they could not lay claim to the special privileges of the *Beamte* and to the working-class right of coalition at the same time.[153] The important question for the future was whether the government could retain authority over its officials, or whether it would remain an "object of civil servant recklessness" *(Spielball der Beamtenwillkür).*[154] With regard to the political implications of the strike the paper suggested that a Communist conspiracy had been behind the conflict. "In the final analysis," the *DAZ* noted, "civil servants had played the game of the Communists," and they had brought Germany to the brink of a civil war which the KPD needed to establish a government of soviets following the Russian example. If the latter ever happened, the paper warned, "civil servant rights would not be a matter of discussion any longer, because there would be no civil servants."[155] It is not surprising that similar views were held in the DNVP press. Here, too, civil servants were accused of having participated in a "Communist conspiracy" and the "*Streikbeamten*" were warned of the dangerous consequences of their activities.[156]

[152] *Germania,* no. 90, February 10, 1922 *(Sozialpolitik oder Politik des Terrors).*

[153] *DAZ,* no. 67, February 9, 1922 *(Lehren des Streiks).*

[154] *Ibid.,* no. 66, February 8, 1922 *(Das Ende des Streiks).*

[155] *Ibid.,* no. 68, February 9, 1922 *(Wem zum Nutz?).* A type-script version of this article was sent by the district government of Düsseldorf to local agencies on February 14, 1922 (letter in HStAD, Reg. Düss., 15618), requesting that the article should be reprinted by the local press. This might indicate, that the original *DAZ* version was "government inspired." The *DAZ,* it may be remembered, was still the semi-official mouthpiece of the German government at that time, although its close ties to the industrial wing of the DVP were well known.

[156] *Korrespondenzblatt* of the DNVP, no. 37, February 13, 1922, copy in ZStAP, RLB Pressearchiv, 5615, Bl. 5.

The Battle Over Disciplinary Measures and the Political Crisis

The response of the Weimar press toward the February Strike and the way it was settled indicates that a conflict which had originally been sparked by economic and social demands had created the seeds of a major political crisis. Such a crisis was indeed to develop in the course of the two weeks immediately following the strike. In its first stage, this political crisis led to a more general (and rather well known) parliamentary battle between coalition and opposition parties over the way in which the government had handled the strike, had negotiated its settlement, and was dealing with its repercussions.[157] In its second stage, the crisis would develop into a (much less known) cabinet crisis, with Chancellor Wirth and Transport Minister Groener as the chief contestants in a battle over how the question of the disciplining of the strikers should be handled.[158] It stands to reasons that civil servant organizations, the Reichsgewerkschaft as well as the DBB, were an important third party in this conflict, which therefore quickly assumed the character of a renewed *social* conflict between government and interest group.

In the morning of February 8, the day after the strike had been called off, RG leaders went to see the chancellor in order to get his reassurance that disciplinary punishments and dismissals of non-tenured civil servants would be handled by the cabinet in the way promised by Wirth in the negotiations of the previous evening. They were told by the state secretary in the Chancellery that, as promised, the full cabinet would adopt guidelines for the disciplining of the strikers this very afternoon.[159] This rather non-committal statement, coupled with the chancellor's unwillingness to receive them, undoubtedly increased the RG leaders' apprehensions and worries that they might have been outmaneuvered when they gave their consent to disciplinary punishments in the first place.

These worries were not totally unfounded. During the cabinet meeting in the afternoon of the same day, Wirth denied that he had made concessions of any consequence to the RG with regard to the disciplin-

[157] On the parliamentary conflict, which will not be explored in depth here, see E. Laubach, *Die Politik der Kabinette Wirth...*, pp. 154 ff., C. Severing, *Mein Lebensweg...*, vol. 1, pp. 344—346, and F. Stampfer, *Die ersten vierzehn Jahre...*, pp. 262 ff.

[158] A brief summary of the cabinet crisis is given by I. Schulze-Bidlingmaier, introduction to *ARK. Kab. Wirth*, p. LVII.

[159] *RG Denkschrift Maßregelungen* (see note 130), p. 12.

ing issue. He argued that the jurisdiction of the Transport Ministry in this matter was not subject for discussion and insisted that he had given his consent only that in singular cases, where "acts of revenge" could be suspected, he, as chancellor, would review the matter. The cabinet then unanimously adopted guidelines suggested by Groener, which called for disciplinary punishment of tenured civil servants, or dismissal of non-tenured civil servants, who had been strike leaders, or had committed acts of sabotage or violence.[160] That Wirth was playing a rather dubious game at this point is borne out by the fact that immediately after the cabinet session he again met with RG representatives. He apparently reassured them regarding his promise that a mass-disciplining of strikers would not take place, and he raised no objections when RG leaders recapitulated the agreement reached the day before. On the other hand, Wirth refused to turn a copy of the guidelines over to the unionists, arguing that some minor stylistic changes still had to be made. Consequently, the RG leaders were left in doubt over the exact content of the directives, and the extent of disciplinary measures to be taken by the Reichsbahn Administration.[161]

Wirth's speech to the Reichstag on the next day must have indicated to RG leaders that the chancellor had embarked on a tougher policy toward the strikers. Wirth spoke of a "revolt of the *Beamtenschaft*" against the government; he categorically denied that civil servants possessed the right to strike and avoided any direct mentioning of how the government would handle the problem of punishment of strikers.[162] On the other hand, railroad civil servants and their union leaders did not really need the chancellor's opinion on the extent of the *Maßrege-*

[160] Cabinet meeting, February 8, 1922, *ARK. Kab. Wirth*, pp. 560—561. In the railroad administration a great number of civil servants were non-tenured *(kündbar)*. They were lower-grade civil servants, usually former wage earners *(Arbeiter)*, who had been promoted to civil service posts on a trial basis.

[161] *RG Denkschrift Maßregelungen* (see note 130), p. 12. The inaccuracy of the wording of the protocols in this document has been mentioned above. They would be subject of a controversy between Wirth and the Reichsgewerkschaft in June 1922, when the Denkschrift was issued and circulated in the Reichstag. (See protocol of a meeting between Wirth, RG representatives, and union leaders in BA, R 43I/2125, Bl. 144—154). As a source of the sequence of the meetings on February 7 and 8, and for the *general* topics that were discussed between Wirth and RG leaders, the *Denkschrift* can be used, however.

[162] The conservative bourgeois press in particular was pleased about the chancellor's tough stance. See, for example, *Germania*, no. 90, February 10, 1922 *(Der Reichskanzler über den Eisenbahnerstreik)* and *DAZ*, no. 69, February 10, 1922.

lungen at this point any longer, because they had been confronted with the hard facts already. Within a matter of a few days, the Railroad Administration and the Transport Ministry had dismissed well over a thousand non-tenured officials; more than three hundred "regular" civil servants had been suspended and were awaiting disciplinary proceedings.[163] What the RG had envisioned of being "limited to a few single cases" had become a mass-disciplining of the worst possible kind. Clearly, the government was determined to reestablish its authority over its unruly servants at all costs.

It must remain a matter of controversy, however, who exactly represented "state authority" on the railroads in the initial days after the strike. Groener, no doubt, was interested in a "more determined" handling of the matter, but it seems unlikely that he personally pressed for reprisals of such magnitude within his administration. Allegations made later by Groener's political foes that he had in fact lost control over "his lieutenants," i. e. the heads of the regional Reichsbahn districts, cannot be totally discounted.[164] They had borne the main brunt of the strike and were very much inclined on a course of "settling the score" with the Reichsgewerkschaft once and for all. The fact that Groener later, on February 15, sent detailed instructions to the Reichsbahn district offices on who was subject to disciplinary action and who was not, might be another indication that initially he was overtaken by overzealous high officials in his own administration.[165] On the other hand, Groener quite emphatically thanked those Reichsbahn employees who had not participated in the strike, but had "remained dutifully in their posts" during what he called "the fateful drama of insubordination."[166] The transport minister's general attitude toward

[163] Figures varied, of course. The *Gemeinschaft* claimed that by February 11 more than 1200 dismissals had been undertaken, and an additional 350 suspensions of tenured personnel was underway (*DG*, February 16, 1922). A partial [!] listing supplied by the Reichsgewerkschaft during the subsequent negotiations mentioned 7315 dismissals and suspensions, 4100 of these in the Frankfurt Reichsbahn District (BA, R 43I/2124, Bl. 364). Figures given by the Transport Ministry later on were considerably lower. A listing drawn up in February 1923 speaks of 182 dismissals, and 483 suspensions or disciplinary proceedings to have taken place immediately after the strike (BA, R 43I/2125, Bl. 238).

[164] Such allegations were made by the USPD Reichstag deputy Dittmann in the strike debate of the Reichstag on February 10. For further details see p. 338 below.

[165] Groener to regional Reichsbahn districts, February 15, 1922. Bundesarchiv-Militärarchiv, Freiburg (hereafter referred to as BA/MA), Nachlaß Groener, 143, Bl. 138—140.

[166] *RVBl.A*, February 13, 1922. The proclamation, issued on February 12, was entitled *Dank!*

the strike and toward those who participated in it no doubt played a role in the determination of the high officials in the Reichsbahn administration to deal with the strikers as harshly as possible.[167]

Whatever its ultimate causes, the consequences of the mass-disciplining were readily apparent. The radical wing of the RG, which had only reluctantly agreed to the calling-off of the strike in the first place, saw a chance to refuel discontent and to ignite a renewed conflict on the railroads.[168] This course found mass support within the rank-and-file of their own organization, as well as within other, radically oriented civil servant associations.[169] On February 10, the RG council decided on a conditional strike vote: if negotiations on the disciplinary question would not lead to a solution within a week, a new strike would be called. A motion to call a strike immediately, sponsored by the radicals, was only narrowly defeated.[170]

These development did not remain unnoticed. On February 10, Groener informed Wirth that the radicals in the Reichsgewerkschaft had not given in and were making preparations for a renewed strike, this time to be spearheaded by a strike-call of the postal civil servant unions. Groener used the occasion to remind Wirth not to deviate from the guidelines adopted by the cabinet. He charged that according to information made available to him, Wirth had again met with a representative of the Reichsgewerkschaft, and had allegedly offered milder terms in the handling of disciplinary cases.[171]

[167] Also, there were the requirements of the first hour, so to speak. On February 8 and 9, civil servants returned to work and it was then that a decision regarding their readmittance to their former work place had to be made.

[168] A flyer, issued by the Reichsgewerkschaft, warned that "in the last hour" the strike was to begin again because of Groener's "campaign of revenge." Copy of the flyer in HStAD, Reg. Düss., 15618.

[169] At a local meeting of the RG in Magdeburg, for example, a vote to resume the strike immediately was taken on February 10 or 11. Undated report of this meeting in BA, R 43I/2124, Bl. 386—387. A resolution adopted by the Soziale Arbeitsgemeinschaft called for solidarity with the disciplined strikers (copy in ZStAP, RMdI, 2185, Bl. 258), and the radical *GBZ* pointed out that civil servants in other administrative branches were being harrassed as well for having shown sympathy with the railroad officials during the strike (*GBZ*, March 15, 1922 — *Gegen die Maßregeln*).

[170] Details on this meeting mentioned in the report from Magdeburg cited above. The main speaker at the Magdeburg gathering had participated in the meeting of the RG council in Berlin as a representative of the radical faction.

[171] Groener to Wirth, February 10, 1922, BA, R 43I/2124, Bl. 254.

Whatever the real danger of a new strike might have been, the political damage had already been done. During the tumultuous parliamentary debate on the government's handling of the strike, which took place in the afternoon of February 10, Wirth found himself attacked from all sides. The right accused him of having been too conciliatory to the strikers during the strike, and for having effectively sabotaged the transport minister's justified efforts to punish the strikers *after* the strike by negotiating behind his back with the Reichsgewerkschaft.[172] The left charged that he had not kept his promises to prevent a "campaign of revenge" *(Rachefeldzug)* by the Reichsbahn administration against those who had participated in the strike.[173] Groener, who had insisted in his introductory statement to the Reichstag that *all* decisions regarding disciplinary measures rested solely with him as the minister in charge of the appropriate department *(Ressortminister)*,[174] became the target of vicious criticisms from the radical left. When the USPD Deputy Dittmann finally called him a scoundrel (a *Hundsfott)*, all hell broke loose and the session had to be closed.[175] Resumed on the following day, the parliamentary debate ended with three motions of no-confidence introduced against the Wirth government, two by the right (DNVP and DVP), and one by the left (USPD/KPD). Wirth then announced that he would make the survival of his cabinet contingent upon a clear vote of confidence, rather than on a defeat of each of the three motions of no-confidence separately, which in view of shifting votes between left and right would have been a rather certain affair. Through a parliamentary maneuver, however, this vote

[172] *Stenographische Berichte...*, vol. 352, pp. 5749—5788, p. 5769 (speaker is the DNVP Deputy Berndt) and p. 5775 (speaker is the DVP Deputy Scholz, who was also the chairman of the Reichsbund der höheren Beamten at that time, an organization vehemently opposed to the strike).

[173] *Ibid.*, p. 5757 (speaker is the MSPD Deputy Otto Wels, i. e. a spokesman of Wirth's coalition partner, who warned that a "malicious policy of revenge" should be avoided), and p. 5788 (speaker is the USPD Deputy Dittmann, who charged that Groener's henchmen *("Groenergesellen")* in the district administrations of the Reichsbahn had already embarked on a policy of revenge and were dismissing civil servants by the thousands.

[174] *Ibid.*, p. 5751.

[175] *Ibid.*, p. 5788. Dittmann's remark was meant to recall Groener's famous anti-strike proclamation during the April strikes of 1917. On this see G. D. Feldman, *Army...*, pp. 344—348. Groener later charged that Dittmann's speech had been prepared by the RG, and he sent documents to Wirth to prove this allegation (Groener to Wirth, February 15, 1922, BA, R 43I/2124, Bl. 337).

was postponed to take place several days later.[176] On February 15, the Reichstag gave the chancellor the desired vote of confidence. The parliamentary crisis, which had been unleashed by the strike and its aftermath, had been averted. The political crisis, however, was to continue at the cabinet level, and the confrontation between the government and civil servant organizations over the disciplining of the strikers was to intensify as well.

Already on February 13, the RG had informed the chancellor that the Transport Ministry and the regional Reichsbahn offices had embarked on a course of revenge: thousands of civil servants had been dismissed, suspended, or reprimanded. In Frankfurt alone 5,000 railroad civil servants had allegedly been dismissed. Warrants had been issued for the arrest of "colleagues who had done nothing except that they belonged to local strike committees." The RG warned that discontent had risen to new and higher levels, which "could very well endanger the general political measures" enacted by the chancellor thus far. The RG reminded Wirth of his own broad interpretation of the disciplinary measures and warned that unless those who had been dismissed were not reinstated immediately, the union would not feel bound to its promises any longer either.[177] In spite of this veiled threat of a possible resumption of the strike, the tone of the letter indicated willingness to negotiate rather than immediate strike action to force the issue.

Like the chancellor, the RG, too, was apparently playing a double-game, or at least pursued a double strategy. Under the pressure of its radical wing, the union had called a special meeting of its executive council to Berlin for February 16. The fact that the representatives of those RG branch associations and regional organizations which had not taken part in the strike, i. e. those in the South and South-West, had *not* been invited, was proof enough to Groener that a decision over a new strike-call was imminent. He insisted, however, that the government would have the better cards in a renewed conflict, because emergency operations could begin at an instant, and several branch associations of the RG, among them the train engineers, had indicated their support of

[176] *Stenographische Berichte...*, vol. 352, p. 5823. The reason given publicly was that too many deputies of the Center Party were absent. It shows that Wirth's Center Party was not sure to survive an immediate vote of confidence.

[177] RG to Reich Chancellor, February 13, 1922, BA, R 43I/2124, Bl. 335—336. The letter was signed by Thieme, a member of the moderate faction, and by Scharffschwerdt, a spokesman of the RG's radical wing.

the government's position in a possible new conflict.[178] Other reports confirmed that internally the RG had indeed slipped into an organizational crisis, and that the power struggle between its radical and its moderate factions was triggering the disintegration of the union.[179] Yet in view of a militancy rapidly increasing within the rank-and-file of the larger branch organizations in response to the mass disciplining, it could not be taken for granted that a renewed strike call would fall on deaf ears among railroad civil servants.

Worried that the radicals in the RG were planning to stage a takeover of the peak association, the DBB entered the scene at this juncture. On February 16, Remmers phoned the Chancellery and urgently requested a meeting with the chancellor. He claimed that the DBB needed an "authentic interpretation" of the guidelines as agreed to by Wirth on February 7. Although he was reminded by the Chancellery official who took the call that the transport minister had clarified the issue already during the Reichstag debate, Remmers insisted on an interpretation by the chancellor himself. Only if such a meeting could be arranged, he said, the DBB would be able to use its influence to act as a controlling force against the rising willingness to strike which had reappeared within large portions of the *Beamtenschaft.*[180]

On the advice of his senior Chancellery official, State Secretary Hemmer, Wirth declined to meet with a DBB delegation.[181] Instead, a meeting between the state secretary, two other high Chancellery officials, and DBB leaders took place in the afternoon of the following day. This meeting turned out to be inconclusive however. DBB Chairman Flügel, who was accompanied by Remmers, reiterated the request for a personal meeting with the chancellor in order to receive the desired "authentic statement" on the disciplining issue. Again, the request was denied. Taken aback by the state secretary's uncompromising attitude, Remmers charged that the DBB was being excluded from negotiations on this important issue, while representatives of the Reichsgewerkschaft were at the same time awaiting outside for a meeting with the chancellor. This, he claimed, was detrimental to the DBB's prestige as a

[178] Groener to Wirth, February 15, 1922, *ibid.,* Bl. 337.

[179] Police report, ZStAP, RköO, 455, Bl. 4. This report, dated February 24, 1922, deals with organizational developments in the RG between February 8 and 14.

[180] Notation on a telephone conversation, February 16, 1922, BA, R 43I/2124, Bl. 343.

[181] This emerges from the marginal notes on the document just cited.

peak organization, and it would in the long run only make the situation more difficult for the government. Hemmer seemed unmoved by these charges, however, and reminded Remmers that not the government, but rather the DBB's own shifting politics during the strike had precipitated the partial erosion of its bargaining power. To this Flügel could only reply that hopefully the government would in the future consult with the DBB at an earlier instance in important matters.[182]

Immediately afterwards, the RG delegation met with the state secretary. They were accompanied by the DVP Reichstag Deputy Seibert, who apparently had arranged the meeting.[183] The RG spokesman charged that mass disciplining had taken place and insisted that it should be stopped immediately. The DVP deputy, who supported these demands, told the state secretary that "the situation had become critical." Hemmer, who was obviously rather impressed with the specifics of what the members of this delegation had to say, and with the supporting materials they had presented to him, agreed to report to the chancellor immediately. A few minutes later, he returned, accompanied by Chancellor Wirth, who had just left a cabinet session. In the meeting which followed the spokesmen of the Reichsgewerkschaft restated their complaints that in spite of Wirth's promises mass-disciplining had taken place. Specifically, they wanted clarification on who should be considered a strike leader *(Urheber)* and thus be subjected to disciplinary punishment or dismissal. Wirth agreed that clarification was needed regarding this point and promised to sent a written statement in a few days. He was less agreeable on the suggestion made by the RG delegates that all dismissed civil servants should be rehired pending the final formulation and interpretation of the strike-leader clause. Politically such a move was impossible, Wirth claimed; already he had been

[182] *Niederschrift über die Besprechung vom 17. Februar 1922, nachmittags 4 Uhr,* BA, R 43I/2124, Bl. 357—360.

[183] *Niederschrift über die Besprechung vom 17. Februar 1922, nachmittags 5 Uhr, ibid.,* Bl. 361—363. It is more than ironic that this meeting was arranged by a member of the same party which in the Reichstag debate had chided the chancellor most sharply for negotiating with the "criminals in the Reichsgewerkschaft." Seibert, a train engineer by profession, was most likely a member of the union of train engineers (Gewerkschaft Deutscher Lokomotivführer), the branch union of the RG headed by Scharffschwerdt, which had played a most prominent part in the strike. The RG delegates handed Hemmer a list with the disciplinary actions taken in the Reichsbahn districts. Although still incomplete (the strike centers of the Ruhr were not listed), the list totalled 7315 cases altogether. *Ibid.,* Bl. 364.

attacked in the Reichstag for having been too conciliatory toward the strikers. He agreed, however, to consult with the transport minister in the entire affair.[184]

Apparently, however, the chancellor forgot (or chose not) to inform the transport minister about the talks in the Chancellery. As a result, Groener learned about them through reports in the morning papers on February 18, in which the Reichsgewerkschaft claimed to have scored a victory against Groener and his policy in the disciplining question. Groener's reaction was predictable; a sharp confrontation between chancellor and transport minister, between Wirth and Groener ensued, nearly triggering-off a cabinet crisis.

In response to Wirth's actions, Groener drafted a letter, to be sent to all cabinet members, in which he demanded a cabinet vote over who should be in charge in the supervision of the guidelines and their execution.[185] Before distributing the letter, however, Groener sent a copy to the Reich President's Office, perhaps in an attempt to get Ebert's support, perhaps in an effort to reach a last-minute compromise, with the Reich President acting as the mediator. The latter happened indeed. On February 21, State Secretary Meissner of the President's Office called the Transport Ministry and relayed the message that if Groener sent the letter to the cabinet, Wirth would be forced to ask for a vote of confidence. Ebert assured Groener that Wirth was not working toward replacing him, since the chancellor agreed that "a change in the Transport Ministry would be disastrous for the authority of the state under the present circumstances."[186] After a meeting with Ebert on February 22, Groener met with the chancellor himself. Wirth, under pressure to avoid further political damage, agreed to Groener's principle demands (1) not to negotiate again with the Reichsgewerkschaft and (2) "to restore the shaken authority of the transport minister" through an "explanation" (i. e. an apology) in the cabinet.[187] When the cabinet met on the following day, the conflict had already been partially defused. Wirth explained that he had no intentions to act as a supreme arbiter in the matter of the disciplining of the strikers, since

[184] *Niederschrift über die Besprechung im Reichskanzlerhaus am 17. Februar 1922, nachmittags 6 1/2 Uhr, ibid.*, Bl. 349—355.

[185] Groener to Cabinet members, draft letter dated February 19, 1922, BA/MA, Nachlaß Groener, 143, Bl. 58—62.

[186] Notation on a telephone conversation, dated February 21, 1922, *ibid.*, Bl. 63.

[187] This emerges from a handwritten notation, written by Groener himself, on the front page of the draft letter, cited in note 185 above.

the full cabinet had the task to watch over the implementation of the guidelines. He informed the cabinet that he had refused to meet with another delegation of the Reichsgewerkschaft, and had sent them to the Transport Ministry instead. Although Groener forced the issue and insisted that "the transport minister had been played against the chancellor" by the union, the great showdown between the two contestants did not take place.[188]

The net effect of the political controversy between Groener and Wirth was that the grievances of the railroad civil servants, and the question of the legality of the mass-disciplining undertaken by the Transport Ministry were not brought up the meeting. In this respect Groener had won out in the conflict, and his policy of toughness toward a possible new strike, in which even passive participants *(Mitläufer)* would be subject to disciplinary punishment, prevailed.[189] His policy seemed to work, because a few days later the RG's executive council decided against a new strike. However, not just political considerations, but serious internal organizational tensions had played a part in the RG's decision against an immediate revival of the strike. It is to these organizational conflicts, which had already surfaced in the unsuccessful struggle against the disciplinary measures, to which we shall now turn in the concluding part of this chapter.

The Organizational Crisis and the Founding of the Allgemeiner Deutscher Beamtenbund (ADB)

The tensions within the DBB over the strike issue, which had already surfaced immediately before the strike, intensified during and after the conflict as a result of the DBB's shifting attitude toward the struggle of the railroad civil servants, and as a result of the unsuccessful policies pursued by the DBB leadership with regard to the disciplining of the strikers. The radical wing of the DBB, led by the radicals in the Reichsgewerkschaft, seized the opportunity for a takeover of the umbrella organization. A first attempt, made in a meeting of the DBB executive on February 23, failed however; the moderates under the leadership of DBB Chairman Flügel received a narrow vote of confidence.[190]

[188] Cabinet meeting, February 23, 1922, *ARK. Kab. Wirth*, pp. 585—590.

[189] This Groener had announced in a directive sent to the regional Reichsbahn districts on February 20, 1922, reprinted in *RVBl.*, A, 1922, p. 83.

[190] *Schulthess...* (1922), p. 27.

But the confrontation between RG and DBB had merely been postponed, not cancelled. Despite some signs of partial organizational disintegration after the strike, the radical leaders of the Reichsgewerkschaft had found similar support of their policies by the RG's executive council.[191] They had established close contacts to the KPD, moreover and plans for a renewed strike had been drawn up jointly between RG and KPD functionaries.[192] In a series of public speeches and mass meetings, lasting through February and March, the two radical exponents of the RG, Chairman Menne and his deputy, Scharfschwerdt, were busy stirring-up emotions against moderates in their own organization and, in addition, against the DBB. General meetings of both organizations were scheduled to be held in early April, and according to Menne, this would become days of reckoning with those who had betrayed the strikers.[193]

The meeting of the RG took place on April 5, 1922. In the elections to the executive committee the radical wing scored a major victory. Menne, Scharfschwerdt, and other radical leaders were reelected to their posts, while those who had opposed the strike lost their seats in the executive committee. Now in full control of the organization, the radical faction announced its determination to step up its opposition to the government's "policy of revenge," as well as to the DBB's policy of non-affiliation with the working class and its rejection of the strike as a trade-union weapon.[194]

The confrontation with the DBB leadership was to take place only two days later, at the DBB's third general meeting in Berlin. The battle began with a programmatic speech by DBB Chairman Flügel, who obviously was determined to settle the strike question once and for all, and to block any attempts to move the DBB closer to the labor movement. "A striking civil servant ceases to be a civil servant," he said. Only in extraordinary cases of self-defense *(Notwehr)* should the civil

[191] Reports on these tendencies of internal disintegration in ZStAP, RköO, 453, Bl. 3—5.

[192] Police report, dated March 29, in *ibid.*, Bl. 35—36. The report claimed that Menne had become a member of the KPD. This is confirmed by another report in *ibid.*, Bl. 8—9, while yet another report (*ibid.*, Bl. 9) suggests that he had retained his membership in the MSPD.

[193] Report on a speech delivered at a RG meeting in Dresden, March 6, 1922, *ibid.*, Bl. 12a—14. Reports on a series of meeting in other cities are contained in a report dated March 29, 1922, *ibid.*, Bl. 22—25.

[194] Report of this meeting in *ibid.*, Bl. 62 and in *DF*, April 10, 1922.

servant resort to "a terrible weapon that destroys the state's authority and leads to political chaos." He similarly rejected the idea of a closer cooperation, or even affiliation of the DBB with the other trade unions. The fact that the civil servant served the general public *(Allgemeinheit)* rather than a private employer precluded his conversion into a regular-type employee *(Arbeitnehmer).* The civil servant occupied a special position in society, Flügel held, which should also find an equivalent in the organizational realm.[195]

Flügel's speech indicated that not only the immediate consequences of February Strike were at issue, but rather the future of the DBB as a trade-union-type interest organization, and its relationship to the labor movement, which had been an unresolved problem since the great controversies of 1921.[196] Finally, the question was raised again whether the social position of the *Beamte* was to be determined primarily by his socioeconomic position as an *Arbeitnehmer,* as proposed by the DBB's left-wing, or, as Flügel claimed, by the civil servant's "higher function" as a servant to the public and to the state.[197]

The debate showed that the fronts had been drawn and that the positions had hardened. Flügel's position was supported emphatically by the conservative South German associations, whose speaker welcomed the fact that the DBB had finally laid at rest the idea of an economic strike *(Lohnstreik).* In addition, speakers for those associations which predominantly organized the "traditional civil servants," i. e. the *Hoheitsbeamte* and teachers, tended to side with Flügel's approach. Opposition came from those organizations which had already supported the strike before it broke out and had always argued for closer relations with blue-collar trade unions, i. e. the postal organizations, associations of lower-grade officials, and, of course, the railroad civil servant union.[198] Several RG delegates emphasized the social dimension of their struggle for the entire *Beamtenschaft* and for all dependently employed. Finally, after repeated invitations, RG Chairman Menne spoke. He charged that the DBB had failed as an "instrument of exerting power." He accused the DBB leadership of only

[195] „Der dritte Bundestag des Deutschen Beamtenbundes." Reported in *Beamtenkorrespondenz,* nos. 4—6, April 7—10, 1922, here no. 4, pp. 1—2. (All further references will be made by citing issue and page number[s]).

[196] Cf. CHAPTER FIVE of this study.

[197] *Beamtenkorrespondenz,* no. 4 (1922), p. 2.

[198] *Ibid.,* no. 4, pp. 3—4.

supporting the interest of the upper ranks of the *Beamtenschaft,* and he warned that the DBB would now have to decide whether it would follow the existing *Vorstand* or the course of the RG.[199] In the vote of contest which followed, the moderates prevailed: Flügel was reelected as chairman by a clear margin. When a spokesman of the right-wing called on the RG delegate to "draw the conclusions" from this vote, a final walkout of the radical wing was only prevented by quickly adjourning the meeting.[200] When the delegates met again on the following day, RG Chairman Menne announced on behalf of his own organization, the postal association, and other DBB affiliates supporting the left wing, that they had decided to remain within the DBB. For the time being, an organizational rupture had been averted.[201]

But in the end, the unresolved strike question and the continuing tensions between a "pro-strike *Arbeitnehmer* wing" and an anti-strike "civil servant wing" proved to be the demise of the DBB. Throughout the next months the RG continued its agitation against the moderate DBB leaders. Contacts with the former rivals in the Socialist trade unions were intensified, and in June 1922 a Socialist "Free" civil servant federation, the Allgemeiner Deutscher Beamtenbund (ADB) was founded at a meeting in Leipzig.[202] The leaders of both DBB and ADGB were presented with a *fait accompli.* The ADGB, which was conducting its own general meeting in Leipzig at the time, only reluctantly agreed to this step, in spite of the fact that some of its own supporters and, above all, the Afa-Bund had played a major part in it.[203] In the end

[199] *Ibid.*, no. 5, p. 2.

[200] *Ibid.*, no. 5, p. 4. The vote was 278 for Flügel and 149 for his rival candidate of the RG. There were 21 abstentions.

[201] *Ibid.*, no. 6, p. 1.

[202] Cf. *Protokoll der Gründungsversammlung des Allgemeinen Deutschen Beamtenbundes am 18. Juni 1922 in Leipzig* (Berlin, n. d.) (hereafter cited as *ADB Protocol 1922*). Invitations to the founding meeting had been sent out by the RG and the Justizbeamtenbund.

[203] See *Allgemeiner Deutscher Gewerkschaftsbund, Protokoll der Verhandlungen des elften Kongresses der Gewerkschaften Deutschlands (1. Bundestag des Allgemeinen Deutschen Gewerkschaftsbundes),* Berlin 1922, pp. 97 ff., and *ADGB Vorstand Protocol,* June 29, 1922, pp. 13—14. During the ADB founding meeting Schumann of the ADGB *Vorstand,* who was at the same time a spokesman for the Verkehrsbund — which, as has been shown in CHAPTER FIVE above, stood in sharp opposition to the "Three-Pillar Principle" — criticized that the step had not been cleared with the ADGB *Vorstand.* Members of the ADGB *Beamtenzentrale,* especially the Afa-Bund, were instrumental in the ADB founding. (*ADB Protocol 1922,* passim).

however, the ADGB acquiesced to the move, especially since it looked as if a majority of the DBB affiliates and some of the DBB's leading personalities were in support of it.[204] About a year later, the ADB would conclude an organizational pact with both ADGB and Afa-Bund, turning the "Three-Pillar-Principle" finally into reality.[205]

Viewed from the side of the DBB, the founding of the ADB and the subsequent secession of some of its largest member associations represented the most critical hour for the survival of the principle of a politically non-affiliated civil servant *Einheitsverband,* and, of course, a test for the survival of the very existence of the DBB as a peak association. And yet, in the crucial meeting of the DBB executive committee on June 22, 1922, the group around DBB Chairman Flügel seemed determined to draw a final line in the ongoing conflict with the left-wing. "A civil servant is not the employee *(Arbeitnehmer)* of a capitalist employer, but of the 'national community' *(Volksgemeinschaft,*" Flügel said, and this alone precluded an economic strike of civil servants. Moreover, it required a certain distance to the blue-collar trade unions, even if the DBB itself was founded on "trade-union principles" as well. A vote then taken by the DBB's executive committee, which implied that the RG had "ceased to be a member of the DBB," ended the internal conflict between the pro-strike and anti-strike factions within the DBB.[206]

The organizational consequences of the February Strike were decisive indeed. Henceforth the newly-founded ADB would be the representative of the strike-supportive, or *Arbeitnehmer* wing, of the civil servant movement. In the organizational realm, the civil servant strike of February 1922 had aided in the schism of the civil servant movement along social and political lines. Whether this would enable civil servants to press with greater vehemence and chances of success for the attainment of those social and economic demands which had orginally triggered off the strike, was doubtful at best.

The February Strike of 1922 was not only a turning point in the organizational development of the civil servant movement, however. It

[204] Albert Falkenberg and Hans Völter both went over to the DBB's new rival organization, Falkenberg becoming its long-time chairman, Völter its chief executive officer and *de facto* head. Initially, the ADB could claim some 350,000 members.

[205] Text of the pact published in the *Allgemeine Deutsche Beamtenzeitung (ADBZ),* the mouthpiece of the ADB, on April 15, 1923.

[206] *Niederschrift über die Sitzung des Bundesvorstands am 22. Juni 1922,* in: *Beamtenkorrespondenz,* no. 9 (1922), pp. 1—5.

also marks the zenith of civil servant protest and civil servant militancy during the inflation period. Since the strike was lost, it was to remain the only attempt by civil servants to press for socioeconomic demands by means of direct collective action. In the subsequent phases of hyperinflation and stabilization a certain "primacy of negotiation" was to reassert itself. In turning now to a discussion of civil servant interest politics during phases of hyperinflation (mid-1922 to late 1923) and stabilization (late 1923 to mid-1924), less militant patterns of collective bargaining with public employers, shifting alliances between social groups, and new patterns of political radicalization among German civil servants will emerge.

CHAPTER SEVEN

From Hyperinflation to Stabilization, July 1922 to June 1924

In mid-1922 Germany moved from 'accelerated' into 'hyper'inflation. This final phase of the German inflation, which would last eighteen months until stabilization was achieved in December of 1923, did much to establish the subsequent "inflation trauma" within German society. The social tensions and recurring political crises that characterized this phase of the inflation, which in the fall of 1923 were seemingly compressed into a general crisis of the Weimar state, were probably as (if not more) important in establishing the "inflation trauma" than the actual economic and monetary process. To be sure, the complete destruction of a currency is a traumatic experience by any account, and the German case was the first of its kind in a modern industrial society. But one would still have to caution that the often redrawn picture of German housewives dragging along carriages full of worthless paper money is but one aspect of the social consequences of inflation, or even of hyperinflation, because it describes the situation prevailing at the very end of the inflation process.[1] Adjustment to hyperinflation occurred in several stages, however, and only in its final stage did this adjustment process push against certain limits. By then, moreover, stabilization was already in the making and presented an entire set of new problems to German society and its various groups. Owing to the close interdependence between the processes of hyperinflation, espe-

[1] Understandably, the year of hyperinflation, i. e. 1923, has loomed large in establishing an "inflation trauma" in German society to this day. On this, see the pertinent remarks made by the German writer Heinrich Böll, in an article for the *New York Times Magazine*, May 2, 1976 entitled "The Specter still haunts in Germany: Inflation." For the general overrating of the hyperinflation as an interpretative framework for the *entire* inflation period, see also the discussion in the INTRODUCTION to this study and the literature cited there, esp. pp. 3—4 above.

cially in its final stages, and the stabilization of the currency, and thus of the economic and political settings, these two intrinsically related subject matters will be dealt with concurrently within this final chapter of our study. In terms of timespan, therefore, this chapter covers a rather long period from mid-1922 to early 1924. Once again, the conduct of civil servant salary policy will play a major role in our story. Within the context of stabilization, however, employment policy will emerge as the most important topic of inquiry. Finally, the political consequences of inflation *and* stabilization will be examined by probing into the civil servants' behavior as voters in the so-called "inflation elections" of 1924.

A word of caution might be in place at the onset, though. The twenty-two months covered by this chapter were months of sustained political and social crisis in Germany. Dealing with these developments in their entirety lies beyond the scope of this study. Our question is a rather more modest and much simpler one: how did civil servants respond and adjust to the impact of hyperinflation, i. e. to a process of *extreme* currency depreciation and its immediate social and economic impact? More specifically, would civil servant interest politics, especially salary policy as it had developed through the preceding stages of the inflation, be capable of adjusting to the new phenomenon of hyperinflation and thus continue to guarantee the economic survival of the *Beamtenschaft,* or would new ways have to be found to reach this goal if, indeed, it was to be reached at all. Finally, as far as the stabilization crisis of 1923-24 was concerned, how would civil servant interest politics fare at a time when public employers were armed with emergency powers and able (and willing!) to suspend rights of bargaining and negotiation which, as we had seen, had developed during the preceding period of inflation.

Into Hyperinflation, July 1922 to January 1923

In the course of the seven months or so between July 1922 and early January 1923 the German economy moved further into hyperinflation. The impact of this transition on the economic and social conditions of civil servants and other dependently employed was dramatic indeed. As the cost-of-living index rose sharply from 54 in July to 446 in November, wages and salaries had to be adjusted to the inflation rate in progressively shorter intervals, if the purchasing power of nominal earnings was to be maintained.[2] For civil servants this entailed an additional burden, since the complicated and longwinded mechanism of salary policy was certainly not conducive to the timely adjustment of pay levels to a rapidly increasing rate of inflation. It was very likely, therefore, that the process of adjustment to hyperinflation would be difficult, if not accompanied by the same type of conflicts which had characterized the preceding months of accelerated inflation. As it turned out, though, this adjustment proved to be less painful and less conflict-ridden than one would have expected. Moreover, the experience of hyperinflation was to lead the major civil servant interest organizations to the formulation of very concrete economic-policy proposals in an effort to participate in the political decision-making process for a future monetary and economic stabilization. In a sense, therefore, hyperinflation prompted civil servant organizations to take the important step from social (i. e. salary) policy to economic policy.

The beginning of hyperinflation in the summer of 1922 interrupted a longer period of recovery of civil servant real income levels. In a series of successive 'salary drives' *(Teuerungsaktionen)* conducted between February and July 1922, civil servant organizations had been able to recapture some of the ground lost in the preceding period of declining salary levels (October 1921 to January 1922) which, as discussed above, had led to the crisis of January and to the February Strike of 1922.[3] In mid-August 1922, the impact of hyperinflation made itself felt, however, and double-digit leaps in the cost-of-living put renewed pressure on the purchasing power of wages and salaries in the public sector. On August 15, the Prussian State Commissar for Public Order warned of a renewed strike of railroad and postal employees, who, interestingly enough, did not demand pay raises, but rather a reduction of the price of food and other commodities.[4] A report sent by Prussian Mining Authority to the Ministry of Trade and Commerce in September 1922, pointed out that in the industrial centers of the Ruhr prices had doubled in the month of August. While the wages of miners had been raised by 97 percent and had thus kept pace with the rate of inflation,

[2] *Zahlen zur Geldentwertung*..., p. 5, and the frequent reports on the wage and salary changes in the public sector published in *Wirtschaft und Statistik*, (1922—1923).

[3] See CHAPTER SIX of this study. See also CHAPTER TWO, pp. 75f. above for the overall movement of civil servant salaries in this period.

[4] State Commissar for Public Order Weismann to Prussian Minister of the Interior, August 15, 1922, ZStAP, RMdI, 2185, Bl. 334.

civil servants had only received a cost-of-living increase of 30 percent during the same period. The report warned of a "revolt of the *Beamtenschaft* against the state," because civil servants had become convinced that their economic plight was a result of the fact that other societal groups had been able to heap the burdens created by the economic circumstances on their shoulders.[5]

Similar views were propounded by the civil servant press. Commenting on the "rules of the race between wages and prices" in the wake of the "catastrophic price increases" of the preceding month, the DBB's mouthpiece wrote, "We realize that we are in the midst of a vicious cycle, but neither can the *Beamtenschaft* remain outside this cycle *(Kreislauf)*, nor can civil servants slow down their actions within it as compared to those of other social groups. We have already been left behind. What needs to be done now is to catch up [with other groups] in order to prevent an even further decline of our economic position." In spite of the fact that paper money had nearly lost its value, a further increase of paper-mark salaries was the only option available to civil servants at the present time, the DBB gazette concluded, in order to catch up with other social groups.[6]

This indeed was the policy which civil servant organizations embarked on in the following two months. In a series of *Teuerungsaktionen*, now conducted as often as twice a month, they were able to recoup some of the lost ground. Interestingly enough, the government itself took the initial step in early September in an effort to bring civil servant pay back into line with the steadily rising cost of living.[7] The results were less encouraging, however. While the inflation rate had increased by 120 percent in September alone, the pay settlement negotiated in mid-September increased the cost-of-living supplement by the average of between 40 and 70 percent only.[8] Once again, the "proletar-

[5] Preußisches Oberbergamt to Minister für Handel und Gewerbe, September 24, 1922, copy in ZStAP, RhB, 52, Bl. 61—64. Report is dated September 1, 1922.

[6] *Der Beamtenbund* (hereafter cited as *DB*), August 31, 1922. (In February 1922 *Die Gemeinschaft* had been renamed into *Der Beamtenbund*).

[7] Details on September actions in ZStAP, RhB, 54. The voluminous files on *Teuerungsaktionen* contained in the RhB deposit (ZStAP, RhB, files 52 through 67) are an invaluable source on the conduct of civil service salary policy in this period, and much of what follows now has been learned from these files, even if specific citations have been kept to a necessary minimum.

[8] *WSt.*, 2 (1922), pp. 614—615; *ADBZ*, September 21, 1922; *ZRhB*, no. 10, 1922, pp. 110—111.

ianization of the civil servants" was depicted as a consequence of insufficient government aid. Protest meetings were held, increasing rank-and-file pressure on the organizational leadership to pursue a tougher line in negotiations with public employers. In Hamburg, for example, civil servants conducted several protest rallies in September and warned that the insufficiencies of civil service pay were about to lead to a "collapse of the state's machinery and thereby to total chaos."[9] The Reichstag Deputy Willy Steinkopf, the SPD's expert in civil service affairs, warned that the uninterrupted increase in prices was forcing civil servant organizations to begin a new salary drive immediately, in spite of the fact that a settlement had just been negotiated and passed by the Reichstag. He emphasized that much would depend on the government's position regarding indexation as a means of adjusting wages and salaries in the public sector, although he did not fail to mention that the labor unions and civil servant associations were at odds in the question of the applicability of the "sliding scale."[10]

In a memorandum, published on September 30, 1922, the Reich Finance Ministry rejected the introduction of the "sliding scale." Aside from many other reasons given for its negative decision, the memorandum made much of the fact that labor unions were opposed to indexation, because it might lessen the unions' influence on the conduct of wage policy. In addition, it would destroy export advantages stemming from low real wages and would thus endanger the high level of employment which this trade advantage had helped to generate. Even one of the major civil servant peak associations had changed its attitude on a

[9] Reported under the heading, *Die Proletarisierung der Beamten* by a local Hamburg paper on September 19, 1922, clipping in StAH, 122-4-3. The meetings were organized by the Hamburg organization of the DBB to alert the public to the *Wirtschaftsnot der Hamburgischen Beamten.* Flyer announcing the meeting, in: *Ibid.*

[10] Willy Steinkopf, *Die Besoldungsfrage,* in: *Volksstimme* (Frankfurt), September 19, 1922, clipping in ZStAP, RhB, 52, Bl. 66. — In April 1922, after a series of public hearings (cf. a report in ZStAP, RhB, 55, Bl. 239—242) the Reichstag had adopted a resolution, which asked the Reich government to respond to the indexation problem in form of a detailed memorandum. As has been mentioned several times already, civil servant associations were the main proponents of an automatic indexation by means of the "sliding scale," and the issue had been one of the goals of the February Strike. A useful summary of the indexation issue and the position of the labor unions is given by Herbert Perrin, *Die Stellung der Gewerkschaften zur Frage der gleitenden Lohnskala,* Diss., Freiburg 1923, Perrin's discussion of the civil servant organizations' opinion (*ibid.*, pp. 115—123) is rather brief, however, and does not do justice to the important role played by these organizations in the struggle for indexation.

"schematic" adjustment of salaries to the inflation, the memorandum noted. During the September negotiations, representatives for this organization had argued that the official cost-of-living index could not be trusted any longer with regard to its accuracy, and that an adjusting of salaries on the basis of "dead figures" would not lead to calmness within the *Beamtenschaft.* This, the government concluded, showed that "even influencial circles within the civil servants' own representative organizations are of the opinion that a smooth adjusting of wages and salaries could not be done by way of a compulsory and mechanical scheme, but only by way of free and unlimited negotiation."[11]

Indeed, civil servant associations were not as upset about the government's negative response as one might have expected in view of their earlier, very emphatic endorsement of the "sliding scale." They, too, had learned to appreciate the value and the intrinsic power of negotiation. As long as the government rejected the sliding scale, one association wrote, they would have to respond with an uninterrupted sequence of salary offensives.[12] While negotiation thus remained the all-important weapon available to civil servants in their struggle against the impact of hyperinflation, the use of this weapon needed to be reclaimed in a persistent struggle with the government.

In mid-October 1922, negotiations between the organizations and the Reich Finance Ministry about a restructuring of the pay scale finally broke down completely, because the government regarded some of the organizations' demands as exorbitant and impossible to fullfil. As a result, a partial revision of the pay scale was undertaken single-handedly by the government and pushed through in the Reichstag. Without much success, the organizations had lobbied at the parliament in an attempt to realize some of the changes sought by them, especially the introduction of a minimum pay standard for the lower grades.[13]

[11] *Denkschrift über die selbstätig gleitende Gehalts- und Lohnskala,* in: *Stenographische Berichte...,* vol. 375, no. 5007, quoted according to a typescript version in BA, R 43I/2564, Bl. 373—374. — Although the memo does not give the organization's name, it is very likely that it was referring to the ADB here. A survey of the relevant files shows that the other peak associations, especially the DBB, had also altered its earlier support of indexation somewhat.

[12] Westfälischer Philologenverein to RhB, Oct. 23, 1922, ZStAP, RhB, 6, Bl. 112. In response to the Reich government's negative evaluation, the Reichstag later dropped legislative action on the sliding scale.

[13] *DB,* October 26, 1922. — The organizations, except the RhB, were enraged that a so-called *Kopfzuschlag* had been dropped, i. e. an across-the-board lump-sum payment favoring the lower groups, and that the government had attempted to differentiate a new

In an attempt to recoup their losses and, no doubt, to cover up their defeat, the organizations went to the Finance Ministry two days after the Reichstag vote had been taken and demanded the immediate beginning of a new round of negotiations to increase the cost-of-living supplement. They were told by a high ministry official that, in view of the pay awards just voted by the Reichstag, talks about new cost-of-living increases were out of the question at this juncture. As they had done at earlier occasions, the organizations took their complaints to the Chancellery. There, they emphatically protested against the Finance Ministry's uncompromising attitude. The plight of their members required immediate action, they told a Chancellery official. Already "civil servants, donning their uniforms, were flocking onto the fields in order to steal potatoes." The authority of the state was suffering as a consequence of such incidents, and in view of the steady rise of the cost of living, new unrest and even strikes were likely to occur.[14]

After some hesitation, the government gave in and a new round of talks commenced in the Finance Ministry on November 1, 1922. The course of these negotiations showed, however, that a serious rift had developed between government and organizations on the underlying principles of collective bargaining for civil service pay. In a take-it-or-leave-it approach, government negotiators offered a pay increase that they had decided upon in advance, and which the organizations viewed as totally insufficient but were forced to accept. Protesting against "an ultimatum" on the part of the government, the organizations declared that they regarded this settlement as "temporary," and that they would come forward with new pay demands "within the next few days."[15]

This conflict has been retold in some length, because it shows that the existing negotiating machinery had finally run its course under the impact of an inflation rate that was leading to drastic changes in price levels within a matter of a few days, rather than weeks or months as had been the case until then. In the fall of 1922 civil servant organizations

supplement for married civil servants on the basis of base pay and location. The latter they were able to prevent. Details on the pay revision in *WSt.*, 2 (1922), p. 709, and in ZStAP, RhB, 58.

[14] Notation on a meeting in the Chancellery, October 25, 1922, BA, R 43I/2565, Bl. 22.

[15] Report in *ADBZ*, November 2, 1922. Declaration of the organizations in ZStAP, RhB, 60, Bl. 7.

were unable to keep pay levels in line with the rising cost of living. In real terms, civil servant salaries dropped sharply in October and November, indeed, in the latter month they reached one of their lowest (in Hamburg *the* lowest) points during the entire inflation period.[16]

A second aspect is important in this context. The breakdown of negotiations and the public declaration issued by the organizations had once again attracted public attention to the salary question, and it had sensitized an already restive public once again to the high costs of wages and salaries in the oversized public service sector. The industry-oriented DAZ emphatically supported the government's position that the costs of the organizations' demands would have run into the "hundreds of billions", and that it was beneath the government's dignity to engage in log-rolling *(Kuhhandel)* with the unions. The paper speculated that the success of yet another salary drive would be "more than questionable in view of the government's tough stance."[17] Even sharper language was used by the *Deutsche Zeitung*, a right-wing paper close to agrarian interests. "Over the past years even the most ignorant have begun to realize," this paper wrote, "that increases in civil service pay are being financed solely by the printing presses." These pay increases, the paper surmised, had been largely responsible for the increase in paper money, for more inflation and further increases in the cost of living, under which the other "productive groups" *(Stände)* of the population were chafing.[18]

It was partially as a counter offensive against mounting criticism of this kind that in mid-November 1922 the two major civil servant federations went public with economic-policy proposals of their own. It was an attempt to break out of the limits of salary policy and to offer propositions for changes in economic policy that would make further *Teuerungsaktionen* superfluous.

In its proposal, sent to the Reich government in early November, the DBB emphasized that the "race between salaries and prices" could ultimately only be ended by a drastic and, above all, controlled reduction of price levels. In this context the DBB raised the demand that

[16] Cf. FIGURES 1 and 2 in CHAPTER TWO of this study.

[17] *DAZ*, no. 481, November 4, 1922, clipping in BA, R 43I/2565, Bl. 39.

[18] *Deutsche Zeitung. Wirtschaftlicher Teil*, no. 521, November 19, 1922, clipping in ZStAP, RhB, 52, Bl. 75. The paper charged that civil servant pay had increased by 700 % in nine months' time, and pointed for the first time to the advantages of the civil servant quarterly prepayment of salaries.

more civil servants be appointed to the staffs of the so-called 'price control agencies' *(Preisprüfungsstellen)*, which were in charge of supervising pricing practices at the local and regional levels. The main emphasis of the DBB's economic program was, however, to offer suggestions on how to arrest the progressively worsening depreciation of the currency. Stabilizing the mark, the DBB claimed, was a precondition for all other economic measures that might be taken by the government. One step toward stabilizing the currency was the curtailing of the huge budget deficits incurred by the Reich. Greater productivity and an "increased rationalization of the entire work process" would be one way to trim government spending. Another would be the implementation of a more equitable tax system, which would distribute the tax burden more evenly on all groups in society. Lastly, the government was called upon to adopt tougher measures aimed against profiteering, excessive consumption of luxuries, speculation on the depreciation of the currency, and the export of capital.[19]

The ADB, too, sent a catalog of economic proposals and social demands to the Reich government in early November. It stands to reason that the proposals advanced by the Socialist civil servant federation would follow in the footsteps of programmatic pronouncements made earlier by its two "parent organizations," ADGB and Afa-Bund.[20] In fact, very few original ideas were contained in the ADB's economic policy proposals. Like the Free Trade Unions, the ADB demanded a reform of the currency by "seizing real assets" *(Erfassung der Sachwerte)*, by preventing the export of capital *(Kapitalflucht)* and the "flight from the mark," a more timely exaction of income taxes withheld from employees' paychecks by employers, and measures against overpricing *(Preistreiberei)* and profiteering. Most importantly, however, the ADB protested against allegations that only an extension of the work hours could lead to a solution of Germany's financial and economic problems. Placing civil servants squarely within a joint front of all *Arbeitnehmer*, the ADB wrote:

[19] *DBB Geschäftsbericht 1924*, pp. 40—41. — The entire section on „Wirtschaftspolitik" in this report (pp. 40—51) is relevant in this context.

[20] In fact, ADGB and Afa-Bund had sent similar demands to the chancellor at the same time. For an appraisal of the earlier programmatic demands made by the ADGB in the summer of 1921, see CHAPTER FIVE, pp. 257 f. above. On the famous 10-point economic program, put forth by the same organization in the fall of 1921, see H. Potthoff, *Gewerkschaften...*, pp. 295—306.

"It must be prevented at all costs that the attempts at restoring the currency are being done *only* by increasing the amount of work performed by the laboring classes, to which civil servants belong as well. In the end, the dependently employed will again be deprived the fruits of their additional labor without receiving any assurances that an actual improvement of the general economic situation will take place at the same time."[21]

Clearly, the ADB had elevated the *general* problems faced by all wage and salary earners above the *specific* ones faced by civil servants. This tendency of integrating civil servant demands into general *Arbeitnehmer* policy was to remain an integral part of the ADB's approach to social and economic policy. During the stabilization crisis, this would create serious problems in interest representation and lead to difficulties in the maintaining of a 'social identity' on the part of the Socialist civil servant federation.[22]

The political impact of the economic proposals made by the two civil servant peak associations in the fall of 1922 was limited, however, not least because they appeared at a time of acute political crisis. Only a few days after the organizations had made their pronouncements, the Wirth government resigned and a "cabinet of industry" under the chancellorship of Wilhelm Cuno, a director of a major German shipping line, was formed.[23] Initially, the civil servant organizations were rather doubtful that the new government would last for any significant length of time.[24] They would soon learn, however, that the appointment of the Cuno government was to be the final turn toward a sustained period of domestic crisis and economic chaos through which German society would have to suffer in 1923.

From Ruhr Occupation to Indexation, January to November 1923

On January 11, 1923 French and Belgian troops invaded the unoccupied sections of the industrial centers of the Ruhr, ostensibly in an

[21] *ADBZ*, November 16, 1922 *(Der Allgemeine Deutsche Beamtenbund zur Wirtschaftspolitik).*

[22] This theme will be further explored in section 3 of this chapter.

[23] For these political developments, which cannot be explored in greater detail here, see the introduction to Karl Heinz Harbeck (ed.), *Akten der Reichskanzlei. Weimarer Republik. Das Kabinett Cuno. 22. November bis 12. August 1923,* Boppard 1968, pp. XIX—XXV.

[24] *DB,* November 30, 1922.

effort to seize real assets in lieu of missing reparation payments. The German government responded with a call for passive resistance, which placed a heavy burden on the population in the Ruhr Region. The situation of public officials was especially precarious; many were arrested or expelled for refusing to "take orders from the enemy," which had been decreed by the government in Berlin as part of passive-resistance policy.[25] The major civil servant organizations cooperated with the government and participated in the *Ruhrhilfe*, a scheme devised to finance passive resistance.[26] Furthermore, a joint "resistance committee" *(Abwehrausschuß)* was formed, in which the (nominally rival) civil servant peak associations cooperated very smoothly. It was one of the signs of a new (but rather short-lived) *Burgfrieden* mentality which the Ruhr Occupation had created within German society.[27]

The economic consequences of the Ruhr occupation and passive resistance would soon place great strains on the newly-discovered social harmony, however. In the wake of the Ruhr invasion, the value of the German currency took another heavy loss. By January the dollar exchange rate had climbed to more than 4,000, i. e. the mark lost more than half of its value if compared to December, when the dollar rate had stood at 1,800. The decline of the mark on foreign exchanges corresponded to an upsurge of domestic price levels. In some regions (and not only in the occupied territories, where prices soared the most) the cost of living was reported to have tripled during the second half of January, an increase which, as one civil servant organization charged, was con-

[25] The relevant documents are contained in BA, R 43I, files 203, 205, 206. A summary of the decrees regulating the "behavior of civil servants toward the occupation forces" is contained in a letter of Reich Minister of Finance Hermes, dated January 20, 1923 in: *Ibid.*, 203, Bl. 176—177. A summary of the situation of civil servants, containing a list of civil servants arrested as of February 1, is given in a letter sent by the DBB regional association of the Rhineland to the Chancellor, February 4, 1923, *ibid.*, 206, Bl. 406—419.

[26] See *ADBZ*, January 15, 1923, where the famous trade-union proclamation, *Mitten im Frieden* is reprinted. The DBB issued its own proclamation reprinted in *DB*, January 25, 1923, as did the RhB, whose proclamation (copy in BA, R 43I/203, Bl. 147) was filled with the most rabid nationalist pathos.

[27] These brief remarks do not, of course, aspire to offer an exhaustive treatment of the Ruhr Occupation and its political and social consequences. On this, see H. Rupieper, *The Cuno Government*..., passim, G. D. Feldman, *Iron and Steel*..., Chapter 6, and Ch. S. Maier, *Recasting*..., pp. 355—386. For a succinct summary of the activities of the German civil servant organizations in the Ruhr Conflict, see *DBB Geschäftsbericht 1924*, pp. 74—90.

cealed by the official Reich index for political purposes.[28] With the help of the Reichsbank, the German government embarked upon a stabilization of the mark in February and March of 1923. Although these efforts proved to be temporarily successful, with the dollar exchange rate dropping slightly in March and remaining stable through April, domestic price levels did not follow suit, but continued on their upward climb.[29] As a consequence, pressures for an adjusting of wage levels to steadily rising prices increased again by March 1923, and civil servant organizations demanded pay increases to offset the previous price hikes.[30]

The "struggle for the March Supplement"[31] was to be the last major conflict between government and civil servant organizations over the conduct of salary policy during the inflation period. Characteristically, it occurred at a time when the government had embarked on a stabilization course. The conflict thus followed a pattern which had been established at previous instances of attempted monetary stabilization.[32] However, the Ruhr Crisis and its political implications, as well as the specifics of hyperinflation, added a special dimension to this final "salary struggle" of the inflation period. The pay offensive of March 1923 was to set the stage for the frequent (and relatively) smooth salary negotiations of spring and summer of 1923, which were to prevail until indexation would finally take the place of negotiation in July 1923. For these reasons, it deserves to be reexamined in greater detail.

On March 1, the peak organizations approached the Reich government and demanded a pay increase for the month of March.[33] After

[28] Westfälischer Philologenverein to RhB, February 3, 1923, ZStAP, RhB, 65, Bl. 16, and RhB to Reich Finance Ministry, February 3, 1923, *ibid.*, Bl. 19.

[29] ADB to Reich Chancellor, March 7, 1923, BA, R 43I/1152, Bl. 86, where the ADB points to the discrepancy between the "stable" exchange rate and continuously rising prices, arguing that business circles were taking advantage of the situation through an aggressive price policy. The same organization publicly claimed that the entire stabilization effort was "dubious" *(faule Stabilisierung), ADBZ,* March 12, 1922. The government had raised the cost-of-living supplement twice in January and February. Cf. *WSt.*, 3 (1923), pp. 53—54, 156—157.

[30] Reichsgewerkschaft to Reich President, Reich Chancellor, and other ministries, March 13, 1923, BA, R 43I/2565, Bl. 170.

[31] *Der Kampf um die Märzzulage,* in: *ADBZ,* March 12, 1923.

[32] See, for example, the discussion in CHAPTER FOUR of this study.

[33] The source of the following account is a confidential circular (no. 5 a/23), sent by the RhB to its affiliated organizations on March 19, 1923 (copy in ZStAP, RhB, 66, Bl. 63—64). This source is more accurate than any of the press reports published later on

some foot-dragging on the part of the government, negotiations began on March 7 in the Reich Finance Ministry. Placing great emphasis of the confidentiality of the meeting, Ministerial Councillor von Schlieben of the Reich Finance Ministry told the organizational representatives that the success of the entire Ruhr Action depended on a further stabilizing of the mark against the dollar and on the future price reductions. The support of the mark, he said, required huge sums of money. These efforts and the planned price reductions would be seriously endangered if the public were alarmed by a renewed drive for a cost-of living increase on the part of government employees. Moreover, the circulation of notes would be expanded to intolerable levels, since the (quarterly) salaries for April, May and June would have to be paid out almost immediately afterwards. For these reasons, the Reich cabinet had decided against a renewed cost-of-living increase a few days earlier. The finance minister would be willing, though, to meet with organizational leaders at a later date. After the organizations had voiced their "gravest objections" to the government's position, the meeting was adjourned.

Since Finance Minister Hermes had fallen ill, the meeting with the organizations could not take place as had been scheduled. On March 9, the State Secretary in the Finance Ministry, Schroeder, received the organizational leaders on behalf of the minister. In the intervening days government negotiators had conducted separate talks with organizational leaders in order to receive their support for a compromise solution which, as in earlier cases, called for a prepayment of regular salaries. Several organizations, among them the RhB, had indicated their support for what they considered to be an acceptable compromise between the political viewpoint of the government and the economic demands of the *Beamtenschaft.*

This solution was then offered by State Secretary Schroeder on March 9. In a follow-up meeting, Schlieben conceded that as far as the Reich government was concerned the entire affair was a veiled salary movement. "In view of the political situation and the concerns of the public one could not call it by its right name," he said, but had to "throw dust in the public's eyes." Three days later, on March 12, the organizations and the government made final the details of their agreements. The sharp criticism of an alleged *Diktat* of the government in the salary question, which the civil servant press expounded in the days

by the organizations. Moreover, it could be verified against minutes taken by RhB delegate during the meetings. (*Ibid.*, Bl. 52—62.)

after the negotiations,[34] may safely be interpreted as part of the scheme to deceive the public about the real extent and implications of the previous settlement. Public disclaimers notwithstanding, which also contained the usual organizational bickering, a relationship of mutual dependency had been established between government and the organizations by mid-1923. One of the consequences of this interdependence was that the *Beamtenschaft* was able to recover some of the economic losses it had suffered since the previous fall. In the spring of 1923 civil servant salaries began to show an upward trend again in real terms.[35] The by then very smoothly operating negotiating machinery was, no doubt, partially responsible for this recovery.[36]

The failure of the stabilization effort, and the renewed collapse of the mark in May 1923 pushed the negotiating machinery to its limits, though. In view of the catastrophic depreciation of the currency, and of price increases that were now measured in five and six digit figures within a matter of days, there was little room left for an actual bargaining for wages and salaries. The foremost goal became the adjustment of pay levels in a more timely fashion, and, since one could not negotiate continuously, on the basis of some kind of permanent and more durable footing. The attaining of greater stability of value *(Wertbeständigkeit)* of wages and salaries emerged as the most important goal of civil servant interest politics in the summer of 1923. It called for a more effective adjustment of pay rates (and of tax rates as well) to the depreciation of the currency on the basis of a price index which would be recalculated and constantly revised in shorter time spans than before.[37] Civil servant organizations seemed aware of the limitations of these endeavors. Ultimately, the ADBZ warned, only a stable currency could lead to stable value pay. In this sense, therefore, stability of value based on an indexation of paper mark salaries was a misnomer and likely to create illusions of a kind of stability which in reality did not exist.[38]

[34] E. g., *Gegen die Gehaltspolitik der Regierung,* in: *ADBZ,* March 20, 1923.

[35] Cf. CHAPTER ONE, pp. 75—76 above.

[36] The DBB later stressed this aspect in its report of salary policy in the inflation years. Cf. *DBB Geschäftsbericht 1924,* pp. 53—54. The documents contained in the RhB files confirm this impression. (ZStAP, RhB, 63 and 67).

[37] *Für wertbeständige Gehälter und Steuern,* in: *ADBZ,* June 23, 1923.

[38] *Wertbeständige Gehälter und Währungspolitik,* in: *Ibid.,* June 30, 1923. A similar assessment, although in retrospect, is given in *DBB Geschäftsbericht 1924,* p. 58. To this day, there is a great argument among economists on the functional value of indexation.

The organizations began their offensive for an indexation agreement in late June of 1923. The issue and the timing of negotiations was, to some degree, forced upon them because talks on indexation of wages and salaries in the private sector were already underway in the Reich Labor Ministry.[39] On July 12, 1923 negotiations for the public sector resumed in the Finance Ministry. After a series of difficult and increasingly complicated sessions on the mechanics of indexation, an agreement was reached on July 19. It provided for a review of wage levels in the public sector on a weekly, for civil servant salaries initially on a bi-weekly basis. A number of the rather complicated provisions allowed for a partial projection of *future* increases in the cost-of-living and their computing into wage and pay levels.[40] For civil servants, who were paid in advance on a monthly or even three-months basis, this entailed the advantage of receiving a larger sum of money at a point in time when its purchasing value was still higher than the estimated cost-of-living index figure on which the tabulation of this pay had been based. Moreover, *pre*payment of pay at a time of hyperinflation entailed another advantage. At a time when the index figures at the day of payment, and the instant conversion of money wages into tangible items became crucial variables, the stipulation of the Indexation Agreement that prepaid salaries would be deducted from scheduled supplementary payments *at face value* only was an advantage indeed. It led to the fact that civil servants received a higher pay in real terms than blue-collar workers or contractual employees with the same paper-mark salary.[41]

An assumed example may clarify this point: A civil servant receives a pay check for the forthcoming month at the beginning of the month of 100 accounting units. In the middle of the month his salary is retabulated, on the basis of a new index figure, to be 1000 units. The civil servant would then receive a supplementary payment of 900 units although the 100 units deducted (at face value) represented a much greater value on the day they had originally been paid out. It is for this reason that the principle of prepayment of salaries, one of the civil

[39] ADB to Reich government, June 27, 1923, BA, R 43I/1152, demanding the resumption of immediate talks on indexation in the public sector.

[40] *Verhandlungen über wertbeständige Löhne und Gehälter,* July 12, 1923, ZStAP, RhB, 526, Bl. 30—31. For a summary of the complicated mechanisms of indexation which was finally agreed upon, see *Die Technik der Gehaltsanpassung,* in: *ADBZ,* no. 26, 1923, p. 166.

[41] See the discussion in CHAPTER ONE, and TABLE 21 on p. 89 above.

servant's "well earned rights," was to come under sharp attack in the fall of 1923.[42] While the terms of the Indexation Agreement of July 1923 thus gave to civil servants an advantage over other social groups, indexation as such brought a temporary respite only. Ultimately, the "stability agreement failed because of the instability of the currency," the DBB later correctly observed.[43]

It was one sign of the progressively worsening condition of the German currency that in September, 1923 the cost-of-living supplement had to be replaced by a so-called "measuring figure," with which all portions of civil servant pay were from then on simply to be multiplied. Set at 388 at the day of its first introduction in September 1923, this figure had risen to 35,000 by the second week of October, only to reach two million (!) by the end of that month. In real terms, however, civil servant salaries went on a sharp downward spin during the autumn months of 1923.[44]

As money was rapidly losing its function as a device to purchase the essentials of life, procurement of food, coal, and other items directly from producers increased in importance. Like other organized social groups, civil servants possessed the organizational framework for activities in the area of economic self-help.[45] Throughout the preceding years, civil servants had employed means of economic self-help to withstand the acute economic dislocations and shortages of the inflation period. The system employed was quite simple and efficient. Civil servants associations, or civil servant cooperatives, purchased large amounts of food-stuffs, especially potatoes, from agrarian producers, or heating fuels from industrial producers or wholesalers. These items were then sold to their members at substantial savings entailed by bulk-purchase. The financing was handled by credit institutions controlled by the organizations, the so-called *Beamtenbanken,* which in turn obtained non-interest loans from the government to finance these purchases.[46]

[42] This will be explained in greater detail in section 3 below.

[43] In retrospect, i. e., *after* stabilization, civil servant organizations acknowledged this advantage, which *during* the inflation they had disavowed. See *DBB Geschäftsbericht 1924,* p. 58.

[44] *WSt.,* 3 (1923), pp. 610—611, 671.

[45] The most important central organization was the *Beamtenwirtschaftsbund* (BWB), founded in 1919, in which the peak organizations held shares. Local and regional organizations were an important factor as well.

[46] Documentation on these activities at the regional level in Baden, in GLAK, 233, 3505 a and 3496.

In mid-1923, however, these credit practices came under closer scrutiny by the government. Since the loans would usually be repaid several weeks or even months later (after deductions had been made from civil servants' paychecks), the government was paid back in depreciated currency as the inflation progressed. In July 1923, the Reich government finally introduced a currency depreciation factor *(Entwertungsfaktor)*.[47] Two months later the Reich government stopped the credit program entirely.[48] By then calculations had become almost impossible anyway, and sellers of commodities increasingly demanded hard currencies as payment. Reluctantly, some governmental agencies supplied civil servant banks with foreign currencies to enable them to continue with their efforts at a somewhat reduced scale.[49] On the whole, therefore, the practices of economic self-help provided a shelter against the impact of the inflation at first, but in the final stages of hyperinflation it, too, became a victim of the collapse of all monetary relationships and methods of accounting, and of a general credit crisis which had developed by then.

Nothing illustrates the destruction of the German currency more drastically, perhaps, than the fact that in November, 1923 the German government was forced to pay portions of the salaries of its own employees in other, i. e. stable currencies than the paper mark. As of November 23, 1923, fifty percent of civil servants' salaries were paid *wertbeständig*, i. e. in other currencies or forms of legal tender than the by then worthless official currency.[50] Yet despite the fact that significant portions of civil servant pay were paid in "stable currencies," the real value of civil servant salaries decreased by nearly one-third in November alone. The suspension of the prepayment mode, which had come into effect by then, was one of the reasons for this decline, but it may also have come as a consequence of the general collapse of traditional forms of monetary relationships, and thus of salary policy as well.

[47] Minutes on a meeting in the Chancellery, (July 10), 1923, BA, R 43I/2636, Bl. 61.

[48] Baden Minister of Finance to Badischer Beamtenbund, September 6, 1923, GLAK, 233, 3505 a, informing the organization that the Baden State Government would suspend its credit program as well.

[49] Ortskartell Karlsruhe of the Badischer Beamtenbund to local leaders, November 6, 1923, GLAK, 233, 3496. The letter mentions that the Baden State Government had given 2,000 U.S dollars to the credit union of the Badischer Beamtenbund to finance purchases of food stuffs. Whether this was a credit or a straight purchase of foreign currency does not emerge from the source.

[50] *WSt.*, 3 (1923), pp. 736—737.

A new chapter in civil service salary policy would begin with the stabilization of the German currency on the *Rentenmark* basis in mid-November, and with the setting of "Goldmark" salaries in December of 1923. This, as well as some of the other developments that have just been sketched out briefly, were already part of an exceedingly painful and acrimonious process of economic stabilization, which had been underway since mid-August 1923. It is to the "crisis of stabilization" in the fall and winter of 1923-24, and its impact on the *Beamtenschaft* that we shall now have to turn to in the following sections of this chapter.

Confronting Stabilization, Fall 1923 to Spring 1924

Stabilization is a necessary consequence, if not an integral part of a period of prolonged economic inflation. In the economic sphere, stabilization marks the point of the inflation process when the tasks of currency reform and the attaining of greater economic and fiscal stability have become paramount. In the political sphere, stabilization requires (and usually goes hand in hand with) a new government, whose task it is to prepare and to enforce the cluster of stabilization policies necessary to redirect a society on a course of austerity after a period of prolonged, but largely "apparent" prosperity caused by inflation. In the social-political realm, lastly, stabilization presents itself as period of intense struggle between, the "stabilizing authorities" and the relevant social groups over the terms of stabilization and the distribution of its social burdens. A similar conflict of distribution may occur between and even within the groups themselves, as the "inflation consensus" that has guided interest alliances during the years of inflation disintegrates without a new "stabilization consensus" there to take its place. From the perspective of the various groups of a society undergoing stabilization, this process often entails a defensive battle against carrying an allegedly disproportionate share of the burdens created by stabilization.[51]

In the fall of 1923 German society appeared in roughly the kind of state just outlined above in rather abstract terms. After a "stabilization government" had taken office in late August 1923, a Great Coali-

[51] This discussion owes much to the insightful analysis of the socioeconomic and political preconditions for stabilization given by Ch. S. Maier, *The Politics of Inflation*..., in: F. Hirsch: J. Goldthorpe (eds.), *The Political Economy*..., pp. 67—69 and passim.

tion government under the chancellorship of Gustav Stresemann,[52] a sharp battle over the conduct and the course of stabilization ensued. In the course of this battle, civil servants, like other social groups, were forced to defend their economic positions and interests in an increasingly bitter struggle over the distribution of the burdens created by stabilization politics. *Abbau* (retrenchment) became one of the catchwords of the political conflicts and social tensions created by stabilization. For civil servants, these conflicts were not just a question of whether a rollback of social policy gains made since 1918 could be prevented, but whether they would be able to withstand one of the most serious challenges made to the principles and inviolability of civil servants' "well-earned rights." From this angle, the struggle against stabilization (or rather against its social impact) appears as a defensive battle against attempts to undermine the very foundations on which the German civil service rested, a foundation which had been reclaimed in 1919 under the most difficult circumstances.[53] For a civil servant movement shaken by internal strife and weakened by the erosion of its financial capabilities in the wake of hyperinflation, the waging of this battle of defence would not be easy.[54] This was the case even more so, because the position of its foremost adversary, the Reich government, had been strengthened by a broader parliamentary base and, later on, as a consequence of emergency powers granted to it by the Reichstag.[55] This shifting of the balance of power between government and interest group would play a major role in the defeat which civil servants were to suffer in two key battles waged during the stabilization crisis of 1923-

[52] An excellent summary of the political background of the Stresemann government and its policies is given in the introduction to Martin Vogt and Karl Dietrich Erdmann (eds.), *Akten der Reichskanzlei. Weimarer Republik. Die Kabinette Stresemann I und II*, Boppard 1978, pp. XIX ff., esp. LXXX—LXXXVIII.

[53] Cf. CHAPTER TWO of this study, esp. pp. 156—158 above.

[54] The DBB's business report for 1922—1924 notes this in retrospect. As of midsummer 1923, the financial situation of the DBB had become increasingly precarious since membership fees owed to the central organization by the affiliates were paid late and in depreciated currency. In August 1923, the DBB had been forced to launch a drive among the membership for the economic survival of the organization. *DBB Geschäftsbericht 1924*, pp. 23—25. See also *Der Beamtenbund*, August to November 1923, where the appeals for financial contributions were published. By October, the paper itself was cut down in size for financial reasons to two pages and two issues per month (rather than four).

[55] Martin Vogt/Karl Dietrich Erdmann, introduction to *ARK. Kab. Stresemann*, pp. XXXIII—XXXV.

24: the struggle for the preservation of quarterly pay, and the struggle against personnel cutbacks, the notorious but, as we shall see, partially misnamed *Beamtenabbau* of 1923-24.[56]

The Struggle for Quarterly Pay

The first phase in the civil servants' defensive battle against the policies of stabilization was the struggle against the suspension of quarterly pay. As has been mentioned above, quarterly pay (or prepayment of monthly salaries) had given civil servants an economic advantage over other employee groups. Moreover, quarterly pay was considered an inviolable "well-earned right," and civil servants suspected —not without good reason, as it turned out — that its suspension was only to serve as a first step in a series of violations of constitutionally guaranteed civil servant privileges.[57] This fact, rather than the increasingly elusive economic advantages, might explain the fierceness with which civil servant organizations fought against the suspension of the quarterly pay mode in August and September of 1923.

Public criticism of quarterly pay had been mounting in the summer of 1923, especially after the Indexation Agreement of July 1923 had led to the non-sensical (but economically advantageous) prepayment of supplementary payments. "The entire German press, regardless of its political persuasion, has identified this method as a source of the inflation," the *Soziale Praxis* judged in early September, and the same paper alleged that higher civil servants in particular had misused the advanced payment of huge sums of money to engage in currency speculation.[58] These charges of a "public scandal of the greatest magnitude," which once again had been spearheaded by the business-oriented *DAZ* did two things: it forced the government to speed up its preparations for legislative action designed to suspend quarterly pay, and it prompted civil servants and their organizations to mobilize their forces against the government's plans and the "malicious anti-civil servant

[56] Some aspects of the discussion which follows have been dealt with previously by this author in a separate article. See Andreas Kunz, *Stand versus Klasse. Beamtenschaft und Gewerkschaften im Konflikt um den Personalabbau 1923/24*, in: *Geschichte und Gesellschaft*, 8 (1982), pp. 55—86.

[57] *DB*, August 30, 1923.

[58] *SP*, September 9, 1923, which presents a good survey of the public press campaign against quarterly pay.

campaign" *(Beamtenhetze)* conducted in the public press.[59] Civil servants were quick to point out where the originators of this campaign were to be found and what their motives were. "Business circles have finally realized that the situation of the economy is leading into a catastrophy," a civil servant organization in Cologne wrote, and the public "is being led to believe that civil servants are responsible for economic chaos produced by the alliance of industry, agriculture, trade and commerce." Yet the "gravediggers of the state are to be found in other circles than within the *Beamtenschaft*," the resolution concluded.[60] Another civil servant organization called it a "stupidity" to claim that the prepayment of quarterly salaries was the main cause for the collapse of German public finances, while in reality it had been caused by "the currency speculations of big industry and high finance," and by the "insane pricing policies of producers and traders."[61] There were warnings, finally, about a political backlash within the *Beamtenschaft.* A DVP civil service committee in Berlin sharply criticized that one of this party's semi-official organs (i. e. the *DAZ*) had been on the forefront in the attack against the *Beamte.* In a personal letter to DVP Chairman (and Reich Chancellor) Stresemann the committee's chairman warned that as a consequence "civil servants will turn their backs to our party" and move further to the right, to the Nationalists.[62]

The further course of events would show, however, that the government was unmoved by outside pressures on this issue. The suspension of the quarterly pay mode was an integral part of the Stresemann government's stabilization policy, and the way this issue was handled shows that civil servant organizations had already lost part of their influence on the political decision making process. On September 1, 1923 a decision was reached in Reich Finance Ministry that quarterly pay would have to be suspended by a special enabling law to be passed

[59] The *ADBZ* spoke of a "civil servant pogrom" *(Beamtenpogrom)* committed by the *DAZ* (*ADBZ*, September 1, 1923). In its article, which had started the campaign, the *DAZ* had alleged that there existed a conspiracy between civil servant organizations and high officials in the Reich Finance Ministry with regard to the pay issue. Several documents concerning the same allegations are cited in *ARK. Kab. Stresemann,* pp. 128—129, note 10.

[60] *Entschließung der Beamtenausschüsse... in Köln,* dated August 30, 1923, copy in StAH, 122-4, 3.

[61] Beamtenarbeitsgemeinschaft Rhein-Ruhr to Reich Chancellor, August 31, 1923, BA, R 43I/2566, Bl. 9.

[62] Brüggemann to Stresemann, August 31, 1923, *ibid.,* Bl. 11—14.

by the legislature.[63] Three days later, on September 4, the cabinet agreed to this procedure, and a bill was sent to the Reichsrat on the same day.[64] When on the following day the peak associations appeared at the Finance Ministry, they were presented with a *fait accompli.* There was nothing to be negotiated, since the government had already made its decision. Surprisingly, though, their response was relatively mild. Assured by Reich Finance Minister Hilferding that the measure would be temporary, the organizational leaders had apparently reconciled themselves to the fact that a further defence for quarterly pay was pointless.[65] To be sure, they still regarded it as a violation of civil servants' protected rights and warned that civil servants should not be singled out as a group to bear a greater proportional share of the burdens of stabilization. More importantly, they remained suspicious that the attack against quarterly pay was only "the first round in a battle of overly powerful economic groups" against constitutionally-guaranteed well-earned rights.[66] Rumors of an impending personnel reduction scheme in the public service, effecting the *Beamtenschaft* as well as other public employees, were already circulating at this point. As had been predicted by the DBB at an earlier instance, the notorious *Beamtenabbau* would become the second round in a "battle against the *Beamtenschaft,*" during the stabilization crisis of 1923-24.[67]

The Politics of *Abbau*

In late August 1923, rumors of an impending sweeping reduction of personnel employed by the Reich government had begun to intensify.[68]

[63] Report on a meeting in the Reich Finance Ministry. September 1, 1923, *ibid.*, Bl. 5—6.

[64] *ARK. Kab. Stresemann*, p. 186.

[65] Reports on this meeting in *DB*, September 13, 1923, and in *ADBZ*, September 8, 1923. The latter paper gave indirect support to the Social Democratic Finance Minister Hilferding by pointing out that "civil servants experienced in trade union affairs" would refrain from "fruitless criticisms."

[66] Resolution of the DBB executive of September 4, 1923, printed by *DB*, September 13, 1923.

[67] From the very beginning of the struggle the DBB had charged that the issue of quarterly pay was being used to whip up public support for the *Beamtenabbau*, which was in the planning stage then. *DB*, August 30, 1923.

[68] On the quantitative dimension of the Abbau problem, see CAPTER ONE of this study, esp. pp. 53—58 above. The following discussion will be limited to the political and social aspects of the *Beamtenabbau*.

In view of the rigorous way in which the Stresemann government had handled the question of quarterly pay, civil servant organizations were becoming alarmed that a streamlining of public employment could lead to mass dismissals of civil servants in disregard of the protection provided by the principle of life-tenure, one of the most cherished "well-earned rights." Their worries were compounded by the fact that the preparations for a 'Personnel Reduction Law' *(Personalabbaugesetz)*, which were known to be underway in the Reich Finance Ministry, had been conducted with the utmost secrecy.[69] Repeatedly, the organizations had demanded to be informed and consulted in the matter. Since civil servants were an "equally interested party" in a future reduction of public personnel, the DBB wrote in a letter to the Finance Ministry, they should have the right "to know under which guiding principles and methods the *Abbau* will be conducted."[70] But for the time being, the government remained firmly committed to its policy of secrecy and non-consultation with the organizations on the *Abbau* question.

On August 23, the very same day the DBB had asked to be informed, Reich Finance Minister Hilferding submitted a first comprehensive proposal for a reduction-scheme to the Cabinet. It called for the forced retirement of civil servants above the age of sixty, and for the "temporary retiring of dispensable civil servants." Hilferding pointed out that the existing legal provisions were not sufficient to conduct a streamlining of the civil service, and he hinted that special legislation and the

[69] The initial preparations had already been made by the Cuno government as early as November 1922. The Ruhr Conflict and the increased importance of the *Beamtenschaft*'s goodwill and support had forced the government to suspend these initial plans temporarily, which were geared toward forced retirement and a hiring freeze. In June 1923, however, the Finance Ministry was put in charge of preparing a comprehensive draft for a Personnel Reduction Law. Interministerial preparatory work had already been done when the Stresemann government came into office in August 1923. While the *Beamtenabbau* certainly fit squarely into its stabilization policies, and was to become an important part of it, the Stresemann government did not invent the idea of the *Abbau*, and it is pointless to argue whether the Socialist Hilferding or the Centrist Luther should take the blame (or the laurels) for having originated it. On Hilferding, see C.-D. Krohn, *Helfferich contra Hilferding*..., in: *VSWG*, 62 (1975), pp. 62—92; on Luther's role, see K.-B. Netzband/H. P. Widmaier, *Währungs- und Finanzpolitik*..., pp. 120—131.

[70] DBB to Reich Finance Ministry and Ministry of the Interior, August 23, 1923, printed by *DB*, September 13, 1923. The DBB responded to a note published in the KPD's *Rote Fahne* that the Reich government was planning to dismiss more than 400,000 civil servants.

suspension of civil service laws would be necessary "to rid the administration of dispensable and obstructive [!] forces."[71]

As had been urged by Minister Hilferding, the matter was discussed by the full cabinet two weeks later. The finance minister reiterated his point that the matter was urgent and a *sine qua non* for the planned financial reform. The minister of interior, the Social Democrat Sollmann, raised objections, however, with regard to some of the specifics of the proposed measures, as well as on a more general level. He feared that proposed Reduction Law would produce a negative impact on the mood of the *Beamtenschaft* and thus on the general domestic situation. In view of these differences, the decision was deferred until such a time when an agreement between the two ministers could be reached.[72]

Since in the meantime speculations on the content of the draft proposal and the extent of the planned reduction measures had mushroomed in the press, civil servant organizations increased their pressure for a "meeting of clarification" with the chancellor.[73] On September 18, such a meeting took place, although it failed to produce as much clarification as the organizations had hoped for. Stresemann himself left the meeting after a few introductory remarks, leaving the further conduct of the talks to Finance Minister Hilferding. The organizations complained that thus far they had not been informed, much less been consulted, on an issue of such bearing for the fate of their members. Although they were subsequently informed by Hilferding about the main thrust of the planned *Abbau* measures, and reassured that the integrity and special rights of the civil service would, in the long run at least, not be impaired, the civil servant leaders were dissatisfied with the meagre results of the meeting, which was broken off somewhat abruptly by the finance minister.[74]

The Stresemann government's request for an "Enabling Law" to solve the economic problems Germany was facing in the fall of 1923

[71] Finance Ministry to State Secretary in the Reich Chancellery, August 23, 1923, ZStAP, RMdI, 2554, Bl. 31—37. The political connotations of the phase "obstructive forces," a hidden suggestion to retire conservative high officials, were duly noted by the state secretary, who underlined the word *hemmend* (obstructive) and put a questions-mark into the margins.

[72] Cabinet meeting, September 10, 1923, *ARK. Kab. Stresemann*, pp. 230—231.

[73] On September 4, 1923 the DBB had adopted a resolution on basic principles of economic policy and had sent it to the chancellor two days later, requesting a meeting. DBB to Reich Chancellor, September 6, 1923, BA, R 43I/2436, Bl. 85—86.

[74] Meeting with the civil servant peak associations, September 18, 1923, *ARK. Kab. Stresemann*, pp. 296—298.

increased the worries of civil servant leaders that the government was planning to infringe upon constitutionally guaranteed civil servant rights in its drive for financial reform. On October 9, one day after the proposed bill for an Enabling Law had reached the Reichstag, the DBB demanded that it be consulted before any decrees were passed under the emergency law that involved civil servant affairs.[75] In a rather belated response considering the urgency of the matter, and only after the bill had already passed the Reichstag and had been signed into law, the Reich Ministry of the Interior replied that the government was indeed willing and prepared to "deviate from constitutional rights" in implementing all measures it deemed necessary to improve the financial and economic situation of the Reich. Since a reduction of the size of the civil service was one option that had already been considered in the solving of the financial crisis of the state, application of the special powers provided by the Enabling Law was likely to happen, although the government would refrain from using its powers in a one-sided and indiscriminate way. He finally mentioned that the organizations would soon be called into the Finance Ministry, where they would be able to express their grievances more fully.[76]

This meeting had, in fact, already taken place, but as far as the organizations were concerned, it had not fulfilled its purpose. On October 15, the Finance Ministry had sent letters of invitation to the civil servant peak associations and the trade union federations for a discussion of the *Abbau* question in the ministry. To the organizations it must have appeared as if the government had finally suspended its policy of non-negotiation.[77] During a cabinet meeting two days later the new finance minister, Hans Luther, came under attack, though, for his willingness to negotiate with the civil servant interest organizations and the unions. Reich Labor Minister Brauns argued that it would be impossible to discuss a legislative proposal with interest organizations, while at the same time the parliament had been excluded from any further influence on the bill as a result of the Enabling Law. Brauns rejected the Finance Ministry's contention that negotiations with the organizations might lead to the political advantage of receiving the support of groups most affected by the emergency measures. He sug-

[75] DBB to Reich government, October 9, 1923, ZStAP, RMdI, 2554, Bl. 59—60.

[76] Reich Ministry of the Interior to DBB, October 22, 1923, *ibid.*, Bl. 63.

[77] Reich Ministry of Finance to organizations, October 15, 1923, ZStAP, Büro RP, 85, Bl. 21.

gested that the organizations should merely be informed of the general content of the planned measures, and articulate their wishes regarding these measures; it would be left to the government whether or not it was inclined to consider the organization's requests.[78]

This new style of "negotiation," which entailed a marked departure from the type of bargaining that had prevailed during the preceding years, was indeed followed through by representatives of the Finance Ministry in two meetings, held with the organizations on October 21 and 22, 1923. Organizational delegates were informed verbally about the plans of the government, but government negotiators refused to supply them with written materials, e. g. a draft of the proposed emergency decree which the organizations had still not been able to study. Left only with their own notes taken during the meeting, the organizations were given twenty-four hours to formulate a response and the meeting was adjourned.[79]

It is not surprising that when consultations were resumed on the following day, the style of negotiation employed by the government became a major point of criticism in itself. Speaking for all organizations present at the meeting, DBB Chairman Flügel claimed that the government had obviously tried to overrun the organizations in an attempt to block constructive criticisms and proposals that could have been made by them if they had had more time and better supporting materials. The further course of the meeting shows that the organizations had indeed been taken by surprise and, no doubt due to the shortness of time and the still-existing uncertainty about the exact extent of the *Abbau* measures, had been unable to formulate a joint rebuttal that would do justice to the common interest of *all* public employees, i. e. workers, salaried employees, and civil servants. In spite of their common objections to the *Abbau* as such — or at least as proposed by the government — speakers representing the three different employee groups were obviously eager to minimize the impact of the impending reduction measures, which they could not prevent, on their own group, if need be at the expense of another group. The civil servant speaker insisted that contractual employees would have to be

[78] Cabinet meeting, October 17, 1923, *ARK. Kab. Stresemann*, pp. 608—611. During this meeting the specifics of the *Abbau* were discussed as well, and an overall reduction of 25 percent was tentatively agreed upon.

[79] This and the following account is based on the notes taken by the RhB delegate at these meetings, which are contained in ZStAP, RhB, 1, Bl. 111—118.

dismissed first,[80] while the representative of the white-collar Afa-Bund charged that the greater employment security enjoyed by civil servants should not lead to a disproportional dismissal of contractual employees in government service. A joint resolution issued by the organizations after the talks had been broken off, because the government had refused to make any concessions at all, could not conceal the fact that serious internal differences had weakened, if not rendered impossible, an alliance of public employees across social lines.

The worries of the *Soziale Praxis* that a 'united battle front' *(gemeinsame Kampffront)* of civil servant organizations and labor unions might prevent the *Beamtenabbau* in a last-minute forceful push, were thus unfounded.[81] Rather, the major civil servant organizations and the labor unions made separate last-minute attempts to modify the forthcoming regulations in favor of their own constituents.[82] While these efforts reflected rather well the disintegration of the social alliance among public employee groups under the impact of stabilization policies, they failed to produce concrete results. On October 27, 1923 the Reich government issued the "Decree for the Reduction of Public Personnel" *(Personalabbauverordnung*—PAV).[83] The conflict over the implementation of the measures set by the emergency decree would become the second phase in the civil servants' struggle against the policy of *Abbau.* While the struggles in preparatory phase had led to a collapse of established bargaining practices in the public sector, and to a

[80] This idea had surfaced in the precedings weeks. In a petition to the Reich government the Association of Municipal Civil Servants had demanded in mid-September already that any dismissals of civil service personnel could only be undertaken if *contractual* employees were laid off first. *Rundschau für Kommunalbeamte,* October 10, 1923, reprints the petition. A more detailed discussion of the *Abbau* from the perspective of the *öffentliche Angestellte* is contained in A. Kunz, *Stand versus Klasse...,* in: *GG,* 8 (1922), pp. 65 ff.

[81] *SP,* November 11, 1923.

[82] Deputy Breunig (an ADGB functionary) to Reich Minister of the Interior Sollmann, October 25, 1923, ZStAP, RMdI, 2554, Bl. 91—93, requesting that the decision for lay-offs of workers and contractual employees not be made solely on the basis of bureaucratic evaluation, i. e. not be based on decisions made by civil servants as superiors of contractual workers. DBB circular of October 22, 1923, StAH, 122-4-102, informing members of the far-reaching infringement on well-earned rights and suggesting a last-minute campaign, which, among other things, should emphasize that contractual workers would have to be laid off before any civil servant could be dismissed.

[83] *Verordnung zur Herabminderung der Personalausgaben des Reichs (Personal-Abbau-Verordnung),* in: *RGBl.,* I, 1923, pp. 999—1010.

disintegration of the social alliance between public employee groups, the second phase was to lead to partial restoration of these negotiating practices, but also to a partial disintegration of the civil servant alliance.

The response of the three major civil servant peak associations to the problem of the *Beamtenabbau* had never been entirely uniform. In its inital stages, when the Social Democrat Hilferding had still been in office as finance minister, the Socialist ADB had viewed the trimming of the civil service as a "very real problem" which one had to face at a time of economic stabilization.[84] Later on, once Hilferding had left his post and was replaced by Luther, the ADB had stepped up its criticism of the planned measures, which it then tended to view as part of the general rollback of social policy conducted by the government at the insistence of business interests. To avert such a general rollback, of which the attack against the eight-hour day was the most consequential feature, the ADB proposed the integration of civil servants in common front of defence of all wage and salary earners, in order to wage a battle against all rollbacks undertaken by the government in the area of social and civil service policy.[85] After this attempt had failed because of the insurmountable differences that existed between the interests of civil servants and those of other public employees in the *Abbau* question, the ADB's attention shifted again to the more specific problems and grievances faced by the *Beamtenschaft.* The Socialist civil servant federation now proposed the establishing of a second "front of defence", comprised of the major civil servant peak associations.[86] In a letter sent to the other peak associations on October 25, i. e. shortly before the PAV was issued, the ADB proposed to undertake "joint action" against the menaces of *Abbau* and longer work-hours.

The other organizations had viewed the ADB's shifting attitude toward the *Abbau* with unconcealed hostility, because they suspected that organizational politics rather than the defence of civil servant interests were the main motives of the ADB's moves. They remained opposed to the idea of engaging in joint action, which would ostensibly imply a strike, or at least a strike threat, on the part of the *Beamtenschaft.* The two conservative organizations, the Federation of Higher Civil Servants (RhB) and the Christian Trade Union affiliated GDB, had rejected the idea of a *Kampffront* immediately when it became known

[84] *ADBZ,* September 9, 1923.
[85] *Ibid.,* October 13, 1923.
[86] *Ibid.,* November 3, 1923.

that the ADB was planning on a strike vote. The remaining two organizations, the DBB and the national-liberal RDB continued to negotiate with the ADB, but they insisted that the conduct of a strike vote within the *Beamtenschaft* was out of the question. As a consequence, the talks were broken off.[87] Moreover, the DBB informed the government about these talks and offered its services "to stem the tide against the radical tendencies within the *Beamtenschaft.*"[88] As a reward, so to speak, the DBB requested that its own proposals regarding the current situation of the *Beamtenschaft* be accepted as the basis of a meeting with the chancellor in the immediate future. In a message to the chancellor, Chairman Flügel suggested that a speedy acceptance of his proposals would be of great help in the DBB's attempt of putting together a working alliance *(Gemeinschaft)* of the civil servant associations, which under its own leadership would be committed to perform "positive work on a legal basis." Should a meeting with the Chancellor be arranged, he would let the Chancellery know in advance and confidentially about the main demands that would be raised by the organizations.

Whether the cooperation strategy proposed by the DBB, and the rapprochement between interest organization and the government would be of help in the civil servants' struggle against the vicissitudes of stabilization remains to be seen. At this juncture it may be viewed as a clear indication that after the failure of the "public employee alliance", the civil servant alliance had partially disintegrated as well.

Political Repercussions: Civil Servants and the "Inflation Elections" of May 1924

Thus far we have examined the struggles conducted by civil servant organizations in the critical phase in which stabilization was prepared and first implemented, i. e. in the autumn and winter of 1923. Seen from the perspective of the civil servants, it had been a defensive and ultimately losing battle against what was regarded as an attack on the economic and social survival of the *Beamtenschaft,* and on the continued existence of the career civil service, the *Berufsbeamtentum,* with

[87] *DBB Geschäftsbericht 1924,* pp. 12—13.

[88] Notation on a telephone conversation (with DBB Chairman Flügel), November 7, 1923, BA, R 43I/2612, Bl. 160, for this and the following.

its special rights and privileges.[89] The suspension of the quarterly pay mode in September 1923, the Personnel Reduction Decree of October 1923, and the not-so-golden "Goldmark Salaries" of December 1923 — not without some justification civil servants viewed these pay levels as "starvation salaries" *(Hungergehälter)* and as the final blow to their economic survival — these three events were the milestones in the civil servants unsuccessful struggle against what they tended to view as a disproportional share of the social burdens created by stabilization. Some of the social and organizational consequences of this losing battle have been discussed already, i. e. the final disintegration of those social alliances that had characterized the inflation years. With regard to civil servants, the disruption of the alliance with other public employee groups and the unions which represented them, i. e. the blue and white collar trade unions, must be viewed as one of the most significant consequences. Stabilization and the inter-group conflicts it created brought the final separation of the great majority of the civil servant movement, represented by the DBB, from the organized working class and from *Arbeitnehmer* politics.[90] If the joint struggle against inflation had brought civil servants, white-collar salaried employees, and blue-collar workers together in a kind of "Emergency Coalition," stabilization was to drive them apart again as each group began to view its own situation as most critical and tried to soften the impact of stabilization, if need be at the others' expense. The conflicts between civil servants and public contractual employees during the *Abbau* is an illustrative, albeit by no means the only example of this tendency of social segregation *(soziale Abgrenzung)*.[91] In the case of the *Beamtenschaft*, it was to lead to its complete social isolation in the struggles against the impact of economic depression and renewed financial stabilization some five years later.[92]

[89] This was stressed by DBB Chairman Flügel in an second meeting with Stresemann, which took place on November 14, 1923 (protocol in BA, R 43I/2612, Bl. 201—202). Concerning the career civil service, Flügel is reported to have said: „Das Berufsbeamtentum muß unter allen Umständen erhalten bleiben. Es seien Kräfte am Werk, die es in seinem jetzigen Inhalt zu unterhöhlen versuchten."

[90] This was articulated forcefully by Flügel at the DBB's first general meeting in the post-inflation period in 1924, where he said, „Die besondere Stellung der Beamten im Staate macht eine reine Arbeitnehmerpolitik unmöglich." *DBB Protocol 1924*, p. 12.

[91] A more exhaustive discussion of the tendencies toward social segregation and its long-range consequences is contained in A. Kunz, *Stand versus Klasse...*, in: *GG*, 8 (1982), pp. 80—86.

[92] For a probing analysis of the politics pursued by civil servant organizations during

It seems appropriate to end the discussion of civil servant interest politics during hyperinflation and stabilization with some observations on the political behavior of civil servants in these periods. The question needs to be raised whether the combined impact of hyperinflation and stabilization, and the dissatisfaction and embitterment against "being singled out" (in a negative sense) during stabilization found an expression in a political as well as a social reorientation of the *Beamtenschaft.*

That the onerous burdens placed on civil servants during stabilization might result in a renewed political radicalization of civil servants to the extreme right and left, was noted in several reports drawn up during the preparatory stages of the Personnel Reduction Decree, and voiced repeatedly by the minister of the interior during cabinet sessions in which the PAV was discussed. In a cabinet meeting on October 10, 1923, for example, the "civil service minister" had warned that the planned personnel reduction law would produce an immediate impact on the already deteriorating mood within the *Beamtenschaft.*[93] A report drawn up in the Interior Ministry on October 26, i. e. the day before the PAV was to come into effect, stressed that the parties of the extreme left and right had been "raking the fire" within the *Beamtenschaft* and were trying to gain mileage from the "course of austerity" placed upon civil servants by the stabilization policy. The report urged to watch current developments and the prevailing mood within the civil servant organizations with greater attention "so that the difficult domestic situation will not be made even more critical by battles ignited by the *Beamtenschaft.*"[94]

Whatever politically-motivated unrest might have already developed by then within the *Beamtenschaft,* it was not yet reflected by the politics and tactics of its organizations. In the days of the great political crises of late October and early November 1923, their support of the duly-elected, constitutional government was unwavering. On November 9, the day Hitler staged his abortive putsch in Munich, DBB Chairman Flügel informed the chancellor that his organization would protect the constitutional government with all means at its disposal.[95] A public

this period, see Hans Mommsen, *Staat und Bürokratie in der Ära Brüning,* in: *Tradition und Reform in der deutschen Politik. Gedenkschrift für Waldemar Besson,* Gotthard Jasper (ed.), Frankfurt 1976, pp. 81—137.

93 Cabinet meeting, October 10, 1923, *ARK. Kab. Stresemann,* p. 230.

94 Report dated October 26, 1923, in ZStAP, RMdI, 2325, Bl. 149—150.

95 Notation on a telephone conversation, November 9, 1923, BA, R 43I/2650, Bl. 56.

proclamation in support of the government was issued by the DBB on the following day.[96] It is characteristic of the approach of the interest organization that it made its support quasi-dependent on the goodwill of the government to listen to *its* complaints: Flügel urged the chancellor to agree to the long-overdue meeting with the organizations as soon as the political situation had improved.[97]

Even after the overall political and economic situation had improved with the final stabilization of the currency in December 1923, and a new government under the chancellorship of the Centrist Wilhelm Marx had taken office to oversee the continuation of the stabilization effort, complaints voiced by civil servant organizations increased that the burdens of stabilization carried by their constituents were disproportionally great.[98] In response to the government's persistent refusal to decrease the social burdens carried by the civil servants, particularly its categoric refusal to soften the impact of the detested *Beamtenabbau*, which was running in full gear by then, the organizations brought partisan politics into play. "We are convinced that the *Beamtenschaft* will furnish the receipt for the way it has been treated in the forthcoming elections," the DBB warned in late February of 1924.[99] That these warnings were not just rhetoric, the political parties supporting Marx's coalition cabinet and the other political and social forces in Germany were to learn after the so-called "inflation elections" of May 1924 had been held, which once again brought a noticeable electoral shift to the political right.

As had been the case in the 1920 Reichstag elections, the May elections of 1924 led to shifts in electoral support from the liberal parties of the center to the conservative and radical parties of the right, and from the moderate to the extreme left of the political spectrum. Once again, moreover, civil servants became an important target group for the appeals of both radical wings. During the acrimonious election campaign that was conducted in the spring of 1924, the civil servant

[96] *DBB Geschäftsbericht 1924*, pp. 32—33, where the proclamation is reprinted in full length.

[97] Notation ... (see note 95 above). The meeting took place on November 14, 1923.

[98] This was pointed out in the first petitions, which DBB and ADB sent to the newly installed Marx government on January 15 and January 18, 1924, respectively (BA, R 43I/2613, Bl. 353—359, 368—369). A meeting with the new chancellor, which took place on February 19, 1924, failed to produce a clear result on the most pressing problems (*ARK. Kab. Marx I*, pp. 381—383).

[99] DBB to Reich government, February 26, 1924, BA, R 43I/2613, Bl. 105—106.

press warned that "the attack of all groups against the *Beamtenschaft*" would be a major factor in the civil servant vote.[100] Still, the organizations did not support attempts to form a special 'Civil Service Party' *(Beamtenpartei)* which were being seriously discussed in some circles of the civil servant movement.[101] The fact that this option was discussed at all, though, confirms the impression that stabilization led to a disenchantment of major social groups most affected by it with the established political parties, and thus to the rise of special interest parties and to the partial dissolution of the Weimar party system.[102] To civil servants, too, it seemed plausible that the political representation of civil servant interests should be taken away from parties which had only betrayed these interests during the stabilization crisis.

If the creation of a *Beamtenpartei* did not take place, at least not on a nationwide basis, this was to no small measure due to the opposition of the major civil servant associations to such a step. What did take place, however, was an obvious voting endorsement of those political parties which were least implicated with the politics of *Abbau,* i. e. those who had not participated in the Great Coalition of 1923. The DNVP made the "attack civil servant rights," the *Abbau,* and the insufficient "goldmark salaries," principle issues in its electoral campaign, and since the DNVP did not have to assume political responsibility for any of these measures, it was relatively easy for this party to profit from a protest vote on the part of the civil servant.[103] The position of the DVP, the party which in 1920 had profited from a shift in the civil servant vote, was much more difficult. Its appeals to civil servant constituents that the DVP had helped to put the currency back into order, and that it had "resurrected the authority of the state,"[104] may well have been true, but they hardly fulfilled the desired function of garnering the vote of the civil servant who had only suffered as a result of the state's new

[100] *Zur Reichstagswahl,* in: *DB,* April 1, 1924.

[101] *Ibid.,* where these attempts are discussed in some length.

[102] On this see Larry E. Jones, *Inflation, Revaluation, and the Crisis of Middle-Class Politics,* in: *CEH,* 12 (1979), pp. 143—168.

[103] Many campaign flyers issued by the DNVP, and addressed to civil servants play on this theme. One pamphlet, for example, ends with the following appeal: „Beamte, wollt Ihr Eure wohlerworbenen Rechte schützen, wollt Ihr die Aufhebung der rigorosen Bestimmungen der Personalabbauverordnung, wollt Ihr Abrechnung halten mit den Parteien, dann wählt am 4. Mai: Deutschnational!" (GStA, XII, HA IV, no. 186, contains this flyer and other DNVP election materials).

[104] These claims were made in DVP campaign materials, contained in: *Ibid.,* no. 167.

authority. Both liberal parties, DVP and DDP, were now being forced to conduct a defensive battle, and while civil servants had lost their struggle in 1923, the two liberal parties lost theirs in May of 1924.[105] In much greater numbers than before civil servants cast their ballots for the one bourgeois party untainted by stabilization politics: for the DNVP, or for the new political force on the extreme right, the Völkisch Bloc.[106] Lower-grade *Unterbeamte*, moreover, may well have thrown their support to the radical left-wing party, the KDP, which in the spring of 1924 had embarked on a major offensive to increase its support within the lower-middle classes. To reach this goal, the KDP began to place great attention to mobilizing support within the lower ranks of the *Beamtenschaft*, a group which according to a KPD pamphlet issued in early 1924, had been "proletarianized" and thus radicalized to "a greater degree than ever before."[107]

The outcome of the May Elections showed that civil servants had indeed withdrawn their support from the political center — not to mention the moderate left of Weimar's political spectrum. In terms of voting behavior, therefore, hyperinflation and stabilization moved civil servants back to the conservative side of German politics, a side which the *Beamtenschaft* had (all too briefly) abandoned as a consequence of war, revolution, and — initially at least — postwar inflation.

[105] Larry Jones' forthcoming study will contain a thorough treatment of these events from the perspective of the two liberal parties.

[106] This is, of course, an inference based on the drop of civil service support experienced by the other two parties which depended heavily on civil service vote, i. e. the DDP and the DVP. A similar evaluation of the shifting support of the civil service vote prevailed in the contemporary civil servant press. See *DB*, May 20, 1924 where the turn to the right is brought into connection with the conduct of civil service policy during the *Abbau.* On the 1924 elections, see Th. Childers, *Inflation, Stabilization, and Political Realignment* ..., in: G. D. Feldman et al. (eds.), *The German Inflation* ..., who shows that this trend continues beyond 1924.

[107] See a pamphlet entitled *Die Kommunistische Partei Deutschlands und die Beamten*, published in March 1924, copy in GStA, Rep. 90, 2225, Bl. 232—237, which contains specific instructions on how the mobilization of civil service support was to be done.

EPILOGUE

Civil Servants, Economic Crisis, and Weimar Democracy

The stabilization crisis of 1923-24 brought to a close a decade of sustained socioeconomic and political upheaval in Germany. The combined impact of war, political revolution, and economic inflation had left deep imprints on German society. Its political and social institutions, its social groups and their organizations, and lastly its economic system had undergone total — or at least partial — transformation. To some degree it may be said that German society emerged as a different, perhaps a more modern society from the ravages of war, revolution, and inflation. Its traditional structures and perceptions of social and political order had been shattered profoundly as a consequence of a decade of protracted economic inflation, and social and political upheaval. Some of its institutions had been transformed, while others had at least been partially reformed. The civil service may safely be included within the latter category. To contemporary observers, especially those outside of Germany, the Weimar Republic presented itself as a surprisingly advanced and innovative state, particularly in the areas of labor relations and social policy.[1]

It has been one of the aims of this study to show that the reform of labor relations in the public sector — and within the civil service in particular — played an important part in this process of transformation and partial modernization of German society in the early 1920s. Interest politics, collective bargaining procedures, and other forms of conflict resolution, all of which had been virtually non-existent in the authoritarian and paternalistically structured relationship between civil servants and the government as employer in the prewar German Empire, had been firmly established only ten years later in the postwar

[1] See, e. g., Nathan Reich, *Labour Relations in Republican Germany. An Experiment in Industrial Democracy*, New York 1938.

republican setting. By introducing and accepting these essential, and in some sense "modern" principles of labor relations in the public as well as in the private sectors of the economy, Weimar Germany's social system developed some remarkably modern characteristics of an advanced industrial society. Due to a certain infatuation with the residues of the *traditional* elements persisting in Weimar society, historians have until recently tended to overlook these more innovative and modern trends.[2]

This study has tried to show that the German public service participated in a process of social change, and that the contingencies of war and inflation acted as a catalyst for implementing these changes. While the war and the hardships created by wartime inflation provided the important initial stimulus by setting in motion a process of interest articulation, organization, and interest-group formation among German civil servants, the Revolution of 1918/19 brought this process to a close and, at the same time, prepared the ground for the civil servants' forceful entry into interest politics. But it was the postwar inflation and the contingencies of salary policy in a prolonged period of steadily rising prices which led to the introduction and refinement of negotiation procedures in the German public sector in general, and in the civil service in particular. That the adaptation of collective agreements, negotiating practices, and conflict solution was, in part, a painful experience, accompanied as it were by social tensions, sharp confrontations with public employers, and even militant forms of conflict solution has also been shown in the preceding chapters. Despite these conflicts and tensions, however, and despite some temporary setbacks, as, for example, during the stabilization crisis of 1923-24 and, again, during the period of "deflation politics" in the closing years of the Weimar Republic, the patterns of collective bargaining established during the inflation years left a lasting imprint on German society. Even after their forced suspension during the Nazi period, they would reemerge after 1945 to become an integral part of the socio-political

[2] This point has been brought up again in a recent exchange on the role of industrial relations in the Weimar Republic between Hagen Schulze and Gerald Feldman. In a rejoinder to Feldman's scathing critique of his book *Weimar. Deutschland 1917—1933*, Berlin 1982, Hagen Schulze has charged that Feldman misinterprets the history of the Weimar Republic as an episode in the history of industrial relations. See the review by Feldman in *GG*, 9 (1983), pp. 462—470 and the response by Schulze in: *Ibid.*, 10 (1984), pp. 142—146, p. 145.

structure of the West German Federal Republic.[3] The historical roots of collective bargaining and of negotiating patterns and practices in the German public sector, including the peculiar division into a 'civil service' and a 'public employee' branch, are thus to be found in the development of public sector wage policy and civil service salary policy in the First World War and the postwar periods of inflation and stabilization.

If in the area of public sector labor relation lines of continuity can be drawn from the inflation years to present-day Germany, the impact of the inflation on the political behavior of civil servants in the interwar years is of more relevance to the immediate history of the parliamentary democracy of Weimar. As the foregoing study has attempted to show, it was the *termination* of the inflation rather than the inflation itself which prompted some important social-political rearrangements among German social groups. These rearrangements would, in the long run, produce an impact on the political development of the Weimar Republic in the post-inflation period. In taking a necessarily brief look at some post-1924 developments within the German *Beamtenschaft* and their social movement, the long-range impact of inflation and stabilization on the functioning or dysfunctioning of Weimar democracy in periods of relative stability (1924—1928/29) and economic depression (1929—1933) will move into perspective.

Most importantly, the post-inflation period witnessed a change in the system of social alliances in the public sector which had been forged during the inflation years and, in spite of all the pressures placed on public finances, had been generally supportive of the Weimar state. During the stabilization crisis of 1923-24, the interest alliance between civil servants and other public employee groups, an alliance which had contributed to the economic survival of civil servants and other dependently employed groups during the inflation years, disintegrated and was replaced by a course of social segregation, even isolation, pursued by the majority of civil servants and their dominant organization, the DBB. Since the interest coalitions of the inflation period had

[3] On public sector wage policy and civil servant interest politics in the Federal Republic, see Berndt Keller, *Arbeitsbeziehungen im öffentlichen Dienst. Tarifpolitik der Gewerkschaften und Interessenpolitik der Beamtenverbände*, Frankfurt-New York 1983, and idem, *Public Sector Labor Relations in West Germany*, in: *Industrial Relations*, 19 (1978), pp. 18—31. See also the older study by William McPherson, *Public Employee Relations in West Germany*, Ann Arbor 1971.

also been an indication of a more general social and political reorientation of the *Beamtenschaft* to the liberal center, if not to the moderate left-wing of Weimar's political spectrum, the departure from *Arbeitnehmer* policy and from cooperation with the Socialist trade unions also reflected a return to the political right.

The interest struggles connected with the Personnel Reduction Law of 1923-24 were perhaps the decisive step in the civil servants' transition — if not regression — from a broadly-based employee policy *(Arbeitnehmerpolitik)* to a more narrowly defined civil service politic *(Beamtenpolitik).* The inter-group conflicts sparked by the embattled personnel cuts in the public service sector reinforced a latent tendency toward social segregation within the majority of the *Beamtenschaft,* a tendency which war, revolution, and inflation had suspended temporarily in favor of a broader alliance between all employee groups. Already in the wake of the February Strike of 1922, but definitely in connection with the "defensive battle" against stabilization policies in late 1923 and early 1924, the specific interests of civil servants and the protection of traditional social rights and privileges — the coveted "well-earned rights" — moved into the foreground of civil servant interest politics once again. The departure from the common interests of all *Arbeitnehmer* and the renewed insistence on *Beamtenprivilegien* then became the adopted policy of the DBB in the organizational as well as in the social-political spheres. The argument still advanced by the leaders of the trade-union oriented Socialist ADB that only an alliance of *all* public employees would, in the long run, guarantee the civil servants' social position and their material well-being,[4] increasingly lost support within the vast majority of the *Beamtenschaft.*

The decline of the ADB itself can be used to demonstrate the civil servants' disenchantment with trade-union ideology. As TABLE 26 shows, the membership of the Socialist civil servant peak association was halfed between 1924 and 1926 — a reflection of the demise of its most important branch organization, the Reichsgewerkschaft — and continued on its downward path. With a membership of less than 170,000 in 1928, the ADB had by then shrunk in size to a mere splinter organization, while at the same time the DBB had been able to reintegrate most the *Beamtenschaft* under its banner by amalgamating

[4] Cf. Allgemeiner Deutscher Beamtenbund, *Entwurf eines Beamtengesetzes,* Berlin 1926, where civil service law is brought into close connection with general labor law and thus made into a target of general trade union policy.

TABLE 26

Membership in Civil Servant Peak Associations, 1919—1933 (In Thousands)

	1919	1920	1922	1924	1926	1928	1930	1932
DBB	1000	1060	774	845	903	1058	1069	993
ADB	—	—	350	354	178	166	177	171
GDB	—	200	150	200	150	—	—	—
RDB	—	—	30	65	54	32	—	—
RhB	40	55	75	101	100	100	100	100

DBB = Deutscher Beamtenbund. Non-affiliated.
ADB = Allgemeiner Deutscher Beamtenbund. Affiliated with the Socialist Trade Unions (ADGB).
GDB = Gesamtverband Deutscher Beamtenverbände. Affiliated with the Catholic Trade Unions (DGB). Figures are estimate of civil-servant membership. Merges with DBB in 1926.
RDB = Ring Deutscher Beamtenverbände. Affiliated with the national-liberal Hirsch Duncker Unions. Merges with DBB in 1928.
RhB = Reichsbund der höheren Beamten. Non affiliated, organized higher civil servants only.

Source: As in TABLE 23.

with the civil service section of the Catholic trade unions. The ADB's decline and the DBB's success show that the model of the politically non-affilated occupational association *(Berufsverband)* rather than the trade-union oriented civil service union *(Beamtengewerkschaft)* appealed to the vastly greater proportion of the *Beamtenschaft* as the guarantor to recapture, strengthen, and defend their social rights and privileges and thus their special position in German society. While these tendencies certainly ran counter those modernizing trends discussed above, it must be remembered that the DBB, too, employed a modern, in some sense trade union-type of interest politics — albeit with the important exception of an outright commitment to the strike principle.[5]

[5] Although a veiled strike clause was retained in the new statutes adopted by the DBB in 1928 („Der Bund wird zur Erreichung seiner Ziele alle gewerkschaftlichen Mittel anwenden". Quoted in *DBB Ursprung, Weg, Ziel,* p. II/121), the DBB, unlike its rival, the ADB, never again seriously considered going ahead with a strike vote among its members.

It was perhaps a logical parallel development to the social and organizational reorientation of civil servants and of the civil servant movement in the post-1924 period that civil servants tended to support those political forces which from then on claimed to defend civil servant rights most prominantly and vigorously. As has been shown, the right-wing nationalist DNVP was able to profit from a civil-servant protest vote in 1924. Only six years later, in 1930, another "protest party" would be able to draw heavily from civil service support by reinvoking the "inflation (or rather stabilization) trauma" within the *Beamtenschaft.* Faced once again with the prospects of having to carry a disproportionate burden as a result of financial austerity measures implemented in an economic crisis, civil servants as voters gave their support to the one party which had not been "tarnished" with the preparation, formulation, and implementation of a policy of pay cuts and special taxation: Hitler's NSDAP.[6] It was a most accurate description of this trend, and an ominous prophecy indeed, when ADB Chairman Albert Falkenberg warned in early 1931 that civil servants were being driven into the arms of the National Socialists as a consequence of the civil service policies pursued by the Brüning government. The end result would be most damaging to the survival of Weimar Democracy, he predicted, because civil servants would "stand at attention at the open doors of their offices to welcome the dictator" if only he promised to look after their affairs.[7] The events after January 30, 1933 would confirm Falkenberg's dire predictions in many respects.

It would be misleading, however, to infer the politics pursued by the main civil servant interest organizations in the closing years of the Weimar Republic from the voting behavior and the political activities of the civil servants as a political target group. The ADB's fierce opposition to the Nazi movement needs no further explanation, but

[6] On the voting behavior of civil servants in this period, see the article by Thomas Childers already cited above, and the recent, book-length study by the same author, *The Nazi Voter: The Social Foundations of Fascism in Germany, 1919—1933,* Chapel Hill 1983. See also Jane Caplan, *Civil Service Support for National Socialism: An Evaluation,* in: Gerhard Hirschfeld/Lothar Kettenacker (eds.), *The 'Führer State': Myth and Reality,* Stuttgart 1981, pp. 167—193.

[7] Undated manuscript, written by Falkenberg and entitled „Gegen die faschistische Durchsetzung der Beamtenschaft," to be found in ZStAP, RMdI, PA 267, Bl. 30—33. This was most likely the draft for a speech which Falkenberg delivered at a meeting of the ADB Council on March 12, 1931. See the report on the public portion of this meeting in *ADBZ,* March 17, 1931.

even the top leadership of the DBB, while certainly more susceptible to right-wing political currents, remained relatively unaffected by Nazi infiltration. At the DBB's general meeting in 1932, for example, an attempted takeover by a Nazi oriented branch organization was rather easily defeated.[8] The fact that there was such an attempt in the first place, however, may be interpreted as an indication that the DBB leadership was confronted with increased right-wing radicalization of *some* of its member associations as well as among the rank-and-file membership.

The latter can be substantiated by looking once again at the election results to the representative civil service staff boards in the Reichsbahn administration. TABLE 27 presents a long run of the election results to

TABLE 27

*Elections to Representative Staff Boards in the Reichsbahn Administration, 1921—1932**

Electoral Slate	1921	1924	1926	1930	1932
Free Trade Unions (ADGB/ADB)	61 000	132 000	67 000	61 500	43 000
Christian Trade Unions (DGB/GDB)	74 000	60 000	83 000	177 000	62 000
Deutscher Beamtenbund (DBB)	231 000	75 000	95 000		79 000
Railroad Engineers (GDL)	—	—	52 000	54 000	47 000
National Socialists (ANRB)	—	—	—	11 000	43 000

* Returns are for the Central Civil Servant Advisory Board (Hauptbeamtenbeirat) at the Ministry of Transportation.

Sources: 1921, 1924: *Reichsverkehrsblatt,* Ausgabe A (Eisenbahnen), 1921, 1924.
1926: *ADBZ,* October 12, 1926.
1930: *Beamten-Jahrbuch,* 1931, p. 256.

[8] Deutscher Beamtenbund, *Bericht über die Verhandlungen des 8. Bundestages,* Berlin 1932, pp. 54—59, 83—87.

the main civil service advisory board at the Ministry of Transportation, covering the years 1921 to 1932. Two trends become readily apparent. For one, the figures again reveal the drastic decline of the Socialist appeal to civil servants, with the Free Trade Union slate dropping from 132,000 in 1924 to 43,000 in 1932. The DBB/GDB slate reaches a stable level of some 177,000 votes in 1926-1930, but then declines by about 30,000 votes in the 1932 elections. The losses suffered by the politically "non-affilated" organizations (i. e. DBB, GDB and the railroad engineer's union) roughly correspond to the gains scored by a newcomer to scene: a National Socialist slate, supported by the Arbeitsgemeinschaft Nationaler Reichsbahnbeamter (ANRB), an organization which had ties to the NSDAP.[9] The fact that this organization was able to increase its vote from 11,000 in 1930 to 43,000 in 1932 shows that National Socialism had indeed made inroads among railroad civil servants by 1932.

Even if this example covers only one branch of the German civil service — albeit an important one in quantitative terms — it helps to demonstrate that during the economic and social crisis of 1930-32 civil servant protest would gravitate toward the radical right of the political spectrum, while in 1919-24 it had tended to be polarized between the radical left *and* the radical right which was then represented by the DNVP. Moreover, in 1930-32 civil servants would again turn their attention to the one party which had not become "tainted" with the responsibility for the conduct of civil service policy in times of economic crisis. While in 1924 the DNVP had profited from the civil servants' protest vote, in 1930 and 1932 it would be Hitler's NSDAP.

The partial radicalization of the rank and file was to no small measure a consequence of the DBB's failures in the realm of interest politics, especially in salary policy, in the preceding weeks and months. In a series of emergency decrees, the Brüning government had reduced civil servant salaries by nearly 25 percent between 1930 and 1932, and the

[9] There is some material on this organization and on its activities in the 1932 elections in BA, NS 22/261. The documents show that the ANRB was not fully recognized as a subsidiary of the NSDAP party organization, but that serious rivalries existed between the railroad organization and the general Nazi civil service section, headed by the Gauleiter of Hesse, Sprenger. It was typical of these internal tensions that Sprenger in October 1932 advised the party leadership that the ANRB should not have received the party's endorsement in the Reichsbahn elections, not least because National Socialists had appeared on other electoral slates. Hauptabteilung VII (Berufsbeamtentum) to Reichsorganisationsleitung, October 5, 1932, BA, NS 22/261, Bl. 46—47.

DBB had been forced to acquiesce to these measures rather helplessly.[10] It now appeared that social isolation had a price, too. As long as the DBB had been able to score spectacular successes like the Salary Reform of 1927, which had set civil servant salaries above prewar levels (in real terms) for the first time since 1918, the rationale for a course of social segregation on the part of the dominant civil servant organization seemed justified and plausible indeed. However, when in 1930 economic depression and a new financial crisis of the state threatened the withdrawal of gains just made in a period of relative economic stability, and when a new defensive battle seemed imminent, the DBB went on a somewhat frantic search for social allies.

In mid-1930 the DBB approached the Socialist trade unions in an effort to forge an alliance against the pay cuts planned by the Brüning government for the public sector. On June 26, 1930 an interesting and in many ways revealing meeting between DBB officials and trade union leaders took place at the ADGB headquarters in Berlin. In the course of this meeting, the DBB delegates formally proposed the reestablishing of an alliance between civil servants, salaried employees, and blue-collar workers in the public sector. The response of the unionists was mixed, however. Several union leaders reacted to the DBB's interest in an all-encompassing "front of defence" with unconcealed suspicion, or even with open hostility. They argued that only a stiff dose of opportunism had prompted the DBB to make its offer of cooperating with the trade unions. They were irritated further by the fact that DBB Chairman Flügel pledged to attach his organization to the "powerful alliance of all trade unions," but upon further queries refused to consider a more formal organizational pact with the unions. To some trade unionists, this seemed to confirm their conviction that civil servants had not yet learned their lessons; rather than solving *all* social, economic and political problems jointly with the organizations of workers and salaried employees, the DBB, they felt, was merely trying to gather support for the *specific* problems faced by civil servants, not least because it had come under extreme pressure of performance. Although at the end of the meeting a rather vaguely formulated "general understanding of

[10] Deutscher Beamtenbund, *Geschäftsbericht für die Zeit vom Oktober 1928 bis September 1930,* Berlin 1930, pp. 158—186, and idem, *Geschäftsbericht für die Zeit vom Oktober 1930 bis September 1932,* Berlin 1932, pp. 84—206, presents a discussion of the Brüning pay cuts from the DBB's perspective. See also H. Mommsen, *Staat und Bürokratie...,* in: G. Jasper (ed.), *Tradition und Reform...,* pp. 88ff.

future consultation and cooperation" was agreed upon, the overall course of the meeting showed that the "inflation alliance" of the early 1920's could not be restored at will.[11] The self-imposed social isolation of the DBB in the preceding years of relative stability may have added to the high level of mutual suspicion and distrust between the three employee groups in mid-1930.

The failure to draw the conclusions from the positive experiences of the inflation years, and the inability to reconstruct an alliance which had then helped in the struggle for economic survival, would weaken the position of civil servants and other public employees in their battle against the impact of deflation politics during years of economic depression in the early 1930's. More importantly, perhaps, it would also preclude the reconstruction of a *political* alliance of the different employee groups in defence of the Weimar Republic: While in March 1920, during the Kapp-Lüttwitz Putsch, civil servants had joined blue-collar workers and salaried employees in a decisive defeat of the most serious attack on the parliamentary democracy of Weimar in its formative years, they failed to do so, when in its closing years the survival of the state of Weimar, by then a republic besieged from all sides, would be at stake once again.

[11] Minute of a meeting on civil service matters, held in the ADGB Bundeshaus on June 26, 1930, Hiko Berlin, ADGB Restakten, NB 215, Bl. 10. The meeting had been arranged by the leading ADGB unionist Grassmann. Next to ADGB and DBB, delegates for the Afa-Bund and the Hirsch-Duncker unions participated in the meeting. Neither the ADB, nor the Christian trade unions had apparently been invited, or had declined to attend. The specific point of discussion was the policy to be employed to oppose the *Reichshilfe*, a special tax levy on civil servants and other government employees.

BIBLIOGRAPHY

Unpublished Sources

Bundesarchiv Koblenz (BA)

R 43I, Reichskanzlei

2551—2553	Beamtenangelegenheiten, Deutsches Beamtengesetz, 1919—1925
2559—2567	Besoldung der Beamten, 1919—1925
2574—2575	Einordnung der Beamten in die Besoldungsgruppen, 1919—1928
2576	Reichsbesoldungsgesetz, 1919—1926
2578—2580	Besoldung, Eingaben 1919—1930
2583—2585	Teuerungszulagen, 1919—1932
2600	Dienststrafrecht und Strafen, 1919—1925
2612—2614	Beamtenabbau, 1923—1931
2630—2633	Beamtenvertretungsrecht, 1919—1933
2634—2637	Wohlfahrtseinrichtungen, Urlaub
2640	Streikrecht der Beamten, 1919—1923
2642	Bestechungsunwesen, 1919—1930
2650	Beamtenorganisationen, 1923—1932
203—218	Ruhrbesetzung 1923, 1922—1933
990	Beamtenreferat, Reichsamt für Beamtenwesen, 1920
2023—2024	Interessenvertretung der Arbeitgeber und Arbeitnehmer, 1919—1933
2123	Streiks, Einzelfälle, 1920—1932
2124—2125	Eisenbahnerstreiks, 1921—1928

R2, Reichsfinanzministerium

24713	Durchführung der Personalabbauverordnung, 1924—1925
1306—1307	Personal-Abbau-Kommission
22589—90	Spitzenorganisationen der Beamten

R58, Reichssicherheitshauptamt

349	Allgemeiner Deutscher Beamtenbund

Nachlässe
David
Groener (Bundesarchiv/Militärarchiv Freiburg-BA/MA)
Koch-Weser
Saemisch
Südekum

Zentrales Staatsarchiv, Abt. I, Potsdam (ZStAP)

Reichsministerium (Reichsamt) des Innern (RMdI)

2165—2168	Reichsbeamtensachen (allgemeines), 1918—1926
2172	Staatsbürgerliche Rechte der Beamten, 1914—1925
2183	Stellung der Beamten zur Neuordnung des Reiches, 1918—1923
2185—2186	Streikrecht der Beamten, 1919—1925
2215—2217	Erlaß eines Reichsbeamtengesetzes, 1920—1926
2244	Neuregelung des Beamtenrechts, Anträge der Beamtenorganisationen, 1919—1925
2237	Die Pflichten der Beamten zum Schutz der Republik, 1922—1926
2324—2325	Petitionsrecht, Vereinigungsfreiheit, Beamtenvereine, 1913—1926
2554—2558	Beamtenabbaugesetz, 1923—1925
2568	Übersicht über die Beamtenvereine, 1919—1920
2593—2598	Besoldungsgesetz, 1919—1925
2599	Proteste zum Besoldungssperrgesetz, 1920—1925
2600	Besoldungsgesetz, Presseäußerungen, 1914—1925
2613—2615	Anträge der Beamten und Vereine zur Besoldungsreform, 1919—1925
2738—2740	Beamtenvereine, 1914—1925
2741	Beamtenvereine, Presseäußerungen, 1914—1925
2742	Bund der Festbesoldeten, Deutscher Beamtenbund, 1909—1925
2744	Beamtengewerkschaften, 1920—1921
2745	Beamten-Internationale, 1918—1920
PA 267	Falkenberg, Albert (Personalakte)

Reichsjustizministerium (RJM)

469	Streik- und Koalitionsrecht der Beamten, 1922—1925

Reichskommissar für die Überwachung der öffentlichen Ordnung (RköO)

453—454	Reichsgewerkschaft der Eisenbahner, 1922—1929
455	Deutscher Beamtenbund
457	Allgemeiner Deutscher Beamtenbund

Büro des Reichspräsidenten (Büro RP)

85—86	Personalabbau, 1923—1925
92—95	Einkommensverhältnisse der Beamten, 1919—1925
149	Beamtenvereine, 1919—1932

Reichstag (RT)

1951	Organisation von Beamten, Koalitions- und Streikrecht, 1914—1921

Reichsbund der höheren Beamten (RhB)

1—3	Beamtenabbau, 1923—1924
11	Verhandlungsfähigkeit der Beamtenverbände, 1920—1921
15—18	Gehaltskürzungen, 1930—1931
52—67	Besoldung, 1922—1923
70,74	Besoldung, 1924

73	Organisationsverhandlungen
86—86a	Besoldung, 1924
93—96	Schriftwechsel mit den Berufsverbänden, 1920—1933
102—103	dto.
110—111	dto.
120	Berufsverein höherer Verwaltungsbeamter, 1918—1922
193	Verbindung zu den politischen Parteien: DVP
194	Streikbeschluß des DBB 1920
195	Verbindung zu den politischen Parteien: DNVP
196	Verbindung zu den politischen Parteien: DDP
201	Verbindung zu den Gewerkschaften
245	Allgemeiner Schriftwechsel, 1922—1924
310	Organisationsangelegenheiten der Beamten, 1921
332	Verbindung zu den politischen Parteien
526	Wertbeständige Löhne und Gehälter, 1923
544	Zahl der Beamten, 1922—1923

Reichslandbund, Pressearchiv (RLB)

5605	Sozialdemokratische Beamte (Arbeiteraristokratie)
5614	Beamte und SPD, 1922—1931
5616	Streikrecht der Beamten, 1922—1925
5617	Beamte und USPD, 1922

Nachlaß Willy Steinkopf

Geheimes Staatsarchiv, Preußischer Kulturbesitz, Berlin-Dahlem (GStA)

I. HA, Rep. 90, Staatsministerium

470—472	Beamtenvertretungen, 1908—1933
473	Eingaben bezüglich Beamtenvertretungen, 1918—1931
474	Beamtenvertretungen beim Staatsministerium, 1918—1933
475	Beamtenräte bei den Behörden, 1919—1920
478	Beteiligung der Beamten an politisch rechts gerichteten Organisationen, 1924—1930
631	Streikrecht der Beamten, 1919—1926
690—692	Normalbesoldung der Reichsbeamten, 1914—1920
731	dto., 1922—1927
739—744	Personalabbau, 1921—1931
806—809	Kriegsteuerungsbeihilfen, 1915—1923
2324—2326	Politisches Verhalten der Beamten, 1900—1936

I. HA, Rep. 84a, Justizministerium

2718—2724	Beamtenvereine, 1916—1934
3144—3147	Petitions- und Vereinsrecht der Beamten, 1909—1934

XIV. HA, Rep. 180, Regierung Danzig

16883—87	Beamtenrat Danzig
17736	dto.

XII. HA, IV, Flugblätter und Plakate

47—213	Politische Parteien
263	Beamtenorganisationen
266	dto.

Politisches Archiv des Auswärtigen Amtes, Bonn (PA AA)

RM 17

Hauptstaatsarchiv Düsseldorf (HStAD)

Regierung Düsseldorf (Reg. Düss.)

15035—37	Lage im besetzten Gebiet, 1920—1922
15537	Allgemeiner Beamtenbund, 1922
15594	Deutscher Beamtenbund, 1920—1922
15617—18	Eisenbahnerstreik, 1921—1922
15683	Kommunistische Bewegung in der Beamtenschaft, 1922
15717	Nationaler Beamtenbund
15761	Reichsgewerkschaft der Post- und Telegraphen-Beamten, 1921
15762	Reichsgewerkschaft deutscher Eisenbahnbeamten, 1921
15864	Beamtenbewegung
16870	Politische und wirtschaftliche Lageberichte, 1923—1926
15972—73	Politische Agenten-Nachrichten, 1919—1921
16891—92	Eisenbahnerstreik, 1919—1922

Generallandesarchiv Karlsruhe (GLAK)

Abt. 233, Staatsministerium

3420	Beamtenvereine, Beamtenkammer, Beamtenausschüsse, 1897—1923
3478—79	Teuerungszulagen, 1918—1921
3516	Besoldungssperrgesetz
3519	Anpassung der Beamtengehälter an die wirtschaftliche Entwicklung, 1922—1923
3614	Verwendung weiblicher Angestellter
23973	Einwirkung des Krieges auf die Anstellung im öffentlichen Dienst, 1917—1919
23998	Beteiligung der Beamten an Streiks
24012	Unterstützung für abgebaute Beamte
24060	Beamtenkammern und Ausschüsse, 1919—1933
24063	Neuordnung des Beamtenwesens (Beamtenwünsche), 1917—1933
24211—15	Besoldung, 1918—1943
24222	Wirtschaftliche Verhältnisse und Besoldung, 1919—1931
24255—57	Teuerungszulagen, 1907—1925
26294	Beamtenabbau
26320—21	Teuerungszulagen, 1922—1937

Abt. 456, VI. Armeekorps

EV 8 Bd. 70 Zusammenstellung der Monatsberichte der stellvertretenden Generalkommandos, 1916—1917

Staatsarchiv Hamburg (StAH)

122—4 Beamtenrat Hamburg, 1918—1933

Historisches Archiv der Stadt Köln

Nachlaß Wilhelm Marx

Historische Kommission zu Berlin, (West) Berlin (HIKO)

ADGB Restakten

Published Sources

Document Editions and Official Publications

Akten der Reichskanzlei. Weimarer Republik, Das Kabinett Scheidemann. 13. Februar bis 20. Juni 1919, ed. Hagen Schulze, Boppard 1971.

Das Kabinett Bauer. 21. Juni 1919 bis 27. März 1920, ed. Anton Golecki, Boppard 1980.

Das Kabinett Müller I. 27. März 1920 bis 21. Juni 1920, ed. Martin Vogt, Boppard 1971.

Das Kabinett Fehrenbach. 25. Juni 1920 bis 4. Mai 1921, ed. Peter Wulf, Boppard 1972.

Die Kabinette Wirth I und II. 10. Mai 1921 bis 26. Oktober 1921. 26. Oktober 1921 bis 22. November 1922, ed. Ingrid Schulze-Bidlingmaier, 2 vols., Boppard 1973.

Das Kabinett Cuno. 22. November 1922 bis 12. August 1923, ed. Karl Heinz Harbeck, Boppard 1968.

Die Kabinette Stresemann I und II. 13. August 1923 bis 6. Oktober 1923. 6. Oktober 1923 bis 30. November 1923, ed. Karl Dietrich Erdmann, Martin Vogt, 2 vols., Boppard 1978.

Die Kabinette Marx I und II. 30. November 1923 bis 3. Juni 1924. 3. Juni 1924 bis 15. Januar 1925, ed. Günther Abramowski, 2 vols., Boppard 1973.

Denkschrift über die Entwicklung der Besoldung der Reichsbeamten von 1897 bis Dezember 1924, in: *Reichsbesoldungsblatt,* 4 (1925), pp. 11—50.

Deutsche Sozialpolitik 1918—1928. Erinnerungsschrift des Reichsarbeitsministeriums, Berlin 1929.

Material for a Study of Germany's Economy, Currency and Finance. By Order of the German Government, Berlin 1924.

Reichsarbeitsblatt, Sonderhefte, Berlin 1909 ff.

Reichsgesetzblatt, 1914 ff.

Reichsbesoldungsblatt, 1922 ff.

Reichsverkehrsblatt, Ausgabe A: *Eisenbahnen,* 1920 ff.

Statistik des Deutschen Reichs, Berlin 1919 ff.

Statistisches Jahrbuch für das Deutsche Reich, 1914 ff.

Statistisches Reichsamt, *Deutschlands Wirtschaft, Währung und Finanzen,* Berlin 1924.

Statistisches Reichsamt, *Germany's Economic and Financial Situation: An Exhibit of After-effects of the World War*, Berlin 1923.

Statistisches Reichsamt, *Deutsche Wirtschaftskunde. Ein Abriß der deutschen Reichsstatistik*, Berlin 1933.

Statistisches Reichsamt, *Der Personalstand der öffentlichen Verwaltung im Deutschen Reich am 31. März 1927*, in: *Wirtschaft und Statistik*, 9 (1929), Sonderbeilage.

Statistisches Reichsamt, *Personalstand der öffentlichen Verwaltung im Deutschen Reich am 31. März 1928 und 31. März 1927. Ergebnisse der Reichsfinanzstatistik* (= Einzelschriften zur Statistik des Deutschen Reichs, no. 18), Berlin 1931.

Statistisches Reichsamt, *Die deutsche Finanzwirtschaft vor und nach dem Kriege* (= Einzelschriften zur Statistik des Deutschen Reichs, no. 14), Berlin 1930.

Statistisches Reichsamt, *Das deutsche Volkseinkommen vor und nach dem Kriege* (= Einzelschriften zur Statistik des Deutschen Reichs, no. 24), Berlin 1932.

Statistisches Reichsamt, *Personalstand und Personalausgaben der öffentlichen Verwaltung im Deutschen Reich* (= Einzelschriften zur Statistik des Deutschen Reichs, no. 26), Berlin 1933.

Verhandlungen des Reichstags. Stenographische Berichte und Anlagen. I. Wahlperiode 1920 bis 1924, Berlin 1920 ff.

Verhandlungen der Verfassunggebenden Deutschen Nationalversammlung. Stenographische Berichte und Anlagen, vols. 1—18, Berlin 1919 ff.

Wirtschaft und Statistik, 1921 ff.

Zahlen zur Geldentwertung, in: *Wirtschaft und Statistik*, Sonderheft 1, Berlin 1925.

Newspapers and Periodicals

Allgemeine Deutsche Beamtenzeitung, 1922—1924.

Archiv für Sozialwissenschaft und Sozialpolitik, 1910—1924.

Beamten-Jahrbuch. Vierteljahrsschrift für die gesamte Beamtenbewegung, 1914—1920.

Berliner Tageblatt, 1921—1922.

DBB-Korrespondenz, 1921.

Der Beamte. Vierteljahreshefte für Beamtenrecht und Beamtenpolitik, 1914—1924.

Der freie Beamte. Mitteilungsblatt der Zentralstelle für Beamtenagitation, 1920—1922.

Deutsche Allgemeine Zeitung, 1921—1922.

Deutsche Beamtenrundschau, 1914—1919.

Die Gemeinschaft/Der Beamtenbund, 1917—1924.

Die Freiheit, Berliner Organ der USPD, 1921—1922.

Germania, 1921—1922.

Gewerkschaftliche Beamtenzeitung, 1919—1923.

Korrespondenzblatt des Allgemeinen Deutschen Gewerkschaftsbundes, 1919—1922.

Rote Fahne, 1921—1922.

Rundschau für Gemeindebeamte, 1914—1919.

Rundschau für Kommunalbeamte, 1920—1924.

Soziale Praxis, 1914—1924.

Vorwärts, 1921—1922.

Zeitschrift des Bundes (Reichsbundes) der höheren Beamten, 1919—1924.

Protocols, Yearbooks, etc. of Civil Servant Associations and Trade Unions

Allgemeiner Deutscher Beamtenbund, *Protokoll der Gründungsversammlung des Allgemeinen Deutschen Beamtenbundes am 18. Juni 1922 in Leipzig*, Berlin n. d. (1922).

Allgemeiner Deutscher Beamtenbund, *Für die neue Beamtenbewegung. Tatsachenmaterial gegen den Deutschen Beamtenbund* (= Schriften des Allgemeinen Deutschen Beamtenbundes, no. 1), Berlin 1923.

Allgemeiner Deutscher Beamtenbund, *Um die Einheitsfront der Beamtenschaft und Arbeitnehmerschaft* (= Schriftensammlung des Allgemeinen Deutschen Beamtenbundes, no. 5), Berlin 1924.

Allgemeiner Deutscher Beamtenbund, *Geschäftsbericht des Allgemeinen Deutschen Beamtenbundes*, Berlin 1925.

Allgemeiner Deutscher Gewerkschaftsbund, *Beschlüsse der 1.—12. Sitzung des Ausschusses des Allgemeinen Deutschen Gewerkschaftsbundes. Auszug aus den ungedruckten Protokollen der Ausschußsitzungen vom Juli 1919 bis März 1921*, Berlin 1928.

Allgemeiner Deutscher Gewerkschaftsbund, *Ausschuß des Allgemeinen Deutschen Gewerkschaftsbundes, Protokolle der Sitzungen*, printed for internal use, Berlin 1921—1923.

Allgemeiner Deutscher Gewerkschaftsbund, *Protokoll der Verhandlungen des elften Kongresses der Gewerkschaften Deutschlands (1. Bundestag des Allgemeinen Deutschen Gewerkschaftsbundes) abgehalten in Leipzig vom 19. bis 24. Juni 1922*, Berlin 1922.

Allgemeiner Deutscher Gewerkschaftsbund, *Jahrbuch des Allgemeinen Deutschen Gewerkschaftsbundes 1922*, Berlin 1923.

Allgemeiner Deutscher Gewerkschaftsbund, *Handbuch der Deutschen Gewerkschaftskongresse (Kongresse des Allgemeinen Deutschen Gewerkschaftsbundes)*, ed. Salomon Schwarz, Berlin 1930.

Allgemeiner freier Angestelltenbund, *Protokoll vom 1. Gewerkschaftskongreß des Allgemeinen freien Angestelltenbundes in Düsseldorf am 2. und 3. Oktober 1921*, Berlin n. d. (1921).

Allgemeiner freier Angestelltenbund, *Angestelltenbewegung 1921—1925. Deutsche Wirtschaftsgeschichte, Sozialpolitik und Gewerkschaftsentwicklung aus bewegter Zeit*, Berlin 1925.

Deutscher Beamtenbund, *Bericht über die Hauptversammlung und die Verhandlungen des 1. Vertretertages am 11., 12. und 13. Mai im Lehrervereinshaus in Berlin*, n. p., n. d. (Berlin 1919).

Deutscher Beamtenbund, *Bericht über die Verhandlungen auf dem außerordentlichen Vertretertag am 26., 27. und 28. Mai 1920*, Berlin n. d. (1920).

Deutscher Beamtenbund, *Bericht über die Verhandlungen des 4. Bundestages des Deutschen Beamtenbundes*, Berlin 1924.

Deutscher Beamtenbund, *Geschäftsbericht des deutschen Beamtenbundes für die Zeit vom April 1922 bis September 1924*, Berlin 1924.

Deutscher Beamtenbund, *Geschäftsbericht des Deutschen Beamtenbundes für die Zeit vom September 1924 bis Oktober 1926*, Berlin 1926.

Deutscher Beamtenbund, *Die Besoldungsbewegung des Deutschen Beamtenbundes* (= Flugschriften des Deutschen Beamtenbundes, no. 4), Berlin 1921.

Deutscher Beamtenbund, *Stellungnahme des Deutschen Beamtenbundes zur Denkschrift des Reichsfinanzministers über die Besoldung der Reichsbeamten*, Berlin 1925.

Deutscher Eisenbahner Verband, *Berichte der Bezirksleiter und Protokoll der Verhandlungen der 1. Generalversammlung in Jena, 25.—31. Mai 1919*, Berlin 1919.

Deutscher Eisenbahner Verband, *Protokoll der Verhandlungen der außerordentlichen Generalversammlung in Dresden, 12.—18. September 1920*, Berlin 1920.

Deutscher Eisenbahner Verband, *Protokoll über die Verhandlungen der zweiten ordentlichen Generalversammlung in München 11.—16. September 1922*, Berlin 1922.

Deutscher Eisenbahner Verband, *Protokoll der Verhandlungen der dritten ordentlichen Generalversammlung des Deutschen Eisenbahner Verbandes, 21. bis 26. Juni 1925 in Köln. Protokoll der gemeinsamen Tagung des Deutschen Eisenbahner Verbandes und der Reichsgewerkschaft Deutscher Eisenbahnbeamten am 27. Juni 1925 in Köln*, Berlin 1925.

Gewerkschaftsbund Deutscher Eisenbahnbeamten, *Geschäftsbericht des Gewerkschaftsbundes Deutscher Eisenbahnbeamten für die Zeit vom 1. Juli 1919 bis zum 1. Juli 1920*, n. p. n. d. (Berlin 1920).

Internationales Handwörterbuch des Gewerkschaftswesens, 2 vols., Berlin 1932 f.

Published Literature

A) *Contemporary Books and Articles Cited**

Aufhäuser, Siegfried, *Weltkrieg und Angestelltenbewegung*, Berlin 1919.

Bälz, Karl, *Beamtenrecht und Familie. Ein Beitrag zur sozialen Frage* (= Der deutsche Krieg. Politische Flugschriften, vol. 89), Berlin 1917.

Barteld, A., *Die deutsche Beamtenbewegung*, in: Anton Erkelenz (ed.), *Zehn Jahre deutsche Republik*, Berlin 1928.

Bendix, Ludwig, *Das Streikrecht der Beamten*, Berlin 1922.

Bendix, Ludwig, *Zum Streikrecht der Beamten. Ein Wort zur Verständigung*, in: *Der Freie Beamte*, 3 (1922).

Braun, Adolf/Richard Seidel, *Die Stellung der Beamtenschaft in der Gewerkschaftsbewegung*, Berlin 1925.

Brentano, Lujo, *Die Beamtenorganisationen und ihre wirtschaftlichen Ziele*, Munich 1920.

Bresciani-Turroni, Costantino, *The Economics of Inflation: A Study of Currency Depreciation in Post-War Germany*, London 1937.

Bunzel, Julius (ed.), *Geldentwertung und Stabilisierung in ihren Einflüssen auf die soziale Entwicklung in Österreich* (= Schriften des Vereins für Sozialpolitik, vol. 169), Munich-Leipzig 1925.

Burgdörfer, Friedrich, *Tatsachen und Zahlen zum Behördenabbau*, in: *Allgemeines Statistisches Archiv*, 14 (1923—24), pp. 245—255.

Buss, Else, *Die Frauenarbeit im Dienst der preußisch-hessischen Staatseisenbahnen und ihre Entwicklung während des Krieges*, Diss., Göttingen 1919.

Cahen-Salvador, Georges, *Les Fonctionnaires, leur action corporative*, Paris 1911.

Delius, Karl, *Die Stellung der Beamtenschaft im neuen Staat*, Berlin n. d. (1922).

Die drohende Kohlenkrise und die Eisenbahnbeamtenschaft, Berlin 1919.

* Articles appearing in newspapers have not been listed here.

Die Entwicklung der Beamtenzahl im Deutschen Reich seit 1914, in: *Wirtschaft und Statistik,* 2 (1922), pp. 131—134.
Die Wirkungen der Geldentwertung auf die Gehälter der Beamten und Staatsangestellten in den Jahren 1919 bis 1923, in: *Hamburger Statistische Monatsberichte,* 1 (1924), pp. 77—80.
Die Wirkungen der Geldentwertung auf die Löhne einiger typischer Arbeiterberufe in den Jahren 1921 bis 1923, in: *Hamburger Statistische Monatsberichte,* 1 (1924), pp. 97—100.
Eulenburg, Franz, *Die sozialen Wirkungen der Währungsverhältnisse,* in: *Jahrbücher für Nationalökonomie und Statistik,* 122 (1924), pp. 748—794.
Falkenberg, Albert, *Die deutsche Beamtenbewegung nach der Revolution,* 2nd edn., Berlin 1920.
Falkenberg, Albert, *Die Aufgaben der Beamtenbewegung im modernen Rechtsstaat,* in: *Beamten-Jahrbuch,* 1 (1914).
Falkenberg, Albert, *Die Zukunftsarbeit der deutschen Beamtenverbände,* in: *Beamten-Jahrbuch,* 1 (1914), pp. 65—75.
Falkenberg, Albert, *Zur Vereinheitlichung der deutschen Beamtenbewegung,* in: *Beamten-Jahrbuch,* 2 (1915), pp. 107—111.
Falkenberg, Albert, *Die Organisationsfrage der Beamten. Wege und Ziele,* in: *Beamten-Jahrbuch,* 8 (1921), pp. 131—135.
Falkenberg, Albert, *Der Eisenbahnerstreik 1922,* in: *Beamten-Jahrbuch,* 9 (1922), pp. 47—60.
Finer, Herman, *The Principles and Practice of Remuneration in the British Civil Service,* in: Wilhelm Gerloff (ed.), *Die Beamtenbesoldung im modernen Staat,* T. 1 (= Schriften des Vereins für Sozialpolitik, vol. 184/I), Munich-Leipzig 1932.
Flügel, Wilhelm, *Werden und Wesen des Deutschen Beamtenbundes,* in: Ernst Remmers/Albert Falkenberg (eds.), *Beamtenhandbuch,* Berlin n. d. (1921).
Flügel, Wilhelm, *Die Grundlinie der Politik des Deutschen Beamtenbundes,* Berlin 1924.
Friedl, Hans, *Der deutsche Eisenbahnerstreik,* in: *Archiv für Eisenbahnwesen,* 47 (1924).
Für Sozialpolitik nach dem Kriege (= Schriften der Gesellschaft für sociale Reform, vol. 8), Jena 1918.
Geiger, Theodor, *Die soziale Schichtung des deutschen Volkes,* Stuttgart 1932.
Gruber, Erich/Richard Pfaundler, *Die Besoldungsverhältnisse der Beamtenschaft und die neuere Entwicklung der Besoldungspolitik in Österreich,* in: Wilhelm Gerloff (ed.), *Die Beamtenbesoldung im modernen Staat,* T. 2 (= Schriften des Vereins für Sozialpolitik, vol. 184/II), Munich-Leipzig 1934.
Günther Adolf, *Die Folgen des Krieges für Einkommen und Lebenshaltung der mittleren Volksschichten Deutschlands,* in: Rudolf Meerwarth et. al., *Die Einwirkungen des Krieges auf die Bevölkerungsbewegung, Einkommen und Lebenshaltung in Deutschland,* Stuttgart 1932.
Heiler, Hans, *Die Verelendung des Mittelstands* (= Beiträge zur Statistik Bayerns, no. 106), Munich 1925.
Heyde, Ludwig, *Die Beamten und die künftige Sozialpolitik,* in: *Beamten-Jahrbuch,* 2 (1915), pp. 135—140.
Hintze, Otto, *Der Beamtenstand* (= Vorträge der Gehe-Stiftung), Leipzig 1911. Repr. in: Idem, *Soziologie und Geschichte. Gesammelte Abhandlungen,* vol. 2, ed. by Gerhard Oestreich, 2nd edn., Göttingen 1964.

Hirsch, Arnold, *Weibliche Beamte im Deutschen Reich. Ein Ratgeber für junge Mädchen und deren Eltern*, Baden-Baden 1910.

Kamke, Paul, *Der Streik der Staatsbeamten. Ein Kampf- und Weckruf*, Frankfurt a. M. n. d.

Kessler, Gerhard, *Die Lage der deutschen Arbeiterschaft seit 1914*, in: Bernhard Harms (ed.), *Strukturwandlungen der deutschen Volkswirtschaft*, Berlin 1928.

Keynes, John Maynard, *A Tract on Monetary Reform*, London 1923. Reprinted as vol. 4 of *The Collected Writings* of John Maynard Keynes, London 1971.

Kleinheinz, Thomas, *Neue Gedanken zum Gehaltsproblem der Beamten*, in: *Beamten-Jahrbuch*, 3 (April 1916), pp. 30—36.

Knecht, Hermann, *Die Entwicklung der Löhne und Gehälter der Münchener Arbeiter- und Beamtenschaft in der Kriegs- und Nachkriegszeit bis Ende 1923 mit besonderer Berücksichtigung der Geldentwertung (Inflation)*, Diss., Erlangen 1924.

Kolshorn, Else, *Die Lage der weiblichen Post- und Telegraphenbeamtinnen*, in: *Jahrbuch für Frauenarbeit*, J. Silbermann (ed.), Berlin 1924.

Krüger, Ernst, *Die Gewerkschaftsbewegung der deutschen Beamten, ihr Werdegang und ihre Probleme*, Diss., Frankfurt 1924.

Kuczynski, Robert, *Postwar Labor Conditions in Germany* (= Bulletin of the United States Bureau of Labor Statistics, no. 380), Washington 1925.

Kulemann, Wilhelm, *Die Berufsvereine*, 2 vols., Jena 1908.

Kulemann, Wilhelm, *Die öffentlichen Beamten*, Berlin 1916.

Kulemann, Wilhelm, *Der Gewerkschaftsgedanke in der Beamtenbewegung*, Berlin 1919.

Kulemann, Wilhelm, *Gewerkschaften und Beamte*, Berlin 1921.

Kulemann, Wilhelm, *Der Eisenbahnerstreik im rechtlichen Licht*, in: *Deutsche Juristenzeitung*, (1922), col. 137 ff.

Lederer, Emil, *Die Bewegung der öffentlichen Beamten*, in: *Archiv für Sozialwissenschaft und Sozialpolitik* (hereafter cited as *ASS*), 31 (1910), pp. 660—709.

Lederer, Emil, *Angestellten- und Beamtensozialpolitik*, in: *ASS*, 34 (1911), pp. 940—984.

Lederer, Emil, *Bewegung der öffentlichen Beamten und Beamtensozialpolitik*, in: *ASS*, 35 (1912), pp. 882—912.

Lederer, Emil, *Beamtenorganisationen und -Fragen im Kriege*, in: *ASS*, 41 (1915/16), pp. 903—926.

Lederer, Emil, *Die sozialen Organisationen*, Leipzig-Berlin 1920.

Lederer, Emil/Marschak, Jakob, *Der neue Mittelstand*, in: *Grundriß der Sozialökonomie*, vol. 9, no. 1, Tübingen 1929.

Leger, Bernard, *Les syndicats des fonctionnaires en Angleterre*, Paris 1929.

Linck, Karl, *Die Beamtenbesoldungspolitik des Deutschen Reiches und ihr Einfluß auf den Reichshaushalt von 1871—1927*, Diss., Frankfurt 1928.

Lorenz, Charlotte, *Die gewerbliche Frauenarbeit während des Krieges*, in: *Der Krieg und die Arbeitsverhältnisse* (= Wirtschafts- und Sozialgeschichte des Weltkriegs, German Series), Stuttgart 1928.

Lotz, Albert, *Geschichte des deutschen Beamtentums*, Berlin 1909.

Mendelssohn-Bartholdy, Albrecht, *The War and German Society*, New Haven 1937.

Most, Otto, *Zur Wirtschafts- und Sozialstatistik der höheren Beamten in Preußen*, in: *Schmollers Jahrbuch*, Neue Folge, vol. 39, no. 1 (1915), pp. 181—218.

Nölting, Erik, *Zur Soziologie der heutigen Beamtenschaft*, in: *Der Beamte. Vierteljahreshefte für Beamtenrecht und Beamtenpolitik*, 1 (1929), pp. 226—231.

Oelschig, Martin, *Die neuere Entwicklung der Beamtenschaft, die Entstehung der Beamtenvereine und die Beamtenberufsvereine*, Diss., Halle 1933.

Oppenheimer, Hilde/Radomski, Hilde, *Die Probleme der Frauenarbeit in der Übergangswirtschaft*, Mannheim 1918.

Ostwald, Hans, *Sittengeschichte der Inflation. Ein Kulturdokument aus der Zeit des Marksturzes*, Berlin 1931.

Perrin, Herbert, *Die Stellung der Gewerkschaften zur Frage der gleitenden Lohnskala*, Diss., Freiburg 1923.

Podschun, Albert, *Die Lohn- und Gehaltsbewegung seit der Revolution und ihre bevölkerungspolitische und kulturelle Bedeutung*, Diss., Berlin 1922.

Remmers, Ernst, *Der Beamte im Volksstaat*, Berlin 1919.

Remmers, Ernst, *Die organisatorische Einheit der deutschen Beamten*, Berlin 1928.

Remmers, Ernst/Lockenvitz, Paul, *Die Verhandlungen über die Ortsklasseneinteilung* (= Flugschriften des Deutschen Beamtenbundes, no. 6), Berlin 1921.

Rosenberg, Arthur, *Die Entstehung der Weimarer Republik* (1928), 10th edn., Frankfurt/Main 1968.

Rosenberg, Arthur, *Geschichte der Weimarer Republik* (1935), 15th edn., Frankfurt/Main 1973.

Rothmeier, Karl/Heinrich, Karl, *Die Kriegsbeihilfen für Beamte in Bayern und den anderen Bundesstaaten*, Munich n. d.

Ruthenburg, O., *Das Besoldungsgesetz für die Reichsbeamten vom 30. 4. 1920*, Berlin 1920.

Scharringhausen, D., *Teuerungszulagen und Bevölkerungspolitik*, in: *Beamten-Jahrbuch*, 4 (1917), pp. 122—127.

Scherf, Kurt Ritter von, *Die Entwicklung der Beamtenbewegung und ihre Interessenvertretung*, Diss., Greifswald 1919.

Schmidt, R., *Die Kriegsteuerungszulagen bei der Reichs- Post- und Telegraphenverwaltung*, in: *Archiv für Post und Telegraphie*, 40 (1920), pp. 128—147.

Schreiber, Georg, *Die Not der deutschen Wissenschaft und der geistigen Arbeiter*, Leipzig 1923.

Schröder, Wilhem/Lockenvitz, Paul, *Der soziale Niedergang der deutschen Beamtenschaft* (= Flugschriften des Deutschen Beamtenbundes, no. 5), Berlin 1921.

Schulte, Albert, *Das Neutralitätsprinzip in der Gewerkschaftsbewegung der Beamten*, Diss., Cologne 1922.

Schultze, Ernst, *Not und Verschwendung. Untersuchung über das deutsche Wirtschaftsschicksal*, vol. 1, Leipzig 1923.

Schwarz, Otto, *Die Entwicklung der Ausgaben und Einnahmen Deutschlands, Englands, Frankreichs und Italiens vor und nach dem Weltkriege* (Anhang: *Die Beamtenvermehrung seit Kriegsbeginn)*, Magdeburg 1921.

Schwarz, Salomon (ed.), *Handbuch der Gewerkschaftskongresse*, Berlin 1930.

Schweitzer, Wilhelm, *Die Beamtenorganisationen in Deutschland und ihre Stellung zur Beamtenfrage*, Diss., Würzburg 1928.

Seidel, Richard, *Die Gewerkschaftsbewegung und das Streikrecht der Beamten*, Berlin 1922.

Steiner, Franz, *Begriff und Wesen des modernen deutschen Beamtentums unter Berücksichtigung des Streikrechts*, Diss., Berlin 1934.

Stampfer, Friedrich, *Die ersten vierzehn Jahre der deutschen Republik*, Karlsbad 1935.

Steinkopf, Willy, *Was muß der Beamte vom Besoldungsgesetz wissen?*, Berlin 1920.

Strutz, Georg, *Das Beamtenproblem nach dem Kriege, insbesondere in Preußen*, Stuttgart 1918.

Teuerungszulagen und Besoldungspolitik. Von einem mittleren Beamten, Berlin n. d. (1917).

Verband Deutscher Post- und Telegraphenbeamten, *Die Entwicklung der Personalverhältnisse bei der Reichs- Post- und Telegraphenverwaltung*, Berlin 1923.

Verband Deutscher Post- und Telegraphenbeamtinnen, *Die Frau in der Post- und Telegraphenverwaltung*, Berlin 1917.

Verhandlungen des Vereins für Sozialpolitik Stuttgart 1924, Theorie des Klassenkampfes, Handelspolitik, Währungsfrage (= Schriften des Vereins für Sozialpolitik, vol. 170), Munich-Leipzig 1925.

Völter, Hans, *Beamtentum und Wirtschaft* (= Flugschriften des Deutschen Beamtenbundes, no. 2), Berlin 1920.

Völter, Hans, *Die deutsche Beamtenbesoldung*, in: Wilhelm Gerloff (ed.), *Die Beamtenbesoldung im modernen Staat*, T. 1 (= Schriften des Vereins für Sozialpolitik, vol. 184/I), Munich-Leipzig 1932.

Weber, Alfred, *Der Beamte*, in: Idem, *Ideen zur Staats- und Kultursoziologie*, Karlsruhe 1927.

Weber, Alfred, *Die Not der geistigen Arbeiter* (= Schriften des Vereins für Sozialpolitik, vol. 163), Munich-Leipzig 1923.

Weber, Max, *Wirtschaft und Gesellschaft*, vol. 1 (= Grundriß der Sozialökonomik, vol. 3, part 1), Tübingen 1925.

Weber, Max, *Bureaucracy*, in: H. H. Gerth/C. Wright Mills (eds. and transl.), *From Max Weber: Essays in Sociology*, New York 1946.

White, Leonard D., *Whitley Councils in the British Civil Service. A Study in Conciliation and Arbitration*, Chicago 1932.

White, Leonard D., *The British Civil Service*, in: Idem et al., *Civil Service Abroad*, New York-London 1935.

Windeler, Heinrich, *Der Eisenbahnerstreik vom Februar 1922 als Beamtenproblem. Ein Beitrag zur Beamtenfrage und zur Geschichte der Inflationsperiode*, Diss., Leipzig 1924.

Winters, Fritz, *Geschichte des Verbandes mittlerer Post- und Telegraphenbeamten*, Berlin 1915.

Winters, Fritz, *Die deutsche Beamtenfrage*, Berlin 1918.

Winters, Fritz, *Zur Frage des Streikrechts der Beamten*, Berlin 1919.

Winters, Fritz, *Abriß der Geschichte des Beamtentums*, 2nd edn., Berlin 1929.

Winters, Fritz, *Der Deutsche Beamtenbund. Seine Entstehung und Entwicklung* (= Templiner Kursushefte, no. 3), Berlin 1931.

Winters, Fritz, *Beamtenbewegung*, in: *Internationales Handwörterbuch des Gewerkschaftswesens*, vol. 1, Berlin 1932, pp. 165—170.

Wolffstieg, Friedrich, *Das Beamtenrecht nach Inkrafttreten der Reichsverfassung vom 11. August 1919. Ein Ratgeber für alle deutsche Beamten*, Berlin 1921.

Zeiler, Alois, *Grundsätzliches zur Ordnung des Beamtengehalts*, in: *Beamten-Jahrbuch*, 4 (1917), pp. 97—108.

Zeiler, Alois, *Der Beamtenschaft Not und Rettung*, Munich 1918.

Zeiler, Alois, *Eine selbsttätige Anpassung von Gehalt und Lohn an die Wirtschaftsentwicklung* (= Flugschriften des Deutschen Beamtenbundes, no. 7), Berlin 1922.

B) *Post-1945 Literature*

Abelshauser, Werner, *Verelendung der Handarbeiter? Zur sozialen Lage der deutschen Arbeiter in der großen Inflation der frühen zwanziger Jahre,* in: Hans Mommsen/Winfried Schulze (eds.), *Vom Elend der Handarbeit. Probleme historischer Unterschichtenforschung* (= Geschichte und Gesellschaft. Bochumer Historische Studien, vol. 24), Stuttgart 1981, pp. 445—476.

Abelshauser, Werner/Petzina, Dietmar, *Krise und Rekonstruktion. Zur Interpretation der gesamtwirtschaftlichen Entwicklung Deutschlands im 20. Jahrhundert,* in: Wilhelm Heinz Schröder/Reinhard Spree (eds.), *Historische Konjunkturforschung,* Stuttgart 1981, pp. 75—114.

Albertin, Lothar, *Liberalismus und Demokratie am Anfang der Weimarer Republik. Eine vergleichende Analyse der Deutsche Demokratischen Partei und der Deutschen Volkspartei,* Düsseldorf 1972.

Aldcroft, Derek H., *From Versailles to Wall Street, 1919—1929* (= History of the World Economy in the Twentieth Century, vol. 3), Berkeley-Los Angeles 1977.

Alemann, Ulrich von (ed.), *Neokorporatismus,* Frankfurt/Main-New York 1982.

Armstrong, John, *The European Administrative Elite,* Princeton 1972.

Berger, Suzanne D. (ed.), *Organizing Interests in Western Europe: Pluralism, Corporatism, and the Transformation of Politics,* Cambridge 1981.

Beyme, Klaus von, *Interessengruppen in der Demokratie,* Munich 1969.

Beyme, Klaus von, *Gewerkschaften und Arbeitsbeziehungen in kapitalistischen Ländern,* Munich 1977.

Bieber, Hans J., *Gewerkschaften in Krieg und Revolution. Arbeiterbewegung, Industrie, Staat und Militär in Deutschland, 1914—1920,* 2 vols., Hamburg 1981.

Borch, Herbert von, *Obrigkeit und Widerstand. Zur politischen Soziologie des Beamtentums,* Tübingen 1954.

Bölling, Rainer, *Volksschullehrer und Politik. Der Deutsche Lehrerverein 1918—1933,* Göttingen 1978.

Borchardt, Knut, *Strukturwirkungen des Inflationsprozesses* (= Schriftenreihe des IFO-Instituts für Wirtschaftsforschung, vol. 53), Berlin-Munich 1972.

Borchardt, Knut, *Die Erfahrungen mit Inflationen in Deutschland,* in: Johannes Schlemmer (ed.), *Enteignung durch Inflation?,* Munich 1972.

Borchardt, Knut, *Wachstum und Wechsellagen 1914—1970,* in: *Handbuch der deutschen Wirtschafts- und Sozialgeschichte,* vol. 2, Stuttgart 1978.

Borchardt, Knut, *Wirtschaftliche Ursachen des Scheiterns der Weimarer Republik,* in: Karl Dietrich Erdmann/Hagen Schulze (eds.), *Weimar. Selbstpreisgabe einer Demokratie. Eine Bilanz heute,* Düsseldorf 1980.

Bry, Gerhard, *Wages in Germany,* Princeton 1960.

Büsch, Otto/Feldman, Gerald D. (eds.), *Historische Prozesse der deutschen Inflation. Ein Tagungsbericht* (= Einzelveröffentlichungen der Historischen Kommission zu Berlin, vol. 21), Berlin-New York 1978.

Caplan, Jane, *The Civil Servant in the Third Reich,* Diss., Oxford 1973.

Caplan, Jane, *The Politics of Administration: The Reich Interior Ministry and the German Civil Service, 1933—1945,* in: *The Historical Journal,* 20 (1977), pp. 707—736.

Caplan, Jane, *The 'Imaginary Universality of Particular Interests:' The Tradition of the German Civil Service in German History,* in: *Social History,* 4 (1979), pp. 299—317.

Caplan, Jane, *Civil Service Support for National Socialism: An Evaluation,* in: Gerhard Hirschfeld/Lothar Kettenacker (eds.), *The 'Führer State': Myth and Reality* (= Publications of the German Historical Institute London, vol. 8), Stuttgart 1981.

Childers, Thomas, *The Social Bases of the National Socialist Vote,* in: *Journal of Contemporary History,* 11 (1976), pp. 17—42.

Childers, Thomas, *National Socialism and the New Middle Class,* in: Reinhard Mann (ed.), *Die Nationalsozialisten. Analysen faschistischer Bewegungen* (= Historisch-Sozialwissenschaftliche Forschungen, vol. 9), Stuttgart 1980.

Childers, Thomas, *Inflation, Stabilization, and Political Realignment in Germany 1924 to 1928,* in: G. D. Feldman et al. (eds.), *The German Inflation* ..., pp. 409—431.

Childers, Thomas, *The Nazi Voter: The Social Foundations of Fascism in Germany, 1919—1933,* Chapel Hill 1983.

Craig, Gordon A., *Germany 1866—1945,* New York 1980.

Cullity, John P., *The Growth of Governmental Employment in Germany, 1882—1950,* in: *Zeitschrift für die gesamte Staatswissenschaft,* 123 (1967), pp. 201—217.

Czada, Peter, *Ursachen und Folgen der großen Inflation in Deutschland,* in: Harald Winkel (ed.), *Finanz- und wirtschaftspolitische Fragen der Zwischenkriegszeit* (= Schriften des Vereins für Sozialpolitik, vol. 73), Berlin 1973.

Czada, Peter, *Große Inflation und Wirtschaftswachstum,* in: Hans Mommsen et al. (eds.), *Industrielles System und politische Entwicklung in der Weimarer Republik,* Düsseldorf 1974.

Dahrendorf, Ralf, *Class and Class Conflict in Industrial Society,* Stanford 1959.

Dederke, Karlheinz, *Reich und Republik. Deutschland 1917—1933,* Stuttgart 1969.

Deppe, Frank et al., *Geschichte der deutschen Gewerkschaftsbewegung,* Cologne 1977.

Deutscher Beamtenbund, *Deutscher Beamtenbund. Ursprung, Weg, Ziel,* Bonn-Bad Godesberg 1968.

Deutscher Beamtenbund, *Die Beamten und das Streikrecht* (= DBB-Dokumente, no. 4), Bonn-Bad Godesberg 1969.

Döhn, Lothar, *Politik und Interesse. Die Interessenstruktur der Deutschen Volkspartei,* Meisenheim 1970.

Ellwein, Thomas, *Gewerkschaften und öffentlicher Dienst,* Opladen 1980.

Ellwein, Thomas/Zoll, Ralf, *Berufsbeamtentum. Anspruch und Wirklichkeit,* Düsseldorf 1973.

Erger, Johannes, *Der Kapp-Lüttwitz Putsch. Ein Beitrag zur deutschen Innenpolitik 1919/20,* Düsseldorf 1967.

Eyck, Erich, *A History of the Weimar Republik,* Cambridge 1962.

Feldman, Gerald D., *Army, Industry and Labor in Germany, 1914—1918,* Princeton 1966.

Feldman, Gerald D., *German Business Between War and Revolution: The Origins of the Stinnes-Legien Agreement,* in: Gerhard A. Ritter (ed.), *Entstehung und Wandel der modernen Gesellschaft. Festschrift für Hans Rosenberg,* Berlin 1970.

Feldman, Gerald D., *Economic and Social Problems of the German Demobilization 1918—1919,* in: *Journal of Modern History,* 47 (1975), pp. 1—47.

Feldman, Gerald D., *Die Freien Gewerkschaften und die Zentralarbeitsgemeinschaft,* in: Heinz Oskar Vetter (ed.), *Vom Sozialistengesetz zur Mitbestimmung. Zum 100. Geburtstag von Hans Böckler,* Cologne 1975.

Feldman, Gerald D., *Iron and Steel in the German Inflation, 1916—1923,* Princeton 1977.

Feldman, Gerald D., *Arbeitskonflikte im Ruhrbergbau,* in: *Vierteljahrshefte für Zeitgeschichte,* 28 (1980), pp. 168—223.

Feldman, Gerald D., *German Interest Alliances in War and Inflation,* in: Suzanne D. Berger (ed.), *Organizing Interests in Western Europe,* Cambridge 1981.

Feldman, Gerald D., *Streiks in Deutschland 1914—1933: Probleme und Forschungsaufgaben,* in: Klaus Tenfelde/Heinrich Volkmann (eds.), *Streik. Zur Geschichte des Arbeitskampfes in Deutschland während der Industrialisierung,* Munich 1981.

Feldman, Gerald D., *The Political Economy of Germany's Relative Stabilization during the 1920/21 Depression,* in: G. D. Feldman et al. (eds.), *The German Inflation...,* pp. 180—206.

Feldman, Gerald D., *The Historian and the German Inflation,* in: N. Schmukler/E. Marcus (eds.), *Inflation through the Ages...,* pp. 386—399.

Feldman, Gerald D./Homburg, Heidrun, *Industrie und Inflation. Studien und Dokumente zur Politik der deutschen Unternehmer 1916—1923,* Hamburg 1978.

Feldman, Gerald D./Steinisch, Irmgard, *Die Weimarer Republik zwischen Sozial- und Wirtschaftsstaat. Die Entscheidung gegen den Achtstundentag,* in: *Archiv für Sozialgeschichte,* 18 (1978), pp. 353—439.

Feldman, Gerald D./Kolb, Eberhard/Rürup, Reinhard, *Die Massenbewegung der Arbeiterschaft am Ende des Ersten Weltkriegs (1917—1920),* in: *Politische Vierteljahresschrift,* 13 (1972), pp. 84—105.

Feldman, Gerald D./Holtfrerich, Carl-Ludwig/Ritter, Gerhard A./Witt, Peter-Christian (eds.), *The German Inflation Reconsidered: A Preliminary Balance* (German title: *Die deutsche Inflation: Eine Zwischenbilanz)* (= Veröffentlichungen der Historischen Kommission zu Berlin, vol. 54, Beiträge zu Inflation und Wiederaufbau in Deutschland und Europa 1914—1924, vol. 1), Berlin-New York 1982. Only some of the contributions to this indispensable volume have been cited separately.

Feldman, Gerald D./Holtfrerich, Carl-Ludwig/Ritter, Gerhard A./Witt, Peter-Christian (eds.), *The Experience of Inflation. International and Comparative Studies* (German title: *Die Erfahrungen der Inflation im internationalen Zusammenhang und Vergleich*) (= Veröffentlichungen der Historischen Kommission zu Berlin, vol. 57, Beiträge zu Inflation und Wiederaufbau in Deutschland und Europa 1914—1924, vol. 2), Berlin-New York 1984.

Feldman, Gerald D./Holtfrerich, Carl-Ludwig/Ritter, Gerhard A./Witt, Peter-Christian (eds.), *Adaptation to Inflation* (German title: *Die Anpassung an die Inflation*) (= Veröffentlichungen der Historischen Kommission zu Berlin, vol. 67, Beiträge zu Inflation und Wiederaufbau in Deutschland und Europa 1914—1924, vol. 8), Berlin-New York 1986.

Fenske, Hans, *Monarchisches Beamtentum und demokratischer Staat. Zum Problem der Bürokratie in der Weimarer Republik,* in: *Demokratie und Verwaltung* (= Schriftenreihe der Hochschule Speyer, vol. 50), Berlin 1972, pp. 117—136.

Fenske, Hans, *Beamtenpolitik in der Weimarer Republik,* in: *Verwaltungsarchiv,* 64 (1973), pp. 117—135.

Flemming, Jens, *Landwirtschaftliche Interessen und Demokratie. Ländliche Gesellschaft, Agrarverbände und Staat 1890—1925,* Bonn 1978.

Flora, Peter, et al., *State, Economy and Society in Western Europe 1815—1975. A Data Handbook,* vol. 1: *The Growth of Mass Democracies and Welfare States,* Frankfurt a. M.-London-Chicago 1983.

Furtwängler, Franz Josef, *ÖTV. Die Geschichte einer Gewerkschaft,* Stuttgart 1955.

Gellately, Robert, *The Politics of Economic Despair: Shopkeepers and German Politics 1890—1914,* London-Beverly Hills 1974.

Gossweiler, Kurt, *Kapital, Reichswehr und NSDAP, 1919—1924,* Cologne 1982.

Habedank, Heinz, *Die Reichsbank in der Weimarer Republik. Zur Rolle der Zentralbank in der Politik des Imperialismus, 1919—1933* (= Forschungen zur Wirtschaftsgeschichte, vol. 12), East-Berlin 1981.

Hahn, Claudia, *Der öffentliche Dienst und die Frauen-Beamtinnen in der Weimarer Republik,* in: Frauengruppe Faschismusforschung (ed.), *Mutterkreuz und Arbeitsbuch. Zur Geschichte der Frauen in der Weimarer Republik und im Nationalsozialismus,* Frankfurt/Main 1981.

Halmen, Rainer M., *„Das Berufsbeamtentum muß unter allen Umständen erhalten bleiben." Die deutsche Beamtenbewegung zwischen Etatismus und gewerkschaftlicher Orientierung im Übergang vom Kaiserreich zur Weimarer Republik,* in: *Internationale wissenschaftliche Korrespondenz zur Geschichte der deutschen Arbeiterbewegung,* 18 (1982), pp. 49—77.

Hamilton, Richard, *Who Voted for Hitler,* Princeton 1982.

Hardach, Gerd, *The First World War* (= History of the World Economy in the Twentieth Century, vol. 2), Berkeley-Los Angeles 1977.

Hardach, Gerd, *Klassen und Schichten in Deutschland. Probleme einer historischen Schichtungsanalyse,* in: *Geschichte und Gesellschaft,* 3 (1977), pp. 503—524.

Hardach, Karl, *Wirtschaftsgeschichte Deutschlands im 20. Jahrhundert,* Göttingen 1976.

Hattenhauer, Hans, *Geschichte des Beamtentums* (= Handbuch des öffentlichen Dienstes, vol. 1), Cologne 1980.

Holborn, Hajo, *A History of Modern Germany 1840—1945,* New York 1969.

Hoffmann, Gabriele, *Sozialdemokratie und Berufsbeamtentum. Zur Frage nach Wandel und Kontinuität im Verhältnis der Sozialdemokratie zum Berufsbeamtenum in der Weimarer Zeit* (= Hamburger Historische Studien, vol. 4), Hamburg 1972.

Holtfrerich, Carl-Ludwig, *Die deutsche Inflation. Ursachen und Folgen in internationaler Perspektive,* Berlin-New York 1980 (Engl. edn. *The German Inflation 1914—1923. Causes and Effects in International Perspective,* transl. by Theo Balderston, Berlin-New York 1986).

Holtfrerich, Carl-Ludwig, *Die konjunkturanregende Wirkung der deutschen Inflation auf die US-Wirtschaft in der Weltwirtschaftskrise 1920/21,* in: G. D. Feldman et al. (eds.), *The German Inflation ...,* pp. 207—234.

Holtfrerich, Carl-Ludwig, *Political Factors of the German Inflation 1914—1923,* in: *N. Schmukler/E. Marcus (eds.), Inflation through the Ages ...,* pp. 400—416.

Hughes, Michael L., *Private Equity, Social Inequity: German Judges React to Inflation, 1914—1924,* in: *Central European History,* 16 (1983), pp. 76—94.

Hülden, Arnold, *Die Entwicklung der Beamtenbesoldung in den letzten 50 Jahren,* in: *Deutscher Beamtenbund. Ursprung, Weg, Ziel,* Bonn-Bad Godesberg 1968.

Jones, Larry Eugene, *The 'Dying Middle': Weimar Germany and the Fragmentation of German Politics,* in: *Central European History,* 5 (1972), pp. 23—54.

Jones, Larry Eugene, *Inflation, Revaluation, and the Crisis of Middle-Class Politics: A Study in the Dissolution of the German Party System, 1923—1928,* in: *Central European History,* 12 (1979), pp. 143—168.

Jones, Larry Eugene, *The Dying Middle. German Liberalism and the Dissolution of the Weimar Party System,* Chapel Hill 1986.

Kalmer, Georg, *Vom Staatsdiener zum Staatsbürger. Die Entwicklung der bayerischen Beamtenorganisationen*, in: *Informationsschrift des Bayerischen Beamtenbundes anläßlich seines 50jährigen Bestehens*, Munich 1967.

Kalmer, Georg, *Beamtenschaft und Revolution. Eine sozialgeschichtliche Studie über Voraussetzungen und Wirklichkeit des Problems*, in: Karl Bosl (ed.), *Bayern im Umbruch*, Munich-Vienna 1969.

Kleineberg, Lilian, *Die Entwicklung der wirtschaftlichen Lage der Beamten des Reiches bzw. Bundes von 1909 bis heute*, Diss., Cologne 1954.

Kocka, Jürgen, *Klassengesellschaft im Krieg. Deutsche Sozialgeschichte 1914—1918*, Göttingen 1973.

Kocka, Jürgen, *The First World War and the 'Mittelstand': German Artisans and White Collar Workers*, in: *Journal of Contemporary History*, 8 (1973), pp. 101—123.

Kocka, Jürgen, *Zur Problematik der deutschen Angestellten*, in: Hans Mommsen et al. (eds.), *Industrielles System und politische Entwicklung in der Weimarer Republik*, Düsseldorf 1974, pp. 792—810.

Kocka, Jürgen, *White Collar Workers in America 1890—1940. A Social-Political History in International Perspective.* Translated by Maura Kealey (= Sage Studies in 20th Century History, vol. 10), London-Beverly Hills 1980.

Kocka, Jürgen, *Class Formation, Interest Articulation, and Public Policy: The Origins of the German White-Collar Class in the Late Nineteenth and Early Twentieth Centuries*, in: Suzanne D. Berger (ed.), *Organizing Interests in Western Europe*, Cambridge 1981, pp. 63—81.

Kocka, Jürgen, *Die Angestellten in der deutschen Geschichte 1850—1980*, Göttingen 1981.

Keller, Berndt, *Zur politischen Ökonomie der Besoldungsbeziehungen*, in: *Jahrbuch für Sozialwissenschaft*, 30 (1979), pp. 358—381.

Keller, Berndt, *Zur Interessenpolitik von Beamtenverbänden*, in: *Zeitschrift für Soziologie*, 9 (1980), pp. 194—212.

Keller, Berndt, *Public Sector Labor Relations in West Germany*, in: *Industrial Relations*, 17 (1978), pp. 18—31.

Keller, Berndt, *Determinants of the Wage Rate in the Public Sector: The Case of Civil Servants in the Federal Republic of Germany*, in: *British Journal of Industrial Relations*, 19 (1981), pp. 345—360.

Keller, Berndt, *Arbeitsbeziehungen und öffentlicher Dienst. Tarifpolitik der Gewerkschaften und Interessenpolitik der Beamtenverbände*, Frankfurt/Main-New York 1983.

Krohn, Claus-Dieter, *Stabilisierung und ökonomische Interessen. Die Finanzpolitik des Deutschen Reiches 1923—1927*, Düsseldorf 1974.

Krohn, Claus-Dieter, *Helfferich contra Hilferding. Konservative Geldpolitik und die sozialen Folgen der deutschen Inflation 1918—1923*, in: *Vierteljahrschrift für Sozial- und Wirtschaftsgeschichte*, 62 (1975), pp. 62—92.

Krohn, Claus-Dieter, *Die große Inflation in Deutschland 1918—1923*, Cologne 1977.

Krohn, Claus-Dieter/Flemming, Jens/Witt, Peter-Christian, *Sozialverhalten und politische Reaktionen von Gruppen und Institutionen im Inflationsprozeß. Anmerkungen zum Forschungsstand*, in: O. Büsch/G. D. Feldman (eds.), *Historische Prozesse...*, pp. 239—263.

Kübler, Horst, *Besoldung und Lebenshaltung der unmittelbaren preußischen Staatsbeamten im 19. Jahrhundert. Eine verwaltungsgeschichtliche Analyse*, Nürnberg 1976.

Kunz, Andreas, *Stand versus Klasse. Beamtenschaft und Gewerkschaften im Konflikt um den Personalabbau 1923/24*, in: *Geschichte und Gesellschaft*, 8 (1982), pp. 55—86.

Kunz, Andreas, *Verteilungskampf oder Interessenkonsensus? Einkommensentwicklung und Sozialverhalten von Arbeitnehmergruppen in der Inflationszeit 1914 bis 1924*, in: G. D. Feldman et al. (eds.), *The German Inflation...*, pp. 347—384.

Kunz, Andreas, *Arbeitsbeziehungen und Arbeitskonflikte im öffentlichen Sektor. Deutschland und Großbritannien im Vergleich*, in: *Geschichte und Gesellschaft*, 12 (1986), pp. 34—62.

Kunz, Andreas, *Variants of Social Protest in the German Inflation: The Mobilization of Civil Servants in City and Countryside, 1920—1924*, in: G. D. Feldman et al. (eds.), *Adaptation to Inflation...*, pp. 323—353.

Laubach, Ernst, *Die Politik der Kabinette Wirth 1921/22*, Lübeck-Hamburg 1968.

Laursen, Karsten/Pedersen, Jørgen, *The German Inflation 1918—1923*, Amsterdam 1964.

Lohmann, H. E., *Die Entwicklung der Beamtenbesoldung seit dem Jahre 1909*, in: *Die Selbstverwaltung*, (1953).

Ludewig, Hans-Ulrich, *Arbeiterbewegung und Aufstand* (= Historische Studien, vol. 432), Husum 1978.

Mai, Gunther, *Kriegswirtschaft und Arbeiterbewegung in Württemberg 1914—1918* (= Industrielle Welt, vol. 35), Stuttgart 1983.

Maier, Charles S., *Recasting Bourgeois Europe: Stabilization in France, Germany and Italy in the Decade After World War I*, Princeton 1975.

Maier, Charles S., *The Politics of Inflation in the Twentieth Century*, in: Fred Hirsch/John H. Goldthorpe (eds.), *The Political Economy of Inflation*, London 1978, pp. 37—72.

Maus, Hans, *Die soziologischen Formkräfte und Auswirkungen der deutschen Bürokratie als Sozialgebilde*, Diss., Heidelberg 1950.

Maur, Hans, *Zur Einheitsfrontpolitik der KPD im Eisenbahnerstreik 1922*, in: *Beiträge zur Geschichte der Arbeiterbewegung*, (1972), pp. 237—259.

Maur, Hans, *Zur Rolle der KPD im Februarstreik der Eisenbahnarbeiter und -beamten im Jahre 1922*, in: *Wissenschaftliche Zeitschrift der Ernst-Moritz-Arnst Universität Greifswald. Gesellschafts- und sprachwissenschaftliche Reihe*, 2—3 (1965).

McPherson, William, *Public Employee Relations in West Germany*, Ann Arbor 1971.

Miller, Susanne, *Die Bürde der Macht. Die deutsche Sozialdemokratie 1918—1920*, Düsseldorf 1978.

Moeller, Robert G., *Dimensions of Social Conflict in the Great War: The View from the German Countryside*, in: *Central European History*, 14 (1981), pp. 142—168.

Moeller, Robert G., *Winners as Losers in the German Inflation: Peasant Protest over the Controlled Economy, 1920—1923*, in: G. D. Feldman et al. (eds.), *The German Inflation...*, pp. 255—288.

Moeller, Robert G., *German Peasants and Agrarian Politics, 1914—1924: The Rhineland and Westphalia*, Chapel Hill 1986.

Mommsen, Hans, *Beamtentum im Dritten Reich*, Stuttgart 1966.

Mommsen, Hans, *Die Stellung der Beamtenschaft in Reich, Ländern und Gemeinden in der Ära Brüning*, in: *Vierteljahrshefte für Zeitgeschichte*, 21 (1973), pp. 151—165.

Mommsen, Hans, *Staat und Bürokratie in der Ära Brüning*, in: Gotthard Jasper (ed.), *Tradition und Reform in der deutschen Politik. Gedenkschrift für Waldemar Besson*, Frankfurt/Main 1976, pp. 81—137.

Mommsen, Hans (ed.), *Sozialdemokratie zwischen Klassenbewegung und Volkspartei*, Frankfurt/Main 1974.

Mommsen, Hans/Petzina, Dietmar/Weisbrod Bernd (eds.), *Industrielles System und politische Entwicklung in der Weimarer Republik.* Düsseldorf 1974, Reprint (2 vols.) Kronberg/Taunus 1977.

Mommsen, Wolfgang J., *Die deutsche Revolution 1918—1920: Politische Revolution und soziale Protestbewegung,* in: *Geschichte und Gesellschaft,* 4 (1978), pp. 362—391.

Morsey, Rudolf, *Zur Beamtenpolitik des Reiches von Bismarck bis Brüning,* in: *Demokratie und Verwaltung* (= Schriftenreihe der Hochschule Speyer, vol. 50), Berlin 1972.

Morsey, Rudolf, *Beamtenschaft und Verwaltung zwischen Republik und neuem Staat,* in: Karl Dietrich Erdmann/Hagen Schulze (eds.), *Weimar. Selbstpreisgabe einer Demokratie,* Düsseldorf 1980, pp. 151—167.

Netzband, Karl-Bernhard/Widmaier, Hans Peter, *Währungs- und Finanzpolitik der Ära Luther 1923—1925,* Basel 1964.

Niehuss, Merith, *Arbeitslosigkeit in Augsburg und Linz a. D. 1914 bis 1924,* in: *Archiv für Sozialgeschichte,* 22 (1982), pp. 133—158.

Niehuss, Merith, *Arbeiterschaft in Krieg und Inflation. Soziale Schichtung und Lage der Arbeiter in Augsburg und Linz 1910—1925* (= Veröffentlichungen der Historischen Kommission zu Berlin, vol. 58, Beiträge zu Inflation und Wiederaufbau in Deutschland und Europa 1914—1924, vol. 3), Berlin-New York 1984.

Nocken, Ulrich, *Corporatism and Pluralism in Modern German History,* in: Dirk Stegmann et al. (eds.), *Industrielle Gesellschaft und politisches System. Beiträge zur politischen Sozialgeschichte,* Bonn 1978, pp. 37—56.

Nocken, Ulrich, *Korporatistische Theorien und Strukturen in der deutschen Geschichte des 19. und frühen 20. Jahrhundert,* in: Ulrich von Alemann (ed.), *Neokorporatismus,* Frankfurt/Main-New York 1981, pp. 17—39.

Oltmann, Uwe, *Reichsarbeitsminister Brauns in der Staats- und Währungskrise 1923/24,* Diss., Kiel 1968.

Opitz, Reinhard, *Der deutsche Sozialliberalismus 1917—1933,* Cologne 1973.

Pfleiderer, Otto, *Die Reichsbank in der Zeit der großen Inflation,* in: Deutsche Bundesbank, *Währung und Wirtschaft in Deutschland 1876—1975,* Frankfurt 1976.

Pikart, Eberhard, *Preußische Beamtenpolitik 1918—1933,* in: *Vierteljahrshefte für Zeitgeschichte,* 6 (1958), pp. 119—137.

Potthoff, Heinrich, *Gewerkschaften und Politik zwischen Revolution und Inflation,* Düsseldorf 1979.

Preller, Ludwig, *Sozialpolitik in der Weimarer Republik,* Düsseldorf 1949. Reprint: Kronberg/Taunus 1978.

Priamus, Hans Jürgen, *Angestellte und Demokratie. Die nationalliberale Angestelltenbewegung in der Weimarer Republik,* Stuttgart 1979.

Ringer, Fritz K., *The German Inflation,* New York 1969.

Ritter, Gerhard A., *Staat, Arbeiterschaft und Arbeiterbewegung in Deutschland,* Berlin-Bonn 1980.

Röhl, John C. G., *Higher Civil Servants in Germany, 1890—1900,* in: *Journal of Contemporary History,* 2 (1967), pp. 101—121.

Röhl, John C. G., *Beamtenpolitik im Wilhelminischen Deutschland,* in: Michael Stürmer (ed.), *Das kaiserliche Deutschland,* Düsseldorf 1970, pp. 287—311.

Ruge, Wolfgang, *Deutschland von 1917 bis 1933* (= Lehrbuch der deutschen Geschichte, Beiträge), East Berlin 1974.

Runge, Wolfgang, *Politik und Beamtentum im Parteienstaat 1918—1933,* Stuttgart 1965.

Rupieper, Hermann J., *The Cuno Government and Reparation*, The Hague 1979.
Saul, Klaus, *Konstitutioneller Staat und betriebliche Herrschaft. Zur Arbeiter- und Beamtenpolitik der preußischen Staatseisenbahnverwaltung 1890—1914*, in: Dirk Stegmann et al. (eds.), *Industrielle Gesellschaft...*, pp. 315—336.
Schieder, Wolfgang (ed.), *Faschismus als soziale Bewegung*, Hamburg 1976.
Schmahl, Hermannjosef, *Disziplinarrecht und politische Betätigung der Beamten in der Weimarer Republik*, Berlin 1977.
Schmitter, Philippe C., *Still the Century of Corporatism?*, in: *Review of Politics*, 36 (1974), pp. 85—131.
Schmitter, Philippe C., *Interest Intermediation and Regime Governability in Contemporary Western Europe and North America*, in: Suzanne D. Berger (ed.), *Organizing Interests in Western Europe*, Cambridge 1980, pp. 287—330.
Schmitter, Philippe C., *Democratic Theory and Neo-Corporatist Practice* (= E. U. I. Working Paper, no. 74), San Domenico (FI) 1983.
Schmitter Philippe C./Lehmbruch, Gerhard, *Trends Toward Corporatist Intermediation*, London-Beverly Hills 1979.
Schmitter, Philippe C./Lehmbruch, Gerhard (eds.), *Consequences of Corporatist Policy Making*, London-Beverly Hills 1982.
Schmuckler, Nathan/Marcus, Edward, *Inflation through the Ages: Economic, Social, Psychological, and Historical Aspects*, New York 1983.
Schneider, Michael, *Die Christlichen Gewerkschaften 1894—1933*, Bonn 1982.
Schrön, Ernst, *Deutscher Beamtenbund (DBB) 1918—1933*, in: Dieter Fricke (ed.), *Die bürgerlichen Parteien in Deutschland. Handbuch der Geschichte der bürgerlichen Parteien und anderer bürgerlicher Interessenorganisationen*, vol. 1, Leipzig 1968, pp. 422—428.
Schwabe, Klaus (ed.), *Die Ruhrkrise 1923. Wendepunkt der internationalen Beziehungen nach dem Ersten Weltkrieg*, Paderborn 1984.
Severing, Carl, *Mein Lebensweg*, 2 vols., Cologne 1950.
Speier, Hans, *Die Angestellten vor dem Nationalsozialismus*, Göttingen 1977.
Stegmann, Dirk, *Zwischen Repression und Manipulation. Konservative Machteliten und Arbeiter- und Angestelltenbewegung 1910—1918*, in: *Archiv für Sozialgeschichte*, 12 (1972), pp. 351—432.
Stegmann, Dirk/Wendt, Bernd-Jürgen/Witt, Peter-Christian (eds.), *Industrielle Gesellschaft und politisches System. Beiträge zur politischen Sozialgeschichte. Festschrift für Fritz Fischer* (= Schriftenreihe des Forschungsinstituts der Friedrich-Ebert-Stiftung, vol. 137), Bonn 1978.
Stephan, Werner, *Aufstieg und Fall des Linksliberalismus. Geschichte der Deutschen Demokratischen Partei*, Göttingen 1973.
Sturmthal, Adolf (ed.), *White Collar Trade Unions*, Urbana, Ill. 1966.
Trachtenberg, Marc, *Reparation in World Politics*, New York 1981.
Tschirbs, Rudolf, *Der Ruhrbergmann zwischen Privilegierung und Statusverlust: Lohnpolitik von der Inflation bis zur Rationalisierung (1919—1927)*, in: G. D. Feldman et al. (eds.), *The German Inflation...*, pp. 308—346.
Ullmann, Peter, *Bibliographie zur Geschichte der deutschen Parteien und Interessenverbände* (= Arbeitsbücher zur modernen Geschichte, no. 6), Göttingen 1978.
Varain, Heinz Josef (ed.), *Interessenverbände in Deutschland*, Cologne 1973.
Wendt, Bernd-Jürgen, *Whitleyism — Versuch einer Institutionalisierung des Sozialkonflik-*

tes in England am Ausgang des Ersten Weltkrieges, in: D. Stegmann et al. (eds.), *Industrielle Gesellschaft...,* pp. 337—353.

Wehler, Hans-Ulrich, *Das deutsche Kaiserreich,* Göttingen 1973.

Weisbrod, Bernd, *Schwerindustrie in der Weimarer Republik,* Wuppertal 1978.

Winkler, Heinrich August, *Mittelstand, Demokratie und Nationalsozialismus. Die politische Entwicklung von Handwerk und Kleinhandel in der Weimarer Republik,* Cologne 1972.

Winkler, Heinrich August, *Der rückversicherte Mittelstand. Die Interessenverbände von Handwerk und Kleinhandel im deutschen Kaiserreich,* in: Walther Rüegg/Otto Neuloh (eds.), *Zur soziologischen Theorie und Analyse des 19. Jahrhunderts,* Göttingen 1971.

Winkler, Heinrich August, *Pluralismus oder Protektionismus? Verfassungspolitische Probleme des Verbandswesens im Deutschen Kaiserreich,* Wiesbaden 1972.

Winkler, Heinrich August, *From Social Protectionism to National Socialism: The German Small Business Movement in Comparative Perspective,* in: *Journal of Modern History,* 48 (1976), pp. 1—18.

Winkler, Heinrich August, *Die Sozialdemokratie und die Revolution von 1918/19,* Berlin-Bonn 1979.

Winkler, Heinrich August, *Liberalismus und Antiliberalismus. Studien zur politischen Sozialgeschichte des 19. und 20. Jahrhunderts,* Göttingen 1979.

Winkler, Heinrich August, *Klassenbewegung oder Volkspartei? Zur Programmdiskussion der Weimarer Sozialdemokratie,* in: *Geschichte und Gesellschaft,* 8 (1982), pp. 9—54.

Winkler, Heinrich August, *Von der Revolution zur Stabilisierung. Arbeiter und Arbeiterbewegung in der Weimarer Republik 1918 bis 1924,* Berlin-Bonn 1984.

Witt, Peter-Christian, *Finanzpolitik und sozialer Wandel in Krieg und Inflation 1918—1924,* in: H. Mommsen et al. (eds.), *Industrielles System...,* pp. 395—425.

Witt, Peter-Christian, *Reichsfinanzminister und Reichsfinanzverwaltung. Zum Problem des Verhältnisses von politischer Führung und bürokratischer Herrschaft in den Anfangsjahren der Weimarer Republik (1918/19—1924),* in: *Vierteljahrshefte für Zeitgeschichte* 23 (1975), pp. 1—61.

Witt, Peter-Christian, *Der preußische Landrat als Steuerbeamter 1891—1918. Bemerkungen zur politischen und sozialen Funktion des deutschen Beamtentums,* in: Imanuel Geiss/Bernd-Jürgen Wendt (eds.), *Deutschland in der Weltpolitik des 20. Jahrhunderts. Festschrift für Fritz Fischer,* Düsseldorf 1973, pp. 205—219.

Witt, Peter-Christian, *Tax Policies, Tax Assessment and Inflation. Toward a Sociology of Public Finances in the German Inflation 1914—1923,* in: N. Schmukler/E. Marcus (eds.), *Inflation through the Ages...,* pp. 450—474.

Wishnia, Judith, *French Fonctionnaires: The Development of Class Consciousness and Unionization, 1884—1926,* Diss., Stony Brook 1978.

Zapf, Wolfgang, *Die Verwalter der Macht. Materialien zum Sozialprofil der höheren Beamtenschaft,* in: *Studien zur Soziologie,* 3 (1965), pp. 55—94.

Zapf, Wolfgang, *Wandlungen der deutschen Elite. Ein Zirkulationsmodell deutscher Führungsgruppen 1919—1961,* Munich 1965.

Ziemer, Gerhard, *Inflation und Deflation zerstören die Demokratie,* Stuttgart 1971.

INDEX OF SUBJECTS AND GEOGRAPHIC NAMES

INDEX OF PERSONS

Kirchweg 33 ('Mittelhof'). D-1000 Berlin 38 (Nikolassee)